BERKSHIRE ENCYCLOPEDIA OF SUSTAINABILITY

VOLUME 8

The Americas and Oceania: Assessing Sustainability

Editors Sara G. Beavis, *The Australian National University*; Michael L. Dougherty, *Illinois State University*; Tirso Gonzales, *University of British Columbia Okanagan*

The darkened areas on this map indicate regions covered in this volume.

© 2012 by Berkshire Publishing Group LLC

All rights reserved. Permission to copy articles for internal or personal noncommercial use is hereby granted on the condition that appropriate fees are paid to the Copyright Clearance Center, 222 Rosewood Drive, Danvers, MA 01923, USA, telephone +1 978 750 8400, fax +1 978 646 8600, e-mail info@copyright.com. Teachers at institutions that own a print copy or license a digital edition of *The Americas and Oceania: Assessing Sustainability* may use at no charge up to ten copies of no more than two articles (per course or program).

Digital editions
The *Berkshire Encyclopedia of Sustainability* is available through most major e-book and database services (please check with them for pricing). Special print/digital bundle pricing is also available in cooperation with Credo Reference; contact Berkshire Publishing (info@berkshirepublishing.com) for details.

For information, contact:
Berkshire Publishing Group LLC
122 Castle Street
Great Barrington, Massachusetts 01230-1506 USA
info@berkshirepublishing.com
Tel + 1 413 528 0206
Fax + 1 413 541 0076

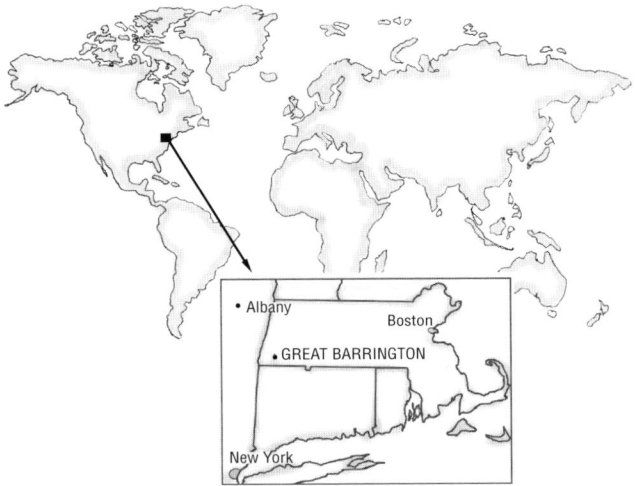

Library of Congress Cataloging-in-Publication Data

Berkshire encyclopedia of sustainability: / The Americas and Oceania: Assessing sustainability, edited by Sara G. Beavis, Michael L. Dougherty, and Tirso Gonzales.
    v. cm.
    Includes bibliographical references and index.
    Contents: vol. 8. The Americas and Oceania: Assessing sustainability —
    ISBN 978-1-933782-18-8 (vol. 8 print : alk. paper)
    1. Environmental quality—Encyclopedias.   2. Environmental protection—Encyclopedias.   3. Sustainable development—Encyclopedias. I. Beavis, Sara. II. Dougherty, Michael. III. Gonzales, Tirso.

Berkshire encyclopedia of sustainability (10 volumes) / edited by Ray Anderson et al.
    10 v. cm.
    Includes bibliographical references and index.
    ISBN 978-1-933782-01-0 (10 volumes : alk. paper) — 978-1-933782-00-3 (10 volumes e-book) — ISBN 978-1-933782-15-7 (vol. 1 print: alk. paper) — ISBN 978-1-933782-57-7 (vol. 1 e-book) — ISBN 978-1-933782-13-3 (vol. 2 print : alk. paper) — ISBN 978-1-933782-55-3 (vol. 2 e-book) — ISBN 978-1-933782-14-0 (vol. 3 print : alk. paper) — ISBN 978-1-933782-56-0 (vol. 3 e-book) — ISBN 978-1-933782-12-6 (vol. 4 print : alk. paper) — ISBN 978-1-933782-54-6 (vol. 4 e-book) — ISBN 978-1-933782-16-4 (vol. 5 print : alk. paper) — ISBN 978-1-933782-09-6 (vol. 5 e-book) — ISBN 978-1-933782-40-9 (vol. 6 print : alk. paper) — ISBN 978-0-9770159-0-0 (vol. 6 e-book) — ISBN 978-1-933782-69-0 (vol. 7 print : alk. paper) — ISBN 978-1-933782-72-0 (vol. 7 e-book) — ISBN 978-1-933782-18-8 (vol. 8 print: alk. paper) — ISBN 978-1-933782-73-7 (vol. 8 e-book) — ISBN 978-1-933782-19-5 (vol. 9 print : alk. paper) — ISBN 978-1-933782-74-4 (vol. 9 e-book) — ISBN 978-1-933782-63-8 (vol. 10 print : alk. paper) — ISBN 978-1-933782-75-1 (vol. 10 e-book)
    1. Environmental quality—Encyclopedias.   2. Environmental protection—Encyclopedias.   3. Sustainable development—Encyclopedias.   I. Anderson, Ray, et al.
    HC79.E5B4576   2010
    338.9'2703—dc22
                                                                                                                                      2009035114

Editors

Editors
Sara G. Beavis
The Australian National University

Michael L. Dougherty
Illinois State University

Tirso Gonzales
University of British Columbia Okanagan

Associate Editors
Ricardo Braun
Centre for Environmental Analysis (Nasa)

Muhammad Aurang Zeb Mughal
Durham University

Mark Wilson
Northumbria University

Advisory Board
Ray C. Anderson, *Interface, Inc.;* Lester R. Brown, *Earth Policy Institute;* Eric Freyfogle, *University of Illinois, Urbana-Champaign;* Luis Gomez-Echeverri, *United Nations Development Programme;* Daniel M. Kammen, *University of California, Berkeley;* Ashok Khosla, *International Union for Conservation of Nature;* Christine Loh, *Civic Exchange, Hong Kong;* Sunita Narain, *Center for Science and Environment;* Cheryl Oakes, *Duke University*

Production Staff

Publisher
Karen Christensen

Project Coordinator
Bill Siever

Copyeditors
Mary Bagg
Kathy Brock
Elaine Coveney
Cindy Crumrine
Carolyn Haley
Elizabeth Laederich
Kristen Osborne
Elma Sanders
Heidi Sias
Catherine Skeen
Vali Tamm
Susan Walker

Editorial Assistants
Ellie Johnston
Ginger Nielsen-Reed
Amanda Prigge

Design
Anna Myers

Information Management
Trevor Young

Composition and Indexing
Aptara, Inc.

Printer
Thomson-Shore, Inc.

Image Credits

Front cover photo by Carl Kurtz.

Inset cover photo is of Silk Caye in the Gladden Spit and Silk Cayes Marine Reserve (GSSCMR), Belize. Photo by Liz Wilkes.

Engraving illustrations of plants and insects by Maria Sibylla Merian (1647–1717).

Photos used at the beginning of each section:

A. *Yellow flowers, Belize.* Photo by Liz Wilkes.

B. *Queen angelfish, Flower Garden Banks National Marine Sanctuary, Gulf of Mexico.* Photo by Joyce and Frank Burek. National Oceanic & Atmospheric Administration (NOAA).

C. *Red flowers, Belize.* Photo by Liz Wilkes.

D. *Community gardens, Detroit, Michigan, USA.* Photo by Larissa Larsen.

E. *Grand Canyon National Park, Arizona, USA.* Photo by Amy Siever.

F. *Iguana in a tree, Belize.* Photo by Liz Wilkes.

G. *Sand castle on Lake Michigan beach, Frankfort, Michigan, USA.* Photo courtesy of United States Environmental Protection Agency Great Lakes National Program office.

L. *Fence line, Huaraz, Peru.* Photo by Ellie Johnston.

M. *Isla de Janitzio, former fishing village, key site for Day of the Dead, Mexico.* Photo by Karen Christensen.

N. *Bladder campions, McAllister Park, Great Barrington, Massachusetts, USA.* Photo by Amy Siever.

O. *Kepirohi Waterfall, Pohnpei, Federated States of Micronesia.* Photo by James Sellmann.

P. *Aerial mountain view, Belize.* Photo by Liz Wilkes.

continued on next page

R. *Copacabana beach from Sugarloaf, Rio de Janeiro, Brazil.* Photo by Liz Wilkes.
S. *Dandelions on Max Patch Bald, North Carolina, USA.* Photo by Ellie Johnston.
T. *Grasses, Heart Lake, Yellowstone National Park, Wyoming, USA.* Photo by Amy Siever.
U. *Earth at Night 2001. Human-made lights highlight particularly developed or populated areas of the Earth's surface, including the seaboards of the eastern United States.* Photo courtesy of NASA/Goddard Space Flight Center Scientific Visualization Studio.
V. *View of Vancouver, British Columbia, Canada.* Photo by Ernest Yanarella.
W. *Ephemeral pool, White Mountains, New Hampshire, USA.* Photo by Ellie Johnston.
Y. *Flathead valley, British Columbia, Canada.* Photo by Harvey Locke.

Contents

Map of the World   ii–iii

List of Entries   viii–x

Reader's Guide   xi–xiii

List of Contributors   xiv–xviii

Series List: The Encyclopedia of Sustainability   xix

Introduction   xx–xxv

"Agriculture, Tropical (the Americas)" through "Yellowstone to Yukon Conservation Initiative (Y2Y)"   1–338

Index   339–344

List of Entries

A

Agriculture, Tropical (the Americas)

Amazon River

Amazonia

Andes Mountains

Appalachian Mountains

Architecture

Auckland, New Zealand

Australia

B

Bogotá, Colombia

Brazil

C

Canada

Caribbean

Central America

Chesapeake Bay

Columbia River

Corporate Accountability

Curitiba, Brazil

D

Detroit, United States

E

E-Waste

Ecotourism (the Americas)

Ecovillages

Energy Efficiency

F

Fair Trade

Forest Management

G

Gender Equality

Great Lakes and Saint Lawrence River

Guatemala City

L

Labor

Las Vegas, United States

Lima, Peru

M

Mackenzie River

Marine Ecosystems Health

Marine Preserves

Mexico

Mexico City

Mining (Andes)

Mining (Australia)

Mississippi and Missouri Rivers

Mobility

Multilateral Environmental Agreements (MEAs)

Murray–Darling River Basin

N

New Orleans, United States

New York City, United States

New Zealand

North American Free Trade Agreement (NAFTA)

Northwest Passage

O

Oceania

Organization of American States (OAS)

P

Pacific Island Environmental Philosophy

Parks and Protected Areas

Perth, Australia

Phoenix, United States

Public Transportation

R

Rio de Janeiro, Brazil

Rio Earth Summit (UN Conference on Environment and Development)

Rocky Mountains

Rural Development (the Americas)

S

Sanitation

Small Island States

Social Movements (Latin America)

Southern Cone

Sydney, Australia

T

Toronto, Canada

Travel and Tourism Industry

U

United States

Urbanization

V

Vancouver, Canada

W

Water Use and Rights

Y

Yellowstone to Yukon Conservation Initiative (Y2Y)

Reader's Guide: Articles by Category

Note: most articles appear in more than one category

BUSINESS AND ECONOMICS

Corporate Accountability

Ecotourism (the Americas)

Fair Trade

Labor

Mining (Andes)

Mining (Australia)

North American Free Trade Agreement (NAFTA)

Northwest Passage

Organization of American States (OAS)

Travel and Tourism Industry

CITIES

Auckland, New Zealand

Bogotá, Colombia

Curitiba, Brazil

Detroit, United States

Guatemala City

Las Vegas, United States

Lima, Peru

Mexico City

New Orleans, United States

New York City, United States

Perth, Australia

Phoenix, United States

Rio de Janeiro, Brazil

Sydney, Australia

Toronto, Canada

Vancouver, Canada

ENVIRONMENTAL HISTORY

Amazon River

Amazonia

Andes Mountains

Appalachian Mountains

Australia

Brazil

Canada

Caribbean

Central America

XI

Chesapeake Bay

Columbia River

Great Lakes and Saint Lawrence River

Mackenzie River

Mexico

Mississippi and Missouri Rivers

Murray-Darling River Basin

New Zealand

Oceania

Pacific Island Environmental Philosophy

Rocky Mountains

Small Island States

Southern Cone

United States

INDUSTRY AND MANUFACTURING

Detroit, United States

E-Waste

Energy Efficiency

Fair Trade

Labor

Mining (Andes)

Mining (Australia)

Public Transportation

Sanitation

Travel and Tourism Industry

Urbanization

NATURAL RESOURCES

Agriculture, Tropical (the Americas)

Forest Management

Marine Ecosystems Health

Marine Preserves

Mining (Andes)

Mining (Australia)

Pacific Island Environmental Philosophy

Parks and Protected Areas

Water Use and Rights

POLITICS, LAW, AND GOVERNMENT

Multilateral Environmental Agreements (MEAs)

North American Free Trade Agreement (NAFTA)

Organization of American States (OAS)

Rio Earth Summit (UN Conference on Environment and Development)

Social Movements (Latin America)

Water Use and Rights

Yellowstone to Yukon Conservation Initiative (Y2Y)

Science, Technology, and Medicine

Architecture

E-Waste

Energy Efficiency

Public Transportation

Sanitation

Urbanization

Society and Social Welfare

Architecture

Corporate Accountability

Ecotourism (the Americas)

Ecovillages

Fair Trade

Gender Equality

Labor

Mobility

Public Transportation

Rural Development (the Americas)

Sanitation

Social Movements (Latin America)

Travel and Tourism Industry

Urbanization

List of Contributors

Abadie, Luis María
Basque Centre for Climate Change (BC3)
Energy Efficiency (co-author: Ibon Galarraga)
Property Rights

Adcock, Christina
University of British Columbia
Northwest Passage

Andreas, Robert
College of Micronesia
Pacific Island Environmental Philosophy
 (co-author: James D. Sellmann)

Beavis, Sara G.
The Australian National University
Sanitation

Beck, Abby
University of Nevada, Las Vegas
Las Vegas, United States (co-author:
 Krystyna Stave)

Becker, Marc
Truman State University
Social Movements (Latin America)

Bennett, Judith A.
University of Otago
Oceania

Brooking, Tom
University of Otago
New Zealand (co-authors: Eric Pawson,
 Hamish G. Rennie)

Buckley, Ralf
Griffith University, Australia
Ecotourism (the Americas) (co-author:
 Fernanda de Vasconcellos Pegas)

Castro, José Esteban
Newcastle University
Southern Cone

Childers, Dan
Arizona State University
Phoenix, United States

Cleary, David
The Nature Conservancy
Amazon River

Crawford, Colin
Tulane University Law School
New Orleans, United States
Rio de Janeiro, Brazil

Dameron Hager, Irene
The Ohio State University
Great Lakes and Saint Lawrence River

Dávila, Julio D.
University College London
Bogotá, Colombia

Dey, Christopher
University of Sydney
Sydney, Australia

Dougherty, Michael L.
Illinois State University
Rural Development (the Americas)
Volume Introduction

Drummond, José Augusto
Universidade de Brasília
Brazil

Eiselen, Sieg
University of South Africa
E-Waste

Evans, Sterling
University of Oklahoma
Central America
Mexico (co-author: Amanda Prigge)

Evenden, Matthew
University of British Columbia
Canada (co-author: Graeme Wynn)

Flippen, J. Brooks
Oklahoma State University
Chesapeake Bay

Gade, Daniel
University of Vermont, Emeritus
Andes Mountains

Galarraga, Ibon
Basque Centre for Climate Change (BC3)
Energy Efficiency (co-author: Luis María Abadie)

Galloway, William David
Environmental Innovators Program, Keio University
Architecture

Hall, C. Michael
University of Canterbury
Murray-Darling River Basin
Small Island States

Himley, Matthew D.
Illinois State University
Mining (Andes)

Hurley, Andrew
University of Missouri, St. Louis
Mississippi and Missouri Rivers

Irvine, Sandy
City of Sunderland College, Emeritus
Rio Earth Summit (UN Conference on Environment and Development)

Kalfagianni, Agni
VU University Amsterdam
Multilateral Environmental Agreements (MEAs)

Kearns, Robin A.
The University of Auckland
Auckland, New Zealand

Keeling, Arn
Memorial University of Newfoundland
Mackenzie River

Knox, John H.
Wake Forest University
North American Free Trade Agreement (NAFTA)

Larsen, Larissa
University of Michigan
Detroit, United States

Lewis, James G.
Forest History Society, Durham, North Carolina
United States

Ling, Christopher
Royal Roads University
Urbanization

Locke, Harvey
Strategic Advisor, Yellowstone to Yukon Conservation Initiative
Yellowstone to Yukon Conservation Initiative (Y2Y)

Lockyer, Joshua
Arkansas Tech University
Ecovillages (co-author: James R. Veteto)

MacDonald, Kate
University of Melbourne
Corporate Accountability (co-author: Shelley Marshall)

Marcotullio, Peter J.
Hunter College, City University of New York
New York City, United States

Marshall, Shelley
Monash University
Corporate Accountability (co-author: Kate MacDonald)

Mateo, Nicolás
Agronomist, San José, Costa Rica
Agriculture, Tropical (the Americas) (co-author: Rodomiro Ortiz)

Mather, Diarmid
Curtin University
Mining (Australia) (co-author: Erkan Topal)

Moberg, Mark A.
University of South Alabama
Caribbean
Fair Trade

Montelongo, Ivett
Gonzales & Asociados (Gonzales & Associates)
Mexico City

Moscoso, Victor J.
Researcher, Daedalus Strategic Advising
Guatemala City (co-author: J. Rodolfo Neutze)

Neutze, J. Rodolfo
Councilman, Guatemala City
Guatemala City (co-author: Victor J. Moscoso)

Ortiz, Rodomiro
Swedish University of Agricultural Sciences (SLU)
Agriculture, Tropical (the Americas) (co-author: Nicolás Mateo)

Pawson, Eric
University of Canterbury
New Zealand (co-authors: Tom Brooking, Hamish G. Rennie)

Pegas, Fernanda de Vasconcellos
Griffith University, Australia
Ecotourism (the Americas) (co-author: Ralf Buckley)

Prigge, Amanda
Berkshire Publishing Group
Mexico (co-author: Sterling Evans)

Reed, Maureen
University of Saskatchewan
Gender Equality

Rennie, Hamish G.
Lincoln University
New Zealand (co-authors: Tom Brooking, Eric Pawson)

Santos, Evandro C.
Jackson State University
Curitiba, Brazil
Mobility
Public Transportation

Sellmann, James D.
University of Guam
Pacific Island Environmental Philosophy (co-author: Robert Andreas)

Shaw, Brian J.
The University of Western Australia
Perth, Australia

Sherman, Benjamin H.
HEEDMD.ORG (Health Ecological & Economic Dimensions of Major Disturbances Program)
Marine Ecosystems Health

Silver, Timothy
Appalachian State University
Appalachian Mountains

Stave, Krystyna
University of Nevada, Las Vegas
Las Vegas, United States (co-author: Abby Beck)

Straka, Thomas J.
Clemson University
Forest Management

Striffler, Steve
University of New Orleans
Labor

Takahashi, Bruno
State University of New York (SUNY-ESF)
Lima, Peru

Taylor, Joseph E., III
Simon Fraser University
Columbia River

Taylor, Laura
York University
Toronto, Canada

Thrasher, Rachel Denae
Boston University
Organization of American States (OAS)

Topal, Erkan
Curtin University
Mining (Australia) (co-author: Diarmid Mather)

Tyrrell, Ian
University of New South Wales
Australia

Veteto, James R.
University of North Texas
Ecovillages (co-author: Joshua Lockyer)

Vrtis, George
Carleton College
Rocky Mountains

Wakild, Emily
Boise State University
Parks and Protected Areas

Ward, Evan R.
Brigham Young University
Travel and Tourism Industry

Whitehead, Neil
University of Wisconsin, Madison
Amazonia

Wise-West, Tiffany
University of California, Santa Cruz
Water Use and Rights

Wowk, Kateryna M.
Global Ocean Forum
Marine Preserves

Wynn, Graeme
University of British Columbia
Canada (co-author: Matthew Evenden)

Yanarella, Ernest J.
University of Kentucky
Vancouver, Canada

Berkshire Encyclopedia of Sustainability

- Volume 1: *The Spirit of Sustainability*
- Volume 2: *The Business of Sustainability*
- Volume 3: *The Law and Politics of Sustainability*
- Volume 4: *Natural Resources and Sustainability*
- Volume 5: *Ecosystem Management and Sustainability*
- Volume 6: *Measurements, Indicators, and Research Methods for Sustainability*
- Volume 7: *China, India, and East and Southeast Asia: Assessing Sustainability*
- Volume 8: *The Americas and Oceania: Assessing Sustainability*
- Volume 9: *Afro-Eurasia: Assessing Sustainability*
- Volume 10: *The Future of Sustainability*

Berkshire Publishing is committed to preserving ancient forests and natural resources. We elected to print this title on 30% postconsumer recycled paper, processed chlorine-free. As a result, we have saved:

10 Trees (40' tall and 6-8" diameter)
5 Million BTUs of Total Energy
830 Pounds of Greenhouse Gases
4,503 Gallons of Wastewater
301 Pounds of Solid Waste

Berkshire Publishing made this paper choice because our printer, Thomson-Shore, Inc., is a member of Green Press Initiative, a nonprofit program dedicated to supporting authors, publishers, and suppliers in their efforts to reduce their use of fiber obtained from endangered forests.

For more information, visit www.greenpressinitiative.org

Environmental impact estimates were made using the Environmental Defense Paper Calculator. For more information visit: www.edf.org/papercalculator

Introduction to Volume 8

This volume, titled *The Americas and Oceania: Assessing Sustainability*, is the second of three regional volumes of the *Encyclopedia of Sustainability*. (Volume 7 focuses on China, India, and East and Southeast Asia; Volume 9 deals with Africa and Eurasia.) The regional volumes have a particular focus on the assessment of sustainability in each of these regions, which allows the reader to understand the variability of sustainability at a regional scale. This volume has a range of important articles—from the general to the specific in both topical and geographic terms. This volume also represents a very interdisciplinary take on sustainability with entries written by natural scientists, social scientists, philosophers, and humanists.

From the Earth Summit to Rio+20

The United Nations promoted the concept of sustainable development beginning in the 1980s as a way to address the dual crises of environmental degradation and persistent poverty in the developing world. In 1983 the United Nations convened the World Commission on Environment and Development, commonly referred to as the Brundtland Commission. Its 1987 report, *Our Common Future*, laid out a series of global challenges including uneven growth, food insecurity, species decline, and energy and resource depletion, and put forward a model of sustainable development as the solution. The Brundtland report's definition of sustainable development, "development that meets the needs of the present without compromising the ability of future generations to meet their own needs," remains the standard definition today.

The 1992 United Nations Conference on Environment and Development in Rio de Janeiro, Brazil (commonly known as the Earth Summit), built upon the work of the Brundtland Commission, further establishing concrete mechanisms to achieve sustainable development. Additionally, the conference produced the nonbinding Rio Declaration on Environment and Development, which put forth the twenty-seven principles, known as the Rio Principles, intended to guide future sustainable development. The Earth Summit succeeded in changing the discussion around environmental issues from government regulation to market provision of sustainable growth. The Rio Declaration, in large part, has made sustainability the dominant environmental discourse of recent decades. Yet, the outcomes of the Earth Summit and the sustainable development model in general for biodiversity conservation and environmental protection have been mixed. In this volume, Sandy Irvine's article, "Rio Earth Summit," does an excellent job of documenting and discussing this mixed record.

In 2012 we are celebrating the twentieth anniversary of the Earth Summit and the Rio Principles. It is, therefore, no coincidence that these final volumes of the *Berkshire Encyclopedia of Sustainability* are being published at this precise historical moment—to commemorate the Earth Summit and celebrate Rio+20, the United Nations Conference on Sustainable Development that took place in Rio de Janeiro, Brazil, in June of 2012. This conference—like its namesake the 1992 Earth Summit—brought together representatives of governments around the world (including heads of state) along with international institutions, organizations, researchers, and members of civil society to develop strategies for advancing poverty reduction and sustainability.

The original Earth Summit was vaguer than Rio+20 in the way it conceived sustainable development. Where the original Earth Summit was focused on conceptually linking environmental stewardship and economic growth more generally, Rio+20 specifically focused on honing and reaching consensus around strategies of the so-called green economy to stem the tide of climate change. The United Nations identified seven critical axes that made up the focus of the Rio+20 meetings: jobs, energy, cities, food, water, oceans, and disasters. The model of the green economy—economic revitalization through transforming our energy, waste management, and transportation infrastructures—is a set of ideas that captures the spirit of the original Rio Principles but with much more coherence and specificity. Further, where the original conference was focused on environmental issues more broadly, Rio+20 focused more specifically on the urgent issue of global climate change. Because the emphasis of these meetings was more specific, and because climate change is such an urgent and salient issue today, there was hope that Rio+20 would produce concrete and binding resolutions that would bring us closer to the elusive goal of sustainable development. Unfortunately, though, this does not appear to have happened. Although it is too soon to judge the long-term outcome of Rio+20, many commentators seem to be of the opinion that the meeting had low expectations for any real change in global climate change governance, and that even these low expectations were not met; the consensus on the meeting's legacy appears to be that the major changes in environmental behavior that the world desperately needs must be made first by individuals and groups, rather than waiting for governments to act.

Rio de Janeiro (Rio), Brazil's second-largest and best-known city, was a fitting site for this meeting, as it was for the original Earth Summit in 1992. Rio is located in an ecologically important stretch of Atlantic rain forest, a global biodiversity hotspot. In addition, Rio is a massive, industrial city with sprawling slums (*favelas*) ringing the urban core. Being both a biodiversity hotspot and a source of a great deal of contamination and ecosystem degradation made Rio an ideal site, both symbolically and practically, for this conference. Rio represents the contradictions of development and is a place where sustainability must be worked out and put in place. Further, under Brazilian President Luiz Inácio Lula da Silva (in office from 2003–2010), cash transfer programs and social policies helping the poor succeeded in dramatically reducing inequality during a period of high economic growth (Seidman 2010). Achieving economic growth and economic justice simultaneously has been a rare outcome throughout modern world history. Therefore, Brazil serves as a symbol of growth with justice and was thus further appropriate as a site for Rio+20. In this volume, Colin Crawford's article, "Rio de Janeiro," captures many of these complex issues in great detail.

Toward *Developing Sustainability*

The Rio+20 United Nations Conference on Sustainable Development, like its predecessors, made it clear that the emphasis in the term *sustainable development* is on the noun, *development*, and that *sustainability* is relegated to adjective status. This focus has changed little since the original Rio Principles stated, "Human beings are at the center of concerns for sustainable development." Terminology used throughout the original Rio Declaration—"production, exploitation, technology, and free trade"—underscored the intent of the doctrine to address environmental ills as spillovers of advocating economic growth. The Earth Summit took the position that both poverty and wealth were leading causes of environmental degradation, and therefore framed economic growth itself as a solution to environmental ills as well as a cause. As the Rio Principles suggest, sustainable development is a model in which environmental stewardship and economic growth are understood not simply as complementary but as codependent. One cannot exist without the other.

Because sustainable development treats economic growth and environmental stewardship as correlated, it has wide appeal across the political and geographic spectrums. Further, since *sustainable* is used widely to apply to a broad range of institutions, the meaning has become so diluted as to be virtually meaningless. The win-win framing of sustainable development, as well as its definitional ambiguity, has imbued sustainability with a near-universal appeal. As the sociologists Craig Humphrey, Tammy Lewis, and Frederick Buttel (2002, 224) point out, no politician has ever come out in favor of "unsustainable development."

Regarding the definitional problem, economist Herman Daly (1996, 2003) has pointed out that it is unclear what exactly is being sustained in discussions about sustainability. Is it the economic growth that we are sustaining or is it the Earth's stocks of biophysical resources? Daly calls the former of these interpretations *the utility definition*, and the latter *the throughput definition*. The utility definition suggests that the happiness of future generations is to be non-declining. This is the common definition bequeathed by Brundtland, Rio, and subsequent conferences. Daly's favored definition, the throughput definition, takes nature as its focal point rather than human society. The throughout definition holds that resource inputs into economic production be returned to nature's resource stocks in the same proportions in which they are extracted.

Following the throughput definition, then, is human society practicing sustainability? Regrettably, we haven't been converting proportional amounts of outputs into inputs (throughput) since the late 1970s. In 1961, human society was consuming approximately half of what the Earth could provide in terms of energy and material resources, but we crossed the sustainability threshold in the late 1970s. By 2010, human civilization was consuming approximately one and a half times what the Earth could sustainably supply. We are drawing down nature's stocks 50 percent faster than they can be replenished, and this pattern is intensifying every year (Ewing et al. 2010).

In light of our wildly unsustainable current rate of resource consumption, we must move beyond the Brundtland utility definition. We must shift the focus away from the phrase *sustainable development*—where *sustainable* merely modifies the noun *development*—to a focus on *developing sustainability*, where *sustainability* itself becomes the operative noun. Many hoped that Rio+20 would have taken such a revised conceptual framework seriously, although (admittedly) this would have been difficult to accomplish at a conference designed for broad appeal and intended to achieve consensus among the world's diverse heads of state. As Sandy Irvine highlights in the article titled "Rio Earth Summit" in this volume, neither the original Earth Summit nor Rio+20 were focused on reducing consumption as a centerpiece of the agenda.

The Value of This Volume

Nowhere are questions of sustainability more acute and salient than in Latin America and Oceania—the two regions with the greatest stocks of biological capacity remaining in the world. Australia and South America, together with Canada, comprise the densest concentrations of biological capacity. Yet Australia—like the United States, Canada, and Scandinavia—has one of the largest per capita ecological footprints in the world. This means that Australia, with very high levels of biocapacity and a deep ecological footprint, is a crucial nexus for reversing global patterns of unsustainable consumption. Oceania overall, despite its tremendous biocapacity, has a per capita ecological footprint of more than double the global average, a majority of which is contributed by Australia (Ewing et al. 2010).

In Latin America, biocapacity is high relative to its levels of consumption. As a region, residents of Latin America are below the global average per capita ecological footprint, although this varies greatly by nation. Haiti has the smallest per capita footprint in the region, and Paraguay has the largest. To a large extent, the considerable biocapacity of Brazil, Argentina, Uruguay, Paraguay, and Bolivia compensate for high levels of consumption in the region, maintaining Latin America as "by far the largest regional ecological remainder in the world" (Ewing et al. 2010, 64).

Despite Latin America's high concentrations of biomass, the region faces severe environmental issues. The glaciers in Chilean and Argentine Patagonia are thinning at a dramatic rate. Glacial melt from Patagonia alone, over the past half century, has contributed approximately 10 percent to the total increase in the sea level from mountain glacier melt (Glasser, Harrison, Jansson, Anderson, and Cowley 2011).

The Amazon rain forest is giving way to monocultures of soy beans and natural gas fields at an exponential pace, diminishing biodiversity and emitting a great deal of carbon. As infrastructure in the Amazon improves, more and more of the rainforest is being cleared for soy production. Brazilian soy production exploded in the 1990s and has been increasing exponentially since. In 2006, Brazilian exports outpaced US exports for the first time in history with a record 26.1 million metric tons as compared to US exports of only 24.8 million metric tons (USDA 2006).

Further, the so-called political turn to the left in Latin America in the first decade of the twenty-first century has not meant greater environmental protections for this vulnerable region. Extractive industries—mining and petroleum—continue to expand in the region under weak regulatory institutions. Matthew D. Himley's article, "Mining (The Andes)," in this volume discusses this in detail as does Erkan Topal and Diarmid (Dinty) Mather's entry, "Mining (Australia)." For these and many other reasons, assessing sustainability in the Americas is crucial at this particular historical moment.

The economies of Oceania range from advanced industrial world leaders like Australia, to traditional smallholder agricultural economies on many small islands. Agriculture is a small part of the overall economy of the region but accounts for the majority of foreign exchange earnings. Agriculture is more important on smaller islands such as Vanuatu and Fiji. Across Oceania, the largest economic sector is service, owing to the large tourism industry.

Glacial melt from Patagonia links sustainability concerns in Latin America with Oceania in visceral ways that highlight the global dimensions of the climate crisis. Smaller islands in the Pacific Ocean are losing surface area at an alarming rate as a result of sea level rise, yielding the world's first climate-change refugees and serving as symbols of the urgency of addressing greenhouse gas emissions. Between 1979 and 2008 the average global rate of coastline erosion has increased by 300 percent. Because of their unique position as the world's first climate change refugees, the governments and civil society in many parts of Oceania are on the cutting edge of climate change activism. As of 2009, for example, Fiji derived 66 percent of its energy from renewable sources (Bohane 2009).

Not only are many islands in Oceania losing surface area, but the encroachment of the sea salinizes agricultural land, making farming more difficult, forcing residents to change their traditional diets, and creating new dependencies on foreign food aid. Further, neighboring areas must absorb these refugees, creating fiscal stress for local governments and generating social conflict. In this volume, C. Michael Hall's "Small Island States" explores this phenomenon of sea level rise in Oceania as part of a larger discussion of small island ecosystems and the particular sustainability challenges these small island nations face. In many parts of Oceania, non-Western cosmologies are still strong but are increasingly threatened by displacement and social change wrought by climate change. James D. Sellmann and Robert Andreas have an article in this volume titled "Pacific Island Environmental Philosophy," which provides a well-informed and elegant discussion of this issue, among many other topics.

In addition to their connection via sea level rise, both Latin America and Oceania are home to a variety of indigenous peoples and minority ethnic groups that bear disproportionate amounts of the global environmental burden. More frequent and more intense droughts (as well as the increased frequency of tropical cyclones and their associated devastating effects) impact subsistence farmers disproportionately, and indigenous and remote rural settlements are increasingly being asked to absorb waste-treatment facilities, extractive projects, and hydroelectric dams that transform the landscape and take a toll on traditional social relations.

About This Volume

These regional volumes of the *Berkshire Encyclopedia of Sustainability* series are additionally important because they serve to highlight the fact that human civilization's unsustainable rates of growth do not impact all regions and all countries evenly. In fact, one of the great tragedies of advanced global capitalism is that those countries with the smallest ecological footprints often face the costs of unsustainability most acutely. Parts of Latin America and Oceania, in particular, face new challenges wrought by overconsumption in the wealthy countries of Europe, North America, and parts of Asia.

These regional volumes also are important because of their emphasis on assessment. As discussed above, there is no definitional consensus for sustainability. The meaning of the term varies widely depending on the intentions of the speaker. For this reason, sustainability is difficult to assess and even harder to measure. These volumes lead us incrementally toward those elusive goals of a consensual definition of sustainability and a standard for assessment.

In this volume we have included a wide range of country-specific articles as well as many more general topical articles that span the focal regions. There are a rich series of pieces herein dealing with the environmental history of key countries and subregions within the geographic compass of this volume. We have also included a number of articles on key geologic and hydrogeologic resources within the scope of this volume. For North America, we have provided articles on the Chesapeake Bay—the world's largest estuary—the Mississippi and Missouri Rivers, the Appalachian Mountains, and the Great Lakes, among others. Regarding Latin America, we have articles on the Andes Mountains, the Southern Cone (the southern tip of the continent), and the Amazon River, among others. Regarding Oceania, articles such as that on the Murray-Darling Basin and those on the environmental histories of Australia, New Zealand, and Oceania in general, highlight key focuses of regional sustainability. This volume also offers a series of excellent articles on urban sustainability in major urban centers within the target region—from New York City and Detroit, to Guatemala City and Bogotá, to Vancouver, Sydney, and Auckland. Finally, the volume also offers a variety of more general articles on sustainability issues as wide-ranging as fair trade, rural development, gender equality, and parks and protected areas.

We have sought to strike a balance between the geographically specific and topically broad in this volume, yet no single volume encompassing such a wide swath of world geography can be entirely comprehensive. There are inevitable omissions in our coverage here, but the geographic range, the cross-cutting focuses on urban and rural issues, the transdisciplinarity, and the combination of specific and general topics provides a useful reference guide for understanding and assessing sustainability in the Americas and Oceania.

It is urgent that human civilization achieve sustainability—in throughput terms rather than utility terms—in the immediate future. Already we have begun to witness irreversible environmental degradation as a product of global climate change, and nowhere are these changes more visible and urgent than in the ecological toll on Latin America and the human toll in Oceania. Since the original Earth Summit in 1992, the considerable amount of debate, research, and advocacy undertaken has failed to resolve the tensions in human society between the drive for economic growth and material satisfaction and the need to shepherd our biophysical world. The Rio+20 conference was a landmark meeting and an opportunity to reach a binding consensus on the steps toward sustainability. This volume, and indeed the entire ten-volume *Berkshire Encyclopedia of Sustainability* series, serves as a comprehensive inventory of themes, issues, and phenomena related to understanding, assessing, and achieving these goals. Thank you for using this reference.

Michael L. DOUGHERTY
Illinois State University

Note: sources and further reading appear under the Acknowledgements section below.

Acknowledgements

Berkshire Publishing is saddened by the loss, during production of this volume, of Neil Whitehead, chair of the Anthropology Department at the University of Wisconsin–Madison. We are grateful for his contributions to this volume and other Berkshire publications. We would also like to thank the following people for their help and advice in various matters. In a project of this scope there are many to acknowledge, of course, but these people deserve our special thanks:

Daniel Gade, *University of Vermont, Emeritus.*

Ibon Galarraga, *Basque Centre for Climate Change (BC3).*

Ralf Buckley, *Griffith University.*

Terje Oestigaard, *The Nordic Africa Institute.*

Frederick R. Steiner, *The University of Texas at Austin.*

Elizabeth Allison, *California Institute of Integral Studies.*

Nazim Muradov, *Florida Solar Energy Center.*

Frank Rosillo-Calle, *Imperial College London.*

Molly Anderson, *College of the Atlantic.*

Charles E. Flower, *University of Illinois, Chicago.*

Julio Dávila, *University College London.*

Warren Neilson, *World Green Building Council.*

Irene Dameron-Hager, *The Ohio State University.*

Elizabeth Gingerich, *Valparaiso University.*

Paul Rosier, *Villanova University.*

Sue McNeil, *University of Delaware.*

Kirsten Grorud-Colvert, *Oregon State University.*

Evan Ward, *Brigham Young University.*

Jose Juan González Márquez, *Metropolitan Autonomous University.*

Gavin Mudd, *Monash University.*

Peter Pettengill, *University of Vermont.*

Edward Broughton, *Johns Hopkins University.*

Jan Thulin, *International Council for the Exploration of the Sea.*

Ralf Buckley, *Griffith University.*

Rachel Denae Thrasher, *Pardee Center for the Study of the Longer-Range Future, Boston University.*

Robert Andreas, *College of Micronesia.*

Sadeka Halim, *Dhaka University.*

Margarita del Rosario Ramirez Vargas, *Universidad del Valle de Guatemala.*

Charles L. Redman, *School of Sustainability, Arizona State University.*

Orin G. Gelderloos, *University of Michigan, Dearborn.*

Steve Striffler, *University of New Orleans.*

Evandro C. dos Santos, *Jackson State University.*

José Augusto Drummond, *Universidade de Brasília.*

Graeme Wynn, *University of British Columbia.*

David A. Sonnenfeld, *Wageningen University; State University of New York.*

Vernon Tava, *University of Auckland.*

Melissa Goodall, *Yale University Office of Sustainability.*

Ian Spellerberg, *Lincoln University.*

Nathan Nadramija, *Metis Gaia, Lima, Peru.*

Victor J. Moscoso, *Daedalus Strategic Advising.*

Tenley Conway, *University of Toronto, Mississauga.*

Paul Adam, *University of New South Wales.*

David Christian, *Macquarie University; Ewha Womans University*

Sources and Further Reading

Bohane, Ben. (2009). Climate change's first refugees. *The Diplomat.* Retrieved May 23, 2012, from http://the-diplomat.com/2009/12/26/climate-changes-first-refugees/

Ewing, Brad, et al. (2010). *The ecological footprint atlas 2010.* Oakland, CA: Global Footprint Network.

Daly, Herman E. (1996). Sustainable growth: An impossibility theorem. In Herman E. Daly and Kenneth Townsend (Eds.), *Valuing the Earth: Economics, ecology, ethics.* Cambridge, MA: The MIT Press.

Daly, Herman E. (2003). Sustainable economic development: Definitions, principles, policies. In Norman Wirzba (Ed.), *The essential agrarian reader: The future of culture, community, and the land.* Lexington: University Press of Kentucky.

Glasser, Neil F.; Harrison, Stephen; Jansson, Krister N.; Anderson, Karen; & Cowley, Andrew. (2011). Global sea-level contribution from the Patagonian Icefields since the Little Ice Age maximum. *Nature Geoscience 4*(5), 303–307.

Humphrey, Craig R.; Lewis, Tammy L.; & Buttel, Frederick H. (2002). *Environment, energy, and society: A new synthesis.* Belmont, CA: Wadsworth Thomson Learning.

Seidman, Gay. (2010). Brazil's "Pro-poor" strategies: What South Africa could learn. *Transformation: Critical Perspectives on Southern Africa, 72,* 86–103.

United States Department of Agriculture (USDA). (2006). *Brazil replaces the US as the top soybean exporter in 2005/06* (USDA Foreign Agricultural Service Circular Series FOP 2-06). Retrieved April 7, 2012, http://www.fas.usda.gov/oilseeds/circular/2006/06-02/FULL06FEB.pdf

A

Agriculture, Tropical (the Americas)

Diversity is the key word to describe agriculture in tropical America. The ever-changing climate, the varied natural and human geography, increased urbanization, and new consumption patterns give rise to different types of agriculture, which often coexist in the same territories. There are about 15 million farms and over 100,000 small- to medium-sized agriculture-related enterprises. Strong agricultural growth is closely related to export markets.

Altitude, soils, rainfall, temperature, winds, natural vegetation, and human factors such as population density, proximity of cities, infrastructure, income, and market demands determine the presence and the practice of extremely different types of agriculture in what is often referred to as the Americas tropical belt, an area between 23.5° N (the Tropic of Cancer) and 23.5° S (the Tropic of Capricorn). This area encompasses the lower half of Mexico, the Caribbean, Central America, and the top half of South America, ending at the bottom of Bolivia and Brazil. The region possesses important resources, particularly abundant freshwater and good soils, which offer comparative and competitive advantages for the future; however, some resources are also threatened and need to be better protected in order to assure long-term sustainability. A significant regional tendency is the shift, particularly in those countries where income is higher, toward a more diversified diet (more animal protein and more fruits and vegetables). This tendency has important implications for the way food production and markets will be organized and carried out in the future.

The relative importance of agriculture in tropical America, when compared to other economic activities in terms of the gross domestic product, has decreased since the 1980s. Despite this fact and according to the Inter-American Institute for Cooperation in Agriculture (IICA), if forward and backward linkages (input manufacturing, product transformation, value added, packaging, and transport) are considered, the weight of agriculture in the total economy of some countries could reach up to 30 percent (IICA 2007). There is no consensus on how to classify agriculture in tropical America; however, for practical purposes a relatively straightforward classification, with subcategories and specific characteristics, is offered below.

Market-Oriented High-Input Agriculture

High-input agriculture—involving large inputs of water, fertilizers, and pesticides—is common practice in crops and animals intended for high-end markets, including vegetables for export (asparagus, snap beans, paprika, mini-vegetables), fruits (avocado, mango, melon, pineapple, and others), nuts (macadamia), ornamentals, aquaculture (fish and crustaceans produced in fresh or brackish water), nutraceuticals (plants that provide components with health benefits), and forest products (teakwood and others). Additionally, production of coca leaves, intended for drug manufacturing or legal indigenous traditional consumption (by chewing) in the South American Andes, occupy approximately 0.1 percent of arable land.

The areas used for high-input agriculture may be large or small, but they show common characteristics: resource use (water, fertilizers, or agrochemicals) and labor are high-intensity, and production and post-harvest technologies are imported or are developed and adapted locally by companies. The main objective is to satisfy national or international markets. Risks are high (pests, diseases, transport losses, market price fluctuations), but also incomes are high when everything goes well. Finally, due to the intensity of resource use, the pollution of natural resources such as soil and water can be significant and may require constant monitoring and remediation practices.

There are several activities and fields of interest for high-input agriculture practitioners: value added, food safety, quality control, nutritive value, optimization of resource use, certification, market information, and well-managed value chains.

Traditional Commercial Agriculture

Before the substantial agricultural diversification undertaken by most tropical countries in the last decades of the twentieth century, a few commodities were the mainstays and key sources of income and employment for the rural sector, especially the growing of bananas, cacao, coffee, cotton, sugarcane, and beef production. These are still important but have lost ground to other economic activities and to the highly diverse products of market-oriented high-input agriculture.

Traditional commercial agriculture is, in general, undertaken in large areas of land and involves significant numbers of individuals and families. The term *traditional commercial* is more appropriate than *plantation* agriculture because beef production and crops such as coffee or cotton can also be found in medium-scale holdings, not just large plantations, throughout the American tropics.

Production technology in traditional commercial agriculture can be the responsibility of national research programs or, as is often the case, is conducted by private companies or producers' associations that contribute an agreed tax on production or export volumes to support their own research and development. Technological inputs can be very intensive, as in the case of bananas, or it can be more environmentally friendly, as it is for shaded coffee and cacao, which are planted with other species in succession systems. Beef production, while critically important as a source of income and nutrition, has been controversial and often associated with deforestation, essentially the clearing of forested land in order to respond to market demands for beef.

Similarly to market-oriented high-input agriculture, traditional commercial agriculture attempts to better position itself in world markets by such initiatives as brand recognition, certificates of origin, food safety, environmental safeguards, and value added.

Agro-Silvo-Pastoral Systems

Although agro-silvo-pastoral (ASP) systems have existed since the early times of agriculture, they are a relatively newly recognized agricultural category—for example, in Central American countries—that includes crops, animals, and trees in various time and space combinations. They have shown significant advantages in terms of optimizing resource use and in terms of better protecting the natural resource base. Common arrangements include trees and pastures that allow cattle to grow and develop while tree growth is enhanced by the addition of manure. Also, the combination of crops in the early stage of tree development brings mutual benefits (nitrogen fixation, water use, pest and disease tolerance) to the various species. Some ASP, particularly those based in coffee and cacao associated with shade trees, tends to be permanent, often lasting thirty to fifty years.

Other advantages of ASP include the diversification of income and the time and spatial distribution of labor throughout the year; in essence ASP tends to be less risky than single crop or single animal production systems. Additionally, ASP may be part of national efforts to enhance environmental services and initiatives to promote agritourism.

Family Agriculture

In terms of the number of people involved, family agriculture is the predominant type of exploitation found in tropical America. It continues to be so, despite the increasing importance of other economic activities and the intensity and impact of world trade. Family agriculture is not easily defined; however, it is easily recognized. Of the different categories and definitions available, a number of common elements are shared by family agriculture: all or most of the labor required in the farm is provided by the family; the farms are often located in marginal lands (on slopes, with poor soils, having inadequate infrastructure and services); the use of outside inputs is limited or nonexistent; significant amounts of the goods produced are consumed by family members; poverty and vulnerability runs high, particularly in those cases where access to markets is severely limited; and family agriculture tends to be highly diversified in terms of the number of species grown or maintained and the prevalence of a variety of domestic animals.

Family agriculture falls generally into three categories: subsistence, transitional, and consolidated. At the subsistence level, it often involves the poorest of the poor, families with insecure land tenure for whom agriculture may be only a part-time activity and a partial source of income and nutrition. Additional income, if available, is found off farm as hired labor or in nonfarm work. People involved in subsistence farming are highly vulnerable and often require assistance from government-supported programs. This type of agriculture includes the well-known practice of slash and burn, whereby a piece of forested land is burned to make room for crops, also taking advantage of higher soil fertility present after burning trees and shrubs; once the land loses its initial fertility, it is left fallow for several years before it can be used again. Slash and burn, as a production system, is not capable of providing sustenance to large populations, not productively sustainable over time, and often results in serious negative impacts to the environment.

Family agriculture at the transitional level constitutes an intermediate category where families are relatively better off in terms of availability of services and infrastructure, are able to grow most of what is consumed by family members, and may be able to sell part of the produce in local markets, securing some income to fulfill other family needs. In this category, land titles are often available, which provides security and, if needed, limited access to credit. As in the case of subsistence agriculture the level of diversification is high regarding the number of crops, trees, and animal species present in the farm. For example, in the South American Andes, potato, quinoa, cereals such as barley, maize, and wheat, and some pulses such as broad beans, lupins, and peas, are very important for food security, and any harvest surplus may provide extra income. Also, raising livestock such as llamas and alpacas and dairy production are helping to build assets for small rural businesses and provide a major source of income for farming households.

Families in the consolidated category of family agriculture normally have better or secured access to markets; may need to hire one or a few outside workers at peak times in order to fulfill planting, harvesting, or processing needs; and enjoy better infrastructure and services. These farms, while still diversified, tend to specialize in one or two products with market demand—such as grains, fruits, vegetables, beef, or coffee—that are the leading sources of family income. The use of outside inputs and improved technologies and cultivars is much more common. Income security is significantly higher in this condition, and families are less vulnerable.

Going Forward

According to the World Development Report (World Bank 2007), Latin America and the Caribbean is now an urbanized region, where agriculture accounts for a small share of national growth, even though several subsectors have sustained spectacular growth, for example soybeans in Brazil, rice in Peru, and vegetables in Guatemala. The report described key structural features of the region, in particular, the supermarket revolution (higher incomes and rapid urbanization have increased the demand for higher-value products); the stubbornly high rural poverty and inequality; and the overall weak governance of public organizations. The agenda set forth by the World Development Report for urbanized countries supports and promotes the inclusion of smallholders in the new food markets, enhancing productivity in subsistence agriculture, and following a territorial approach to promote the rural nonfarm economy and enhance skills to give access to jobs and investment opportunities.

In a 2010 paper, Bernard Hubert, senior scientist at the National Institute for Agricultural Research, and his colleagues predicted stable economic growth rates (3.5–4.5 percent per year on average) for Latin America and the Caribbean through the early twenty-first century. The region will therefore experience a significant increase in daily per capita calorie consumption and decline in child malnutrition by 2050. Meat exports will increase, whereas average grain yield growth will be slightly up (1.25 percent per year), and total cereal areas will grow by 9 percent. In 2050, however, about one hectare of land will be needed to feed one person (compared to 0.7 and 0.5 in 2000 and 1965, respectively). Hence, sustainable intensification of agro-ecosystems leading to higher productivity will be required to meet the increasing demands for food, feed, fiber, and fuel, particularly in Mesoamerica and the South American Andes, where climate change will negatively affect food output and quality due to a higher occurrence of extreme events such as droughts and floods. Diversification with high-value crops should also enhance farmers' income, generating new jobs both in rural and urban areas, improving the long-term sustainability and profitability of agro-ecosystems. Agro-biotechnology is expected to contribute sustainably to the agriculture of this region by conserving agro-biodiversity, reducing pesticide use, and improving competitiveness by lowering farming and processing costs. Innovations in agriculture should provide solutions to farmers and the agricultural industry and respond to social requirements of end users. Enabling policies, secure land rights, output markets, sharing new knowledge and technology with farmers, and public–private partnerships will be among the various factors needing attention in order to succeed in the short and long terms.

In sum, while tropical agriculture in the Americas faces important challenges, the region is well positioned not only to feed its future population but also to contribute surplus food production to the rest of the world. The astonishing diversity of environments and ecosystems found in Mesoamerica and South America, as well as the abundance of freshwater and relatively good soils point to a bright future, provided good stewardship of natural resources becomes the norm, and sufficient resources for infrastructure, services, and research and development are consistently invested now and in the future.

Nicolás MATEO
Agronomist, San José, Costa Rica

Rodomiro ORTIZ
Swedish University of Agricultural Sciences (SLU)

See also Amazonia; Brazil; Caribbean; Columbia River; Ecotourism (the Americas); Fair Trade; Forest Management; Labor; Multilateral Environmental Agreements (MEAs); North American Free Trade Agreement (NAFTA)

FURTHER READING

Hubert, Bernard; Rosegrant, Mark; van Boekel, Martinus A. J. S.; & Ortiz, Rodomiro. (2010). The future of food: Scenarios for 2050. *Crop Science, 50,* S33–S50.

Inter-American Institute for Cooperation on Agriculture (IICA). (2007). *Agriculture and the new challenges of development. Summary: The state of and outlook for agriculture and rural life in the Americas, 2007.* San José, Costa Rica: IICA.

Ortiz, Rodomiro. (2010, March 3). Biotechnology-assisted crop genetic improvement for food security and sustainable agriculture: Perspectives for the Latin American and Caribbean region. (paper, Agricultural Biotechnologies in Developing Countries: Options and opportunities in crops, forestry, livestock, fisheries and agro-industry to face the challenges of food insecurity and climate change [ABDC-10]). Guadalajara, Mexico. Retrieved October 4, 2011, from http://www.fao.org/fileadmin/user_upload/abdc/documents/iicaredbio.pdf

Pomareda, Carlos, & Hartwich, Frank. (2006). *Agricultural innovation in Latin America: Understanding the private sector role.* Washington, DC: International Food Policy Research Institute.

World Bank. (2006). *Institutional innovation in agricultural research and extension systems in Latin America and the Caribbean.* Washington, DC: The International Bank for Reconstruction and Development/The World Bank.

World Bank. (2007). *Agriculture for development. World Development Report 2008.* Washington, DC: The International Bank for Reconstruction and Development/The World Bank.

Berkshire's authors and editors welcome questions, comments, and corrections. Send your emails about the *Berkshire Encyclopedia of Sustainability* in general or this volume in particular to: sustainability.updates@berkshirepublishing.com

Amazon River

The Amazon River, the world's largest, is part of a basin that, by some standards, hosts the planet's highest levels of biodiversity. Its climate has fluctuated between wet and dry periods since the last ice age. The more recent effects of colonization have been largely negative for its ecosystems, although large areas of the basin remain intact. The future effects of climate change and human interference remain unclear.

The Amazon River basin is the largest river system in the world, draining approximately 7 million square kilometers (40 percent of the South American landmass) and accounting for almost a third of the world's freshwater. Although the Nile is marginally longer, the Amazon is the world's largest river in terms of water volume. The main stem of the river, flowing from the Andes eastward into the Atlantic, is nourished by a complex network of headwaters in the eastern Andes and very large tributary rivers to both the north and south. The Amazon's largest tributary, the 2,400-kilometer-long Rio Negro (Black River), which joins the Amazon at the city of Manaus, is itself the world's second largest river by volume (Pollard 2010, 22). The Amazon flows through eight countries (Venezuela, Colombia, Ecuador, Peru, Bolivia, Brazil, Suriname, and Guyana), but approximately 60 percent of its basin falls within Brazil, whose modern history has been the most important determinant of recent environmental trends. At its mouth, the Amazon is so wide that it surrounds the world's largest freshwater island (Marajó Island), which, at 48,000 square kilometers, is roughly the size of Switzerland.

Geology and Prehistory

In geological terms the Amazon River is young, having assumed its current form around 4 million years ago, when tectonic plate shifts in the Earth uplifted the Andes Mountains to the point where they blocked off the Amazon's original westward drainage into the Pacific Ocean, creating an enormous lake in the heart of the South American landmass. Around 2 million years ago a new channel developed, draining eastward into the Atlantic Ocean, and the Amazon River basin assumed something like its present form. The climatic fluctuations of the Quaternary Period (2 million year ago to the present), and especially of the last million years, subsequently altered Amazonian geography. During the ice ages, when temperatures and sea levels were lower, the Amazon's estuary lay 320 kilometers farther out into the Atlantic from its present position and flowed into the ocean through a network of high and narrow drainage channels. The Amazon River during the ice ages, then, was quite unlike the modern Amazon. Its current large delta, broad main channel, and meandering flow are also temporary and will undoubtedly change again during the next ice age.

Pollen cores from lake sediments, marine cores from the Amazon delta, ice cores from the Andes, and carbon isotope data from soil analyses all suggest the climate of the Amazon basin has been unstable, fluctuating between wet and dry periods since the last ice age ended around 13,000 years ago (Mayle and Beerling 2004). The Amazon's high levels of biodiversity (biological diversity as indicated by numbers of species of animals and plants), by some standards the most elevated on the planet, may have been even higher during the early Holocene Epoch (around 8,000 years ago), when mean temperatures were some 5°C lower, the Andean snowline was about 0.6 kilometers lower, and there were cold-adapted tree species at lower elevations in the western Amazon. At that time, what is now steamy jungle would have been more similar to a temperate forest (Behling 1997).

This climatic instability led scientists concerned with the origins of Amazonian biodiversity to formulate the Pleistocene refuge theory, which dominated models of Pleistocene Amazonian environmental history until the 1990s. This theory asserted that the Amazon was dry, even arid, during the portion of the Pleistocene Epoch spanning from 100,000 years ago to about 10,000 years ago, and that patches of forests were separated by the more dominant savannas, so that there existed multiple "islands," or species reservoirs, wherein allopatric (isolated) speciation occurred. When the forests expanded during wetter periods, species spread over a wider area, only to be isolated again as the forests retracted. Repetition of this process was believed to be the reason for the high biodiversity. More recently, however, the scientific consensus has been that the Pleistocene refuge theory is mistaken and that Amazonian biodiversity is better explained by a combination of high levels of natural disturbance, the presence of river barriers, and the stability of forest ecosystems over time (Brew 2005).

Early Human Colonization

The precise date of human colonization of the Amazon is unknown. The earliest reliable radiocarbon dates are from 11,500 years ago, but the earliest sites, coastal and riverine by definition, have been destroyed by changing sea levels and river courses. Most specialists accept early penetration by humans at around 15,000 years ago, or even earlier. Some genetic and linguistic evidence suggests a human presence as long as 20,000 years ago, but this is controversial. The archaeological record suggests that human impacts on Amazonian ecosystems were more intense and longer lasting than previously thought. By the late prehistoric period, there were few parts of the Amazon that had not been occupied at least sporadically, and sophisticated cultures had evolved in both floodplain and upland areas. These cultures supplemented agriculture by gathering, especially of palm products; they created large patches of fertile artificial soils throughout the basin and intensively exploited aquatic and marine ecosystems. Although population densities were lower than in Andean and Central America, total populations were probably comparable to either (Denevan 1992). Jewelry, metalwork, and other evidence from grave sites also suggest the existence of extensive trade networks linking the central Amazon to the Caribbean.

Consequently, there was considerable human impact on ecosystems even before the arrival of Europeans. Forest burning was probably sufficient to cause greater seasonality and local decrease in rainfall in the late prehistoric period, and at least one complex prehistoric culture, the Marajoara, may well have collapsed through overexploitation of its natural resource base. The arrival of Europeans and the colonial experience paradoxically reduced human impacts on the floodplain through the destruction or enslavement of its indigenous population. Much of the floodplain, which had been an intensively exploited landscape in the sixteenth century, was reclaimed by forest. Much less is known about environmental change in the upland areas during the colonial period, but it is likely that there was a similar advance in forest cover. The greater productivity brought on by metal tools was counterbalanced by the long-term decline of the indigenous population. It is one of the great ironies of Amazonian history that these young forests were construed by early European science as primeval and as uninhabited rather than as having undergone a process of depopulation.

Environmental Change in the Modern Period

Large-scale colonization has dominated the modern history of the Amazon. The first wave of settlement grew out of the rubber boom of the late nineteenth century; at this time, the new influx of people into both floodplain and upland areas raised the Amazon's population back up to late prehistoric levels. Far-reaching environmental impacts were brought about when the demands of rapidly growing urban centers drove settlers to cut back forests on a large scale for the first time through slash-and-burn agriculture and ranching. Belém and Manaus, in Brazil, and Iquitos, in Peru, had populations of more than 100,000 in 1900—the first time there were cities of such size in the Amazon basin; Belém and Manaus would have populations of well over 1 million just a century later.

The composition of the region's population also changed: many of the indigenous groups that had previously withdrawn from the floodplain to the uplands, to avoid enslavement during the colonial period, were incorporated, often violently, into the rubber economy. As their numbers declined and the flow of outsiders increased, an even greater proportion of the Amazon's population was of European descent.

After 1912, the environmental impacts of the rubber boom subsided along with the rapid collapse of the demand for Amazonian rubber, which was replaced in world markets by plantation rubber from southeastern Asia (grown from stolen Amazonian seedlings). Colonization of the Amazon stopped and people began to leave the region, with many parts of the basin reverting to secondary forest. Not until the 1960s did national societies renew their penetration of the Amazon, this time with far more dramatic environmental consequences.

Beginning in the late 1960s the construction of a network of highways linked the Amazon to the national hinterlands of the states that shared the basin and funneled millions of migrants into the region. Road building was most extensive in Brazil, where it had the most far-reaching effects, but all Amazonian countries experienced a similar cycle of frontier development. The consequences were largely disastrous. Some 12 percent of the Amazon's forest cover was removed by the end of the twentieth century, replaced largely by low-productivity ranches and subsistence smallholdings. Many of these enterprises lasted less than a generation before the declining pasture quality forced their abandonment. The destruction was concentrated mostly in the uplands; the floodplain remained relatively unaffected by colonization.

In the early twenty-first century, partly owing to improved governance (with more effective satellite monitoring of land clearance in Brazil), and partly owing to gradually increasing productivity in the beef industry and in agriculture in general, deforestation rates declined from their peak in the 1980s. Consumer concern over deforestation and greater state presence in Brazil have encouraged commercial farming and ranching to intensify rather than expand, starting a transition to production systems that make fewer demands on the land. At least in Brazil, reclaiming degraded pasture may in the future allow agricultural expansion with minimal to no land clearance. The growth of extensive and robust protected areas and indigenous reserve networks in a number of Amazonian countries is another positive development.

Outlook

It is too soon to be confident about the future. There is already strong evidence of climate change in some parts of the Amazon basin linked to forest clearance, with declines in rainfall and greater seasonality. This change will likely be permanent. The long-term effect of global warming will be to increase drought stress and make many parts of the Amazon more flammable. Local and global climate change may feed into each other, to the detriment of forest cover and biodiversity. Some climate models suggest that "forest drying," combined with more intense fires, could shift significant areas of the Amazon to savanna-type vegetation during the course of the next century or two.

Equally important is the fact that improvements in Brazil could be offset by accelerated land clearances elsewhere. Improvements in security in Peru and Colombia could see those countries invest more in road building and further development of oil and gas reserves; this development could touch off a largely uncontrolled influx of migrants along the lines of the influx into the Brazilian Amazon from the 1960s to the 1980s. Eastern Bolivia is well suited for large-scale ranching and commercial agriculture, but has nothing approaching the governance levels or monitoring systems of much of the Brazilian Amazon. Increasing urbanization and demand for clean energy in all the Amazonian countries will inevitably expand the number and scale of hydroelectric projects in the Amazon, including their potential to affect riverine environments downstream and pose challenges for relations between the countries sharing the basin. On the other hand, the basin's enormous size and the resilience of its ecosystems may buffer human influences. It is a gamble whose outcome remains to be seen.

David CLEARY
The Nature Conservancy

See also Agriculture, Tropical (the Americas); Amazonia; Andes Mountains; Bogotá, Colombia; Brazil; Caribbean; Colombia; Curitiba, Brazil; Forest Management; Labor; Lima, Peru; Mining (Andes); Rio de Janeiro, Brazil; Urbanization

FURTHER READING

Bates, Henry Walter. (1863). *The naturalist on the River Amazon.* London: John Murray.

Cleary, David. (2001). Towards an environmental history of the Amazon: From prehistory to the nineteenth century. *Latin American Research Review, 36*(2), 65–96.

Behling, Hermann. (1997). Late quaternary vegetational and climate changes in Brazil. *Review of Palaeobotany and Palynology, 99*(2), 143–156.

Brew, Alex. (2005). Why the Amazon rainforest is so rich in species. Retrieved April 12, 2012, from http://earthobservatory.nasa.gov/Newsroom/view.php?id=28907

Dean, Warren. (1987). *Brazil and the struggle for rubber.* Cambridge, UK: Cambridge University Press.

Denevan, William. (Ed.). (1992). *The native population of the Americas in 1492.* New York: Wiley.

Mayle, Francis E., & Beerling, David J. (2004). Late quaternary changes in Amazonian ecosystems and their implications for global carbon cycling. *Palaeogeography, Palaeoclimatology, Palaeoecology, 214,* 11–25.

Medina, Jose Toribio. (Ed.). (1988). *The discovery of the Amazon.* New York: Dover.

Meggers, Betty. (1996). *Amazonia: Man and culture in a counterfeit paradise* (rev. ed.). Washington, DC: Smithsonian Institution Press.

Moran, Emilio F. (1993). *Through Amazonian eyes: The human ecology of Amazonian populations.* Iowa City: Iowa University Press.

Pollard, Michael. (2010). *The Amazon: A journey along some of the world's great rivers.* London: Evans Brothers.

Roosevelt, Anna Curtenius. (1991). *Moundbuilders of the Amazon: Geophysical archaeology on Marajo Island, Brazil.* San Diego, CA: Academic Press.

Schmink, Marianne, & Wood, Charles H. (1984). *Frontier expansion in Amazonia.* Gainesville: University of Florida Press.

Amazonia

The tropical regions of South America were once thought to have been unfavorable for sustained human occupation on a large scale. That picture in the twenty-first century is rapidly changing. The archaeological recovery of ancient artifacts has revealed complex adaptations and management of Amazonian environments for at least twelve thousand years, while anthropogenic soils have proved to be far more widespread and of greater antiquity than previously thought.

As the largest tropical rain forest on the planet, Amazonia holds a unique place in both world environmental history and the imagination of South America. A vast region that extends through present-day Brazil and seven other South American nations (Colombia, Ecuador, French Guiana, Guyana, Peru, Surinam, and Venezuela), it symbolically stands for the dominance of nature over humans and as a source of still-unknown plants and animals. In fact Amazonia has been an intensively managed, human-made environment for many hundreds of years. The current perception of Amazonia as one of the last wildernesses reflects not the rain forest's pristine nature, but rather the colonial conquest's erasure of the native population through violence.

The Amazon River basin is considered, at a minimum, to comprise 96 million hectares; the Amazon River itself is the largest (by volume) in the world, nearly 160 kilometers wide at its mouth. The civilizations that arose there were functionally isolated from the rest of the world. Evidence for these past civilizations has emerged slowly, given the absence of stone building and the sheer scale of the Amazon as a context for research.

Any definition of Amazonia as an ecological, cultural, or political unit therefore proceeds more by a process of exclusion than by reference to broad uniformities in the Amazonian environment because such uniformities are illusory. The definition of Amazonia employed here reflects the conventions established in the US anthropologist Julian H. Steward's *Handbook of South American Indians* (1946–1963) and carried over into twenty-first-century anthropological usages. Amazonia comprises the whole of the Amazon River drainage system, including the right-bank tributaries of the Orinoco, to which the Amazon River has two connections: one permanent (via the Casiquiare Canal) and one seasonal (via the flooding of the upland savannas between the Rio Branco and the Essequibo River). This latter connection effectively unites the Atlantic coastal region of the Guianas with the Amazon River basin, giving rise to the designation "Guayana" or "Guianas" (in Steward's *Handbook*) for this area encircled by the Atlantic, Orinoco, and Amazon, which anthropologists consider a subregion of Amazonia. Steward (1946–1963, 3:885) also hypothesized that Guiana was a center of dispersal for the "tropical forest-complex" of agriculture of the manioc plant—a tuber whose pulp became a staple of the regional diet—although later anthropologists challenged this view.

Steward connected these conventions in the geographical criteria for the delimitation of regions to a wider classificatory scheme in the *Handbook*. In an attempt to give some analytical shape to the mass of ethnological, historical, and archaeological information that the *Handbook* brought together, anthropologists thought these contrasting geographical zones delineated cultural regions. As the Austrian-born US anthropologist Robert Lowie put it in his introductory essay to volume 3 of the *Handbook*, "The Tropical Forest complex is marked off from the higher Andean civilizations by lacking architectural and metallurgical refinements, yet outranks cultures with the hunting-gathering economy" (Lowie 1948, 1). Accordingly, experts assigned "advanced" sociocultural status to the Andean and Colombian-Venezuelan regions, fitting their status as the locale of the Incan Empire and other gold-working chiefdoms of the Circum-Caribbean and Colombia sierras, on the basis of cultural traits, such as hierarchical organization, metalworking, burial practices, and so forth. Because these cultures lay outside the agriculturally poor region of the tropical forests of Amazonia, anthropologists accepted their complex and large-scale character as a logical result of an environment conducive to the development of human civilization.

A "Counterfeit Paradise"

In the Amazonian region, archaeologists and historians rejected any evidence of advanced civilizations as the exaggeration of an unreliable historical record or as a result of extraneous origins, the result of cultural diffusion from the Colombian or Andean regions. They dismissed the evidence because they assumed the Amazon region was ecologically unfavorable to human settlement on a large scale, despite its dense vegetation and variety of fauna—it was a "counterfeit paradise" (Meggers 1992). Archaeologists took as evidence the poverty of soils away from the floodplain deposits, the small scale of contemporary indigenous societies, and the absence of major archaeological sites, except in the case of the mound builders of Marajó Island at the mouth of the Amazon. They explained this sophisticated culture as a result of a downriver migration from a more complex center in the Peruvian or Colombian Andes. They saw the apparent decline of this cultural complex, almost from the point of its establishment on Marajó, as "proof" that higher sociocultural forms could not sustain themselves in the lowland tropics where manioc agriculture was practiced. In contrast, other experts championed the idea of the Amazon basin as a cradle of migration across the rest of the continent, a view supported by a significant proportion of research as of 2011.

Whether or not Amazonia was, or is, in fact a "counterfeit paradise," therefore, remains at the heart of scholarly dispute. Because there have been insufficient archaeological data to resolve this dispute, historians and ethnographers have added their voices to the debates on native ecology and agriculture, demography, and population levels. The eventual outcomes of such research are of profound significance in answering questions not just about human–environmental relationships, but also about the place of Amazonia in the overall development of New World society and culture.

Early Settlement

Human occupation of Amazonia is much more ancient and more extensive than experts had once assumed. By about 9000 BCE two lithic (using stone tools) traditions had become widespread in Amazonia. These stone implements included arrowheads and edged cutting tools for processing animal game and grindstones for preparing maize. By 5000 BCE two more practices had emerged. First, there is evidence that by 2000 BCE—or even earlier (Whitehead, Heckenberger, and Simon 2010)—groups on the Atlantic coast were using domesticated plants, with maize use emerging in the Minas Gerais region by about 1500 BCE. Second, research as of 2011 indicates that occupation of the lower Amazon began by at least 10,000 BCE. Archaeologists have made a dramatic discovery of ceramics from around 6000 BCE in a site along the lower Amazon, making this the earliest example of pottery in the Americas.

Close examination of this early period in northeastern Amazonia, along the Guiana coastal region, illustrates the close relationship between agricultural adaptation to a complex environment and a resultant development of appropriate lithic technologies. The development of the lithic repertoire directly reflects transitions from gathering to the horticulture of certain plants, particularly the *ite* palm (*Mauritia flexuosa*) and the *mora* tree (*Mora excelsa*), as well as other utilitarian species. Although anthropologists have theorized that these subsistence techniques are ancestral to the emergence of tropical forest horticulture in the region, the developmental analogies are probably stronger with the *sambaqui* (shell-mound) peoples of coastal Brazil than with the occupants of the tropical forests because their horticultural and foraging repertoires are quite distinct. This development suggests that progressive adaptation to the complexities of the Amazonian environment was a process repeated across the whole region.

Various ancient societies also practiced relatively intensive forms of agriculture, evidenced by widespread landscape modification throughout Amazonia. In fact, some experts have argued that the landscape of Amazonia, as it is seen today and as it has been for the last 350 years or so, is the historical product of a return to a semiwilderness consequent on the colonial depopulation of the native inhabitants. Moreover, the current evidence for the existence of prehistoric roads and causeways in both the *llanos* (prairies) of Bolivia, Colombia, and Venezuela and in the heart of Amazonia itself indicates that these landscape modifications were related to the presence of large and complex societies.

Recently investigated systems of extensive ridged fields and agricultural mounds along the Atlantic coast of the Guianas, for example, underline how limited knowledge of the "tropical forest" region really is. The presence of complex agricultural techniques to deal with the low-lying, swampy conditions in this region, as well as the use of intensive farming practices from at least 700 CE, shows how people made complex adaptations to the variety of Amazonian environments. Archaeological evidence thus fits well with the historical sources that report both significant population and a complex agricultural repertoire among the indigenous groups.

Soil Holds Clues

Apart from this physical manipulation of the landscape, research interest in ancient Amazonia has focused on anthropic or anthropogenic soils (that is, soils whose formation is directly related to human activity)—or at least on trying to assess what kind of soils in Amazonia human activities may have generated, how widespread the soils actually are, and to what extent such soils were intentionally fomented. The banks of the main channel of the Amazon as well as of many of its tributaries are replete with black earth sites, illustrating both the continuity and antiquity of human presence. The use of such sites for agricultural purposes thus illustrates both sophisticated knowledge of soil properties and systems of agricultural management that were stable over many generations.

These kinds of soils, particularly *terra preta* (black earth), which is black anthropogenic soil with enhanced fertility because of high levels of soil organic matter and nutrients, are common throughout Amazonia. Humans created the valuable soil either through direct agricultural fertilization or as a consequence of intense settlement—human waste materials enrich the soil with nitrogen. The historical evidence shows that there was no one-to-one relationship between the presence of agriculturally favorable soils and the past existence of complex polity or an extensive cultural repertoire. Scientists' investigation of anthropogenic soils seems to provide evidence that human occupation of an area was not dependent on conducive environmental conditions. Archaeological investigation of the many well-documented *terra preta* deposits along the main Amazon channel, as well as along its tributaries, is still in the early stages, however.

Agriculture and diet anthropologists have studied the addition of maize to modes of subsistence that previously centered on palms and manioc, as well as the systematic exploitation of other food plants. Interest in the advent of maize cultivation results from seeing maize use as a token of social and cultural complexity, however, given its easy storage and high nutritional value. Evidence of its use in Amazonia, where the use of manioc varieties predominates in the historic and ethnographic reports of aboriginal horticulture, is especially significant. This apparent predominance of manioc agriculture in ethnographic and historical materials about Amazonia, however, may result from the way in which manioc use increased over the last five hundred years as a result of indigenous access to steel tools through trade with the Europeans. Steel axes would have permitted much greater clearance of forest for the cultivation of manioc, a root that must be dug from the earth, than stone axes would have. As a result, and also stimulated by European trading interest in manioc flour, there were distinct advantages for domestic groups to opt out of the systems of intensive agricultural production that sustain large civilizations. Consequently the dietary use of manioc, as opposed to maize, may well have increased substantially during the historic period.

Basic Questions Remain

The nature of these transformations over the last five hundred years is critical to an understanding of ancient Amazonia, but the sheer size of the region and the lack of sociocultural continuity between past and present society and culture, as a result of colonial depopulation, make comprehensive study of the environmental history of the region especially challenging. Many of the basic questions of Amazonian prehistory remain open, not least of which are those of the scale and longevity of human occupation. It seems likely that ethnography and history, as much as archaeology, will continue to play a role in the discussion of human adaptations to the Amazonian environment. Work in progress that emphasizes ethnoarchaeological techniques, systematic survey, and interpretation of historical records, as well as the deployment of new technical resources, such as geophysical survey, seems well positioned to do justice to the complexity of Amazonian antiquity.

As researchers deploy these techniques and the database grows, it already seems likely that they will cast issues of human environmental adaptation in a different framework to that which produced the idea of Amazonia as some kind of false paradise whose apparent botanical bounty belied the actual poverty of its soils for human usages. Already much of the work there suggests that Amazonia is too complex an environment, and its human adaptations too various, to be adequately characterized as either utterly unfavorable or uniformly conducive to human settlement. The very uncertainties about the definition of an Amazonian region reflect the fact that the conceptualization of Amazonia as a homogeneous entity is in itself flawed. As actual investigation of human adaptations through time replaces debates about models of the Amazonian environment, researchers will be in a far better position to appreciate the variety and complexity of human adaptation to both the challenges and the potential of the Amazon basin proper, as well as of the surrounding regions.

Neil L. WHITEHEAD
University of Wisconsin, Madison

See also Agriculture, Tropical (the Americas); Amazon River; Brazil; Bogotá, Colombia; Caribbean; Central America; Curitiba, Brazil; Ecotourism (the Americas); Fair Trade; Forest Management; Guatemala City; Parks and Protected Areas; Rio de Janeiro, Brazil; Rio Earth Summit (UN Conference on Environment and Development); Social Movements (Latin America); Southern Cone; Urbanization

FURTHER READING

Acuña, Cristobal de. (1859). A new discovery of the great river of the Amazons. In C. R. Markham (Ed.), *Expeditions into the valley of the Amazons* (pp. 44–142). London: Hakluyt Society.

Denevan, William. (2002). *Cultivated landscapes of native Amazonia and the Andes*. New York: Oxford University Press.

Lowie, Robert. (1948). The tropical forests: An introduction. In Julian H. Steward (Ed.), *Handbook of South American Indians: Vol. 3. The tropical forest tribes* (pp. 1–57). Washington, DC: US Government Printing Office.

Meggers, Betty. (1992). Amazonia: Real or counterfeit paradise? *The Review of Archaeology, 13*(2), 25–40.

Posey, Darrell, & Balée, William. (Eds.). (1989). *Resource management in Amazonia: Indigenous and folk strategies* (*Advances in economic botany: Vol. 7*). New York: New York Botanical Garden.

Roosevelt, Anna. C. (1980). *Parmana: Prehistoric maize and manioc subsistence along the Amazon and Orinoco*. New York: Academic Press.

Roosevelt, Anna. C. (1991). *Moundbuilders of the Amazon: Geophysical archaeology on Marajó Island, Brazil*. New York: Academic Press.

Steward, Julian. H. (Ed.). (1946–1963). *Handbook of South American Indians* (Vols. 1–6). Washington, DC: US Government Printing Office.

Whitehead, Neil. L. (1994). The ancient Amerindian polities of the lower Orinoco, Amazon and Guayana coast: A preliminary analysis of their passage from antiquity to extinction. In Anna C. Roosevelt (Ed.), *Amazonian Indians from prehistory to the present: Anthropological perspectives* (pp. 33–54). Tucson: University of Arizona Press.

Whitehead, Neil L.; Heckenberger, Michael J.; & Simon, George. (2010). Materializing the past among the Lokono (Arawak) of the Berbice River, Guyana. *Antopológica, 11*(4), 87–127.

Share the *Encyclopedia of Sustainability*: Teachers are welcome to make up to ten (10) copies of no more than two (2) articles for distribution in a single course or program. For further permissions, please visit www.copyright.com or contact: info@berkshirepublishing.com

Andes Mountains

A strong geographical personality characterizes the Andes as manifested in the adaptations of rural peoples to a vertical landscape. Substantial ecological deterioration has occurred in the region, and the key sustainability issue of the twenty-first century is how peasant land use will be transformed. Trends suggest that some aspects of environmental well-being and quality of life have improved but that water problems loom ahead.

The environmental history of the Andes has unfolded in the context of spectacular natural diversity and notable cultural achievement. The Andes form a complex of mountain ranges in western South America that extends 7,000 kilometers from Venezuela to Tierra del Fuego. Because the Andes, the world's longest mountain system, stretch from the equator to within nine degrees of the Antarctic Circle, and rise more than 6,000 meters in some places, there is a wide range of climate and vegetation types, from humid rain forest in the north to arid desert farther south. Soils also vary a great deal, from fertile alluvium in many valleys to thin soils on steep slopes. Vegetation removal makes the latter susceptible to erosion. Glaciers occur in different places throughout the Andes, but it is in the sparsely populated far south, most notably in Argentina's Los Glaciares National Park, in Patagonia, where glaciers cover 2,600 square kilometers of land. Few people have lived in the southern Andes, where conditions make it difficult to sustain human life. In contrast, the portion of the Andean Highlands that lies within tropical latitudes has fertile valleys and sharply telescoped vertical habitats that have favored agricultural diversification over short distances.

One distinctive feature of the Andes are patches of *Polylepis* forest (a genus of trees in the rose family), which are located at altitudes up to 4,500 meters from Venezuela to northern Chile and Argentina, with a large concentration in Bolivia. The Andean people use the Polylepis trees primarily as firewood. The remaining fragments of forest are vulnerable to the increasing expansion of roads, which allows woodcutting to take place on a large scale and trucks to haul the wood away.

History

Pre-Columbian Andean peoples domesticated a wide range of plants, of which the potato is the best known, permitting a sedentary form of life that goes back to at least 4000 BCE. The consolidation of local societies into larger polities started around 1000 BCE. At a much later time, the Inca Empire (c. 1100–1532 CE) absorbed people of different cultures into an intricately organized state apparatus based on sustainable farming and the raising of llamas and alpacas. At different periods in the pre-Columbian era, people constructed earthworks that dramatically reshaped certain landscapes. Stone bench terraces on steep slopes enabled crops to be irrigated with little loss of soil to erosion. Elsewhere, systems of artificial ridges made it possible to grow crops in swampy terrain. The Spanish conquered the Inca Empire in 1532 and introduced most of the inventory of European crops, animals, technology, religion, and political organization. Native people of the Andes have long resisted wholesale absorption into Spanish culture. To this day, the cultures of the highland peasantry reflect a mixed heritage of indigenous and introduced folkways.

The Andes manifest both continuity and discontinuity from their pre-Columbian past. Highland deforestation is the most visible human impact, but the bulk of the tree cover had been removed already during the Inca period. Colonizing Spaniards stripped most remaining woodland to meet the increased demand for firewood and timber and to accommodate the grazing needs of cattle, sheep, goats, and equines. The fortuitous introduction of eucalyptus after 1860 provided an alternative wood supply, although plantations of exotic species have created vulnerable monocultures of one kind of tree that have taken massive quantities of water out of the soil.

Sustainability Issues

The contemporary Andean landscape must be seen not as a simple response to biophysical factors but as a product of human interventions in the past. Desertification, especially severe in Bolivia, reflects overgrazing, not climatic change. Soil erosion and water pollution are not recent but are of growing severity. Unrestrained cultivation of steep slopes and the negative effects of mining and roads on streams and forests continue to take their toll on land and water quality. An environmental consciousness emerged in the latter part of the twentieth century that was largely inspired by the movement in industrialized countries. Local and international advocacy groups formulated conservation agendas, promulgated correctives to counter past abuses, passed laws, and established natural areas to preserve what is left of a greatly diminished flora and fauna.

The most important sustainability issue in the Andes is striking a balance between population growth and resource use. This issue requires an understanding of the peasant way of life that has dominated rural livelihoods and how this way of life has been changing over the past half century. Known in the highlands as *campesinos*, peasants are, by definition, agriculturalists who raise food for both themselves and urban dwellers. In the Central Andean core of Ecuador, Peru, and Bolivia, peasants form the largest concentration of indigenous people in the Western Hemisphere. They maintain traditional lifestyles, including their own Indian languages, of which Quechua is the most widely spoken. With cultural roots in the pre-Columbian era, these rural folk have nevertheless adopted some Spanish beliefs, customs, and practices. Isolation, poverty, and conservativeness have combined to make much of the Andean cultural landscape a living museum of the past. They have been cautious in accepting innovations, preferring traditional technologies and methods that they know to work.

Peasant families in the Central Andes have small plots on which many crops are grown as a way of hedging their bets on a satisfactory harvest. If frost, drought, or disease destroys one crop, a different crop will yield. Their choice of crops depends on climatic differences, which correspond to altitude above sea level. In conjunction with food crops, farmers also raise domesticated animals, most notably sheep, llamas, cattle, swine, chickens, and guinea pigs. Pastoral activities become more important in areas above 3,500 meters elevation. High inputs of manual labor characterize the typical farm unit in which all family members, including small children, participate. When peasants sell their products to wholesalers in the city, they often have to accept prices so low they can scarcely make a profit. Perceiving that they are being exploited by powerful elites, Andean peasants have developed a worldview in which they see themselves, in part, as victims.

Most Andean country people no longer labor as peons on landed estates as they did for four hundred years. Agrarian reform programs instituted in Bolivia in the 1950s and in Peru in the 1970s broke up the large estates that held most of the good land and distributed that land to workers. Moreover, several kinds of migration have relieved the demand for access to cultivable land. Most of the explosive growth in Quito, Cuenca, and Guayaquil (Ecuador); Lima, Huancayo, Cusco, and Arequipa (Peru); and La Paz, Cochabamba, and Santa Cruz (Bolivia) is the result of younger people leaving the countryside to move to the city. Other migration has involved highlanders of these three countries carving out farms in the jungle. Finally, people of peasant background have migrated at an increasing rate to other countries, notably Chile, Argentina, Spain, and the United States, to find work. Employment opportunities in other economic sectors such as mining and tourism create another safety valve against land hunger. The manufacture of handicrafts, closely tied to tourist demand, supports many families. Weaving, in particular, is a traditional source of alternative income for Andean farmers.

Peasant farming in the Andes no longer has an abundant labor supply, and that reality has begun to transform old assumptions and practices. Among the rural transformations that Andeanist scholars have witnessed over the past half century are a cash economy supplanting barter, a decline in birthrates and infant mortality, and incursions of new religious forms competing with the longstanding Catholic influence.

As individualistic values come to the fore, the old assumptions of communal organization that once regulated much daily life wither away. At the same time, rural folk are increasingly adept at harmonizing efforts to voice their concerns to local, regional, and national governments. Nongovernmental organizations have also taken up their causes; indeed these groups, funded largely from foreign sources, have often been the first to articulate community needs. No longer passive, rural Andean people regularly demonstrate and strike to gain road access, electricity, schools, and health clinics. Meanwhile, national governments are in a better financial position to respond to these demands than was once the case.

Outlook

Although conditions of rural life have improved, by first world standards the Andean Highlands are nevertheless a region of poverty. Narrowing the economic gap is a function not just of rising aspirations, but of acculturation toward the Western model. Through knowledge gained about the world outside the local community, those who stay have developed expectations of better health and greater material prosperity. Most trends now point to a scenario for the Andean core of a more productive and less ecologically vulnerable land use. In the decades ahead, most marginal cropland will be abandoned, especially fields on steep slopes cultivated in a long-fallow system. Fertile alluvial soils on the valley floors will undergo intensification through regular application of fertilizers. Water issues, however, will become increasingly prominent as forecasted changes in the global climate will lead to the melting of glaciers that have traditionally fed the irrigation canals. Farms will increase in size as tiny properties are consolidated. At some point, the economy of scale will justify the acquisition of machines to replace some kinds of manual labor. Like twentieth-century Europe, the Andes will experience in the twenty-first century the transition away from a peasantry with its own set of assumptions. One of the casualties will be the decline or elimination of indigenous lifestyles that have long made the Andes a unique cultural realm. The search for sustainability in these mountains of South America will involve trade-offs whose outcomes are freighted with ambiguities.

Daniel W. GADE
University of Vermont, Emeritus

See also Agriculture, Tropical (the Americas); Appalachian Mountains; Bogotá, Colombia; Brazil; Forest Management; Lima, Peru; Mining (Andes); Rocky Mountains; Southern Cone

Further Reading

Gade, Daniel W. (1999). *Nature and culture in the Andes.* Madison: University of Wisconsin Press.

Mayer, Enrique. (2001). *The articulated peasant: Household economies in the Andes.* Boulder, CO: Westview Press.

Mörner, Magnus. (1985). *The Andean past: Land, societies, and conflicts.* New York: Columbia University Press.

Berkshire's authors and editors welcome questions, comments, and corrections. Send your emails about the *Berkshire Encyclopedia of Sustainability* in general or this volume in particular to: sustainability.updates@berkshirepublishing.com

Appalachian Mountains

The Appalachian Mountains span more than 3,000 kilometers of eastern North America, from Newfoundland in Canada to Alabama in the southern United States. They harbor a rich cultural heritage and an abundance of natural resources. The region has been dramatically changed by coal mining and lumbering but continues to provide home to a wide range of biologically diverse ecosystems and vast tracts of protected forests.

The Appalachian Mountains stretch from the coasts of Newfoundland and Labrador in Canada to northern Alabama in the United States, spanning more than 3,000 kilometers and fifteen degrees of latitude (Orme 2002, 291). The basic contours of the range developed 500 million years ago, giving the Appalachians distinction as the continent's oldest mountains. Once higher than the Himalaya in Asia, the mountains have been worn down by hundreds of millions of years of erosion into the mostly rounded (with some exceptions) mountains that they are today (Skelton 2011). With rainfall that can exceed 180 centimeters per year in places, the Appalachians are home to the most extensive and diverse forests in eastern North America. To the north and west, the mountains touch the Saint Lawrence Lowlands of the Great Lakes region. To the south and east, they extend down to the Fall Line at the Coastal Plain. The highest point in the range is Mount Mitchell in North Carolina, which stands at 2,037 meters. In April of 1934, wind speeds of 372 kilometers per hour were measured at the top of Mount Washington in New Hampshire, which remains the highest wind speed ever recorded on Earth (Mount Washington Observatory 2012). The range includes diverse climates, thus offering varied and plentiful vegetation and a variety of physical landscapes (Orme 2002, 302–303).

History

Humans probably migrated into the Appalachians eight thousand years ago. The region's indigenous populations included the maritime Beothuk people of Newfoundland, the hunting and gathering Micmacs of northern New England, and the farming people of the eastern woodlands, notably the Iroquois confederacy in upstate New York and the Cherokees of the southern highlands. Since the earliest human settlement, people have altered the mountain environment in subtle but important ways. They used fire to clear agricultural fields and open the woods for travel and other purposes.

Hernando de Soto, in 1540 in what is now North Carolina, was the first European to traverse the Appalachians. In the first decades of the nineteenth century, rampant land speculation, the discovery of gold in Georgia, and the tragic government removal of southern indigenous populations led to the rapid influx of European settlers. These settlers sold surplus crops, cattle, and hogs to merchants in the emerging cities along the Atlantic coast. Such development led to increased erosion, and free-roaming livestock damaged Appalachian hardwood forests.

The most extensive and destructive alterations in the Appalachian environment have occurred since the mid-nineteenth century. By 1910 a growing network of railroads and the burgeoning steel industry created an insatiable demand for coal; steel companies in Pennsylvania and Ohio—predominantly US Steel, owned in part by Andrew Carnegie, J. P. Morgan, and Charles M. Schwab—developed vast mining operations in Virginia, West Virginia, and Kentucky along the Allegheny and Cumberland plateaus. The coal industry also took a toll on the region's forests as nearby trees were cut for mine timber and construction.

The lumber industry followed the railroads into the mountain forests. By the 1890s loggers had largely depleted the forests of Maine, New York, and Pennsylvania, which forced them to move south. Between 1914 and 1918, lumber companies removed more timber from the southern Appalachians than in all the years before 1900. Rapid deforestation from lumbering and mining greatly increased erosion and flooding. Cutover regions became susceptible to devastating forest fires. Beginning in 1904, an exotic fungus introduced from Asia spread throughout the Appalachians, killing American chestnut trees by the thousands. The blight and salvage logging by lumber companies eventually reduced the once-majestic tree to little more than a forest shrub.

In the second half of the twentieth century and into the twenty-first, deforestation and the abandoning of farmland has caused invasive species to colonize much of eastern North America, including the Appalachian region. Japanese honeysuckle and privet are just two such invasive species. Exotic trees such as Norway spruce, weeping willow, and Lombardy poplar have also begun to appear (Orme 2002, 298).

The mining and logging industries also created within the Appalachian Mountains a colonial economy that supplied raw materials to urban centers and made local people dependent on urban capital. This economic dependency on the demand for natural resources outside of Appalachia has caused severe poverty in some areas when that demand goes away. Efforts are under way throughout Appalachia to diversify economies and localize them. Parts of West Virginia have been successful in attracting outdoor recreational tourism, while areas of eastern Kentucky and southern West Virginia are still heavily dependent on the coal industry and are very economically depressed.

Conservation Efforts

In 1898 Gifford Pinchot, the first chief of the United States Forest Service, and Carl Alwin Schenck, a forestry educator, established a forestry school on a 73,000-hectare forested tract near Asheville, North Carolina, and the southern Appalachians became the birthplace of modern US forestry. The nationwide growth of the conservation movement led to the setting aside of national forests throughout the range, and by 1940 the US Forest Service became the single largest landowner in southern Appalachia.

The entire length of the Appalachian range is threaded by the Appalachian Trail, a 3,500-kilometer trail conceived by New Englander Benton MacKaye in 1921 and completed in 1937. The trail, which stretches from Mount Katahdin in Maine to Springer Mountain in Georgia, remains a popular destination for residents and visitors alike. MacKaye conceived of the trail (which he proposed in the *Journal of the American Institute of Architects*) as a "new approach to the problem of living" (King 2000). The National Park Service, which administers the trail, estimates that 4 million people a year enjoy the trail (National Park Service 2012). The trail has been extended to Crow Head in Newfoundland, Canada, where it is called the International Appalachian Trail/Sentier International des Appalaches (IAT/SIA). The extension adds a further 2,900 kilometers to the trail (Browning 2012.)

Great Smoky Mountains National Park, the Blue Ridge Parkway, and a host of state parks prospered with the post–World War II boom in families taking vacations by automobile. During the last half of the twentieth century, some of Appalachia began a pronounced shift from agriculture and extractive industries toward an economy based on tourism. The change has brought new environmental problems. Air pollution and acid rain resulting from automobile traffic and emissions from coal-fired power plants in places like the Ohio Valley and Tennessee Valley currently threaten the remaining high-elevation forests. Ozone levels in the Great Smoky Mountains routinely exceed those in the nation's largest cities. State and federal governments have thus far been slow to respond, and the Appalachian forests remain an environment at risk.

Demands on Natural Resources and the Future

In the late-twentieth century, due to continued demand for coal, the practice of mountaintop removal coal mining began. This process removes mountain summits and ridges to get at seams of coal that were too thin or otherwise uneconomical to mine. Mountain summits are detonated with high-powered explosives and then dumped in nearby valleys, ruining water sources and compromising entire ecosystems. In 2009 the US geographer Ross Geredien (2009, 2) estimated that "at least 500 mountain ridges in the region have been partially or completely leveled." Efforts are under way to ban the practice of mountaintop removal, but they face resistance from the coal industry.

Out of the diverse indigenous communities that originally settled in Appalachia plus the European settlers who arrived later, a rich culture has developed in this mountain region. At times exploited and forgotten, local peoples and the emerging tourism economy are recognizing this unique regional culture, thus bringing renewed strength to communities in Appalachia and movements toward sustainability. Old time and bluegrass music are becoming increasingly popular and bringing communities together where they had become fractured. Local cuisine is also on the rise as farmers find markets for their heirloom crops in local tailgate markets and restaurants. As destructive resource extraction continues in order to supply cities along the East Coast, areas of Appalachia must continue to address environmental issues if they are to sustain the variety and richness of their ecosystems and cultural and natural resources. There are signs—from the arts and craft community of Berea, Kentucky, that is training the next generation of local craftspeople, to the burgeoning solar energy companies of Asheville, North Carolina—that Appalachia is rising to the challenges of the twenty-first century.

Timothy SILVER
Appalachian State University

See also Andes Mountains; New York City, United States; Ecotourism (the Americas); Forest Management; Great Lakes and Saint Lawrence River; Parks and Protected Areas; Rocky Mountains; Travel and Tourism Industry

This article was adapted by the editors from Timothy Silver's article "Appalachian Mountains" in Shepard Krech III, J. R. McNeill, and Carolyn Merchant (Eds.), *Encyclopedia of World Environmental History*, pp. 60–61. Great Barrington, MA: Berkshire Publishing (2003).

FURTHER READING

Brooks, Maurice (1965). *The Appalachians*. Boston: Houghton Mifflin.

Browning, L. M. (2012). L. M. Browning interviews Don Hudson of the International Appalachian Trail. Retrieved February 22, 2012, from http://hiraethpress.com/l-m-browning-interviews-don-hudson-of-the-international-appalachian-trail/

Geredien, Ross. (2009). Post–mountaintop removal reclamation of mountain summits for economic development in Appalachia. Natural Resources Defense Council. Retrieved February 24, 2012, from http://www.ilovemountains.org/reclamation-fail/mining-reclamation-2010/MTR_Economic_Reclamation_Report_for_NRDC_V7.pdf

King, Brian B. (2000). Trail years: A history of the Appalachian Trail Conference. Special 75th anniversary issue of *Appalachian Trailway News*. Retrieved February 24, 2012, from http://www.appalachiantrail.org/docs/atj/00-trailyears.pdf

Maine Department of Environmental Protection. (2011). Frequently asked questions—Air quality. Retrieved January 7, 2012, from http://www.maine.gov/dep/air/faqs.htm

Mount Washington Observatory. (2012). About the Mount Washington Observatory. Retrieved February 24, 2012, from http://www.mountwashington.org/about/

National Park Service. (2012) Appalachian National Scenic Trail. Retrieved February 24, 2012, from http://www.nps.gov/appa/index.htm

Orme, Antony R. (Ed.). (2002). *The physical geography of North America*. Oxford, UK: Oxford University Press.

Pickering, John; Keys, Roland; Meier, Albert; Andrew, Susan; & Yatskievych, Kay. (2002). The Appalachians. In P. R. Gil et al. (Eds.), *Wilderness: Earth's last wild places*. Chicago: University of Chicago Press. Draft version retrieved January 7, 2012, from http://www.discoverlife.org/co/

Science Daily. (2011, November 16). Acid pollution in rain decreased with emissions, long-term study shows, *Science Daily*. Retrieved January 7, 2012, from http://www.sciencedaily.com/releases/2011/11/111116162244.htm

Silver, Timothy. (2003). *Mount Mitchell and the Black Mountains: An environmental history of the highest peaks in eastern America*. Chapel Hill: University of North Carolina Press.

Skelton, Rose. (2011, January 23). On top of Old Smokey: Across the Appalachians with a banjo. *The Observer*. Retrieved January 5, 2012, from http://www.guardian.co.uk/travel/2011/jan/23/music-appalachian-mountains-kentucky-america?INTCMP=SRCH

United States Environmental Protection Agency (EPA). (2010). EPA issues comprehensive guidance to protect Appalachian communities from harmful environmental impacts of mountaintop mining. Retrieved January 5, 2012, from http://yosemite.epa.gov/opa/admpress.nsf/e77fdd4f5afd88a3852576b3005a604f/4145c96189a17239852576f8005867bd!OpenDocument

Weidensaul, Scott. (1994). *Mountains of the heart: A natural history of the Appalachians*. Golden, CO: Fulcrum Publishing.

Wheeler, Quentin. (2010, August 28). New to nature no 18: Urspelerpes brucei. *The Observer*. Retrieved June 25, 2012, from http://www.guardian.co.uk/science/2010/aug/29/new-to-nature-lungless-salamander

Willcox, Kathleen. (2009, March 20). Eating Appalachia: The pursuit of fried squirrel. *Eat Me Daily*. Retrieved January 7, 2012, from http://www.eatmedaily.com/2009/03/eating-appalachia-the-pursuit-of-fried-squirrel/

Williams, J. A. (2002). *Appalachia: A history*. Chapel Hill: University of North Carolina Press.

Share the *Encyclopedia of Sustainability*: Teachers are welcome to make up to ten (10) copies of no more than two (2) articles for distribution in a single course or program. For further permissions, please visit www.copyright.com or contact: info@berkshirepublishing.com

Architecture

In the Americas and Oceania, architecture is significant because the construction it dictates is one of the largest consumers of raw resources, energy, and land. Architecture is also significant for the types of social patterns and behavior it allows and encourages. Once focused almost exclusively on resource conservation, the scope of sustainable architecture is now expanded to include adaptation and the creation of resilient communities.

Architecture is broadly defined as the purposeful design and construction of the built environment. In terms of sustainability, it is intricately linked with the larger concept of sustainable development, and as such it includes not only buildings but also landscapes and small-scale urban environments.

The raw materials, energy, and financial capital needed to construct and maintain the built world are enormous. Nearly half of all carbon dioxide emissions in the United States, for example, can be traced to the energy consumed by buildings, linking them directly to one of the chief causes of climate change (Mazria and Kershner 2008). This is true of almost every industrialized nation, and as a result one of the core ambitions of sustainable architecture is to reduce energy consumption in order to minimize greenhouse gas emissions.

Because it is ultimately a product built for use by families, businesses, and communities, sustainable architecture is equally defined by its capacity to affect social and economic issues. The manner in which a building is constructed can impact employment and even the local knowledge base as skills are taught and transferred to users and residents. Similarly, when a building is completed, the way it fits into its surroundings can affect the kinds of social activities that take place. If undertaken along with other social-oriented projects, such as transportation infrastructure, education, and economic development, its impact can be amplified significantly.

It is difficult to generalize across regions as large as the Americas and Oceania, but broadly speaking, the role of sustainability in architecture at that scale seems to fall along economic lines. Wealthier countries tend to be focused on technological advances designed to reduce energy and resource use, while less wealthy nations use architecture more progressively to improve social equity, access to education, employment, and social infrastructure. More recently the use of architecture to build "resiliency" (an ability to bounce back from environmental and other disasters) in communities can be found in both developed and developing nations in the Americas and in Oceania. This new direction is in response to the increasing frequency of natural disasters in all regions but also reflects the emerging emphasis on adaptation policies in the face of climate change (UNFCCC 2007).

Sustainable architecture was once viewed almost entirely through the lens of conservation and mitigation. The social impact of design and the ability to transform behavior at the scale of communities is now more openly recognized, however. This shift suggests a new direction in the way that sustainable architecture will be used, judged, and measured.

From Mitigation to Adaptation

The exhaustion of nonrenewable resources such as oil is a major motivation for the development of more energy-efficient infrastructure, compatible with alternative sources of energy and focusing on conservation.

Origins

The role of sustainability in architecture has expanded continuously since its inception in the 1970s, loosely paralleling the changing ideals of sustainable development. Its origin is found in the oil shock of the 1970s, a global energy crisis orchestrated for political and economic reasons by the Organization of the Petroleum Exporting Countries (OPEC). For many, the oil crisis seemed to confirm worries already stirred by the Club of Rome in their controversial 1972 publication, *The Limits to Growth*, which warned that a culture of consumption could not be sustained indefinitely (Bardi 2011). In energy dependent nations in particular, such as the United States, Brazil, and Australia, the political need to quickly reduce energy consumption led to a number of radical transformations of energy use at the national level. It was at this time, for instance, that Brazil began its switch from gasoline to ethanol-blended automobile fuels. In that context it was quickly understood that the way buildings were designed and built could be used to reduce energy consumption and help to minimize dependence on energy sources controlled by hostile groups and nations. In the United States the government began programs to better insulate low-income homes, while architects began to experiment with passive energy and other techniques, kick-starting decades of research devoted to both energy and material conservation.

Benefits of Conservation and Mitigation

In the 1980s these lessons were absorbed into the global environmental movement and confirmed by the Brundtland Report, which emphasized the use of sustainable development to mitigate the effects of global climate change (WCED 1987). Although it was not intended, in practice this advancement also confirmed a scientific and technical approach to sustainability in architecture that tended to neglect the social contribution architecture could make (Guy and Shove 2000). With the original impetus for change lying in economics and politics, it is not surprising that research and development of sustainable architecture continued to be both funded and justified largely through economic arguments. Environmental and social benefits were realized as a kind of secondary benefit. The approach nonetheless has helped to bring sustainable architecture into the mainstream.

Since the 1970s ways to build sustainably have increased dramatically, and several systematic approaches have emerged, including the Smart House, the Passivhaus, and more recently the Zero-Carbon building, which promises to free buildings from carbon dioxide emissions entirely. These are all based on resource efficiency and make use of a similar group of technologies and strategies, including passive heating and cooling, efficient mechanical systems, day-lighting and natural ventilation, solar orientation, rainwater harvesting, graywater recycling (i.e., reusing wastewater generated from such activities as dishwashing and bathing), waste reduction, green roofs, indoor air quality, and the use of sustainable materials. The technologies, when coupled with renewable energy sources such as solar power, wind power, and geothermal heat pumps, make it possible to create integrated systems that reduce energy use and simultaneously conserve resources such as potable water and building materials. In areas where water scarcity is approaching a crisis point, such as Australia or the southern parts of the United States, the addition of landscape design can take the gains further, even having a regional impact.

The technological know-how related to energy efficiency in architecture has become remarkably advanced. Some energy researchers even argue that oil dependence could be virtually eliminated if the technology was adopted at the national scale (Lovins 2012). In the realm of architecture, the limitations are no longer technical. Even in one of the world's coldest cities, Winnipeg, Canada, we can find the twenty-one-story office building Manitoba Hydro Place by Kuwabara Payne McKenna Blumberg Architects, which is one of the most energy efficient buildings in North America, if not the world (Linn 2010). Using a mix of technical approaches, including geothermal heating and cooling, natural ventilation, and computerized control of the building management, the integrated design was able to create a comfortable working environment in a region that sees a temperature range extending from $-50°C$ in the winter to $+40°C$ in the summer (Kuwabara et al. 2009).

Similar examples can be found across both Oceania and the Americas. Notable buildings include the California Academy of Sciences in San Francisco by Renzo Piano (completed 2008) and the Medellín Sports Coliseum in Colombia by Mazzanti and Plan:B, both of which make use of natural ventilation and lighting as well as other technological systems to reduce their energy impact. The economic benefits of adopting energy-saving technology are clear. Over the lifetime of the building, running costs are significantly lower, while users are treated to better environmental conditions, improving productivity and satisfaction.

Alternatives

Building on the same principles, a growing number of builders use mundane materials in construction to offset the cost of building with energy efficient technology. These include building from straw bales, tires, aluminum cans, and rammed earth, along with stucco and soil in order to create highly insulated homes that are easy to heat with solar energy and achieve a certain amount of energy independence especially in milder climates such as the southern United States. The company Earthship Biotecture is an example of this approach to building practice. Their particular model is based on using recycled materials such as tires filled with compacted dirt, aluminum cans, and glass or plastic bottles. Just as in more obviously hi-tech projects, the buildings are designed to be energy efficient and as self-sustaining as possible (Earthship Biotecture 2012a and 2012b).

It is also possible to renovate and update older buildings to improve their energy efficiency and comfort and to preserve the embodied energy they represent. The United States has had a program to improve the insulation in older buildings since the 1970s. It is possible, however, to take things much further and to invest in a "deep energy retrofit," where energy savings are improved through a holistic approach that renovates all the systems in a building simultaneously. Perhaps the most-well-known example of this type is the Empire State Building in New York City, which will update every window, replace lighting, and introduce more natural lighting and better control of the heating and cooling systems. Taken together, these and other efforts are expected to reduce energy use by some 38 percent (Lockwood 2009). The benefits, however, are expected to go beyond the running costs of the building and include more productivity for workers in the upgraded building as well as the potential for higher rents. The amount of energy that can be saved is perhaps not as large in a retrofitted building as in a newly constructed building (construction of the Empire State Building was started in 1930 and completed a year later). Because there are many more older buildings than new ones in use in almost any city or town, however, the potential impact can be substantial. Financing remains the main obstacle to a rapid increase of renovations of this type, largely due to the short track record of new technology and the uncertainty of a return on investment from the point of view of banks and investors.

Beyond the Building

In contrast to the technology-driven approach to building sustainable architecture, a growing body of work in Central and South America uses architecture to challenge profound social and economic problems. The most advanced version of this effort can be seen in Medellín, Colombia, where the mayor, Sergio Fajardo, began a project in 2003 that combined investments in education, transportation infrastructure, and architecture to transform some of the most violent areas in the city into centers for education and economic growth. The project has been successful by all measures, leading to reduced crime, new investments by businesses, and access to education and economic opportunity for the residents. Fajardo's program includes several buildings and parks. Perhaps the most representative of these is the Parque España library, completed by Giancarlo Mazzanti in 2007. Connected to the new cable metro system, it is literally embedded into the existing slum, forming a new public space but also working as a training center for the residents. The focus of this work is not on the technological sophistication but rather the social impact, which can be profound. Similar social-driven projects can be found in São Paulo, Brazil, in Iquique, Chile, and elsewhere in Central and South America.

The benefits of this expanded version of architecture are not as easy to measure and require more negotiation between diverse groups, which may explain why it is not so commonly attempted. It differs most significantly from the technological approach to sustainable design in that the end goal is not mitigation, but *social sustainability*. Its effects are deliberately felt far beyond the walls of the buildings.

The Need for Adaptation

Natural disasters are not uncommon, but the lessons architects take from them have begun to change. In the wake of events such as the flooding in New Orleans (2005), the tsunami at Constitución, Chile (2010), and the earthquake that damaged Christchurch, New Zealand (2010), architects have taken the stance that sustainability cannot be achieved through simple replacement of the original buildings and urban organization. They argue instead for long-term plans that will improve on previous buildings and cities, so they will be more adaptive and able to withstand future disasters and conditions. A robust community is widely regarded as a prerequisite for resiliency in the face of disaster. Architects working on the rebuilding of these structures are required to create not only new architectural typologies and technology, but also to facilitate public participation in the design process. The shift from design that is based on mitigation and energy efficiency toward design based on a capacity for adaptation and resiliency is difficult because it necessarily involves dealing with social sustainability, not only conservation. It has the benefit, however, of having a larger impact on communities for just the same reason.

Measuring Sustainability in Architecture

The effectiveness of sustainable architecture can be invisible and difficult to measure. Several programs have been created to evaluate, rate, and certify buildings on their environmental, social, and economic performance.

LEED

In North America the most popular tool for measuring sustainable design is Leadership in Energy and Environmental Design (LEED), an accreditation system that verifies that a building or community conforms to a set of interconnected criteria thought to be necessary in a sustainable "green" project. The criteria include sustainable site development, energy efficiency, water efficiency, material selection, and indoor environmental quality. A building is given a certain number of points for meeting the requirements of each category, which allows it to advertise a particular rating. Similar programs exist in Australia (National Australian Built Environment Rating System [NABERS] and Green Star), New Zealand (Green Star NZ) and Canada (LEED Canada), and are used in other countries as well.

Critique

The critical response to LEED certification is that the systematic approach encourages practice that is too prescriptive and becomes nothing more than a checklist. In response, an alternative measuring system recently emerged called the Living Building Challenge. It is explicitly designed to tackle social equity and requires proof of net-zero energy use over a year of real inhabitation. More radically, it is performance based rather than prescriptive in order to leave room for innovation. An example that fulfills the ambition of that system is the Van Dusen Botanical Gardens in Vancouver, Canada, by the architecture firm Perkins and Will (completed 2011).

The Future

A number of trends are emerging in the field of architecture and sustainability. In general the direction is toward recognizing a more holistic approach to design that is flexible and able to accommodate complexity. For example, "cradle to cradle" is a concept that looks to the process of creating materials and suggests that instead of aiming for recycling, it would be more useful to create a system that allows a product to be broken into component parts to be reused in new configurations. At the same time, it requires a production process that is entirely nontoxic. An example can be seen in the NASA Sustainability Base designed by William McDonough + Partners (2012) in Moffett Field, California.

Biomimicry represents a technical evolution in sustainable architecture. It explores the potential of natural materials and processes in order to translate them into building materials with unexpected but useful properties. A building skin could be designed to mimic the self-regulating properties of a pine cone, for example, by its construction from materials that automatically open and close in response to moisture in the air.

Challenges

Sustainable architecture faces adversity on three main fronts: scaling, costs, and access.

Scaling

Sustainable architecture has made impressive inroads, but faces several challenges. Chief among them is the difficulty of scaling successful solutions in order to maximize their impact. While individual buildings can be quite successful, the problems that sustainable architecture is intended to address are regional, if not global, and it is necessary to find a way to have an effect at that level.

Costs

Similarly, although building technology is often adopted to reduce long-term costs by investors, some costs cannot be accommodated without subsidies from the government. In the face of that vulnerability, adoption is risky, and progress slowed as a result. Such issues may be resolved only by cultural innovations. At the same time not all communities are able to invest in the required technology. In less wealthy regions more research is necessary to find inexpensive ways to achieve the same goals.

Access

Finally, unequal access to technology and knowledge makes it difficult for some nations to pursue the best strategies. Knowledge-sharing agreements can help to improve that situation; innovation, however, is required in areas where industrial abilities are not sufficient to build according to best practices.

William David GALLOWAY

Environmental Innovators Program, Keio University

See also Ecovillages; Energy Efficiency; Mobility; Public Transportation; Urbanization

FURTHER READING

Bardi, Ugo. (2011). The Limits to Growth *Revisited*. New York: Springer.

Benyus, Janine. (2002). *Biomimicry: Innovation inspired by nature*. New York: Harper Perennial.

Davis, Mike. (2006). *Planet of slums*. London: Verso.

Earthship Biotecture. (2012a). Homepage. Retrieved May 23, 2012, from http://earthship.com/

Earthship Biotecture. (2012b). Construction materials. Retrieved May 23, 2012, from http://earthship.com/construction-materials

Gauzin-Müller, Dominique. (2002). *Sustainable architecture and urbanism: Concepts, technologies, examples* (Kate Purver, Trans.). Boston: Birkhäuser.

Girard, Luigi Fusco; Forte, Bruno; Cerreta, Maria; De Toro, Pasquale; & Forte, Fabiana. (Eds.). (2003). *The human sustainable city: Challenges and perspectives from the habitat agenda*. Aldershot, UK: Ashgate.

Guy, Simon, & Shove, Elizabeth. (2000). *A sociology of energy, buildings, and the environment: Constructing knowledge, designing practice*. London: Routledge.

Hyde, Richard. (2008). *Bioclimatic housing: Innovative designs for warm climates*. London: Earthscan.

International Living Future Institute. (2010). *Living building challenge 2.1: A visionary path to a restorative future*. Retrieved March 20, 2012, from https://ilbi.org/lbc/LBC%20Documents/lbc-2.1

Kaye, Leon. (2011). New ideas for sustainable architecture in the Americas. *The Guardian*. Retrieved December 2, 2011, from http://www.guardian.co.uk/sustainable-business/sustainable-architecture-south-america

Kuwabara, Bruce; Auer, Thomas; Gouldsborough, Tom; Akerstream, Tom; & Klym, Glenn. (2009, June 22–24). *Manitoba Hydro Place: Integrated design process exemplar*. Quebec City, Canada: PLEA 26th Conference on Passive and Low Energy Architecture.

Linn, Charles. (2010, October 13). Innovation 2010: Is Manitoba Hydro the most energy efficient building in North America? *Architectural Record*. Retrieved May 21, 2012, from http://www.kpmb.com/index.asp?navid=19&layid=29&fid3=5&fid2=159

Lockwood, Charles. (2009, November–December). Building retro. *Urban Land* (pp. 46–57). Washington, DC: Urban Land Institute. Retrieved May 22, 2012, from http://www.esbnyc.com/documents/sustainability/uli_building_retro_fits.pdf

Lovins, Amory. (2012). *Reinventing fire: Bold business solutions for the new energy era*. White River, VT: Chelsea Green Publishing Company.

Main, Hamish, & Williams, Stephen Wyn. (Eds.). (1994). *Environment and housing in third world cities*. New York: John Wiley & Sons.

Mazria, Edward, & Kershner, Kristina. (2008). *Meeting the 2030 challenge through building codes*. Santa Fe, NM: 2030, Inc./Architecture 2030.

McDonough, William, & Braungart, Michael. (2002) *Cradle to cradle: Remaking the way we make things*. New York: North Point Press.

Mesa R., Miguel. (2010). A manifesto for Medellín. *Domus, 937*, 50–66.

Peters, Terri. (Ed.). (2011, November–December). Experimental green strategies: Redefining ecological design research; *Architectural Design, 214*. New York: Wiley.

Ratti, Carlo, & Townsend, Anthony. (2011, September). The social nexus. *Scientific American, 305*, 42–48.

Truelove, James. (2003). *The smart house*. New York: Harper Design International.

United Nations (UN). (1992). *Agenda 21*. New York: UN.

United Nations Framework Convention on Climate Change (UNFCCC). (2007). *Impacts, vulnerabilities, and adaptation in developing countries*. Bonn, Germany: UNFCCC.

World Commission on Environment and Development (WCED). (1987). *Our common future*. Oxford, UK: Oxford University Press.

Berkshire's authors and editors welcome questions, comments, and corrections. Send your emails about the *Berkshire Encyclopedia of Sustainability* in general or this volume in particular to: sustainability.updates@berkshirepublishing.com

Auckland, New Zealand

1.5 million est. pop. 2012

Auckland, the largest city in a country known worldwide for its breathtaking natural beauty, has a growing, multiethnic population, a new definition of its city limits—with the formation in 2010 of an Auckland "Super City"—and an inadequate public transport system. The Auckland Plan, launched in 2012, is the city's thirty-year strategy to deal with social inequalities, environmental quality, economic growth, and infrastructure planning, and to help achieve its goal of becoming the world's most liveable city.

Auckland, the largest urban area in New Zealand, is situated toward the north of the country's North Island. It is centered on a narrow volcanic isthmus lying between Waitemata and Manukau harbors, which extend in from the Pacific Ocean and Tasman Sea respectively, and includes a number of offshore islands. Much of the city is bordered by coastline, as well as expanses of land to the north and south that are devoted to pastoral farming and horticultural activity, and the steep and heavily forested Waitakere Ranges. The city has a temperate climate with warm, humid summers and mild, damp winters. Rainfall is relatively frequent throughout the year, and average daily maximum temperatures range from 23°C in February (summer) to 14°C in July (winter) (Cameron, Hayward, and Murdoch 2008).

The city's colonial past is reflected in its name. In 1840, William Hobson, New Zealand's first governor, named the city after George Eden, the first earl of Auckland. Since the 1990s its Māori name, Tamaki Makau-rau ("many people") has come back into informal usage. To found the capital city, Hobson acquired a 1,200-hectare site around the volcanic Mt. Eden (Maungawhau) from the local Ngati Whatua Māori chiefs. Within a few years there were more than 2,000 residents. Auckland's tenure as capital was brief, however; the nation's political center moved to Wellington in the southwestern end of the North Island in 1865 (King 2003).

By the early twentieth century, the many fragmented settlements dispersed across the Auckland isthmus had amalgamated to form an early version of the city. Expansion and modernization characterized the first half of the century as road, tram, and rail links were developed, and water and electricity boards were established to respond to the swelling demands associated with population growth. Suburbanization in the post–World War II period resulted in a diminished prominence of the city's central core as a residential area. As the residential population declined and moved away from the city's center, employment opportunities also declined (Bush 1998). This decentralization of both population and employment has been an enduring characteristic of the city, leading to numerous challenges and changes in its approaches to governance across the region.

Until the first decade of the twenty-first century, Auckland's status was ambiguously defined. It was referred to both as a metropolitan region (made up of four independently named cities) and as the most centrally located of the four composite cities. Auckland City comprised the isthmus area (including the central business district and the older, more densely settled residential neighborhoods). The metropolitan area comprises Auckland City as well as some adjoining urban jurisdictions (principally North Shore, Manukau, and Waitakere). In November 2010, however, an Auckland "super city"—a unitary metropolitan area of 5,600 square kilometers that also includes significant tracts of rural land and a number of offshore islands—was formed.

The 2012 population estimate was 1.5 million, or almost one-third of the nation's population (Auckland

Council 2012a). There was a 6.5 percent population growth rate in the years 2006–2010, a rate that exceeded that of most other urban areas in New Zealand. This growth has placed considerable pressure on infrastructure and generated debate over the merits of establishing a metropolitan limit and identifying locations in which to target future, and more intensified, urban development. Despite this growth, Auckland is a very green city with many public open spaces. Although the city's central core is relatively densely constructed, the majority of urban Auckland is very low density and features numerous parks and reserves. Another key characteristic of the city is its growing multiculturalism. Whereas three decades ago there were few numerically significant cultural groups in addition to the indigenous Māori, the descendants of the British settlers, and migrants from Pacific Islands, recent changes in immigration policy have seen Auckland emerge as New Zealand's destination of choice for over one hundred nationalities. Two of the major groups contributing to the population increase (since the late 1980s) have been emigrants from China and Indians from the subcontinent (Friesen 2008).

Infrastructure and Economic Development

The city's expansion and retail development was initially triggered by tramway development on the isthmus, but the private motor vehicle remained the principal form of transport in the later decades of the twentieth century. Decisions concerning transport options have been highly influential in the city's development and subsequent form. Established infrastructure succumbed to the dominance of the private automobile, and Auckland's tramways were removed by 1956. A proposed electric rail system never eventuated, although the central government has made a commitment to electrify the existing metropolitan rail network that currently runs on diesel. The bridge crossing Waitemata Harbour (also referred to as Auckland Harbour), now an iconic symbol of the city, was opened in 1959 but only to cars. Its initial designs included pedestrian/bicycle and rail lanes, but these aspects were shelved because of the cost involved (Mees 2010). The bridge opened the way to considerable suburbanization on the northern side of the harbor, as did subsequent highway development in the 1970s that penetrated areas to the city's west and south and continues to be extended. By the end of the twentieth century, and contrary to common erroneous perceptions overseas, Auckland had become an increasingly car-congested city. Car use is deeply ingrained in the national psyche, and achieving a reorientation toward more sustainable travel modes has proved to be notoriously difficult despite increased public awareness of environmental problems caused by the overdependence on cars (Bean, Kearns, and Collins 2008).

As the Australian planning expert Paul Mees (2010, 21) points out, Auckland's transport system "is untouched by the environmental activism for which New Zealanders are renowned." While both city politicians and planners alike have talked of public transport initiatives, until recently neither has seemed able to convert rhetoric into reality. In the new "Super Auckland," however, previously elusive goals are finally finding some traction with a modest expansion of the suburban rail lines, the prospect of integrated ticketing (that allows riders to make transfers and use different modes of transport on a single ticket) slated for a November 2012 launch, and annual increases in public-transport patronage.

Other infrastructural challenges have led to crises that have had profound impacts on the city and triggered changes. In 1994, a water shortage (precipitated as much by rising demand as by drought) led to the expensive development of a major pipeline that brings water from the Waikato River. Following this, the 1998 power failure that cut electricity to central Auckland for more than a week led to a reassessment of the viability of the city's infrastructure (Bush 1998). This crisis led to major upgrading and reinforcement of the supply into Auckland. Lurching from infrastructure crisis to crisis has been at least partly associated with a fragmented governance structure across the region and contributed to the drive for more "joined-up" governance of Auckland (whose multiple and geographically dispersed jurisdictions have been colloquially referred to as a series of villages connected by a sewage line). A decade into the new millennium, this drive culminated in the establishment of a unified Auckland Council that has signaled a new chapter in Auckland's history.

Auckland is the country's principal city and largest commercial center, and has a diverse economic base, primarily composed of commercial services, light industry, and the import and export activities of the city's sea and air ports. The city developed its industrial base through a national-level project of economic growth, involving industrial tariff protection. A critical break occurred in 1984, however, when New Zealand embarked on an extensive program of economic liberalization. Auckland was heavily impacted; many of Queen Street's historic buildings were destroyed, for example, and the fine Georgian and Victorian architecture was replaced with 1980s-style high-rise buildings. Although many negative impacts undoubtedly have stemmed from this shift, New Zealand continues to be a strongly economically liberal country. Auckland's urban and regional economy reflects the city's position both within the Pacific Rim and within global economic networks (Le Heron and Pawson 1998).

Outlook

The recently released thirty-year Auckland Plan involves a bold quest to "make Auckland the world's most liveable city" (Auckland Council 2012). While Auckland is consistently highly rated on surveys like the Mercer Quality of Living Survey—it was ranked third out of 221 cities in 2011 (Mercer 2011)—such ratings overlook local expressions of inequality such as the persistence of relatively deprived households and suburbs, especially in the state-housing areas of south Auckland. Ultimately the health and well-being of Aucklanders relies on developing an urban environment that takes into account connections between transport, urban design, energy use, and adequate housing, among other issues.

Sustainability involves the capacity to endure in environmental, social, and economic terms, and Auckland faces challenges at the intersection of these domains. Housing offers a good example. The conventional "kiwi" (the nickname for New Zealanders) dream is a freestanding dwelling on a modestly sized block of land including a lawn and garden. Urban sprawl inevitably undermines the viability of public transport and walkable retail and service centers, contributes to car dependence, and consumes fertile farmland and natural heritage on the urban periphery. Although in the new millennium there have been experiments with "new urbanism" and more compact city forms, the jury is still out as to the acceptability and viability of higher-density living, especially for family life and child rearing. The central business district, for instance, has undergone a radical repopulation in the last decade. This growth has predominantly been linked with the construction of new apartments, with significant numbers of these also caught up in the "leaky building" crisis. These buildings were designed for singles and couples but are now housing families, particularly new immigrant families, many of whom are struggling to offer their children opportunities for independent exercise and leisure. Public perception of such developments is largely negative and challenging to overcome.

Another key challenge related to the ethic of inclusiveness, which itself is associated with sustainability, is how Auckland "should consider, provide for, and support the development of Māori land" (Livesey 2010, 41). In Auckland, as in the nation's other cities, there are considerations, which are not optional, to maintain and improve opportunities for Māori to contribute to local government decision-making processes. Properly implemented, this may help to create a culturally and economically sustainable future. In Auckland, as in the nation's other cities, these considerations are not optional, given the strong ethic of partnership arising from the founding treaty between the peoples of New Zealand.

The city has a strong tradition of activism. Over the years, the streets have been intermittently occupied for protests that have ranged from the fierce opposition that greeted the racially selected South African rugby union team that toured New Zealand in 1981 to support for the nation's antinuclear stance that led to the New Zealand's Nuclear Free Zone, Disarmament, and Arms Control Act of 1987.

At the neighborhood level, small-scale activism continues, and new developments signal steps toward sustainability. First, a number of "Transition Towns" groups are flourishing, encouraging residents to begin—literally in their own backyards—to use resources wisely and to develop community resilience such as support for community-gardening initiatives and organic food markets. Second, initiatives such as "Twin Streams" are local government-supported projects that engage residential and school communities in water catchment restoration. Locals who live near streams are involved in activities as diverse as native-tree planting, art projects, stream cleanups, water-quality monitoring, and household sustainability audits. Third, within school communities, walking school bus (WSB) initiatives that provide structured, parent-supervised group walks to and from school have become established, and within a decade well over one hundred new WSB programs were offering children a mode of safe, active, healthy, and sociable travel while concurrently contributing to traffic decongestion (Collins and Kearns 2008). Fourth, Auckland localities, such as Hobsonville and Tamaki, are undergoing transformations through private-public partnerships (i.e., businesses and government) that have the stated aims of being sustainable and communal places. These developments also illustrate an evolving culture of innovative partnership between the state, private developers, and communities.

Transport is one of the major challenges that Auckland still faces in its attempt to become a sustainable city. With its high car-ownership rates, for example, and relatively weak emissions controls, central Auckland suffers from an undesirable level of pollutant emissions. Because the city is surrounded by water, there is an underdeveloped potential for passenger ferry transport, and debate still rages regarding any increased investment in rail.

The national-level requirement that city councils develop long-term plans (through the Local Government Act of 2002) offers local government and members of the public an opportunity to reflect on the future effects of contemporary decisions. As the Auckland Council's publicity says, "[I]t is easy to keep rates down this year by putting off essential works like replacing bridges or footpaths. But the bridges and footpaths must still be replaced" (Auckland Council 2012b). As the twenty-first century unfolds, the overarching challenge will be to develop and enact strategies for the now-extensive Auckland Council area that manage and use resources efficiently, reflect local needs and aspirations, are socially inclusive, and environmentally friendly while they allow the economy to remain competitive and resilient and infused with a distinctive New Zealand cultural flavor.

Robin A. KEARNS
The University of Auckland

See also Australia; Mobility; New Zealand; Oceania; Parks and Protected Areas; Perth, Australia; Public Transportation; Sydney, Australia; Travel and Tourism Industry; Urbanization; Water Use and Rights

FURTHER READING

Auckland Council. (2012a, January 2). News release: Auckland welcomes its 1.5 millionth citizen. Retrieved May 11, 2012, from http://www.aucklandcouncil.govt.nz/EN/News/NewsArticles/Pages/aucklandwelcomesits15millionthcitizen.aspx

Auckland Council. (2012b). What is the Auckland plan? Retrieved May 11, 2012, from http://www.aucklandcouncil.govt.nz/EN/AboutCouncil/PlansPoliciesPublications/theaucklandplan/Pages/theaucklandplan.aspx

Bean, Catherine E.; Kearns, Robin A.; & Collins, Damian C. A. (2008). Exploring social mobilities: Narratives of walking and driving in Auckland, New Zealand. *Urban Studies, 45*(13), 2829–2848.

Bush, Graham W. A. (1998). *Decently and in order: The centennial history of Auckland City Council*. Auckland, New Zealand: Collins.

Cameron, Ewen; Hayward, Bruce; & Murdoch, Graeme. (2008). *A field guide to Auckland: Exploring the region's natural and historic heritage*. Auckland, New Zealand: Godwit Press.

Collins, Damian C. A., & Kearns, Robin A. (2010). Walking school buses in the Auckland region: A longitudinal assessment. *Transport Policy, 17*(1), 1–8.

Friesen, Wardlow. (2008). *Diverse Auckland: The face of New Zealand in the 21st century?* Wellington, New Zealand: Asia New Zealand Foundation.

King, Michael. (2003). *The Penguin history of New Zealand*. Auckland, New Zealand: Penguin Books.

Le Heron, Richard B., & Pawson, Eric. (1998). *Changing places in New Zealand: A geography of restructuring*. Auckland, New Zealand: Longans.

Livesey, Biddy. (2010). Do urban growth strategies support the development of Māori land for residential use? In Keriata J. Suart & Michelle Thompson-Fawcett (Eds.), *Taone Tupu Ora: Indigenous knowledge and sustainable urban design*. Wellington, New Zealand: Steele-Roberts.

Mees, Paul. (2010). *Transport for suburbia: Beyond the automobile age*. London: Earthscan.

Mercer Consulting. (2011). 2011 Quality of Living worldwide city rankings: Mercer survey. Retrieved May 11, 2012, from http://www.mercer.com/press-releases/quality-of-living-report-2011

Share the *Encyclopedia of Sustainability*: Teachers are welcome to make up to ten (10) copies of no more than two (2) articles for distribution in a single course or program. For further permissions, please visit www.copyright.com or contact: info@berkshirepublishing.com

Australia

22 million est. pop. 2012

Notwithstanding urban environmental concerns, Australia's greatest challenges, in terms of development and sustainability, have always been tied to the limits imposed by its harsh physical traits, especially its scarcity of water and the poor quality of its soils. These, together with the profound effects of the El Niño–La Niña cycle, continue to pose challenges to those trying to fashion a living out of a wild landscape.

Australia (the Commonwealth of Australia) is a country of nearly 7.7 million square kilometers, comprising the mainland of the Australian continent and the island of Tasmania, which lies about 250 kilometers south of the continent's southeastern corner, as well as numerous smaller islands. Its population of approximately 22 million (US CIA 2012) is mostly of European origin but, since the 1960s, also includes many Asian immigrants. A large percentage (26 percent) of this population is foreign born. The country's official language is English, and Protestantism and Catholicism are the two predominant religions. Buddhism and Islam are also practiced.

Australia's capital city is Canberra; other main cities are Sydney, Melbourne, Perth, and Brisbane. Australia's major cities are found in the east, with the exception of Perth, the capital of Western Australia. Although Australian society is primarily urban, industries include the key commodity exports of iron ore, coal, and gold mining. In addition, the country produces wheat and cotton and is home to cattle and sheep ranching. Tourism, the urban-based service sector, and manufacturing industries (which are on the decline) also contribute to the country's economy.

Australia has a federal constitution, with a national government, six state governments, and several territories. The political system is based on the Westminster tradition. Following democratic elections, a majority parliamentary vote chooses the prime minister and his or her government; they are answerable to Parliament.

Natural and Pre-European Features

Australia is the driest of all the continents, with the poorest soils, the least amount of water (except Antarctica), and the lowest mountain ranges. About 10 percent of the total landmass is forested. The largest river system is the Murray-Darling, which carries less water than most comparable rivers of its size in other parts of the world (e.g., the Sacramento–San Joaquin River of California). Much of the continent, apart from the fertile east coast, the southeastern crescent, and the southwestern part of Western Australia, is covered by scrub, native grasses, and deserts. The continent is profoundly affected by the El Niño–La Niña climatological cycle and is subject to debilitating droughts. By European standards, the climate is generally mild, merging to tropical in the north. Its unique flora and fauna, especially its marsupials and eucalyptus trees, have attracted much attention.

Europeans were not the first to leave their mark on the Australian landscape. For sixty thousand years before the arrival of European settlers, Australian Aborigines had settled on the continent from Southeast Asia. These people burned forest undergrowth to promote better grass cover and encourage game. Some forests, such as the Pilliga of western New South Wales, have become more extensive and changed composition since the decline of the Aboriginal population.

Aboriginal Australians also changed the environment by introducing the dingo (a native dog). Through their hunting practices, they may have been responsible for eliminating large marsupials such as the giant wombat (*Diprotodon*) and, on the mainland, the Tasmanian tiger, or thylacine (*Thylacinus cynocephalus*). The thylacine was rendered extinct on the mainland by a combination of native hunting, dingo depredations, and possible climate change in the distant past. In the nineteenth century decimation of the Aboriginal populations in eastern Australia (by disease and through the violence of the white settlers) led to plagues of possums and kangaroos in some areas.

European Perceptions

The foreignness of the flora and fauna profoundly influenced the attitudes and practices of Europeans following the establishment of the first white settlement in 1788. Although they had some appreciation of indigenous species and of the grandeur of those landscapes that resembled the stately parks of large English estates, the European settlers viewed nature mostly as a resource rather than as something to be preserved. They thought of the Australian landscape as deficient because it did not conform to European standards of beauty. The dearth of deciduous trees, the dull appearance of the eucalyptus forests, and the lack of distinct seasons disturbed or repelled many settlers. Although late-nineteenth-century European painters displayed a greater appreciation of Australia's natural environment, the landscape they depicted was pastoral and, in essence, a celebration of the settler's triumph over nature. It was not until the 1930s that artists prominently assimilated the harsher tones of the "red center"—the arid and often desertlike outback in the center of Australia—and arid lands into art of the region.

Land Settlement

Following colonization, the colonial governments intervened on a large scale to develop land, causing considerable environmental change. These governments gave governors the authority to make "land grants," that is, to confer title upon an area of land, often to prominent members of the British-Australian community such as colonial officials and army officers, usually for farming or grazing purposes. Beginning in 1831, these land grants began to be replaced with sales of the land belonging to the British Crown, in an effort to further encourage settlement. Until the 1860s, however, large landholders called "squatters," occupied most land, and they grazed large herds of sheep and cattle that eroded native vegetation. These squatters had no legal hold on the land they occupied, but gained use of it by virtue of the fact that they were the first whites to occupy it. From the 1860s to the 1920s colonial governments tried, largely unsuccessfully, to encourage small-scale development, first through land legislation for "free selection" (1860s) and then, in the 1880s and after 1900, through irrigation policies.

In 1885 Alfred Deakin, the minister of water supply in the state of Victoria and a future prime minister, traveled overseas to study foreign irrigation policies and practices. While in California, he met the Canadian engineer George Chaffey, who, together with his brother William B. Chaffey, had successfully implemented irrigation programs in California. Deakin was impressed by these programs and, in his comprehensive report on his findings, recommended that the Australian government provide assistance in bringing water to arid regions. Deakin then encouraged the Chaffey brothers to go to Australia to work on what later became known as the Mildura and Renmark programs. The two accepted, and the colonial governments gave them 300,000 hectares of land grants to establish planned towns on the Murray River in Victoria and South Australia. Although the Chaffey brothers got into financial difficulties in the 1890s, their settlements and Deakin's legislation became the foundation of Australian irrigation-based farming, which continued to grow in importance.

Irrigation systems were established to promote "closer," that is, intensive, settlement on the assumption that a sound and prosperous society with a stable social structure required sturdy yeoman farmers; it was increasingly accepted that the state would be required to support these ideals with advice, cheap finances, and suitable laws. Further developments along these lines were implemented by the US engineer Elwood Mead, who was chairman of the Victorian State Rivers and Water Supply Commission from 1907 to 1915 and advocated irrigation as a tool for advancing planned rural settlement.

Irrigation, however, led to a plethora of problems: overuse of water, especially contentious after the development of cotton farming in the 1970s in northwestern New South Wales; interference with natural river systems through the erection of dams in the Murray-Darling River basin (after the 1920s) and on the Ord River in Western Australia (after the 1960s); and salinization of soil and water. Irrigation was only one of the agricultural factors negatively affecting the environment.

The demand for land and agricultural production was such that sometimes land use clashed with the limits nature imposed. In the marginal land of South Australia, north of the so-called Goyder's line (a boundary said to separate a region to the north where rainfall levels are so low that the land is suitable only for grazing from an area to the south where rainfall is sufficiently high to support farming), wheat farming was initially successful in the 1870s only to be defeated by severe droughts in the 1880s.

Agricultural activities were the source of more environmental damage than were pastoral activities, some of which were compatible with the survival of some native vegetation and extensive tree cover. Extensive clearing of trees through ringbarking (or girdling—the practice of thinning forests by removing a ring of bark from the entire circumference of the trunk or branch of a tree so that wood tissues beyond the ring will die) occurred after the 1850s to promote denser settlement. Removal of trees has caused great salinity problems. Although apparent by the 1940s, these effects were largely ignored, and by the late-twentieth century much of Western Australia's wheat belt and the Murray-Darling River basin were severely affected by salinity due to the excessive removal of native trees.

Furthermore, overgrazing led to the removal of native grasses and vegetation, robbed the soil of nutrients, and spread weeds introduced from Europe and South Africa through the physical transportation of seeds by hoofed animals. Extinction of animal species, notably the thylacine, in Tasmania, also occurred as farmers killed them in an effort to protect their flocks and crops from predators.

Imprudent agricultural methods triggered large numbers of dust storms. In her book *Flying Fox and Drifting Sand*, the Australian zoologist and conservationist Francis Ratcliffe (1938) alerted the public to the impact of soil erosion, exacerbated by drought, rabbits, and the combination of overgrazing and wheat farming. The absence of a national policy hampered farmers and governments in their responses to these problems. Unlike the United States, which under the New Deal advanced programs to recapture millions of hectares from soil erosion, Australia had no policy. It was not until after 1938 that Australian states began to follow the US lead and establish a more coordinated approach to soil conservation services in its states.

A vast range of invasive animals and plants, linked mainly to European agricultural and pastoral occupations, spread across Australia. In the mid-nineteenth century, homesick English colonists introduced exotic birds and trees throughout the colonies to provide hunting for the gentry under the acclimatization movement (a movement that exchanged exotic plants and animals for economic, scientific, and aesthetic "improvement" of the land). Most damaging of the invasive species were the European wild rabbit, introduced in 1859 for hunting, and the prickly pear cactus from Central America, first cultivated in 1839 as an ornamental. By 1900, the cactus covered millions of hectares of land in Queensland and New South Wales; rabbits spread across all areas except the far tropics. Both the prickly pear cactus and rabbit invasions were facilitated by low human-to-land ratios under pastoral occupation, and they threatened the viability of that pastoral economy, as well as the prospects for broadacre agriculture (large-scale crop operations) and small-scale farming. By the 1920s, demands for biological control were growing. In 1924, introduction of the *Cactoblastis* moth proved successful against the prickly pear cactus. In her book *Silent Spring*, US marine biologist Rachel Carson (1962) lauded this introduction as an outstanding example of how biological alternatives to pesticides could be found. The vastly greater exploitation of new synthesized insecticides, such as dichlorodiphenyltrichloroethane (DDT), however, outweighed the use of biological controls after 1945 in Australia.

Although the rabbit gravely damaged the flora of Australia, no objection was made to the comparable damage done by sheep—it was the competition for pasture by the 1880s that led to the search for controls. Eventually the myxomatosis virus, introduced from South America, decimated the rabbit population after its release between 1949 and 1950. Rabbits subsequently gained partial immunity, and myxomatosis had to be supplemented in the 1990s with calicivirus, finally allowing larger areas of the inland to be revegetated.

Conservation and Restoration

Although Australia's European population has always been predominantly urban based, there has been relatively little historical writing on urban environmental problems and little evidence of organized urban environmental movements until the 1970s. For one thing, the image that Australians had of themselves—until the 1960s—was one that emphasized an important connection with the "bush" (rural Australia). Moreover, Australia was urbanized, but not heavily industrialized, and even the (few) big cities were, apart from certain inner city areas, relatively free of the congestion-induced environmental problems present in Britain and elsewhere. Because Australia was not industrialized until the 1940s (with the exception of the regional towns of Newcastle and Port Kembla, in New South Wales,

Botany, in Sydney, and some parts of Victoria), problems of pollution in urban areas tended to be those stemming from small industry, homes, and some power stations. There were also occasional poverty- and congestion-related health problems (such as the notorious outbreak of plague in The Rocks area in central Sydney in the first few years of the twentieth century).

In the nineteenth century, the most notable Australian impacts upon the land were those wrought by farming and mining, although these impacts included, to be sure, the demands for timber and other raw materials required by urban growth.

In the mid-nineteenth century people began to recognize the damage being wrought on the land by European agricultural methods. Conservation sentiment that emerged after the Australian gold rushes brought to the fore the negative impacts of the deforestation that had been carried out to aid the mining industry and provide fuel for growing towns in Victoria. Ideas about the changing impacts of human activities on nature were also stimulated by the US diplomat and philologist George Perkins Marsh in his book *Man and Nature* (1864). Important authorities such as Ferdinand Mueller, the director of the Victorian Botanic Gardens, and John Ednie Brown, the South Australian conservator of forests, emphasized the value of tree cover as a means of conserving moisture. These men favored extensive reforestation and afforestation, including planting imported Monterey pines from California. Brown elevated the attributed role that trees play in climate control from one that is merely influential to one that fully controls climate.

At the same time the government established the first national parks, not as wilderness preserves, but as recreation areas, especially for the cities of Sydney and Melbourne. In 1878, Audley, south of Sydney, became the second officially designated "national park" in the world and was stocked with European deer for the benefit of hunters, bushwalkers (hikers/wilderness campers), and picnickers.

The forestry administration services operating from within the colonial lands or mines departments—and the fragmentation of authority through the colonial sovereignty of Crown lands—stymied conservation policies. This fragmentation of authority continued even after federation (the union of the six colonies under a federal constitution) in 1901, as water policies and Crown lands were under control of the state governments (unlike the situation in the United States, where public lands were under control of the federal government). Water regulation between states for the Murray-Darling River basin—the river system that covered four of the six states—was thus ineffective despite later interstate agreements.

After the 1880s, conservation-minded foresters such as George Perrin and his supporters, influenced by European and Indian forestry service practices, advocated state forests for the colonies and experimented with exotic trees in plantations. Royal commissions (a formal government-appointed judicial inquiry with legal powers to subpoena witnesses and recommend criminal contempt charges for false testimony) on forestry in Victoria (1897–1901) and New South Wales (1908–1909) led to the enactment of laws regulating the cutting of timber and promoting state forestry services. The services thus formed, with government administration, were established in each colony through acts of parliament, and the regulations controlling logging and planting then spread to other states. Conservation movements with popular support had roots in ornithology through the Gould League of Bird Lovers, founded in 1909 by the Australian schoolteacher Jessie McMichael in Victoria, and named after the nineteenth-century English ornithologist John Gould. This organization enrolled hundreds of thousands of young children, encouraged the study of Australian birds, and enjoyed the prestige of having Prime Minister Alfred Deakin as its first president.

Conservation sentiment was in part a product of federation and nationalism. The Australian Forest League raised pride in Australian trees and their wood products; by the 1910s and 1920s bushwalker clubs were established. Led by such early conservationists as Myles Dunphy in New South Wales, these clubs promoted greater appreciation of nature and the creation of additional national parks.

During the years between the world wars, conservation meant efficient use of resources, especially of timber, through the Imperial Forestry Conferences, the development of a Commonwealth Forestry School (in 1926), and water conservation measures. The most ambitious plans to harness the country's natural resources involved the push for irrigating the deserts by turning coastal streams inland. The outlandish Bradfield scheme (a plan for diverting the coastal rivers of Northeastern Australia back inland through huge tunnels under the Great Dividing Range, in order to irrigate the dry interior of the continent) was advocated without success between 1938 and 1942, and the writings of journalist Ion Idriess championed this approach without success. Efforts to harness the country's resources were eventually partially attained, however, with the creation of the Snowy Mountains program, modeled on the Tennessee Valley Authority in the United States. The Snowy Mountains Authority was forged by the Labor federal government and in the 1950s advanced a program to divert water from the coast, producing hydroelectric power, flood control, and recreational lakes in the Snowy Mountains and supplying irrigation water to the Murray-Darling River basin. These vast changes were accepted by Australians eager to realize the promised efficiency and economic benefits and to put the depression of the 1930s and wartime austerity behind them.

Modern Environmentalism

The new ecological consciousness of the 1960s heightened Australians' awareness of the environmental consequences of national development proposals. Dam projects were subject to bitter controversy. When, in the 1960s, the Tasmanian government decided to push ahead with more dams for its power grid, it met resistance. The decision of Tasmania's Hydroelectric Commission to build a dam in the middle of Lake Pedder National Park in 1967 led to the founding of the Tasmania Wilderness Society and greater emphasis on wilderness preservation. Although Lake Pedder was flooded in 1972, despite widespread protests, the Tasmania Wilderness Society led a successful effort in 1983 to save the Franklin River from a similar fate, an achievement that catapulted Green Party leaders such as Bob Brown into national prominence and gave them political representation in the federal and state parliaments from the late 1980s onward.

The rebirth of the conservation movement in the United States in the 1960s, together with mining projects and dam building, fostered a similar rebirth in Australia. Plans to drill for oil near the Great Barrier Reef and to mine the sand dunes of Fraser Island on the Queensland coast produced pioneering modern environmental movements in the 1960s and 1970s. The Australian Conservation Foundation (1965) was active in the leadership of the Great Barrier Reef struggle. Mining on the Fraser Island sand dunes was outlawed in most parts in 1975, and a world heritage area was eventually established in 1992. At the same time (1975), the federal National Parks and Wildlife Conservation Act and the legislation for the creation of the Great Barrier Reef Marine Park were enacted.

The election of Prime Minister Gough Whitlam's Labor federal government in 1972 aided conservation efforts, as did a new, more socially and environmentally conscious urban middle class that was university trained, committed to environmental values, and strongly backed by elements within the left-wing section of the trade union movement and the Labor Party. Labor and trade unionists took the lead on urban environmental issues.

The growth of Australia's cities was substantial after 1950, and controlling air pollution and conserving the new environment became major campaigns by the 1970s. Trade unions established "green bans" to prevent destruction of important buildings and streetscapes, and some freeway construction was halted. Smoke from factories and exhaust fumes from the steadily building traffic in Sydney and Melbourne had produced a decline in air quality during the 1960s and 1970s that led to the establishment of environmental protection agencies within the state governments. Power stations were moved out of the cities, transferring pollution to regional communities such as the Hunter River Valley, in New South Wales, and Latrobe Valley, in eastern Victoria. Major environmental battles continued to rage in the 1980s and 1990s over the destruction of old-growth forests for wood chips (used in making paper pulp—an industry established in the 1960s, principally in New South Wales and Tasmania) and over uranium mining in the outback. Australia remained without nuclear power, except for one small research reactor, although much uranium was exported from a selected handful of mines.

The conservative Liberal Party government that assumed power in 1996 moved away from the more environmentally conscious policies pursued by the Labor Party governments from 1983 to 1996. In 2001, for example, Prime Minister John Howard's Liberal Party government refused to endorse the Kyoto Protocol on greenhouse gases on the pretext that it would damage Australia's coal industry. The government stopped fuel excise indexation as the cost of living rose, thus making car transport effectively cheaper over time. (Australia eventually ratified the agreement under Kevin Rudd's Labor Party government in 2007, leaving the United States as the only other industrial nation not to ratify the protocol; Canada abandoned the treaty in December of 2011.)

Atmospheric pollution continues to threaten human health, although the decline of heavy industry and prevalent climatic conditions make skies clearer and cleaner than those in many countries. Air pollution in the cities improved in the 1980s, but impending environmental disasters lie ahead for Australia with the massive growth of Sydney, as well as the swelling size of Melbourne and Brisbane. Pollution problems associated with this growth, especially in western Sydney, are now apparent, with industry and housing spreading to the Blue Mountains some 80 kilometers to the west, in a manner comparable to the urban sprawl of Los Angeles.

Outlook

Notwithstanding urban environmental concerns, the most significant issues remain those of water, salinity, tree clearing, and other land-use practices. Urban intrusion on bushland has enhanced the risks to property and life from the massive bushfires that are endemic to eucalyptus forests. The fire in Victoria on 7 February 2009 took 173 lives and devastated communities in an unprecedented disaster known as Black Saturday (Disaster Assist 2011). These issues continue to be raised by the impact of a European (and increasingly US-influenced) culture and economy on a natural world that has always been characterized by harsh physical constraints. The continued deterioration of water supplies in the Murray-Darling Basin, the crucial food bowl of the country, is a phenomenon tied to El Niño–related climate variations and is accentuated by apparent longer-term warming trends in the regional climate.

Since 2007, the issue of population pressure has burst back into contention. Although Australia is not heavily populated by world standards, many believe its population level and its population growth rate (one of the higher rates in the developed world owing to strong immigration) should be cut back as drier conditions limit both agricultural potential and city water supplies. In 2010, the federal government appointed a minister for the Department of Sustainability, Environment, Water, Population and Communities in an attempt to square the circle—between tackling the nation's water crisis and acceding to business and mining industry demands for ever more supplies of labor, which can come only from migration. There is no foreseeable end to this dilemma, and Australia's population will most likely continue to grow at levels incompatible with life support systems of water and soils.

Ian TYRRELL
University of New South Wales

See also Auckland, New Zealand; Forest Management; Mining (Australia); Murray-Darling River Basin; New Zealand; Oceania; Perth, Australia; Sydney, Australia; United States; Water Use and Rights

FURTHER READING

Bolton, Geoffrey. (1981*). Spoils and spoilers: Australians make their environment, 1788–1980.* Sydney: Allen and Unwin.
Bonyhady, Tim. (2001). *The colonial Earth.* Melbourne, Australia: Miegunyah Press.
Carson, Rachel. (1962). *Silent spring.* New York: Houghton Mifflin.
Dargavel, John. (1995). *Fashioning Australia's forests.* Melbourne, Australia: Oxford University Press.
Disaster Assist. (2011). Victorian bushfires January February 2009. Retrieved May 16, 2012, from http://www.disasterassist.gov.au/www/disasterassist/disasterassist.nsf/Page/Currentdisasters_VictorianBushfiresJanuaryFebruary2009
Flannery, Tim. (1994). *The future eaters: An ecological history of the Australasian lands and people.* Sydney: Reed Books.
Griffiths, Tim. (2002). *Forests of ash: An environmental history.* Melbourne, Australia: Cambridge University Press.
Hutton, Drew, & Connors, Libby. (1999). *A history of the Australian environmental movement.* Sydney: Cambridge University Press.
Marsh, George Perkins. (1864). *Man and nature: Or physical geography as modified by human action.* New York: Charles Scribner.
Powell, Joseph Michael. (1976). *Environmental management in Australia, 1788–1914.* Melbourne, Australia: Oxford University Press.
Pyne, Stephen J. (1991). *Burning bush: A fire history of Australia.* New York: Henry Holt.
Ratcliffe, Francis. (1938). *Flying fox and drifting sand: The adventure of a biologist in Australia.* London: Chatto and Windus.
Robin, Libby. (2008). *How a continent created a nation.* Sydney: University of New South Wales Press.
Rolls, Eric C. (1969). *They all ran wild.* Sydney: Angus and Robertson.
Rolls, Eric C. (1981). *A million wild acres.* Melbourne, Australia: Thomas Nelson.
Tyrrell, Ian. (1999). *True gardens of the gods: Californian-Australian environmental reform, 1860–1930.* Berkeley and Los Angeles: University of California Press.
United States Central Intelligence Agency. (US CIA). (2012). The World factbook: Australia. Retrieved May 18, 2012, from https://www.cia.gov/library/publications/the-world-factbook/geos/as.html

Bogotá, Colombia

7.5 million est. pop. 2011

Despite its long distance from the sea, Bogotá has historically been the richest city in Colombia, with a diversified economy and a skilled population. Since the 1990s, successive governments have made decisive governance and environmental interventions in public transportation, public space, walking, cycling, risk reduction, and social welfare. Informal growth, poverty, and income inequality, as well as coordination with neighboring municipalities about future growth, remain substantial challenges.

Bogotá is the capital city of Colombia, with a population estimated at 7.5 million in 2011 (Bogotá Mayor's Office 2010). The city's origins may be traced to small, dispersed settlements of the indigenous Muisca people in the Sabana de Bogotá—the fertile plateau on which the city sits in the Andes mountain range, at 2,640 meters above sea level. It was founded as Santa Fe de Bogotá in 1538 by Spanish conquistadors searching for gold (some say spurred on by the legendary El Dorado tale of untold riches). The town eventually became the seat of government for the vast viceroyalty of Nueva Granada in the colonial era (mid-1500s to early 1800s), which provided a rich source of indigenous manual labor, tributes, and income from textiles, agriculture, emeralds, and precious metals for the European invaders. It retained its status as capital of Colombia upon independence from Spanish rule in the early nineteenth century, when its name changed to Bogotá.

For centuries, the city's population grew very slowly, largely a reflection of its physical isolation from the rest of the country. Reaching the Caribbean-fortified port of Cartagena, some 1,000 kilometers to the north, involved a trip lasting several weeks down the steep Andean slopes and long boat journeys in the sticky heat of the Magdalena River. The Spanish Empire brought with it an array of occupations, including administrators, craftspeople, and religious orders, who set up some of the oldest schools and universities in the Americas. By 1900, the city had a population of 100,000, mostly contained in a small area surrounding the Plaza de Bolívar, the city's administrative and religious heart. Population rose rapidly after 1950, when the country's economic and social torpor was shaken by a combination of a largely rural, nondeclared civil war (known as La Violencia) that claimed hundreds of thousands of lives and increased the concentration of agricultural land in fewer hands, and the effects of protectionist policies to stimulate agricultural and industrial production of consumer and capital goods previously imported from Europe and the United States. Migrants from the countryside and smaller towns moved in vast numbers to Bogotá and other regional capitals in search of jobs and protection from rural violence. The population of the city rose to 3 million by 1973 and to more than 4 million by 1985. Migration soon subsided, and nowadays expansion comes largely from natural population growth (Safford and Palacios 2002; Bogotá Mayor's Office 2010).

Today 90 percent of the city's population is contained in a continuously built-up area of some 35,000 hectares within a single large administrative jurisdiction known officially as Bogotá Distrito Capital (with a total area of 1,732 square kilometers) (Bogotá Mayor's Office 2010). Much of the city's future expansion will take place in neighboring municipalities to the north, west, and southwest of the city, where, as of 2012, some 10 percent of the population lives.

Economy and Society

Unemployment, poverty, and income inequality have been key challenges for successive city administrations. During the decades of rapid population growth, the city did create vast numbers of jobs, though not all were stable, involving good working conditions and a monthly paycheck. Close to half of the labor force toiled away in the *informal sector*—unstable, poorly paid jobs in precarious working conditions as street vendors, construction workers, and porters. This split has not altered dramatically in the early twenty-first century, though now most workers, even in the informal sector, are covered by a social security system, while their children are guaranteed a free place in a state school. At 10 percent in 2010, the city's rate of unemployment has been among the lowest of the country's largest cities, a measure of Bogotá's diversified economy attracting both national and foreign investment, and of a young, skilled labor force (Banco de la República and DANE 2010).

Bogotá's economy grew at a non-negligible rate of 4.5 percent per year between 2000 and 2009. Even when adjusted for population growth, a 30 percent increase in real incomes (to US$8,000 per capita in 2009) is remarkable for a city that owes much of its earlier growth to its preeminence as the national capital and largest domestic market (Banco de la República and DANE 2010). But then Bogotá has never been a strong exporter. In value, exports were the equivalent of US$188 per capita in 1991 and US$450 in 2008, and comprised a combination of textiles and chemicals produced in its factories, as well as minerals and cut flowers from surrounding municipalities but flown out of the city's El Dorado airport. At over $1 billion a year, Colombia's cut-flower export industry is the second largest in the world after the Netherlands, and is an important source of jobs mainly for women in small municipalities (Asocolflores 2010; Banco de la República and DANE 2010; Dávila 1996).

Like many large cities around the world, as Bogotá's economy has become integrated into the world economy, the financial and property services industries have grown faster than traditional sectors such as government services and manufacturing. Together with commerce, these five sectors currently represent close to 60 percent of the city's economy (Banco de la República and DANE 2010). Globalization also seems to have entrenched another feature of most Latin American societies: income inequality, which in Colombia stands among the highest in the world (with a Gini coefficient—a commonly used measure of inequality, with 0 indicating complete equality and 1, complete inequality—for the thirteen largest cities of 0.53 in 2010) (DNP 2011). Despite this, the city's sustained economic growth helped halve poverty levels in the decade after 2000 (to 15.5 percent of the total in 2010 according to one official measure), a trend reinforced by the city government's social welfare programs (health, nutrition, and education for the poorer strata) (DNP 2011).

Environment and Transportation

Bogotá is well-known internationally for the remarkable turnaround from a poorly managed, chaotic city with a high murder rate and decaying infrastructure in the 1970s to a "model city" by the first decade of the twenty-first century, with a highly successful mass-transportation system built in record time, significant drops in violent deaths and in car dependency, public spaces (including sidewalks) recovered for public enjoyment, 334 kilometers of permanent bicycle paths built since 1998, and a modest increase in open spaces and neighborhood parks. This transformation was the result of a combination of national and local factors, including decentralization reforms allowing the election of city mayors by popular vote and an increase in mayoral terms (from two to four years); strengthening of city finances and a more effective and equitable property tax system; the active participation of a mature electorate composed of voters now born in the city with a growing sense of belonging (particularly compared with previous generations of in-migrants); and a succession of enlightened administrations led by charismatic mayors supported by honest and skilled officials in charge of a single large local authority (compared to five municipalities in Caracas, Venezuela; four provinces in Santiago de Chile; and three states in Greater Mexico City). Reforms also built on the sturdy physical and institutional legacy created in the 1960s by highly capable administrations, which included a record of sound, nonpoliticized management of publicly owned utility companies, such as the electricity and water supply companies, and a remarkable coverage of basic services among the city's population, including its poorest settlements as well as eleven neighboring municipalities. Since its introduction in 2000, Transmilenio, a mass-transit system using bus rapid transit (BRT) technology with dedicated lanes and fixed bus stations, has helped transform the city and improved quality of life among commuters (especially the poor) by significantly reducing travel times and emissions. Fuel-efficient, articulated buses replaced thousands of buses chaotically vying for passengers in traffic-clogged roads. An unintended effect of the BRT is that it has promoted greater levels of physical activity in a city where only 44.7 percent of the adult population regularly engages in any form of physical exercise. Accounting for 25 percent of daily public transport trips in 2010, the BRT prompts users to walk longer distances to stations compared to the previous system, when bus drivers stopped whenever asked to (Cervero et al. 2009; Gómez et al. 2010). Physical improvements to sidewalks and public spaces introduced with the BRT system have also encouraged greater use of public spaces by pedestrians.

Risk Prevention and Urban Planning

Perhaps less well-known are efforts at creating a system of risk-prevention and reduction measures that have been integrated into a long-term city development plan. This plan identifies areas of the city subject to landslides or particularly vulnerable to earthquakes and flooding and steers new development away from them. Especially problematic are already established informal settlements, where the poor buy or rent a dwelling with prices markedly lower, largely due to the area's vulnerability to such risks. In a context of high levels of poverty, where new development is likely to take place spontaneously in such precarious conditions, channeling development is a challenge, as relocating vulnerable families is very complicated. Despite their reach, many of the measures that have made Bogotá a success story have increasingly fallen short of the needs of a city where the number of private vehicles (especially motorcycles) grows at a rate far outstripping population growth. The formally constituted metropolitan government will not be politically viable as the city's population spills out of Bogotá's jurisdiction. As a result, it will be up to an alliance of local authorities to face up to the challenge of sustaining the remarkable social and environmental gains made between 1990 and 2010.

Julio D. DÁVILA
University College London

See also Amazon River; Amazonia; Andes Mountains; Brazil; Caribbean; Central America; Guatemala City; Labor; Lima, Peru; Mexico City; Mobility; Poverty; Public Transportation; Southern Cone; Urbanization

FURTHER READING

Asociación Colombiana de Exportadores de Flores (Asocolflores). (2010). *Noticias frescas no. 200* (2nd trimester) [Fresh news no. 200]. Bogotá, Colombia: Asocolflores.

Banco de la República, & Departamento Administrativo Nacional de Estadística (DANE). (2010). *Informe de coyuntura económica regional: Bogotá y Cundinamarca* [Report of regional economic conditions: Bogotá and Cundinamarca]. Bogotá, Colombia: DANE.

Berney, Rachel. (2010). Learning from Bogotá: How municipal experts transformed public space. *Journal of Urban Design, 15*(4), 539–558.

Bogotá Mayor's Office. (2010). *Revisión al plan de ordenamiento territorial de Bogotá. La construcción de un territorio más competitivo. Equidad, productividad y sostenibilidad* [Review of the land-use plan of Bogotá: Building a more competitive territory; Equality, productivity and sustainability]. Bogotá, Colombia: Secretaría de Planeación Distrital.

Cervero, Robert; Sarmiento, Olga L.; Jacoby, Enrique; Gómez, Luis F.; & Neiman, Andrea. (2009). Influences of built environments on walking and cycling: Lessons from Bogotá. *International Journal of Sustainable Transportation, 3*(4), 203–226.

Dávila, Julio D. (1996). Bogotá, Colombia: Restructuring with continued growth. In Nigel Harris & Ida Fabricius (Eds.), *Cities and structural adjustment* (pp. 136–160). London: UCL Press.

Dávila, Julio D. (2004). La transformación de Bogotá [The transformation of Bogotá]. In Fernando Cepeda Ulloa (Ed.), *Fortalezas de Colombia* [Colombia's strengths] (pp. 417–439). Bogotá, Colombia: Editorial Planeta.

Departamento Nacional de Planeación (DNP). (2011, October 6). Incidencia de la pobreza por ingresos y Gini [Incidence of income poverty and Gini] (spreadsheet). Retrieved April 4, 2012, from www.dnp.gov.co

Gilbert, Alan. (2006). Good urban governance: Evidence from a model city? *Bulletin of Latin American Research, 25*(3), 392–419.

Gilbert, Alan. (2008). Bus rapid transit: Is Transmilenio a miracle cure? *Transport Reviews, 28*(4), 439–467.

Gilbert, Alan, & Dávila, Julio D. (2002). Bogotá: Progress within a hostile environment. In David J. Myers & Henry A. Dietz (Eds.), *Capital city politics in Latin America: Democratization and empowerment* (pp. 29–63). Boulder, CO: Lynne Rienner Publishers.

Gómez, Luis F., et al. (2010). Characteristics of the built environment associated with leisure-time physical activity among adults in Bogotá, Colombia: A multilevel study. *Journal of Physical Activity and Health, 7*(2), 196–203.

Martin, Gerard; Escovar, Alberto; Martin, Marijke; & Goossens, Maarten. (Eds.). (2007). *Bogotá: El renacer de una ciudad* [Bogotá: The rebirth of a city]. Bogotá, Colombia: Instituto Distrital de Patrimonio Cultural.

Osorio, Gustavo. (2009). *Prevención y reducción de riesgos a través de los instrumentos de planificación territorial en Bogotá* [Prevention and risk reduction through territorial planning instruments in Bogotá]. Lima, Peru: PREDECAN, Secretaría de la Comunidad Andina.

Safford, Frank, & Palacios, Marco. (2002). *Colombia: Fragmented land, divided society.* Oxford, UK: Oxford University Press.

Skinner, Reinhard. (2004). City profile: Bogotá. *Cities, 21*(1), 73–81.

Brazil

205.7 million est. pop. 2012

As the world's largest tropical country, with a rich biodiversity and a well-documented history of the interactions between people and its natural resources, Brazil offers rich lessons in environmental history. Doubts exist about whether these lessons will be heeded and, if so, how they will shape the country's future, in terms of biodiversity protection and of the economic uses of this biodiversity in fields such as medicine and genetic engineering.

Brazil is the largest country in South America, occupying nearly 48 percent of the landmass of South America and 20 percent of the landmass of North and South America put together. With an area of 8.5 million square kilometers, it is the world's fifth largest country (behind the Russian Federation, Canada, China, and the United States) and the largest country in the Southern Hemisphere. More than 92 percent of the country is located in the intertropical zone, making it the world's largest tropical country as well.

The Brazilian population of 205.7 million (US CIA 2012) is the fifth largest in the world (behind China, India, the United States, and Indonesia). Eighty-four percent of Brazilians are considered urban dwellers because they reside within city limits, however these limits extend into rural areas where a fair portion of people live in very small towns and engage in rural productive activities. In the 1950s and 1960s, Brazil's population, which up to that point had been mostly rural, grew rapidly and became urbanized faster than the populations of almost all other countries. The growth rate fell sharply after the 1980s, however, and today it is continuing to decline. Brazilians are distributed unevenly over the enormous national territory, with a large majority of the people and almost all large cities located along, or close to, its Atlantic coastline. Vast central and western areas have low population densities.

Brazil is a fully industrialized country, although it is not considered as "developed" because of its relatively low per capita income, its strongly skewed wealth distribution, and its severe social inequalities. In 2010, its gross domestic product (GDP), at $2,023,528 million, was the sixth largest in the world, after that of the United States, China, Japan, Germany, and France, and followed by the United Kingdom and Italy. In the same year, Brazil was also the world's seventh largest consumer of energy, and ranked ninth in energy production (Enerdata 2011a and 2011b).

Almost every type of modern industry can be found in Brazil. It is a world-class producer of steel and metallurgical products, motor vehicles and parts, airplanes, motors and machinery, chemical products, electronics, paper and cardboard, clothes, plastics, and shoes. It also has a vast, although uneven, agricultural and animal husbandry sector. Soybeans, corn, rice, sugarcane, coffee, citric fruits, cassava, cotton, and processed and unprocessed meat are some of its major agricultural products. In 2009 Brazil had the world's second largest cattle herd, with approximately 190 million head (Brazilian Beef 2009), and the world's leading chicken exporter and third-largest chicken producer (Peer 2008) *and* the world's third largest hog producer (NationMaster.com 2012). Its service sector is also diversified and dynamic.

The economic system is mixed, including both private enterprise (foreign and multinational companies) and strong state investments and companies. Since the mid-1990s, however, private firms have taken over or advanced strongly into many economic sectors previously dominated by the state (such as oil and natural gas production, telecommunications, steel production, mining, railroads, electricity, gas, phone utilities, and financial institutions). Brazil's economy, which was built mostly on the voracious (and often wasteful) extraction and transformation of natural resources, is dynamic and attains high growth rates.

Colonized by Portugal, Brazil has been an independent country since 1822. Until 1889 it was the only monarchy in the Americas. Today it is a federated republic, with twenty-six states and a federal district that hosts the national capital, Brasília. The national language is Portuguese. Brazilian culture is a blend of European (specifically Iberian), African, and native influences. The European and African contributions were diversified in their respective origins, however, and formed many blends with each other and with the also diverse native cultures. Ethnically, Brazilian society is a rich amalgamation of these interactions, and includes a remarkable degree of miscegenation and cultural exchange. Racial tensions and conflicts, for this reason, range from moderate to weak. Brazil has the largest number of Catholics in the world, although lately several Protestant and evangelical denominations have gained numerous followers. Afro-American religions are more openly practiced than they had previously been. Brazilians have a tolerant attitude about religion, however, and many people follow more than one orientation, thereby lessening religious conflict.

Brazil's Relevance to Environmental History

Brazil is highly relevant to the world's environmental history and future for at least seven reasons:

1. The national territory is large, spanning about 37 degrees of latitude and about 38 degrees of longitude (corresponding to four time zones), an expanse that makes for sharp variations in ecological processes, ecosystems, and landscapes.
2. Most of Brazil is tropical, and biodiversity (biological diversity within an environment) is richest in the warmer and moister areas of the planet. Indeed, because Brazil is tropical, and because it is so large and moist, it is frequently cited as being endowed with a "megabiodiversity," along with Colombia, Peru, Ecuador, Mexico, and Indonesia, among others.
3. The variety and distribution of biomes (major biological community types) enhance this biodiversity. The biologically rich tropical rain forests, in their Amazon and Atlantic formations, cover or covered approximately 55 percent of the Brazilian territory, interfacing with the extensive and also biologically rich savannas (the Cerrado), which make or made up 25 percent. Other biomes include the more confined and less diverse desert scrub formations (the Caatinga) (13 percent), and tropical and temperate grasslands (2.5 percent). The freshwater wetlands biome (the Pantanal) is relatively small (1 percent) but biologically rich. Finally, extensive coastal mangroves and shoreline scrub formations account for about 3.5 percent of the Brazilian territory, along the almost 8,000 kilometers of Atlantic coastline and complemented by the Atlantic Ocean's own marine life forms.
4. The Americas in general, and Brazil in particular, were among the last areas of the globe to be occupied by populations of *Homo sapiens*. The oldest undisputed records of human presence in Brazil date back to a maximum of only eight thousand years, which is quite recent in relative terms. This means that in Brazil, as in the rest of the Americas, Australia, and Oceania (islands of the Pacific Ocean), the window of time wherein human activities have been able to have an effect on natural processes and landscapes is shorter than it is in the Old World (the mainlands of Africa, Asia, and Europe) and, consequently, their cumulative effect is less significant. Brazil's rich tropical formations are therefore considered to be, in the broad sense of the word, wilder.
5. The bulk of the prehistoric human experience in the Americas, and in Brazil in particular, occurred under the regimes of small groups of nomadic hunter-gatherers or small, semipermanent villages of tropical gardeners, and not under complex civilizations based on intensive agriculture, specialized social classes, centralized states, professional armies, permanent towns and cities, and organized religions. This holds true even if the Mexican, Mayan, and Inca civilizations are taken into account, together with other more complex societies prevailing for some time in other parts of the Americas, including the Brazilian Amazon. In fact, many of the remaining peoples of the world still influenced by, or actually experiencing, the "traditional," low-impact lifestyles of hunting, gathering, and tropical gardening live in Brazil. Over the last few centuries there has been ample opportunity to record their forms of interaction with, and adaptation to, the natural environment.
6. The European colonization of Brazil and other New World countries left relatively abundant evidence of the interactions between the numerous types of colonizers and colonized peoples within many ecological settings and under many socioeconomic and cultural circumstances. The sharp cultural distinctions between natives and colonizers, including African slaves transferred by force to Brazil, are in themselves a rich source of documented lessons in environmental history—exchanges of domesticated and semidomesticated plants and animals, deliberate and accidental introductions of new plants and animals, spread of contagious diseases, uses

of fire, extraction of floral resources, hunting and fishing, gardening, agricultural expansion, values and perceptions, religions, and technology, among others.
7. Brazil is rich in many of the natural resources most useful to humanity, particularly in freshwater (the Amazon River basin alone holds 20 percent of the world's freshwater) and in the associated hydroelectric potential of its numerous long rivers. It also has extensive deposits of the world's most useful ores and minerals (iron, aluminum, manganese, tin, copper, and kaolin) as well as gold, silver, and precious stones. Its tropical forests, the most extensive in the world, yield wood and dozens of other products; it also has a vast stock of agricultural soils, in addition to its flora and fauna, and their respective genetic endowments.

Nature and Society Shaping Each Other

Brazilian prehistory and history encompass many episodes in the unfolding of environmental history in the form of eloquent exchanges between natural landscapes, processes and features, and human societies.

History of a Name

Brazil is reportedly the only modern nation named after a tree. The brazilwood tree, *pau-brasil* in Portuguese and *Caesalpinia echinata* in scientific nomenclature, was the first commodity the Brazilian natural treasure chest sent out to the rest of the world in modern times. The striking red color of the dense hardwood of this tree, endemic to the coastal formations of the Atlantic Forest, was not easy to collect or transport but, eventually, the name *brazil* grew so much in commercial importance that, in addition to being used for the tree and the commodity, it was used as the name of the colony, its inhabitants, and the country.

Of course, the economic importance of the tree, more than any preservationist sensitivity on the part of the pragmatic Portuguese colonizers, led them to name the country after the tree. The wood yielded a highly valued, deep-red dye used in carpets, drapes, and, most importantly, garments for nobles and clergy. It was also used in cabinetmaking and crafts. The brazilwood trade began immediately after the arrival of the Portuguese in 1500 and continued all the way to the 1870s, when its dye was replaced by synthetic dyes created in European laboratories. Selected for its commercial value from among hundreds of tree species of the Atlantic Forest, the brazilwood tree became the country's national tree. Today, although it is hard to find mature individuals in the wild, the species is protected, cultivated in botanical gardens and in small plantations and nurseries, and used for landscaping.

Only a residual trade in brazilwood remains, mainly for cello and violin bows.

Recent Arrivals and Recent Extinctions

The very fact that human occupation of the Brazilian territory is so recent relates to many matters of environmental history. As humans expanded into the Americas, they found a vast and diverse territory in which biological processes had been evolving, untouched by human intervention. Life had by no means been static, of course. Plants, animals, ecosystems, and landscapes had undergone many changes over time—migration, expansion or shrinkage of ranges, speciation (formation of new species), adaptation, extinction, erosion, climate shifts, and rising and falling of sea levels. Not until about eighteen thousand years ago were humans present in the Americas to influence, or merely witness, these changes. Several species of large land animals (megafauna), such as mastodons, giant sloths, armadillos, felines, horse-like, and camel-like species became extinct shortly after the first humans spread through the continent. Brazil is one of the areas in which the fossilized remains of these species are commonly found. A likely explanation for this is that, because these animals evolved in settings that had no human hunters, once they were exposed to them, they were easy prey to the newcomer's keen hunting skills. Combined with other factors, such as climate and ecosystem change and the slow reproduction rates of these large animals, human hunting may thus have contributed decisively to the impoverishment of the continental fauna in relatively recent times.

New Plants and Animals

A distinct aspect of the timing of the original human migration into the Americas is that it preceded the domestication of certain plants and animals in the Old World, thereby setting the stage for independent domestication of plants and animals in the New World (i.e., the Western Hemisphere, especially the Americas). If the dates of early migrations into the Americas and of the domestication of plants and animals in the Old World are correct, it can safely be said that the original migrants entered the Americas without the support of the plants and animals that were domesticated only later in Eurasia and North Africa.

Whereas several Old World populations, starting around eleven thousand years ago, began to master the cultivation of the more famous and lasting of the domesticated plants (such as wheat and rice) and the domestication of animals (such as cattle, goats, pigs, horses, and sheep), populations in the Americas, arriving without these resources, had to start domestication from scratch, in an entirely different natural setting, with a different set of plants and animals. Nonetheless, archeologists have identified at least three major centers of plant and animal domestication in the Americas—two in the high plateaus of present-day Mexico and the high plateaus of Peru and Bolivia, and one in the present-day eastern United States. Corn (*Zea mays*), beans (*Phaseolus* sp.), potatoes (*Solanum tuberosum*), sweet potatoes (*Ipomoea batatas*), squash (*Cucurbita pepo*), peanuts (*Arachis hypogaea*), tomatoes (*Lycopersicum esculentum*), cotton (*Gossypium hirsutum* or *G. barbadense*), the llama (*Lama glama*—the only large animal native to the New World to be domesticated before contact with Europeans), and the turkey (*Meleagris gallopavo*), among others, were all domesticated in these centers.

In contrast, the vast lowlands of South America, in which Brazil is located, contributed much less to the stock of regionally or globally significant domesticates. Manioc (*Manihot esculenta*) and sweet potatoes (*Ipomoea batatas*) seem to be the only food plants from the lowlands (although not necessarily from Brazilian territory) to have been domesticated before European contact and to have gained wider importance as sources of food, spreading to Africa, Asia, and Oceania. Besides these, several other native or transplanted Mesoamerican or South American species of food plants, yams (*Dioscorea* sp.), squash, and beans were already found by Europeans in or around the modest gardens of the tribal natives of Brazilian lowlands, but they gained only local importance. Other useful plants, such as cotton, tobacco (*Nicotiana tabacum*), and gourds (*Crescentia cujete*), were also cultivated or protected by Brazilian natives, and some of them became world-class commodities. Not a single domesticated animal taken from the lowland fauna was recorded, however, although some native groups confined modest flocks of Muscovy ducks (*Cairina moschata*) and several species of freshwater turtles, such as *Podocnemis unifilis* and *Podocnemis expansa*.

Bounty of the Wild

One lens through which it is possible to examine the relations between humans and nature in Brazil is the contrast between its relatively meager contribution to the portfolio of humanity's cultivated plants and animals and its rich biodiversity. Indeed, Brazil's contribution has been primarily in the form of useful wild plant and animal products. Among the more famous of these are rubber and the Brazil nut, products of the rubber tree (*Hevea brasiliensis*) and the Brazil nut tree (*Bertholletia excelsa*) respectively, both endemic to mature Amazonian forests. But there are many other extractive goods that have been important Brazilian products as well: any number of ornamental and medicinal plants; fibers; the hides of caimans (*Melanosushus niger*, reptiles similar to alligators, once a targeted species); the pelts of several wild animals, such as the peccary (*Tayassu tajacu* and *Tayassu pecari*), the jaguar (*Pantera onca*), and the otter (*Pteronura brasiliensis*); bird feathers; fish; and whale oils. Moreover, Brazil participates prominently as a supplier in a contemporary and dynamic global trade—most of it illegal—in live animals such as tropical fish, birds (*Psittacidae* parakeets, parrots, and macaws, *Ramphastidae* toucans, and many songbirds, among others), tamarin monkeys and other primates, felines, reptiles (such as iguanas), scorpions, tarantulas, and butterflies.

Brazil is also the source of accidental exports of "unwanted" species. This is eloquently illustrated by the infamous "fire ant" (*Solenopsis invicta*). Probably hidden in the crevices of tropical tree trunks imported through the port of Mobile, Alabama, in the 1930s, this aggressive species native to Brazil, Argentina, and Paraguay spread throughout the South of the United States and became a major problem for urban dwellers, farmers, and wildlife managers. The so-called African bee (*Apis mellifera adansonii*), another notorious insect invader of the United States and other countries of the Americas (although not native to Brazil), started its decades-long spree starting from the city of São Paulo. In 1956, a set of these highly aggressive bees, under study in a Brazilian lab, was accidentally released and spread over tropical America and parts of temperate America, either blending with or extinguishing the western honey bee (*Apis mellifera*) populations, introduced much earlier from Europe, creating havoc in beekeeping industries and killing hundreds of people and livestock. Many natural elements found in Brazil (including reproductive and genetic materials like the seeds of the rubber tree *Hevea brasileinsis*) are still regularly taken from their natural settings and integrated into wider social and economic networks, bypassing local domestication and sometimes even local knowledge (showing that this knowledge, despite arguments to the contrary, is not necessarily required for the identification and use of components of biodiversity).

Domestication in the Making

Brazil's rich flora and fauna also provide the opportunity for contemporary and fairly well-documented episodes of successful or attempted domestication. The world's most important acts of domestication were prehistoric and thus left meager traces, inferred from archeological sites, myths, and genetic information. The exact details of the domestication of, for example, wheat, corn, and rice (humanity's three most important and widely cultivated foods today), or cattle, chickens, and sheep, may never be known. But latter-day episodes of domestication reveal much about the demands that societies place on nature. Brazil provides several opportunities for examining such episodes. The floral dye *urucum*, for example, made from seeds of the native bush *Bixa orellana*, was once an entirely extractive product, intensively used by Native Brazilians for body adornment, protection against insects, and other needs. The plant was domesticated and planted in Brazil and elsewhere in the early twentieth century. Starting in the 1940s, however, synthetic dyes devalued *urucum* plantations, until the 1980s when *urucum* made a strong agricultural and commercial comeback as a natural dye, after its synthetic substitutes were proven to be carcinogenic.

Domestication of the Brazilian rubber tree (*Hevea brasiliensis*) was not achieved in Brazil, nor by Brazilians, but rather by scientists and technicians in Europe and by colonial administrators and plantation owners in South and Southeast Asia. For many decades the rubber tree had been exploited in Brazil exclusively as an extractive product, based on widespread areas of its growth as a wild plant throughout vast sections of Amazonia. Domestication, mastered in England and executed in Asia, virtually extinguished the commercial importance of extractive rubber production in Brazil. The huge economic importance of natural rubber in the late 1800s made the tree's domestication one of the best documented episodes in the human quest for mastering plants, especially because the global scope of production and consumption of rubber created equally global alliances and rivalries.

Three other examples of domestication with remarkable commercial success are the domestication of the cashew tree (*Anacardium occidentale*), the *guaraná* vine (*Paullinia cupana*), and the cocoa tree (*Theobroma cacao*), all of which are also native to Brazil and were also once exploited in entirely extractive modes. These trees were domesticated at different times and planted in extensive plantations in Brazil (and, in the case of cocoa, in other countries as well) that cultivated fruit, pulp, seeds, and nuts. The *jaborandi* tree (*Pilocarpus microphyllus*) is an even more recent example: this native tree yields bark and leaves with important medicinal uses, including in the treatment of glaucoma. Since the 1990s, its production, once entirely extractive, shifted toward cultivation. The Amazonian palm tree *açaí* (*Euterpe oleracea*) is collected or managed in its wild stands, but soon plantations may prevail over wild populations to feed an expanding market of energy drinks. Two other Amazonian fruit trees that are going through processes of domestication are *cupuaçu* (*Theobroma grandiflorum*) and *graviola* (*Annona muricata*).

Brazilian research and environmental agencies, in association with farmers, also are trying to domesticate, or at least establish captive breeding for, a variety of wild native animals, such as the capybara (*Hidrochaeris hydrochaeris*, the world's largest rodent), several species of freshwater fish and turtles, and caimans.

Historical Introductions

After European contact, Brazil's soils were systematically and extensively used for the cultivation of many non-native plants introduced by colonizers. The sugarcane plantations and mills of *Saccharum* sp., originally located in the Brazilian Northeast, concentrated on a plant domesticated in Southeast Asia or New Guinea. These plantations were the first permanent, large-scale, and commercially successful economic activity developed by Europeans anywhere in the Americas. They began in the 1550s and later spread to other parts of Brazil, which has been a world-class producer of sugar for almost five centuries. The coffee plant (*Coffea arabica* and *Coffea robusta*), a native of Africa and possibly domesticated in Arabia, also began a successful career in plantations in Brazil's mid-south in the 1770s and has now spread into the country's midwest and even into southern Amazonia. For about 160 years (1790–1950), Brazil was the largest coffee producer and exporter in the world, and coffee cultivation today is expanding once again.

A more recent and less durable introduction was the Asian fiber plant jute (*Corchorus capsularis*). Introduced to the Amazonian floodplains in the 1930s, it grew well and expanded for about forty years, but its use for making fiber bags for coffee and other grains was quickly outdated in the 1970s by the development of plastic fibers.

This string of successful introductions continues to this day. Soybeans (*Glycine hispida*), introduced on a large scale only in the 1970s, have prospered, as have Brazil's herds of cattle, chickens, and hogs. Brazil is also a world-class producer of introduced citrus fruits, namely oranges

(*Citrus aurantium*), lemons (*Citrus limonum*), and tangerines (*Citrus reticulata*). Tropical fruit species introduced from other areas of the world, such as mangoes (*Mangifera indica*) and jackfruit (*Artocarpus integra*), also grow well. Recently, Brazil started to produce large yields of temperate fruits such as grapes, apples, and melons.

Rushing for Gold and Precious Stones

The mining of gold and precious stones in Brazil had a profound impact on the country's environmental history. These mineral riches were discovered by Portuguese explorers in the 1690s, after almost two hundred years of frantic searches all over Brazil. Gold and precious stones were found throughout a vast and unsettled area deservedly named Minas Gerais (general mines), now the name of a Brazilian state.

This vast frontier of gold and precious stones produced well for about one hundred years, with different locations reaching peaks at different times. Most of the digging and sifting was done manually in rivers and along their banks and floodplains, uprooting native vegetation, silting rivers and changing their courses, churning soils, and creating scarred landscapes. Each location successively attracted, was settled by, and then left behind by tens of thousands of Portuguese, Brazilian Creoles, and African slaves involved in mining, transportation, government, supervision, farming, and support activities. Besides inundating Portugal and the rest of Europe with tons of gold and precious stones, and accelerating commercial and industrial changes there, this gold rush was the impetus behind the surveying and mining of thousands of square kilometers of the Brazilian backlands, with massive environmental transformations of the topography, humid forests, savannas, and scrub forests. Such transformations, many of them almost invisible today to the untrained eye, remain to be studied and compared to the transformations of smaller, contemporary frontiers of gold and precious stone in other areas of the country, such as Amazonia.

Frontiers into the Twenty-First Century

Brazil is one of the few countries of the world in which extensive frontiers remain to be settled by, or fully incorporated into, the core of the national society. A vast portion of Brazil's immense Amazon region and a fair percentage of Brazil's midwestern region still display characteristic frontier features, such as low population density, strong population influx, difficulty of access, unassigned and abundant natural resources, weak societal norms, and loose governmental controls. These features attract big government and private initiatives, as well as migrations of small-scale settlers, soldiers of fortune, and adventurers, all of whom consider these frontiers as tabula rasa areas to be made over swiftly.

The social and environmental dimensions of this process have been strong enough to earn Brazil a bad reputation among many contemporary environmentalists, particularly concerning recent policies and moves toward the occupation of the Amazonian frontier. The economy of Brazil's settled areas, together with the needs of other countries, create strong and multiple demands for ores, water, wood, energy (in the forms of firewood, charcoal, and hydroelectric dams), agricultural soils, land for agrarian reform and colonization, roads, and railroads to these frontiers, and governments respond to these demands. This leads to local social and environmental impacts such as deforestation, encroachment on native peoples' homelands, migrations, displacements, conflicts over land, and new and often turbulent social arrangements. These impacts have been harshly criticized by international public opinion. Although population increase and resource use are still limited for the Amazon frontier as a whole, certain areas are indeed ridden with personal drama, social conflict, and environmental wastefulness.

One Tropical Forest Down

Brazil can be singled out as the country that erased the world's largest continuous stretch of tropical rain forest, the Atlantic Forest. Despite the fact that it took many years to eliminate more than 90 percent of this forest, and the fact that Brazilian society is richest and most developed inside its former range, the Atlantic Forest is nevertheless mostly gone. During the five hundred years of Brazil's national history, this forest, which occurred in seventeen of Brazil's current twenty-six states (with an original and mostly continuous range of 1.1 million square kilometers), took most of the brunt of the new and expanding human demands created by European colonization and lifestyles. There are many lessons to be learned from this forest—its exhaustion, its resilience, its recovery, its reclamation, and its conservation—lessons to be learned both by Brazilians and by peoples of other countries who have their own tropical or temperate forests.

Until 1971 only 1 percent of Brazil's vast Amazon rain forests had been deforested. By 2010 deforestation had climbed to 18 percent. Will deforestation proceed or will the lessons of the Atlantic Forest be heeded? This is a major topic for investigation by environmental historians.

Exploration of Biodiversity

The organisms of Brazil's rich but poorly studied biodiversity offer many subjects for research, but Brazil's installed capacity for investigating this part of its natural endowment remains limited. International cooperation by multinational networks of scientists, companies, universities, and government agencies will be needed.

Prospecting, researching, and manipulating genetic resources, in particular, may have significant consequences for humanity. Although the future is not usually the domain of historians, the possibilities of new cultivated plants (or new variants of already cultivated plants), new active principles to be used in medication and treatments, transplantable genes, and other promises of genetic engineering should not be ignored. Brazil's biodiversity is a major source of the biological and genetic materials required for the fulfillment of such promises.

An important branch of biodiversity research is the study of so-called emerging diseases. Brazilian public health institutions are researching at least a dozen contagious, fatal, or potentially fatal diseases that are suspected to have infected human beings only quite recently. These diseases are apparently linked to the opening of new frontiers (through deforestation) or to the settlement of denser populations in recently opened frontiers, in as much as they were recorded mostly among individuals living along roads or in mining camps, particularly in Amazonia, and among missionaries and in personnel stationed at remote military outposts. Much like the Ebola virus in Africa, these diseases probably have unidentified wild animals as hosts and transmitters. These native diseases, originating in frontier areas, seem to be a counterpoint to the Old World infectious diseases that once ravaged Native American populations everywhere, including Brazil. For all its bright promises, Brazilian biodiversity also seems to harbor diseases that threaten humans.

Urban Environmental Issues

As an urbanized and industrialized country, Brazil displays almost every known urban-industrial environmental problem. Large- and medium-size cities, especially in the southeast and along the Atlantic coast, suffer from polluting industries, circulation of hazardous materials, toxic wastes, poor sanitation and related waterborne diseases, poorly managed garbage collection and disposal, dirty air and water, noise, and intensive traffic. One measure to control or overcome these problems deserves attention; the city of São Paulo, in Brazil's industrial heartland, conducts the world's largest and most aggressive program for limiting the use of private automobiles in an attempt to control air pollution. On any given day during the part of the year when the program is in effect, 20 percent of the city's private car fleet is banned from a large central area.

Many cities located in the Atlantic Forest biome suffer from serious, regular floods in the rainy seasons. The more modernized agricultural areas of Brazil are also afflicted by problems such as the excessive use of chemicals, outbreaks of pests, erosion, and silted rivers.

Environmental Laws and Management

Brazil is going through a "third generation" of environmental laws, agencies, and policies. Since the 1930s Brazil progressed from loose regulations on specific resources to today's encompassing laws concerning water, ores, genetic materials, flora, and fauna, and from multiple federal agencies in charge of regulation and management to a single federal executive agency created in the 1990s under the Secretariat for the Environment. Every state has a similar secretariat and environmental control agency. Since the late 1980s hundreds of environmental-impact statements have been drafted as part of the requirements for licensing many kinds of productive and infrastructural activities. An encompassing management system allows the cooperation of federal and state agencies, workers, scientists, businesses, and nongovernmental organizations through the National Environmental Council and equivalent councils in each state. Sixty-four national parks and hundreds of other federal and state conservation units have been created and managed since 1937. At least two extensive and lasting animal conservation programs in Brazil have achieved success, one focused on the golden-lion tamarin (*Leontopithecus rosalia*) and another focused on several species of marine turtles (such as *Dermochelys coriacea* and *Chelonia mydas*).

The United Nations Conference on Environment and Development, held in Rio de Janeiro in 1992 and also known as the Rio Earth Summit, spurred Brazilians to become concerned with environmental issues, resulting in the creation of hundreds of citizen groups that have legal standing to make use of the judicial system in the defense of the environment. Many other international and national meetings of scientists, managers, and activists have kept this concern alive. Brazil was also host to the largest multilateral environmental program in the world, the Pilot Program to Conserve the Brazilian Rain Forests, supported by the G-7 countries (the world's seven richest countries—the United States, Japan, Canada, United Kingdom, France, Italy, and Germany). The program had many fronts that included community-based demonstration projects, renewal of scientific institutions, personnel training in state environmental agencies, management of indigenous homelands, sustainable practices in logging and fishing, and others.

For all of this, Brazil should continue to be a focal point for the study of past and current events and processes that make up the fabric of environmental history.

José Augusto DRUMMOND
Universidade de Brasília

See also Agriculture, Tropical (the Americas); Amazon River; Amazonia; Curitiba, Brazil; Ecotourism (the Americas); Ecovillages; Forest Management; Gender Equality; Mobility; Organization of American States (OAS); Rio de Janeiro, Brazil; Rio Earth Summit (UN Conference on Environment and Development); Rural Development; Social Movements (Latin America); Southern Cone; Urbanization; Water Use and Rights

FURTHER READING

Becker, Bertha K., & Egler, Claudio A. G. (1992). *Brazil: A new regional power in the world economy*. Cambridge, UK: Cambridge University Press.

Brazilian Beef. (2009). The Brazilian livestock. Retrieved May 10, 2012, from http://www.abiec.com.br/eng/3_pecuaria.asp

Dean, Warren. (1987). *Brazil and the struggle for rubber: A study in environmental history*. Cambridge, UK: Cambridge University Press.

Dean, Warren. (1995). *With broadax and firebrand: The destruction of the Brazilian Atlantic Forest*. Berkeley: University of California Press.

de Onis, Juan. (1992). *The green cathedral*. New York: Oxford University Press.

Diamond, Jared. (1998). *Guns, germs and steel: The fate of human societies*. New York: Norton.

Dillehay, Thomas D. (2000). *The settlement of the Americas: A new prehistory*. New York: Basic Books.

Enerdata. (2011a). Global energy statistical yearbook 2011: Total energy consumption. Retrieved May 10, 2012, from http://yearbook.enerdata.net/#/2010-energy-consumption-data.html

Enerdata. (2011b). Global energy statistical yearbook 2011: Total primary production. Retrieved May 10, 2012, from http://yearbook.enerdata.net/#/2010-energy-primary-production.html

Goulding, Michael; Smith, Nigel J. H.; & Mahar, Dennis J. (1996). *Floods of fortune: Ecology & economy along the Amazon*. New York: Columbia University Press.

Guimaraes, Roberto. (1992). *Politics and the environment in Brazil*. Boulder, CO: Tynne Rienner.

Hall, Anthony L. (1989). *Developing Amazonia: Deforestation and social conflict in Brazil's Carajás Program*. Manchester, UK: Manchester University Press.

Miller, Shawn William. (2000). *Fruitless trees: Portuguese conservation and Brazil's colonial timber*. Stanford, CA: Stanford University Press.

NationMaster.com. (2012). Agriculture statistics: Hog production (most recent) by country. Retrieved May 10, 2012, from http://www.nationmaster.com/graph/agr_hog_pro-agriculture-hog-production

Peer, Melinda. (2008, September 18). Tyson plucks Brazilian poultry producers. Retrieved May 10, 2012, from http://www.forbes.com/2008/09/18/tyson-foods-closer-markets-equity-cx_mp_0918markets36.html

United States Central Intelligence Agency (US CIA). (2012). The world factbook: Brazil. Retrieved April 16, 2012, from https://www.cia.gov/library/publications/the-world-factbook/geos/br.html

Share the *Encyclopedia of Sustainability*: Teachers are welcome to make up to ten (10) copies of no more than two (2) articles for distribution in a single course or program. For further permissions, please visit www.copyright.com or contact: info@berkshirepublishing.com

C

Canada

33.4 million est. pop. 2010

Canada had a population of a half million indigenous people and an ecologically diverse environment on the eve of European contact. Subsequent trade and settlement led to increasing exploitation of various resource staples. With the twentieth century came piecemeal implementation of conservation and sustained yield management policies, but early twenty-first century Canada lags many other nations in the development of sustainable energy capacity and the stringency of its commitment to environmental protection. Canada became the only ratifying nation to formally abandon the Kyoto Protocol in December of 2011.

Canada encompasses North America between the United States and the Arctic islands and from the Atlantic to the Pacific oceans. Intense cold, aridity, and thin soils pose significant challenges to agriculture and settlement. Covering 9,203,054 square kilometers, this area was sparsely inhabited by indigenous peoples (except on the Pacific coast, which accounted for 200,000 of the estimated precontact population of 500,000) and was only slowly brought within the realm of European settlement. Fewer than 3 million people of European descent occupied this area in the 1850s. By 1901 the total Canadian population was 5.3 million, and in 1951, 14 million. In 2010 its population was estimated to be 33.4 million. Canada is a plural society, with two official languages (English and French), a complex regional and immigrant background, and diverse forms of religious observance.

Colonialism, Settlement, and Resource Development

As in all settler societies, the occupation and development of the land was a significant part of the colonization process. Early interactions between Europeans and aboriginal peoples led to sizable demographic shifts. Epidemic diseases reduced populations on both the Atlantic and Pacific coasts and in the St. Lawrence Valley before extensive trade networks or settler colonialism developed. As European trade connections extended into the interior and north, patterns of demographic collapse and rapid cultural change followed.

From the banks of the Saint Lawrence River in the seventeenth century to the western plains in the twentieth, immigrants and their descendants cleared forests and turned prairie sod to establish farms and families. The cumulative impact was enormous. By 1911, forest covered less than 10 percent of once heavily treed southern Ontario. Settlers drained many wetlands and swamps. A grid of roads and farms lay over much of southern Canada. Fields of wheat replaced grasslands, and cattle roamed the short-grass prairie. Settlers introduced new plant and animal species and displaced indigenous flora and fauna. These changes brought the introduction of pests, drove some native species to extinction (the passenger pigeon) and dramatically reduced others (the bison).

As Atlantic and world commerce brought early Canada into their expanding orbit, they began to see its environment as a storehouse of valuable resources open to exploitation. These resources supplied external markets and yielded valuable returns to developing colonial and Canadian economies, but they were soon exploited. Cod, beaver, timber, and minerals were the most notable of the Canadian staples, but wheat and other agricultural products can be counted among them.

In the sixteenth and seventeenth centuries explorers believed the codfish stocks of the western Atlantic were inexhaustible. As a rising European population and an ever greater number of religious fast days pushed up the demand for fish, the banks of Newfoundland and the waters of the Gulf of Saint Lawrence attracted hundreds of fishing voyages from Portugal, France, and England each year. By the early eighteenth century, much of the catch came from small settlements that fished inshore. Some local stocks showed signs of depletion. Communities sought to control exploitation through a loose form of moral economy, but changing economic, social, and demographic circumstances eventually undermined most such efforts to limit exploitation. With the introduction of new technologies throughout the twentieth century, the diffuse, loosely structured, and difficult-to-control fishery began overfishing cod stocks. Despite efforts to regulate the catch by extending jurisdiction over international waters to 320 kilometers, the Newfoundland fishery fell into crisis. In 1993 the Canadian government closed the Atlantic cod fishery.

In contrast to the fishery, which had a broadly radial structure, the fur trade was linear in its organization and easier to control. Heavily but not exclusively focused on the beaver, it ran into the northern heart of the continent through two portals, the Saint Lawrence–Great Lakes and Hudson Bay. In Montreal the Northwest Company established the command center of a trade carried inland along the waterways of the Canadian Shield and beyond across the prairies. From posts on the shores of the northern entry to the continent, the Hudson's Bay Company (HBC) also engaged aboriginal people in this trade. With new markets for beaver and other pelts, and new goods (from copper kettles to blankets, axes, and beads) to be acquired in exchange, aboriginal exploitation of fur-bearing animals increased markedly. Pressure on the resource only increased as trade expanded and HBC and Montreal traders competed with each other for native suppliers. By 1840, parts of northern Ontario, once rich in beaver, were virtually hunted out. Only a few years later, and well aware of the need for conservation, the HBC encouraged the devastation of beaver stocks in an area beyond the Rocky Mountains in an effort to reduce their value and attractiveness to US rivals.

Devastation of another sort followed the fur trade. Commercial networks brought new diseases among aboriginal peoples. Between the last decades of the eighteenth century and the middle years of the nineteenth, the common cold, measles, and other common Western ills killed tens of thousands of aboriginal peoples who lacked previous exposure to and immunity from these virulent invaders.

Gold and silver brought to Europe from Spanish America inspired hopes that the north would also yield mineral wealth, but mining was slow to develop. Gold rushes occurred in several places in the mid nineteenth century, but most were small and ephemeral. The most significant was in British Columbia, where discoveries along the Fraser River in 1858 brought some thirty thousand placer miners (who mined alluvial deposits). Demographic, economic, social, and environmental transformations occurred in short order. Some forty years later, the Klondike rush to the Yukon repeated the basic patterns of extraction and environmental transformation.

Coal fueled the Canadian industrial revolution in the late nineteenth century, but there were significant reserves only in limited places. In parts of Nova Scotia, mining towns, hills of refuse shale, and later land subsidence (sinking or settling) mark the environmental legacies of the industry. Less evident were the pollutants spread across the land and into human lungs by the industries that burned local coal. Late in the nineteenth and through the twentieth century, deep, expensive new mines in the hard rock of the Canadian Shield and the western cordillera yielded fortunes in gold, silver, and other metals such as lead, zinc, copper, nickel, and eventually uranium. In Alberta, oil and natural gas development expanded massively after 1945; today the tar sands of northern Alberta hold one of the richest unrealized oil sources in North America. Again, environmental impacts have been largely local, but toxic materials released or utilized in the processing of ore and petroleum products sometimes destroyed downwind vegetation and/or poisoned streams and lakes. Technological innovation is changing modes of bitumen extraction and reducing the ecological footprint of production on a per-barrel basis, but output is being ramped up, and recent estimates place greenhouse gas emissions from the production of synthetic crude oil at two to three times those from the production of conventional oil (Charpentier, Bergerson, and MacLean 2009). Extracting oil from the tar sands is a complex, multistage operation that requires large amounts of water and energy to extract bitumen (which amounts to only about 10–12 percent of the total material) from the mix of sand, silt, clay and water that make up the "sands," and then upgrading it to crude oil that requires further refining to produce gasoline. On average, surface mining entails the removal of 2 tonnes of overburden and then processing 2 tonnes of tar sands (using 2–5 barrels of freshwater and 250 cubic feet of natural gas) to extract a barrel of oil, which, when upgraded to gasoline (through further energy inputs), would allow a large sport-utility vehicle (SUV) to travel about 500 kilometers.

In situ oil extraction, used at depths greater than 100 meters, is less disruptive to the land surface but requires even larger energy inputs. In 2012, industry consumption of natural gas approached 2 billion cubic feet per day (Royal Society of Canada 2010; Shenker 2008; Woynillowicz, Severson-Baker, and Raynolds 2005). In 2011 the Canadian government began referring to the tar sands as a source of "ethical oil," contrasting it with "conflict oil," which comes from less democratic states (Hickman 2011). When the proposed Keystone XL pipeline intended to carry Alberta bitumen to undersupplied upgraders on the Gulf Coast of Texas met serious environmental opposition, particularly related to its passage through the ecologically sensitive sand hills of Nebraska, in 2011, and further environmental impact assessments were mandated by the US State Department, the Canadian government moved to promote development of Enbridge's Northern Gateway pipeline, intended to carry Alberta oil to Kitimat in British Columbia. Opposed by a large number of First Nations bands whose traditional territories it will cross, as well as by many environmental groups, the proposal is, as of 2012, the subject of public hearings. Frustrated by the number of registered interveners, members of the government spoke out against the efforts of "foreign funded radicals" to stop the project and moved to amend Canada's already limited environmental protection legislation. Facing reelection, and pressure from the political right, in 2012 the US president Barack Obama was moved to offer a public expression of support for "fast-tracking" development of that section of the proposed pipeline between Cushing, Oklahoma, and the Gulf of Mexico, now known as the Gulf Coast project (Alberts 2012; Goldenberg 2011).

The forest has been one of Canada's richest and most enduring resources. Its exploitation underpinned much nineteenth-century development because of British and US demand for lumber. In the twentieth century, pulp mills depended on hitherto underutilized species such as spruce, and the logging frontier expanded west and north. British Columbia and, in time, the boreal forests became major producers. Conservation initiatives and the natural resilience of the forest have sustained the resource into the twenty-first century. Today Canada has more land in forest (over 45 percent of the national land area) than in 1900. Forest products accounted for approximately 14 percent of Canadian manufacturing in the 1990s. Since 1980 the industry has changed dramatically. Rapidly altering economic conditions, changing societal expectations, and strong opposition to prevalent logging practices have forced the government to introduce new regulations and greater levels of public participation in decision making to achieve more sustainable forest practices.

Water became an especially important resource in the twentieth century. Hydroelectric dams provided energy for resource development in remote regions and for urban industrial and consumer demand. Cheap electricity underwrote growth in mineral and pulp and paper industries that required large amounts of energy. Although some conservationists advocated hydroelectricity as a green fuel, critics pointed to the deleterious consequences of reservoir flooding and damming on wildlife, fisheries, and human settlements. Water development has also been an important driver of agricultural intensification. By extending irrigation systems, semiarid portions of the Prairie Provinces and of British Columbia were incorporated into range and cattle operations and developed for crops as diverse as stone fruits and sugar beets. Irrigated agriculture accounts for a significant portion of total water consumption in the Prairie Provinces and faces increasing criticism as population and urban growth pushes domestic consumption levels upward.

Canada's two largest cities, Montreal and Toronto, created commercial linkages across the continent and commanded transportation corridors, particularly after the advent of the transcontinental railroad in the 1880s. By the late nineteenth century, the power of metropolitan centers in Canada, steam-powered technologies, and new transportation connections facilitated the rise of a national economy based upon industrial resource extraction. By 1940, most Canadians lived in cities on the southern fringe of the country. Canada's vast land increasingly came under the power of an industrial extractive economy, supporting local development and feeding international markets for raw and semiprocessed natural resources.

Environmental Policy

The problems of jurisdiction in a federal state have shaped environmental policy in Canada. Since Canadian Confederation, the federal government and the provinces have split jurisdiction over natural resources. Sections 92 and 102 of Canada's foundational constitutional legislation, the British North America Act (1867), assign broad powers over land and resources to the provinces. The act also gives the federal government jurisdiction over ocean-based and anadromous fisheries (fisheries that carry fish such as salmon, which live in saltwater and spawn in freshwater) and over navigable and international rivers. Section 91 grants the federal government significant powers related to natural resources, particularly in trade and commerce, taxation policy, and, most broadly, in "Peace, Order and good Government." Before constitutional changes in 1982, the basic outlines of Canada's provincial-federal division of powers gave rise to an environmental policy regime marked by "provincially led intergovernmental collaboration" (Hessing and Howlett 1999). Policy analysts argue that the division of powers under the constitution has hindered environmental management at the national level. A national parks program created Rocky Mountain Park (later Banff National Park) in 1885, however, and by the 1930s a national system of parks extended across the country. In the early twentieth century, a federally led commission of conservation organized inventories of forests, rivers, fur-bearing animals, and other resources, but its effects on policy were limited. Federal jurisdiction over fisheries was one of the strongest national levers in environmental policy and had important implications for conservation and habitat planning. Beyond these examples, provinces cooperated in areas such as water planning. Primarily, however, the provincial level manages and regulates resources; a diverse body of legislation and policy shapes environmental issues and resource development across the country.

Canada and the United States

Canada's relationship with the United States has also shaped the evolution of environmental issues and policy in the twentieth century. Canada and the United States share a boundary across North America that interrupts north–south aligned ecological zones and crosses major rivers and lakes. Most Canadians live within 160 kilometers of this boundary, and much Canadian economic activity revolves around cross-border trade.

Managing nature and shared resources across the Canada-US boundary has produced a number of innovative policies and institutions. Many of these attempts died in negotiation, but the Migratory Birds Treaty (1916), which seeks to protect migratory birds over a wide continental space, represents an early and enduring achievement. Other institutions have sought to coordinate transboundary development. The International Joint Commission (IJC), established in 1909, has overseen a cooperative approach to water development. It supplies national governments with expert recommendations on shared water resources and air pollution disputes. The IJC has been particularly important in shaping major transnational development projects, such as that embodied in the Columbia River Treaty (1964), and in addressing water and air pollution problems in the Great Lakes region. Like other transboundary institutions, however, the IJC has limited jurisdiction and authority. It has operated primarily as a diplomatic instrument to provide arm's length recommendations. The Commission for Environmental Cooperation of the North American Free Trade Agreement (NAFTA) bears the same promise and limitations.

The two nations also have somewhat similar positions towards the Kyoto Protocol, the international climate change pact that entered into force in February 2005. At that point, 141 countries had ratified the binding protocol, including every major industrialized country except the United States and Australia. Monaco ratified the accord in February 2006, and Australia did so in 2007 under its new Labor government. Canada—whose Liberal government, led by Jean Chretien, ratified the accord on December 17, 2002—became the only ratifying nation to formally abandon the Kyoto Protocol in December 2011, when Stephen Harper's Conservative government withdrew from the protocol. Supporters of the Canadian Alliance party (a precursor of the Harper Conservatives) had opposed the Kyoto arrangements, describing them as late as 2002 as a "socialist scheme" based on "contradictory" data. The Harper government's decision abandoned Canada's original Kyoto commitment to reduce greenhouse gas emissions by six percent from 1990 levels by 2008–2012. Acknowledging that Canada's emissions had increased by 24 percent in less than four years since ratification, the government announced in 2011 that it would adopt the less ambitious target—agreed to by the United States under the Copenhagen Accord—of a 17 percent reduction from 2005 levels by 2020 (Dion 2011, 31a; Government of Canada 2010).

Other resource sectors have produced seemingly as much conflict as cooperation. Disputes over appropriate catch levels between national fisheries have torn the Pacific salmon fishery of British Columbia, the US Pacific Northwest, and Alaska. Early twentieth-century attempts to coordinate fisheries regulations and set national limits failed. Only in 1937, after years of diplomatic effort and signs of resource decline, did the Pacific Salmon Convention establish a binational commission to study the resource and recommend catch levels. Despite fifty years of constructive activity, intense political pressure dissolved the institution in the mid-1980s. Since that time, a new Treaty and Pacific Salmon Commission has sought to address national and regional demands within the context of a continuously declining fishery. Conflict and high-level diplomacy remain constant.

Canada's economy and natural resource trade progressively integrated with that of the United States. During

World War II and after, the two national economies increasingly intertwined. Exports of strategic minerals spiked, and all natural resources were more intensively developed and traded. Despite several bouts of protectionism in the 1930s and 1970s, continental integration advanced during the twentieth century. In 1989, Canada and the United States signed a Free Trade Agreement (FTA) to remove tariff barriers to trade and to establish agreements about specific sectors, such as energy. In 1992, NAFTA extended the FTA to include Mexico. A side agreement established the Commission for Environmental Cooperation (CEC).

There have been several implications of closer integration for environmental issues. Trade in natural resources has soared over the last hundred years, hindering, to some extent, the development of secondary manufacturing in Canada while driving expansionist development policies, particularly in less-settled interior regions and the middle north. Since the 1970s, for example, Quebec Hydro has expanded its hydroelectric energy supply in northern Quebec, flooding Cree hunting territories, to profit from energy markets in the United States and particularly New York State. Second, the United States has pressured Canada to harmonize environmental and trade policies with the United States in order to level the playing field in competitive resource sectors (such as forestry products), and to insure resource security for the United States in fields such as energy and strategic minerals. The Canadian export trade in softwood lumber has been particularly contentious. Before and after the NAFTA, US competitors and legislators charged that the pattern of resource tenure rights in Canada constituted unfair trading practices. Canadian exporters and governments have, in turn, fought these charges and decried US protectionism.

Matthew EVENDEN and Graeme WYNN
University of British Columbia

See also Columbia River; Forest Management; Great Lakes and Saint Lawrence River; Mackenzie River; Mexico; Multilateral Environmental Agreements (MEAs); North American Free Trade Agreement (NAFTA); Organization of American States (OAS); Northwest Passage; Parks and Protected Areas; Rocky Mountains; Toronto, Canada; United States; Vancouver, Canada; Yellowstone to Yukon Conservation Initiative (Y2Y)

FURTHER READING

Alberts, Sheldon. (2012, March 22). Obama trumpets decision to proceed with part of Keystone pipeline. *Ottawa Citizen*. Retrieved on March 26, 2012, from http://www.canada.com/technology/Obama+trumpets+decision+proceed+with+part+Keystone+pipeline/6343040/story.html#ixzz1qFOYF1zE

Charpentier, Alex D.; Bergerson, Joule A.; & MacLean, Heather L. (2009). Understanding the Canadian oil sands industry's greenhouse gas emissions. *Environmental Research Letters, 4*(1). doi:10.1088/1748-9326/4/1/014005

Dion, Stéphane. (2011). The fight against climate change: Why is Canada doing so little? *The Tocqueville Review / La Revue Tocqueville, 22*(2), 21a–46a. Retrieved July 6, 2012, from http://www.utpjournals.com/blog/wp-content/uploads/2011/12/03a_32.2dion-Eng.pdf

Environment Canada. (2011). Homepage. Retrieved February 5, 2012, from www.ec.gc.ca

Goldenberg, Suzanne. (2011, November 4). Q&A: Keystone XL oil pipeline. *The Guardian*. Retrieved November 22, 2011, from http://www.guardian.co.uk/environment/2011/nov/04/qa-keystone-xl-oil-pipeline?INTCMP=SRCH

Government of Canada. (2010). Canada's action on climate change. Retrieved July 9, 2012, from http://www.climatechange.gc.ca/cdp-cop/default.asp?lang=En&n=C4BD2547-1

Harris, Cole. (1997). *The resettlement of British Columbia: Essays on colonialism and geographical change*. Vancouver, Canada: University of British Columbia Press.

Hessing, Melody, & Howlett, Michael. (1999). *Canadian natural resource and environmental policy: Political economy and public policy*. Vancouver, Canada: University of British Columbia Press.

Hickman, Leo. (2011, July 28). Canadian campaign puts spin on "ethical oil." *The Guardian*. Retrieved November 22, 2011, from http://www.guardian.co.uk/environment/blog/2011/jul/28/oil-tar-sands-canada-ethical

Innis, Harold A. (1978). *The cod fisheries: The history of an international economy*. Toronto: University of Toronto Press. (Original work published 1940)

Kiy, Richard, & Wirth, John D. (Eds.). (1998). *Environmental management on North America's borders*. College Station: Texas A&M University Press.

MacEachern, Alan Andrew. (2001). *Natural selections: National parks in Atlantic Canada*. Montreal: McGill-Queen's University Press.

Mitchell, Bruce. (1995). *Resource and environmental management in Canada: Addressing conflict and uncertainty*. Toronto: Oxford University Press.

Nelles, H. V. (1974). *The politics of development: Forests, mines & hydroelectric power in Ontario, 1849–1941*. Toronto: Macmillan of Canada.

Rajala, Richard A. (1998). *Clearcutting the Pacific rainforest: Production, science and regulation*. Vancouver, Canada: University of British Columbia Press.

Ray, Andrew J. (1974). *Indians in the fur trade*. Toronto: University of Toronto Press.

Royal Society of Canada. (2010, December). *Expert panel: Environmental and health impacts of Canada's oil sands industry*. Retrieved March 26, 2012, from http://www.rsc.ca/creports.php

Shenker, Sarah. (2008, December). Canada's black gold oil rush. *BBC News*. Retrieved November 22, 2011, from http://news.bbc.co.uk/1/hi/world/americas/7762226.stm

Wood, J. David. (2000). *Making Ontario: Agricultural colonization and landscape re-creation before the railway*. Toronto: University of Toronto Press.

Woynillowicz, Dan; Severson-Baker, Chris; & Raynolds, Marlo. (2005). *Oil sands fever: The environmental implications of Canada's oil sands rush*. Drayton Valley, Alberta: Pembina Institute.

Wynn, Graeme. (1981). *Timber colony: A historical geography of early nineteenth century New Brunswick*. Toronto: University of Toronto Press.

Caribbean

Human settlement has transformed the natural environment of the Caribbean islands. The first settlers introduced non-native species of plants and animals to the islands, a process that accelerated during European colonization from the fifteenth century. In modern times, tourism and intensive agriculture continue to contribute to environmental and social instability.

The Caribbean region extends 4,000 kilometers along an arc from northwestern Cuba to the southern tip of Trinidad. This arc forms the northern and eastern boundaries of the Caribbean Sea, a basin of 2.7 million square kilometers. To the west, the sea is bounded by the Yucatán Peninsula of Mexico, Belize, Guatemala, Honduras, Nicaragua, and Costa Rica, and to the south by Panama, Colombia, and Venezuela. The hundreds of islands that make up the Caribbean region are highly diverse in size, landforms, geology, and climate. Cuba, for example, occupies an area of more than 110,000 square kilometers, whereas the smallest of the region's independent island nations, such as St. Kitts and Nevis, occupy an area of scarcely 258 square kilometers. Geographers conventionally divide the region into the Greater Antilles (the large islands of Cuba, Hispaniola, Jamaica, and Puerto Rico) and the much smaller but more numerous Lesser Antilles to the east, which run in a north–south axis separating the Caribbean Sea from the Atlantic Ocean.

The Caribbean is a polyglot (using several languages) region whose history includes centuries of imperial conflict over the land, resources, and people of the region. Most of the population is descended from non-native peoples brought to the region between the sixteenth and twentieth centuries as slaves or indentured laborers. Little remains of the region's indigenous peoples, other than some Carib native communities on St. Vincent and Dominica. Despite the common circumstances of coerced migration that populated the Caribbean following European conquest and the collapse of native societies, the now-independent nations of the Caribbean reflect the linguistic, cultural, and political characteristics of their colonizing powers, whether Spain, France, Britain, or the Netherlands. In many instances, islands repeatedly changed hands between rival imperial powers during the colonial era, giving rise to contemporary societies such as St. Lucia and Dominica whose official language is English but whose spoken vernacular is a French patois.

Geography and Climate

Landforms throughout the Caribbean tend to be mountainous and plunge into deep oceanic trenches. With the exception of the Bahamas, Barbados, Antigua, and Trinidad, flat, low landscapes are uncommon in most of the region. The interiors of the Greater Antilles islands are geological extensions of the highlands of southern Mexico and reach elevations of more than 2,700 meters in the Dominican Republic, which shares the island of Hispaniola with Haiti. Most of the Lesser Antilles lie along the intersection of two tectonic plates that yield both mountainous uplifting and geological instability. Earthquakes occur with some frequency on these islands, such as the January 2010 earthquake that devastated Haiti, killing more than 300,000 people and leaving more than a million homeless. Dramatic and occasionally destructive volcanic eruptions have also occurred on some islands: the 1902 eruption of Mount Pelée on Martinique killed nearly all of the 30,000 inhabitants of St. Pierre, the island's largest town; and a 1997 volcanic eruption on Montserrat forced the evacuation of most of that island's 11,000 residents.

Natural vegetation patterns on the islands are likewise diverse, ranging from tropical rain forest, tropical seasonal forest, and mountain forest to savanna, dry scrub, and even desert. Maximum rainfall usually occurs from June through November, yielding to a comparatively dry season in the first half of the year. Rainfall generally increases from north to south throughout the Caribbean, but island topography is at least as critical as latitude in determining climate and associated vegetation. The high peaks on many islands trigger rainfall from easterly winds, whereas low-lying islands receive less rainfall and may experience frequent drought. Because of the mountainous terrain throughout the Lesser Antilles, entirely distinct climatic patterns are often found in close proximity even on small islands. In general, wetter, more heavily forested zones face the Caribbean (leeward) sides of the Lesser Antilles islands, and drier zones occupy the windward sides facing the Atlantic. As important as latitude and topography are in determining climate and vegetation, the biogeography (geographical distribution of plants and animals) of each island has been massively affected by ecological changes wrought by five hundred years of European colonialism and settlement.

Pre-Columbian Human Environments

Prior to human settlement, forest cover throughout the Caribbean region was extensive, although it was periodically diminished by natural environmental disturbances. Forces such as hurricanes and volcanic eruptions precluded the development of climax forests (stable plant communities achieved through long-term ecological adaptation) and associated fauna and in some instances led to complete recolonization by floral and faunal species of adjacent islands. Before the arrival of humans, the only mammal species north of Trinidad consisted of bats and rodents.

Earliest human settlement in the Caribbean was by a variety of preceramic (nomadic, pre-agricultural) foraging and fishing peoples who sailed or drifted to the Greater Antilles from Central America as early as 5000 BCE. Much later, around the first century CE, Native Americans from Venezuela and Guyana migrated northward through the Lesser Antilles in pursuit of the region's aquatic resources (primarily fish, turtles, and sea mammals). These peoples, collectively known as Taino (formerly Arawaks), brought about the first significant human modification of Caribbean island environments. The Taino introduced South American cultigens (cultivated varieties or species for which a wild ancestor is unknown) such as cassava, sweet potato, yams, peanuts, beans, and maize, all of which were grown on plots (*conucos*) under tropical forest shifting cultivation. Caribbean peoples also made extensive use of inshore mammal and fish species, as well as birds and lizards.

After 1200 CE the Taino were steadily supplanted by more militaristic island Caribs, who swept northward through the Lesser Antilles by incorporating existing populations through conquest and intermarriage. At the time of European conquest, indigenous populations of the Caribbean were estimated at 2–4 million. In some areas of high population density, soil erosion apparently resulted from native cultivation techniques. Yet, most indigenous peoples in the Caribbean appear to have lived in relative harmony with their environments, if not always with each other.

Ecological Effects of Conquest

Hispanic colonization of the Caribbean commenced in 1493 but entailed small numbers of actual settlers: the entire Spanish population of the region never exceeded ten thousand during the fifteenth and sixteenth centuries. Similarly, Britain, France, and the Netherlands did not seek to populate the Caribbean extensively with their citizens, however much they fought each other over the region's resources. Yet, the ecological consequences of European conquest were immediate and irreversible and were felt through a massive depopulation of the region. Horrified colonial-era chroniclers such as Spanish historian Fray Bartolome de las Casas graphically documented the mistreatment of Caribbean natives forced to mine gold for the Spanish in the sixteenth century. It is likely, however, that Old World diseases such as plague, smallpox, measles, and malaria, to which indigenous populations lacked any acquired immunity, exacted a far greater toll than did European slavery and other abuses. By 1524 all of the native populations of the Greater Antilles and the Bahamas, as well as most of those of the Lesser Antilles, had been extinguished.

As native populations died out, their agricultural lands were abandoned and quickly reverted to forest cover, a process that occurred in other former aboriginal areas of the Americas as well. In the Caribbean, this process was extraordinarily rapid, and most traces of native agriculture and even settlements were quickly swallowed by encroaching forest. Barbados, for example, had been one of the most heavily populated of the Lesser Antilles during the pre-Columbian period. Yet, when the first English settlers arrived one hundred years after the demise of the native population, they encountered nothing but dense forests growing down to the shoreline. Although the Spanish introduced many non-native plant species into the region, most were initially unable to establish themselves in the new environment, primarily because of direct competition with species from the encroaching forest or because of the lack of available space within it. Non-native plants did not gain a foothold until the later removal of island forests to make way for sugarcane. Introduced faunal species, however, multiplied rapidly in habitats that lacked natural predators and had known no previous hoofed animals. The Spanish left pigs on virtually every island as a potential food source for colonists, and these animals adapted readily to Caribbean forests. By 1514 more than thirty thousand pigs, most of them wild, were reported on Cuba. Pigs, in particular, competed with the declining native human population and may have hastened its demise by rooting up *canucos* and destroying native crops. Spanish cattle also thrived on Caribbean islands, further compounding long-term environmental problems. The hooves of both cattle and pigs compacted the soil along their trackways, resulting in severe gully erosion in the form of *barrancas* (ravines or gorges) on Cuba and Hispaniola by the late sixteenth century.

As readily accessible sources of gold were depleted, together with the native population compelled to mine it, colonists sought other sources of wealth during the sixteenth century. Throughout the Caribbean, European settlers and Crown authorities turned to an array of agricultural commodities. Tobacco, cotton, indigo, and ginger were introduced with varying levels of success, typically among the few thousand European yeoman farmers who settled in the region. None of these crops, however, transformed human–environmental relations in the Caribbean as much as sugarcane did. Originally domesticated in Asia from a wild grass species, sugarcane was introduced by the British to Barbados and by the French to St. Kitts in the 1640s. The crop grows well throughout all but the driest parts of the Caribbean, but its demands posed sweeping environmental consequences for the islands of the region. Intolerant of competition for sunlight, water, and nutrients, sugarcane could be successfully cultivated only after the clear-cutting of native forest, followed by continuous weeding. Lowland seasonal forest soils provided the best soil and nutrient combinations for cane cultivation, and consequently these areas were most extensively cleared to make way for the crop. Soon the only areas remaining under forest cover were the highland zones of mountainous islands; low-lying islands were rapidly stripped of all forest cover. Even higher elevations were rarely spared the effects of sugar cultivation because the boilers used to refine sugar were usually fueled by firewood cut from upland forests. In Barbados virtually all of the island's seasonal forests had been cut and replanted with cane by 1665, just twenty years after English settlement. St. Kitts, Nevis, and Montserrat followed suit by the 1680s; Antigua, Guadeloupe, Martinique, and lowland Jamaica by the 1750s; and the Spanish territories of Santo Domingo, Cuba, Puerto Rico, and Trinidad by 1800.

Consequences of Sugar Production

The ecological consequences of sugarcane cultivation in the Caribbean would be difficult to overstate. It is estimated that hundreds, or even thousands, of plant and animal species were driven to extinction in this process. On Barbados, writers of the 1650s commented on the marked absence of songbirds compared to other islands. Indeed, by that time all forest-based birds, other than several hummingbird species, had already disappeared, together with their forest habitats. The region's shift to a monocrop plantation economy also accentuated ecological problems as varying metropolitan demands for sugar dictated cultivation practices and intensity. When European markets became glutted with sugar or prices fell, Caribbean planters typically fallowed some of their land, opening a niche for other plant species on their farms. After the native forest cover had been decimated, more often than not these niches were filled by weed species introduced (usually unwittingly) from abroad. The legacy of this pattern is an extraordinarily high level of non-native plant species on most of the islands of the Caribbean. On Barbados, a large percentage of the wild plant species recorded in the 1960s originated from outside the island, one of the highest levels of non-native vegetation of any country in the world.

The clearing of native forest and the cultivation and harvest of sugarcane required vast quantities of human labor, a vexing problem for colonists witnessing the virtual extinction of native populations. The demand for agricultural labor was resolved in the sixteenth century by the start of the Atlantic slave trade, during which an estimated 1.7 million Africans were transported to Britain's Caribbean holdings alone. The presence of African slaves and demand for plantation land quickly swallowed the small-scale tobacco and subsistence farms earlier established by European yeoman farmers. On the sugar-growing islands, African populations soon vastly outnumbered European settlers. Because of the sheer size of the workforce required for cane production and the devotion of virtually all arable land to sugarcane, the Caribbean came to rely heavily on imported food. In some instances, however, plantation owners allotted gardens to their slaves to defray some of the costs of their subsistence.

Throughout the Caribbean, the era of slavery was marked by a continual hemorrhage of labor through defection and flight as slaves sought refuge in maroon (fugitive slave) communities created in remote upland areas. With the formal end of slavery, plantation owners sought other mechanisms to bind workers to their farms, but many freed slaves were reluctant to resume work on sugar plantations. Because the end of slavery was not accompanied by a redistribution of land, however, former slaves who wished to cultivate farms of their own were forced to do so in areas of marginal productivity, such as swamps and hillsides. Such farming was all but impossible on islands such as Montserrat and Barbados, where there simply was no land apart from that owned by the planter class. Elsewhere, however, subsistence farming on hillsides produced erosion and topsoil loss within a few decades of the end of slavery. Planters' efforts to recruit replacement laborers through indentured servitude (primarily of natives of the East Indies) in the late nineteenth century further aggravated the already high person-to-land ratios, food deficits, and environmental problems associated with farming in marginal zones. For many residents of the Caribbean, environmental pressures and the absence of occupational opportunities apart from estate labor stimulated a rising tide of emigration. By the early twentieth century, numerous Afro-Caribbean communities had been formed along the coast of Central America by migrants seeking work on the Panama Canal or the region's banana plantations. High levels of emigration continue in the twenty-first century. Most families in the English-speaking Caribbean can identify numerous close relatives living in the United States, Britain, or Canada, and many are heavily dependent on the money sent home by migrants living abroad.

Contemporary Environmental Issues

Although few nations in the Caribbean, other than Cuba, the Dominican Republic, and Haiti, rely heavily on sugar any longer as their primary export, the legacies of sugar production continue to plague the region. A highly inequitable pattern of land ownership (much of it now under absentee control) and extremely high population density continue to result in destructive hillside farming, the loss of topsoil, and outmigration. Beginning in the early 1950s, the eastern Caribbean islands of St. Lucia, St. Vincent, Dominica, and Grenada developed export-oriented banana industries based exclusively on peasant production. Although Caribbean fruit is of high quality, the small scale and labor intensive nature of production means that per hectare yields are typically only one-third those of Central American plantations. A complex tariff-quota system limited the access of Central and South American producers to the UK market, in effect guaranteeing higher prices and a stable market share for Caribbean growers. The production of bananas on steep hillside slopes in the Caribbean has resulted in many cases of soil erosion and siltation of waterways. Yet eastern Caribbean farmers inflict less damage on the environment than their Central American counterparts, where plantation monocrop production requires an array of toxic chemicals that Caribbean farms use less frequently, or not at all. Following a 1998 World Trade Organization ruling against the tariff-quota system, banana production throughout the Caribbean has plummeted as island producers must now compete on the basis of price with Latin American fruit marketed by Chiquita, Dole, Del Monte, and other large banana corporations. Accordingly, migration from the islands, unemployment, crime, and drug trafficking have increased on the former banana-producing islands. Since the early 1990s, the number of active banana growers on the islands has declined by nearly 90 percent, with the remainder managing to stay in production by seeking fair-trade certification of their products.

In much of the Caribbean, local livelihoods and government revenues since the 1960s have been tied ever more closely to tourism. The region's famed expanses of white beaches and turquoise water have encouraged a proliferation of hotels, all-inclusive resorts, port facilities for ocean liners, and casinos. Within the Caribbean, the heavy reliance on foreign tourists as a primary source of hard currency remains an issue of much debate, given that the frequently changing tastes of the tourist industry often preclude long-term national economic planning. Critics assert that the transformation of Afro-Caribbean residents into maids, cooks, and sex workers who cater to the needs of affluent whites creates an unwanted parallel with the era of slavery. There seems little doubt that tourism has caused already high land prices to skyrocket, further excluding many local residents from access to farming. Apart from such questions, the development of Caribbean coastlines to accommodate millions of visitors each year poses formidable environmental problems of its own. The filling of estuaries and mangrove swamps to create resorts and golf courses contributes to siltation of the once-crystalline waters eagerly sought by tourists and has dire consequences for coral reefs and local fisheries. Few islands possess adequate sewage and solid-waste disposal infrastructure to maintain large-scale tourist facilities on an environmentally sustainable basis. Perhaps the most ironic illustration of this process was the decision of the government of Barbados to construct a new landfill during the late 1990s, mostly to accommodate waste from tourist hotels and ocean liners. The site chosen for the new landfill was a national park once promoted by the tourist industry as one of the island's most scenic natural environments.

Mark A. MOBERG
University of South Alabama

See also Agriculture, Tropical (the Americas); Amazonia; Bogotá, Colombia; Brazil; Central America; Ecotourism (the Americas); Fair Trade; Forest Management; Labor; Marine Ecosystems Health; Marine Preserves; Mexico; Organization of American States (OAS); Parks and Protected Areas; Small Island States; Social Movements (Latin America); Travel and Tourism Industry

FURTHER READING

Collinson, Helen. (Ed.). (1996). *Green guerrillas: Environmental conflicts and initiatives in Latin America and the Caribbean: A reader.* London: Latin American Bureau.

Grossman, Lawrence S. (1998). *The political ecology of bananas: Contract farming, peasants and agrarian change in the eastern Caribbean.* Chapel Hill: University of North Carolina Press.

Josling, Timothy E., & Taylor, Timothy G. (Eds.). (2003). *Banana wars: The anatomy of a trade dispute.* Cambridge, UK: CABI Publishing.

Lentz, David L. (2000). *An imperfect balance: Landscape transformations in the Precolumbian Americas.* New York: Columbia University Press.

Mintz, Sidney. (1985). *Sweetness and power: The place of sugar in modern history.* New York: Viking.

Moberg, Mark. (2011). *Slipping away: Banana politics and fair trade in the eastern Caribbean.* New York: Berghahn.

Richardson, Bonham. (1983). *Caribbean migrants: Environment and human survival on St. Kitts and Nevis.* Knoxville: University of Tennessee Press.

Watts, David. (1990). *The West Indies: Patterns of development, culture, and environmental change since 1492.* Cambridge, UK: Cambridge University Press.

Watts, David. (1995). Ecological responses to ecosystem shock in the island Caribbean: The aftermath of Columbus, 1492–1992. In Robin Alan Butlin & Neil Roberts (Eds.), *Ecological relations in historic times* (pp. 267–279). Oxford, UK: Blackwell.

Share the *Encyclopedia of Sustainability*: Teachers are welcome to make up to ten (10) copies of no more than two (2) articles for distribution in a single course or program. For further permissions, please visit www.copyright.com or contact: info@berkshirepublishing.com

Central America

Central America is unique geographically, a bridge between two continents, an isthmus between two oceans. Rich in biodiversity, poor in natural resources, and rugged in terrain, it has absorbed colonization, exploitation, and foreign investment and has been left with a tradition of dependence on the outside world. Today there is a rising determination to profit from its tropical situation through export agriculture and ecotourism.

Central America comprises seven small countries—Belize, Guatemala, El Salvador, Honduras, Nicaragua, Costa Rica, and Panama—and forms an isthmus, roughly the size of Italy, connecting South America with North America. In its role of bridge between two continents and two oceans (the Atlantic and the Pacific), the isthmus is one of the most distinctive places in the world. It was formed between 3 and 4 million years ago, during the Pliocene Epoch. A range of volcanic mountains (many of which are still active), as high as 4,267 meters, dominates this bridge and has historically been a barrier to transportation and communication. Different life zones (regions characterized by specific plants and animals) prevail on these mountain slopes, ranging from dry deciduous to wet tropical forests and, in the higher elevations, cloud forests. A lack of major navigable rivers has also hindered travel and communication throughout the region.

Central America's two coasts, east and west, have different climates and ecosystems. The Atlantic side features tropical lowland plains with high rainfall, dense forests, and banana plantations. Historically covered with deciduous forests, the Pacific side is drier and today has been mostly cleared for farmland and pasture. The variety of elevations and tropical life zones, combined with the region's being both intercontinental and interoceanic, has created a high degree of biodiversity (biological diversity as indicated by numbers of species of animals and plants). There are hundreds of species of birds, mammals, fishes, reptiles, and amphibians, thousands of species of plants, and hundreds of thousands of species of insects. Many of these life forms are endemic to the region.

Urban centers have risen in the many intermontane valleys and plateaus. The coastal regions where the heat, humidity, insects, and tropical storms have retarded urban development lack good ports or deep harbors. But even in the valleys, residents have been exposed to a variety of natural disasters such as earthquakes and volcanic eruptions. As one Costa Rican historian has written, "living with earthquakes and volcanoes has been an inescapable part of Central American life for centuries" (Pérez-Brignoli 1989, 2).

Indigenous Mesoamerica (Middle America)

In this diverse setting a variety of peoples learned to survive and gave rise to vibrant cultures. Some anthropologists claim there was an immigration of people from Asia thirty to forty thousand years ago, but many of today's native peoples feel that they originated from a specific place within the region—that they are, in fact, indigenous. Either way, the region became densely populated in Belize, Guatemala, and Honduras by people under the hegemony of Mayan culture. El Salvador and Nicaragua were settled, although less densely, by Pipil and Nicarao natives, tracing their roots to the Nahua (Aztecs) from Mexico. The Miskito native peoples populate the Caribbean coast of Honduras and Nicaragua. A variety of native peoples such as the Guaymí and Cabécar, who were related to tribes from South America and who formed more nomadic societies than the sedentary, technologically advanced Maya, populate Costa Rica and Panama.

The Maya, who today still speak more than fifty dialects, formed an advanced civilization based on city-states that were only loosely unified. Individual cities such as Tikal, in Guatemala, or Copán, in Honduras, which were also ceremonial centers with great temples and pyramids, retained self-rule. Sustaining such large population centers meant developing an agricultural system that provided not only sufficient food for daily use, but a surplus for lean times as well. Corn (maize), which became the vital staple, was grown under a slash-and-burn cultivation system. Also known as "swidden agriculture," it required the clearing and burning of forests for cornfields (milpas). Natives planted nitrogen-fixing beans, whose vines could climb cornstalks, between corn rows; they also planted squashes whose leaves provided shade cover for the beans and acted as natural pest control. Native peoples used this efficient intercropping system throughout the Americas, which helped them survive for thousands of years. A variety of fruits, vegetables, fish, mammals (especially deer), and chocolate from cacao further supplemented their diet.

Nature figured prominently in Mayan cosmology. The Maya believed the ceiba tree (*Ceiba pentandra*) held up the four corners of the world and was the tree under which people's souls went after they died. Many people planted them in their homes and in communal plazas and would not cut them down in the forests—a practice many Mayan Indians, but certainly not all, continue even today. They also considered animals such as the jaguar sacred.

All native groups in Central America left their mark on the environment. Scholars believe that before the arrival of the Europeans, many native civilizations cleared great sections of forests for milpas and new cities, which could have been part of the reason for the Maya's eventual decline. Some research attempts to show how the Maya exceeded their carrying capacity (the population that an area will support without deterioration), but the decline of native civilizations in the region overall seems to have been a question of scale and lifestyle. Most indigenous groups were small enough to avoid exceeding their resources, and in areas where this was not the case, they simply moved on, allowing for natural replenishment.

Arrival of Europeans and the Colonial Period

European explorers, with their very different perspectives on the environment, entered this world in the early-sixteenth century. Christopher Columbus, on his fourth trip to the New World in 1502, explored Central America's Atlantic coast and named part of it "Costa Rica" (rich coast) for the mineral wealth he was hoping to find. The fixation with extracting riches underscored the European state of mind. In 1513, Vasco Núñez de Balboa and his men crossed the Isthmus of Panama and "discovered" the Pacific Ocean, setting in motion Spain's eventual need to secure the isthmus as a strategic crossing point in its gold trade from Peru, on the continent, to Europe.

As early as 1519, the incoming Spanish settlers established cities in the region, the first garrisons for Spanish control of the land, which, in great part, were built by local native peoples whom the Spaniards had brutally enslaved. At the same time, the newcomers introduced the diseases that would, over time, constitute the most enduring biological change to the region. What has been called "the Columbian exchange" (Crosby 1972, 2) included the microbial invasion that caused epidemics of smallpox, typhus, dysentery, pneumonia, and the plague to decimate native populations who had no natural immunities to the diseases.

Europeans during the colonial period (1500–1800) saw Central America, unlike mineral-rich Mexico and Peru, as a kind of backwater, not attracting as many immigrants as other parts of the Spanish Empire. But those who did move there discovered that Central America had other commodities to export. Indigo and cochineal dyes were in high demand in Europe and became Central America's first colonial exports. Sugar, cotton, and tobacco later became important crops. But these monoculture crops altered the environmental and social landscapes. They required a huge conversion of native vegetation and depended on the slave labor system the Spaniards introduced. Under this system, known as the *encomienda*, Spanish planters were "entrusted" with native peoples to work the fields and tend the cattle. The idea of private land ownership was in complete contrast to the native communal farming system.

Certainly not all of Central America was changed in this way. The Spanish preferred to settle in climates and terrains that reminded them of home, such as the central valley of Costa Rica and the highlands of Guatemala. In those places, referred to as "neo-Europes" (Crosby 1986, 134), Spaniards could create wheat and barley fields, olive and fruit orchards, vineyards, and cattle pastures to provide them with the commodities they were used to in Europe. The coastal lowlands and montane forests (relating to the biogeographic zone of moist, cool upland slopes below the timberline dominated by large coniferous trees) were not easily adaptable for this kind of agriculture and were thus avoided.

Independence and the Nineteenth Century

Independence came to Central America in 1821. After a two-year period of incorporation by Mexico (during which the state of Chiapas elected to remain a part of the country), leaders in the region formed the United Provinces of Central America with Guatemala City as the capital. Unity, however, was fleeting—Guatemalan predominance, territorial jealousies, and the environment itself thwarted its success. The combination of mountainous terrain and slow communications prevented political cohesion, so that by 1838 Nicaragua and Costa Rica had withdrawn from the union, and the other three provinces soon followed their lead. Five small nations thus emerged on the isthmus, with Guatemala having the greatest population (660,000) and Costa Rica the smallest (70,000).

The new nations and the majority of the people in them were poor. Because the region lacked large quantities of natural resources, most Central Americans maintained a subsistence economy. That changed in the 1850s, when Europeans discovered that the volcanic soil of the highlands and plateaus was perfect for the production of coffee beans. The coffee industry thrived, setting Central America on an even more export-dependent pathway and converting a great many hillsides in Guatemala, El Salvador, and Costa Rica into coffee plantations. This new agro-economy thrived for decades, but disease eventually threatened coffee trees. Rust (or *roya* in Spanish) could devastate entire fields, and scientists worked with coffee growers in an effort to deal with the problem (McCook 2009). The introduction of bananas in the late-nineteenth century accelerated the pattern. To meet a growing demand for the fruit, US investors converted millions of acres of coastal lowlands into banana plantations, developed railroads around the region to transport the fruit to shipping ports, and established a multinational export network. Leading this effort was the United Fruit Company, which by 1910 came to control 75 percent of the international banana trade and made Costa Rica the world's largest banana producer. Honduras and Guatemala became close competitors. But, as the historian John Soluri (2005) has so eloquently explained, *sigatoka* (a leaf blight) and Panama disease (a root fungus), which thrive in plantation settings, destroyed many thousands of acres, causing the banana producers to move on and convert other lowland areas into plantations. For diseases in both coffee and banana plantations, growers and scientists turned to a high use of chemical insecticides, fungicides, and herbicides—acts that worsened environmental and agricultural conditions in both crops and often caused a great deal of human illness as well.

Much of this late-nineteenth- and early-twentieth-century development was spawned by a belief in the philosophy of science known as positivism. As advanced by economists in Europe, this theory held private property, scientific education, technological advancement, and modernization in the highest regard, which meant for Central America a large degree of foreign investment to pay for the changes taking place in the region. Foreign investment set in motion a tradition of dependence on outside areas for a variety of local development projects, which, as in the case with bananas, often brought severe environmental change.

The Twentieth Century

Construction of the Panama Canal in the early-twentieth century created one of the biggest environmental changes in Central America. Opened in 1914, the canal was an engineering masterpiece that people in the United States viewed as an important commercial and military advantage. But no one seemed to worry about the environmental impact of digging the ditch and creating locks, dams, and diversion weirs in this tropical and biologically sensitive area. Perhaps this would not have been the case in a time less focused on economic development, but we can look back now and clearly see many of the problems. First, cutting a canal directly through a mountain ridge (the Culebra Cut) necessitated vast amounts of energy, from both humans and steam. A workforce was imported from the Caribbean, thousands of Afro-Caribbeans from Jamaica and elsewhere in the region who not only were incredibly sturdy workers, but who could withstand one of the greatest environmental threats to the creation of the canal: the anopheles mosquito that carried yellow fever and malaria. Battling this ecological threat was no easy task, especially because the canal's construction created pools of standing water, and hundreds of white workers became ill, were quarantined, and died. As the historian Paul Sutter (2007) has shown, the battle against mosquitoes became a monumental project involving entomologists, virologists, epidemiologists, naturalists, as well as government and health officials in Panama—all to battle the tiniest of creatures in the construction of what was the world's largest project at the time.

Vast amounts of wood from local forests fueled the boilers that generated the steam to power the shovels that dug out the canal's walls and rechanneled water between the oceans. No environmental impact statements would have been conducted at that time to assess the damage caused to the Panamanian environment, but the damage to the tropical biodiversity can be imagined from the amount of wood burned. Even more lumber was needed to build the railroad that ran alongside the canal. The rail line was important for removing the soil from the trench, bringing workers to the work sites, and delivering construction supplies and food. But it was also a monumental engineering feat, complete with bridges and trellises and innumerable railroad ties—all made of wood.

All in all, the Panama Canal was undoubtedly a great accomplishment of engineering and construction, especially against such odds as mosquito-borne diseases. The locks that lifted the ships up through the Culebra Cut and then down toward the Pacific were nothing short of genius, but their utility today is still debated. A much more efficient Central American canal could have been built on the San Juan River, which divides Costa Rica from Nicaragua, with short land-level canals connecting the waterway to Lake Nicaragua, Lake Managua, and then to the Pacific Ocean. Political reasons against a Nicaraguan canal precluded that plan, and the United States gained economic and militarily strategic advantages and a territorial prize (the Canal Zone—five miles of land on either side of the canal that constituted US territory until 2000) because it was built across Panama. The canal also fostered construction technology that was later utilized in other large-scale earthmoving projects like the Hoover and Grand Coulee dams in the American West. But by the late-twentieth century, the Panama Canal had become almost obsolete. It is not wide enough to support large oil tankers, it can be backlogged with ship traffic slowing transportation, and it is not easily modernized. Talk consequently has once again surfaced about constructing another transoceanic canal, possibly through Nicaragua or even across the Tehauntepec Isthmus of southern Mexico.

The canal not only transformed the isthmus but also set the stage for an even larger US presence in the region. That presence was manifested in policies that supported Central American leaders (often dictators) friendly to US business. Like their positivism-oriented predecessors, these leaders were eager to continue modernization and development strategies that hastened economic growth without benefiting the majority of their people. Such were the cases especially in Nicaragua, El Salvador, and Guatemala in the early and middle parts of the twentieth century. In

Guatemala, United Fruit's empire was threatened when Jacobo Arbenz, an avowed socialist with plans to nationalize foreign holdings through land reform, was elected president in 1950. His land reform efforts were cut short, however, when the United States acted on behalf of United Fruit and on the fear that Arbenz represented a "communist" threat to the region. The Central Intelligence Agency engineered a coup that ousted Arbenz and propped up a government friendlier to US interests (Schlesinger and Kinzer 1999). The result was the beginning of a civil war that lasted thirty years and left hundreds of thousands of Guatemalans dead and the land scorched from constant warfare.

Other wars and revolutions in the region in the 1970s and 1980s had similar causes and effects. As one scholar has explained, the root of these upheavals "can be summed up in one word: land" (Weinberg 1991, 5). The inequitable uses and ownership of land and resources prompted the revolts for political and economic reforms in Nicaragua and El Salvador in those years. And while the revolts raged, prolonged in Nicaragua by US support of the Contras (counterrevolutionaries opposed to the Sandinista government that came to power in 1979 by ousting the Somoza dictatorship), the tropical forests and agricultural fields suffered great damage.

Out of all this turmoil, there developed a move to conserve tropical resources and environments. Costa Rica has been a regional leader in this area, with more than 25 percent of its land dedicated to preservation through national parks and biological reserves. There are many pressures (i.e., logging, mineral exploration, and cattle grazing) on this "model," but at least it represents a framework for future environmental protection. Costa Ricans have also been in the forefront of inventorying their biodiversity with the understanding that protecting nature means first fully understanding the exact extent of their biological resources. Panama has been a newer player in national park development (emulating Costa Rica in terms of number of "protected" parks and reserves) and biodiversity inventorying, and has made worthwhile strides in conserving its biological treasures. To make the parks "pay their way," ecotourism is now a flourishing industry. This industry, however, also puts other pressures on the environment, albeit, perhaps, in gentler ways. Belize, Guatemala, Panama, and Nicaragua are also marketing their tropical beauty and archaeological riches to foreign tourists. Nicaragua has been trying hard in the twenty-first century to shed its image of political instability, to market its tropical wonders (forests, mountains, and lakes) to North American tourists interested in getting off the more well-known Costa Rican or Panamanian treadmill and to show how it is different, special, and, especially, how it has less known and trammeled natural areas. That effort has not been entirely successful as yet—old images and stereotypes die slowly, but the government has increased spending for marketing ecotourism there. The same can be said of Honduras, whose government in the 1990s earmarked all areas above a certain elevation as "national parks" (although for the most part that meant a great deal of inaccessible mountain peaks). While that country has always enjoyed the benefits of tourism in the beautiful tropical islands off its Caribbean coast (especially in the tourist resort of Roatán), North American tourists have eschewed the mainland. Nicaragua and Honduras are the poorest nations in the region, so infrastructure inadequacies, the very real threat of crime (especially in urban areas), and a general lack of tourist facilities have hindered the growth of tourism in both countries. A highly publicized outburst of gang-related violence has marred life in Honduras and hindered the country's tourism efforts even further. Many of the gang members in Tegucigalpa and San Pedro Sula (the country's largest cities) are returning youth from Los Angeles—immigrants from Honduras to the United States, many of whom became involved in gang life there and then returned home, bringing that lifestyle with them.

Outlook

Tourism, now the leading industry in Costa Rica and a growing industry in other nations, will need to be monitored closely for its environmental side effects. Despite the fact that it has been greatly exaggerated or exploited in a variety of ways (Honey 2008), ecotourism—a buzz term for more than twenty years—can still lead to local economic growth while attempting to preserve the tropical environment.

Central Americans are also concerned about energy production and consumption, improved tropical conservation, effects of export agriculture (including chemical pesticide dependence), and mining. Each nation has a department of *medio ambiente* (environment), an agency focused on natural resources and the environment that monitors many of these issues. They are all strapped economically, however, and thus have drawn much international attention from nongovernmental organizations wanting to assist in the environmental protection of such an ecologically diverse and rich region. Some of those organizations have promoted "carbon trading" initiatives based on the idea of making nations (or corporations or individual citizens) that use high amounts of energy pay Central American nations for storing carbon, through conservation of tropical forests, to make up for their own carbon footprints (made from polluting factories, jet travel, or other fossil fuel–depleting industries). The thought is that if the wealthy, energy-consuming North could pay for the production and storage of carbon in the South, there could be trade-off benefits for all involved. Although that may be the case, the carbon trading initiatives surely do not decrease pollution in the North.

"Sustainability" has become a common term in Central America for environmental groups and government agencies in dealing with these kinds of problems, but it is often confused with the term "sustained economic growth." The two can be complementary, but only with the right safeguards in place, often missing in this region. There are countless conferences, symposia, and meetings about solar and other alternative energy resources, for example, and there is often great talk of pollution control and increased enforcement of environmental standards. But without adequate funding, the talks become pipe dreams and are never realized. The successful alternative community of Gaviotas in Colombia (complete with a variety of solar energy devices and other environmentally and socially responsible alternative technologies) has exported ideas, advice, and concepts to a variety of places in Central America, but with only measured and sporadic success rates. Yet local successes can be multiplied on national scales, and with no Central American nation producing its own oil, solar power and other alternative energy sources will be required in the near future.

In the same vein, urban issues such as congestion, sprawl, pollution, expanding greenbelts and parks, improving mass transit, and dealing with waste and recycling are all urgent issues facing Central American cities as they continue to grow rapidly. Every year millions of campesinos (rural farm workers) looking for work and a better life migrate to Guatemala City, San Salvador, Tegucigalpa, San Pedro Sula, Managua, San José, and Panama City, where they are often forced to live in marginalized housing or slums without access to public services. Municipal and national leaders thus have many responsibilities and planning challenges ahead. Governments in all Central American nations will have to focus more on cities, with their enormous environmental challenges, and will have to direct even greater attention to conserving the tropical forests than in the past.

Sterling EVANS
University of Oklahoma

See also Agriculture, Tropical (the Americas); Caribbean; Ecotourism (the Americas); Fair Trade; Forest Management; Guatemala City; Labor; Marine Ecosystems Health; Marine Preserves; Mexico; Multilateral Environmental Agreements (MEAs); Organization of American States (OAS); Parks and Protected Areas; Public Transportation; Social Movements (Latin America); Travel and Tourism Industry; Urbanization

FURTHER READING

Adams, Richard E. W. (1991). *Prehistoric Mesoamerica*. Norman: University of Oklahoma Press.
Barry, Tom. (1987). *Roots of rebellion: Land and hunger in Central America*. Boston: South End Press.
Barry, Tom, & Preusch, Deb. (1986). *The Central America fact book*. New York: Grove Press.
Barzetti, Valerie, & Rovinski, Yanina. (Eds.). (1992). *Toward a green Central America: Integrating conservation and development*. West Hartford, CT: Kumarian Press.
Bonta, Mark. (2003). *Seven names for the bellbird: Conservation geography in Honduras*. College Station: Texas A&M University Press.
Brockett, Charles D. (1998). *Land, power, and poverty: Agrarian transformation and political conflict in Central America*. Boulder, CO: Westview Press.
Carrasco, Davíd. (1990). *Religions of Mesoamerica*. San Francisco: Harper San Francisco.
Castro Herrera, Guillermo. (1996). *Naturaleza y sociedad en la historia de latinoamérica* [Nature and society in Latin American history]. Panama City, Panama: CELA.
Castro Herrera, Guillermo. (2008). Isthmus in the world: Elements for an environmental history of Panama. *Global Environment, 1*(1), 10–55.
Coatsworth, John H. (1994). *Central America and the United States: The clients and the colossus*. New York: Twayne Publishers.
Cole-Christensen, Darryl. (1997). *A place in the rain forest: Settling the Costa Rican frontier*. Austin: University of Texas Press.
Collins, Joseph. (1986). *Nicaragua: What difference could a revolution make (food and farming in the new Nicaragua)*. New York: Grove Press.
Collinson, Helen. (Ed.). (1997). *Green guerrillas: Environmental conflicts and initiatives in Latin America and the Caribbean*. Montreal, Canada: Black Rose Books.
Crosby, Alfred W. (1972). *The Columbian exchange: Biological and cultural consequences of 1492*. Westport, CT: Greenwood Press.
Crosby, Alfred W. (1986). *Ecological imperialism: The biological expansion of Europe, 900–1900*. Cambridge, UK: Cambridge University Press.
Evans, Sterling. (1999). *The green republic: A conservation history of Costa Rica*. Austin: University of Texas Press.
Franke, Joseph. (1993). *Costa Rica's national parks and preserves: A visitor's guide*. Seattle, WA: Mountaineers.
Gallini, Stefania. (2008). Los agrosistemas y la consolidación del paradigm agro-exportador en Guatemala, 1873–1898 [Agricultural ecosystems and the consolidation of the agricultural exporter paradigm in Guatemala]. In Reinaldo Funes Monzote (Ed.), *Naturaleza en declive: Miradas a la historia ambiental de América Latina y el Caribe* [Nature in decline: A glimpse at the environmental history of Latin America and the Caribbean] (pp. 125–158). Valencia, Spain: Centro Francisco Tomás y Valiente, UNED Alzira-Valencia, Fundación Instituto de Historia Social.
Honey, Martha. (2008). *Ecotourism and sustainable development: Who owns paradise?* Washington, DC: Island Press.
Johnson, Melissa A. (2003, October). The making of race and place in nineteenth-century British Honduras. *Environmental History, 8*(4), 598–617.

Karnes, Thomas L. (1961). *The failure of union: Central America, 1824–1960*. Chapel Hill: University of North Carolina Press.

LaFeber, Walter. (1993). *Inevitable revolutions: The United States in Central America*. New York: W. W. Norton.

Marañón, Jon. (2001). *The gringo's hawk*. Eugene, OR: Kenneth Group Publishing.

McCook, Stuart. (2009). La roya del café en Costa Rica: Epidemias, inovación y medio ambiente, 1950–1995 [Coffee rust in Costa Rica: Epidemics, innovation, and the environment, 1950–1995]. *Revista de Historia, 59–60*, 99–117.

McCullough, David. (1977). *The path between the seas: The creation of the Panama Canal, 1870–1914*. New York: Simon & Schuster.

Meza Ocampo, Tobías A. (1999). *Costa Rica: Naturaleza y sociedad* [Costa Rica: Nature and society]. Cartago: Editorial Tecnológica de Costa Rica.

Pérez-Brignoli, Héctor. (1989). *A brief history of Central America*. Berkeley & Los Angeles: University of California Press.

Picado Umaña, Wilson; Díaz, Rafael Ledezma; & Granados Porras, Roberto. (2009). Territorio de coyotes, agroecosistemas y cambio tecnológico en una region cafetalera de Costa Rica [Coyote territory, agricultural ecosystems, and technological change in a coffee-growing region of Costa Rica]. *Revista de Historia, 59–60*, 119–165.

Schlesinger, Stephen, & Kinzer, Stephen. (1999). *Bitter fruit: The story of the American coup in Guatemala*. Cambridge, MA: Harvard University Press.

Soluri, John. (2005). *Banana cultures: Agriculture, consumption, and environmental change in Honduras and the United States*. Austin: University of Texas Press.

Sutter, Paul. (2007). Nature's agents or agents of empire? Entomological workers and environmental change during the construction of the Panama Canal. *Isis, 98*, 724–754.

Wallace, David Rains. (1992). *The quetzal and the macaw: The story of Costa Rica's national parks*. San Francisco: Sierra Club Books.

Weinberg, Bill. (1991). *War on the land: Ecology and politics in Central America*. London: Zed Books.

Weisman, Alan. (2008). *Gaviotas: A village to reinvent the world*. White River Junction, VT: Chelsea Green.

Woodward, R. Lee. (1985). *Central America: A nation divided*. New York: Oxford University Press.

Chesapeake Bay

Chesapeake Bay is the United States' largest estuary. Some of the earliest colonists built settlements along the bay. The bay has played an important role in the history of the United States, and is home to one of the world's largest naval bases. While pollution was once a problem, efforts such as the Chesapeake Bay Program have worked to clean and restore the bay to a healthy state.

An estuary is a body of freshwater fed by rivers and streams that meets the ocean. Chesapeake Bay is the largest such body of water in the United States, and the third largest in the world. The bay has played an important role in the nation's economic, political, and environmental history. Bounded by Virginia and Maryland, the bay is 297 kilometers long but only 56 kilometers at its greatest width. Draining a watershed of over 155,000 square kilometers, which covers portions of six states, the bay flows to the Atlantic Ocean through a 27-kilometer-wide opening just north of Cape Henry, Virginia, at the bay's southern extreme. Although the bay is large, with several thousand kilometers of shoreline, it is not deep. The average depth is just over 6 meters, with its deepest point only 53 meters.

History and Features

Great Shellfish Bay, the English translation of the name the Native Americans gave Chesapeake Bay (Tschiswapeki), has played a prominent role in American history. Famed Jamestown colonist John Smith first noted the bay's abundant resources. The English established their earliest settlements in the seventeenth century along its wide tributaries. The emergent colonies developed extensive fishing industries. Tobacco as well as widespread crab and oyster populations solidified the area's reputation. Protected from coastal storms, port cities such as Norfolk, Virginia, and Baltimore, Maryland, prospered and remain terminals of trade with Europe and the rest of the world.

Today more than 15 million people live in the bay's watershed, and the population is still growing. The economy still largely depends upon the bay. Approximately 90 million tonnes of imports and exports pass through its major ports annually. Recreation and tourism are critical to the local economies. The shipbuilding industry in the Virginia's Hampton Roads area is one of the largest in the world. Norfolk is home to one of the world's largest naval bases.

With many marshes and wetlands, the bay is home to approximately 3,500 species of plants and animals, including over 300 species of fish. Its waters are vital to seasonal bird migrations along the Atlantic Seaboard. As humpback, minke, and pilot whales make their way along the Atlantic coast, people often spot them in the north of the bay during their migration. The sandbar shark is the most common shark inhabiting the bay's waters, but it is harmless to humans. Other sharks enter the bay on occasion for food as they too migrate along the coast (Chesapeake Bay Program 2009).

Sustainability Issues

Centuries of growth, however, have threatened the fragile ecosystem of the bay. Today the federal Environmental Protection Agency (EPA) includes the bay on its list of impaired waterways, its most damaged tributaries including the Patapsco, Anacostia, and Elizabeth rivers. With environmental regulations since the 1980s constraining direct industrial discharge, the greatest threat to the bay today comes from nonpoint (diffuse) pollution. A variety of human activities, including agriculture and construction, wash contaminants or toxins into the bay's tributaries. Excess nutrients have led to eutrophication (excess algal growth that blocks sunlight from the underwater grasses critical to the bay's ecosystem). The condition of the bay has prompted public and private efforts at conservation since the 1980s. In 1983 local governments created the Chesapeake Bay Program to coordinate restoration efforts, with private initiatives such as the Chesapeake Bay Foundation assisting. Thanks to such efforts, the bay has begun to show improvements.

Today the bay is the site of projects to improve water quality, restore habitats, manage fish stocks, protect watersheds, and create an educational site for the public (Chesapeake Bay Program 2011b). It is one of the most biologically diverse areas of the United States. A 6 percent improvement of water quality, however, does not indicate that the bay is in good health. Serious problems remain; its overall health was only about 45 percent of total health in 2009 (Chesapeake Bay Program 2011b).

The "world's longest running carbon dioxide experiment in Maryland" has taken place on the bay. Scientists are re-creating salt marshes in the bay that simulate a possible future environment (O'Brien 2010). With rising sea levels, low-lying islands and countries around the world, such as Bangladesh and the Maldives, run the risk of disappearing completely. Ice caps melt as increased carbon dioxide levels heat up the planet. This excess water raises sea levels, which then erode coastlines. Tangier Island, located in the bay, 148 kilometers southeast of Washington, DC, is disappearing because rising sea levels have caused erosion. Although it once had a population of more than 1,200 people, it is now below 500 (BBC 2011).

Outlook

Increased levels of carbon dioxide are the biggest cause of global warming, but scientists in the bay have discovered that increased carbon dioxide levels also make some plants grow faster, which keeps pace with the increased atmospheric levels. This new plant growth then causes soils to rebuild, which reclaims land from the sea. Patrick Megonigal, a senior biogeochemist with the Smithsonian Environmental Research Center, states that the "marsh can actually build soil through root growth and more soil means this marsh can rise upwards and therefore keep pace with rising sea levels" (O'Brien 2010).

Ongoing efforts, such as the Chesapeake Bay Program and the EPA's Total Maximum Daily Load, which restricts the amounts of pollutants that can enter the bay (US EPA 2010), aim to restore the bay to a healthier state.

J. Brooks FLIPPEN
Oklahoma State University

See also Columbia River; Marine Ecosystems Health; Marine Preserves; Mississippi and Missouri Rivers; United States; Water Use and Rights

This article was adapted by the editors from the article "Chesapeake Bay" in Shepard Krech III, J. R. McNeill, and Carolyn Merchant (Eds.), the *Encyclopedia of World Environmental History*, pp. 210–211. Great Barrington, MA: Berkshire Publishing (2003).

FURTHER READING

British Broadcasting Company (BBC). (2011, October 26). The disappearing island in the Chesapeake Bay. Retrieved November 18, 2011, from http://www.bbc.co.uk/news/magazine-15395685

Chesapeake Bay Program: A Watershed Partnership. (2009). Bay FAQ. Retrieved November 18, 2011, from http://www.chesapeakebay.net/bayfaq.aspx?menuitem=14589

Chesapeake Bay Program: A Watershed Partnership. (2011a). Bay health. Retrieved November 18, 2011, from http://www.chesapeakebay.net/status_bayhealth.aspx?menuitem=15048

Chesapeake Bay Program: A Watershed Partnership. (2011b). Bay restoration. Retrieved November 18, 2011, from http://www.chesapeakebay.net/bayrestoration.aspx?menuitem=13989

Curtin, Philip D.; Brush, Grace S.; & Fisher, George W. (2001). *Discovering the Chesapeake: The history of an ecosystem*. Baltimore, MD: Johns Hopkins University Press.

Dorbin, Ann E. (2001). *Saving the bay: People working for the future of Chesapeake*. Baltimore, MD: Johns Hopkins University Press.

Lippson, Alice Jane, & Lippson, Robert L. (1984). *Life in the Chesapeake Bay*. Baltimore, MD: Johns Hopkins University Press.

O'Brien, Jane. (2010, November 4). The world's longest running carbon dioxide experiment. Retrieved November 18, 2011, from http://www.bbc.co.uk/news/world-us-canada-11685516

Shubel, Jerry R. (1981). *The living Chesapeake*. Baltimore, MD: Johns Hopkins University Press.

United States Environmental Protection Agency (US EPA). (2010). Chesapeake Bay Total Maximum Daily Load (Fact sheet). Retrieved January 2, 2012, from http://www.epa.gov/reg3wapd/pdf/pdf_chesbay/BayTMDLFactSheet8_6.pdf

Wennersten, John R. (2001). *The Chesapeake: An environmental biography*. Baltimore: Maryland Historical Society.

Columbia River

The Columbia River basin is arguably the most ecologically and socially diverse watershed in North America. The basin encompasses one Canadian province and seven US states. It is ecologically very diverse, containing the largest wilderness area in the continental United States, extensive irrigation farming, major urban centers, and intensive industrialization with all its attendant environmental problems including damming, habitat change, and pollution.

The Columbia River is 1,953 kilometers long and is the second-largest US river by volume. Along with its largest tributary, the Snake River, the Columbia drains 668,220 square kilometers of the Pacific Northwest and western Canada, an area roughly equal to the size of France. Its major tributaries include the Bitterroot, Blackfoot, Bruneau, Canoe, Clarks Fork, Clearwater, Cowlitz, Deschutes, Flathead, Grande Ronde, John Day, Kootenai, Malheur, Okanogan, Owyhee, Pend d'Oreille, Salmon, Spokane, Umatilla, Wenatchee, Willamette, and Yakima rivers. The river's power is exemplified at the Columbia Gorge, the only place where water breaches the great mountain barriers of the western United States. Six species of Pacific salmon, several species of western trout, two species of sturgeon, the sardine-like eulachon, and beaver are historically important native species. Since the late nineteenth century, many additional species have invaded the watershed on their own or were introduced by humans. Among the more prominent newcomer species are invertebrates such as green crabs and the New Zealand mud snail, warm-water fishes like pike and largemouth and smallmouth bass, anadromous species (species that spawn in freshwater but mature in saltwater) such as striped bass and shad, and aquatic animals like the nutria, Virginia opossum, and bullfrog.

The Columbia basin is arguably the most ecologically and socially diverse watershed in North America. The basin includes the tundra-like environs of the Canadian Rockies and the desert-like conditions of the world's largest basaltic plateau and the Great Basin of Utah and Nevada, and it extends from the Continental Divide in Yellowstone to the rain-drenched forests surrounding the entrance to the Pacific Ocean. The region's peoples are equally diverse. Aboriginal groups varied from the densely settled salmon specialists along the lower Columbia to small, migratory bands at the edge of the Great Basin and buffalo-hunting horse tribes that skirted the Rockies. Contact with Euro-Americans brought tremendous social and environmental change to the basin. Native American populations declined and were forced to shift away from subsistence activities, like fishing and hunting, but some groups obtained treaties that enabled them to maintain their historic ties to salmon despite mounting social and ecological obstacles. Present-day non–Native American settlements range from mining communities such as Libby, Montana, and Mica, British Columbia, to agricultural areas in the Yakima River, upper Snake River, Hood River, and middle Willamette River valleys, the ever-growing urban centers of Portland, Oregon, and Spokane, Washington, and recreational and tourist meccas such as Jackson, Wyoming, and Bend, Oregon. The basin contains both the largest wilderness area in the continental United States and the most polluted sites in North America, and an immensely complex governance structure controls the sprawling geography. The Columbia encompasses one province (British Columbia), two nations, seven states (Oregon, Washington, Idaho, Montana, Nevada, Wyoming, and Utah), and many tribes, while management of its salmon, some of which migrate far out into the Pacific Ocean, has necessitated treaties with Canada, Russia, South Korea, Japan, and Taiwan to regulate high-seas harvests of runs that spawn as far inland as eastern Idaho and southern British Columbia.

Environmental Challenges

The basin's socioeconomic complexity makes dealing with environmental issues difficult. Industrial, military, and agricultural development bolstered economies in western Canada and the United States throughout the twentieth century, but such developments altered habitat and produced pollution that now threatens humans and nature alike. Contamination by nuclear wastes at Hanford, Washington, and Arco, Idaho, and chemical and heavy-metal deposits from mining around Coeur d'Alene, Idaho, and Butte, Montana, eventually led to designating these areas as Environmental Protection Agency Superfund sites because the scale of pollution required federal funding to clean up hazardous wastes. This support has been calculated to cost several billion dollars. Long-term changes to habitat and intensive harvesting by industrial and sport fishers extinguished many individual runs—though no species—of salmon, and many runs have been listed as threatened and endangered under the US Endangered Species Act of 1973. Resolving environmental problems poses daunting political and technical challenges because the region's economy is intrinsically dependent on the very activities that cause environmental degradation.

The complexity of the Columbia River basin's political ecology is most conspicuous in its famed dam system. Damming is an ancient activity in the basin. For millennia, Native peoples constructed rock weirs and wooden lattices to obstruct and harvest adult fish during spawning migrations, but these were temporary structures that served a seasonal need and then were disassembled or destroyed by floods. Soon after arrival in the late 1830s, settlers began to build very different structures as part of the process of resettlement. Farmers and miners built many small irrigation dams, wing dams, and dikes to constrain the flow of streams. Loggers erected splash dams to build a head of water so they could float timber to mills. Urbanites buried tributary creeks, stripped banks of vegetation, and entombed shorelines in riprap or concrete. None of these dams included effective fishways (provision for migrating fish), raising concerns about the obstruction of salmon migrations even during Oregon's territorial period before 1859. Larger structures appeared starting at Willamette Falls on the Willamette River in 1888 and at Swan Falls on the Snake River in 1901. Cities as varied as Portland, Oregon; Spokane, Washington; and Lewiston, Idaho, built structures to provide hydroelectricity, drinking water, flood control, and water transportation. All these dams decreased fish populations by thwarting migrations and increasing pollution.

The first efforts to build very large dams across the Columbia came in the 1920s. The first to be completed were Rock Island Dam (1931) by the Chelan County Public Utility District in Washington State, Bonneville Dam (1937) by the US Army Corps of Engineers, and Grand Coulee Dam (1941) by the US Bureau of Reclamation. Many more dams rose during the Cold War to coordinate flood control and hydroelectric generation across five states and one province, and to enable commercial river traffic from the Pacific Ocean to Lewiston. There are now more than forty of these very large dams in the basin. Since 1937, the sale of electricity has been handled by the Bonneville Power Administration. The system is regulated nationally by the Federal Columbia River Power System and internationally with Canada through the 1964 Columbia River Treaty. For decades, environmental issues were largely an afterthought. The impact of dams on salmon were expected to be mitigated by artificial propagation through a system of hatcheries established the 1938 Mitchell Act.

The balance between environmental and industrial demands in the basin has shifted remarkably since 1980. Dams did not just obstruct migrating eel, salmon, shad, and sturgeon populations; they also slowed currents, inundated refuges and reproductive habitat for aquatic and avian species, and warmed waters in ways that make large parts of the basin friendlier to non-native species such as bass and pike than to salmonids (salmon and their relatives). By the 1970s, the only remaining free-flowing stretch of river, adjacent to the Hanford Nuclear Reservation, had the only remaining resilient populations in the basin. Naturally reproducing fish were declining rapidly nearly everywhere other than in the Hanford Reach, so in 1980 Congress passed the Northwest Electric Power Planning and Conservation Act to create balance between commercial and environmental interests when managing dams. The new agency, known at first as the Northwest Power Planning Council and now called the Northwest Power and Conservation Council, is guided by a group of scientists, lawyers, and politically appointed representatives from the basin states. Since its beginning, members have found it easier to agree on power policies than to protect fish. By the late 1990s, the Environmental Protection Agency listed a number of salmon and other aquatic species as threatened or endangered. Authority over river management shifted from agencies to courts at this point as interested parties battled over implementation of the Endangered Species Act–mandated Biological Opinion (colloquially known as the Bi-Op) on river management.

Since 2002, these contests have been institutionalized in the US District Court for the District of Oregon, presided over by Judge James A. Redden. Lawyers representing a variety of interests have challenged plans put forth by the administrations of George W. Bush and Barack Obama, and in general federal agencies have been forced repeatedly to revise their management to give greater accommodation to nature. A ruling in August 2011 once again forced the National Oceanic and Atmospheric Administration to give more attention to salmon habitat restoration, yet this ruling also approved at least portions of the existing approach. Redden's ruling sent mixed signals to all parties. Pro-dam forces were frustrated that the judge continued to entertain arguments about breaching some dams, especially the lower four dams on the Snake River, to help fish, yet Redden's support of the existing plan through 2013 also suggested that success in habitat restoration beyond 2013 could undermine arguments for the necessity of breaching dams. Given the cultural and economic complexity of the Columbia basin, it is not clear that interests at either end of the political spectrum can realize their vision of a river continuing to operate by the outmoded industrial model or an extensively re-wilded river.

Joseph E. TAYLOR III
Simon Fraser University

See also Canada; Parks and Protected Areas; Rocky Mountains; United States; Vancouver, Canada; Water Use and Rights; Yellowstone to Yukon Conservation Initiative (Y2Y)

FURTHER READING

Lang, William L., & Carriker, Robert C. (Eds.). (1999). *Great river of the west: Essays on the Columbia River.* Seattle: University of Washington Press.

Meinig, Donald W. (1968). *The great Columbia Plateau: A historical geography, 1805–1910.* Seattle: University of Washington Press.

Taylor, Joseph E., III. (1999). *Making salmon: An environmental history of the Pacific salmon crisis.* Seattle: University of Washington Press.

White, Richard. (1995). *The organic machine: The remaking of the Columbia River.* New York: Hill and Wang.

Share the *Encyclopedia of Sustainability:* Teachers are welcome to make up to ten (10) copies of no more than two (2) articles for distribution in a single course or program. For further permissions, please visit www.copyright.com or contact: info@berkshirepublishing.com

Corporate Accountability

Since the early 1990s, increasing social pressure has been mobilized to make business practices more socially and environmentally responsible. Corporate accountability *can refer to both legal and nonjudicial sources of regulatory pressure, while* corporate social responsibility *often refers to more collaborative and discretionary approaches to transforming corporate decision making. Success in reforming business practices through regulation and activism has been mixed.*

Since the 1990s, a range of initiatives led by businesses, social organizations, and governments have aimed to pressure companies to behave in more socially and environmentally responsible and accountable ways. This is a new development for many parts of the business world. Previously, the state (or government) was assumed to establish standards and behavioral norms for most businesses. When community organizations and interest groups wanted to change business behavior, they focused on changing the law. But since the 1990s, new alliances and influences emerged to affect business norms by linking together consumers, communities, workers, and producers.

Corporate Social Responsibility vs. Corporate Accountability

The terms *corporate responsibility*, *corporate social responsibility* (CSR), and *corporate accountability* are sometimes confused or viewed as synonymous. Corporate responsibility and corporate accountability are typically distinguished in several ways, however. Corporate responsibility, in its broadest sense, refers to the belief that corporations have responsibilities beyond generating profit for their shareholders. Such responsibilities include the negative duties to refrain from causing harm to the environment, individuals, or communities, as well as the positive duties to safeguard society and the environment, such as by protecting the human rights of workers and communities affected by business activities, or actively incorporating principles of environmental sustainability into day-to-day business practices. Such responsibilities are generally considered to extend beyond direct social and environmental impacts to the more indirect effects resulting from relationships with business partners, such as those involved in global production chains.

In contrast, corporate accountability commonly refers to more confrontational or enforceable ways to influence corporate behavior. Often, the term *corporate responsibility* is used to indicate voluntary approaches, even those supported by market-based incentives. The term *corporate accountability*, however, typically implies that pressure is being exerted by social and governmental actors outside the company. Such actors can adopt a range of strategies, including, but not limited to, enacting laws and regulations to enforce social standards.

Innovations in the Americas and Oceania

Initiatives to pressure companies to conform to standards of social responsibility have taken a number of forms: (1) "soft" collaborative approaches where companies have worked together with nongovernment organizations (NGOs) and other social groups to try to improve the sustainability of their behavior; (2) "hard" approaches involving coercive pressure from confrontational activist campaigns and/or traditional forms of government regulation; and (3) mixed strategies in which collaborative approaches have been combined with greater involvement of workers and communities affected by corporate behavior in shaping corporate decision making. Often these approaches have interacted in important ways, both in shaping the way the approaches have developed over time and in influencing the sustainability of business behavior.

Activist Campaigns

Activist campaigns advocating corporate responsibility began gaining momentum in the 1990s. These campaigns took advantage of increasing mobilization within prominent consumer sectors such as garments and coffee. They focused on improving working conditions and raising wages for workers in developing countries through a series of public campaigns that targeted both companies and consumers in industrialized countries, including North America.

The emergence of such campaigns was facilitated by the increasing capacity of activists in the global North to communicate directly with workers in distant factories, together with broader changes in the focus of NGOs in the United States after the end of the Cold War. As the corporate accountability agenda emerged and developed through the success of campaigns focused on prominent brands such as Nike in 1998, a broad range of social and political organizations began to mobilize around the corporate responsibility issue, including NGOs, unions, immigrant workers, and a wide range of individuals and organizations linked through email lists, student groups, and religious institutions.

As a result, such campaigns sometimes took on interesting cross-regional dynamics in which NGOs, unions, and other social groups in consumer and investor countries joined forces with workers or communities to pressure companies to change their behavior. One example of such alliances between the Americas and Oceania is a campaign that was launched in 2001 in support of workers at the Taiwanese-owned Chentex factory in Nicaragua's Las Mercedes Free Trade Zone, with the support of both local unions and a range of labor and human rights NGOs (Macdonald 2007). In Taiwan, the participating coalition of labor activists, Taiwan Solidarity for Nicaraguan Workers, pressured the Taiwanese owner of the Chentex factory (the Nien Hsing consortium) by protesting outside the stock market and at the company's annual meeting. In Nicaragua, the Sandinista-based labor union at Chentex pressured local management directly with widespread protests and strikes. In the United States, labor campaigners organized consumer boycotts and protests at retail outlets across the country, directed against major clients of the Chentex factory. Coordinated action in all segments of the global production chain was thus used as a basis for corporate accountability.

Collaborative Multi-Stakeholder Programs

Often, these activist campaigns have prompted companies to join into "partnerships" with NGOs and others to bring about sustainable changes in corporate behavior in accordance with the social and environmental standards championed by the campaigns. These partnerships are often built around principles of voluntary action, dialogue, and collaboration. They call for governments, businesses, and workers to engage in a process of mutual learning and to increase compliance through preventive and cooperative efforts.

An example from the United States of one such multi-stakeholder corporate accountability program is the Fair Labor Association (FLA), in which a number of high-profile apparel and sportswear companies work together with universities and NGOs to promote compliance with core international labor standards within their global supply chains. The FLA was initiated by the Clinton administration in response to ongoing activist pressure during the 1990s. The administration coordinated a series of meetings between representatives of companies in the apparel and sportswear sectors and the labor and human rights groups involved in activist campaigns, which ultimately led to the establishment of the association. As in many similar initiatives, the multi-stakeholder character of the FLA is reflected in the broad range of actors who participate: companies involved in the design and marketing of branded apparel and sportswear products, universities who license many of these products, and North American NGOs concerned with labor and human rights issues. The central goal of the FLA is to promote compliance with international labor standards. To do this, it has developed a range of regulatory mechanisms—including setting standards and implementing monitoring and audit systems and some "soft" forms of enforcement—to change corporate behavior (Macdonald 2011).

Government Regulation

Although multi-stakeholder initiatives like the FLA are seen as an improvement on wholly voluntary approaches to generating corporate social responsibility, some people continue to call for strengthening national, regional, and international legislation and regulation to ensure compliance.

Such "hard" corporate accountability agendas have two objectives. One is to reform state-based regulation in order to better operate within global systems of production. This entails legally formalizing nonstandard working arrangements—extending the reach of regulation outside the traditional workplace or factory—as well as providing new rights to consumers. It also involves extending regulation beyond national jurisdictions. Efforts toward this goal include the ongoing work resulting from John Ruggie's mandate as the United Nations Secretary General's Special Representative on Business and Human Rights that seeks to clarify the responsibilities of businesses under international human rights law (Human Rights Council 2007 and 2008).

Governments in the Americas and Oceania have, in fact, intervened to strengthen private initiatives. In some cases, national legislative bodies have succeeded in inserting voluntary codes in national and international laws that require companies to be more transparent and report on social or environmental performance. The California Cooperative Compliance Program adopted by California's Occupational Health and Safety Administration, for example, includes a provision for litigation to enforce standards that may be in breach (Vogel 2005).

In other cases, existing regulations have been used creatively—often in ways that go beyond the original intentions of the relevant provisions—as a way to more stringently enforce norms of corporate responsibility. In Los Angeles, the LA City Sweatfree Procurement Ordinance initiative has been very successful in requiring private companies to demonstrate compliance with national labor standards in order to have their bids for municipal work considered by the city. Where business activities involve labor standards of subcontractors in countries other than the United States, the ordinance also requires those subcontractors to comply with local minimum standards and the payment of a "procurement living wage" assessed on the basis of local wages, time spent working, and conditions (Owen-Smith, Coast, and Donovan 2010, 340–341).

"Hard" regulatory approaches have often been used by activists in inventive ways to try to enforce principles of responsible corporate practice against major transnational corporations such as Nike and Walmart. Activists have used unfair competition and false advertising legislation to try to hold companies accountable for claims made in their CSR marketing material, such as in the California case of *Kasky v. Nike* (45 P.3d 243 (CA 2002)). The US Alien Tort Claims Act (28 U.S.C. 1350 (1789)), which allows civil lawsuits to be brought in the US judicial system for extraterritorial actions "committed in violation of the law of nations or a treaty of the United States," has also been used repeatedly to enforce international corporate responsibility (Vogel 2005, 168). Such lawsuits are sometimes successful in gaining publicity and providing greater corporate transparency, partly through the discovery processes by which claimants have been able to gain access to documents previously unavailable to the public. These private law mechanisms require substantial financial and time commitments from the claimants, however, and they have not succeeded in bringing about the desired lasting and meaningful change in corporate practices.

Following another legal avenue, many social alliances that promote corporate accountability have pressured governments to regulate corporate behavior in ways that reflect standards of social responsibility. For example, the Fair Wear Campaign in Australia, an alliance between religious and community organizations and unions, has, for many years, pressured the state and federal governments to strengthen the regulation of sweatshops and home-based workers. Fair Wear has pressured governments to enact innovative regulation that extends beyond the standard employer/employee relationships to cover business entities that do not themselves manufacture but instead organize and outsource production. Successful campaigning by this alliance has led to the introduction of a range of highly innovative supply-chain regulations (Fenwick et al. 2008).

The Asia Wage Floor Alliance is another example of a movement for new regulatory techniques to increase corporate accountability. It campaigns for an enforceable minimum wage for workers in the Asian garment industry and fair pricing for suppliers across Asia. It insists on both the role of the state in mediating labor standards and production prices and consistent transnational standards that reflect the global nature of the contemporary garment industry.

Impact and Outlook

What, then, has been achieved to date by corporate accountability initiatives of these various kinds? It would be a mistake to overstate the extent or impact of this shifting agenda with respect to mainstream corporate practice. Globally, very few businesses have adopted the practices promoted by corporate accountability movements, including the implementation of social auditing or joining established corporate accountability mechanisms such as the Fair Labor Association. Furthermore, the corporate accountability agenda's impact on business practices with regard to labor standards or environmental sustainability has in many cases been very limited. In the same period in which the idea of corporate accountability has gained prominence in the media and society, real wages for many vulnerable workers have continued to fall. In December 2007, Neil Kearney of the International Textile, Garment, and Leather Workers' Federation noted that since 2000, real wages in the textiles sector have fallen by 25 percent and working hours have increased by 25 percent (cited by Mantovan et al. 2010).

Nevertheless, such initiatives have brought about some important changes in businesses in a range of economic sectors. In understanding the scope and limits of such change, it is useful to examine how impacts have differed across the spectrum of "soft" and "hard" corporate accountability.

Soft vs. Hard Approach Impacts

Softer approaches, focused more on collaboration and learning to bring about change, have certainly made some contributions to influencing corporate behavior in the positive direction of achieving greater sustainability. In particular, collaborative initiatives that offer forums for stakeholder dialogue and participation can strengthen communication, trust, and shared learning in areas of potentially common interests. Additionally, participating directly in consultative and decision-making processes associated with new forms of standard setting and enforcement strengthens NGOs and affected groups that participate. The learning and dialogue can also contribute to organizational and cultural change within companies. NGOs can be especially effective in influencing complex features of organizational culture such as discrimination and health and safety regulatory systems where normative change and participatory engagement are often important prerequisites for effectiveness.

But such soft approaches to corporate accountability have been widely criticized as ineffective and unresponsive to the concerns of workers and communities affected by corporate activity. Because they lack a way to impose penalties on companies that do not change, improvements achieved as a result of soft approaches are typically unevenly implemented across sectors and companies. Such approaches have also been subject to strong criticism for enabling corporations to unilaterally adopt, implement, and enforce particular codes of conduct. There is also widespread concern that businesses might use these soft corporate accountability approaches to deflect attention from more controversial practices, thereby undermining improved, sustainable corporate behavior in the longer run.

Alternatively, where governments have implemented strong regulatory approaches to underpin corporate accountability strategies, stronger and more consistent enforcement of CSR norms has been achieved in some cases. Precisely because the "business case" for compliance is often weak, legal sanctions can provide the incentive for compliance that would otherwise be absent. The strength of legal enforcement mechanisms reflects the distinctive capacity of law to both counter underlying power imbalances among social actors and provide for greater consistency, as tensions between competing interests may be resolved on a normatively principled and consistently applied basis.

On the other hand, critics of mandatory approaches continue to highlight possible high costs to businesses of excessive regulatory burdens and the difficulties of designing regulations capable of accommodating the diverse contexts of business activity. Moreover, many states have not matched new legal clout with resources for the departments and unions responsible for monitoring and prosecuting (Marshall 2010), thereby undermining enforcement capabilities of governments.

Somewhere between these two approaches lie those corporate accountability campaigns and initiatives that seek to engage a broader range of nonbusiness actors and strengthen the nonmarket incentives underpinning compliance with CSR norms. The involvement of a broader range of stakeholders often enables more robust systems of monitoring and compliance to be established. In some cases, enhanced transparency and participation can also improve the perceived legitimacy of such programs.

Area of Greatest Impact

Perhaps the most important innovation of the corporate accountability movement has been its demands for increased participation by affected groups. This has been shown to be extremely important in many contexts as a basis for effective compliance with specified norms. In the few and often short-lived cases in which workers' organizations or representatives have been included, positive outcomes for workers have often been achieved, both in factory settings and among home-based workers.

Lasting changes to social power relationships can be made through the potential of initiatives to create sustainable social alliances between workers, producers, and communities affected by transnational business activity. Such participatory, multi-stakeholder processes do, however, confront a range of practical challenges associated with both a weak capacity among key stakeholder groups to engage effectively and, in some cases, the inherent difficulty in mediating conflicting priorities of affected stakeholders.

Clearly, significant challenges continue to confront all these different strategies of corporate accountability. To view these initiatives as static, institutional arrangements, however, misinterprets their purpose and impact as both experimental, learning processes in specific governance contexts and as broader vehicles for social transformation gained through provision of ongoing sources of knowledge and pressure that can contribute to progressive change within wider social and political institutions. Much uncertainty remains, and a great deal more experimentation will be needed as corporate accountability initiatives continue to be formed and improved, either as stand-alone forms of corporate regulation or in conjunction with other strategies.

Shelley MARSHALL
Monash University

Kate MACDONALD
University of Melbourne

See also E-Waste; Fair Trade; Labor; Mining (Australia); Mining (Andes); North American Free Trade Agreement (NAFTA); Organization of American States (OAS); Social Movements (Latin America); Travel and Tourism Industry; Urbanization; Water Use and Rights

FURTHER READING

Fenwick, Colin; Howe, John; Marshall, Shelley; & Landau, Ingrid. (2008). Labour and labour related laws in small and micro enterprises: Innovative regulatory responses (SEED Working Paper 81). Geneva: International Labour Organisation.

Human Rights Council. (2007). Business and human rights: Mapping international standards of responsibility and accountability for corporate acts (A/HRC/4/035). Geneva: United Nations Human Rights Council.

Human Rights Council. (2008). Promotion and protection of all human rights, civil, political, economic, social and cultural rights, including the right to development (A/HRC/8/5). Geneva: Human Rights Council.

Macdonald, Kate. (2007). Globalising justice within coffee supply chains? Fair trade, Starbucks and the transformation of supply chain governance. *Third World Quarterly, 28*(4), 793–812.

MacDonald, Kate. (2011). Fair labor association. In Thomas Hale & David Held (Eds.), *Handbook of transnational governance: Institutions & innovations* (pp. 243–251). Cambridge, UK: Polity Press.

Mantovan, Franco; Ausserhofer, Dietmar; Huber, Markus; Schulc, Eva; & Them, Christa. (2010). Interventions and their effects on informal caregivers of people with dementia: A systematic literature review. *Pflege, 23*(4), 223–239.

Marshall, Shelley. (2010). Australian textile clothing and footwear supply chain regulation. In Colin Fenwick & Tonia Novitz (Eds.), *Human rights at work: Perspectives on law and regulation* (pp. 555–585). Oxford, UK: Hart Publishing.

Owen-Smith, Amanda; Coast, Joanna; & Donovan, Jenny. (2010). Are patients receiving enough information about healthcare rationing? A qualitative study. *Journal of Medical Ethics, 36*(2), 88–92.

Vogel, David. (2005). *The market for virtue: The potential and limits of corporate social responsibility*. Washington, DC: Brookings Institution Press.

Berkshire's authors and editors welcome questions, comments, and corrections. Send your emails about the *Berkshire Encyclopedia of Sustainability* in general or this volume in particular to: sustainability.updates@berkshirepublishing.com

Curitiba, Brazil

1.7 million est. pop. 2010

Curitiba, the capital of Paraná State in southeastern Brazil, has become a global model for urban conservation, environmental preservation, and public transportation. Curitiba pioneered bus rapid transit and transit oriented development (urban and metropolitan planning), which has resulted in high quality of life and influenced later efforts in some South American cities such as Bogotá and Santiago, and also in North American cities including Portland, Oregon; San Francisco; and Los Angeles.

Curitiba, the Paraná State capital city located in southern Brazil, was founded in 1693; but it was in the 1940s that effective urban planning began to guide the city's physical expansion and economic development. By 1940, the population of Curitiba was 127,000 (IPPUC 2006). By 1950, the number had jumped to 180,000; by 1960, it had doubled to 361,000; and by 2010, it reached a population of more than 1.7 million (IBGE 2010). The international and rural-to-urban population migration that marked most Brazilian cities also caused Curitiba's exponential population growth.

Some common urban problems, like downtown traffic congestion, emerged in Curitiba with this population growth. It should be noted, however, that *Curitibanos* use about 25 percent less fuel per capita than other Brazilians (IPEA 1998), even though they are actually more likely to own cars. This is due to a very efficient public transportation system and plentiful nonmotorized transportation options, including 119 kilometers of bikeways crisscrossing almost the entire urban area (IPPUC 2004).

The success of Curitiba's famous urban planning is not measured through award-winning United Nations' prizes, references in planning magazines, or newspaper accounts, but through the city's livability. The most important characteristics of this livability are due to the successful implementation of sequential master plans. The first comprehensive master plan, known as Agache's Plan, was put in place in the 1940s, but it was much compromised by urban growth pushed by the expansion of the automobile industry (Santos 2011). During this era, the design of the city centered around automobiles, incorporating wide avenues. The official development plan called for widening the main streets of the city to add more traffic lanes, which would have resulted in the destruction of many turn-of-the-century buildings downtown. One urban planner, Jaime Lerner, was vocal in opposition to this trend. He eventually became Curitiba's mayor in 1971 at the age of thirty-three, serving three terms over two decades.

Jaime Lerner's emphasis on remaking Curitiba for people, not cars, profoundly shaped the city. The transformation of Curitiba's urban design began during his era and began with its central street, XV de Novembro, which had been almost obliterated by an overpass. Lerner insisted that it become an exclusively pedestrian mall. The first in Brazil, this pedestrian mall is emblematic of Lerner's drive for a human-scaled city. He also made forceful efforts to increase public space in the urban environment. In twenty years, even as the population exploded, green space per capita grew from about 1.7 to more than 42 square meters (IPPUC 2004). Stone quarries and flood planes were converted into magnificent parks and green public areas.

Since the early 1970s, Curitiba has systematically focused on the three most important conceptual pillars of urban planning: land use, road networks, and mass transit. All three require large investments in public transportation to create effective traffic patterns. Bus expressways with articulated buses that could carry 270 passengers were one addition to the urban landscape.

The successive Master Plans of 1966, 1975, 1993, 2000, and 2004 gradually transformed Curitiba from a small and disarticulated town into a very organized and competitive metropolis. Even before the petroleum crisis of the 1970s, Curitiba had prioritized mass transit over single-occupancy automobiles. The public transportation system, for example, carries the same number of passengers as any subway system and costs less to ride. The surface, bus-based public transportation system known as bus rapid transit (BRT) is a showcase. More than just a transit system, the BRT system links with nonmotorized urban transportation, represented by pedestrian and bicycle pathways. These nonmotorized modes of transportation are important in both community and economic development.

The "wise vision" thus became a reality in designing and rebuilding the city through urban planning and public transportation. Wide and efficient mass transportation corridors and rigid control of urban land use and occupation developed high-quality, well-designed neighborhoods. This approach, known as transit-oriented development (TOD), was a result of the often-cited successful urban planning collaboration. Curitiba is a dynamic and engaging city for both community development and environmental protection by modern standards, as plans set in motion in the 1970s continue to bear fruit. The city continues to evolve, balancing new population needs with fast changes stemming from sudden and intensive urbanization.

Curitiba's pioneering experience can be evaluated against later experiences of other South American cities like Bogotá, Colombia (the TransMilenio project), and Santiago, Chile (the Transantiago project). Some US cities, including Los Angeles, Houston, San Diego, Boston, Las Vegas, and Portland, Oregon, have looked to Curitiba's experience in development planning.

The city's futuristic vision institutionalized an urban design approach in which public transportation interacting with planning guidelines structures urban growth. The holistic vision of urban planning is then transformed into practical solutions for most urban issues. The decision-making process generates a synergetic flow, with beneficial actions in turn creating more fertile conditions for implementing additions and improvements. Curitiba's success was in part possible because the city was growing and changing rapidly, providing opportunities to intervene with progressive master plans. Curitiba provides an example of the effective coordination of urban land use and transportation development. Its successes are models for developing BRT systems and transportation infrastructure, as well as sustainable urban planning for livable cities worldwide.

Evandro C. SANTOS
Jackson State University

See also Architecture; Bogotá, Colombia; Brazil; Las Vegas, United States; Public Transportation; Rio de Janeiro, Brazil; Urbanization

FURTHER READING

Del Rio, Vicente, & Siembieda, William. (2008). *Contemporary urbanism in Brazil: Beyond Brasilia*. Gainesville: University Press of Florida.

Del Santoro, Roberto D. V. (2002). *Curitiba: Um modelo em evolução* [Curitiba: A model in evolution]. Curitiba, Brazil: Foco Editorial.

Instituto Brasileiro de Geografia e Estatística (IBGE) [Brazilian Institute of Geography and Statistics]. (2010). *Censo 2010* [Census 2010]. Retrieved February 27, 2012, from http://www.ibge.gov.br/cidadesat/topwindow.htm?1

Instituto de Pesquisa e Planejamento Urbano de Curitiba (IPPUC) [Institute of Urban Planning and Research]. (2006). Homepage. Retrieved September 4, 2006, from http://www.ippuc.org.br

Instituto de Pesquisa Econômica Aplicada (IPEA) [Institute of Socio-Economic Research and Planning]. (1998). *Brasil em desenvolvimento: Estado, planejamento e políticas públicas* [Developing Brazil: State, planning and public policies]. Retrieved April 5, 2007, from http://www.ipea.gov.br/bd/pdf/Livro_BrasilDesenvEN_Vol04.pdf

Santos, Evandro C. (2009). Curitiba, Brazil: Systems planning pioneer. In Gary Hack, Eugénie Birch, Paul Sedway & Mitchell Silver (Eds.), *Local planning: Contemporary principles and practice* (pp. 385–387). Washington, DC: International City / County Management Association (ICMA) Press.

Santos, Evandro C. (2011). Curitiba, Brazil: Pioneering in developing bus rapid transit and urban planning solutions. Saarbrücken, Germany: LAP Lambert Academic Publishing.

Wright, Lloyd. (2004). *Bus rapid transit: Sustainable transport: A sourcebook for policy-makers in developing cities*. London: University College London.

PIERCE COLLEGE LIBRARY

Detroit, United States

713,777 city est. pop. 2010; 4.3 million metropolitan area est. pop. 2010

The rapid growth of Detroit, Michigan, in the early twentieth century was largely due to the city's concentration on automotive manufacturing. The decline in the economic vitality of this industry has amplified problems of poverty and segregation. The city, whose population has decreased by half since 1950, faces major challenges involving regional transportation, vacant property, air pollution, and water pollution. Grassroots community-based strategies are leading efforts to rethink the city's future.

In the 2010 US Census, Detroit, Michigan, had a population of 713,777 people within the city and a population of 4,296,250 within the nine-county metropolitan area (also referred to as Metro Detroit). The dominance of the automobile manufacturing industry has shaped this city and region in many ways. Although the work opportunities provided by industrialization initially led to the diversification of the city's population by attracting foreign immigrants and African American workers from the South, the decline of the US automotive industry has since been accompanied by a reduction of the city's population by more than one-half (down from a high of almost 1.9 million in 1950) (Linebaugh 2011). The region's long-standing pattern of racial segregation has led to an isolated black central city surrounded by whiter suburbs and a lack of regional planning.

Geography and History

Detroit is located on the west side of the Detroit River between Lake Huron and Lake Erie, two of the five Great Lakes. The Great Lakes constitute one-fifth of the world's freshwater (84 percent of US surface water) and supply drinking water to more than 40 million people in the United States and Canada. The lakes moderate Detroit's temperatures, and the city's location on the westward shore (relative to the prevailing westerly winds) protects it from receiving large amounts of lake-effect snow. In January, Detroit has an average temperature of $-5.1°C$ and in July, it has an average temperature of $22.4°C$. Detroit receives 83 centimeters of annual precipitation and only 103.4 centimeters of annual snowfall (climate-zone.com n.d.).

Although archaeological evidence indicates that indigenous people long frequented the shoreline area that later became Detroit, European settlement dates back to 1701. By 1810, this early fur-trading post had evolved into a town serving the needs of the surrounding farming communities (Zunz 1982). Advancements in water transportation, such as the first steam vessel (1818) and the steam barge (1848), significantly increased activity on the Great Lakes. Detroit's importance as a regional center was strengthened when the Erie Canal opened in 1825. The Erie Canal connected Lake Erie at Buffalo, New York, to the Hudson River and the Atlantic Ocean and allowed ships to move between the Great Lakes system and the Atlantic Ocean.

Although Detroit was the eighteenth-largest city in the United States in 1880 with 116,340 residents, its diverse economic activities were relatively small in scale and more consistent with a regional trading center than a specialized industrial hub. Detroit's position relative to the area's many natural resources—including coal, timber, limestone, iron ore, and other mineral deposits—permitted the movement of raw materials by ship through the Great Lakes system to the city. These resources were crucial to the stove production that began in Detroit in 1861 and flourished during the 1870s. In 1870, an innovation in steel production known as the Bessemer process was rapidly adopted in Detroit. The new process blew air through the molten iron to remove impurities in the pig iron and enabled the inexpensive mass production of steel. In addition to stove production, Detroit had many horse-drawn carriage makers.

As Detroit emerged as an industrial center beginning in the 1890s, its physical settlement pattern was consistent with that of Pittsburgh, Buffalo, Cleveland, and Milwaukee. These "newer" industrial cities had a different spatial gradation from their core to their periphery when compared to older US cities such as New York, Chicago, and Philadelphia. In these newer cities, population density rapidly declined outside of the central business district. In Detroit, open space was particularly abundant outside of the central business district, because single-family houses were the pervasive residential typology (as opposed to multifamily structures), and industry was scattered throughout the area (Zunz 1982). Annexation of surrounding townships between 1880 and 1918 increased Detroit's physical size to an expansive 336 square kilometers and lessened the need for dense development. Two municipalities, Hamtramck and Highland Park, remained encapsulated islands within Detroit's boundaries.

The Automotive Industry and Immigration

Between 1900 and 1908, 501 automotive companies started in the United States; a critical mass of these companies, including Hudson, Nash, Fraser, Briggs, Kaiser, Packard, Chrysler, Dodge, Studebaker, and Ford, was located in Detroit. More than 60 percent of these early automotive start-ups failed within several years, however, including Henry Ford's first two efforts. It was Detroit's higher ratio of truck relative to car production that established the city's dominance in automobile manufacturing relative to other Midwestern cities in the 1910s (Farley, Danziger, and Holzer 2000). As the system of railroads in the United States became congested, truck transportation, responsible for moving armaments and munitions to the East, became increasingly important. In 1914, Detroit's 43 car manufacturers built 25,000 trucks per year. By 1918, the last year of World War I, they were producing 227,000 trucks annually.

As the early city experienced explosive economic development, Detroit attracted multiple waves of domestic and international immigrants. The first significant wave comprised foreign-born immigrants from eastern and southern Europe. Beginning in the 1870s, a significant number of Polish, Russian, and Italian immigrants arrived. Polish immigrants worked in Detroit's stove-manufacturing facilities, and by 1925 Poles constituted 10 percent of Detroit's population and were the city's largest foreign-born ethnic group. As automotive production increased in the first two decades of the twentieth century, automakers actively recruited foreign-born immigrants. In 1915, Ford employed workers from forty-nine different countries. In 1925, approximately half of Detroit's 1,242,044 residents had been born outside the United States. At this time, Detroit had the highest percentage of foreign-born residents of any city in the country (Bak 2003). In these first few decades of the twentieth century, Detroit's neighborhoods were divided into ethnic enclaves and bluntly assigned names such as Poletown, Germantown, Jewtown, Hunkytown, Corktown, Greektown, and Black Bottom (Jacoby 1998).

The second important wave of immigration to Detroit began in the 1920s when US immigration laws tightened, thereby making it difficult for foreign-born immigrants to enter the country. With the continuing expansion of local industries, Detroit's employers began recruiting workers from within the United States. It was during this second major wave of immigration that a significant number of African Americans arrived from the South (as part of what was termed the Great Migration) and white migrants arrived from the Appalachian Mountains. New African American migrants faced more difficulties in securing housing and good jobs in the area relative to their white counterparts from Appalachia. Although the African American population of Detroit comprised only 1 percent of the city's population in 1900 (4,000 residents), it increased to 33 percent in 1960 and 44 percent in 1970 (Farley, Danziger, and Holzer 2000). After New York and Chicago, Detroit had the third largest concentration of African Americans in the North (Jacoby 1998).

World War II created tremendous demand for Allied armaments and munitions. Automakers and their suppliers produced US$30 billion worth of military equipment from 1942 to 1945. But when the automakers built new factories to meet this demand, many were located outside Detroit's boundaries.

In the 1950s until the late 1960s, expressways transformed the urban landscapes of US cities and helped trigger the initial stages of the suburban exodus. After the war, large numbers of predominantly white residents left Detroit for newer and larger homes in the suburbs, relying on cars to commute to work. Undoubtedly influenced by the automobile industry, city leaders saw highways as a method by which to ease traffic congestion, remove "blighted areas," and increase the downtown's competitiveness with the emerging suburbs (Thomas 1997). The large swaths of land required for highway construction within the city, however, were generally taken from poorer neighborhoods and the neighborhoods that people of color occupied. The construction of highways to the city's downtown core required on- and off-ramps that reduced pedestrian comfort in the city and created physical barriers within existing neighborhoods. Detroit's overdevelopment of highway infrastructure within the city came at the expense of mass transit alternatives.

Detroit's "peacetime" automotive manufacturing operations peaked in 1965. In this year, 11.1 million cars, trucks, and buses were built in the United States, and automotive-related parts and products composed approximately 10 percent of all US manufacturing shipments. Approximately one in every six employees in the United States at this time had an automobile-related job. But the dominance of US manufacturing firms began to fade as foreign manufacturers grew. Between 1960 and 1970, America's contribution to world trade declined by 16 percent. In the 1970s, America's contribution declined by another 23 percent (Bluestone and Harrison 1982). Although specialized manufacturing permitted Detroit to flourish in the first half of the twentieth century, that specialization made the city and region vulnerable to changing world markets in the second half of the twentieth century (Sugrue 1996).

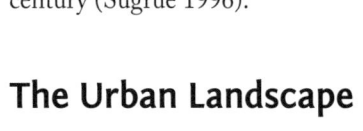

The Urban Landscape

While racially exclusionary suburbanization was a trend throughout the postwar US urban landscape, its continuing impact has been extremely damaging to Detroit and the economic diversity of its remaining residents. In 1950, 1,546,000 of the city of Detroit's almost 2 million residents were categorized as white. By 1990, only 220,000 white residents remained in the city. The 2000 census determined that of 951,270 residents, 81.6 percent were black and 12.3 percent were white; the 2010 census results indicate that 10.6 percent of the severely diminished number of residents were white. Both residents of Hispanic or Latino origin and residents who were foreign born accounted for 5 percent of the city's population in 2000, although the percentage of Hispanic residents had increased to 6.8 percent by 2010. Many of the remaining residents are extremely poor. The wealthier, suburban communities lack interest in regional planning efforts. With little tax base and many poor residents, the city in 2012 is approaching bankruptcy. With the city's constraints, community-based organizations are important actors, helping move neighborhoods toward stability and rethinking grassroots approaches in order to improve residents' quality of life.

Improving the public-transportation system is one of the city's greatest sustainability challenges. Now, four out of every five jobs in the region is located in the suburbs. Detroit is the largest metropolitan area in the United States without a regional transit authority. Currently, the public transportation systems are limited to a small, one-way loop of elevated train in the downtown core (the People Mover), an urban bus system, and an independent suburban bus system. Efforts in 2011 to build a light-rail system down Woodward Avenue, the city's spine, stalled because of the city's worsening financial situation. Some improvements have been seen in the development of nonmotorized greenways and the establishment of dedicated bicycle lanes on city streets.

Today, Detroit is more defined by its voids than by a discernible urban fabric of structures. With the loss of more than half of the city's residents since 1960, vacant land and abandoned properties are a problem. The 2009 Detroit Residential Parcel Survey (published in 2010) determined that of the city's 343,849 residential parcels, 91,488 (26.6 percent) were either vacant or contained abandoned structures. Of the 91,488 unused residential parcels, 23,645 (26 percent) were "improved," meaning that the abandoned house had been demolished and 67,843 (74 percent) contained an unused structure (Detroit Residential Parcel Survey 2010). The city's physical form, outside the downtown core, always had an open spatial character unlike that of many other cities, but the loss of population has amplified these openings. City administration began a planning process, called the Detroit Works, in 2010 in an effort to think about how best to cluster the remaining residents and efficiently provide public services.

The 1993 North American Free Trade Agreement (NAFTA) has had a significant impact on the city. NAFTA lowered or eliminated trade tariffs between the

United States, Canada, and Mexico. In the ten years following NAFTA's signing, Canada's exports to the United States doubled and now represent one-third of all Canada's worldwide exports. This has dramatically increased freight movement through Detroit. Each year, US$160 billion in trade passes through Michigan's two main land ports: Detroit, Michigan, and Port Huron, Michigan. Detroit is responsible for US$100 billion of this trade and 93 percent of US-Canada trade is conducted with the adjacent province of Ontario.

Sustainability Challenges

Unfortunately this traffic has worsened Detroit's air pollution problems. Despite economic decline, steel production, automobile manufacturing, and oil refining continue in the city, particularly in southwestern Detroit. These point-source pollutants combine with mobile (nonpoint) sources from the increased truck traffic at the border. Currently, more than eight thousand trucks cross the Ambassador Bridge linking Detroit with Windsor, Ontario, every day (MDOT 2011), and the state estimates that that number will significantly increase over the next twenty years. The cumulative impacts of emissions from mobile and point sources are not well characterized, but research documents their negative health impacts (Dvonch et al. 2009; Keeler et al. 2007). Of particular concern to human health is fine particulate matter that is less than 2.5 micrometers (μm) in aerodynamic diameter ($PM_{2.5}$) because these small particles can penetrate deep into the human respiratory system. From 1999 to 2010, quarterly and annual average concentrations of $PM_{2.5}$ at the Michigan Department of Environmental Quality air monitoring site at Southwest High School in Delray have been consistently at or above the annual average regulatory standard of 15 micrograms per cubic meter of air ($\mu g/m^3$) (Michigan DEQ n.d.). Both acute and long-term exposure can result in increased hospitalizations and mortality due to respiratory distress (e.g., asthma) and cardiovascular disease (Fernandez et al. 2003; Lewis et al. 2005; Schulz et al. 2005).

Detroit's Great Lakes location has always been important. While water quantity is not a major concern for the city, water quality is threatened by the region's reliance on a combined sewer system (CSO) as opposed to a separated waste and stormwater system. During heavy precipitation, the CSO fills to capacity and all the untreated waste and stormwater must be discharged directly into the receiving waters. These discharges of untreated wastewater pose serious threats to water quality and public health. With the increased area of impervious surfaces due to low density development in the watershed and the increasing intensity of precipitation events due to global climate change, the annual number of untreated discharges is expected to increase.

The Future

The city's vacant land, inexpensive housing stock, and wide streets have resulted in the rise of urban agriculture, new creative enterprises, and an emerging biking culture. Between 2000 and 2010, the number of college-educated residents under thirty-five increased by 59 percent. Although Detroit was once the symbol of industrial advancement, today the community-based sustainability and social justice efforts are resourcefully rethinking what constitutes community and economic development.

The Greening of Detroit, a local nonprofit organization, estimates that, as of 2012, there were 1,600 gardens of various sizes within the city. This organization was initiated to replace trees and shrubs in city streets and parks that had been lost over the last fifty years due to age and Dutch elm disease. Replanting efforts have expanded, however, and the organization now has a strong community development component that sees the establishment of urban gardening, green employment opportunities, and environmental education as key program areas. They are currently collaborating with Eastern Market, a large and well-established wholesale and retail food market, to create a two-acre demonstration farm next to the market.

Southwest Detroit Environmental Vision (SDEV) is an example of a small grassroots environmental justice organization working hard to address the immediate challenges of air pollution and lead contamination within southwest Detroit while advocating for long-term community investment. SDEV works with local trucking and industrial facilities to retrofit older engines to reduce diesel air pollution and to plant vegetation to reduce the problem of fugitive dust (solid airborne particulate matter). They annually spearhead neighborhood cleanups to remove garbage and tires that are dumped in the poorest neighborhoods. The Greening of Detroit and SDEV are only two examples of many community-based organizations that wrestle with the challenges of advancing social justice and sustainability in Detroit neighborhoods.

Larissa LARSEN
University of Michigan

See also Canada; Great Lakes and Saint Lawrence River; Labor; Las Vegas, United States; Mexico; Mobility; New Orleans, United States; New York City, United States; North American Free Trade Agreement (NAFTA); Phoenix, United States; Public Transportation; Sanitation; United States; Urbanization; Water Use and Rights

FURTHER READING

Bak, Richard. (2003). *Henry and Edsel: The creation of the Ford empire*. Hoboken, NJ: John Wiley Press.

Bluestone, Barry, & Harrison, Bennett. (1982). *The deindustrialization of America: Plant closings, community abandonment, and the dismantling of basic industry*. New York: Basic Books.

climate-zone.com. (n.d.). Homepage. Retrieved May 14, 2012, from www.climate-zone.com

Detroit Residential Parcel Survey. (2010). 2009 survey report. Retrieved May 14, 2012, from http://www.detroitparcelsurvey.org/interior.php?nav=reports

Dvonch, J. Timothy, et al. (2009). Acute effects of ambient particulate matter on blood pressure: Differential effects across urban communities. *Hypertension, 53*(5), 853–859.

Farley, Reynolds; Danziger, Sheldon; & Holzer, Harry J. (2000). *Detroit divided*. New York: Russell Sage.

Fernandez, Art, et al. (2003). Inhalation health effects of fine particles from the co-combustion of coal and refuse derived fuel. *Chemosphere, 51*(10), 1129–1137.

Jacoby, Tamer. (1998). *Someone else's house: America's unfinished struggle for integration*. New York: Basic Books.

Keeler, Gerald J.; Morishita, Masako; Wagner, James G.; & Harkema, Jack R. (2007). Characterization of urban atmospheres during inhalation exposure studies in Detroit and Grand Rapids, Michigan. *Toxicologica Pathology, 35*(1), 15–22.

Lewis, Toby C., et al. (2005). Air pollution-associated changes in lung function among asthmatic children in Detroit. *Environmental Health Perspectives, 113*(8), 1068–1075.

Linebaugh, Kate. (2011, March 23). Detroit's population crashes: Census finds 25% plunge as blacks flee to suburbs; Shocked mayor seeks recount. Retrieved June 11, 2012, from http://online.wsj.com/article/SB10001424052748704461304576216850733151470.html#project%3Ddetroit0311%26articleTabs%3Dinteractive

Michigan Department of Environmental Quality (DEQ). (n.d.). PM 2.5 information and documents. Retrieved May 14, 2012, from http://www.michigan.gov/deq/0,1607,7-135-3310_30151_30154_30156-211669--,00.html

Michigan Department of Transportation (MDOT). (2011). *New international trade crossing proposal overview*. Available at http://partnershipborderstudy.com/

Schulz, Amy J., et al. (2005). Social and physical environments and disparities in risk for cardiovascular disease: The healthy environments partnership conceptual model. *Environmental Health Perspective, 113*(12), 1817–1825.

Sugrue, Thomas J. (1996). *The origins of the urban crisis*. Princeton, NJ: Princeton University Press.

Thomas, June Manning. (1997). *Redevelopment and race: Planning a finer city in postwar Detroit*. Baltimore, MD: The Johns Hopkins Press.

United States Department of Transportation (US DOT), Federal Highway Administration. (2009). *Record of decision: Proposed Detroit River international crossing Wayne County, Michigan*. Lansing, MI: US DOT. Retrieved May 14, 2012, from http://www.partnershipborderstudy.com/pdf/2009-01-14%20DRIC%20Final%20ROD.pdf

United States Environmental Protection Agency (US EPA). (2008). National emissions inventory. Retrieved May 14, 2012, from http://www.epa.gov/ttnchie1/net/neip/appendix_8.pdf

Zunz, Olivier. (1982). *The changing face of inequality: Urbanization, industrial development, and immigrants in Detroit, 1880–1920*. Chicago: University of Chicago Press.

Share the *Encyclopedia of Sustainability*: Teachers are welcome to make up to ten (10) copies of no more than two (2) articles for distribution in a single course or program. For further permissions, please visit www.copyright.com or contact: info@berkshirepublishing.com

E-Waste

Redundant electronic products, e-waste, have become an environmental problem of huge proportions, not only in developed countries such as the United States and Canada, but also in developing countries such as Nigeria and India, where hazardous e-waste is being dumped or recycled in adverse conditions. E-waste contains highly toxic substances that necessitate special care to prevent health hazards to humans and environmental damage. International conventions and national legislation are regulating the handling of e-waste as the focus has shifted from dealing with toxic waste to the recycling of valuable resources.

E-waste refers to electronic products ranging from calculators, cell phones, and computers to television monitors, microwaves, and refrigerators that have become redundant. Most of these products have a relatively short lifespan of between three and five years due to constant technological innovation rendering older products obsolete very quickly. E-waste is the fastest growing stream of waste in developed countries, placing greater strain by sheer volume on already overburdened waste disposal systems and sites.

E-waste is the fastest growing new waste stream in the Americas and Oceania (Boon 2006, 731). In the United States about 400 million units of consumer electronics are scrapped annually (ETBC n.d.a). The US Environmental Protection Agency (EPA) estimated that in 2007 more than 3 million tons of e-waste were generated, of which only 13.6 percent was collected for recycling (ETBC n.d.a). Between 50 and 80 percent of the e-waste collected is exported to countries such as China, India, Ghana, and Nigeria (ETBC n.d.a). The US government alone discarded an estimated ten thousand computers per week in 2011, but so far there is little control over the disposal and recycling of this e-waste (ETBC 2012).

In the United States there is no federal legal regime aimed at reducing the effects of e-waste as of yet, but most individual states have introduced mandatory legislation or are in the process of doing so. Even so, recyclers who are willing to export e-waste to Asian countries provide an easy way to circumvent these regulatory controls (GAO 2008, 6–7).

E-waste contains a number of highly toxic substances such as lead, mercury, and cadmium, which all have the potential to cause serious harm to the environment and to human health. These products should be dealt with separately from normal household waste in order to prevent the harmful chemicals and heavy metals from contaminating the environment, water sources, and the air. The cost of recycling e-waste has led developed countries to export their e-waste to developing countries that often do not have the capability to properly treat e-waste. E-waste in the United States is being exported to countries such as India, China, and Nigeria, often illegally (GAO 2008, 5–8). In 2011 the federal government brought the first charges against illegal exporters (Avery 2011). The exporters would pose as recyclers, but then dump the e-waste in developing countries (Avery 2011).

E-waste also contains a number of valuable resources such as gold, silver, copper, and palladium. As of 2012, 90 percent of these valuable nonrenewable resources go to waste because e-waste is not being recycled. The focus of e-waste treatment has steadily shifted to the recycling of these resources. The United Nations Environment Programme (UNEP) has played an important part in this process.

The Nature of E-Waste

There is a general consensus that e-waste includes a wide range of domestic devices ranging from refrigerators, washing machines, and television sets to mobile phones, personal computers, fax machines, printers, and toys. Apart from their use in normal households, these products are used by medicine, education, communications, security, and entertainment industries and in businesses. The steady growth in e-waste is set to continue as emerging markets catch up to the markets in the developed world (UNEP 2009a, 1–2).

It is estimated that between 20 and 50 million metric tons (depending on inclusions and exclusions of products) of electronic waste are generated each year (NEMA 2010). These huge volumes of waste, which decay much slower than household waste, take up much space in waste dumps that are already stretched to their limit by other forms of household waste (Hull 2010, 5–6).

E-waste consists of a wide range of components. Some of these components are bulky such as the steel and aluminum in refrigerators and washing machines, the plastic compounds in televisions, the computer and printer housings and keyboards, and the glass in television sets. Some components make up minor parts of e-waste bulk but contain significant amounts of valuable or toxic materials. Modern electronics can contain up to sixty different elements. Printed wiring boards and mobile phones contain the most complex mix of substances and are major consumers of base metals such as copper and tin, many precious metals such as gold, silver, and palladium, and special metals such as cobalt, indium, and antimony. A tonne of mobile phones without batteries contains 130 kilograms of copper, 3.5 kilograms of silver, 340 grams of gold, and 140 grams of palladium. The lithium-ion (Li-ion) batteries add another 3.5 kilograms of cobalt (UNEP 2009b, 7–8).

Some e-waste is highly toxic because it contains significant amounts of metals such as lead, mercury, cadmium, hexavalent chromium, beryllium, barium, and nickel. Many of the plastic compounds as well as the brominated flame retardants used in computer and television housings, cables, and printed circuit boards cause toxic fumes upon incineration, creating health hazards for workers in informal recycling processes (Templeton 2009, 766–768).

A substantial part of US e-waste is exported to Ghana (BAN 2010). A 2008 Greenpeace analysis found that soil and sediment taken from two e-waste scrapyards in Ghana contained severe hazardous chemical contamination. Samples were taken from open-burning sites at Agbogbloshie market in the capital city, Accra, the main center for e-waste recycling in Ghana, and from a site in the city of Koforidua, as well as from a shallow lagoon at the Agbogbloshie. "Many of the chemicals released are highly toxic, some may affect children's developing reproductive systems, while others can affect brain development and the nervous system," said Kevin Brigden, a British scientist at Greenpeace International (Greenpeace 2008). In Ghana, China, and India, workers, many of them children, may be exposed to substantial levels of these hazardous chemicals.

Recycling Need and Potential of E-Waste

The UNEP states that "E-waste is usually regarded as a waste problem, which can cause environmental damage if not dealt with in an appropriate way. However, the enormous resource impact of electrical and electronic equipment (EEE) is widely overlooked" (UNEP 2009a, 6). Beyond the need simply to reduce the amount of waste as with other recyclable products such as glass and paper and to avoid the toxic elements from polluting the environment or creating health hazards, there is also a need to recycle the valuable minerals, which are not a renewable resource. It requires significantly lower amounts of energy to recycle these metals than to mine them, resulting in many fewer carbon emissions. It is still much more expensive, however, to recycle these materials than to mine them.

The electronics industry in the Americas and Oceania is a major consumer of base metals, precious metals, and special metals, which are mined at great environmental cost by primary producers in places such as Canada, Australia, Russia, China, and South Africa. The use of special minerals, called rare earth elements (REE), in the production of electronic products has become contentious, as 95 percent of these minerals are mined in China and exported to the rest of the world (Hurst 2010). Although significant new deposits have been found in South Africa (Yahoo Finance 2011), Greenland (Greenland Minerals and Energy 2012), and in the seabed near Hawaii (Arthur 2011) and will be developed by countries such as Korea and Japan, the current shortage of REE and the dependence on China will remain for a number of years. REE will likely be in short supply until these sources are exploited (Humphries 2011, 3–4).

The electronics industry consumes the following estimated amounts of metals produced annually: gold, 3 percent; silver, 3 percent; palladium, 13 percent; cobalt, 15 percent; indium, 80 percent; ruthenium, 80 percent; and antimony, 50 percent. (UNEP 2009a, 7–8). Potentially there are more than 40 million tonnes of base and precious metals that can be recycled annually based on 2009 volumes.

Whereas mining for base metals (such as iron and copper) and precious metals are quite widespread, current REE mining is located primarily in China. In 2010 China upset world markets when it suspended export to Japan due to a diplomatic dispute (Folger 2012). Since 2010 China has also been reducing its exports to protect its own electronics industries, as its current known deposits are sufficient for only twenty years at current production levels (Folger 2012). Most of the mining of REE takes place in the Bayan Obo district of Inner Mongolia in China and comes at a heavy environmental cost. Air and water pollution is widespread in the immediate vicinity, contaminating the Huang (Yellow) River and the water sources of many villages. Soils around the mines are dangerously polluted with toxic or radioactive heavy metals (Hurst 2010).

Recycling in the Americas and Oceania

E-waste recycling consists of collection, dismantling, processing, and end-processing. E-waste collection depends on consumer awareness and cooperation in sorting waste and disposing of e-waste separately. Consumers can use special containers and curbside collections of e-waste by authorities; sellers or producers can provide special dump sites and collection containers. Dismantling and preprocessing consists of sorting e-waste into different components, removing valuable items such as chips and processors that can be reused, removing hazardous materials, and shredding and crushing bulk materials. This process can be very labor-intensive. End-processing usually requires expensive high-tech equipment relying on big volumes to be economically viable. Regionalization of such facilities therefore makes economic sense. Low-tech informal end-processing often leads to the kind of environmental damage and health risks illustrated by the Ghanaian example.

In the United States, redundant electronic equipment that is still serviceable may be donated to organizations such as the National Christina Foundation of the World Computer Exchange. Although there are still many questionable recyclers in the United States, the recyclers belonging to the e-Steward network do not export to developing countries and follow high standards in recycling (ETBC n.d.b).

Because responsible recycling is expensive, there is a lucrative illegal trade in e-waste where primary producers responsible for recycling simply export their e-waste to developing countries such as the Philippines, Ghana, Nigeria, India, and China to be dumped or recycled. Recycling costs in these countries are much lower due to lower labor costs and far fewer if any regulations imposed on recycling operations (Templeton 2009, 763–764). The restrictions of international and national regulations, aimed at preventing the cross-border export of hazardous waste, have led to a lucrative illegal trade in e-waste that has been hard to contain.

The market for recycling e-waste is enormous. For example, it is estimated that the treatment of e-waste produced in the United States alone is worth in excess of $5 billion annually (Majmudar 2011). This estimate provides a strong indication of the size of the e-waste recycling market as a whole and will increase as the price of REE rises. Stricter controls and decreasing costs of recycling may lead to the development of viable recycling industries in the developed nations and a decrease in the illegal trade and dumping of e-waste.

International Agencies and E-Waste

A number of international agencies or organizations promote responsible recycling of e-waste. The United Nations established UNEP in 1972 to advocate global environmental protection. The responsible recycling of e-waste has become an important part of UNEP's focus. As part of their Solving the E-Waste Problem (StEP) initiative, UNEP published a 2009 report *Recycling: From E-waste to Resources*, which was a major contribution to the debate and knowledge about the responsible treatment of e-waste.

The Basel Action Network (BAN) is a nongovernmental environmental action group based in the United States but is focused on confronting the global environmental injustice and economic inefficiency of toxic trade (toxic wastes, products, and technologies) and its devastating impacts. BAN first raised awareness about the plight of the Guiyu, China, residents who suffered grave health damage, including lead poisoning, skin diseases, and higher-than-normal rates of miscarriage, from the toxic waste of what may be the world's largest e-waste dump site. It has reported on similar situations in Ghana, Nigeria, India, and the Philippines (BAN 2004).

The Electronics TakeBack Coalition (ETBC) is a similar organization situated in the United States aiming to promote green design and responsible recycling in the electronics industry. Their goal is to protect the health and well-being of electronics users, workers, and the communities where electronics are produced and discarded by requiring consumer electronics manufacturers and brand owners to take full responsibility for the life cycle of their products.

These and many other similar organizations play an important role in raising the awareness of the responsible treatment of e-waste and confronting the illegal dumping of e-waste in developing countries.

Regulatory Landscape

A number of international, regional, and national regulations are relevant to the management of e-waste. These compulsory instruments determine the extent to which e-waste is regulated.

On the International Front

There is no international convention specifically aimed at e-waste. Instead there are a number of conventions that deal generally with the cross-border transportation of toxic waste. E-waste is a fairly new phenomenon that can be considered within the scope of the broader definition of toxic waste contained in the conventions. The problem has not been a lack of regulation, but a lack of proper implementation. The European Union's WEEE (waste electrical and electronic equipment) Directive is one such initiative to ensure proper implementation and compliance with its obligations under the Basel Convention of 1989. The US Responsible Electronics Recycling Bill of 2011 is an instrument aimed at ensuring that the United States addresses the issues, although the United States has not yet ratified the Basel Convention.

Numerous countries have national legislation specifically addressing e-waste management, including the exportation of e-waste. In the United States, about half the states have now introduced e-waste legislation and more are considering it (ETBC 2011).

Basel Convention 1989 The Basel Convention on the Transboundary Movement of Hazardous Waste is the most important multilateral convention for controlling the movement of hazardous wastes across international boundaries. It entered into operation in 1992 (Pratt 2011, 156ff). Its main objective is to ensure that the export of hazardous waste between countries is done in a way that is environmentally responsible. There are 179 parties to the convention, but three original signatories—Afghanistan, Haiti, and the United States—have not ratified it yet. A 1995 amendment to the convention, the Basel Ban Amendment, aims at a ban of all export of hazardous waste between developed and developing countries. Due to its controversial nature, which in part concerns the lack of regulations about what constitutes recycling, it had not yet been in force by the end of 2011.

The Basel Convention has not yet been successful in eliminating the large-scale exportation of e-waste, partly because the United States is not a party to the convention and partly due to strategies circumventing the convention, such as exporting e-waste under the guise of equipment destined for reuse in the importing country. The US legal associate Shaza Quadri (2010, 468–469) remarks that e-waste continues to be dumped in India despite India's ratification of the convention.

Bamako Convention 1991 African nations were not satisfied with the Basel Convention because it did not contain a total ban on the export of toxic waste. The Bamako Convention of 1991, Convention on the Ban of Import into Africa and the Control of Transboundary Movement and Management of Hazardous Wastes within Africa, mirrors the Basel Convention in many respects, but contains an all-out ban on the importation of toxic waste into Africa from outside of Africa. The convention entered into force in 1998 and has been ratified by twenty-four African nations.

The European WEEE Directive 2002/96/EC

Although the European WEEE Directive is applicable only within the European Union, it has had a beneficial influence on the regulatory provisions and on changes in policy in South Korea, which adopted the principle of Extended Producer Responsibility. This principle requires the producers of electronic products to take greater responsibility to collect and properly dispose of e-waste.

The Regulatory Landscape in the Americas and Oceania

There is no federal legislation in the United States dealing with e-waste, but there are a growing number of states that have implemented specific e-waste legislation. The ETBC provides an up-to-date overview of all existing and proposed legislation on their website (ETBC n.d.c). By October 2011, twenty-five states had enacted some kind of e-waste legislation, and six more had introduced bills for adoption. Of these, twenty-nine had producer responsibility regulations while two had consumer fee or advanced recycling fee models. Producer responsibility regulations require manufacturers of electronics products to be responsible for the end-of-life collection and disposal of their products.

The Federal Responsible Electronic Recycling Bill (HR 2284) was introduced into Congress during June 2011 and is aimed at prohibiting US companies from exporting hazardous electronic waste to developing nations.

In Canada, a number of provinces (Alberta, Saskatchewan, British Columbia, Nova Scotia, and Ontario) have introduced advanced recycling fees similar to those of the pioneering California electronic waste recovery and recycling program. In 2007 Manitoba issued the Electrical and Electronic Equipment Stewardship Regulation, by which the sale of regulated products is forbidden unless covered by the stewardship program. Products covered under this legislation include televisions, desk- and laptop computers, and scanners (Fezty 2007).

In Australia, the Australian and New Zealand Environment and Conservation Council (now incorporated in the Council of Australian Government's standing Council on Environment and Water) was the first body to identify e-waste as a concern. In 2002, the council declared that e-waste needed action. The Product Stewardship Act and Regulations 2011 were adopted to deal with the problem. The industry-run and funded National Television and Computer Recycling Scheme was launched in 2012 under these regulations. The national e-waste recycling program provides free pickup of computers, hard drives, keyboards, printers, and televisions to households and businesses. The e-waste will be recycled in an environmentally friendly manner and valuable nonrenewable resources reclaimed (Nguyen 2012).

Outlook

There is a growing awareness of the problems that e-waste management poses to waste management in general, the management of toxic waste, and the export to and dumping of e-waste in developing countries that do not have the capacity to properly deal with such waste. There is a need for better enforcement of the international and national regulations that restrict the dumping of e-waste. Consumer awareness will play a key role in the more effective collection and recycling of e-waste. Organizations like UNEP also will play an important role in this regard. There are indications that the United States, one of the largest producers of e-waste, will exercise stricter control over the dumping of e-waste in developing nations. This will have a similar beneficial effect to the stricter measures that have been imposed by the members of the European Union.

Sieg EISELEN
University of South Africa

See also Corporate Accountability; Energy Efficiency; Fair Trade; Labor; Mining (Australia); Mining (Andes); Multilateral Environmental Agreements (MEAs); Rio Earth Summit (UN Conference on Environment and Development)

FURTHER READING

Arthur, Charles. (2011, July 4). Japan discovers "rare earth" minerals used for iPads. *The Guardian.* Retrieved February 13, 2012, from http://www.guardian.co.uk/technology/2011/jul/04/japan-ipads-rare-earth

Avery, Greg. (2011, September 16). Executive recycling execs indicted; Environmental crimes alleged. *Denver Business Journal.* Retrieved May 14, 2012, from http://www.bizjournals.com/denver/news/2011/09/16/executive-recycling-execs-indicted-for.html?page=all

Badger, Emily. (2011, July 1). Why e-waste should be kept, recycled in US. *Pacific Standard.* Retrieved May 14, 2012, from http://www.psmag.com/environment/why-e-waste-should-be-kept-recycled-in-u-s-33233/

Basel Action Network (BAN). (2003, February 24). China serves as dump site for computers. Retrieved March 28, 2012, from http://www.ban.org/ban_news/china_serves.html

Basel Action Network (BAN). (2004, April 6). Dante's digital junkyard. Retrieved March 28, 2012, from http://www.ban.org/ban_news/dantes_digital_040406.html

Basel Action Network (BAN). (2010, November 15). Ghana. Retrieved May 14, 2012, from http://ban.org/ban_news/2010/101115_ghana_dangers_escrap.html

Basel Action Network (BAN). (2012). Toxic trade news/current news. Retrieved May 14, 2012, from http://www.ban.org/toxic-trade-news/

Boon, Joel. (2006, Spring). Stemming the tide of patchwork policies: The case of e-waste. *Transnational Law and Contemporary Problems, 15*(2), 731–757.

Council of Australian Government (COAG). (2011). Product stewardship (televisions and computers) regulations 2011. Retrieved May 15, 2012, from http://www.environment.gov.au/settlements/waste/ewaste/publications/pubs/fs-regulations.pdf

Council of Australian Government (COAG). (2012). National television and computer recycling scheme. Retrieved May 15, 2012, from http://www.environment.gov.au/settlements/waste/ewaste/index.html

Courtney, Rob. (2006, July). Evolving hazardous waste policy for the digital era. *Stanford Environmental Law Journal, 25,* 199–227.

Drayton, Heather L. (2007, Fall). Economics of electronic waste disposal regulations. *Hofstra Law Review, 36*(1), 149–183.

E-waste hazardous to human life. (2010, February). *ReSource, 12*(1), 37–39, 41.

Electronics TakeBack Coalition (ETBC). (n.d.a). Responsible recycling vs global dumping. Retrieved May 14, 2012, from http://www.electronicstakeback.com/global-e-waste-dumping/

Electronics TakeBack Coalition (ETBC). (n.d.b). Recycle it right. Retrieved May 14, 2012, from http://www.electronicstakeback.com/how-to-recycle-electronics/

Electronics TakeBack Coalition (ETBC). (n.d.c). Promote good laws. Retrieved May 16, 2012, from http://www.electronicstakeback.com/promote-good-laws/

Electronics TakeBack Coalition (ETBC). (2011). Brief comparison of state laws on electronics recycling. Retrieved May 14, 2012, from http://www.electronicstakeback.com/wp-content/uploads/Compare_state_laws_chart.pdf

Electronics TakeBack Coalition (ETBC). (2012). Feds appear clueless about their own e-waste. Retrieved May 14, 2012, from http://www.electronicstakeback.com/2012/03/21/feds-appear-clueless-about-their-own-e-waste/

Ezroj, Aaron. (2010). How the European Union's WEEE & RoHS directives can help the United States develop a successful national e-waste strategy. *Virginia Environmental Law Journal, 28,* 45–72.

Fehm, Sarah. (2011, Fall). From iPod to e-waste: Building a successful framework for extended producer responsibility in the United States. *Public Contract Law Journal, 41*(1), 173–192.

Fezty, Katalin. (2007, February 19). E-waste legislation grows in Canada. *EE Times.* Retrieved May 14, 2012, from http://eetimes.com/electronics-news/4182411/E-waste-legislation-grows-in-Canada

Folger, Tim. (2012, April). Rare earth elements. *National Geographic.* Retrieved March 28, 2012, from http://ngm.nationalgeographic.com/2011/06/rare-earth-elements/folger-text

Government Accountability Office (GAO). (2008, August). Electronic waste: EPA needs to better control harmful US exports through stronger enforcement and more comprehensive regulation. Retrieved May 14, 2012, from http://www.gao.gov/new.items/d081044.pdf

Greenland Minerals and Energy Ltd. (2012). Rare earth elements at Kvanefjeld. Retrieved February 13, 2012, from http://www.ggg.gl/rare-earth-elements/rare-earth-elements-at-kvanefjeld/

Greenpeace. (2008, August 5). European, American and Japanese electronic waste poisoning the environment in Ghana. Retrieved May 14, 2012, from http://www.greenpeace.org/international/en/press/releases/european-american-and-japanes/

Hull, Eric V. (2010). Poisoning the poor for profit: The injustice of exporting electronic waste to developing countries. *Duke Environmental Law and Policy Forum, 21*(1), 1–48.

Humphries, Marc. (2011, September 6). Rare earth elements: The global supply chain (Congressional Research Service Report). Retrieved February 13, 2012, from http://www.fas.org/sgp/crs/natsec/R41347.pdf

Hurst, Cindy. (2010, November 15). The rare earth dilemma: China's rare earth environmental and safety nightmare. *The Cutting Edge.* Retrieved February 13, 2012, from http://www.thecuttingedge-news.com/index.php?article=21777

International Business Times. (2010, November 3). China's dream for rare earths rests on grim costs. Retrieved February 13, 2011, from http://www.ibtimes.com/articles/78461/20101103/rare-earth-china.htm

International ICT Policies and Strategies. (2011, June 25). E-waste law and regulatory framework in India. Retrieved May 15, 2012, from http://ictps.blogspot.com/2011/06/e-waste-law-and-regulatory-framework-in.html

INTERPOL Pollution Crime Working Group. (2009, May). Electronic waste and organized crime: Assessing the links. Lyon, France: INTERPOL.

Kellner, Rod. (2009). Integrated approach to e-waste recycling. In Ronald E. Hester & Roy M. Harrison (Eds.), *Issues in environmental science and technology: Vol. 27. Electronic waste management.* London: Royal Society of Chemistry.

Knee, Jeremy. (2009, Fall). Guidance for the awkward: Outgrowing the adolescence of state electronic waste laws. *Environs Environmental Law and Policy Journal, 33*(2), 157–187.

Kutz, Jennifer. (2006). You've got waste: The exponentially escalating problem of hazardous e-waste. *Villanova Environmental Law Journal, 17,* 307–329.

Luther, Linda. (2007, September 10). Managing electronic waste: An analysis of state e-waste legislation (CRS Report for Congress). Washington, DC: Congressional Research Service.

Majmudar, Nishad. (2011, September 18). E-waste: Recyclers, scrap haulers vie to keep US computer trash home. *Washington Post.* Retrieved March 29, 2012, from http://www.washingtonpost.com/business/economy/e-waste-recyclers-scrap-haulers-vie-to-keep-us-computer-trash-home/2011/09/15/gIQAJi7EdK_story.html

Manasvini, Krishna, & Kulshrestha, Pratiksha. (2008). The toxic belt: Perspectives on e-waste dumping in developing nations. *U.C. Davis Journal of International Law and Policy, 15*(1), 71–93.

McCrea, Hannah. (2011, Summer). Germany's take-back approach to waste management: Is there a legal basis for adoption in the United States? *Georgetown International Environmental Law Review, 23*(4), 513–529.

National Environmental Management Authority (NEMA). (2010). *Guidelines for management of e-waste in Kenya.* Nairobi, Kenya: NEMA. Retrieved February 13, 2012, from http://gesci.org/assets/files/Knowledge%20Centre/E-Waste%20Guidelines_Kenya2011.pdf

Nguyen, Diana. (2012, May 15). E-waste recycling scheme launches in Canberra. *Computerworld.* Retrieved May 15, 2012, from http://www.computerworld.com.au/article/424620/e-waste_recycling_scheme_launches_canberra/?fp=4&fpid=1398720840

Pratt, Laura A. W. (2011, Winter). Decreasing dirty dumping? A re-evaluation of toxic waste colonialism and the global management of transboundary hazardous waste. *Texas Environmental Law Journal, 35*(2), 147–178.

Proactiveinvestors Australia. (2009, June 18). Greenland Minerals and Energy confirms huge rare earth resource in Greenland. Retrieved February 13, 2012, from http://www.proactiveinvestors.com.au/companies/news/1767/greenland-minerals-and-energy-confirms-huge-rare-earth-resource-in-greenland-1767.html

Quadri, Shaza. (2010). An analysis of the effects and reasons for hazardous waste importation in India and its implementation of the Basel Convention. *Florida Journal of International Law, 22*(3), 468–493.

Royal Society of Chemistry (RSC). (2011, July 13). Manufacturers targeted by India's e-waste laws. Retrieved May 15, 2012, from www.rsc.org/chemistryworld/News/2011/July/13071101.asp

Templeton, Nicola J. (2009, Spring/Summer). The dark side of recycling and reusing electronics: Is Washington's e-cycle program adequate? *Seattle Journal for Social Justice, 7*(2), 763–797.

Tladi, Dire. (2000). The quest to ban hazardous waste import into Africa: First Bamako and now Basel. *Comparative and International Law Journal of South Africa, 33*(2), 210–222.

United Nations Environment Programme (UNEP). (2009a, January 28). Solving the e-waste problem (StEP) white paper: E-waste take-back system design and policy approaches. Retrieved December 14, 2011, from http://www.google.com/url?sa=t&rct=j&q=&esrc=s&source=web&cd=1&ved=0CE4QFjAA&url=http%3A%2F%2Fwww.step-initiative.org%2Ftl_files%2Fstep%2F_documents%2FStEP_TF1_WPTakeBackSystems.pdf&ei=dsK7T5idNrT8iQLhgaGGDg&usg=AFQjCNEnRzPZzWgUamR2z9AWnZigH2aRlw

United Nations Environment Programme (UNEP). (2009b, July). *Recycling: From e-waste to resources.* Retrieved December 14, 2011, from http://www.unep.org/PDF/PressReleases/E-Waste_publication_screen_FINALVERSION-sml.pdf

Widawsky, Lisa. (2008). In my backyard: How enabling hazardous waste trade to developing nations can improve the Basel Convention's ability to achieve environmental justice. *Environmental Law, 38*(2), 577–626.

Yahoo! Finance. (2011, July 13). Frontier Rare Earths and Korea Resources Corporation sign definitive strategic partnership agreement. Retrieved May 29, 2012, from http://finance.yahoo.com/news/Frontier-Rare-Earths-and-ccn-3926911672.html?x=0&.v=1

Ecotourism (the Americas)

The success of ecotourism depends on socioeconomic factors such as political support, social stability, cultural ties to natural resources, and economic profitability. In some locations, ecotourism has the potential to reduce threats to the environment and to the people who live there by providing alternative ways to use resources and generate income, thus contributing to the well-being of people and the conservation of nature.

Ecotourism is a subsector of the global tourism industry that, in some cases at least, aims to foster social involvement and provide incentives for protecting biodiversity (Buckley 2009; Honey 1999). The term *ecotour* originated in the 1960s but did not gain prominence until the 1990s (Buckley 2003; Weaver and Lawton 2007). Since 2000, the role of ecotourism as a tool in conservation and sustainable development has strengthened, with events such as the 2002 International Year of Ecotourism, including the World Ecotourism Summit. Both the demand for and supply of ecotourism continue to grow, enhancing its role as a significant segment of the tourism industry, an effective tool in sustainable development, and a valid field of research.

Significance for Sustainability

Sustainability of livelihoods, culture, and biodiversity is interlinked with the ways in which the environment is conserved and protected. Environmental conservation helps sustain our basic survival needs, from the water we drink to the air we breathe. Despite an understanding of these vital roles and the establishment of protected areas, ecosystems remain threatened by urban and agricultural expansion, illegal land settlement, large-scale deforestation, and the poaching of wildlife. In some locations, ecotourism can reduce these threats by providing alternative ways to use resources and generate income, contributing to the well-being of people and conservation of nature (Buckley 2003 and 2010; Durham 2008). Such cases are currently few, but with appropriate attention to socioeconomic and political pressures, ecotourism can continue to contribute to sustainable development.

Dynamics among Regions

The demand for ecotourism has historically come from the wealthier nations, with developing countries as the main destinations. Within Latin America, Costa Rica, Belize, Bolivia, Ecuador, and Peru are currently the most popular destinations. A number of other countries, notably Brazil, are currently developing their ecotourism potential. Ecotourism activities in North America are not as widespread as in Latin America and are largely focused on First Nations indigenous lands in the far north. Community-based ecotourism, where local communities own the land and are involved in both conservation and tourism management, is restricted to areas with communal land tenure. This approach is especially widespread in the greater Amazon basin region, with examples such as the Tambopata Lodge in the Community of Infierno in Peru (Stronza 2010) and the Mamirauá Sustainable Development Reserve in Brazil (Charity and Materson 1999).

People and Organizations

The Americas are characterized by socioeconomic and environmental contrasts that influence the implementation and sustainability of ecotourism. International organizations such as the United Nations Environment Programme (2011) and the International Union for the Conservation of Nature (2011) have helped to establish policies, quality-control standards, and implementation of individual projects that target conservation, livelihoods, and sustainable economic development at regional and global levels. Multilateral nongovernmental organizations (NGOs) such as Conservation International (CI), the Nature Conservancy (TNC), and the World Wide Fund for Nature (WWF) have provided financial and technical support and fostered resources and conservation (Buckley 2003 and 2010). For example, Conservation International (2011) is active in Bolivia and Brazil. National-scale NGOs, such as SOS Mata Atlântica in Brazil, also play a vital role. A number of individual tour operators, such as Horizontes Nature Tours and Costa Rica Expeditions in Costa Rica and Natural Habitat Adventures and Off the Beaten Path in the United States, have gained recognition for their efforts to raise support for conservation (Buckley 2003 and 2010). Some tour operators have also established partnerships with indigenous communities. Rainforest Expeditions in Peru, for example, established a twenty-year partnership agreement with the indigenous Community of Infierno (Stronza 2010).

Controversial Issues

Controversies persist over the factors that lead some ecotourism enterprises to falter in fulfilling their socioeconomic and environmental promises. There are debates, for example, over ways to involve local communities in decision making, and whether economic benefits are sufficient incentives for conservation (Pegas and Stronza 2010; Weaver and Lawton 2007). Even renowned ecotourism destinations, such as the Galapagos Islands, are challenged by socioeconomic issues associated with land-use practices and tourism management strategies (Durham 2008). In other locations, local cultural practices, such as hunting and whaling, may clash with tourists' expectations and values (Parsons and Draheim 2009). These cultural clashes can be reduced by incorporating resource management strategies that take into consideration the needs of local residents while fulfilling tourists' expectations (Stronza 2010). In the longer term, however, these new forms of resource use may lead to losses of cultural identity and traditional knowledge (Pegas and Stronza 2010).

Future Outlook

The future of ecotourism as an industry and a tool for conservation and sustainable development is promising but not free of challenges. The success of ecotourism depends on factors such as political support, social stability, economic profitability, sociocultural ties with nature, and the conservation status of relevant resources. A lack of any of these factors may have a lasting impact on local livelihoods and resources. Since 2005, for example, Brazil, Guatemala, Haiti, Costa Rica, Peru, and Chile were hit heavily by natural disasters, while Mexico, Colombia, and Venezuela were subject to social instability. In 2009, health concerns associated with the H1N1 virus and the financial-economic crisis that began in 2008, led to a 5 percent decline in overall tourism revenues among Latin American countries (UNWTO 2010). The sustainability of ecotourism depends not only on implementation and management at the local level but also on large-scale external socioeconomic changes.

Fernanda de Vasconcellos PEGAS and
Ralf BUCKLEY
Griffith University, Australia

See also Amazonia; Bogotá, Colombia; Brazil; Caribbean; Central America; Corporate Accountability; Curitiba, Brazil; Ecovillages; Fair Trade; Forest Management; Guatemala City; Marine Preserves; Mexico; Mexico City; Parks and Preserves; Rio de Janeiro, Brazil; Southern Cone; Travel and Tourism Industry

FURTHER READING

Buckley, Ralf. (2003). *Case studies in ecotourism*. Wallingford, UK: CABI.
Buckley, Ralf. (2009). *Ecotourism principles and practices*. Wallingford, UK: CABI.
Buckley, Ralf. (2010). *Conservation tourism*. Wallingford, UK: CABI.
Charity, Sandra, & Materson, Don. (1999). Mamirauá sustainable development reserve, Brazil. In Sue Stolton & Nigel Dudley (Eds.), *Partnerships for protection: New strategies for planning and management of protected areas* (pp. 109–117). London: Earthscan.
Conservation International (CI). (2011). Homepage. Retrieved August 8, 2011, from http://www.conservation.org/learn/culture/communities/Pages/successes.aspx
Durham, William H. (2008). Fishing for solutions: Conservation and ecotourism in Galapagos National Park. In Amanda Stronza & William Durham (Eds.), *Ecotourism and conservation in the Americas* (pp. 66–90). Wallingford, UK: CABI.
Honey, Martha. (1999). *Ecotourism and sustainable development: Who owns paradise?* Washington, DC: Island Press.
International Union for the Conservation of Nature (IUCN). (2011). Projects. Retrieved August 8, 2011, from http://www.iucn.org/about/work/programmes/water/wp_where_we_work/wp_our_work_projects/
Parsons, E. Christien, & Draheim, Megan. (2009). A reason not to support whaling—a tourism impact case study from the Dominican Republic. *Current Issues in Tourism, 12*(4), 397–403.
Pegas, Fernanda de Vasconcellos, & Stronza, Amanda. (2010). Ecotourism and sea turtle harvesting in a fishing village of Bahia, Brazil. *Conservation and Society, 8*(1), 15–25.
SOS Mata Atlântica. (2011). SOS Mata Atlântica Foundation. Retrieved August 8, 2011, from http://www.sosmatatlantica.org.br/english.html
Stronza, Amanda. (2010). Commons management and ecotourism: Ethnographic evidence from the Amazon. *International Journal of the Commons, 4*(1), 56–77.
United Nations Environment Programme (UNEP). (2011). Great apes survival partnership. Retrieved August 8, 2011, from http://www.unep.org/grasp/Activities_and_Projects/pf_EC.asp#fp
United Nations World Tourism Organization (UNWTO). (2010). UNWTO world tourism barometer. Madrid, Spain: UNWTO.
Weaver, David B., & Lawton, Laura J. (2007, March 7). Twenty years on: The state of contemporary ecotourism research. *Tourism Management, 28*, 1168–1179.

Ecovillages

In the first decades of the twenty-first century, growing environmental, social, and economic crises compel societies to seek more sustainable ways of living. A global movement of experimental communities that refer to themselves as ecovillages has taken up this formidable challenge. Although the impact of this movement has been small, its efforts provide an entry point for considering and moving toward greater sustainability.

Ecovillages are intentional human communities that use integrative design, local economic networking, cooperative and common property structures, and participatory decision making to minimize members' ecological footprint and provide as many of life's basic needs as possible in a sustainable manner. Ecovillages are often rooted in a bioregional approach and use permaculture design to achieve their sustainability goals. Permaculture (a global grassroots sustainable development philosophy and movement that encompasses a set of ethical principles and design guidelines and techniques for creating sustainable, permanent culture and agriculture); agroecology and organic agriculture; alternative energy systems such as solar, wind, and microhydro; and natural and green building methods are common features of ecovillages. Some ecovillages have their roots in the communes and intentional communities of the 1960s, but most came into being during and after the 1990s as the ecovillage model became a worldwide phenomenon. The Global Ecovillage Network (GEN) is currently tracking 522 ecovillages around the world, including 234 in the Americas (114 in the United States) and 40 in Oceania (21 in Australia) (GEN 2011). Hundreds of other ecovillages are either forming or exist that are not documented by GEN. The ecovillage movement is largely centered in the United States and western Europe, but it has spread to seventy-two countries around the world. The government of Senegal in Africa, for example, has recently instituted a Minister of Ecovillages and plans to convert all of its fourteen thousand traditional villages into ecovillages. In the global North in recent years, the ecovillage trend has started slowing down due to difficulties such as high land prices, prohibitive zoning and building codes, and an economic system in recession in which control of life's basic necessities (land, water, food, and air) is increasingly in the hands of private corporations and financial institutions. At the same time, decreasing jobs and access to economic resources for nonelites has made the formation of additional ecovillages and the expansion of those already existing increasingly difficult. Numerous ecovillages have transformed themselves into local and regional hubs and educational centers in the transition movement, which focuses on turning communities, towns, and cities into sustainable human habitations that are resilient to global crises such as peak oil, climate change, and economic recession and collapse.

The ecovillage movement represents an attempt to move beyond the widespread Western worldview that not only separates nature from culture but implicitly holds that humans can control nature and continue to use it to meet their growing needs and desires without consequence. Ecovillagers attempt to live in ways that reduce the patterns of social and environmental injustice resulting from uneven distribution of resources and resource use among rich and poor on both local and global levels. Ecovillagers are essentially attempting to internalize what economists refer to as externalities; they recognize that in a global economy the processes of production and consumption produce far-flung social and environmental consequences that are not accounted for in the costs of things they consume. They are attempting to make these costs more visible by bringing production and consumption processes within a more local sphere. At a fundamental level, ecovillagers are trying to put environmental and social justice ethics into action by creating communities that are more locally self-reliant and premised on the notion that each person and each community must take responsibility for the social and ecological impacts of fulfilling their economic and subsistence needs.

Ecovillages in Practice

Examples of well-known and established ecovillages in North America and Oceania illustrate concrete ways in which ecovillagers attempt to put environmental and social justice ethics into action. Dancing Rabbit Ecovillage is a community of approximately fifty members located on 280 acres of degraded farmland in northeastern Missouri. Their stated goal is "to live ecologically sustainable and socially rewarding lives, and to share the skills and ideas behind that lifestyle" (Dancing Rabbit Ecovillage 2012). The members of Dancing Rabbit have agreed to organize their lives around defined lists of ecological covenants and sustainability guidelines. Because they recognize the impacts of fossil fuel extraction on ecosystems and communities and the implications of high levels of fossil fuel use for global climate change, they have agreed not to use fossil fuels to power vehicles, heat or cool homes, provide refrigeration, or heat domestic water supplies. The members of Dancing Rabbit have put in place renewable energy systems that use locally produced biofuels, passive building design (using solar energy to heat and cool buildings), renewable and community-scale energy sources, and decreased energy demand in order to lessen their dependence on fossil fuels and, by extension, their contributions to further ecological degradation and social and environmental injustice.

In addition to addressing energy use, Dancing Rabbit has policies in place that specify the sourcing of lumber used in constructing their buildings. Ecovillage members agree to use only lumber harvested within their own bioregion for use in building projects. Recognizing that this is difficult in the rolling prairies of northeastern Missouri, they allow exceptions for recycled and reclaimed lumber. As a result, Dancing Rabbit members frequently participate in building demolitions in their local area and harvest the reclaimed lumber for use in the growing number of residential and community buildings in their village. In addition to seeking more sustainable patterns of energy and material consumption, the members of Dancing Rabbit address ways to deal with their waste as well. Another of their ecological covenants states that all organic and recyclable material used in the village will be reclaimed for use by the community. One manifestation of this is the extensive food-waste composting Dancing Rabbit practices. They use compost to build soils, thus contributing to their goals of becoming more food self-reliant while also restoring the fertility of the degraded farmland that they inherited from previous generations. Numerous other ecovillages exist throughout the Americas. Some of the most well-known among them include Ecovillage at Ithaca (United States), Earthaven Ecovillage (United States), Los Angeles Ecovillage (United States), Ecoaldea Huehuecoyotl (Mexico), Nashira Ecovillage and Sasardi Ecovillage (Colombia), O.U.R. Ecovillage (Canada), and Whole Village (Canada).

Many similar attributes characterize Crystal Waters Ecovillage in Queensland, Australia. Crystal Waters is a community of approximately two hundred residents established in 1988 on 650 acres of degraded pasture land. Sustainable development at Crystal Waters is based on permaculture design principles: residents agree to live in ecologically sustainable ways that make the connections between consumption, waste, and ecological degradation readily visible. Most resident dwellings are owner designed, built using non-toxic and sustainably harvested building materials, and rely upon good design and small-scale sustainable technologies for producing electricity. Clean and fair food is a priority, and some members produce all of their own food. Members harvest water for household needs and agriculture on-site using rainwater catchment systems and small-scale earthen storage dams. Much like Dancing Rabbit Ecovillage, the members of Crystal Waters have created a number of small businesses that serve as a base for local economic networking both within the community and with local neighbors. Crystal Waters has created facilities to host visitors from around the world. These facilities are designed to demonstrate ecovillage and permaculture values, principles, and practice through tours and by offering educational courses and consultancies in sustainable agriculture, ecovillage design, and conflict resolution, among other topics. In 1996, Crystal Waters received the United Nations World Habitat Award in recognition of its pioneering work in demonstrating new practices of low-impact living and has been listed on the United Nations' Best Practices database. Few ecovillages in the Oceania region are as well established and well-known as Crystal Waters, but the website of the Global Ecovillage Network hosts a growing list (GEN 2011).

The ecovillage and associated permaculture movements in the Americas and Oceania have engaged in mutual cross-fertilization. For example, the Australian biologist Bill Mollison and his student David Holmgren first developed the philosophy and practice of permaculture, which is foundational to many ecovillages, in Tasmania in the 1960s and 1970s. In subsequent years, Mollison and Holmgren toured the United States and other parts of the world, sharing their philosophy and design practices with interested audiences. A number of people from these audiences went on to found prominent ecovillages throughout the Americas. The Global Ecovillage Network was founded by ecovillagers in the Americas and Europe as a way to share and coordinate efforts around the world. Soon after, Asia and Oceania was added as a third region in the Global Ecovillage Network and, in recent years, the number of ecovillages in Oceania has grown considerably, sometimes drawing inspiration from existing ecovillages in the other regions. Crystal Waters Ecovillage has hosted the Oceania office of the Global Ecovillage Network for many years and serves as a regional networking hub for the broader global ecovillage movement.

Ecovillage Futures

Outside academic analysts and participants in the ecovillage movement itself have debated the effectiveness of the ecovillage movement in creating changes in the broader society. A running debate between the Greek political philosopher and economist Takis Fotopoulos (2000, 2002) and the US sociologist Ted Trainer (2000, 2002) in the journal *Democracy and Nature* illustrates the different perspectives adopted by outside analysts. Both scholars recognized the need for broad-scale social change in order to move toward greater sustainability. Trainer argued that the ecovillage movement provided a foundation upon which to build such changes. Fotopoulos argued that the ecovillage movement was too small in scale and limited in its political vision to serve as a catalyst for broader change. In recent years, leading members of the global ecovillage movement have recognized the limited impact twenty years of ecovillage building has had on the broader society. They have sought to reorient the philosophy and goals of the movement in turn. Prominent members of the movement have indicated that their current goal is not to encourage a proliferation of ecovillages, but rather to use existing ecovillages as research, training, and demonstration centers for citizens around the world as they seek to transform existing communities toward more sustainable entities (Christian 2008). This work continues today, in part, through international offerings of Ecovillage Design Education courses and through Gaia University, whose courses are often located at existing ecovillages.

As we move into the second decade of the twenty-first century, developments in the ecovillage movement give cause for both hope and caution. The existence of a growing, globally aware, ethically motivated, and international movement of people who are voluntarily engaged in fundamentally changing the way they go about their lives in order to bring about a more just and sustainable world is an encouraging development. On the other hand, in the broader society, consumption patterns continue in unsustainable directions—ecological degradation continues unabated, the divide between the rich and the poor continues to grow, and continuing ecological, economic, and humanitarian crises suggest that the world faces a situation too dire for a relatively small number of well-meaning ecovillagers to solve. It will be telling to observe the degree to which broader publics and, perhaps more importantly, governments take advantage of the opportunity to learn from and scale up the natural experiments in sustainable living being offered by existing ecovillagers. Initiatives by a number of governments in countries like Senegal and Canada are encouraging, but missed opportunities remain in both the poorest and richest countries of the world.

Joshua LOCKYER
Arkansas Tech University

James R. VETETO
University of North Texas

See also Architecture; Australia; Canada; Ecotourism (the Americas); Energy Efficiency; Fair Trade; Labor; Mobility; Oceania; Pacific Island Environmental Philosophy; Public Transportation; Rural Development (the Americas); United States; Urbanization

FURTHER READING

Bang, Jan Martin. (2005). *Ecovillages: A practical guide to sustainable communities*. Gabriola Island, Canada: New Society.

Christian, Diana Leafe. (2002). *Creating a life together: Practical tools to grow ecovillages and intentional communities*. Gabriola Island, Canada: New Society.

Christian, Diana Leafe. (2008). The ecovillage movement today. *Ecovillages Newsletter.* Retrieved March 12, 2012, from http://www.ecovillagenews.org/wiki/index.php/The_Ecovillage_Movement_Today

Dancing Rabbit Ecovillage. (2012). Homepage. Retrieved April 20, 2012, from http://www.dancingrabbit.org/

Dawson, Jonathan. (2006). *Ecovillages: New frontiers for sustainability.* Totnes, UK: Green Books.

Fotopoulos, Takis. (2000). The limitations of life-style strategies: The ecovillage "movement" is NOT the way towards a new democratic society. *Democracy & Nature, 6*(2), 287–308.

Fotopoulos, Takis. (2002). The transition to an alternative society: The ecovillage movement, the simpler way and the inclusive democracy project. *Democracy & Nature, 8*(1), 150–157.

Global Ecovillage Network (GEN). (2011). Homepage. Retrieved October 22, 2011, from http://gen.ecovillage.org/

Kirby, Andy. (2003). Redefining social and environmental relations at the ecovillage at Ithaca: A case study. *Journal of Environmental Psychology, 23*(3), 323–332.

Lindegger, Max, & Oliver, Val. (2003). Crystal waters: 15 years on. *Permaculture Magazine, 38,* 28–32. Retrieved March 3, 2012, from http://gen.ecovillage.org/iservices/publications/articles/Crystal%20Waters%20PM38.pdf

Lockyer, Joshua. (2010). Intentional community carbon reduction and climate change action: From ecovillages to transition towns. In Michael Peters, Shane Fudge & Tim Jackson (Eds.), *Low carbon communities: Imaginative approaches to combating climate change locally* (pp. 197–215). Cheltenham, UK: Edward Elgar.

Metcalf, Bill. (2004). *The Findhorn book of community living.* Forres, UK: Findhorn Press.

Sargisson, Lucy, & Sargent, Lyman Tower. (2004). *Living in utopia: New Zealand's intentional communities.* Burlington, VT: Ashgate.

Trainer, Ted. (2000). Where are we, where do we want to be, how do we get there? *Democracy & Nature, 6*(2), 267–286.

Trainer, Ted. (2002). Debating the significance of the global ecovillage movement: A reply to Takis Fotopoulos. *Democracy & Nature, 8*(1), 143–149.

Veteto, James R., & Lockyer, Joshua. (2008). Environmental anthropology engaging permaculture: Moving theory and practice toward sustainability. *Culture & Agriculture, 30*(1), 47–58.

Walker, Liz. (2005). *Ecovillage at Ithaca: Pioneering a sustainable culture.* Gabriola Island, Canada: New Society.

Energy Efficiency

Concern about energy consumption and its environmental damages has led to improving energy efficiency. This reduces the amount of energy required to provide a number of products and services and consequently emitting less greenhouse gases, decreasing nonrenewable resource consumption, and reducing environmental impacts. All this directly and positively contributes to sustainability. Programs and policies for improving energy efficiency in the United States, Brazil, and Australia provide positive examples of various measures adopted worldwide.

Energy efficiency (EE) is a condition that results when individuals, businesses, organizations, and governments develop and use products and services for society with reduced amounts of energy and as little waste as possible. Examples of EE include the replacement of incandescent lightbulbs by more-efficient alternatives such as light-emitting diodes (LEDs) or improving insulation of buildings to reduce energy consumption for cooling and heating. EE measures, together with other structural changes, can lead to reductions in per capita energy consumption. In the same way, energy intensity (the amount of energy used per dollar of real gross domestic product, or GDP) can also be reduced. Efforts to achieve energy efficiency have been particularly strong in the United States, Brazil, and Australia—and comparable to best international practices—with a variety of programs and polices instituted by governments and businesses alike.

EE measures can provide significant economic and environmental benefits, such as reductions in fossil fuel consumption, which in principle should result in lower prices; improvements in security of supply; reductions in emissions of greenhouse gases, which are primary suspects for projected global climate change; reductions in air pollution; reduction in water consumption and water pollution; reductions in the balance of trade deficit (or increases in the surplus) for energy-importing countries; modernization of industrial plants and greater competitiveness; positive image effects for companies; and creation of specialist jobs. Investment in EE is encouraged both by high fuel prices and by concerns for protecting the Earth's environment.

International Efforts

In the thirty-four member countries (as of 2011) of the Organisation for Economic Co-operation and Development (OECD), EE measures have helped limit growth in energy consumption (Geller et al. 2006). The International Energy Agency (IEA) recommended the adoption of EE measures at the summit meetings of the Group of 8 (the eight major economies of the world: Canada, France, Germany, Italy, Japan, Russia, the United Kingdom, and the United States, also known as the G8) in 2006, 2007, 2008, and 2009, covering twenty-five areas of action in seven priority areas. The McKinsey Global Institute, the research institute of the McKinsey management-consulting firm, estimates that investment in existing technologies could reduce growth in energy demand by at least half by 2020 (McKinsey Global Institute 2007).

Awareness of the need for improvement in EE led to the establishment in May 2009 of the International Partnership for Energy Efficiency Cooperation (IPEEC). The overall goal of this organization is to provide global leadership on energy efficiency by identifying and facilitating government implementation of policies and programs that yield high energy-efficiency gains. The IPEEC also aims to promote information exchange on best practices and facilitate initiatives to improve energy efficiency. As of May 2010, its members were Australia, Brazil, Canada, China, the European Union, India, Japan, Mexico, Russia, South Korea, and the United States, with its member countries accounting for about 75 percent of global GDP and energy consumption.

Means and Effects

Primary areas in which improvements in energy efficiency are gained include efficiency of appliances and lighting; energy savings in residential, commercial, and government buildings; efficiency of industrial manufacturing plants; and efficiency of electric power delivery and end use (Dixon et al. 2010). Economic measures to encourage investment in EE include tax credits, subsidies, energy labeling, compulsory standards in the manufacturing of energy-consuming appliances, support for EE research, interest rate subsidies, and lower social security contributions. EE measures have also been favored by developments in information and communications technology (ICT), as the use for monitoring and measuring systems contributes to reducing uncertainty and increasing energy savings, managing systems more efficiently using real-time information.

In general, it is easier to achieve rapid improvements in efficiency in those items with short useful lifetimes. For expensive, long-lived elements (such as power plants, power lines, refineries, and gas transportation and storage facilities) the rate of improvement is usually much slower. In the case of buildings, EE measures are implemented at the time of construction and as equipment deteriorates and is replaced; here also the scope for improving efficiency in the stock of existing buildings is limited in the short and medium term.

One of the effects closely linked to energy efficiency is the so-called rebound effect, which occurs when increases in efficiency are accompanied by increases in consumption. For instance, the improved energy efficiency of a household appliance may encourage increased use of the appliance, thus increasing the total energy consumption. If this effect is significant, the energy-efficiency benefit is limited, although the quality of life of the consumer is improved. The rebound effect needs to be taken into consideration when designing and implementing policies to promote EE. It can be a direct effect when consumers or companies spend the money saved via EE investment on further consumption, for example switching to more-efficient lamps but then leaving more lights on; or an indirect effect, as when savings are spent on purchasing additional energy-consuming equipment; or a market or dynamic effect, as when EE measures result in a decrease in demand for certain fuels or for electricity. This might cause energy prices to drop, making appliances affordable that previously were not and consequently increasing energy demand. The rebound effect might also affect the efficiency of policies intended to reduce greenhouse gas (GHG) emissions.

EE efforts often generate what is known as the energy efficiency paradox, in which investments in EE that at first sight appear highly beneficial are not actually carried out. This effect has been well documented in the United States (Anderson and Newell 2004). Generally speaking, almost 40 percent of potential energy savings worldwide are not achieved (IEA 2007). Many factors contribute to this inaction, such as information barriers, when consumers and company managers lack the information (or knowledge) required to assess the investment properly; principal-agent issues that lead to decisions to maximize short-term profit rather than commit to long-term strategies; uncertainty regarding savings compared to certainty regarding costs and the irreversible nature of the investment required; lack of liquidity; lack of financial capacity; difficulties accessing funding; transaction costs; and energy-using behavior (Charles 2009).

Policies in the United States

Energy efficiency measures are promoted at federal and state levels in the United States. Notable legislation includes the Energy Independence and Security Act of 2007 (EISA) for the development of energy conservation and efficiency measures (Dixon et al. 2010). Among other things, these measures would help renewables acquire a greater share of the market. Also worthy of mention is the National Action Plan for Energy Efficiency (NAPEE), which is a public–private partnership to create a sustainable, aggressive national commitment to energy efficiency through the collaborative efforts of gas and electric utilities, utility regulators, and other partner organizations. Measures developed by the US Environmental Protection Agency (EPA) related to energy efficiency include building codes for EE (commercial and residential); EE portfolio standards; public benefit funds; and state appliance efficiency standards.

Another notable measure is the Industrial Assessment Centers (IAC) program for small and medium manufacturing enterprises in the United States, which receive assessment from the US Department of Energy (DOE). This program has been in place since 1976, with the main aim of getting industry to increase productivity and reduce its environmental impact through energy efficiency, waste minimization, and the prevention of atmospheric pollution. In spite of the apparent benefits of EE measures suggested, only around 50 percent of the recommendations made to firms between 1984 and 2009 were implemented, possibly for reasons related to the energy efficiency paradox.

Energy Star is a voluntary labeling program set up in 1992 by the EPA and jointly administered by the EPA and the DOE since 1996. Its objective is to promote energy-efficient products and practices and thus reduce the cost of energy consumed and the amount of GHGs emitted. The information on the label helps consumers and organizations choose energy-efficient products and adopt suitable practices. The label was first used for computers and monitors and later extended to items such as office equipment, consumer electronics, heating/ventilation/air-conditioning (HVAC) equipment, lighting, residential appliances, commercial appliances, and others, in a list that now includes sixty product categories. By 2002 its use was extended to energy-efficient production processes. Official information on the program shows that with its help, the energy saved in 2009 was worth $17 billion, and GHG emissions equivalent to those from 31 million cars were avoided. The label recognizes the top 25 percent of products in terms of energy efficiency, so competition among the manufacturers of the remaining 75 percent to attain label standards can lead to significant improvements in efficiency, and consequently in sustainability. In 2009, the Energy Star program saved the equivalent of 5 percent of US electricity demand, which translates to a monetary saving of $17.1 billion, and an environmental saving of 46.3 million metric tons of carbon dioxide equivalent not emitted (US EPA 2010).

Policies in Brazil

Brazil has extensive experience in demand-side management as was demonstrated by the successful implementation of energy conservation policies during the country's 2001 energy crisis (World Bank Group 2010). These policies fostered EE measures for residential, industrial, and commercial sectors.

For the residential sector the measures include switching from incandescent lightbulbs to energy-saving, compact fluorescent lamps (CFLs) (2010); adoption of stricter mandatory efficiency standards (starting in 2015); a substitution program of older refrigerators in low-income communities; stricter mandatory standards for air-conditioning (starting in 2015); substitution of electric water-heating systems with solar-powered systems on top of 1 percent of homes in south, southeast, and center-west Brazil each year, with a goal of 22 percent by 2030.

For the industrial and commercial sectors, EE measures include optimization of combustion processes; processes heat-recovery systems; furnace waste heat recovery; steam systems optimization; switching to more modern and efficient processes; and operations maintenance and control (World Bank Group 2010).

The main EE policy makers in Brazil are the National Electrical Energy Conservation Program (PROCEL) designed to combat electricity waste; the CTEnerg sectoral fund to invest in energy-efficiency research and development programs; PROESCO (Brazilian National Development Bank's program to fund energy-efficiency projects that contribute to saving energy, increasing the overall efficiency of the energy system, and promoting the replacement of fossil fuels for renewable sources), devoted to financing energy-economy projects for various areas and final uses; and the National Agency for Electric Energy (ANEEL) Program.

Policies in Australia

The government of Australia promotes EE policies through the Department of Climate Change and Energy Efficiency. Their efforts mainly center on regulating for more-efficient industries, providing incentive programs, developing a more efficient kind of energy supply, providing a wide range of information resources, and working on improving the energy efficiency of the government's own operations.

Australian energy efficiency policy is based on the National Strategy on Energy Efficiency (originated in 2009), a coordinated effort between state and territory governments. It is supported by joint government groups to implement the National Framework for Energy Efficiency (first stage in 2004, second stage in 2007), which is overseen by the Ministerial Council on Energy (the national policy and governance body for the Australian energy market) and with the support of the Energy Efficiency Working Group that advises on the performance of Australia's end-use energy efficiency policies and programs. In addition to this, the prime minister established an advisory group called the Task Group on Energy Efficiency (2010).

Energy efficiency allows using less energy for the same level of services required, so it does contribute to energy saving. This in turn means less GHG emissions, lower nonrenewable resource consumption, and fewer environmental impacts. All this directly and positively contributes to sustainability.

In terms of EE, energy-importing countries are usually more efficient due to higher energy prices and also due to the higher cost of not having been efficient (such as energy cost, emissions permits, and/or other negative impacts). In this regard countries in the Americas and Oceania, although EE improvements have been significant, are low in the twenty-eight IEA member countries energy-intensity ranking. In particular the United States is in the fourteenth position; Australia in the eighteenth; New Zealand, twenty-first, and Canada, twenty-fourth (in terms of market exchange rates). In terms of purchasing power parity (PPP), the results are even worse for most of Americas and Oceania (IEA 2009).

Luis María ABADIE and Ibon GALARRAGA
Basque Centre for Climate Change (BC3)

See also Architecture; Australia; Brazil; Canada; Mobility; Multilateral Environmental Agreements (MEAs); Public Transportation; United States; Urbanization

Further Reading

Abadie, Luis María, & Chamorro, Jose M. (2010). Toward sustainability through investments in energy efficiency. In W. H. Lee & V. G. Cho (Eds.), *Handbook of sustainable energy* (pp. 735–774). New York: Nova Science Publishers.

Anderson, Soren T., & Newell, Richard G. (2004). Information programs for technology adoption: The case of energy-efficiency audits. *Resource and Energy Economics, 26,* 27–50.

Ang, Beng Wah; Mu, A. R.; & Zhou, Peng. (2010). Accounting frameworks for tracking energy efficiency trends. *Energy Economics, 32,* 1209–1219.

Ansar, Jasmin, & Sparks, Roger. (2009). The experience curve, option value, and the energy paradox. *Energy Policy, 37,* 1012–1020.

Banerjee, Abhijit, & Solomon, Barry D. (2003). Eco-labeling for energy efficiency and sustainability: A meta-evaluation of US programs. *Energy Policy, 31,* 109–123.

Bigano, Andrea; Ortiz, Ramon Arigoni; Markandya, Anil; Menichetti, Emanuela; & Pierfederici, Roberta. (2011). The linkages between energy efficiency and security of energy supply in Europe. In Ibon Galarraga, Mikel Gonzalez-Eguino & Anil Markandya (Eds.), *The handbook of sustainable energy* (pp. 60–83). Cheltenham, UK: Edward Elgar.

Charles, Dan. (2009). Leaping the efficiency gap. *Science, 325,* 241–250.

Clinch, J. Peter, & Healy, John D. (2001). Cost-benefit analysis of domestic energy efficiency. *Energy Policy, 29,* 113–124.

Dixon, Robert K.; McGowan, Elizabeth; Onysko, Ganna; & Scheer, Richard M. (2010). US energy conservation and efficiency policies: Challenges and opportunities. *Energy Policy, 38,* 6398–6408.

Fleiter, Tobias; Worrell, Ernst; & Eichhammer, Wolfgang. (2011). Barriers to energy efficiency in industrial bottom-up energy demand models—A review. *Renewable and Sustainable Energy Reviews, 15,* 3099–3111.

Galarraga, Ibon; González-Eguino, Mikel; & Markandya, Anil. (2011, August). Willingness to pay and price elasticities of demand for energy-efficient appliances: Combining the hedonic approach and demand systems. *Energy Economics, 33*(Suppl. 1), S66–S74. doi:10.1016/j.eneco.2011.07.028

Geller, Howard; Harrington, Philip; Rosenfeld, Arthur H.; Tanishima, Satoshi; & Unander, Fridtjof. (2006). Polices for increasing energy efficiency: Thirty years of experience in OECD countries. *Energy Policy, 34,* 556–573.

Industrial Assessment Centers (IAC) Program. (2011). Homepage. Retrieved July 17, 2011, from http://iac.rutgers.edu/

International Energy Agency (IEA). (2007). Mind the gap: Quantifying principal-agent problems in energy efficiency. Paris: Organisation for Economic Co-operation and Development/IEA.

International Energy Agency (IEA). (2009). Implementing energy efficiency policies: Are IEA member countries on track? Paris: Organisation for Economic Co-operation and Development/IEA.

Jackson, Jerry. (2010). Promoting energy efficiency investments with risk management decision tools. *Energy Policy, 38,* 3865–3873.

Kanoglu, Mehmet; Dincer, Ibrahim; & Rosen, Marc A. (2007). Understanding energy and energy efficiencies for improved energy management in power plants. *Energy Policy, 35,* 3967–3978.

Kounetas, Kostas; Skuras, Dimitris; & Tsekouraseller, Kostas. (2011). Promoting energy efficiency policies over the information barrier. *Information Economics and Policy, 23,* 72–84.

Liu, Tibin; Lu, Jiao; & Xieounetas, Honglian. (2011). Study on the appliances energy efficiency label and multi-dimensional thinking under low-carbon economic development. *Energy Procedia, 5,* 577–580.

Morrissey, John, & Horne, R. E. (2011). Life cycle cost implications of energy efficiency measures in new residential buildings. *Energy and Buildings, 43,* 915–924.

Mahlia, T. M. I, & Saidureves, R. (2010). A review on test procedure, energy efficiency standards and energy labels for room air conditioners and refrigerator-freezers. *Renewable and Sustainable Energy Reviews, 14,* 1888–1900.

McKinsey Global Institute. (2007). Curbing global energy demand growth: The energy productivity opportunity. Chicago: McKinsey & Company.

Office of Energy Efficiency (OEE). (2011). Homepage. Retrieved July 17, 2011, from http://oee.nrcan.gc.ca/english/

Office of Energy Efficiency and Renewable Energy (EERE). (2011). Homepage. Retrieved August 3, 2011, from http://www.eere.energy.gov

Oikonomou, Vlasis; Becchis, F.; Steg, L.; & Russolillo, D. (2009). Energy saving and energy efficiency concepts for policy making. *Energy Policy, 37*, 4787–4796.

Schipper, Lee. (2000). On the rebound: The interaction of energy efficiency, energy use and economic activity. *Energy Policy, 28*, 351–353.

Schleich, Joachim, & Gruberahlia, Edelgard. (2008). Beyond case studies: Barriers to energy efficiency in commerce and the services sector. *Energy Economics, 30*, 449–464.

Thollander, Patrik; Danestig, Maria; & Rohdinurner, Patrik. (2007). Energy policies for increased industrial energy efficiency: Evaluation of a local energy programme for manufacturing SMEs. *Energy Policy, 35*, 5774–5783.

Turner, Karen, & Hanley, Nick. (2011, September). Energy efficiency, rebound effects and the environmental Kuznets Curve. *Energy Economics, 33*(5), 709–720.

United States Environmental Protection Agency (EPA). (2010). *Energy Star and other climate protection partnerships 2009 annual report*. Retrieved March 12, 2012, from http://www.energystar.gov/ia/partners/publications/pubdocs/2009%20CPPD%20Annual%20Report.pdf?ee42-ac16

Varone, Frédéric, & Aebischer, Bernard. (2001). Energy efficiency: The challenges of policy design. *Energy Policy, 29*, 615–629.

The World Bank Group. (2010). Brazil low-carbon country case study. Retrieved September 30, 2011, from http://siteresources.worldbank.org/BRAZILEXTN/Resources/Brazil_LowcarbonStudy.pdf

F

Fair Trade

Fair trade is an international movement to alleviate poverty in the developing world by creating a market for products grown under sustainable conditions. Fair trade producers must abide by stringent social and environmental criteria in exchange for higher product prices and higher wages. Activists have criticized the movement for its willingness to certify the products of global corporations as fair trade goods.

Since the deregulation of many commodity markets in the 1980s, the need for fairer international trade became increasingly evident in much of the developing world. The abandonment of long-standing efforts to stabilize commodity prices, such as the International Coffee Agreement, forced producer prices to unprecedented lows during the 1990s. Coffee prices fell in that decade to their lowest point in a generation, creating enormous economic hardship in coffee-producing regions of Central and South America.

Fair trade arose in response to such trends. It is an international movement that seeks social justice and environmental sustainability through retail markets themselves. In the words of one advocate, "Fair Trade is a trading partnership, based on dialogue, transparency, and respect, that seeks greater equity in international trade. It contributes to sustainable development by offering better trading conditions to, and securing the rights of, marginalized producers and workers" (Moore 2004, 73). By labeling the products of family farmers, cooperatives, and ethically run commercial farms as fair trade goods, fair trade organizations encourage consumers to buy products originating in socially just and environmentally sustainable conditions. Fair trade goods usually sell at a higher retail price than their conventional counterparts, which is intended to generate greater earnings for family farmers and living wages on commercial farms. In addition, a portion of every purchase is returned to the producer's organization itself as a "social premium" to be invested in a community project of local design. In 2009, 1.2 million farmers or workers worldwide were involved in the production of fair trade goods, generating nearly US$75 million of social premiums for producer communities in that year alone.

The Fairtrade Labelling Organizations International (FLO) is the largest fair trade organization. FLO has established global certification standards for producers of coffee, tea, cacao, a large number of fresh fruits and vegetables, sugar, honey, juice, wine, cut flowers, spun cotton, as well as some manufactured goods. European and UK supermarkets prominently display these items on their shelves, and broadcast and print advertising in those regions heavily promotes them. Fair trade is less conspicuous in North American retail stores, although the United States currently represents the second largest share of fair trade sales in absolute terms. Retail sales of fair trade goods have undergone nearly exponential growth since 2000: by mid-decade, total fair trade sales worldwide reached US$1.45 billion, increasing to US$4.58 billion in 2009. Despite this growth, the higher retail prices of fair trade goods have limited their purchase mostly to consumers with above-average discretionary income. Producers estimate that potential supplies of fair trade coffee are about seven times greater than actual demand.

Latin America and the Caribbean represent the single largest segment of fair trade producers, accounting for 313 out of the 847 fair trade producer groups worldwide. Although coffee remains the region's largest fair trade export, the region also exports fair trade cocoa, bananas, honey, processed foods, and wine and spirits. Oceania is comparatively much less prominent as a fair trade producing region and is home to only 34 groups that produce fair trade coffee, cocoa, and coconut oil. All of these organizations are located on the island nation of Papua New Guinea. On the other hand, Australia and New Zealand are now the fastest-growing retail markets for fair trade goods, with sales going from AU$51 million in 2009 to almost AU$150 million by 2010 (*Probono Australia News* 2011).

Producers must satisfy FLO criteria to benefit from fair trade prices. The farmers must grow their products under socially equitable and sustainable conditions. Small-scale farmers must belong to democratically governed producers' associations, in which participation is open to all regardless of ethnicity, gender, religion, or political affiliation. Larger-scale fair trade commercial farms should abide by International Labor Organization (ILO) standards affirming the right to association, freedom from discrimination, prohibition of child labor, and workplace safety. Environmental practices designed to minimize the impact of farming on watersheds, soil, and wildlife also apply to the production of fair trade goods. Chemicals are limited to a narrow range of approved inputs, and each farm records the amount and frequency of their use. Certifiers based in the developed countries monitor compliance through on-site audits. Farmers seeking certification are subject to standards with little or no modification. Although fair trade is premised on reciprocity in consumer-producer relations, some Caribbean farmers have criticized the standards as arbitrary or authoritarian (Moberg 2008 and 2010). Researchers working in Central America (Lyon 2008 and 2010) have noted a gap between the movement's promises of gender equity and actual practices on the ground. Some Costa Rican farmers have become disillusioned with stagnant fair trade prices and have abandoned that market for the more lucrative specialty coffee market (Smith 2010). The rebound in specialty coffee prices in recent years has stymied the growth of the fair trade coffee market.

Activists have criticized mainstream fair trade organizations such as FLO because they oppose the certification of products that large corporations such as Nestlé, Chiquita, Cadbury, and Proctor and Gamble market. Fair trade's sustained 30-plus percent annual growth in sales since the late 1990s has attracted the interest of these and other companies eager to enter new markets and to rehabilitate their corporate images.

FLO's decision to certify Nestlé's Nescafé Partners Blend coffee in 2005 initiated a widening rift within the movement. Because Nestlé's dominance in the global coffee market has enabled it to maintain low producer prices, some regard the company as responsible for the poverty that sparked the fair trade movement in the first place. Some activists fear that FLO's certification of a corporation's single product signals to consumers that FLO certifies the whole company as "ethical." Nestlé in fact acquires just 0.1 percent of its coffee through fair trade channels (UNICEF and Baby Milk Action n.d.).

Other segments of the movement, including FLO's North American affiliate, welcome the marketing opportunities arising from the desire of multinational corporations to acquire fair trade certification of some of their products.

Outlook

Many trade activists consider this willingness to engage with global corporations to violate the movement's original intention to reform the global trading system. Some have split from the FLO umbrella to organize independent fair trade organizations. A team of experts from I-DEV International, an organization for market-based sustainable development, traveled to remote villages in Sumatra, Indonesia, where they found that workers had no concept of how their products were used around the world or what kind of income the products were generating. The weaknesses this team found in fair trade show a window of opportunity for a new movement to take over. Direct Trade has surfaced in response to dissatisfaction with current FLO practices. For FLO and fair trade to survive, they will need to be restructured, such as implementing a tiered system (similar to LEED building certification, which uses points to satisfy specific green building criteria). They must be stricter in their certification of companies and keep a continuous scorecard of the company's performance (SSIR 2011).

Mark A. MOBERG
University of South Alabama

See also Agriculture, Tropical (the Americas); Australia; Brazil; Caribbean; Central America; Corporate Accountability; Gender Equality; Labor; New Zealand; North American Free Trade Agreement (NAFTA);

Oceania; Rural Development (the Americas); Social Movements (Latin America)

FURTHER READING

Fridell, Gavin. (2007). *Fair trade coffee: The prospects and pitfalls of market-driven social justice.* Toronto: University of Toronto Press.

Jaffee, Daniel. (2007). *Brewing justice: Fair trade coffee, sustainability, and survival.* Berkeley & Los Angeles: University of California Press.

Lyon, Sarah M. (2008). We want to be equal to them: Fair trade coffee certification and gender equity within organizations. *Human Organization, 68*(3), 258–268.

Lyon, Sarah M. (2010). *Coffee and community: Maya farmers and fair trade markets.* Boulder: University Press of Colorado.

Lyon, Sarah M., & Moberg, Mark. (Eds.). (2010). *Fair trade and social justice: Global ethnographies.* New York: New York University Press.

Moberg, Mark. (2008). *Slipping away: Banana politics and fair trade in the eastern Caribbean.* New York: Berghahn Books.

Moberg, Mark (2010). A new world? Neoliberalism and fair trade farming in the eastern Caribbean. In Sarah M. Lyon & Mark Moberg (Eds.), *Fair trade and social justice: Global ethnographies* (pp. 47–71). New York: New York University Press.

Moore, Geoff. (2004). The fair trade movement: Parameters, issues, and future research. *Journal of Business Ethics, 53*(1), 73–86.

Murray, Douglas L.; Raynolds, Laura T.; & Taylor, Peter L. (2006). The future of fair trade coffee: Dilemmas facing Latin America's small-scale producers. *Development in Practice, 16*(2), 179–192.

Probono Australia News. (2011, March 10). Fairtrade sales in Australia skyrocket. Retrieved May 25, 2012, from http://www.probonoaustralia.com.au/news/2011/03/fairtrade-sales-australia-skyrocket

Smith, Julia. (2010). Fair trade and the specialty coffee market: Growing alliances, shifting rivalries. In Sarah M. Lyon & Mark Moberg (Eds.), *Fair trade and social justice: Global ethnographies* (pp. 28–46). New York: New York University Press.

Stanford Social Innovation Review (SSIR). (2011, June 6). The future of fair trade . . . is there one? Retrieved May 25, 2012, from http://www.ssireview.org/blog/entry/the_future_of_fair_tradeis_there_one/

United Nations Children's Fund (UNICEF), & Baby Milk Action. (n.d.). Why boycott Nestlé Fairtrade Kitkat? Retrieved May 25, 2012, from http://www.babymilkaction.org/pdfs/nestlefairtrade0210.pdf

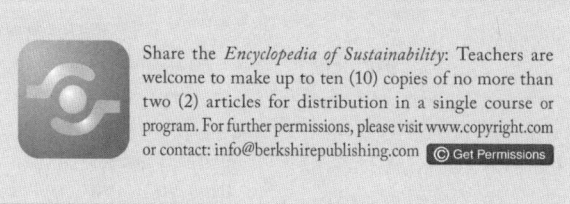

Forest Management

The Americas and Oceania account for 44 percent of the world's forest area and 54 percent of its total timber volume, reflecting highly productive forest land and effective forest management over much of the region. Intensive forest management, including a sizable forest industry, is common in many countries of the Americas and Oceania, and sustainable forest management is commonly practiced, especially in the developed nations.

The Americas and Oceania include some of the most important forest regions and forest economies of the world. In terms of managed forests and wood output, major nations include Australia, Brazil, Canada, Chile, New Zealand, and the United States. These same countries are some of the world's most important in terms of forest plantations. The region contains 44 percent of the world's forest area, but that area cultivates over half of the world's growing stock (timber volume) and produces nearly half of its industrial wood. It produces only 19 percent of the world's fuelwood, a relatively low portion as many of its economies are developed and rely on other fuels.

Consumers and governments have recognized and expect sustainable forest management (SFM) on lands that produce forest products. The United Nations Forum on Forests found that countries within this region increasingly have adopted SFM systems and practices since about 2000. Much of the forest area in the region is considered critical in terms of biological diversity and conservation, and where SFM is adopted, it contributes to the protection of these forests' biodiversity and soil and water resources.

Forest Area

Forests cover about one-third of North America's land area, nearly one-half of Latin and South America and the Caribbean, and nearly 23 percent of Oceania. Respectively, that represents 17 percent, 22 percent, and 5 percent of the world's forest area. (See table 1 on the next page).

Between 1990 and 2010, forest area in North America experienced a slight increase. Mexico lost some forest area, but gains in the United States outweighed these losses. These gains and losses were mainly due to shifts in production, multiple use, and protected forest land classifications. Latin America is heavily forested and experienced significant declines in forest area in this period, due mainly to deforestation caused by conversion of land to agricultural use and urbanization. Brazil ranks in the top five counties globally in terms of forest area (13 percent of global forest) and has the world's largest area of tropical forests. The largest declines in forest area occurred in South America, centering on clear-cutting in the Amazon River basin, and the largest declines on a percentage basis occurred in Central America. Forest area in the Caribbean increased due to conversion of abandoned agricultural lands to forest. Oceania lost forest area also, mainly due to a severe drought and massive forest fires in Australia in the latter half of this period.

Globally, about 7 percent of the forest area is planted forests. (See table 1). North America contains about 14 percent of the world's forest plantation area; Latin America and the Caribbean about 6 percent; and Oceania

TABLE 1. Forest Area

Region	Forest Area 2010 (1,000 ha*)	Annual Change Forest Area 1990–2010 (%)	Planted Forest Area 2010 (%)	Production and Multiple-Use Forest Area (%)
Canada	310,134	0.00	2.9	88
Mexico	64,802	−0.41	4.9	87
United States	304,022	0.13	8.3	76
North America	**678,958**	**0.02**	**5.5**	**82**
Caribbean	6,932	0.81	7.9	32
Central America	19,499	−1.40	3.0	29
South America	864,351	−0.45	1.6	25
Latin America and Caribbean	**890,782**	**−0.47**	**1.7**	**25**
Oceania	**191,384**	**−0.19**	**2.1**	**38**
World	4,032,905	−0.17	6.5	54

Source: FAO (2011).
*ha = hectare

about 2 percent. Some countries stand out within regions in terms of planted forests; in terms of regional planted forest area, in North America it is the United States (68 percent), in South America it is Brazil (54 percent), in the Caribbean it is Cuba (89 percent), in Central America it is Costa Rica (41 percent) and Guatemala (30 percent), and in Oceania it is Australia (46 percent) and New Zealand (44 percent) (FAO 2011). Increased planted forests resulted from afforestation projects to combat problems like desertification. Nations with large areas of planted forests tend to be those with sustainable forestry programs. One measure of the intensity level of forest management within a region is the percentage of forest designated for production of wood and non-wood forest products; in addition, forest land designated as multiple-use commonly also allows for production of forest products (see table 1 above). Multiple-use lands may have secondary production goals and make larger contributions to biodiversity and sustainability. About 54 percent of the world's forest area is designated as production or multiple-use forest and about 48 percent in the Americas and Oceania is likewise designated. This is heavily influenced by North America with almost two-thirds of the designated forest area being in the Americas and Oceania.

Timber Volume

Large volumes of usable timber, or growing stock, occur in both North and South America, but most of North America's growing stock is considered of commercial quality, compared to just over one-third of South America's. (See table 2 on the next page.) Growing stock per hectare is highest in the moist tropical forests of South America, but high timber volumes also occur in the boreal and temperate forests.

TABLE 2. Growing Stock

Region	Total Growing Stock 2010 (million m³)	Growing Stock 2010 (m³/ha)	Commercial Growing Stock 2010 (%)	Coniferous Growing Stock 2010 (%)	Annual Change in Growing Stock 1990–2010 (%)	Annual Change in Growing Stock/ha 1990–2010 (%)
Canada	32,983	106	—	77	—	—
Mexico	2,870	44	—	35	—	—
United States	47,088	155	92	73	—	—
North America	**82,941**	**122**	**92**	**73**	**0.5**	**0.5**
Caribbean	584	84	78	9	1.4	0.5
Central America	2,891	148	17	11	−1.4	0.0
South America	177,215	205	36	1	−0.4	0.1
Latin America and Caribbean	**180,690**	**203**	**36**	**1**	**−0.4**	**0.1**
Oceania	**20,885**	**109**	**17**	**17**	**−0.1**	**0.1**
World	527,203	131	62	39	−0.03	0.1

Source: FAO (2010).

As indicated in table 2, about 39 percent of the world's growing stock is coniferous species (usually have evergreen needles) and the remainder is broadleaved species (deciduous). Around 62 percent of the world's growing stock is of commercial quality. Total growing stock generally decreased around the world from 1990 to 2010. North America and the Caribbean were exceptions to this trend. Of course, total growing stock is correlated with forest area—less forest area means less ground on which to grow trees. Growing stock per hectare is a better indicator than total growing stock of the amount of wood on the existing forest (forest stocking). Forest stocking has been increasing in this period in all regions of the Americas and Oceania. (See table 2.)

Wood Removals

Wood removed (harvested) from forests and other woodlands is an indication of forest productivity. Various factors impact wood removals, but in general wood removals equate to economic value and social utility of the forest resources and thus contribute to national and local economies. In 2008, wood removals in the Caribbean and Central America were mostly for fuelwood. (See table 3 on the next page.) In North America and Oceania, removals were used mainly for industrial purposes (lumber, paper, and panels). In South America removals were about evenly divided between industrial and fuel uses. Three of the countries with the greatest volume of wood removals were in the Americas (United States, Brazil, and Canada) (FAO 2010).

North and Central America showed stable trends in wood removals from 1990 to 2005. Oceania showed a steady increase in removals (mostly from Australia, New Zealand, Papua New Guinea, and the Solomon Islands). The trend was down in South America, primarily due to decreased logging of Brazil's tropical forests. Forest plantations account for increased removals in New Zealand, Australia, Brazil, Chile, Argentina, and Uruguay. Much of the world's increased wood supply comes from these countries that have developed forest plantations over this period. Globally, wood removals are 0.7 percent of growing stock, and half of removals are used for fuelwood.

Sustainable Forest Management

Traditional forest management has several key concepts that relate to sustainable forest management. A sustained yield approach is one of the foundations of forestry. Under this management system the proportionate land

TABLE 3. Wood Removals

Region	Total Wood Removed 2008 (1,000 m³)	Industrial Wood Removed 2008 (1,000 m³)	Fuelwood Removed 2008 (1,000 m³)	Annual Change Industrial Wood Removals 1990–2005 (%)	Annual Change Fuelwood Removals 1990–2005 (%)
Canada	134,947	132,232	2,715	0.8	−5.4
Mexico	45,101	6,425	38,676	−1.6	2.9
United States	380,509	336,895	43,614	−0.2	−4.4
North America	**560,557**	**475,552**	**85,005**	**0.0**	**−4.4**
Caribbean	6,263	1,359	4,904	0.0	0.0
Central America	44,696	3,281	41,415	2.7	0.0
South America	386,601	185,385	201,216	1.0	−1.1
Latin America and Caribbean	**437,560**	**190,025**	**247,535**	**1.0**	**−1.0**
Oceania	**68,259**	**52,378**	**15,881**	**3.4**	**−13.5**
World	3,410,357	1,541,971	1,868,386	−0.1	0.1

Source: FAO (2010).

or timber volume that can be cut annually on a perpetual basis is determined. This ensures a steady supply of wood or other products from the forest. A second system uses what are called a *reserve growing stock* and a *cutting cycle* to regulate or control timber harvests to ensure a regular flow of timber. For example, a forest that has 12,000 cubic meters per hectare (m³/ha) and has a growth rate of 5 percent annually will produce growth of 3,315 m³/ha. The first year growth is 600 m³/ha, but tree growth compounds, like interest at the bank, thus the extra 315 m³/ha. If this is a 10,000-hectare forest, and the cutting cycle is five years, then every five years one-fifth of the area will be cut. The fifths would be staggered so that only one area is at the end of the five-year cutting cycle each year. Each year the excess growth over reserve growing stock would be cut, thus 1,000 hectares each year, with a total wood volume of 3,315,000 cubic meters. This yield would be obtainable every year on a perpetual basis and is referred to as the *allowable cut*.

Starting in the 1980s, forest sustainability came to the forefront as a global concern. Organizations developed to accredit forest certification programs that promoted SFM, thus providing support of sustainability by offering market incentives for good forest management. Two leading international organizations that promote SFM and provide certification are the Programme for the Endorsement of Forest Certification (PEFC) and the Forest Stewardship Council (FSC).

Two approaches to SFM are common. One is ecosystem management, in which land, water, and living resources are integrated to promote conservation and sustainability. The other, developed at a meeting held in Montreal in 1993, is called the Montreal Process. It uses seven key criteria, which are tied to seven thematic areas that are now considered fundamental to SFM. These provide a structure for systems that certify forest sustainability and are now generally accepted as defining characteristics for SFM. The seven thematic areas are (1) extent of forest resources, (2) biological diversity, (3) forest health and vitality, (4) productive functions of forest resources, (5) protective functions of forest resources, (6) social and economic functions, and (7) legal, policy, and institutional framework.

Outlook

SFM has been widely adopted over the Americas and Oceania. Forest certification is playing a large role in increasing the forest area that is under SFM. The forest area managed under certified sustainable forestry has grown steadily, and the approach has found strong support from environmental groups, nongovernmental organizations, and even forest industry investment groups. The original impetus for increased SFM was to control tropical deforestation, though most of the growth in SFM has been in North America and Europe. Increased pressure is needed for wider application of SFM in the tropical forests.

Progress toward SFM objectives has been generally positive in North America, Central America, and the Caribbean, with the exception of areas impacted by wildfires and insects. Oceania has lost some forest area. Progress toward SFM in South America has been mixed, with a net loss of forest area but increased areas devoted to conservation and protection functions. South America has seen increased planted forests and has increasing forest area under management plans. Progress toward SFM goals thus can help mitigate loss of forest area.

Globally, there are still major problems on which forest management can have a positive impact. Deforestation remains an alarming trend. Some regions are being impacted by droughts and insects. Wood removals and related economic activity has been mixed, resulting in less than stable economic trends. At the same time, however, the rate of deforestation has been slowing. Much forest area is moving into conservation and protection status. More forest area is being planted, and this takes the pressure off other forest areas in terms of required production of forest products. The legal framework is increasingly supportive of SFM and more forest area is being brought under management plans.

Thomas J. STRAKA
Clemson University

See also Agriculture, Tropical (the Americas); Amazonia; Andes Mountains; Appalachian Mountains; Architecture; Brazil; Canada; Caribbean; Central America; Ecotourism (the Americas); Labor; Mexico; Multilateral Environmental Agreements (MEAs); Organization of American States (OAS); Parks and Protected Areas; Rocky Mountains; United States

Further Reading

Bettinger, Peter; Boston, Kevin; Siry, Jacek; & Grebner, Donald L. (2009). *Forest management and planning.* Oxford, UK: Elsevier.

Burton, Philip J.; Messier, Christian; Smith, Daniel W.; & Adamowicz, Wiktor L. (Eds.). (2003). *Towards sustainable management of the boreal forest.* Ottawa, Canada: National Research Council of Canada Research Press.

Dana, Samuel T., & Fairfax, Sally K. (1980). *Forest and range policy: Its development in the United States* (2nd ed.). New York: McGraw-Hill.

Davis, Lawrence S.; Johnson, K. Norman; Bettinger, Peter S.; & Howard, Theodore E. (2001). *Forest management: To sustain ecological, economic, and social values* (4th ed.). New York: McGraw-Hill.

Ferguson, Ian S. (1996). *Sustainable forest management.* Melbourne, Australia: Oxford University Press Australia.

Food and Agricultural Organization of the United Nations (FAO). (2010). *Global forest resources assessment 2010: Main report* (FAO Forestry Paper 163). Rome: Food and Agricultural Organization of the United Nations.

Food and Agricultural Organization of the United Nations (FAO). (2011). *State of the world's forests 2011.* Rome: Food and Agricultural Organization of the United Nations.

Hillstrom, Kevin, & Hillstrom, Laurie C. (2003a). *Australia, Oceania, and Antarctica: A continental overview of environmental issues.* Santa Barbara, CA: ABC-CLIO.

Hillstrom, Kevin, & Hillstrom, Laurie C. (2003b). *North America: A continental overview of environmental issues.* Santa Barbara, CA: ABC-CLIO.

Hillstrom, Kevin, & Hillstrom, Laurie C. (2004). *Latin America and the Caribbean: A continental overview of environmental issues.* Santa Barbara, CA: ABC-CLIO.

International Tropical Timber Organization (ITTO). (2009). *Annual review and assessment of the world timber situation, 2009* (Document GI-7/09). Yokohama, Japan: International Tropical Timber Organization.

Lugo, Ariel E.; Schmidt, Ralph; & Brown, Sandra. (1981). Tropical forests in the Caribbean. *Ambio, 10*(6), 318–324.

National Geographic Society. (2011). Eye in the sky: Human impact: Deforestation and desertification. Retrieved June 20, 2011, from http://www.nationalgeographic.com/eye/deforestation/deforestation.html

Poore, Duncan. (1989). *No timber without trees: Sustainability in the tropical forest.* London: Earthscan.

Putz, Francis E.; Blate, Geoffrey M.; Redford, Kent H.; Fimbel, Robert; & Robinson, John. (2001). Tropical forest management and conservation of biodiversity: An overview. *Conservation Biology, 15*(1), 7–20.

Rametsteiner, Ewald, & Simula, Markku. (2003). Forest certification— an instrument to promote sustainable forest management? *Journal of Environmental Management, 67*(1), 87–98.

Schelhas, John, & Greenberg, Russsell. (Eds.). *Forest patches in tropical landscapes*. Washington, DC: Island Press.

Siry, Jacek P.; Cubbage, Frederick W.; & Ahmed, Miyan R. (2005). Sustainable forest management: Global trends and opportunities. *Forest Policy and Economics, 7*(4), 551–561.

United Nations Forum on Forests. (n.d.). Homepage. Retrieved June 20, 2011, from http://www.un.org/esa/forests

Wadsworth, Frank H. (1997). *Forest production for tropical America* (Agricultural Handbook 710). Washington, DC: USDA Forest Service.

World Commission on Forests and Sustainable Development. (1999). *Our forests, our future*. Cambridge, UK: Cambridge University Press.

G

Gender Equality

Gender equality and sustainability are inherently linked, even in the wealthy countries of North America and Oceania. Understanding gender difference can help explain the challenges faced by women and men who seek to become involved in decisions about the environment and sustainability. Feminist scholarship can be used to investigate other forms of inequality that may affect sustainability.

Many people living in the United States, Canada, or Australia take for granted the fact that women and men alike are active and visible in public life. In these industrialized countries, women and men do not typically rely directly on extraction or consumption of environmental goods and services to sustain their basic livelihood. For example, relatively few people are employed as fishers, coal miners, and loggers. Furthermore, women and men in industrialized countries engage almost equally in practices that have a direct impact on the environment, such as driving cars, drinking bottled water, and purchasing clothes made in far-off places. In relation to environmental sustainability, then, are women and men "created equal"? The simple answer is no. Environmental (un)sustainability is experienced differently by women and men, even in industrialized countries.

Gender and Environmental Sustainability

Gender refers not only to the reproductive organs and structures associated with an individual, but also to the functional and behavioral differences between males and females that are socially and culturally influenced. While our biological sex is usually established at birth, scholars who study gender contend that we become masculine or feminine through a combination of biologically determined sex differences (chromosomes, anatomical structures, hormone levels) and socially influenced characteristics. While men, on average, are larger and stronger than women, for example, their greater physical strength is reinforced from a young age, since boys are traditionally encouraged to engage in active sports and other forms of physical activities while girls are traditionally encouraged to develop their fine motor and nurturing skills. These expectations and attributes are then carried forward into our daily lives, affecting choices, behaviors, and interpretations in our households, worksites, communities, and governing institutions.

If we understand that gender is not "given" to us at birth, but rather is "enacted" in our everyday lives, we can consider gender as a lens that can be used to interpret how women and men come to understand environmental sustainability and take action to achieve it. Studies conducted in North America since the 1990s, for example, found that women express higher levels of concern than men for the protection of the environment (Mohai 1992; Tindall, Davies, and Mauboules 2003). Women also typically express greater aversion to risk and greater concern about climate change than men do (Davidson, Williamson, and Parkins 2003). And, yet, it is unusual to see women in positions of leadership of mainstream environmental organizations.

Researchers have puzzled about this apparent paradox for some time. What they found is that women were more likely than men to get involved in informal or grassroots organizations, but they were less likely to hold positions of authority in large-scale, formal organizations. Indeed, national- or international-level environmental organizations were similar to forestry companies, government departments (especially in resource or financial sectors), or resource sector unions in the fact that their leadership was male dominated. Women were simply far less likely than men to hold leadership positions in a range of occupations that might influence decisions about the environment. Instead, the attention of women has been focused on environmentally friendly behaviors that can be integrated into everyday life, such as recycling, conserving energy, picking up litter, and composting organic waste (Tindall, Davies, and Mauboules 2003). Researchers thus have concluded that, even in countries where the roles and relations of women and men may be viewed as "egalitarian," involvement in activities to protect the environment and to advance sustainability is influenced by gender.

Examples from Canada and Australia

These conclusions have been supported by a number of studies. In a 2007 study of forest management and decision making in Canada, for example, the geographer Maureen Reed and the sociologist Jeji Varghese used gender as a category to analyze a national survey of 102 Canadian forest sector advisory committees. These advisory committees were established across the country to provide input to companies and government agencies about "community perspectives" related to forest management in their regions. The participants did not require special knowledge about forest management. The analysis revealed that women comprised less than 20 percent of the advisory committee memberships. Part of the reason for this is that the committees were primarily composed of participants with a direct economic interest in timber production, even though this was not a requirement of participation. Consequently, there was a bias toward values that supported ongoing resource exploitation. Women who did participate held values that were significantly different from those held by the men, and they rated their experiences as committee members less favorably than did the men.

Follow-up research involving interviews with participants in two different committees found that men often simply did not think it important to include women, while women who participated often felt nervous about participating because they were the only women on the committee and they were concerned that they were not really taken seriously (Richardson et al. 2011). In tandem, these studies suggested exclusion of women likely reinforced a timber extraction bias and restricted women's contributions to advancing the aims of sustainable forestry.

Another study conducted in 2007 in Australia by the geographers Julie Davidson and Elaine Stratford focused on the development of water policy in Tasmania. This study found that economic values and the perspectives of water consumers took precedence over other values that might be associated with "feminist ethics," such as "care" and "responsibility," in the development of water policy. The researchers found that economic values that are typically associated with masculine attributes gained primary consideration while social values typically associated with feminine attributes were not considered at all. They concluded, therefore, that the debates about sustainability of water resources in Australia were subject to gender differences. They suggested that the introduction of "feminist ethics" based on care and responsibility would allow new ideas and new groups of people to be included.

These examples show that efforts to achieve environmental sustainability are subject to differences in the way, and the extent to which, women and men get involved in decisions about the environment. While there has been quite a lot written about gender inequalities in developing countries and how this inequality affects the (un)sustainability of ecological and social relations, there is relatively less discussion about these issues in industrialized countries.

These examples illustrate that gender affects sustainability in countries of North America and Oceania as well.

Population Growth Rates and Gender Empowerment

The effect of human population growth on resource consumption has become a common subject of study. By 2011 the global population had reached 7 billion. Because rates of population growth since the Second World War have historically been much higher in the "developing" world than they have been in industrialized countries, attention on curbing population growth has been focused on the developing countries. In the Americas, however, we now see birth rates that are less than the rate of replacement (2.1 births per couple; the figure is 2.1, rather than the more logical 2.0, to take into account the slightly higher birth rate of boys, over girls, among human populations). Birthrates in Canada (1.0), the United States, (1.4), Mexico (1.9), Costa Rica (1.7), and Brazil (1.8), for example, are all below those of natural replacement (US CIA 2011). These birthrates include some amazing declines, for example, in Brazil. As a primarily Catholic community, abortion is illegal, and there has never been an official government policy regarding birth control. Even so, declines are occurring across all social classes, a phenomenon that is traced back to the early 1970s to "tough, resilient women who set out . . . without encouragement from the government and over the pronouncements of their bishops, to start shutting down the factories any way they could" (Gorney 2011). The *movimento das mulheres* (women's movement) of the 1970s and 1980s gave rise to a generation of women who "decided they didn't want more children. . . . Brazilian women are tremendously strong. It was just a matter of them deciding, and then having the means to achieve it" (Gorney 2011). Low birth rates are often accompanied by higher levels of formal education, particularly for girls. This is viewed as a positive sign of empowerment for women and for the sustainability of resources if it means that there will be fewer people that will have to be supported by the Earth's resources.

Experience in industrialized countries suggests, however, that these trends in population birth rates do not necessarily translate into more sustainable use of resources. The above-listed countries with the lowest birth rates—Canada and the United States—also are among the greatest consumers of the Earth's resources. In addition, higher levels of education among women do not necessarily translate into higher numbers of influential positions held by women. In rural areas of North America, for example, where resource extraction is highest and most of the resource-based communities are located, women are more likely to have higher levels of formal education than men. Their higher education levels, however, do not necessarily translate into greater influence in decisions about the allocation and use of resources. One reason for this is that, while barriers to women's participation have fallen across many urban areas, they persist across rural communities and in environmental resource sectors. Both men and women living in rural places continue to assume the "rightful" place of men is in the workforce, and the "rightful" place of women is in the home (Reed 2003). This assumption goes hand in hand with a range of others, such as those dictating the appropriate behavior of women and men in public settings, those determining who is more knowledgeable about resources and environment, and those presuming who should remain home to take care of the children. These assumptions are often unintentional and taken for granted. They are, nevertheless, counterproductive to the involvement and influence of women in decisions about the use and management of the environment, even in places where the most obvious barriers have broken down.

Tools for a New Generation

Feminist scholars have provided important critiques and frameworks for understanding gender. Their insights and criticisms have helped inform present-day understanding of sustainability. Indeed, they have demonstrated that achievement of sustainability is unlikely without gender equality. Yet, we can no longer assume that gender is the only or even the most important category of analysis when considering social inequalities and sustainability. It is indelibly linked with other forms of inequality, including race or ethnicity and socioeconomic status. Indeed, not only are people of color and people of lower socioeconomic status less likely to be included or effective in decision-making processes that aim to advance sustainability, they are also more likely to be seriously affected by unsustainable practices—even in wealthy countries—and the women in these groups are particularly vulnerable. In the South Coast Air Basin region of the Los Angeles area, for example, it was estimated in the mid-2000s that over 71 percent of African Americans and 50 percent of Latinos reside in areas with the most polluted air, while only 34 percent of whites live in highly polluted areas (Bullard 2005). In Canada, aboriginal peoples living outside of urban areas are more vulnerable to the negative effects of mega-project development, are more likely to be exposed to unsafe drinking water, and are typically not influential in decisions made about environmental resources.

Feminist scholars have been among the first to point out these other forms of social inequality. Tools provided by them and by feminist activists, in general, can help inform a new generation of research and action aimed at understanding conditions for those who are marginalized and to determine steps that will advance environmental and social sustainability for men and women from all walks of life.

Maureen G. REED
University of Saskatchewan

See also Australia; Brazil; Canada; Corporate Accountability; Fair Trade; Forest Management; Labor; Mobility; Oceania; Rural Development (the Americas); Social Movements (Latin America); United States; Water Use and Rights

FURTHER READING

Bullard, Robert. (Ed.). (2005). *The quest for environmental justice: Human rights and the politics of pollution*. San Francisco: Sierra Club Books.

Davidson, Debra J.; Williamson, Tim; & Parkins, John R. (2003). Understanding climate changer risk and vulnerability in northern forest-based communities *Canadian Journal of Forest Research*, *33*(11), 252–261.

Davidson, Debra J., & Hatt, Kierstin. (Eds.). (2005). *Consuming sustainability: Critical social analyses of ecological change*. Blackpoint, Canada: Fernwood Publishing.

Davidson, Julie, & Stratford, Elaine. (2007). En(gender)ing the debate about water's management and care: Views from the Antipodes. *Geoforum, 38*, 815–827.

Gorney, Cynthia. (2011, September). Brazil's girl power. *National Geographic*. Retrieved April 18, 2012, from http://ngm.nationalgeographic.com/2011/09/girl-power/gorney-text

MacGregor, Sherilyn. (2006). *Beyond mothering Earth: Ecological citizenship and the politics of care*. Vancouver, Canada: University of British Columbia Press.

Mohai, Paul. (1992). Men, women and the environment: An examination of the gender gap in environmental concern and activism. *Society and Natural Resources, 5*(1), 1–19.

Reed, Maureen G. (2003). *Taking stands: Gender and the sustainability of rural communities*. Vancouver, Canada: University of British Columbia Press.

Reed, Maureen G., & Varghese, Jeji. (2007). Gender representation on Canadian forest sector advisory committees. *Forestry Chronicle, 83*(4), 515–525.

Reed, Maureen G., & Christie, Shannon. (2009). We're not quite home: Reviewing the gender gap in environmental geography. *Progress in Human Geography, 33*(2), 246–255.

Reed, Maureen G., & George, Colleen. (2011). Where in the world is environmental justice? *Progress in Human Geography, 35*(6), 835–842. doi:10.1177/0309132510388384

Richardson, Kristyn; Sinclair, A. John; Reed, Maureen G.; & Parkins, John R. (2011). Constraints to participation in Canadian forestry advisory committees: A gendered perspective. *Canadian Journal of Forest Research, 41*(3), 524–532.

Tindall, David B.; Davies, Scott; & Mauboules, Céline. (2003). Activism and conservation behavior in an environmental movement: The contradictory effects of gender. *Society and Natural Resources, 16*(10), 909–932.

United States Central Intelligence Agency (US CIA). (2011). The world factbook. Retrieved April 17, 2012, from https://www.cia.gov/library/publications/the-world-factbook/fields/2054.html

Share the *Encyclopedia of Sustainability*: Teachers are welcome to make up to ten (10) copies of no more than two (2) articles for distribution in a single course or program. For further permissions, please visit www.copyright.com or contact: info@berkshirepublishing.com Get Permissions

Great Lakes and Saint Lawrence River

Much of North America's freshwater reserves are contained in the Great Lakes and Saint Lawrence River basin, which are protected by several agreements between the United States and Canada. Heavy shipping traffic, industrial and agricultural runoff, invasive species, and withdrawal of water from the system are all threatening the basin's sustainability. But through negotiation and legislation, progress has been made toward returning the lakes and river to ecological health.

The Great Lakes and Saint Lawrence River are a vast, invaluable shared resource whose sustainability is directly linked to the successful collaboration of two nations, two provinces, and eight states. Forming part of the US-Canadian border, the Great Lakes (244,100 square kilometers) comprise Lakes Superior, Michigan, Huron, Erie, and Ontario. These lakes contain roughly 18 percent of the world supply of fresh surface water (84 percent of North America's supply) and are the largest system of fresh surface water on Earth. They are home to 34 million people in the United States and Canada and generate many billions of dollars in trade, shipping, manufacturing, fishing, forestry, agriculture, mining, energy, and tourism. The Great Lakes historically have provided water for consumption, transportation, and fishing.

Created by erosion and deposition during the glacial movements of the Pleistocene epoch (1.6 million years ago), the Great Lakes are interconnected by rivers, straits, and canals. The Saint Lawrence Seaway (completed in 1959) links the lakes with the Atlantic Ocean via the Saint Lawrence River (the primary outlet of the ecosystem), which is directly affected by the quality and quantity of water from the Great Lakes. Except during icy months, the seaway serves as one of the world's busiest shipping corridors, with more than 50 million tonnes of freight passing through each year.

This high volume of traffic is currently threatening the lakes' ecological sustainability. Big ships emit 17 percent of the air pollution from what are known as mobile sources, such as cars, trucks, and ships. These emissions include vast amounts of nitrogen and sulfur oxides that contribute to acid rain, particulate matter, and ground-level ozone. Poor air quality from these emissions can be especially harmful to children, the elderly, and people with respiratory disorders; the US Environmental Protection Agency (EPA) classifies diesel exhaust as a likely carcinogen. The EPA is proposing a ban on the use of high-sulfur fuel within 200 miles of US coasts as well as along rivers and lakes and nitrogen oxide controls on new engines in the United States (Marrero 2009).

Another shipping problem is the introduction of invasive species. Unwanted stowaways in ship-steadying ballast tanks have been blamed for some of the Great Lakes' most troublesome invaders since the Saint Lawrence Seaway created an artificial shipping link to the Atlantic Ocean a half century ago. The list includes the quagga mussels that now smother the bottom of Lake Michigan, choking out native fish species and spawning noxious algae outbreaks that routinely pile up in stinking mounds on some of Wisconsin's most prized beaches. The EPA has agreed in an out-of-court settlement to draft new pollution standards for ballast discharges under the landmark 1972 Clean Water Act (*Milwaukee Riverkeeper* 2011).

Before the arrival of Europeans in the 1500s, the region was home to numerous Native American groups. They used the lakes for fishing, trading, and transportation, but their relatively small population and low-impact transportation methods did not threaten the ecological sustainability of the lakes. The water was cool, clean, and clear. Early settlers in the 1700s, however, deforested the basins for agriculture and timber, leading to erosion, sedimentation, and high nutrient loads. Eventually, more than two-thirds of the surrounding wetlands were also drained, depriving the basin of its natural water purification system. By the late 1800s, unregulated industries and rapidly growing municipalities were using the lakes as dumping grounds for untreated wastes. Industrial pollutants (especially polychlorinated biphenyls [PCBs]) and agricultural runoff (pesticides, such as dichlorodiphenyltrichloroethane [DDT]) added to water quality problems. Because there are few outflows from the Great Lakes, these pollutants remained in the lakes and became more concentrated with time. Additionally, the large surface area of the lakes made them susceptible to increasing atmospheric pollutants of the twentieth century, such as acid rain.

Fish populations also changed dramatically in the twentieth century, first through overfishing and then through the introduction of non-native species such as the parasitic sea lamprey, which virtually eliminated lake trout in Lakes Huron and Michigan. In 1986, zebra mussels, which filter and clean water by consuming algae, were introduced from Europe. The mussels ingest toxic substances and are then eaten by birds and animals, causing increasing toxic buildup higher in the food chain.

As a result of pollution, many beaches were closed, fish were contaminated, and lake water became undrinkable, raising public alarm. With increasing pollution loads and few natural pollution sinks (bodies that act as storage devices or disposal mechanisms for pollution, such as forests and wetlands), the Great Lakes water quality was in danger. In 1950, Lake Erie was declared "dead," which means unable to support aquatic life.

Recognizing the ecological importance of sustaining the Great Lakes basin, the United States and Canada had signed the Boundary Waters Treaty of 1909 in an unprecedented move of international cooperation. The two governments pledged to work together to restore and sustain the water quality of this priceless natural resource. By 1950, though, it was obvious that the treaty needed updating.

In response to the challenge, the Great Lakes Water Quality Agreements (GLWQA) of 1972 and 1978, expressing the renewed commitment of the United States and Canada to maintain the sustainability of the Great Lakes, replaced the original Boundary Waters Treaty of 1909. (See sidebar on page 118.) The International Joint Commission (IJC) formed under the original Boundary Waters Treaty retained its responsibilities to maintain the chemical, physical, and biological integrity of the waters of the Great Lakes.

The Great Lakes Water Quality Agreement

The GLWQA designated geographic areas of concern (AOC), defined in Annex 2 as a "geographic area that fails to meet the General or Specific Objectives of the Agreement where such failure has caused or is likely to cause impairment of beneficial use or of the area's ability to support aquatic life" (IJC Canada and United States 2011). Examples of such impairments include making water unpotable and fish inedible, ruining aesthetics, closing beaches, the appearance of bird or animal deformities, and reproduction problems. There are a total of forty-three of these Areas of Concern, with twenty-six in the United States, seventeen in Canada, and five shared by the two countries.

Each AOC has a unique set of characteristics that have contributed to its ecological impairment, and as a result, a separate Remedial Action Plan was developed for each area to identify the causes of impairment and then bring sustainability to each area. Some of the causes of impairment the remedial action plans identify are invasive species, point-source pollution (pollution that comes from a specific source, such as a pipe), nonpoint-source pollution, and atmospheric pollution. The goal is to bring about the delisting of each waterway from the list of Areas of Concern.

Amending the Agreement

The Great Lakes Water Quality Agreement was amended by protocol in 1987, and a review of the agreement was begun at that time. The findings were released in 2007. The results are documented in the *Great Lakes Water Quality Agreement Review 2007: Final Agreement Review Report* (Review of the Canada–US Great Lakes Water Quality Agreement 2007a, 2007b, and 2007c). The key finding was that although there have been many successes, the GLWQA is outdated and is unable to address current threats, which include climate change and water withdrawal as well as those mentioned earlier. These threats will have serious environmental, social, and economic implications if they are not addressed.

Recognizing the need to update the GLWQA again to address and resolve the current threats to the ecological sustainability of the lakes, Canadian Minister of Foreign Affairs Lawrence Cannon and US Secretary of State Hillary Clinton announced on 13 June 2009, at the Boundary Waters Treaty Centennial Celebration at Niagara Falls, that the two countries would begin negotiations to amend the agreement in January 2010. On 8 April 2010, senior officials from Environment Canada, Foreign Affairs, and International Trade Canada and the US

> ### GREAT LAKES "AREA OF CONCERN"
>
> For the Parties to the Great Lakes Water Quality Agreement (GLWQA) to designate an Area of Concern (an environmentally degraded area), the area must have at least "one beneficial use impairment which means that it has undergone a change in the chemical, physical, or biological integrity of the water body." These include:
>
> - Restrictions on fish and wildlife consumption
> - Tainting of fish and wildlife flavor
> - Degradation of fish and wildlife populations
> - Fish tumors or other deformities
> - Bird or animal deformities or reproduction problems
> - Degradation of benthos (organisms that live on the bottom of the water body)
> - Restrictions on dredging activities
> - Eutrophication or undesirable algae
> - Drinking water restrictions or taste and odor problems
> - Beach closings
> - Degradation of aesthetics
> - Added costs to agriculture or industry
> - Degradation of phytoplankton and zooplankton
> - Loss of fish and wildlife habitat
>
> *Source:* Great Lakes Information Network (GLIN). (2007). Areas of concern (AOCs): Pollution. Retrieved October 28, 2011, from http://www.great-lakes.net/teach/pollution/aoc/aoc2.html

Department of State and the US Environmental Protection Agency met for the second formal negotiating session. No formal agreement had been reached as of January 2012.

Two Controversies

Two controversies have emerged that had existed but had not been given much importance. They are water withdrawal by industry and communities and pollution abatement from industries surrounding the lakes.

Water Withdrawal

For many years, as communities and industries grew near the lakes, so did the need for water from them. States and provinces have diverted or withdrawn various amounts of both surface water and groundwater. Unregulated withdrawals have caused rising tensions over water levels and the sustainability of the ecosystem; Wisconsin and Illinois feel the greatest tension due to limited water in their aquifers in populous areas.

Once again realizing that the old water compacts were not protecting the basin, Canada and the United States came together to form the Great Lakes–St. Lawrence River Basin Water Resources Compact. This agreement differs from many others, which deal mostly with water quality, because it intends to keep the basin from unauthorized water withdrawals and diversions. The basin's water is necessary to the environment and wildlife, so humans and industry must use the water sustainably (Great Lakes–St. Lawrence River Basin Water Resources Compact 2005; National Wildlife Federation n.d.).

After several years of negotiations, legal mechanisms were adopted to achieve these goals. Many people feel that this compact will be a model for future water negotiations throughout the world. Unfortunately, although the well-designed compact technically became law in December 2008, the Great Lakes states had not developed and put in place the required water conservation and management programs by 2012.

Pollution Abatement

Another current source of tension has been the IJC's twenty-five-year-old ambitious effort to reduce water pollution in the Great Lakes region. Since 2000, the IJC has pursued several contentious policy recommendations: the "virtual elimination" of persistent, bio-accumulative toxins; the phase-out of chlorine and chlorine-containing compounds extensively used by industry; and the adoption of the principle of "reverse onus," whereby the manufacturer or user of a suspected persistent toxic substance carries the burden of proving that it is not and will not be harmful (Smith 1997). The chlorine recommendation in particular sparked a debate that polarized governments, industry, and environmentalists.

Also driving the region's discontent with water management is the EPA's Great Lakes Water Quality Initiative (GLI). Launched in 1995, the GLI includes proposals that would considerably tighten controls on point-source pollution across the Great Lakes Basin. To help substantiate the need for the GLI, the EPA prepared a benefit analysis that estimated the benefits of the program to be $17,000 for each $1 million invested (Smith 1997).

Conversely, an analysis of the EPA's data by Daniel W. Smith (1997) of Smith Technology Corporation, a US environmental consulting, engineering, and on-site remediation service provider, concluded that the agency drastically overestimated the benefits of the program. Smith said, "Benefits accrue from the estimated reduction in human cancer risk as a result of the decrease in point-source loading due to the initiative." By eliminating the estimated reductions and using more tangible, realistic values, Smith determined the benefits to be only $5 for each $1 million invested in the GLI. Each analysis has many strong supporters. As a result of the controversy, no progress has been made.

Outlook

Over the years, the United States and Canada have created many laws, policies, and commissions to keep the Great Lakes healthy and free of pollution. Although they willingly share the responsibility for protecting this invaluable resource, maintaining its sustainability has been challenging, mostly because of the difficulties in enforcing the laws and regulations binationally. The problem is generally due to lack of consensus, money, and political will on both sides of the border. Still, in the face of such challenges, the United States and Canada have managed through various agreements to achieve obvious benefits that continue to develop: beaches have reopened, water is drinkable and clear, and most fish are edible, Lake Erie has thriving fish populations again, and most point-source pollution has been controlled.

Irene DAMERON HAGER
The Ohio State University

See also Canada; Corporate Accountability; Detroit, United States; Ecotourism (the Americas); Forest Management; Mackenzie River; Marine Ecosystems Health; Mississippi and Missouri Rivers; Multilateral Environmental Agreements (MEAs); North American Free Trade Agreement (NAFTA); Northwest Passage; Toronto, Canada; United States; Water Use and Rights

FURTHER READING

Abell, Robin A.; Olson, David M.; Dinerstein, Eric; & Hurley, Patrick. (2000). *Freshwater ecoregions of North America: A conservation assessment*. Washington, DC: Island Press.

Ashworth, William. (1987). *The late, Great Lakes: An environmental history*. Detroit, MI: Wayne State University Press.

Dempsey, David. (2008). *Great Lakes for sale: From whitecaps to bottle caps*. Ann Arbor: University of Michigan Press.

Government of Canada & United States Environmental Protection Agency (EPA). (1995). *The Great Lakes: An environmental atlas and resource book* (3rd ed.). Chicago: Great Lakes National Program Office.

Great Lakes Information Network. (2007). Areas of Concern (AOCs): Pollution. Retrieved October 28, 2011, from http://www.great-lakes.net/teach/pollution/aoc/aoc2.html

Great Lakes–St. Lawrence River Basin Water Resources Compact. (2005, December 13). Homepage. Retrieved May 13, 2012, from http://www.cglg.org/projects/water/docs/12-13-05/Great_Lakes-St_Lawrence_River_Basin_Water_Resources_Compact.pdf

International Joint Commission (IJC), Canada & United States. (2011). Treaties and agreements: About the Great Lakes Water Quality Agreement. Retrieved April 30, 2012, from http://www.ijc.org/rel/agree/quality.html

Marrero, Diane. (2009, October 12). Obey measure could block new EPA ship pollution regulations. Retrieved April 30, 2012, from http://www.jsonline.com/news/wisconsin/64057622.html

Milwaukee Riverkeeper. (2011, March 11). Stiffer pollution regulations expected for Great Lakes ships. Retrieved April 30, 2012, from http://www.mkeriverkeeper.org/content/stiffer-pollution-regulationsexpected-great-lakes-ships

National Wildlife Federation. (n.d.). Great Lakes Water Resources Compact. Retrieved May 11, 2012, from http://www.nwf.org/Wildlife/Policy/Great-Lakes-Restoration/Great-Lakes-Compact.aspx

Olson, James M. (2006). Navigating the great lakes compact: Water, public trust, and international trade agreements. Retrieved April 30, 2012, from http://commonslearningalliance.org/sites/default/files/Olson.pdf

Review of the Canada–US Great Lakes Water Quality Agreement. (2007a). Report to the Great Lakes Binational Executive Committee: Volume 1. Retrieved November 3, 2011, from http://binational.net/glwqa/v1_glwqareview_en.pdf

Review of the Canada–US Great Lakes Water Quality Agreement. (2007b). Report to the Great Lakes Binational Executive Committee: Volume 2. Retrieved November 3, 2011, from http://binational.net/glwqa/v2_glwqareview_en.pdf

Review of the Canada–US Great Lakes Water Quality Agreement. (2007c). Report to the Great Lakes Binational Executive Committee: Volume 3. Retrieved November 3, 2011, from http://binational.net/glwqa/v3_glwqareview_en.pdf

Smith, Daniel W. (1997). Environmental policy analysis, peer reviewed: A critical review of the benefits analysis for the Great Lakes Initiative. *Environmental Science & Technology News, 31*(1), 34A–38A.

Sproule-Jones, Mark. (2002). *Restoration of the Great Lakes: Promises, practices, and performances*. Vancouver, Canada: University of British Columbia Press.

Guatemala City

988,100 est. pop. 2010 (official city); 3.1 million est. pop. in the Department of Guatemala

Guatemala City is the largest Central American capital and is one of the region's most cosmopolitan cities. Its metropolitan area comprises several surrounding municipalities, but there is weak coordination among them. Guatemala City remains the center of economic, political, and cultural activities in Guatemala. The region faces environmental and social challenges such as poverty and crime. Although initiatives exist to address environmental and urban problems, more coordinated public policies and larger infrastructure investments will be required.

Founded under the Spanish rule in 1776 in the area known as the Valley of la Ermita, Guatemala City was initially the capital for the entire Central American region and has been the most important urban center in Central America for the last two centuries. Shortly after gaining independence from Spain in 1821, each new country in Central America established its own capital, but Guatemala City remained the largest and more modern and diverse one of the previously unified region. The rich variety of Guatemala City is exemplified by Kaminal Juyú, an ancient Maya city and trade center in the highlands, located within its borders (Schele and Miller 1986). In addition, the city is home to the national palace, government and business offices, museums, and a historic center that features important architectural structures (Gorry 2009). In modern times, Guatemala City, the capital of both the Republic of Guatemala and the Department of Guatemala, remains the most cosmopolitan city in Central America, but also faces significant economic, environmental, and security challenges.

Although a population of approximately 1 million resides within Guatemala City's official limits, the city's services and resources support most of the 3.1 million people living in the Guatemala Department (22 percent of the national population), and thus are under pressure (UNDP 2011). The human density in the city is 5,264 people per square kilometer, although there are density disparities among the twenty-five city zones or zip codes (PNUMA et al. 2012). Guatemala City proper, along with most municipalities within the Guatemala Department (Villa Nueva, Mixco, Chinautla, San José Pinula, and Santa Catarina Pinula), creates a large urban area in the center of Guatemala. According to the Guatemalan economist Eduardo Velásquez, the population growth around Guatemala City fostered "the creation of new concepts and categories, such as the Metropolitan Area of the City of Guatemala" (2011). Even though there is a constitutional mandate for an organized administration for the entire metropolitan area, Guatemala City and the surrounding municipalities nonetheless have weak or close to no coordination when dealing with their multiple common challenges.

This process of agglomeration around Guatemala City began during the middle of the 1970s due to two extreme events in the country's history. The first and more dramatic event was a massive earthquake in 1976 that brought destruction and despair to several areas, more dramatically in the rural regions, forcing displaced residents to seek refuge in the city. The other important event was the country's long civil war, which lasted from 1960 to 1996. Because the main theater of this war was the rural areas, refugees fled to the city, leading to rapid urbanization.

As the main urban center of the country, the City of Guatemala offers the best educational and labor opportunities in the country, hence providing more fairness than the rural settings. Not surprisingly, the human development index, which measures standard of living and quality of life, in Guatemala City is 0.826 (on a scale of 0 to 1), significantly higher than in the Guatemalan rural areas (PNUD 2011). As the space where the most important companies, services, and industries (food processing, apparel, chemical products) are located, the area in and around Guatemala City produces the majority of the country's gross domestic product (GDP) (PNUMA et al. 2012). In the metropolitan area, the average monthly salary, which is equivalent to US$335, is 36 percent higher than the national average, and women account for 40 percent of the labor force, more than the national average (INE 2011). As a result, about 35 percent of Guatemala City's residents belong to middle and upper classes, compared to only 14 percent nationwide (PNUD 2010).

Guatemala City is a city of contrasts. Although Guatemala's GDP grew, on average, 3.4 percent annually in the first decade of the twenty-first century (MINECO 2012), the poverty level remained at 16.4 percent in the metropolitan area (the national average was 51 percent) (INE 2006). Although increases in the GDP built up affluent areas with high-rise buildings, modern malls, top-quality hospitals, and the country's best educational institutions, the city's poorer areas have not flourished. Frequently located around the hillsides of river basins, hundreds of settlements (similar to the Brazilian *favelas*, or shantytowns) have limited basic services (housing, water, sewage, and parks) and higher crime rates than in areas of the city. Since 2004, Guatemala City has seen an increased emphasis on an intensive gardening and cleaning campaign. But it is perceived as an effort only for the "rich" zones.

The mayor and the city council lead Guatemala City's government, as is the case in all municipalities in the country. Guatemala City's mayor is elected together with three syndics, or city officials, but the ten council members are elected based on the number of votes gained by each political group, encouraging the representation of minorities in the planning and controlling of all the municipal governments in the country.

A priority for public officials is the reduction of crime and violence that has spread throughout the country, particularly during the first decade of the twenty-first century, primarily as a consequence of drug trafficking and the proliferation of gangs. As homicide rates increased during that decade, the country's citizens increasingly perceived a higher vulnerability to violence (Matute and García 2007). The estimated cost of violence and crime, highly concentrated in Guatemala City, was equivalent to 7.3 percent of Guatemala's GDP in 2005 (World Bank 2011).

Social and Environmental Challenges

The lack of coordination among municipalities and the central government, ineffective urban policies, and insufficient financial resources are evident as critical social and environmental problems diminish the quality of life in Guatemala City.

Water management is critical in Guatemala's capital. No major rivers cross the city, which is a highland settlement. Empresa Municipal de Agua (EMPAGUA), the municipal company in charge of the water and sewer services in the city, pumps over 450,000 cubic meters of water per year from adjacent rivers and underground aquifers that are diminishing their potential as sustainable water sources (SEGEPLAN and BID 2006). EMPAGUA's coverage is concentrated in the older parts of the city, where residents complain about the quality and quantity of water received. One compelling problem is that the newly occupied areas, mainly the ones formed by huge popular movements from inside the country, have grown enormously, and EMPAGUA does not provide them with regular service, forcing people to get their water by truck to be dispensed into containers. The metropolitan area also has environmental pollution concerns. For example, a large proportion of the domiciliary and industrial residues from factories in and around Guatemala City are the main source of pollution for Lake Amatitlán, affecting livelihoods and restricting recreational and productive uses (AMSA 2012).

In 2012, the Guatemalan metropolitan area generates an estimated 2,424 tonnes of solid waste daily, most of which is discharged in an open-air landfill that lacks any environmental and sustainable management (PNUMA et al. 2012). Private individuals run the waste collection services, and although city authorities approve the individuals' collection trucks, they do not supervise the service. The landfill is a major source of pollution inside the city and significantly affects the surrounding neighborhoods and creates environmental liabilities for the future. There is huge concern for these matters, and there are several initiatives to promote recycling, particularly for paper, plastics, and metals, primarily run by the private sector and educational institutions, that will initiate the demise of this huge environmental problem.

As the center of Guatemala's logistical corridor, Guatemala City houses La Aurora International Airport and is the connection among the key transit routes in the region. Even so, the city lacks an efficient and secure mass transit system; crowded privately operated buses, which are under city supervision and central government subsidy, transport users who can spend as many as four hours per day traveling through the city. There are more than 700,000 vehicles, mostly those of commuters, using Guatemala City's streets (Obregón n.d.). Because the administration of transit is run by each of the metropolitan area's municipalities, this sometimes creates contradictory transit plans and conflicts among mayors. The importance of tackling the problem from a more macro approach is evident, especially for prioritizing future infrastructure projects to remedy bottlenecks not only in the center of the city, but on the outskirts. In 2007, the city launched a new bus rapid transit system, Transmetro, to address the transit congestion and reduce robberies in the public transport system (Municipality of Guatemala City 2012a). Transmetro, financed by the Guatemalan municipality, was created to emulate similar initiatives in the South American cities of Bogotá, Colombia, and Curitiba, Brazil. Routes operate between the city center and the southern areas, and future expansions are expected toward the northern and eastern extensions of the metropolitan area.

Other challenges that affect the quality of life in Guatemala City are the frequent natural disasters that beset the region. Eruptions of nearby volcanoes, earthquakes, and landslides are common. In 2010, ash from the eruption of the volcano Pacaya covered the city and interrupted operations at La Aurora airport. A 1976 earthquake was responsible for the deaths of more than twenty thousand people and major damages in infrastructure and private homes (Sandoval 2006). A similar catastrophe could have a higher toll in Guatemala City, since poor areas are precarious and located in landslide areas.

There are, nevertheless, positive trends in improving the air quality and the access to recreational areas around Guatemala City. Although fossil fuels consumed by vehicles are the main source of greenhouse gases produced by the energy sector in Guatemala City, the use of biofuels is increasing (Castellanos and Guerra 2008). Additionally, vehicle emissions control has been instrumental in mitigating air pollution in Guatemala City. Although air pollution is higher in areas of heavy transit (IARNA 2009), the Environmental Performance Index reports positive trends for Guatemala in the control of airborne suspended particles and carbon dioxide emissions per capita (Benavides 2012).

Forest coverage in Guatemala City is scarce, with most trees located in the hillsides. Out of the 222 square kilometers of forest that covered Guatemala City and surrounding areas in 1954, only 20.7 percent remained four decades later (Martinez 1996). To reverse that trend, nongovernmental organizations (NGOs) like Fundaeco and the Municipality of Guatemala are promoting the conservation of "green zones" in the city, such as the Cayalá ecological park and the Kanajuyú forest reserve (Fundaeco 2012). In other efforts to increase environmental awareness among citizens, several NGOs, such as Defensores de la Naturaleza, Fundación Solar, and Fundaeco, along with the national Ministry of Environment and Natural Resources, have developed different environmental education initiatives, particularly through schools

Another city project, the Aurora-Cañas Central Corridor, as part of a territorial planning plan initiative, aims to revitalize Guatemala City's central area, attracting new residents and businesses with an integral approach aimed at preventing the flow from citizens to the adjacent suburbs (Municipality of Guatemala City 2012b)

Winds of Change

Guatemala City and the surrounding municipalities face multiple daunting challenges in efforts to enhance the quality of life for their citizens and improve conditions for the development of business and services in Guatemala's capital.

Not surprisingly, in the 2011 elections, mayors who traditionally were reelected in Guatemala's metropolitan areas either experienced a huge decline in the popular vote or were unseated. This change may signal winds of change, where new mayors do not have old grudges between them and thus might decrease the traditional lack of communication between their offices. These alliances will definitely enhance the chances for fundamental problems to be tackled, instead of continually being delayed.

More coordination between Guatemala City and the surrounding municipalities, as well with the central government, is required to address the multiple environmental and social challenges that impact the metropolitan area. The annual public budget for the municipality of Guatemala, which equals about US$120 million (Municipality of Guatemala City 2010), is clearly insufficient to provide basic services and fund the required investments in infrastructure and large-scale projects (sanitation, waste management, public transportation).

There is a growing sense that it has become urgent to rearrange the present independent structure to a more coordinated urban setting, like those in cities such as London, Santiago de Chile, and Caracas, Venezuela, where individual territories become part of a larger urban entity called "The City." It is the only way to solve important problems like transit, water, and sewage and trash disposal.

J. Rodolfo NEUTZE
Councilman, Guatemala City

Victor J. MOSCOSO
Researcher, Daedalus Strategic Advising

See also Bogotá, Colombia; Central America; Curitiba, Brazil; Forest Management; Gender Equality; Lima, Peru; Mexico; Mexico City; Mobility; Public Transportation; Sanitation; Social Movements (Latin America); Urbanization; Water Use and Rights

Further Reading

Autoridad para el Manejo Sustentable de la Cuenca de Lago de Amatitlán (AMSA). (2012). *¿Qué es AMSA?* [What is AMSA?]. Retrieved March 1, 2012, from http://www.amsa.gob.gt/blog/?page_id=22

Benavente, Claudia. (2007, March 5). Ciudad de Guatemala asentada sobre fallas [Guatemala City is set on failure]. *elPeriódico*. Retrieved March 5, 2012, from http://www.elperiodico.com.gt/es/20070305/actualidad/37422/

Benavides, Jorge. (2012). *Desempeño ambiental* [Environmental performance]. Guatemala City, Guatemala: Fundación para el Desarrollo de Guatemala (FUNDESA).

Castellanos, Edwin, & Guerra, Alex. (2008). *El cambio climático y sus efectos sobre el desarrollo humano en Guatemala* [Climate change and its effects on human development in Guatemala]. Guatemala City, Guatemala: Programa de las Naciones Unidas para el Desarrollo (PNUD).

Congreso de la República de Guatemala [Congress of the Republic of Guatemala]. (1985). Constitución política [Constitution]. Guatemala City, Guatemala: Congress of the Republic of Guatemala.

Fundación para el Ecodesarrollo y la Conservación (FUNDAECO). (2012). ¿Donde trabajamos? Cinturón ecológico metropolitano [Where do we work? Metropolitan green belt]. Retrieved February 28, 2012, from http://www.fundaeco.org.gt/mapa.php?selectedmap=51&title=Cinturon+Ecologico+Metropolitano.com

Gorry, Conner. (2009). *Guatemala, great destinations*. Woodstock, VT: The Countryman Press.

Instituto de Agricultura, Recursos Naturales y Ambiente (IARNA). (2009). *Perfil ambiental de Guatemala 2008–2009: Las señales ambientales críticas y su relación con el desarrollo* [Environmental profile of Guatemala 2008–2009: Critical environmental signals and their relation with development]. Guatemala City, Guatemala: Universidad Rafael Landívar (URL), IARNA.

Instituto Nacional de Estadística (INE). (2006). *Encuesta nacional de condiciones de vida (ENCOVI): Principales resultados* [National survey of living conditions (ENCOVI): Main results]. Guatemala City, Guatemala: INE.

Instituto Nacional de Estadística (INE). (2011). *Mercado laboral: Encuesta nacional de empleos e ingresos (ENEI) 2011* [Labor market: National survey of employment and income (ENEI) 2011]. Guatemala City, Guatemala: INE.

Matute, Arturo, & García, Ivan. (2007). *Informe estadístico de la violencia en Guatemala* [Statistical report on violence in Guatemala]. Guatemala City, Guatemala: Programa de Seguridad Ciudadana y Prevención de la Violencia del PNUD Guatemala.

Martínez, José. (1996). *Servicios públicos urbanos: El caso de los residuos sólidos en la Ciudad de Guatemala* [Urban public services: The case of solid waste in Guatemala City]. Guatemala City, Guatemala: Universidad de San Carlos de Guatemala, Dirección General de Investigación (DIGI).

Ministerio de Economía (MINECO). (2012). *Agenda nacional de competitividad: Facilitando empleos formales para los guatemaltecos* [National competitiveness agenda: Facilitating formal jobs for Guatemalans]. Guatemala City, Guatemala: MINECO.

Morán Mérida, Amanda. (1998). *Area metropolitana de la Ciudad de Guatemala: A propósito del proyecto de ley de creación del distrito metropolitano* [Metropolitan area of Guatemala City: The purpose of the bill creating the metropolitan district]. Puerto Barrios, Guatemala: Universidad de San Carlos de Guatemala, Centro de Estudios Urbanos y Regionales (CEUR).

Municipality of Guatemala City. (2010). *Guatemala, una ciudad para invertir* [Guatemala, a city to invest in]. Guatemala City, Guatemala: Municipality of Guatemala City.

Municipality of Guatemala City. (2012a). *Transmetro*. Retrieved March 12, 2012, from http://transmetro.muniguate.com

Municipality of Guatemala City. (2012b). *Corredor Central Aurora Cañas* [Aurora Cañas Central Corridor]. Guatemala City, Guatemala: Municipality of Guatemala City

Obregón, Oliver. (n.d.). *Transporte y sostenibilidad en Ciudad de Guatemala* [Transportation and sustainability in Guatemala City]. Guatemala City, Guatemala: Dirección de Infraestructura, Municipality of Guatemala City.

Programa de Naciones Unidas para el Medio Ambiente (PNUMA); Municipality of Guatemala City; Fundación para el Ecodesarrollo y la Conservación (FUNDAECO); & Secretaría General de Planificación Económica (SEGEPLAN). (2012). Perspectivas del medio ambiente urbano: Geo Ciudad de Guatemala [Prospects of the urban environment: Geo Guatemala City]. Panama City, Panama: PNUMA.

Programa de las Naciones Unidas para el Desarrollo (PNUD). (2011). *Cifras para el desarrollo humano: Guatemala. Colección estadística departamental* [Figures for human development: Guatemala. Departmental statistics collection]. Guatemala City, Guatemala: PNUD.

Sandoval, Marta. (2006, February 5). Lo que el terremoto nos dejó [What the earthquake left us]. *elPeriódico*. Retrieved March 5, 2012, from http://www.elperiodico.com.gt/es/20060205/actualidad/24361/

Schele, Linda, & Miller, Mary. (1986). *The blood of the kings: Dynasty and ritual in Maya art*. New York: George Braziller, Inc., & Kimbell Art Museum.

Schlesinger, María Elena. (2012, February 18). *La fundación de la ciudad* [The foundation of the city]. *elPeriódico*. Retrieved March 5, 2012, from http://www.elperiodico.com.gt/es/20120218/lacolumna/208199/

Secretaría de Planificación y Programación de la Presidencia de Guatemala (SEGEPLAN) & Banco Interamericano de Desarrollo (BID). (2006). *Estrategia para la gestión integrada de los recursos hídricos en Guatemala: Diagnóstico* [Strategy for integrated management of water resources in Guatemala: Diagnosis]. Guatemala City, Guatemala: SEGEPLAN & BID.

United Nations Development Programme (UNDP). (2011). *Cifras para el desarrollo humano: Guatemala; Informe nacional de desarrollo humano* [Numbers for human development: Guatemala; Human development report]. Colección estadística departamental. Guatemala City, Guatemala: Serviprensa, S.A.

Velásquez Carrera, Eduardo (2011, June 15). La ciudad y su área metropolitan: Un estudio sobre la capital [The city and its metropolitan area: A study of the capital]. *elPeriódico*. Retrieved March 5, 2012, from http://www.elperiodico.com.gt/es/20110615/opinion/196825/

World Bank. (2011). *Violence in the city: Understanding and supporting community responses to urban violence*. Washington, DC: World Bank.

Berkshire's authors and editors welcome questions, comments, and corrections. Send your emails about the *Berkshire Encyclopedia of Sustainability* in general or this volume in particular to: sustainability.updates@berkshirepublishing.com

L

Labor

The Industrial Revolution, by greatly expanding the capacity of human beings to transform and consume the environment, is a key moment for understanding the histories and relationships between labor and environmental sustainability in the Americas and Oceania. The view of this relationship has evolved over time, but currently there is growing recognition that the economic well-being of workers and the health of the environment are intimately related.

How does human labor—the productive engagement of people with the environment—transform the natural world? For most of history, this question has been framed largely in terms of survival. The intertwined histories of labor and sustainability in the Americas and Oceania date back to when these areas were first colonized. Before the Industrial Revolution, low population levels and limited productive capacity meant that people spent a lot of time working for food, shelter, and other basic needs, but at the same time their impact on the environment was relatively limited by modern standards.

The Industrial Revolution

European colonization, coupled with the industrialization that began in the 1800s, transformed both the labor forces and the environments of the Americas and Oceania. Agrarian societies were fundamentally disrupted as colonization and industrialization displaced millions of people from agricultural communities, often by force, in order to either work in factories or supply them with raw materials. In the process they created large cities that demanded increased production and exploitation of resources. Industrial centers in Europe, then the United States, Australia, Canada, and New Zealand, followed by other parts of the Americas and Oceania, required everything from coal, cotton, and coffee to sugar, wood, oil, and rubber. The heartlands of industry also turned much of the rest of the world, including Latin America and parts of Oceania, into suppliers of natural resources and basic commodities.

Certain regions (such as the northeastern United States) became industrial centers characterized by a "modern" industrial labor force, increased levels of consumption, rapid urbanization, and associated pollution. Others (such as northeast Brazil, the Caribbean Basin, and northern Mexico) became suppliers of industrial raw materials like rubber and oil, and tropical commodities such as sugar, coffee, and bananas. Still others (such as regions of the Amazon and many of the islands of Oceania) remained on the margins of industrial capitalism.

As the Industrial Revolution transformed people and their environments, it also changed how people thought about labor and the natural world. Labor no longer meant just work as a productive activity, a particular task or job. Labor became a class of workers, a body of people created by and for industry. Whether they were employed in a Detroit automobile factory, a Buenos Aires meat-processing plant, a Honduras banana plantation, or a gold mine in Papua New Guinea, workers as a class shared a common set of conditions and interests. In becoming a class, labor also became identified as both a sociopolitical problem (in the form of political threats like unions or political parties) and as a socioeconomic problem (in the form of the poor who needed welfare, health care, and education). Indeed, prior to World War II, most workers in the Americas and Oceania were in fact poor, unhealthy, and lacking in formal education.

As the process of industrialization allowed human beings, through their labor, to produce and consume on much larger scales, environments also underwent profound transformation and stress, leading to a host of environmental problems that resulted from rapid urbanization, large-scale mining, massive factories, and agro-industry. After these consequences of the Industrial Revolution became apparent, people began to see the natural world as more than something to master through productive labor—it began to be seen as a potentially limited resource that could be permanently damaged or even destroyed by labor. In this sense, it can be said that the concept of environmental sustainability began with efforts to preserve forests and limit factory pollution during the Industrial Revolution. Like labor, however, the environment has come to be seen as a social problem: something in need of political advocacy or state protection.

World War II to 1973

Between the end of World War II and 1970, workers throughout the Americas and in much of Oceania saw their economic fortunes improve as most governments pursued Keynesian policies that promoted economic growth, full employment, and gradual improvements for working people. In the United States, the real wages of the average American worker more than doubled between the end of World War II and 1973. By 1970 only 10 percent of American working families were classified as poor, in contrast to about 40 percent in 1945. Perhaps most importantly, income inequality declined during this time (Krugman and Lawrence 2008).

Workers in the rest of the Americas and in a large part of Oceania experienced similar improvements during the postwar period, as governments adopted policies aimed at expanding the economy and decreasing income equality. Policy makers took for granted that workers had to be employed and well paid if they were to stimulate the economy through consumption. These types of policies also drove economic planning throughout Latin America, as governments attempted to develop domestic industries with well-paid labor forces, although the results there were less dramatic than in other regions.

In this postwar era of economic expansion and steady wage increases, workers in the United States, Australia, and Canada were often some of the earliest environmental advocates—at first due to public-health concerns about air and water pollution, and later as proponents of wilderness preservation. Union support for environmental regulations in the United States varied in intensity, but lasted through the early 1970s: organized labor backed both the Clean Air Act and the Clean Water Act (Obach 2004).

1973 to Present

After 1973 a deep recession abruptly ended decades of postwar economic growth, and labor's relationship with the environment and environmentalism became more strained. Geographic variations aside, the real wages of workers throughout the Americas and Oceania have declined or stagnated since 1973, even as productivity has increased dramatically. In the United States wages grew by only 6 percent from 1973 to 2008, with virtually all of the gains going to highly educated workers—the real earnings of blue-collar workers actually declined during that period (Krugman and Lawrence 2008). In Australia workers have fared slightly better, though within a context of increased unemployment and declining public services, since the government exerts considerably more control over wages. Wages for Canadian workers stagnated between 1980 and 2005, and in New Zealand real wages for workers declined by about 25 percent between the early 1980s and mid-1990s, with little or no recovery since. Meanwhile, the 1980s are referred to simply as "the lost decade" in Latin America, where workers throughout the region have experienced a significant decline in living standards since the mid-1970s. The past four decades have not been good for labor.

Under these conditions, some US workers and much of the labor movement began to see environmental regulations variously as a luxury, or of secondary importance, or even as an active threat to job creation. Job-loss concerns have made it difficult for workers to embrace environmental issues, and they are not alone in seeing environmental protection and regulations as conflicting with job creation and economic expansion. Many people have come to see the interests of labor and the environment as inherently opposed, since the "health" of our economic system (particularly in terms of job creation and retention) depends on the continual growth of the economy. Perpetual growth places ever-greater stress on ecosystems, however. Industrial capitalism's capacity to harness human labor to produce ever-greater quantities of goods has created an economic system that is environmentally unsustainable and responsible for a range of environmental problems, from air pollution, acid rain, and global climate change to water pollution, hazardous waste, and rain forest destruction. This conflict between labor and environmental sustainability has played out in the Americas and Oceania in different areas and at different times.

Timber

An early—and perhaps quintessential—conflict that pitted labor against the environment occurred during the early 1980s, in the Pacific Northwest forests of the United States. Many saw environmental regulations designed to protect old-growth forest and the northern spotted owl as a threat to thousands of jobs in the timber industry. The combination of sensational media coverage and the actions of radical environmentalists captured the national attention, solidifying the notion that jobs and environmental regulations were diametrically opposed and that environmentalists posed a threat to unions and job creation.

Outside of the United States, the tension between workers and forest-protection programs generally has been less intense, although conflicts over deforestation have at times been quite volatile. The Australian "forest wars" of the past two decades have involved similar debates, and deforestation in New Zealand has been a hugely contentious issue, as environmentalists and indigenous peoples have secured legal protection for native forests. In Papua New Guinea, the poverty level means that economic growth and job creation often trump environmental concerns, but a recent report concluded that the country's forests were being logged so quickly that half of its trees could be gone by 2021.

Mining

The clash between the environment and jobs has been particularly contentious in the case of large-scale mining ventures. In places like Appalachia, where the coal industry is in decline and jobs are disappearing, miners often side with mine operators using mountaintop removal, and against environmentalists. In other areas (such as northern Colombia) though, miners and indigenous communities have forged alliances to monitor labor, environmental, and human rights and ensure that coal mining is done better. In the meantime, dangerous working conditions, low wages, and environmental degradation in Chile's copper mines and Peru's gold mines have brought workers and environmentalists together. In Central America, activists have tried to block mining completely because they feel mine operators do not respect the rights of workers or the environment. Likewise, the large multinational-owned copper and gold mines that have existed in Papua New Guinea since the 1970s have put labor, communities, and the environment at odds with each other.

Green Labor

Since the late 1990s these ongoing conflicts, coupled with the increasingly poor state of both the environment and working people, have effected more explicit attempts to bring labor and the environment into alliance. The "green-collar" jobs favored by a range of politicians, activists, and economists demonstrate that productive labor and environmental responsibility don't need to be mutually exclusive—for example, the new energy economy has the potential to improve the environment while creating jobs installing solar panels, weatherizing buildings, and constructing wind turbines. During the same time period workers and environmentalists have tried hard to find common ground, particularly since the protests at the 1999 World Trade Organization meetings in Seattle, when organized labor and the environmental movement worked together to oppose what they perceived to be an unfair system of global trade. In 2002 the United Steelworkers (the largest industrial labor union in the United States) and the Sierra Club (the largest US environmental organization) announced the formation of the BlueGreen Alliance; its motto is "Good jobs, a clean environment, and a safer world." In Canada and Australia, such alliances between labor and environmentalists are perhaps even further developed—and institutionalized to an extent through the Green Party. All of these developments suggest the (uneven) emergence of a broader notion of sustainability throughout the Americas and Oceania, one that recognizes that both good jobs and clean environments are necessary for the long-term health of society.

Steve STRIFFLER
University of New Orleans

See also Amazonia; Appalachian Mountains; Australia; Canada; Ecotourism (the Americas); Fair Trade; Mining (Andes); Mining (Australia); Mobility; Multilateral Environmental Agreements (MEAs); North American Free Trade Agreement (NAFTA); Oceania; Parks and Protected Areas; Rural Development (the Americas); Social Movements (Latin America); United States

FURTHER READING

Bennett, James. (2004). *Rats and revolutionaries: The labour movement in Australia and New Zealand 1890–1940*. Dunedin, New Zealand: University of Otago Press.

Dubofsky, Melvyn, & Dulles, Foster Rhea. (2010). *Labor in America: A history* (8th ed.). Wheeling, IL: Harlan Davidson.

Hutton, Drew, & Connors, Libby. (1999). *History of the Australian environment movement*. Cambridge, UK: Cambridge University Press.

Kline, Benjamin. (2000). *First along the river: A brief history of the US environmental movement* (2nd ed.). San Francisco: Arcada Books.

Krugman, Paul, & Lawrence, Robert Z. (2008, October 13). Trade, jobs, and wages. *Scientific American.* Retrieved October 5, 2011, from http://www.scientificamerican.com/article.cfm?id=krugman-trade-jobs-wages (Original work published April 1994)

Obach, Brian K. (2004). *Labor and the environmental movement: The quest for common ground*. Cambridge, MA: MIT Press.

Pissarides, Christopher. (1991). Real wages and unemployment in Australia. *Economica, 58*(229), 35–55.

Rogers, Thomas D. (2010). *The deepest wounds: A labor and environmental history of sugar in northeast Brazil*. Chapel Hill: University of North Carolina Press.

Rose, Fred. (2000). *Coalitions across the class divide: Lessons from the labor, peace, and environmental movements*. Ithaca, NY: Cornell University Press.

West, Paige. (2006). *Conservation is our government now: The politics of ecology in Papua New Guinea*. Durham, NC: Duke University Press.

Las Vegas, United States

2 million est. pop. 2010

The rapid growth of Las Vegas, Nevada, that began in the 1970s led to urban sprawl, air pollution, and water demand that have compromised the area's environmental and economic sustainability. With economic growth paused, opportunities have arisen to refocus on long-term sustainability, which will depend on expanding the area's economic base beyond its current focus on tourism.

The metropolitan area known as Las Vegas, Nevada, comprises five cities in the southwestern United States—Las Vegas, Henderson, North Las Vegas, Boulder City, and Mesquite—plus unincorporated land in Clark County. The urban area, with a total population of approximately 2 million people, is contained in a basin that measures about 4,200 square kilometers, is bounded by mountains that reach about 3,600 meters to the west, and drains east to the Colorado River at Lake Mead (Huntington 2010). The valley floor slopes from about 1,070 meters elevation at the western foothills to about 300 meters on the eastern edge. Its Mojave Desert climate is arid, with average annual precipitation of 10 centimeters and high temperatures that are often over 42°C in the summer. Sparse vegetation and intermittent desert washes characterize the desert landscape.

Like most cities worldwide, Las Vegas sustains its population by importing resources. No food is grown on a commercial scale within the city's boundaries, and few consumer goods are manufactured in the city. A quarter of Hoover Dam's hydroelectric power goes to the state of Nevada, but most of the region's energy comes from natural gas–based power plants. Casino-focused tourism dominates the region's economy. In 2010, with the lure of in-house gaming, the Las Vegas leisure and hospitality industry (includes gaming) attracted more than 37 million tourists (LVCVA 2010) and $16 billion of revenue, which accounted for about 19 percent of the local economy (US-BEA 2011). Growth and newness have been dominant themes throughout the city's development, with local culture celebrating new and contemporary artifacts and ideas and developers regularly imploding old buildings to make way for new ones. Although there is a budding movement to preserve the city's history, the general narrative of Las Vegas is forward looking rather than grounded in its past.

Until 2008, the future of Las Vegas seemed bright. The tourist economy was vibrant, the cost of living was low, and the job market provided lucrative opportunities for workers lacking advanced education or even a high school degree. There was plenty of money to import needed resources. The growth, together with the city's cultural emphasis on the new and fresh, attracted visitors and residents and created a mood of optimism about the future. Economic sustainability was based on maintaining an image of excitement and change.

The 2008 recession was a serious check to both the region's growth and the local concept of sustainability. Fewer visitors led to a decline in tourism-related jobs, which reduced demand for homes. Casino and housing construction all but stopped. Unemployment, which remained above 10 percent between January 2009 and 2012, peaked at 15.7 percent in July 2010 (US-BLS 2012). As residents abandoned Las Vegas for jobs elsewhere, the region experienced its first-ever decrease in population in 2008 (Clark County Nevada 2009). In January 2012 alone, owners of one in every 172 homes in Clark County filed for foreclosure, and between 2008 and 2012 Nevada had the highest rate of foreclosure of any US state (RealtyTrac 2012). Poor economic conditions, together with empty homes and neglected yards, began to tarnish the shine of the Las Vegas image.

Another obstacle to regional sustainability stems from residents' lack of a strong sense of community connection to Las Vegas. A recent survey of Las Vegas neighborhoods found that most residents moved to the Las Vegas Valley from another state or country (Futrell et al. 2010); only 8 percent reported they were born in Las Vegas; fewer than half (37 percent) reported feeling a strong sense of belonging to the city; and 40 percent of respondents reported they would leave Las Vegas if they could. The city's low ranking in a variety of social indicators affects how connected residents feel. High school graduation rates in Clark County were 44.3 percent in 2008 (National Center for Education Statistics 2011). Almost 20 percent of the population twenty-five years and older in Las Vegas lack a high school diploma, while only 7.5 percent of residents hold a graduate or professional degree (City of Las Vegas 2012). Only 37 percent of residents surveyed believe the quality of life will improve over the next decade (Futrell et al. 2010).

In the first few years of the twenty-first century, sustainability discussions focused on how to support the growth in population and the economy—specifically, how best to manage land development, traffic congestion and related air quality problems, and water demand. In the second decade of the twenty-first century, the focus of sustainability discussions has shifted from how to manage the environmental consequences and infrastructure of growth to how best to restore the region's economic and social vitality.

Historical Development

Development of the present-day metropolitan area began in the mid-1800s around artesian springs in the center of the valley. Travelers called the area Las Vegas, Spanish for "the meadows." Mormon missionaries were the first documented non–Native American settlers. By 1875 several ranches were established near the Las Vegas springs. A railway from Salt Lake City to Los Angeles crossed through Las Vegas, and it was officially declared a town in 1905.

Subsistence ranching and services for travelers formed the economic base of the community until the 1930s and 1940s, when a magnesium processing industry developed and Hoover Dam was built to create Lake Mead on the Colorado River. Population grew modestly in response to these industries, reaching 8,422 in 1940. After casino gambling was legalized in 1931 (City of Las Vegas 2012), population growth accelerated. By 1970 the Las Vegas metropolitan area had a population of nearly 275,000, more than one million by 1995, and 2 million by 2009 (Clark County Nevada 2012). The region had the fastest rate of population growth in the United States in the late 1990s and the early-twenty-first century—averaging 5.95 percent per year between 1995 and 2005. After a brief decline in 2008, the population began to grow again at approximately 1 percent per year.

Resource Management Issues

Urban sprawl, air quality, and water management are the region's major resource management and environmental issues. The rapid population growth since the 1970s led to residential development that pushed the boundaries of the city outward from the center. (See figure 1 below.) Although the metropolitan area is surrounded by public land managed by the US Bureau of Land Management (BLM), exchanges of land between the city and the BLM allowed the urban footprint to expand beyond a seemingly fixed boundary (Sonoran Institute 2010). In leapfrog fashion, developers established large-scale master-planned communities on large parcels of inexpensive land at the outskirts, leaving smaller, more central plots undeveloped. The most extreme example is Coyote Springs, a golf course–centered community more than 80 kilometers from the developed edges of the Las Vegas valley.

Growth of the urban area has led to air quality problems. During the housing construction boom, disturbance of large areas of sensitive desert soils generated significant coarse particulate matter (PM_{10}) in the air. The sprawling pattern of development plus the growing population increased the total vehicle miles traveled (VMT) in the valley and, with it, transportation-related air pollution. As the urban area grew, the area was listed

Figure 1. Urban Land Use Change in the Las Vegas Valley

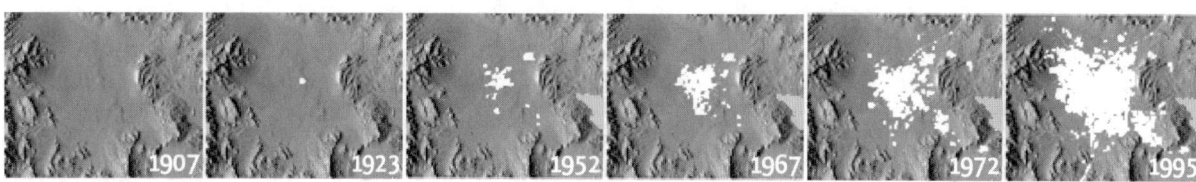

Source: Acevedo et al. (2003).

Urban expansion over an eighty-eight-year time frame, accelerating rapidly since the 1970s. (The dark area on the right-hand side of the four images to the right side of the series of pictures is the edge of Lake Mead, created after the Hoover Dam was built in the 1930s.)

as a nonattainment area (not attaining the National Ambient Air Quality Standards) for carbon monoxide (CO) and ozone (smog) in addition to PM_{10} (EPA 2010). Pollen problems from residential and commercial landscaping increased. The hot, dry climate exacerbates air pollution problems by keeping dust and allergens in the air and promoting smog formation. Urban development has contributed to temperatures warmer inside the city than in nearby rural areas due to the urban heat island (UHI) effect (City of Las Vegas 2010). This temperature rise led to an increased focus in building techniques to mitigate heat absorption and increase tree canopy cover to provide both cooling and air quality benefits. The recent foreclosure crisis and subsequent loss of residential landscaping has negatively contributed to the heat island issue.

Water supply comes primarily from the Colorado River at Lake Mead, which annual snowmelt from the Rocky Mountains supplies. Las Vegas receives an allocation of 300,000 acre-feet (370 million cubic meters) from the river, an amount set in the 1920s when population was low. In addition, however, the city receives return flow credit when water used and processed through the water treatment system is returned to the lake. Return flow credits increase the supply by approximately 200,000 acre-feet (246 million cubic meters) per year (SNWA 2012).

Extravagant fountains and other casino water features, as well as golf courses in the desert, leave visitors with the impression that these account for a large portion of the valley's water use. In fact, these sectors represent only about 14 percent of total water consumption. Residential users consume the greatest amount, accounting for 60 percent of the valley's water consumption (SNWA 2009). Two-thirds of that is used outdoors, mostly for residential landscaping, which often reflects ideas brought by people moving from less arid climates. The architecture of most homes reflects a Tuscan or Mediterranean design, despite the desert climate. Palm trees (a naturally tropical species) are common, and lush green lawns have been a staple of most yards. In the first decade of the twenty-first century, however, xeriscaping—landscaping specifically for dry climates—became more widely adopted and was actively supported by direct payments from the water district. Per capita residential water use in 2002 was 314 gallons per capita per day (GCPD), among the highest in the United States, but due in part to xeriscaping and other conservation methods, consumption has been reduced to 223 GCPD (SNWA 2012).

In the early years of the twenty-first century, the US Southwest has experienced a drought, which has diminished the amount of water flowing from the Colorado River. As a result, the level of Lake Mead has dropped by 30.5 meters since 2000 (LVVWD 2012). A third intake pipe is being constructed should levels drop below the current penstocks. Other water procurement plans include an approved pipeline from east-central Nevada to provide more than 80,000 acre-feet (98 million cubic meters) of water per year to southern Nevada. This project compromises relations between northern and southern areas of the state because of potential environmental harm associated with the construction of the pipeline and because reducing water resources in the north could constrain their future economic and population growth.

Sustainability Efforts

In the 1990s and the early-twenty-first century, when steady growth seemed likely to continue unchecked, several initiatives addressed land use, air quality, water supply, and other environmental concerns. The Clark County Department of Air Quality and Environmental Management successfully instituted measures to bring coarse particulate matter and carbon monoxide levels into attainment (acceptable levels) and developed plans for ozone management. Conservation programs of the Southern Nevada Water Authority reduced per capita water demand by 29 percent between 2002 and 2012.

The Southern Nevada Regional Planning Commission was formed, bringing together the cities of Las Vegas, North Las Vegas, Henderson, and Boulder City, as well as the Southern Nevada Water Authority, Transportation Commission, and Clark County Comprehensive Planning, to address growth management.

Following the economic crash of 2008, efforts were directed toward environmental and social needs along with economic redevelopment. A private-public partnership, Green Chips, formed to assist the business community in reducing their environmental impact while holding conferences to establish and implement best practices for a social, environmental, and economic stabilization (Green Chips 2012).

In 2010, one of the largest projects in the world to be certified environmentally friendly by Leadership in Energy and Environmental Design (LEED), City Center, was built in Las Vegas. It helped push Nevada to number one in square feet of LEED-certified buildings per capita (USGBC 2012). Many strip hotels, including the water feature at the Bellagio, use sophisticated graywater (nonindustrial, nonsewage wastewater) systems (Bellagio 2012). Low-flow fixtures are becoming more common in new residential design. Xeriscaping is now required for all new home construction, and rebates offered to owners of existing homes have helped reduce outdoor water consumption (SNWA 2012).

The region is trying to develop renewable energy technology. Because of the area's abundance of open space and sunny days, development of solar energy may lessen the region's dependence on fossil fuel–based energy and at the same time diversify the economy. A limiting factor is the vast extent of federally owned land where development for energy is discouraged by fragile ecosystems and protected status.

Outlook

Although the economy is now the focus of most sustainability discussions, efforts to save money through water and energy conservation will likely benefit environmental sustainability. Promoting development on vacant land in central areas (infill development) would alleviate pressures on infrastructure and reduce VMT. According to a growth model the Sonoran Institute developed, the city could accommodate as many as 500,000 more people within the current development boundary (Sonoran Institute 2010). Continued investment in green building practices could make the Las Vegas area a leader in water- and energy-efficient design.

Sustainability challenges remain. Public transportation use is low, partly because of a strong cultural preference for use of private cars, and partly because urban sprawl hampers the efficiency of public transportation. Uneven residential density and the separation of residential and commercial development have reinforced reliance on the automobile. Although renewable energy development has the potential to reduce environmental pollution and promote economic stabilization, concern remains about how solar panel arrays might affect local ecosystems. Finally, the effect of climate change on the region is highly uncertain but must be considered in sustainability discussions, as increasing temperatures quickly exacerbate water and air quality concerns.

Economic downturn has reduced some of the pressure on land use, infrastructure, and resources for growth. How the city responds to this opportunity to refocus from a growth-focused culture to a broader concept of development that considers other aspects of quality of life will play a large part in its long-term sustainability.

Krystyna STAVE and Abby BECK
University of Nevada, Las Vegas

See also Detroit, United States; Energy Efficiency; Lima, Peru; Mobility; New Orleans, United States; New York City, United States; Perth, Australia; Phoenix, United States; Public Transportation; United States; Urbanization; Water Use and Rights

Further Reading

Acevedo, William, et al. (2003). Urban land use change in the Las Vegas Valley. US Geological Survey. Retrieved February 6, 2012, from http://geochange.er.usgs.gov/sw/changes/anthropogenic/population/las_vegas/

Bellagio Hotel. (2012). Bellagio environmental commitment. Retrieved March 11, 2012, from http://www.bellagio.com/hotel/sustainability.aspx

City of Las Vegas, Nevada. (2009). Educational achievement based on 2005–2009 American Community Survey 5-year estimates. Retrieved March 11, 2012, from http://www.lasvegasnevada.gov/files/Educational_Attainment.pdf

City of Las Vegas, Nevada. (2010). Summary report: Urban heat island effect. Retrieved March 28, 2012, from http://www.lasvegasnevada.gov/files/UHI_Report_2010-2.pdf

City of Las Vegas, Nevada. (2012). History. Retrieved March 11, 2012, from http://lasvegasnevada.gov/FactsStatistics/history.htm

Clark County Nevada. (2009). Historic population and housing data. Retrieved February 6, 2012, from http://www.clarkcountynv.gov/depts/comprehensive_planning/demographics/pages/default.aspx

Clark County Nevada. (2012). Demographics. Retrieved February 6, 2012, from http://www.clarkcountynv.gov/depts/comprehensive_planning/demographics/pages/default.aspx

Futrell, Robert, et al. (2010). Las Vegas metropolitan area social survey. Las Vegas: University of Nevada.

Green Chips. (2012). Our mission and goals. Retrieved February 9, 2012, from http://greenchips.org/about-us/mission/

Huntington, Jena. (2010). Conceptual understanding and groundwater quality of the basin-fill aquifer in Las Vegas Valley, Nevada. In Susan Thiros, Laura Bexfield, David Anning & Jena Huntington (Eds.), *Conceptual understanding and groundwater quality of selected basin-fill aquifers in the southwestern United States*. Reston, VA:

USGS. Retrieved March 11, 2012, from http://pubs.usgs.gov/pp/1781/pdf/pp1781_section6.pdf

Las Vegas Convention and Visitors Authority (LVCVA). (2010). 2010 Vegas FAQs. Retrieved February 9, 2012, from http://www.lvcva.com/getfile/106/2010%20Vegas%20FAQs.pdf

Las Vegas Valley Water District (LVVWD). (2012). Drought and restrictions. Retrieved March 11, 2012, from http://www.lvvwd.com/conservation/drought.html

National Center for Education Statistics. (2011). *Public school graduates and dropouts from the common core of data: School year 2007–2008*. Retrieved February 21, 2012, from http://nces.ed.gov/pubsearch/pubsinfo.asp?pubid=2010341

NV Energy. (2012). Power facts. Retrieved February 9, 2012, from https://www.nvenergy.com/company/energytopics/where.cfm#southern

Pavelko, Michael T.; Wood, David B.; & Laczniak, Randell J. (1999). Las Vegas, Nevada: Gambling with water in the desert (US Geological Survey Circular 1182). Retrieved February 6, 2012, from http://pubs.usgs.gov/circ/circ1182/pdf/08LasVegas.pdf

RealtyTrac. (2012) National real estate trends. Retrieved March 11, 2012, from http://www.realtytrac.com/trendcenter/trend.html

Sonoran Institute. (2010). Growth and sustainability in the Las Vegas Valley. Tucson, AZ: Sonoran Institute.

Southern Nevada Water Authority (SNWA). (2009). Water resource plan 2009. Retrieved March 28, 2012, from http://www.snwa.com/assets/pdf/wr_plan.pdf

Southern Nevada Water Authority (SNWA). (2012). Conservation. Retrieved March 11, 2012, from http://www.snwa.com/consv/conservation.html

United States Department of Commerce Bureau of Economic Analysis (US-BEA). (2011). GDP by metropolitan area. Retrieved February 21, 2012, from http://www.bea.gov/iTable/iTable.cfm?ReqID=70&step=1

United States Department of Labor Bureau of Labor Statistics (US-BLS). (2012). Local area unemployment statistics. Retrieved March 11, 2012, from http://data.bls.gov/timeseries/LAUMT32298203?data_tool=XGtable

United States Environmental Protection Agency (EPA). (2012). Air actions, Nevada. Retrieved March 11, 2012, from http://www.epa.gov/region9/air/actions/nv.html

United States Green Building Council, Nevada Chapter (USGBC). (2012). LEED in Nevada. Retrieved February 6, 2012, from http://www.usgbcnv.org/leed-in-nevada

Share the *Encyclopedia of Sustainability*: Teachers are welcome to make up to ten (10) copies of no more than two (2) articles for distribution in a single course or program. For further permissions, please visit www.copyright.com or contact: info@berkshirepublishing.com

Lima, Peru

8.8 million est. pop. 2012

The city of Lima, capital of Peru and the fifth largest in Latin America, faces a variety of environmental problems linked to its explosive population growth, geographic characteristics, and the recent economic prosperity of portions of its population. Despite improvements in infrastructure and services, major problems in respect to air and water quality, transportation, urban planning, and waste management are still widespread.

The city of Lima, originally called "The City of Kings" by Spanish founder Francisco Pizarro in 1535, is the economic and political capital of Peru. Lima is located on the central coastal region of the country, at the shores of the Pacific Ocean. Its centrality, equidistant from the northern and southern borders with Ecuador and Chile, respectively, favors its international relations.

The city is adjacent to the constitutional province of Callao, both of which form the larger metropolitan area (281,165 hectares). Callao has the largest seaport in the country, which is the main hub for imports and exports. The metropolitan area accounts for approximately 50 percent of all the production of goods and services in the country.

Lima is the fifth most populous city in Latin America, with a population close to 8.8 million people, about one-third of Peru's population (US CIA 2012). Starting in the 1950s, the city, as has been the case in most large Latin American cities, has experienced a fast population growth, mostly originating from the rural areas. This migration, mostly due to economic constraints, has created a variety of social and economic problems. Additionally, the city faces overwhelming environmental challenges despite the infrastructure and economic improvements the city has experienced since the 1990s. A recent report ranked Lima, along with Guadalajara, well below average among seventeen main Latin American cities in a green city index that included indicators of air and water quality, energy use, waste disposal, and transportation, among others (*The Economist* 2010).

Urban Planning and Risks

The influx of migrant populations still represents a challenge to local authorities that struggle to provide them with basic services and infrastructure. Unlawful appropriation of land in the periphery of the city has created unsanitary and unsafe conditions for its inhabitants. This growing population, as well as the dry weather conditions of the city, has contributed to making Lima one of the Latin American cities with the least green coverage per habitant. The fast population growth has now brought the average to fewer than 3 square meters per habitant, far from the 8–9 square meters recommended by the World Health Organization. The lack of thoughtful urban planning under these conditions also contributes to the extreme levels of risk due to natural disasters and infectious diseases.

Lima is located in close proximity to major tectonic plates, making the city highly vulnerable to seismic activity. A major earthquake, such as the one that hit the city in 1746, would have considerable consequences to many areas of the city that are not prepared to support such events. These areas include the historic downtown, which has several buildings from the Spanish colonial era. The United Nations Educational, Scientific, and Cultural Organization (UNESCO) declared the historic center a World Heritage Site.

Lima, as well as most of the central and northern coastal areas of Peru, is affected by weather conditions associated with El Niño. This seasonal weather event creates the circumstances for the spread of bacterial diseases such as cholera and dengue. In 1991 and 1998, Lima, as well as other major Peruvian cities, experienced cholera epidemics that affected thousands of people, events that had not occurred in the previous hundred years (Goldman 2004).

Transportation and Air Pollution

The deregulation of the transportation sector in the 1990s created the conditions for the disordered public system that currently operates in the city. Multiple microbusinesses flooded the market with highly polluting vehicles that quickly exceeded the city's infrastructure capacity. In the early twenty-first century, the World Bank calculated that the inefficiencies in the system cost the city approximately $500 million in person-hours and operational costs (Gómez 2000). Some estimates place this figure as high as $1 billion, but reliable data are difficult to come by. Some projects and initiatives by the city and the national government have started to mend these problems, however.

In the mid-1980s, Peruvian president Alan García spearheaded the construction of an elevated railway line project (the electric train) that was intended to connect the city periphery, but the project was halted due to insufficient funds. More than twenty years passed before the project's first phase was finally completed during Garcia's second term (2006–2011). The first 22 kilometers that connect the poor southern suburb, Villa El Salvador, and the city's center became operative in 2011 (*The Economist* 2012).

In addition, the Municipality of Lima started the implementation of a bus rapid transit (BRT) system, following the successful examples of other South American cities such as Bogotá, Colombia, and Curitiba, Brazil. The BRT system, called El Metropolitano (The Metropolitan), is already operating its first main route (north-south), covering sixteen districts of the city. Additional routes are planned in the next decade.

The Municipality of Lima plans to integrate the BRT system with nonmotorized modes of transportation. In this respect, the city has started to make some progress in promoting the use of bicycles. This includes new bike path construction, which now total 120 kilometers, according to the Municipality of Lima. Several barriers, however, such as insufficient bike paths, bicycle theft, social stigma associated with the poor, and unsafe biking conditions due to a lack of a road-sharing culture, have prevented the popularization of this mode of transportation.

On the other hand, a booming economy has made it possible for many city residents to afford newer vehicles. According to the Ministry of Transportation and Communications, Lima and Callao had a total of 1.3 million vehicles in 2011, a considerable increase from the 855,000 vehicles existent in 2004 (MTC 2005). This increase has created heavy traffic congestion throughout the city, however, especially during the peak hours of the early morning and the evening.

In addition to the inefficiencies in the system, the transportation sector is also the main source of air pollution. The old units of public transportation are aged and polluting. Additionally, despite having a smaller population and a smaller automotive fleet than other large Latin American metropolises, such as Mexico City, São Paulo, and Santiago, Lima has higher levels of air pollution due to the high levels of sulfur in their diesel. Sulfur levels before the year 2010 were 5,000 parts per million (ppm), well above the 50 ppm or less of ultralow sulfur diesel used in many countries. Legislative and technological innovations are under way to address this problem, including the conversion of vehicles to natural gas and improvements in oil refining. The topography of the city also prevents the dispersion of such contaminants; especially particulate matter less than 10 micrometers in diameter. The city's northern and eastern areas are surrounded by rocky hills, which act as barriers for the winds blowing from the west. This pollution is responsible for acute respiratory diseases such as asthma, which were credited with more than 10 percent of all deaths in Lima and Callao in the year 2000 (Defensoría del Pueblo 2008).

Water Issues

The city of Lima receives very limited rainfall, with an average of 9 millimeters per year (*The Economist* 2010). The main water supply for the city is the Rimac River, which originates in the high Andes and drains into the Pacific Ocean. Mining and industrial operations continuously contaminate the headwaters of the Rimac River by disposing their effluents without major treatment. Additionally, the recurrent state of drought, the deforestation around the headwaters of the rivers, and the intensive use of water for industrial, mining, energy production, agriculture, and human consumption place a considerable amount of pressure on the hydric systems, affecting the quantity and quality of the resource. These problems are expected to become exacerbated in the context of global climate change, which is linked to the melting of tropical glaciers. The resultant decrease in water availability will affect the energy sector, which is mostly based in hydroelectric power.

Water treatment is uncommon in the city, with only 9 percent of its wastewater being treated (*The Economist* 2010). Only some districts, such as Santiago de Surco and San Borja, utilize biochemical processes to reuse the wastewater for the irrigation of public parks and other green spaces. The rest of the city disposes the wastewater without any treatment directly into the Pacific Ocean, in many cases close to recreational beaches and to the main rivers: Rimac, Chillon, and Lurin. In 2005, 15 percent of the beaches in the city's shoreline were classified as unsuitable for recreational use (UNEP et al. 2005).

Waste Disposal

According to the Peruvian Ministry of the Environment, the metropolitan area of Lima produces 30 percent of the daily amount of waste produced in Peru (7,605.57 tonnes per day) (Buendía 2008). Waste is disposed in five landfills around Lima and Callao. These landfills, however, do not have the capacity to manage all of the waste produced by the city residents and industries, and more than 20 percent is not recollected or properly disposed (Buendía 2008). Each of the forty-nine districts in the metropolitan area is responsible for its own waste disposal program. Poorer districts therefore suffer the most; waste is oftentimes disposed on the streets and not picked up for several days, incinerated in open fields, directly deposited into bodies of water, or informally recycled.

Recycling is not a mandatory or common practice in the city. There is a lack of recycling programs among the districts, with no adequate infrastructure to process recyclable material. Only a few districts, such as Santiago de Surco, have conducted experimental recycling programs geared toward its residents. Some businesses and industries promote recycling practices within their facilities, but these are few and not significant in terms of volume. Waste pickers conduct most of the informal recycling in the city, and efforts are under way to organize and formalize these individuals.

Outlook

Environmental governance at the city level in Lima is fragmented and inadequate. Most of the responsibilities and technical capacity have been left in the hands of the newly created Ministry of the Environment. This includes the promotion of eco-efficient measures among polluting industries. Despite some significant efforts to alleviate the most noticeable environmental issues, such as air pollution associated with the transportation sector, many issues still require attention. The booming economy represents a challenge to the city because of the growing population, as well as its associated services and increasing levels of consumption. It also represents an opportunity for thoughtful planning that could take Lima into a sustainable future.

Bruno TAKAHASHI

Michigan State University

See also Amazonia; Andes Mountains; Bogotá, Colombia; Brazil; Curitiba, Brazil; Las Vegas, United States; Mining (Andes); Mobility; Perth, Australia; Phoenix, United States; Public Transportation; Rio de Janeiro, Brazil; Sanitation; Social Movements (Latin America); Urbanization; Water Use and Rights

FURTHER READING

Andean Airmail & Peruvian Times. (2009, February 18). World Bank approves $330 million loan to help Peru mitigate climate change. Retrieved May 16, 2012, from http://www.peruviantimes.com/18/world-bank-approves-330-million-loan-to-help-peru-mitigate-climate-change/1730/

Buendía, José M. (2008). Informe de la situación actual de la gestión de residos sólidos municipales [Report of the current status of the management of municipal solid waste]. Retrieved May 15, 2012, from http://sinia.minam.gob.pe/admDocumento.php?accion=bajar&docadjunto=337

Defensoria del Pueblo [The Office of the People's Advocate]. (2008). La calidad del aire en Lima y su impacto en la salud y la vida de sus habitantes: Seguimiento de las recomendaciones defensoriales [Air quality in Lima and its impact on the health and lives of its inhabitants: Compliance with the recommendations of Defensoria]. Retrieved May 15, 2012, from http://www.defensoria.gob.pe/modules/Downloads/informes/defensoriales/informe_136.pdf

The Economist. (2010). Latin American green city index: Assessing the environmental performance of Latin America's major cities. Retrieved May 14, 2012, from http://www.siemens.com/entry/cc/features/greencityindex_international/all/en/pdf/report_latam_en.pdf

The Economist. (2012). Lima's metro: The train leaves platform one at last. Retrieved May 15, 2012, from http://www.economist.com/node/21542801

Goldman, Erica. (2004). Forecasting cholera outbreaks. Retrieved May 15, 2012, from http://news.sciencemag.org/sciencenow/2004/02/17-01.html

Gómez, Lara M. (2000). Gender analysis of two components of the World Bank transport projects in Lima, Peru: Bikepaths and busways. Retrieved May 14, 2012, from http://siteresources.worldbank.org/INTGENDERTRANSPORT/Resources/handout.pdf

Ministerio del Ambiente (MINAM) [Ministry of the Environment]. (2011). Más empresas son reconocidas con premio a la ecoeficiencia empresarial, impulsado por el MINAM y la UCSUR. [More companies are recognized with award for corporate eco-efficiency, driven by MINAM and UCSUR]. Retrieved May 15, 2012, from http://www.minam.gob.pe/index.php?option=com_content&view=article&id=1413:mas-empresas-son-reconocidas-con-premio-a-la-ecoeficiencia-empresarial-impulsado-por-el-minam-y-la-ucsur&catid=1:noticias&Itemid=21

Ministerio de Transportes y Comunicaciones (MTC) [Ministry of Transportation and Communication]. (2012). Estadísica: Transporte carretero. [Statistics: Road transportation]. Retrieved May 15, 2012, from http://www.mtc.gob.pe/estadisticas/index.html

United Nations Educational, Scientific and Cultural Organization (UNESCO). (2012). Historic centre of Lima. Retrieved May 15, 2012, from http://whc.unesco.org/en/list/500

United Nations Environment Program (UNEP); el Grupo de Emprendimientos Ambientales (Grupo GEA) [Environmental Enterprise Group]; Municipalidad Metropolitana de Lima [Metropolitan Municipality of Lima]; & Municipalidad Constitucional del Callao [Municipality of Callao]. (2005). *GEO Lima y Callao: Perspectivas del medio ambiente urbano.* [GEO Lima and Callao: Perspectives of the urban environment]. Retrieved May 15, 2012, from http://sinia.minam.gob.pe/index.php?accion=verElemento&idElementoInformacion=87&verPor=&idTipoElemento=8&idTipoFuente=&idfuenteinformacion=94

United States Central Intelligence Agency (US CIA). (2012). The world factbook: Peru. Retrieved June 8, 2012, from https://www.cia.gov/library/publications/the-world-factbook/geos/pe.html

United States Geological Survey (USGS). (2011). Earthquakes of Peru. Retrieved May 15, 2012, from http://earthquake.usgs.gov/earthquakes/world/peru/history.php

Mackenzie River

The Mackenzie River basin drains one-fifth of Canada's landmass, northward to the Arctic Ocean. The basin's environmental concerns include activities such as mining, forestry, natural gas and oil extraction, and plans for a gas pipeline. As federal, territorial, and aboriginal governments address policy development and resource management, the effects of global climate change are of special concern in this northern climatic region.

The Mackenzie River, known to Canada's aboriginal Dene people as Deh Cho and to the Inuvialuit people as Kookpaic, is North America's second-longest river system, flowing northward 4,266 kilometers from its farthest source, the headwaters of the Finlay River in British Columbia, to the Beaufort Sea. The river basin drains 1.8 million square kilometers, or 22 percent of Canada's landmass. The Mackenzie proper, below Great Slave Lake, about 1,800 kilometers long, is named for Alexander Mackenzie (1763–1820), the fur trader who in 1789 became the first European to descend to the river's Arctic Ocean delta. Long at the periphery of settler society in North America, the Mackenzie basin since the mid-twentieth century has seen expanding industrial exploitation of resources, including mining, forestry, and energy developments. This activity has generated both profit and controversy and has made the Mackenzie an important battleground for debates about sustainability in the Canadian north.

Much of the Mackenzie system traverses a subarctic region notable for long, cold winters, discontinuous permafrost, and low precipitation falling mainly as snow. As a result, spring breakup of ice and snowmelt flooding are the major hydrological events shaping the river and its immediate surroundings. The basin includes three very large lakes (Athabasca, Great Slave, and Great Bear) as well as three major deltas (the Peace and Athabasca rivers, Slave River, and the Mackenzie). A region of overall low biological productivity and species diversity, the lower Mackenzie River valley consists largely of muskeg soil with stunted spruce and fir trees; its glacial soils and short growing season make the area unsuited to agriculture. The Mackenzie delta region nevertheless supports the northernmost groves of coniferous trees in North America at about 70° north latitude. The massive delta is a maze of alluvial islands, lakes, and back channels, and the estuary is an important habitat for beluga whale. The system's large lakes contain up to two dozen species of freshwater fish and have variously supported subsistence, commercial, and recreational fisheries for whitefish, lake trout, inconnu, and arctic grayling, among others.

Aboriginal peoples of the Mackenzie region generally consider their occupancy of these lands to date from "time immemorial" or the "time of the Creator." Modern archaeologists consider aboriginal occupancy of the delta to begin about 2500–2000 BCE; the original Paleo-Eskimo and Dorset (designations for the prehistoric peoples occupying the region before 1000 BCE) cultures were replaced after 1000 CE by eastward-migrating Thule whaling people, forebears of the contemporary Inuit. The Mackenzie valley was probably occupied earlier by northward-migrating Paleo-Indians following the most recent glaciation. Precontact Inuit were highly mobile, marine-oriented people adapted to the harsh Arctic environment, whereas Athapaskan (a linguistic designation referring to a number of northern aboriginal groups, including those of the Mackenzie valley, speaking similar languages) speakers mainly hunted the Mackenzie basin's large terrestrial mammals.

Sustained contact between the region's first peoples and Europeans began with the extension of the fur trade from Hudson Bay and accompanying explorations by Europeans, such as those of Mackenzie and Samuel

Hearne, the English naturalist and author, in the late 1700s. Native peoples trapped muskrat, beaver, and arctic fox for furs and provisioned forts with "country food" in return for manufactured goods. This trade dominated the region's economy and society until World War II. Hunting and trapping remain significant subsistence and cultural activities for aboriginal people. A rapacious whaling industry arose in the Mackenzie delta in the 1880s, severely disrupting Inuit society and quickly depleting whale stocks. Today the Mackenzie region remains sparsely settled, its northern sections comprised of remote, mostly aboriginal settlements and southern portions dominated by a few larger centers such as Yellowknife (the territorial capital), the Northwest Territories, and Fort McMurray, Alberta.

Environmental Challenges

Since the late nineteenth century, the Mackenzie region has occupied a contradictory place in the Canadian environmental imagination, signifying both vast, unspoiled wilderness and a nation-building industrial resource frontier. Industrial development began with an oil discovery at Fort Norman in the 1920s. It intensified during and after World War II, driven both by US security operations (especially the Distant Early Warning Line) across northern Canada and growing markets for minerals and oil. Major postwar developments in the basin included radium and uranium mining on Great Bear Lake, uranium mining on the north shore of Lake Athabasca, and several gold mines in the area of Yellowknife. For these early developments the river system served as the major transportation artery for industrial freight during the busy summer shipping season, although aviation and eventually a railway northward from Alberta became increasingly important links. In the lower basin, forestry operations and a major hydroelectric dam on the Peace River in British Columbia in the 1960s significantly altered hydrological regimes and migratory bird habitat in the Peace-Athabasca delta, one of the world's largest freshwater deltas.

The often negative social and environmental changes that resulted from industrial development went largely unexamined until the Mackenzie Valley Pipeline Inquiry in 1975–1976. Public hearings on a plan to pipe gas from arctic fields southward along the valley gave voice to local concerns and stimulated opposition among southern Canadians. Justice Thomas Berger's inquiry report, which recommended the pipeline's delay, was a watershed in Canadian aboriginal and environmental issues. The most significant result, besides a moratorium on the project, was the launch of modern aboriginal land claims processes that have since begun to transform environmental management in the region through the inclusion and empowerment of aboriginal governments. A shorter crude oil pipeline was built, however, from Norman Wells to Northern Alberta in the 1980s.

Contemporary environmental sustainability concerns in the Mackenzie region surround water quality and the revived Mackenzie valley pipeline proposal. The Canadian government, three provinces, and two northern territories signed a water management compact in 1997 to create the Mackenzie River Basin Board. It aimed to establish integrated watershed management based on principles of sustainable development and ecological integrity. In practice, however, detailed water stewardship and monitoring plans have remained elusive, and major industrial developments—including water withdrawals and pollution from oil sands development in Alberta and the proposed expansion of hydroelectric generation on the Peace River in British Columbia— threaten the downstream water supply in the Northwest Territories. The territorial government produced a water stewardship strategy that declared all water flowing into, within, and through the territory should remain "substantially unaltered in quality, quantity, and rates of flow," but this declaration lacks enforceability (GNWT 2010).

In the twenty-first century, the revival of plans to transport natural gas extracted from under the Beaufort Sea to southern markets via a pipeline along the Mackenzie River renewed concerns about the environmental and social impacts of megaproject development. In 2004 federal, territorial, and aboriginal governments launched a joint review panel to study the C$16.2 billion project. Significantly, in its review the panel focused on the cumulative impacts of industrial developments along the pipeline corridor and adopted an explicit principle of "contribution to sustainability" in its evaluation of the project (Gibson 2011). The panel's 2009 report, *Foundation for a Sustainable Northern Future*, approved the project, subject to a series of recommendations aimed at achieving long-term economic and environmental sustainability while monitoring and avoiding cumulative environmental impacts and social equity impacts. In response, both federal and territorial governments rejected or revised many of these recommendations; in any case, the project's medium-term feasibility is doubtful due to low prices in the North American natural gas market, and it remains on hold despite regulatory approvals.

Outlook

The development changes and challenges facing the Mackenzie region are magnified by those related to climate variability and change. Evidence from previous warming periods and models of future climate change indicate that northern latitudes will experience especially strong warming through the twenty-first century (Barry and Sereze 2012). Such changes are likely to have complex effects on vegetation, animal resources, hydrology, lake, river, and sea ice conditions, sea levels, and permafrost regimes along the Mackenzie River system. Considerable research activity is under way to assess possibilities of community vulnerability and adaptation to climate variability and change in the river basin, ranging from challenges to infrastructure (such as roads and other transportation facilities) to the impacts of change on traditional livelihoods and diets.

Arn KEELING
Memorial University of Newfoundland

See also Canada; Columbia River; Great Lakes and Saint Lawrence River; Marine Ecosystems Health; Mining (Andes); Mining (Australia); Mississippi and Missouri Rivers; Murray-Darling River Basin; Northwest Passage; Rocky Mountains

Further Reading

Barry, Roger, & Sereze, Mark. (2012). The changing climates. In Hugh French & Olav Slaymaker (Eds.), *Changing cold environments: A Canadian perspective*. Oxford, UK: Wiley Blackwell.

Berger, Thomas R. (1988). *Northern frontier, northern homeland: The report of the Mackenzie Valley Pipeline Inquiry* (Rev. ed.). Vancouver, Canada: Douglas and McIntyre.

Bone, R. M. (2009). *The geography of the Canadian North: Issues and challenges* (3rd ed.). Toronto: Oxford University Press.

Cohen, Stewart J. (Ed.). (1997). *Mackenzie Basin Impact Study (MBIS) final report*. Downsview, Canada: Environment Canada Atmospheric Environment Service.

Gibson, Robert. (2011). Application of a contribution to sustainability test by the Joint Review Panel for the Canadian Mackenzie Gas Project. *Impact assessment and project appraisal, 29*(3), 231–244.

Government of the Northwest Territories (GNWT). (2010). *Northern voices, northern waters: The NWT water stewardship strategy*. Yellowknife, Canada: GNWT.

Mackenzie River Basin Board (MRBB). (n.d.). Homepage. Retrieved March 27, 2012, from http://www.mrbb.ca

Piper, Liza. (2009). *The industrial transformation of subarctic Canada*. Vancouver, Canada: UBC Press.

Sabin, Paul. (1995). Voices from the hydrocarbon frontier: Canada's Mackenzie Valley Pipeline Inquiry (1974–1977). *Environmental History Review, 19*(1), 17–48.

Wynn, Graeme. (2007). *Canada and Arctic North America: An environmental history*. Santa Barbara, CA: ABC-Clio.

Berkshire's authors and editors welcome questions, comments, and corrections. Send your emails about the *Berkshire Encyclopedia of Sustainability* in general or this volume in particular to: sustainability.updates@berkshirepublishing.com

Marine Ecosystems Health

Major disturbances affecting ecosystem health in Oceania and in the twenty-four large marine ecosystems (LMEs) in the Americas include shifting food-chain associations, loss of habitat, pollution impact, diseases, harmful algal blooms, climate extremes, invasive species, and overfishing. By measuring the changing baseline condition of impact-sensitive indicator species, resource managers can assemble disturbance regimes to better compare, mitigate, and track changes in marine ecosystem health.

In a perfectly sustainable world, ecosystems are resilient, changes are anticipated, and co-evolved plants, wildlife, and human interdependent systems rapidly adapt to short-term anomaly events. Conversely, when marine ecosystems lose their self-regulatory functions, can no longer recycle nutrients to sustain anticipated production, become brittle in the face of disturbance and susceptible to dramatic shifts in biotic community structure from dominance by relatively large, long-lived native species to dominance by smaller short-lived exotics, then resource managers consider marine ecosystem health impaired.

Unprecedented and widespread structural and functional changes observed by scientists in the 1980s motivated teams of epidemiologists, resource economists, and climate and marine scientists to reassemble information by-products of a century's worth of fragmented time-series studies to establish marine health baselines. The following methods and health outcome examples come from within the twenty-four large marine ecosystems (LMEs) of the Americas and an area called the Warm Pool region (Oceania) within the western and southern Pacific.

Predicting Disturbance Impacts

Disturbance surveillance and observation networks began to systematically document oil spills from the late 1960s and early 1970s, harmful algal blooms (HABs) from the mid-1970s, coral system collapses from multiple marine ecological disturbances (MMEDs) from the 1980s, and beach closures and human illness in the 1990s.

Syntheses of these disturbance studies successfully documented the rise of morbidity, mortality, and disease disturbance events along the eastern coast of North America, in the Gulf of Mexico, and in the Caribbean Sea. Scientists found unexpected correlations among HAB events, shellfish mortality, shellfish toxicity, human gastroenteritis, respiratory distress among water workers and the beach-going public, and hospital visits by those who had eaten fish. They found El Niño–Southern Oscillation (warming of the Pacific Ocean) indices statistically linked with coral bleaching events and fish range extensions as well as sea grass and invertebrate declines associated with green crab invasions. Brown tide events became associated with sea grass decline, coincident not only with shading and anoxia (an absence of oxygen), but also the spread of disease. Documenting connections can be slow, as professional resource scientists lack systematic surveys and literature syntheses throughout the Pacific and South American LMEs. Journalists, nongovernmental organizations, beach stranding networks, epidemiologists, and the concerned public have since mobilized to observe and report on disturbances, bridging official information gaps. Motivated by the consequences from disturbance events, they volunteer effort hoping that predictions and forecasts will improve.

Methodologies

The occurrence of multiple marine ecological disturbances has emerged as a useful organizing principle for marine health studies. Numerous anomaly events co-occurring in specific places signify an ecosystem under stress, trending in unhealthy directions. Fewer co-occurring anomalies speak better of a system's resilience to stress. The public perceives dramatic isolated cases of human illness and multispecies mortalities involving charismatic organisms as, by analogy, a "coal miner's canary" for ocean health. Disturbance frequency and duration alter public perceptions and influence management policy and action.

Most science-based marine time-series studies are short-lived and more often produce research publications rather than sustained data streams and ecosystem assessment reports. In the late twentieth century, rigor borrowed from systems, landscape, and forest ecology together with information science disciplines has guided researchers to reorganize data from the scattered published sources along spatial/temporal scales to form new data products. Geologic and climate scientists use metadata (pooled data regarding other data) by proxy techniques to help researchers fill gaps in derived time-series, substituting one indicator for another iteratively, until a disturbance regime statistically forms. Benefitting from this new kind of data archeology, for each place-specific regime scientists can now select the best representative indicators of impact from disturbance observations. Candidate sentinel species (representative species that reflect changes in marine health) can, in turn, forewarn ecologists of impending ecosystem change. Researchers have also employed numerical simulation models with complicated names such as "unsupervised expert 'chunking' algorithms" and "black-box semantic neural network models" to find statistically coherent (predictable) associations between impacts and phenomena. The newer metadata techniques complement long-term marine indicator data surveys such as the international mussel watch, beach surveys, annual shorebird counts, buoy networks, and continuous observations from satellites and ship logs.

Borrowing again from climate and geological science techniques, marine epidemiologists and resource economists are now able to pool data on organism morbidity and mortality events, hospital records, favored fisheries economic data, and climate correlates, allowing more flexible associations among observational data sources never before combined. Rather than leave large spatial regions uncharacterized due to insufficient scientific study, information scientists have also factored anecdotal and mass-media observations of disturbance into MMED assessments (being careful to classify source quality).

From Indices to Trajectories

Resource managers require indices common among all the marine ecosystems they wish to compare. There are eight MMED disturbance indices associated with LME pollution and ecosystem health studies. Index values come from enumeration of anomaly events comprised of thousands of similarly co-occurring impacts. Some occurrences represent (1) acute *biotoxin/exposure* events occurring within a short time span; others are protracted, taking time to evolve, such as (2) *anoxic/hypoxic* (oxygen depletion) events. (3) *Chronic conditions involving keystone species* (species whose presence or absence is crucial within their ecosystem) are the longest to manifest. Other indices describe (4) *trophic magnifications,* where toxins pass through food chains. (5) *Climate forcing factor disturbances* can also alter and drive ecosystem dynamics particularly in extreme circumstances. In response to location stress, (6) anomalous widespread species' *mass mortalities* can signal structural changes to come. (7) *New, novel, or invasive* disturbances capture the first occurrence (beachhead) of a new event type or colonization within a geographic area. (8) *Disease* disturbances account for widespread morbidity and mortality and are associated with pathogen translocation. These eight generic disturbance types complement other indicators, human illness, and fishery and beach closures that individual nations, nongovernmental organizations, small island developing states, and local jurisdictions track to characterize marine health.

The vigor, organization, and resilience of an ecosystem can be expressed using six characteristics: constancy, inertia, elasticity, amplitude, stability, and porosity. *Constancy* is a measure of occurrence frequency. *Inertia* represents resistance to state changes. *Elasticity* represents the speed of an ecosystem's recovery. *Amplitude* is the amount of deviation from a baseline. *Stability* is an ecosystem's resilience to perturbation. *Porosity* is a flow rate of material and energy through a system or the ecosystem's susceptibility to invasion. Ecologists use these six characteristics to determine vulnerability to disturbance using available sentinels. Scientists' concept and perception of changing ecosystem health baselines throughout the Americas and Oceania are built from the following indexed observations.

Biotoxin/Exposure Events

Biotoxin disturbances include algal blooms, cyanobacteria, or diatom blooms that kill fish, invertebrates, and mammals and directly cause human illness. Exposure disturbances include mortality of seabirds, lesions on fish, or toxicity due to bloom by-products such as domoic acid, which causes human eye irritation, memory loss, or neurological damage, and respiratory and skin irritation in humans and wildlife. Toxic dinoflagellates are responsible for a majority of major marine mortalities of fish and birds from blooms. Less frequent toxic diatom blooms (e.g., *Pseudo-nitzschia*) are of concern to ecologists, not only because of direct impacts upon migratory waterfowl populations but also because they cause severe, debilitating illnesses in humans from casual exposure (e.g., *Pfiesteria piscicida*). Cyanobacteria blooms have been implicated in marine mammal mortality and associated with Florida Bay sponge mortality and recruitment failure (young organisms' failure to survive and join the adult population) of spiny lobsters. Red tides, which result from algal blooms, result in widespread mortalities of near-coastal populations of fish, shellfish, and crustaceans. Along the Pacific Rim since the 1980s exposure mortalities of shellfish and finfish species supporting mariculture (culturing of marine organisms in their natural environment) have occurred with greater frequency.

Humans are part of marine ecosystems, too. Exposure events include gastroenteritis, hepatitis, cholera, swimmer's itch, cellulitis, conjunctivitis, otitis externa, seabather's eruption, and jellyfish stings. Though biotoxin- and exposure-related impacts are statistically short-lived, if blooms and exposures persist and expand they may cause longer-term changes in ecosystem structure and use. Beach closures and negative publicity in tourist and fishing economies from exposure events has calculable financial impact.

Biotoxin and exposure impacts occur with greater constancy once an ecosystem has become porous enough to allow a large diversity of potential toxic and noxious seed species to enter and establish themselves.

Anoxia/Hypoxia Events

Frequent blooms of nontoxic microalgae and nuisance macroalgae are harmful because they dramatically reduce sunlight penetration into the water. Large and long blooms can also draw a substantial amount of oxygen from the bottom water at night during respiration. When spent cells decompose, microorganisms remove even more oxygen, creating hypoxia. Prolonged anoxic and hypoxic conditions give sulfur-reducing bacteria a foothold, which accelerates mortality among bottom-dwelling organisms. Subsequent fish and invertebrate death provides more substrate for this decomposition disturbance regime, resulting in dead zones.

The northern Gulf of Mexico's permanent dead zone has steadily grown in size since 1985, contributing to declining fisheries. In the Gulf of Alaska, plankton blooms leading to oxygen depletion impact king crab fisheries. Anoxia from persistent lower nutrient "brown tide" picoplankton (unusually small plankton) blooms makes it harder for filter feeders to sustain their energy requirements per square meter of effort. Recurrent and persistent brown tides within the Peconic Bay of Long Island (United States), for example, devastated oyster fisheries in the 1990s because the tides reduced the sea grass structural habitats, starving them for light. Chronic nutrient overenrichment from runoff and sewers further impairs elasticity following anoxic events.

Trophic Magnification Events

A trophic disturbance is one attributed to interspecies food-web relationships. Species impact increases geometrically as concentrations of toxins pass from one organism to another. Apex (top) predators become sick from the consumption of food stock harboring assimilated toxins. Heavy metals, persistent organic pollution (POP) including 1,1-Dichloro-2,2-bis(p-chlorophenyl) ethylene/dichlorodiphenyltrichloroethane (DDE/DDT), methyl mercury, polychlorinated biphenyls (PCBs), and other biomagnifying (increasing in concentration up the food chain) toxins are an indirect result of near shore water pollution. Naturally occurring biomagnifiers include microalgae biotoxins bioaccumulated (taken in faster than they can be removed) in the tissues of filter-feeding shellfish and fish ingested by larger vertebrate species.

In 1987 domoic acid from a diatom bloom caused amnesic shellfish poisoning (ASP) in humans consuming Scotian Shelf mussels. Short-term and permanent amnesia and even deaths resulted from acute toxicity. Once scientists identified and observed the human etiology in seabirds, they recorded similar events in California, Mexico, and New Zealand.

In the US Northeast Shelf LME, *Alexandrium spp.* causes paralytic shellfish poisoning (PSP) events primarily impacting seabirds, marine mammals, and shellfish themselves. PSP is caused by *Gymnodinium breve* in the Gulf of Mexico and periodically causes toxicity along the Southeastern US Continental Shelf Ecosystem. *Gymnodinium catenatum* is associated with PSP in the Caribbean Sea, Pacific Central American Coastal LME, and off the New Zealand Shelf LME. The dinoflagellate *Pyrodinium* has caused PSP in the Flores Sea (Indonesia), the Philippines, and the Coral (Australia) and Bismarck (Papua New Guinea) seas.

Neurotoxic shellfish poisoning (NSP) affects humans who have consumed shellfish contaminated by *Gymnodinium* dinoflagellates. Brevetoxins impact Florida manatees and seabirds throughout the Gulf of Mexico. This toxin is beginning to take hold within the Southeastern Continental Shelf LME. In the Caribbean Sea LME, bottom blooms of *Gambierdiscus*, *Prorocentrum*, *Ostreopsis*, and *Coolia sp.* are associated with ciguatoxic fish poisoning (CFP). CFP passes from algae to grazers and eventually to large piscivores (fish eaters) within an ecosystem. Tourists have higher body burdens of CFP because of their preferential consumption of larger barracuda and grouper.

Zooplankton and phytoplankton serve as reservoirs for bacteria such as *Vibrio cholerae*. Studies in the Gulf of Mexico, Caribbean Sea, and Humboldt Current LMEs suggest a viable trophodynamic transport mechanism for cholera to humans. Norwalk-type viral diseases, *E. coli*, and shigellosis, all of which can be passed through the food chain, readily spread from one ecosystem to another. In aquaculture areas, antibiotics and nutrient rich feces allow microbes living in biofilms (layers of microorganisms on surfaces) to become more resistant (e.g., salmonella-rich biofilms become more, not less effective vectors for disease) over time.

Mass Mortality Events

Fish are the best-monitored of those species apt to succumb to mass mortality. Anchoveta, herring, mullet, and other reef fish within the Caribbean have inexplicably died in large numbers at separate times. Catfish within the Gulf of Mexico and along the Northeastern Brazilian Shelf Ecosystem have also unexpectedly died in large numbers. Mass mortality disturbances include groups of reports clustered in space or time involving a single-species or multiple-species mortality that scientists have not yet attributed to a particular cause. In retrospect, researchers have found anoxia and HABs as causative agents. Anomalous massive and widespread mortalities indicate brittleness within a system, and die-offs of multiple species at the same time signal state changes in ecosystem health.

A significant and widespread black sea urchin (*Diadema antillarum*) mortality occurred throughout the Caribbean during the 1983 El Niño year. Coincident with the urchin die-off, many Jamaican reef species also collapsed. Sediment and nutrient runoff had already inundated the reefs. Reef fish cleaners depopulated from overfishing could not clear detritus of the newly bleached reefs. A disease controlling overcrowded urchin populations (also reef cleaners) worked in concert to permanently degrade the health of this habitat. Scientists have also observed overlapping disturbance regimes in Canadian green urchin and Pacific kelp populations. Although climate and/or disease etiologies are involved, the driver of system change is the mass mortality event itself. In Jamaica, macroalgal mats now smother the old dead reefs, and populations of all species, particularly fish, remain depressed following just a few massive mortality events.

Marine mammal strandings along beaches in Peru, Chile, the Caribbean, the Gulf of Mexico, Atlantic and Pacific US coastlines, and throughout Oceania have steadily increased since 1970. Due to heightened public awareness, perception of marine health is often linked to beaching events of these charismatic and often threatened species.

Physical Forcing Events

Physical forcing events can refer to the frequency and sometimes the severity of extreme weather events involving extraordinary chemical and physical changes to the properties of water. Recurring seasonal weather patterns (like those associated with the El Niño Southern Oscillation), sudden changes in nutrient or acid concentrations, or circumstances which put more or less freshwater into marine systems are also physically forced events. Dramatic air and sea temperature spikes shift the gradients for species survivability, pushing species outside their tolerance zones and inducing stressors that impact survival. With shifts in seasonality (e.g., earlier springtime) associated with regional climate change, storms and cold-snaps can quickly destabilize species' community structures, which have co-evolved over the years. Populations and communities of organisms adapted to specific tolerance ranges are often ill-prepared for physical extremes. Coral bleaching is the most reported physically forced event type. Scientists have observed this bleaching throughout the Caribbean Sea, the entire Pacific Rim, and the Pacific Central-American

Coastal LME. In particular, reefs have bleached in Ecuador, Costa Rica, Colombia, Chile, Mexico, the Florida Keys, the Bahamas, Bermuda, New Caledonia, Australia, Papua New Guinea, the Philippines, American Samoa, Tokelau, and the Cook, Fiji, Marshall, Society, Tonga and Tuamotu, Palau, Solomon, Vanuatu, and the Turks and Caicos islands. Bleaching occurs when sea surface temperatures exceed 29° C for extended time periods, causing the expulsion of coral polyps.

Extreme climate events in the late twentieth and early twenty-first centuries associated with El Niño cycles have been linked to many unprecedented disturbances. Scientists have used indicator species to better calibrate climate models. Reproductive failure in Oceania's Kiritimati Island seabird populations long precedes dramatic changes to the Humboldt Current LME's Peruvian anchoveta and sardine/mackerel upwelling fishery. The economic impact from the rise and decline of Peruvian anchovy fisheries is well documented. Here, the El Niño–Southern Oscillation disturbance regime is teleconnected (statistically crossing thousands of kilometers) to give Humboldt fisheries managers a chance to pre-adapt, should they heed the early warning. Less predictable have been dramatic cold-stunning events and storm anomalies (sudden pulses of fresh water) that also impact species indicators, particularly marine mammals in proximity to shore and turtles globally burdened with fibroid papilloma virus.

Disease Events

Pathogen pollution refers to the spread of disease throughout an ecosystem from adjacent or faraway sources. The frequency and extent of disease impact has increased since the 1980s. Marine mammal deaths involving agents such as phocine distemper, morbillivirus, and influenza viruses are becoming more common as inter- and intraspecies exchanges increase due to shrinking habitat. The 1997–1998 El Niño–Southern Oscillation event altered food distribution patterns, while severe weather enhanced transmission vulnerability for both crowded mammal and seabird populations. Organisms already stressed provide the perfect hosts for opportunist pathogens.

Epizootic (affecting many animals of the same kind) spread of coral disease underscores the recent increased prevalence theory. Coral white-band, black-band, red-band, and yellow-band / blotch diseases are now found throughout the Caribbean, where they did not previously exist. Sea fan *aspergillus* disease in Colombia, Costa Rica, Panama, Trinidad, and Tobago and ridge mortality disease observed in Mexico continue to spread. Scientists now observe a spreading rapid wasting disease in the Netherlands Antilles and coral neoplasia in Australian waters.

Bivalve and shrimp diseases have also rapidly spread. Taura syndrome, for instance, moved from a single shrimp farm in Ecuador to sites throughout the Americas, likely spread by shrimp-eating birds. The Indo-Pacific hypodermal and hematopoietic necrosis virus regularly causes catastrophic epidemics within aquaculture areas, and both wild and raised shrimp are susceptible. It is not a coincidence that incidences of disease occur in highly polluted areas. The fish disease lymphocystis, as an example, appears to become problematic when heavy rains flush toxic chemicals into fisheries areas.

Novel and Invasive Events

New or novel occurrences are disturbances appearing for the first time in either a species or within an area. Scientists may also include in this classification the first recorded instance of a species invasion, significant change in seasonality or novel distributions (range extensions), or extraordinary new vulnerability of susceptible populations.

Some of the most effective conveyors of bioinvaders from one ecosystem to another are the ballast water of large ships or the results from deliberate fisheries, mariculture, and aquarium-trade translocations. The ecological consequences of these invasions include habitat loss and alteration, altered water flow, short-circuited food webs, the creation of novel and unnatural habitats subsequently colonized by other exotic species, abnormally effective filtration of the water column, hybridization with native species, highly destructive predation, and introductions of pathogens and disease disturbances.

Evolutionary mechanisms such as cyst formation and chemosensitive triggers allow toxic species to more easily spread where disturbances are frequent and/or of sufficient magnitude to permanently establish these opportunists in new ecological niches. Mass mortalities and subsequent species substitutions eventually provide adequate substrate and biofilms to displace predators and competitors.

Natural diffusion of genetic material has evolved as a slow local and gradual process allowing species and ecosystems time to adapt. Scientists identified 367 non-native species in ballast water of ships traveling between Japan and Coos Bay, Oregon, highlighting a fundamental change in diffusion patterns. A novel occurrence tests the elasticity and inertia of a marine ecosystem. The ease with which species invade is a measure of the porosity and vulnerability of the system. Both anthropogenic facilitation and climatic change improve the odds for survival among new, novel, and opportunistic pathogens.

Keystone, Chronic, and Dramatic Events

Algal blooms (red and brown tides), hurricanes, and oil spill events stand apart from long-term impacts recorded from dredging, coastal hydrologic modifications, loss of wetlands and dunes, coral blasting, and fisheries overexploitation. Impact to chronically disturbed keystone species, such as beach-breeding marine turtle populations or the absence of oysters and oyster reefs from the Chesapeake Bay from disease and harvest, can take a long time to manifest. The magnitude of the impact once felt within an ecosystem, rather than the duration of individual occurrences, statistically links event types in the chronic category.

By public perception, oil spills are the most dramatic events for marine ecosystem health. The Santa Barbara Channel spill inspired an environmental movement. The Honolulu/Necker Island, Nantucket Shoals, Tampa Bay, Arthur Kill, Galveston Bay, Bay of Campeche, Tobago, West Indies, and Newfoundland mid-ocean spills did build a case for damage assessment, but these extraordinary spills did not evoke proportionate marine ecosystem health mitigation. Observed but insufficiently assessed spills throughout the twentieth century include spills associated with World War II, Ocean City in New Jersey, Greenpoint/Newtown Creek in Brooklyn (notable for its multidecade duration), Guadalupe, Delaware River, Bermuda, Warrenton in Oregon, San Francisco Bay, the Strait of Magellan, Chile, Brazil, Colombia, and Puerto Rico.

The Cox Bay, Louisiana, and proximal 2006 spills largely went unpunished and unrecorded because of the larger damage Hurricane Katrina caused in the area. The Prince William Sound oil spill (1989), the Gulf of Mexico Deep Horizon oil spill (2010), and the Mississippi Basin Block 252 blowout event (2011) by sheer volume of released oil have restructured these marine ecosystems on the decadal scale of impact.

In the twenty-first century the persistence the petrogenic hydrocarbons from oil spills such as those damaging the Calcasieu River (Mississippi), Makushin and Skan bays (Alaska), Guanabara Bay (Brazil), Guimaras Island (Philippines), Sabine Neches passage (Texas), Mississippi River (multiple spills), Coral Sea (off Australia), and Campos Basin (Brazil) built a stronger case for new forms of litigation on behalf of a marine ecosystem's environmental health. An environmental criminal complaint in Rio de Janeiro named not only corporations but individuals.

Geographic point and nonpoint pollution involve more gradually evolving marine health stressors. These include sewage and nutrient/particulate inundation; warming and cooling of ocean water; salinity gradient changes; acidification from carbon dioxide deposition; micronutrient enrichment from wind-blown Sahel sand; dissolved inorganic nitrogen; phosphates (nutrient overenrichment); endocrine disrupters; new/novel species introductions; disease redistribution; nuisance/noxious algae bloom regimes; military sonic pollution/disruption along migration, feeding, and flyway corridors; and the North Pacific and North Atlantic gyre garbage patches. All are implicated in shifts of marine ecosystems from healthy and stable to those less stable and more brittle, especially for keystone species.

Although impacts are not yet fully known, chronic conditions that could overshadow all other disturbance regimes may include ramifications from a global shift in the acidity of seawater due to increased carbon dioxide in the Earth's atmosphere and its subsequent sequestration (deposition) into the sea. Rapid acidification, which some models predict, could be more than most calcium carbonate–dependent marine organisms (shells and spines) can withstand. Extinctions may be forced by these chronic pressures. Simultaneous large-area changes from warming of water, land, and/or air temperatures include retraction of ice shelves in the Arctic and Antarctic and undermining of ice packs in Greenland, already altering thermohaline stratification, which involves salinity and temperature gradients that can change whole-ocean basin circulation and influence continental weather.

Specific point-in-time events that maintain longer-term persistence include toxin spills, massive hurricanes, cyclones, tsunamis, and human and wildlife exposure to radiation from weapons testing, notably in the Marshall Island atolls, Kiritimati, Amchitka in the Bering Sea (sea otter mortality), and Fangataufa and Moruroa atolls and from depleted uranium around Caribbean military target ranges. These marine ecosystem health impacts include the globally felt nuclear power plant disasters at Chernobyl (Ukraine, 1986) and Fukushima (Japan, 2011) because these event impacts will remain in the geologic record; their persistence is matched only by volcanoes, long-term climate change, pollution, and persistent resource exploitation impacts.

Marine mammals and many other charismatic species are barometers for ecosystem health. Ocean warming threatens polar bear and seal populations as their ice floe habitats and breeding grounds disappear. Invertebrates sometimes lack threatened and endangered species protections; for this reason the less charismatic octopuses of Micronesia, for example, are defined as "keystone" species, those the rest of the community depends on and that may serve as indicators or sentinels for change as well.

Outlook

Even without strict methodology or statistically derived indices, the lay public recognizes marine ecosystem health concerns. People harvest resources and enjoy access to marine aquatic environments unaware of the web of myriad overlapping disturbance regimes keeping them bountiful, stable, and accessible. Even casual news viewers now are aware of mammal strandings, slicks, flotsam, and recreational beach closures. Many have even heard sensationalized mass media accounts of marine and climate disturbances on par with risk of nuclear war and collapse of civilizations. Those repeatedly exposed to marine health media accounts or having anecdotally observed disturbances are inclined to believe marine ecosystem health is more compromised locally, but perhaps healthy somewhere far away in a marine reserve or sanctuary. It is convenient to take for granted stable, bountiful, and resiliently well-functioning ecosystems. It is ever more important for resource managers to identify as a baseline the lack of disturbance noted within a healthy system in order to better assess damages should they occur. With health indices and a better grasp of disturbance regimes, resource managers may compare, monitor, and manage marine ecosystems toward more sustainable conditions.

Adapting to disturbance regime cycles, resource managers have successfully coaxed fishing fleets away from overexploitation, restored wetlands and sea grass habitats, and established large preserves within the Pacific to protect kelp forests and reserve genetic material. Caribbean tourist economies previously noted for sewage inundation and anchor damage are voluntarily rebuilding lost coral, rock, shell reef, and mangrove habitats to return healthy structure and function to otherwise degraded marine ecosystems. Declining marine ecosystem health, although better documented in the last several decades, is not necessarily inevitable.

Benjamin H. SHERMAN
HEEDMD.ORG (Health Ecological & Economic Dimensions of Major Disturbances Program)

See also Amazon River; Caribbean; Ecotourism (the Americas); Marine Preserves; Mississippi and Missouri Rivers; New Orleans, United States; Oceania; Pacific Island Environmental Philosophy; Parks and Protected Areas; Rio de Janeiro, Brazil; Rio Earth Summit (UN Conference on Environment and Development); Sanitation; Small Island States; Water Use and Rights

FURTHER READING

Christensen, Norman L., et al. (1996). The report of the Ecological Society of America Committee on the Scientific Basis for Ecosystem Management. *Ecological Applications, 6,* 665–691.

Committee on Environment and Natural Resources (CENR). (1997). *Integrating the nation's environmental monitoring and research networks and programs: A proposed framework.* Washington, DC: CENR National Science and Technology Council.

Conley, Walt, & Brunt, James W. (1991). An institute for theoretical ecology? Part V: Practical data management for cross-site analysis and synthesis of ecological information. *Coenoses, 6,* 173–180.

Costanza, Robert. (1992). Toward an operational definition of health. In Robert Costanza, Bryan G. Norton & Benjamin D. Haskell (Eds.), *Ecosystem health: New goals for environmental management* (pp. 239–256). Washington, DC: Island Press.

Costanza, Robert, & Mageau, Michael. (1999). What is a healthy ecosystem? *Aquatic Ecology, 33*, 105–115.

Costanza, Robert; Norton, Bryan G.; & Haskell, Benjamin D. (Eds.). (1992). *Ecosystem health: New goals for environmental management.* Washington, DC: Island Press.

Costanza, Robert, et al. (1997). The value of the world's ecosystem services and natural capital. *Nature, 387,* 253–260.

Daszak, Peter; Cunningham, Andrew A.; & Hyatt, Alex D. (2001). Anthropogenic environmental change and the emergence of infectious diseases in wildlife. *Acta Tropica, 78,* 103–116.

Davis, Frank W.; Quattrochi, Dale A.; Ridd, Merrill K.; Lam, Nina S. N.; & Walsh, Stephen J. (1991). Environmental analysis using integrated GIS and remotely sensed data: Some research needs and priorities. *Photogrammetric Engineering and Remote Sensing, 57*(6), 689–697.

Diaz, Robert J., & Rosenberg, Rutger. (2008). Spreading dead zones and consequences for marine ecosystems. *Science, 321*(5891), 926–929.

Ebbesmeyer, Curtis C., et al. (1991). 1976 step in the Pacific climate: Forty environmental changes between 1968-1975 and 1977-1984. In Julio L. Betancourt & Vera L. Tharp (Eds.), *Proceedings of the Seventh Annual Pacific Climate (PACLIM) Workshop, April 1990* (pp. 115–126). (Interagency Ecological Studies Technical Report 26). Sacramento: California Department of Water Resources.

Epstein, Paul R. (1996). Emergent stressors and public health implications in large marine ecosystems: An overview. In Kenneth A. Sherman, Norbert A. Jaworski & Theodore. J. Smayda (Eds.), *The northeast shelf ecosystem: Assessment, sustainability, and management* (pp. 417–438). Cambridge, MA: Blackwell Science.

Epstein, Paul R., & Rapport, David J. (1996). Changing coastal marine environments and human health. *Ecosystem Health, 2*(3), 155–176.

Epstein, Paul R., et al. (1998). *Marine ecosystems: Emerging diseases as indicators of change. Year of the ocean special report on health of the oceans from Labrador to Venezuela.* Boston: The Center for Health and the Global Environment, Harvard Medical School.

Evans, John D. (1997). Infrastructures for sharing geographic information among environmental agencies (Ph.D. dissertation). Cambridge: Massachusetts Institute of Technology.

Fayyad, Usama M.; Haussler, David; & Stolorz, Paul. (1996). Mining scientific data. *Communications of the ACM, 39,* 51–57.

Fisher, William S.; Epstein, Paul R.; & Sherman, Benjamin H. (1999). Overview of health, ecological, and economic dimensions of global change: Tracking marine disturbance and disease. In Thomas J. O'Shea, Randall R. Reeves & Alison Kirk Long (Eds.), *Marine mammals and persistent ocean contaminants: Proceedings of the Marine Mammal Commission Workshop,* October 12-15, 1998. Keystone, CO: Marine Mammal Commission.

Frank, Kenneth T.; Petrie, Brian; Fisher, Jonathan A. D.; & Leggett, William C. (2011). Transient dynamics of an altered large marine ecosystem. *Nature, 477,* 86–89.

French, Jim C.; Jones, Anita K.; & Pfaltz, J. L. (Eds.). (1990). *Scientific database management: Report of the invitational NSF workshop on scientific database management* (TR 90-21). Charlottesville: University of Virginia.

Frithsen, Jeffrey B.; Fabrizio, Mary C.; Holland, A. Frederick; Saul, Gary E.; & Weisberg, Stephen B. (1991). *Example interpretive assessment report for estuaries* (EPA Report 600/04-91/026). Research Triangle Park, NC: US Environmental Protection Agency, Atmospheric Research and Exposure Laboratory.

Gross, Katherine L., et al. (1995). Final report of the Ecological Society of America Committee on the future of long-term ecological data (FLED). Retrieved January 10, 2012, from http://intranet2.lternet.edu/sites/intranet2.lternet.edu/files/documents/Scientific_Reports/Informatics/fledvol1.pdf

Hand, David J. (1998). Data mining: Statistics and more. *The American Statistician, 52,* 112–118.

Harvell, Catherine Drew, et al. (1999). Emerging marine diseases: Climate links and anthropogenic factors. *Science, 285*(5433), 1505–1510.

Holling, C. S. (1995). Sustainability: The cross-scale dimension. In Mohan Munasinghe & Walter Shearer (Eds.), *Defining and measuring sustainability: The biogeophysical foundations.* Washington, DC: World Bank.

Ingersoll, Rick C.; Seasstedt, Tim R.; & Hartman, Michael. (1997). Computers in biology: A model information management system for ecological research. *Bioscience, 47*(5), 310–316.

Jackson, Jeremy B. C., et al. (2001). Historical overfishing and the recent collapse of coastal ecosystems. *Science, 293*(5530), 629–638.

Karr, James R. (1991). Biological integrity: A long-neglected aspect of water resource management. *Ecological Applications, 1,* 66–84.

Levins, Richard, et al. (1994). The emergence of new diseases. *American Scientist, 82,* 52–60.

Likens, Gene E. (1992). The ecosystem approach: Its use and abuse. In Otto Kinne (Ed.), *Excellence in ecology: Vol. 3.* Oldendorf/Luhe, Germany: Ecology Institute.

Lotzehk, Heike K., et al. (2006). Depletion, degradation, and recovery potential of estuaries and coastal seas. *Science, 312*(5781), 1806–1809.

Mack, Richard N., et al. (2000). Biotic invasions: Causes, epidemiology, global consequences and control. *Ecological Society of America, Ecological Applications, 10*(3), 689–710.

Mageau, Michael T.; Costanza, Robert; & Ulanowicz, Robert E. (1995). The development and initial testing of a quantitative assessment of ecosystem health. *Ecosystem Health, 1*(4), 201–213.

Marine Mammal Commission. (1999). *Annual Report to Congress 1998.* Bethesda, MD: Marine Mammal Commission.

McClenachan, Loren; Cooper, Andrew B.; Carpenter, Kent E.; & Dulvy, Nicholas K. (2011, December 13). Extinction risk and bottlenecks in the conservation of charismatic marine species. *Conservation Letters.* doi: 10.1111/j.1755-263X.2011.00206.x

McGowan, John A.; Cayan, Daniel R.; & Dorman, LeRoy M. (1998). Climate-ocean variability and ecosystem response in the northeast Pacific. *Science, 281*(5374), 210–217.

Michener, William K. (Ed.). (1986). *Research data management in the ecological sciences* (Publication no. 16). Columbia: University of South Carolina Press, Belle W. Baruch Library in Marine Science.

Michener, William K.; Brunt, James W.; & Stafford, Susan G. (Eds.). (1994). *Environmental information management and analysis: Ecosystem to global scales.* London: Taylor and Francis.

Michener, William K.; Porter, John H.; & Stafford, Susan G. (Eds.). (1998). *Data and information management in the ecological sciences: A resource guide.* Albuquerque: University of New Mexico, LTER Network Office.

National Marine Fisheries Service (NMFS). (1993). *A special NOAA 20th anniversary report: Estuaries of the United States, vital statistics of a national resource base.* Rockville, MD: US Department of Commerce NOAA.

National Research Council (NRC). (1990). *Managing troubled waters: The role of marine environmental monitoring.* Washington, DC: National Academy Press.

National Research Council (NRC). (1995a). *Review of EPA's environmental monitoring and assessment program: Overall evaluation.* Washington, DC: National Academy Press.

National Research Council (NRC). (1995b). *Finding the forest in the trees: The challenge of combining diverse environmental data.* Washington, DC: National Academy Press.

National Research Council (NRC). (1995c). *Science, policy and the coast: Improving decision making.* Washington, DC: National Academy Press.

National Research Council (NRC). (1997). *Bits of power: Issues in global access to scientific data.* Washington, DC: National Academy Press.

National Science and Technology Council (NSTC). (1997). *Integrating the nation's environmental monitoring and research networks and programs: A proposed framework.* Washington, DC: NSTC.

Paul, John F., & DeMoss, Thomas B. (2001). Integration of environmental indicators for the US Mid-Atlantic region. *Human and Ecological Risk Assessment, 7*(5), 1555–1564

Pauly, Daniel, & Christensen, Villy. (2001). Ecosystem models. In Paul J. B. Hart & John D. Reynolds (Eds.), *Handbook of fish biology and fisheries* (pp. 211–227). Hoboken, NJ: Wiley-Blackwell.

Pimm, Stuart L. (1984). The complexity and stability of ecosystems. *Nature, 307*, 321–326.

Polovina, Jeffrey J.; Mitchum, Gary T.; & Evans, Geoffrey T. (1995). Decadal and basin-scale variation in mixed layer depth and the impact on biological production in the central and north Pacific, 1960–1988. *Deep-Sea Research, 42*, 1701–1716.

Rapport, David J. (1995). Ecosystem health: An emerging integrative science. In David J. Rapport, Connie L. Gaudet & Peter Calow (Eds.), *Evaluating and monitoring the health of large-scale ecosystems* (pp. 5–31). Berlin: Springer-Verlag.

Rapport, David J.; Regier, H. A.; & Hutchinson, T. C. (1985). Ecosystem behavior under stress. *The American Naturalist, 125*, 617–640.

Rosen, Robert. (1977). Complexity as a systems property. *International Journal of General Systems, 3*(4), 227–232.

Roush, Wade. (1995). When rigor meets reality. *Science, 269*(5222), 313–315.

Sherman, B. H. (2001). Assessment of multiple marine ecological disturbances: Applying the North American prototype to the Baltic Sea ecosystem. *Human Ecological Risk Assessment, 7*(5), 1519–1540.

Sherman, B. H., & Epstein, Paul R. (2001). Past anomalies as a diagnostic tool for evaluating multiple marine ecological disturbance events. *Human Ecological Risk Assessment, 7*(5), 1493–1517.

Simon, Herbert A. (1965). Architecture of complexity. *General Systems Yearbook, 10*, 63–76.

United States Environmental Protection Agency (EPA) (1992, March). EMAP Monitor: Newsletter. EPA 600/M-91-051.

United States Global Change Research Program (USGCRP). (2000). *US national assessment of the potential consequences of climate variability and change: A detailed overview of the consequences of climate change and mechanisms for adaptation.* Washington, DC: USGCRP.

Williams, Roy; Bunn, Julian; Moore, Reagan; & Pool, James C. T. (Eds.). (1999). *Interfaces to scientific data archives* (Technical report CACR-160). Pasadena: California Institute of Technology.

Share the *Encyclopedia of Sustainability*: Teachers are welcome to make up to ten (10) copies of no more than two (2) articles for distribution in a single course or program. For further permissions, please visit www.copyright.com or contact: info@berkshirepublishing.com

Marine Preserves

In the Americas and Oceania, marine preserves, areas of the ocean protected through regulations, are valuable tools in addressing impacts to the ocean environment from coastal and offshore development, overfishing, and climate change. When designed and managed effectively, they can sustain marine ecosystems by providing food and other resources, regulating environmental processes including water filtration, and preserving unique habitats such as coral reefs.

It is impossible to attain global sustainability without effective management of human interactions with ocean resources and ecosystems. Oceans provide life-sustaining functions for the planet. They are the primary driver of climate, generate more than half of the world's atmospheric oxygen, provide critical processes for the global cycling of nutrients, and host the majority of the world's biological diversity. Ocean fisheries are essential sources of income that support the livelihoods of hundreds of millions around the globe, employing more people worldwide than does traditional agriculture (FAO 2010). Ocean biodiversity is the basis of a number of important ecosystem services, providing water, fiber, genetic resources, medicines, and cultural products (such as historic shipwrecks, sunken naval vessels and aircraft, or cultural sites that are paramount to a culture's identity) to billions of people.

A number of factors threaten the sustained provision of these services. Long-standing threats, such as overfishing, pollution, and coastal development, are further complicated by emerging issues, such as marine debris and climate change. These threats often interact in harmful ways, severely damaging the health of ocean ecosystems and reducing their resilience and ability to withstand further stress. Failure to implement sustainable oceans management threatens the more than 50 percent of the global population that lives in coastal areas, and, ultimately, the very health of the planet. One tool that is increasingly being used to address these challenges is the designation, implementation, and management of marine preserves.

What Is a Marine Preserve?

Marine preserves take a variety of forms depending on local factors that include variations in geographic area, type of habitat (including ocean, coastal, and/or terrestrial locations), legal status and protective measures afforded to the area, duration of protection (including long- or short-term protection as well as year-round or seasonal protection), and whether laws or regulations governing the area apply to all or part of it. Names given to marine preserves vary, with different names often connoting different types of protection, although this varies among localities.

The most common form of marine preserve is the marine protected area (MPA). The generally accepted definition of an MPA is "an area of intertidal or subtidal terrain, together with its overlying waters and associated flora, fauna, historical and cultural features, which has been reserved by law or other effective means to protect part or all of the enclosed environment" (Kelleher 1999). Other names given to protected areas include marine reserves, parks, sanctuaries, monuments, seascapes, wildernesses, and world heritage sites. These areas enjoy different levels of protection, from MPAs created to protect only one species during a certain time of the year (for example, a particular fish species during spawning season) while allowing other types of extractive or recreational activities to marine reserves where fishing or changing the habitat in any way are strictly prohibited except for scientific monitoring (also known as no-take areas).

On a global scale, only about 0.8 percent of the oceans are protected by a total of about five thousand MPAs. Only 0.08 percent of total ocean area is protected by no-take marine reserves (IUCN and UNEP 2010). These figures are far below the global target—at the 2002 World Summit on Sustainable Development, global leaders agreed to establish "marine protected areas consistent with international law and based on scientific information, including representative networks by 2012" (FAO 2012). More recently, in 2010 the Tenth Conference of the Parties to the Convention on Biological Diversity called for the creation of MPAs in 10 percent of the ocean by 2020. Stewards of the marine environment recognize that, while it is a first step, this modest goal is inadequate to meet the needs of marine conservation. More marine preserves must be created and managed effectively if we are to meet global goals and achieve sustainable oceans. Furthermore, linked and ecologically connected networks of protected areas must be created. These networks can be more resilient to the impacts of human activities than isolated, individual marine preserves, as networks of MPAs can provide protection for a full range of habitats through the placement of individual MPAs that, together, afford the connectivity necessary to maintain ecological integrity for a marine area. For example, functional networks can facilitate the range shifts of populations and the movements of individuals and genes in response to climate change impacts in the ocean. In the Americas and Oceania, although many challenges remain, notable progress has been made.

Preserves by Region

Long-term human impacts such as fishing, pollution, coastal development, dredging, oil and gas extraction, mining, and tourism, as well as newer stresses, including climate change, have adversely affected ocean habitats in the Americas and Oceania. While it would be impractical to note all efforts throughout the region to create and maintain marine preserves, a number of national and regional efforts will serve as examples.

North America

A number of organizations are working to establish marine preserves in North America. Canada, the United States, and Mexico collaborate through the Commission for Environmental Cooperation (CEC), which oversees the implementation of the North American Agreement on Environmental Cooperation (NAAEC). As part of this work, the CEC coordinates the North American MPA Network (NAMPAN), which aims to "enhance and strengthen the conservation of biodiversity in critical marine habitats throughout North America by creating a functional system of ecologically based MPA networks that cross political borders and depend on broad cooperation" (Morgan et al. 2005).

National measures are equally important. In the United States, there are approximately 1,700 MPAs, some of which are managed through a collaborative effort under a national system established in 2009. The objectives and levels of protection for MPAs in the system vary broadly. The majority of sites (72 percent) are multiple-use MPAs that allow human activities, including fishing. Just 28 percent of the sites are no-take, prohibiting the extraction or significant destruction of natural and cultural resources. With coordinated management, this network, with 297 sites and covering an area of 456,491 square kilometers, will provide effective marine stewardship, especially if more connections are made between the preserves (National Marine Protected Areas Center 2011). The Papahānaumokuākea Marine National Monument (PMNM) in the northwest Hawaiian Islands, created in 2006, is the largest conservation area in US territory, and one of the largest in the world, at 362,073 square kilometers. The monument protects exceptional natural and cultural resources, including coral reefs that are home to more than seven thousand marine species. The monument also includes ecological reserves and special preservation areas that together constitute 115,420 square kilometers of no-take areas (PMNM 2011). Both Canada and Mexico also have national initiatives to establish marine preserves, as these countries increasingly recognize the benefits protected areas offer. For example, the Gwaii Haanas National Park Reserve in Canada provides protection to nine-thousand-year-old reefs that are home to a number of associated marine species, as well as to marine birds and mammals—the area is a major passageway for Pacific Coast marine migratory birds (Morgan et al. 2005). In Mexico, the Islas del Golfo de California Flora and Fauna Protection Areas, as well as a number of associated reserves surrounding the islands, afford protection to the so-called Galapagos of Mexico, an area that hosts some of the world's most unique biodiversity and provides spawning areas for an abundance of pelagic fish (Morgan et al. 2005).

Central and South America

Latin America and the Caribbean have also been making efforts toward ocean conservation. By 2008, there were more than seven hundred MPAs offering some type of protection, with a total area of more than 300,000 square kilometers. As is the case in other regions, however, the majority of sites were limited-take MPAs (571 sites covering 51,505 square kilometers), which allowed some or even heavy extractive use of the areas. Mixed-use areas (limited-take MPAs) constituted eighty-seven sites but had the largest area at 236,853 square kilometers. There were ninety-eight marine reserves, but the area under this type of no-take protection was the smallest at 16,862 square kilometers (Guarderas, Hacker, and Lubchenco 2008).

The Bahamas created the first protected park in the region in 1959, and in 1985 the park became the first no-fishing zone in the Caribbean. In 2008, the Bahamas, Jamaica, Grenada, the Dominican Republic, and Saint Vincent and the Grenadines joined the Caribbean Challenge initiative, and agreed to protect almost 20 percent of their marine coastal habitats by 2020, including about 84,984 square kilometers of coral reefs, mangroves, sea grass beds, and other key habitats (The Nature Conservancy 2011). A recently approved grant from the Global Environment Facility for the eastern Caribbean region of about US$8.75 million will help to ensure the long-term conservation of more than 1,000 square kilometers of marine habitat. The sustainable financing and management project, involving Antigua and Barbuda, Grenada, Saint Kitts and Nevis, Saint Lucia, and Saint Vincent and the Grenadines, will implement a system of biophysical and socioeconomic indicators to monitor protected areas (World Bank 2011).

In Central America, the World Wide Fund for Nature (WWF) has been collaborating with the governments of Belize, Guatemala, and Honduras since the 1980s to establish marine reserves and provide management training to protect the Mesoamerican Reef, an ancient system that stretches about 1,127 kilometers from the northern coast of Mexico's Yucatan Peninsula to northern Honduras. The reef is part of a more comprehensive ocean ecosystem that stretches throughout the Caribbean basin and beyond, and benefits communities in the region by providing food and a natural barrier against major storm surges. In 1999, the three countries and Mexico agreed to work with the WWF on an action plan that strengthens the system of protected areas to conserve key species (WWF 2011).

In South America, some of the most productive and diverse ecosystems on Earth are protected through marine reserves or MPAs. In an area surrounding the Galapagos Islands in Ecuador, for example, the Galapagos Marine Reserve was formally established in 1998. It protects 130,000 square kilometers of ocean, home to more than 2,900 marine species, of which about 25 percent are native to the region. The reserve uses a zoning approach to management, allowing certain activities, including diving and fishing, in some zones, and strictly prohibiting all extractive uses in others. The zoned areas are crafted to be fluid, allowing for changing conditions and taking into account that the areas are interrelated and interdependent—a change in one zone may require a different level of conservation in another (Parque Nacional Galapagos 2009). In Colombia, the Seaflower MPA was designated in 2005 to protect more than 65,000 square kilometers along the Archipelago of San Andres, Old Providence, and Santa Catalina, which is a richly diverse area hosting 57 identified coral species, more than 400 fish species, and about 150 bird species (Hance 2010). The Seaflower MPA includes 2,300 square kilometers of no-take area. Marine reserves and MPAs are also in development in Brazil, Chile, and other countries.

Oceania

Marine preserves have existed in Oceania for decades, and ocean conservation in the region is quite advanced. The Phoenix Islands Protected Area (PIPA), established by the Republic of Kiribati and its partners in 2006 and enlarged in 2008, is the largest protected area in the Pacific Ocean. At 408,250 square kilometers, PIPA is critical in protecting one of the world's largest pristine oceanic coral archipelago ecosystems (PIPA 2011). In Fiji, a network of thirteen MPAs protects the area from poaching and destruction. One conservation area, on the small island of Navini, includes a complete ban on the extraction of resources (Niesten and Gjertsen 2010).

Australia was one of the first to take the lead in protecting the marine environment. It established the Great Barrier Reef Marine Park, which today covers an area of 344,400 square kilometers, in 1975. A final management plan for the reef prepared in 2004 set aside 33 percent of the park as marine reserves (no-take areas). In 1991, Australia initiated a broad conservation program through the National Representative System of MPAs (NRSMPA). Today the NRSMPA includes two hundred protected areas that ensure ecological viability and the integrity of populations, species, and communities in 880,000 square kilometers of Australia's ocean (Australian Department of Sustainability 2010).

At the regional level, the Micronesia Challenge and the Coral Triangle Initiative on Coral Reefs, Fisheries and Food Security (CTI) are significant conservation measures. Palau, the Federated States of Micronesia, the Marshall Islands, and the US territories of Guam and the Northern Mariana Islands joined in the Micronesia Challenge with the goal of conserving 30 percent of nearshore coastal waters by 2020. The initiative plays an important role in protecting 61 percent of the world's coral species, 66 threatened species, and more than 1,300 species of reef fish that are found throughout the five jurisdictions (The Nature Conservancy 2011). The CTI was initiated by Indonesia in 2007, and Malaysia, Papua New Guinea, the Philippines, the Solomon Islands, and Timor-Leste joined later. The initiative safeguards more than 75 percent of known coral species, more than 30 percent of the world's coral reefs, and the greatest extent of mangrove forests of any region of the globe. The initiative, supported by the private sector, international agencies, and nongovernmental partners, as well as by the US government through the US CTI Support Program, has the goal of protecting 20 percent of each major marine and coastal habitat in the Coral Triangle by 2020. Individual MPAs are to be scaled up and linked to form an ecologically connected, resilient, and sustainably financed Coral Triangle MPA System. As of 2010, about 64,234 square kilometers in the total Coral Triangle area of 5.7 million square kilometers was under some form of MPA.

Challenges and the Road Ahead

Though much progress has been made toward establishing MPAs and marine reserves in the Americas and Oceania, much remains to be done, and the challenges to further progress are great. Vast coastal and ocean areas remain unprotected. In Central and South America, for example, the seven hundred MPAs established, while they are a first step, cover only 1.5 percent of countries' coastal and shelf waters, with the most stringent protection, marine reserves, covering only 0.1 percent of coastal and shelf waters (Guarderas, Hacker, and Lubchenco 2008). Challenges with implementation, management, and enforcement can often severely hamper the effectiveness of the MPAs. In addition, management is often fragmented between sites, even neighboring sites. Large ocean areas often function as interconnected ecosystems, however. Because water, individuals, and genes ecologically move within and across protected areas, pollution from air, land, and water, the overexploitation of living resources, and natural processes all influence the productivity, resilience, and integrity of the larger ecosystems.

While some progress has been made, more ecologically functional networks of MPAs and marine reserves are urgently needed. Such networks would spread risk (e.g., the threat of catastrophic loss due to the more extreme impacts of climate change could be addressed by protecting a range of habitats and replicating sites that include those habitat types) and increase the viability of the ecosystems (i.e., appropriately sized MPAs could encompass as many habitat types as possible and ensure the potential for self-replenishment of species).

Finally, while national protective measures are critical, there is no international legal framework to protect the 64 percent of the ocean that is beyond national jurisdiction, and there are few MPAs in areas beyond national jurisdiction. If ocean resources and ecosystems are to be sustained in the Americas and Oceania and around the globe, countries must work together to establish international MPAs and marine reserves, including networks that represent all the different types of ocean ecosystems and that are based on the best available science.

As threats to the ocean ecosystem grow, marine preserves are increasingly important tools in an adaptive management strategy. When they are used effectively with a suite of broader conservation tools, they can enhance ecosystem resilience. As long-standing problems and more recent impacts from climate change continue to alter marine ecosystems, habitats, and processes, marine preserves can preserve biodiversity, protect habitats and ecosystem integrity, ensure the ongoing delivery of ecological goods and services, and promote the sustainability of ocean resources and the sustainability of the communities that depend upon them.

Kateryna M. WOWK
Global Ocean Forum

See also Amazonia; Australia; Brazil; Canada; Caribbean; Chesapeake Bay; Ecotourism (the Americas); Marine Ecosystems Health; Multilateral Environmental Agreements (MEAs); New Zealand; Oceania; Parks and Protected Areas; Travel and Tourism Industry; Southern Cone; United States

FURTHER READING

Australian Department of Sustainability, Environment, Water, Population and Communities. (2010). National representative system of marine protected areas. Retrieved October 22, 2011, from http://www.environment.gov.au/coasts/mpa/nrsmpa/

Food and Agriculture Organization of the United Nations (FAO). (2010). *The state of world fisheries and aquaculture: 2010*. Rome: FAO Fisheries and Aquaculture Department. Retrieved October 10, 2011, from http://www.fao.org/docrep/013/i1820e/i1820e00.htm

Food and Agriculture Organization of the United Nations (FAO). (2012). About MPAs. Retrieved April 21, 2012, from http://www.fao.org/fishery/topic/4400/en

Guarderas, A. Paulina; Hacker, Sally D.; & Lubchenco, Jane. (2008). Current status of marine protected areas in Latin America and the Caribbean. *Conservation Biology, 22*(6), 1630–1640.

Hance, Jeremy. (2010, December 1). Environmental and social aggression: Oil exploration threatens award-winning marine protected area. Retrieved October 10, 2011, from http://news.mongabay.com/2010/1201-hance_seaflower_oil.html

International Union for the Conservation of Nature (IUCN) & United Nations Environment Programme (UNEP). (2010). Protect planet ocean: Global facts about MPAs and marine reserves. Retrieved October 10, 2011, from http://www.protectplanetocean.org/collections/introduction/introbox/globalmpas/introduction-item.html

Kelleher, Graeme. (1999). Guidelines for marine protected areas. Gland, Switzerland: IUCN.

Morgan, Lance; Maxwell, Sara; Tsao, Fan; Wilkinson, Tara A. C.; & Etnoyer, Peter. (2005). Marine priority conservation areas: Baja California to the Bering Sea. Montreal: Commission for Environmental Cooperation of North America and the Marine Conservation Biology Institute.

National Marine Protected Areas Center. (2011, March). The National System of MPAs: Analysis of national system sites. Retrieved October 22, 2011, from http://www.mpa.gov/pdf/helpful-resources/factsheets/nss_analysis_march_2011.pdf

The Nature Conservancy. (2011). The Caribbean challenge: The end of paper parks. Retrieved October 22, 2011, from http://www.nature.org/ourinitiatives/regions/caribbean/caribbean-challenge.xml

Niesten, Eduard, & Gjertsen, Heidi. (2010). Economic incentives for marine conservation. Arlington, VA: Science and Knowledge Division, Conservation International.

Parque Nacional Galapagos. (2009). About the Galapagos Marine Reserve. Retrieved October 22, 2011, from http://www.galapagospark.org/nophprg.php?page=reserva_marina_sobre_la

Papahānaumokuākea Marine National Monument (PMNM). (2011). About us. Retrieved October 22, 2011, from http://www.papahanaumokuakea.gov/about/welcome.html

Phoenix Islands Protected Area (PIPA). (2011). Homepage. Retrieved October 22, 2011, from www.phoenixislands.org/

World Bank. (2011). World Bank news: Eastern Caribbean countries to protect 100,000 hectares of fragile marine ecosystems. Retrieved October 22, 2011, from http://web.worldbank.org/WBSITE/EXTERNAL/NEWS/0,,contentMDK:22976130~pagePK:34370~piPK:34424~theSitePK:4607,00.html

World Wide Fund for Nature (WWF). (2011). Mesoamerican Reef. Retrieved October 22, 2011, from http://www.worldwildlife.org/what/wherewework/mesoamericanreef/projects.html

Berkshire's authors and editors welcome questions, comments, and corrections. Send your emails about the *Berkshire Encyclopedia of Sustainability* in general or this volume in particular to: sustainability.updates@berkshirepublishing.com

Mexico

115 million est. pop. 2012

Mexico is the second-largest country in Latin America, after Brazil; its inclusion in the North American Free Trade Agreement (NAFTA) along with the United States and Canada has had a variety of social, economic, and environmental consequences. Mexico faces daunting challenges in the face of environmental and economic sustainability (as well as an ever-worsening drug war), but several social movements, nongovernmental organizations (NGOs), and government policies have risen to address issues like pollution, climate change, and human rights, all of which are indelibly linked to sustainability.

The environmental history of Mexico shows how humans and nature have interacted over time to forge what is today a vibrant and diverse country. Mexico has severe environmental dilemmas, however. Its history helps explain the roots of those dilemmas and the difficulties in resolving them.

Mexico is the second-largest country in Latin America (after Brazil) and is the largest Spanish-speaking country in the world, with an estimated population of 115 million people (US CIA 2012). Its 1.9 million square kilometers cover the area between the United States on the north, Guatemala and Belize on the south, the Gulf of Mexico on the east, and the Pacific Ocean on the west. The Sierra Madre dominate Mexico's physical landscape; the Sierra Madre Oriental run north to south on Mexico's eastern side, and the Sierra Madre Occidental form a spine from north to south on the western side. Between the mountain ranges are plateaus, deserts, and valleys with dry, harsh climates—meaning that only 10 percent of the country is arable, and much of that land requires intense irrigation to make agriculture profitable. In Mexico's southern region are more mountains, some of which are active volcanoes, and dense tropical forests. Like appendages sticking out from both ends, Mexico's two peninsulas have unique characteristics. The Yucatan in the southeast is flat and dominated by low scrub forest, and Baja California in the northwest is characterized by the Sonoran Desert. The deserts, mountains, tropical forests, and lack of any major, navigable rivers have all created geographic barriers to transportation, communication, and development over time. With such a diversity of regions, climates, and ecosystems, however, the country is often considered as "many Mexicos."

The population is equally diverse. Mexico is a federal republic with thirty-one states, the larger ones located in the less-populated north. Mexico City, the nation's capital, is in the Distrito Federal and as of 2012 is the second-largest conurbation in the Western Hemisphere (after São Paolo, Brazil) with 19.3 million people (CIA 2012). Other large urban areas include Guadalajara, Monterrey, and the border cities of Ciudad Juarez and Tijuana. Mexico shares a 3,218-kilometer-long border with the United States, and that means that a great deal of migration to the borderlands has occurred from within the country. The growth has been so swift that social services cannot keep pace with it.

Indigenous Mexico

How Mexico's pre-Columbian indigenous population survived in such diverse environmental conditions merits attention. In the northern deserts, some groups, such as the Chichamecs, were nomadic—they moved around for optimum hunting and gathering. Others, such as the Yaquis, practiced floodgate irrigation by diverting river water for their crops. In southern Mexico, great cities—cities that required considerable quantities of food—flourished in the

Mayan and Aztec empires. To meet those demands for food, the indigenous peoples created an intercropping system: they planted corn (maize) in rows, nitrogen-fixing beans beside the corn to restore nutrients to the soil, and various squashes between the rows. The squash leaves provided cover for the beans and acted as a natural pest control.

In the Valley of Mexico, where the invading Aztecs established the great city of Tenochtitlán (where Mexico City is today), the local natives developed a unique form of agriculture called *chinampas*. This highly productive farming method used beds of mud and decayed plant material in the region's lake shallows to plant an array of grains and vegetables. The natives could get several harvests a year from the *chinampas*, which supported Tenochtitlán—a city of an estimated 235,000 people by the mid-fifteenth century. Further, as one historian notes, "The *chinampas* aided soil and forest conservation by reducing pressures to burn steep wooded hillsides for farming" (Simonian 1995, 25). This efficient farming practice continues today near Xochimilco, but urban sprawl has destroyed much of the *chinampas* land.

Farther south, the Maya of Yucatan and Chiapas (the state bordering Guatemala) used *milpa* (corn plot) farming—fields that were cleared and burned from the tropical forests. Using efficient intercropping, the Maya, too, sustained large populations until the tenth century CE, when their advanced civilization collapsed. Some scholars argue that the Maya had exceeded the carrying capacity (the population that an area will support without deterioration) of the land as their population grew, but others suggest that a cataclysmic event hastened their collapse. Despite these environmental impacts, the Maya, like most indigenous societies, maintained a spiritual relationship with nature. For them, the ceiba tree was sacred—it held up the four corners of the world; also, the souls of their dead went under it, and therefore, it was not to be felled. Their respect and fear of the forest helped to protect it.

Colonial Era

Spanish explorer Hernán Cortés and his crew entered Mexico in 1519. They came in pursuit of riches and domination and set out immediately to conquer Mexico for Spain. Cortés triumphed by 1521 with the help of indigenous groups who had suffered under Aztec control, firearms, horses, and the Aztec belief that Cortés was perhaps a returning deity. The Spanish monarchs then established "New Spain" in Mexico and sent other conquistadors, explorers, and priests to secure the colony. This conquest was facilitated by diseases the Europeans brought with them, against which the natives had no immunities. Epidemics of influenza, measles, typhus, and especially smallpox caused such high mortality that by the mid-seventeenth century, the indigenous population of the region was depleted to between 5 and 10 percent of what it had been in 1500. In great part, the conquest was a biological one.

Other environmental changes occurred when the colonizers introduced crops and livestock to produce the kind of food they knew from Europe. Wheat, malt barley, and wine grapes became new staple crops. Mediterranean fruits and olives replaced some local produce. A variety of weeds competed with, and often overtook, native plant habitats. Cattle and sheep, however, caused the greatest transformations. What has been called "ungulate irruptions" (i.e. upsurges in population of hooved animals; Melville 1994, 6) occurred when livestock exceeded the land's carrying capacity and caused plant communities to crash until a plant-animal accommodation plateau was reached. This result was noted especially with sheep in the Mezquital Valley northeast of Mexico City by the late 1500s when intensive grazing caused severe erosion and deterioration of the environment.

The Spaniards also introduced plantation agriculture in areas that were conducive to growing sugarcane and, with even greater environmental implications, began large-scale mining ventures. Gold and silver were in high demand in Europe, and the Spaniards soon found and exploited Mexico's vast reserves. The colonial labor system for these enterprises was based on the *encomienda*—native labor granted to colonizers to develop the region. Similar to slavery, the process exploited indigenous people and helped transform landscapes. Mining, with its demand for timber to support shafts and food to feed miners, was especially damaging. Finally, exporting sugar, minerals, and other raw materials during the colonial era set Mexico on a dependency pathway that continued after independence.

Independence and the Nineteenth Century

When Mexicans won their independence in 1810, their national map did not look as it does today. It included all of New Spain—from Guatemala to the California-Oregon border. Granted, few Spanish settlements existed in the vast area that is now the US Southwest, only settlements along the California coast and in northern New Mexico. Mexico lost that land, nearly half its territory, however, in the Mexican-American War by 1848—just before the discovery of gold in California. (The Mexican states of Sonora and Chihuahua had been engaged in an increasingly vicious cycle of warfare with Apaches and other Native American tribes for several decades in the sparsely populated region; therefore, some historians maintain Mexico was not entirely loathe to lose the territory to the United States [Aleshire 2001, 306].) The lost resources and land became a boon for an expanding United States.

During the formative years of its new nationhood, Mexico was ruled by General Antonio López de Santa Anna (1794–1876; ruled on and off from 1833–1855), under whose command the country lost tremendous land and suffered from stagnant economic growth. A revolt against his dictatorship brought Benito Juárez to power in 1858; he believed in liberal economic policy. Liberalism in those years implied modernization, material progress, and development of natural resources. Mexico thus began to disburse funds for railroads, mines, and other national projects, which often harmed indigenous communities and altered the natural environment. Forests were cleared, mountainsides often were overgrazed and studded with mining operations and tailings piles, and vast open areas were converted to intensive agriculture.

This pattern accelerated during the dictatorship of Porfirio Díaz (1830–1915; ruled 1876–1911, a period known as the *porfiriato*), whose advisors were schooled in European positivism—a belief that economic development follows private property, modernized agriculture, expanded transportation and communication, and an educational system bent on science and engineering. Díaz's policies therefore converted much native land to plantation agriculture to sell cotton, sugar, henequen (a fiber crop grown in Yucatan and used to make twine and rope), and later, vegetables on the international market. He emphasized mining, especially for copper, which was in high demand due to a growing world market for electrical conduit. He also expanded Mexico's railway system, nearly quadrupling its length, to transport the agricultural and mineral commodities to ports.

Despite the social and ecological changes (e.g., eroded hillsides, clear-cut forests, polluted streams and rivers from mining operations, and dammed valleys) that these developments caused, the expected economic benefits never materialized. The projects were dependent on foreign investment, 80 percent from the United States, meaning that profits went to large land and business owners. By 1910, half of Mexico's land was controlled by three hundred families (seventeen people owned 20 percent of the country) (Brenner 1943, 17; Meyer, Sherman, and Deeds 2002, 398–399). Likewise, the railroads made it easier for people to relocate, as evidenced by the thousands of landless peasants who traveled to the cities to seek work. The newcomers, often having to live in slums on the outskirts of cities, helped Mexico City become a metropolis. A radically changing urban environment, therefore, and all its resource pressures were outcomes of the *porfiriato*.

Twentieth Century

The tyranny and economic malaise of the Díaz years prompted Mexico's revolution and civil war (1910–1920). Along with political reforms that limited presidents to one six-year term, central to the revolution was agrarian reform to return lands that had been taken from *campesinos* (rural peasants) and natives. As a result, Article 27 of the Constitution of 1917 made foreign ownership of land and subsurface resources illegal. It restored much of the land to *ejidos*—communal lands *campesino* or Indian groups cooperatively owned. President Lázaro Cárdenas (1895–1970; in office 1934–1940) accelerated this process by enacting 66 percent of all the agrarian reforms between the revolution and 1940. The largest *ejido* established, 3.2 million hectares, was in the Laguna cotton-growing district of the northern state of Coahuila. Cárdenas further encouraged these communal ventures by creating *ejido* credit banks (which provided loans to purchase seeds and farming equipment) and by supporting large irrigation projects. (By the 1950s and 1960s, dams and hydroelectric projects had sprouted up all over Mexico, forever changing rivers, valleys, and the lives of people who were displaced by the dams' reservoirs.) In 1938, the Cárdenas government nationalized oil reserves to form Petróleos Mexicanos (PEMEX); this move infuriated US oil companies and hastened Mexico to become a petroleum-exploring, -consuming, and -exporting country, with all the ecological changes that those activities bring.

Cárdenas was also the first Mexican president to take an active interest in conservation by pushing for the country's first forest reserves and national parks. He selected Miguel Angel de Quevedo to head the new Department of Forestry, Fish, and Game and assist him in this goal. De Quevedo, who founded the Mexican Forestry Society in 1922, was an expert on hydrology and watershed management and believed strongly in protecting forests. He advocated sustainable logging, and he worked to establish forty national parks.

Mexico continued to modernize its agriculture and to industrialize in the 1940s and 1950s. The country was the first site of the "Green Revolution"—a program developed in the United States to increase crop yields by exporting chemical fertilizers, pesticides, and herbicides to less-developed nations. Most of the program, however, was directed to monocrops for export, and it started Mexico on the road to dependency on synthetic, often foreign-made, chemicals that have caused many health problems and deaths of agricultural workers over the years. As the country further developed its manufacturing industries, millions of citizens flocked to the cities for factory jobs. As Mexico City grew at alarming rates (from an area of 116 square kilometers in 1940 to 1,250 square kilometers by 1990, and then growing at an estimated one thousand persons a day), pollution became a severe environmental and health problem. Smog, an especially visible representation of the problem, accounts for why 80 percent of all days in the Distrito Federal have unacceptable ozone levels, with an estimated 3.9 million tonnes of pollutants emitted into the air every year. Likewise, 40 percent of the city lacks an adequate sewage system (Simon 1997, 77–82). The crisis did spawn the development of an environmental movement in Mexico, however. One of the most active groups is the Grupo de los Cien (Group of One Hundred), which lobbies for environmental policies, such as banning the capture and commercialization of sea turtles, reducing the amount of lead in gasoline, and using media to make the public aware of air quality in Mexico City every day (UNEP 2011). In December 2011, the Grupo de los Cien wrote a plea to Mexico's president, Felipe Calderón (in office since 2006), to cancel mining concessions granted to Canadian companies. The mining concessions threaten territory sacred to the Huichol (Wixáritari) people, specifically in the middle of the Wirikuta Natural Reserve (Grupo de los Cien Internacional 2011; *Huffington Post* 2011).

NAFTA, Immigration, and the Future

Urban, agricultural, and conservation problems will continue to plague Mexico in the twenty-first century. Some scholars cite Mexico's involvement since 1994 in the North American Free Trade Agreement (NAFTA) as a way to improve the nation's economy, but others argue that increased trade means more chemical-dependent export agriculture, ecologically unsound mining and logging, and an increase in the *maquiladora* (foreign-owned assembly plants where workers are paid far less than in the United States) in Mexico's border cities. The *maquiladoras* operate with fewer and less-enforced environmental regulations than factories in the United States.

One example of NAFTA's effects is the increase in factory jobs outsourced from Detroit. Because the passage of NAFTA made it easier to move parts across borders, Detroit shifted manufacturing jobs to Mexico to enjoy the lower labor costs. Detroit's automotive manufacturing sector was hit hard by the US recession, however, and by extension, manufacturing jobs in Mexico suffered layoffs and temporary production shutdowns (Malkin 2009). Detroit's economy has been making a steady recovery as of 2012, which the factories in Mexico will hope to benefit from as well (Malkin 2009; O'Connor 2012).

In 1994, the signing of NAFTA also prompted an uprising by the Zapatista Army for National Liberation in Chiapas that continues off and on into the twenty-first century; the movement is still going as of 2012. The Zapatistas claim that neoliberal economic policies like NAFTA eat away at their natural resources without benefiting the residents of Chiapas. They demand more local control and want to protect the tropical environment of their state.

In response to the criticisms of NAFTA's environmental shortcomings, the United States and Mexico created the Border Environment Cooperation Commission (BECC) and the North American Development Bank (NADB) to prevent the lowering of government environmental standards and to support and fund projects to improve environmental infrastructure such as wastewater treatment and solid waste facilities. By the end of 2011, the BECC had certified 189 projects, 103 of which are in Mexico, and the NADB had committed over US$750 million in loans to fund seventy-nine of the projects in Mexico (BECC and NADB 2011, 15, 19).

Environmental factors also may play an important role in rates of immigration from Mexico to the United States. Although illegal immigration from Mexico has fallen drastically, from approximately 525,000 annually to under 100,000 in 2010, in the wake of the US economic recession (Ewing 2011), climate change may raise those numbers once more. A study conducted by the research associate Shuaizhang Feng and his colleagues found a correlation between crop yields and immigration to the United States. As crop yields decline because of climate change (for instance, due to drought or excessively rainy conditions), for every 10 percent reduction in yields, there is a 2 percent increase in migration across the border. Feng and his colleagues project that by 2080, climate change will induce an additional 1.4–6.7 million people to migrate to the United States (Feng, Krueger, and Oppenheimer 2010). Although Feng and colleagues do not address the mitigation and adaptation strategies that Mexico could apply, their report is a sobering prediction of what could happen if climate change and its effects in Mexico go unchecked.

Finally, as of 2012, tourism is the country's top earner of foreign currency and is at the root of many environmental problems along Mexico's coasts. Environmentalists there worry about its continued effects. Mexico is the eighth most popular tourist destination in the world as of 2012, and tourism rates are projected only to grow in coming years. Mexico is estimated to be the second fastest-growing destination by 2013 (Edward 2006). This projected growth naturally raises concerns about environmental exploitation. In response, many ecotourism groups have risen to promote the combination of tourism and environmental sustainability in Mexico. International websites like Eco Tropical Resorts and the International Ecotourism Society provide information to tourists about environmentally responsible and educational activities available in Mexico. More locally based websites like Visit Mexico not only provide ecotourism information, but also provide links to information about government initiatives and involvement in promoting ecotourism and protecting natural resources (Edward 2006; Mexico Sustainable 2010; Visit Mexico 2011). This increase in tourism awareness on behalf of nongovernmental organizations (NGOs), tourist companies, and government organizations is just one way in which Mexico will be able to address economy and environmental sustainability issues in the future.

Although ecotourism and sustainable tourism are, of course, important issues, much of the news from Mexico in 2012 concerns the escalation of violent incidents surrounding the drug war, which in recent years has seen formerly small-scale gang wars flare into full-scale war involving the Mexican Army. As with any conflict, natural resources and various social and economic issues are intimately tied together. Whether the drug war causes or is caused by environmental degradation (or, most likely, both) is difficult to determine, but the human toll has been staggering. Observers hope that the future of Mexico will be more prosperous, sustainable, and peaceable than is currently the case.

Sterling EVANS
University of Oklahoma

Amanda PRIGGE
Berkshire Publishing Group

See also Canada; Caribbean; Central America; Detroit, United States; Ecotourism (the Americas); Guatemala City; Labor; Mexico City; North American Free Trade Agreement (NAFTA); Social Movements (Latin America); Travel and Tourism Industry; United States

FURTHER READING

Aboites Aguilar, Luis. (1998). *El agua de la nación: Una historia política de México (1888–1946)* [The nation's water: A political history of Mexico (1888–1946)]. Mexico City: CIESAS.

Aleshire, Peter. (2001). *Cochise: The life and times of the great Apache chief*. New York: John Wiley & Sons.

Border Environment Cooperation Commission (BECC), & North American Development Bank (NADB). (2011, December 31). Quarterly status report (BECC/NADB Joint Report). San Antonio, TX: BECC & NADB. Retrieved May 30, 2012, from http://www.becc.org/files/latest_reports/js_status_reports/nadb_becc_report_december_2011_eng_final.pdf

Brenner, Anita. (1943). *The wind that swept Mexico: The history of the Mexican Revolution, 1910-1942*. Austin: University of Texas Press.

Colectivos de Apoyo, Solidaridad y Acción (CASA). (2005). Timeline of Zapatista movement. Retrieved May 30, 2012, from http://www.casacollective.org/content/timeline-zapatista-movement

Collier, George Allen, & Quaratiello, Elizabeth Lowery. (1999). *Basta!: Land and the Zapatista rebellion in Chiapas*. Oakland, CA: Food First Books.

Crosby, A. W. (1972). *The Columbian exchange: Biological and cultural consequences of 1492*. Westport, CT: Greenwood Press.

Eco Tropical Resorts. (2011). Mexico eco lodges. Retrieved May 31, 2012, from http://www.eco-tropicalresorts.com/centralamerica/mexico.htm

Edward, Marion. (2006). Hotel interactive: Where we stand: An overview of tourism in Mexico; The Mexican government is supporting a series of resort development projects to capitalize on the nation's popular tourist economy. Retrieved May 31, 2012, from http://www.hotelinteractive.com/article.aspx?articleID=6674

The Esperanza Project. (2012). Wirikuta archive. Retrieved May 30, 2012, from http://theesperanzaproject.org/tag/wirikuta/

Grupo de los Cien Internacional [Group of One Hundred International]. (2011, December 1). Writers and artists ask Mexico's president to cancel mining concessions in the sacred territory of the Huichol people. Retrieved May 30, 2012, from http://www.dickrussell.org/articles/writers.pdf

Ewing, Walter. (2011). Immigration impact: What does record low migration from Mexico mean for immigration reform? Retrieved May 31, 2012, from http://immigrationimpact.com/2011/07/08/what-does-record-low-migration-from-mexico-mean-for-immigration-reform/

Feng, Shuaizhang; Krueger, Alan B.; & Oppenheimer, Michael. (2010). Linkages among climate change, crop yields and Mexico–US cross-border migration. *Proceedings of the National Academy of Science, USA, 107*, 14257–14262.

Huffington Post. (2011, November 30). Mexico mine protested by famous writers and artists. Retrieved May 30, 2012, from http://www.huffingtonpost.com/2011/12/01/mexico-mine_n_1123226.html

Humphrey, Robert R. (1987). *90 years and 535 miles: Vegetation changes along the Mexican border.* Albuquerque: University of New Mexico Press.

Instituto Nacional de Estadística y Geografía (INEGI) [National Institute of Statistics and Geography]. (2011). *Estadísticas del Medio Ambiente del Distrito Federal y Zona Metropolitana* [Metropolitan Zone of the Mexican Valley Statistics]. Mexico City: INEGI.

The International Ecotourism Society. (2012). Bienvenidos to eco-Destinations Mexico feature! Retrieved May 31, 2012, from http://www.ecotourism.org/mexico

Joseph, Gilbert M. (1988). *Revolution from without: Yucatan, Mexico, and the United States, 1880–1924.* Durham, NC: Duke University Press.

Katzenberger, Elaine. (Ed.). (1995). *First world, ha ha ha: The Zapatista challenge.* San Francisco: City Lights Books.

León-Portilla, Miguel. (1990). *The broken spears: The Aztec account of the conquest of Mexico.* Boston: Beacon Press.

Lorey, David E. (1999). *The U.S.-Mexican border in the twentieth century.* Wilmington, DE: SR Books.

MacLachlan, Colin M., & Beezley, William H. (1999). *El gran pueblo: A history of greater Mexico.* Upper Saddle River, NJ: Prentice Hall.

Mader, Ron. (1998). *Mexico: Adventures in nature.* Santa Fe, NM: John Muir Publications.

Malkin, Elisabeth. (2009, April 23). Saving Detroit, and Mexican jobs. Retrieved May 30, 2012, from http://economix.blogs.nytimes.com/2009/04/23/saving-detroit-and-mexican-jobs/

Melville, Elinor G. K. (1994). *A plague of sheep: Environmental consequences of the conquest of Mexico.* Cambridge, UK: Cambridge University Press.

Mexico Sustainable. (2010). Government institutions. Retrieved May 31, 2012, from http://mexico-sustainable.com/wb/Mex_Sustentable/proyectos_gubernamentales

Meyer, Michael C.; Sherman, William L.; & Deeds, Susan M. (2002). *The course of Mexican history.* New York: Oxford University Press.

Meyer, Michael C., & Beezley, William H. (Eds.). (2000). *The Oxford history of Mexico.* New York: Oxford University Press.

O'Connor, Brian J. (2012, March 30). Michigan economy hits 6-year high. Retrieved May 30, 2012, from http://www.detroitnews.com/article/20120330/BIZ/203300341

Radding, Cynthia. (1997). *Wandering peoples: Colonialism, ethnic spaces, and ecological frontiers in northwestern Mexico, 1700–1850.* Durham, NC: Duke University Press.

Richmond, Douglas W. (2002). *The Mexican nation: Historical continuity and modern change.* Upper Saddle River, NJ: Prentice Hall.

Ross, John. (1995). *Rebellion from the roots: Indian uprising in Chiapas.* Monroe, ME: Common Courage Press.

Ross, John. (1998). *The annexation of Mexico: From the Aztecs to the I.M.F.* Monroe, ME: Common Courage Press.

Ross, John. (2000). *The war against oblivion: The Zapatista chronicles.* Monroe, ME: Common Courage Press.

Ruiz, Ramón E. (1992). *Triumphs and tragedy: A history of the Mexican people.* New York: W. W. Norton.

Simon, Joel. (1997). *Endangered Mexico: An environment on the edge.* San Francisco: Sierra Club Books.

Simonian, Lane. (1995). *Defending the land of the jaguar: A history of conservation in Mexico.* Austin: University of Texas Press.

Sklair, Leslie. (1993). *Assembling for development: The maquila industry in Mexico and the United States.* San Diego, CA: Center for U.S.-Mexican Studies, UCSD.

United Nations Environment Programme (UNEP). (2011). Global 500 environmental program: Grupo de los Cien. Retrieved May 30, 2012, from http://www.global500.org/Roll-of-Honour-/-Laureate-Database/Grupo-de-los-Cien.html

United States Central Intelligence Agency (US CIA). (2012). World factbook: Mexico. Retrieved May 30, 2012, from https://www.cia.gov/library/publications/the-world-factbook/geos/mx.html

Visit Mexico. (2011). Homepage. Retrieved May 31, 2012, from http://www.visitmexico.com/

Wright, Angus. (1992). *The death of Ramón González: The modern agricultural dilemma.* Austin: University of Texas Press.

Zapatista Revolution. (n.d.). Homepage. Retrieved May 30, 2012, from http://www.zapatistarevolution.com/

Share the *Encyclopedia of Sustainability*: Teachers are welcome to make up to ten (10) copies of no more than two (2) articles for distribution in a single course or program. For further permissions, please visit www.copyright.com or contact: info@berkshirepublishing.com

Mexico City

19.3 million est. pop. 2012

Mexico City is the second largest conurbation (after São Paolo, Brazil) in the Western Hemisphere. It has high levels of air pollution, an insufficient quantity of potable water, and waste management and transportation problems. The city has initiated several strategies to ameliorate the various stresses to its environment, but the population and the spread of car use pose a serious challenge to not only the population's health and well-being but also to the city's ambition to become a "green" megacity.

Mexico City, also known as the Distrito Federal (or Mexico DF), is the capital of the United Mexican States (Estados Unidos Mexicanos), and is the union's seat of power. It is the largest and most polluted city in the country. Bordered on the east and west by the State of Mexico and to the south by the State of Morelos, it is located in the Valley of Mexico in an area measuring 1,486 square kilometers and rising to 2,240 meters above sea level. With an estimated population of more than 19.3 million, Mexico City is the second largest conurbation (after São Paolo, Brazil) in the Western Hemisphere (US CIA 2012).

What the world thinks of as Mexico City (which comprises the entire Federal District in the same way that Washington, DC completely comprises the District of Columbia) is actually a conglomerate of fifty-nine municipalities in the State of Hidalgo (one municipality) and the State of Mexico (fifty-eight municipalities) that form the Metropolitan Zone of the Valley of Mexico (Zona Metropolitana del Valle de México) (INEGI 2011).

Geographic Situation

Mexico City's problems are exacerbated by its geographical location. Although the Mexico Valley basin, in which Mexico City is located, occupies only 0.03 percent of the country's total land area, it is home to roughly 22 percent of the country's population. Mountains surround the basin, which has high temperatures and weak or no winds. These conditions prevent pollutant dispersion and are thus agents for thermal inversion—conditions which affect not only the environment but the population's health.

This city is located on a site once made up of many lakes: Texcoco Lake, Xochimilco Lake, and Chalco Lake. These now absent lakes form a closed river basin that makes it difficult to disperse atmospheric pollutants. It is one of several megacities (including Beijing, Cairo, Jakarta, Los Angeles, São Paulo, and Moscow) where the levels of air pollution contaminants exceed the acceptable parameters set by the World Health Organization (WHO) (UNEP 2010; WHO Europe 2005).

Environmental Concerns

Mexico City is one of the largest and one of the most polluted cities in the world and is the most polluted in North America (Economy Watch 2010). Mexico's city and federal governments as well as the local governments of the individual municipalities of the states of Mexico and Hidalgo are responsible for dealing with the Metropolitan Zone's environmental problems and concerns. Constitutionally, federal entities are allowed to act on their own to address issues of pollution, but without cooperation between government entities on federal, municipal, and local levels, effective approaches will be counterproductive.

The region's estimated thirty-five thousand industries generate large quantities of urban waste per year. The city cannot meet the population's enormous demand for potable water with its insufficient supply, and its almost 4 million vehicles contribute to severe environmental problems: health-threatening levels of atmospheric pollution, inefficiency in waste management, and the largest and most crowded highways in the country (CAM 2010; INE 2011).

Population growth continues unchecked, and people live in areas in violation of current land-use laws. The government is forced to allow new housing developments to be built in contradiction to environmental and security considerations.

Industries and Urban Development

Mexico City continues to lead the country's economic activity, currently holding 45 percent of industrial activity, including the most polluting industries (SMA 2007b). According to a case study of the city's Climate Action Plan (CEC n.d.), however, from 1990 to 2000 the city's economic base shifted from industrial production toward the service sector (education, financial services, insurance, textiles, telecommunications, information technology, and transportation). Although the government has tried, through environmental programs, to relocate polluting industries outside Mexico City, there are still a large number of factories that produce not only atmospheric emissions but also hazardous waste, household trash, noise, and wastewater.

On the other hand, Mexico City offers its citizens the best standard of living available in the country. It offers a variety of services, has major industries that provide employment, many commercial options, a variety of banks, the country's best transportation and telecommunications systems, and every level of education, including renowned research institutions and universities.

Rural-to-urban population migration is not a recent phenomenon in Mexico City. During the Spanish domination (1521–1810), the capital (at the time), New Spain, had more than fifty thousand houses and more than one million inhabitants and was even larger and more crowded than cities like Paris, Naples, or Venice. This situation caused serious crowding and even food shortages. Since the 1930s, Mexico City's population growth rate has accelerated, but in the 1980s this rate began to decrease while the city's perimeters continued to expand. Between 1990 and 2000, for example, the Federal District's population growth rate was 0.4 percent, while the Metropolitan Zone of the Valley of Mexico grew in area at an average rate of 2.9 percent per year (CAM 2010, 14, 21; SMA 2010, 9).

Not all the land area is developed, however. Of its total surface, roughly 600 square kilometers constitute urban settlements, and the remainder, 880 square kilometers (59 percent of the city's territory), is designated as conservation land (GDF 2007). These natural areas provide the city with a number of environmental services, such as carbon dioxide capture and mitigation of other contaminants through the process of photosynthesis. Conservation land is located mainly to the south of Mexico City, but the need for additional space to harbor the population, businesses, and industries has produced disorderly and irregular growth of the city, thus creating high-risk zones that encroach on conservation lands. This expansion results in an increased deterioration of the natural resources present in these conservation areas (thus offsetting the environmental advantage offered by having designated and maintained them as natural, unpopulated areas) and a further exacerbation of environmental problems such as the lack of potable water and the exploitation of aquifers. The increase of urban lands in the city has provoked an environmental imbalance between the emission of contaminants and the capacity of the ecosystem to absorb them (SMA 2008).

Vehicle Pollution

The vehicles that circulate in Mexico City contribute to 80 percent of the total amount of the city's air pollution. As of 2012, the total number of vehicles is around 4 million (INE 2011). The increase in car use is linked to the population increase in the Metropolitan Zone of the Valley of Mexico; more people means an increase in car usage, and they travel over longer distances because people live far from their jobs.

This large influx of vehicles has also resulted in an insufficient road infrastructure. New and better roads are needed, but construction takes a long time and causes congestion, noise, and emissions of contaminants—all of which adversely affect the quality of the environment and the quality of life for Mexico City's inhabitants, who already often spend more than two hours per day in their cars at reduced speeds of approximately 6–15 kilometers per hour. To alleviate the congestion and to build additional roads and highways that allow for greater movement of cars and public transport, the city has even resorted to piping away water in order to dry out Mexico City's few existing rivers, such as the Mixcoac River, which is now just a large avenue in the city (Beristain 1999). These new roads prevent the filtration of rainwater through the ground, which instead runs off into the sewer systems.

Thermal inversion is a normal phenomenon in the city. It occurs mostly during the dry season, when clear night skies help heat to leak from the Earth's surface toward the troposphere, resulting in a layer of warm air forming above a layer of cold air, thus causing an accumulation of primary pollutants such as nitrogen oxides and particulate matter that generates a phenomenon known as a "heat island," in which the warmed air is trapped and raises temperatures significantly in a localized area.

Overexploitation of Natural Resources

The river basin in which Mexico City is located used to be rich in natural resources: forests, grasslands, and lakes, with a rich biodiversity and, of course, plentiful supplies of food. Overpopulation, however, has produced an overexploitation of those natural resources and heavy deforestation, thereby eliminating the means to control pollution and maintain an ecological balance. These factors inspired the creation of national parks on the city's outskirts. Another resource used without proper control is water, which is drawn from the majority of Mexico City's existing wells and supplemented with water from other basins, such as the Cutzamala. The lowering of the water table, resulting from water pumping and drainage, has caused the former lake bed to dry out and the clay that made it up to contract. As a consequence, Mexico City sank approximately 9 meters between 1910 and 1990 (SMA 2002).

Environmental Action

Mexico City's first large-scale environmental mobilization effort took place in 1987, with a restriction on driving on a specific day of the week for each private vehicle (controlled by license plate number) under a voluntary program called Day Without a Car (*Un día sin auto*) which in 1990 became mandatory and permanent, and changed its name to Today Don't Drive (*Hoy no circula*). This program is still in force, but the excellent results obtained at the beginning of the program have diminished, and it is no longer an effective instrument of pollution reduction or control (many people circumvented the regulation by buying second and third cars with different license plate numbers, and badly maintained older vehicles did not meet emissions regulations). On the other hand, as of 2012, new highways are being constructed, which should reduce traffic congestion; if the new system helps to reduce the amount of time vehicles are stuck in traffic, it will reduce emissions levels. The city has also begun incorporating better systems of public transportation and extended it to cover more zones. The Metrobus, a rapid transit bus, is a convenient mode of transportation along the city's largest avenues. The system's convenience and affordable prices have inspired twenty-two thousand users to abandon the use of personal cars. Operating Metrobus has resulted in a reduction of carbon dioxide (CO_2) emissions by 73,000 tonnes per year and has reduced traffic congestion and commuting time (Mexico City Experience 2012).

The government implemented more environmental laws in the early part of the twenty-first century. The Federal District Environmental Act came into force in 2002, and people took part in not only voluntary but mandatory environmental regulations. Mexico City's Environment Secretariat was created to oversee the increasingly complex system. In 2004, the Federal District Solid Waste Act began a program to separate waste into organic and inorganic categories—the organic waste destined for reuse as compost for public gardens. Starting in 2006, the Ecobici program promoted the use of bikes, including bike rentals, Sunday rides around downtown, and the construction of a special bike lane on some avenues. Since 2009, the Ecobici program has grown to include ninety bicycle rental stations all over the city, with more than a thousand bikes available. Participants register online, and as of 2012, there were approximately thirty thousand registered users, with a waiting list for new subscribers (Alvarado 2010; Kazis 2012).

Mexico City launched the fifteen-year Green Plan (Plan Verde) on 30 August 2007 to address the city's environmental problems and to provide a framework of various public policy instruments on sustainable development. The policies and actions advanced in Mexico City's overall development program for 2007–2012 assume, as their main objective, a commitment to defend the rights and welfare of the capital's entire present and future populations through the conservation and protection of the environment and the efficient and sustainable management of natural resources. One example of this is the plan to change roofs into green areas (SMA 2007c)

To achieve a sustainable city, the authorities are working in tandem with the population. Since 2008, Mexico City's Environment Secretariat has been certifying buildings that use energy efficiently and promoting the program Green Your City, but all of those efforts are not sufficient. To restore the city's environment to sustainability, it is necessary not only to improve governmental programs but to raise the public's and municipal employees' awareness and to clarify the role of all local, municipal, and federal authorities.

Outlook

Several environmental strategies have been initiated since the 1990s. The first was to create a local legal system that would accompany concrete actions, such improving the city's infrastructure (e.g., highways) and its public transportation. Through the Green Plan (Plan Verde) and various other programs such as the Local Strategy for Climate Action (Estrategia Local de Acción Climática) adopted in 2006 and the 2008–2012 Climate Action Plan (Plan de Acción Climática), the government has attempted to develop an integral environmental policy that affords citizens a better quality of life and a better environment while taking into account a constantly growing population that represents a serious challenge for sustainability (CEC n.d.). Mandatory participation and compliance on the part of Mexico City's citizens has become necessary in order to achieve policy goals. Finally, the city needs more political power and more sovereignty than is currently possible because of its designation as the Federal District. It is a growing city with local problems that must be solved with the participation of city, municipal, and federal authorities. The main challenge is to stop the city's rampant growth—both in area and population—but working together will allow citizens and government representatives to achieve a sustainable city.

Ivett MONTELONGO
Gonzalez & Asociados (Gonzalez & Associates)

See also Architecture; Bogotá, Colombia; Caribbean; Central America; Energy Efficiency; Guatemala City; Mexico; Mobility; Public Transportation; Urbanization; Water Use and Rights

FURTHER READING

Alvarado, Paula. (2010, February). Ecobici: Official bike sharing program launched in Mexico City. Retrieved May 29, 2012, from http://www.treehugger.com/bikes/ecobici-official-bike-sharing-program-launched-in-mexico-city.html

Asociación Nacional de Abogados [National Association of Attorneys]. (1985). *Contaminación ambiental en la frontera entre México y los Estados Unidos de América (II reunión conjunta de la Asociación Nacional de Abogados y el Comité de Derecho Ambiental de la American Bar Association de los Estados Unidos)* [Pollution on the border between Mexico and the United States of America (Second joint meeting of the National Bar Association and the Environmental Law Committee of the United States)]. Mexico City, Mexico: National Association of Attorneys.

Bassols Batalla, Angel; Salazar, Gloria González; & National Autonomous University of Mexico, Institute of Economic Research. (1993). *Zona metropolitana de la ciudad de México: Complejo geográfico, socioeconómico y político. Colección la estructura económica y social de México* [Metropolitan area of Mexico City: Complex geographic, socioeconomic and political development. Collection of economic and social structures of Mexico]. Mexico City, Mexico: Federal District Department, Institute of Economic Research.

Beristain, Javier. (Ed.). (1999). *Los retos de la Ciudad de México en el umbral del siglo XXI* [The challenges of Mexico City in the twenty-first century]. Mexico City: ITAM Program for the analysis of relations between Mexico, the United States, and Canada; Mexico City: Miguel Angel Porrúa Editorial Group.

Carmona Lara, María del Carmen. (2001) Derechos en relación con el medio ambiente: Cámara de Diputados, LVIII Legislatura [Rights in relation to the environment: Chamber of Deputies, LVIII Legislature]. Mexico City: National Autonomous University of Mexico.

Carranco Zúñiga, Joel. (2000). *Régimen jurídico del Distrito Federal* [Federal District legal system]. Mexico City: Miguel Angel Porrúa Editorial Group.

Carrillo Azpeitia, Rafael. (1984). *Historia de la Ciudad de México desde su fundación como capital del Imperio Mexica, hasta su gran desarrollo* [History of Mexico City from its founding as the capital of the Aztec Empire, to its great development]. Mexico City: Panorama Editorial.

Comisión Ambiental Metropolitana (CAM) [Metropolitan Environmental Commission]. (2010). *Agenda de sustentabilidad ambiental para la Zona Metropolitana del Valle de Mexico.* [Environmental sustainability agenda for the metropolitan zone of the Mexican Valley]. Naucalpan, Mexico: CAM.

Commission for Environmental Cooperation (CEC). (n.d.). Best energy management practices in 13 North American municipalities: Case study: Climate action plan energy projects, Mexico City, Federal District, Mexico. Retrieved March 30, 2012, from http://www.cec.org/municipalenergy/docs/Mexico%20City.pdf

Consejo Nacional de Población (CONAPO) [National Population Council]. (1998). *Escenarios demográficos y urbanos de la Zona Metropolitana de la Ciudad de México, 1990-2010 (Síntesis)* [Demographic and urban scenarios of the metropolitan area of Mexico City, 1990–2010 (Summary)]. México, City: CONAPO.

Contreras Bustamante, Raúl. (2001). *La Ciudad de México como Distrito Federal y entidad federative: Historia y perspectivas* [Mexico City as a Federal District and a federative entity: History and perspectives]. Mexico City, Mexico: Miguel Angel Porrúa Editorial Group.

Correa García, Armando. (2004). *Contaminantes atmosféricos en la zona metropolitana de la ciudad de México* [Air pollutants in the metropolitan area of Mexico City]. Mexico City: National Polytechnic Institute and Autonomous Metropolitan University.

Economy Watch. (2010). Population density. Retrieved May 9, 2012, from http://www.economywatch.com/world-country/population-density.html

Gil Corrales, Miguel Ýngel. (2007). *Crónica ambiental: Gestión pública de políticas ambientales en México* [Environmental report: Governance of environmental policies in Mexico]. Mexico City: Economic Culture Fund; Secretariat of Environment and Natural Resources (SEMARNAT); & National Statistics Institute (INE).

Gobierno del Distrito Federal (GDF) [Federal District Government]. (2007). *Programa general de desarrollo 2007–2012* [General program development 2007–2012]. Mexico City: Federal District Government.

Gómez, Laura. (2012). Se triplicó en 20 años el número de autos en las calles: Especialistas [Number of cars on the Street triples in 20 years: Experts say]. Retrieved May 25, 2012, from http://www.jornada.unam.mx/2012/05/03/capital/040n1cap

Instituto Nacional de Ecología (INE) [National Institute of Ecology]. (2011). *Cuarto almanaque de datos y tendencias de la calidad del aire en 20 ciudades mexicanas (2000–2009)* [Fourth almanac data and trends in air quality in 20 Mexican cities (2000–2009)]. Mexico City: INE.

Instituto Nacional de Estadística y Geografía (INEGI) [National Institute of Statistics and Geography]. (2002). *Estadísticas del medio ambiente del Distrito Federal y zona metropolitana* [Environment statistics of the Federal District and metropolitan area]. Mexico City: INEGI.

Instituto Nacional de Estadística y Geografía (INEGI) [National Institute of Statistics and Geography]. (2011). *Estadísticas del medio ambiente del Distrito Federal y zona metropolitana* [Metropolitan Zone of the Mexican Valley Statistics]. Mexico City: INEGI.

Kazis, Noah. (2012, March 22). With a boost from bike-share, cycling surges on Mexico City's mean streets. Retrieved May 29, 2012, from http://www.streetsblog.org/2012/03/22/with-a-boost-from-bike-share-cycling-surges-on-mexico-citys-mean-streets/

McNeill, J. R. (2000). Something new under the sun: An environmental history of the twentieth-century world. New York: Norton & Company, Inc.

Mexico City Experience. (2012). Green living: Transportation. Retrieved May 29, 2012, from http://www.mexicocityexperience.com/green_living/transportation/

Secretaría de Medio Ambiente del Distrito Federal (SMA) [Mexico City's Environment Secretariat]. (2002). *Programa de protección ambiental 2002–2006* [Environmental protection program 2002–2006]. Mexico City: SMA.

Secretaría de Medio Ambiente del Distrito Federal (SMA) [Mexico City's Environment Secretariat]. (2007a). *Agenda ambiental de la Ciudad de México* [The environmental agenda of Mexico City]. Mexico City: Mexico City's Environment Secretariat.

Secretaría de Medio Ambiente del Distrito Federal (SMA) [Mexico City's Environment Secretariat]. (2007b). *Programa de manejo sustentable del agua para la Ciudad de México* [Mexico City's program of sustainable management of water]. Mexico City: Mexico City's Environment Secretariat.

Secretaría de Medio Ambiente del Distrito Federal (SMA) [Mexico City's Environment Secretariat]. (2007c). *Plan Verde de la Ciudad de México* [Mexico City's Green Plan]. Mexico City: Mexico City's Environment Secretariat.

Secretaría de Medio Ambiente del Distrito Federal (SMA) [Mexico City's Environment Secretariat]. (2008). *Programa de acción climática de la Ciudad de México 2008–2012* [Mexico City's climate action program 2008–2012]. Mexico City: Mexico City's Environment Secretariat.

Secretaría de Medio Ambiente del Distrito Federal (SMA) [Mexico City's Environment Secretariat]. (2010). *Inventario de residuos sólidos del Distrito Federal 2010* [2010 Inventory of the solid waste of the Federal District 2010]. Mexico City: Mexico City's Environment Secretariat.

Secretaria de Medio Ambiente del Distrito Federal (SMA) [Mexico City's Environment Secretariat]. (2011). *Quinto informe de trabajo* [Fifth report of employment]. Mexico City: Mexico City's Environment Secretariat.

United Nations Environment Programme (UNEP). (2010). *GEO Latin America and the Caribbean outlook GEO LAC 3*. Nairobi, Kenya: United Nations Environment Programme, Regional Office for Latin America and the Caribbean.

United States Central Intelligence Agency (US CIA). (2012). The world factbook: Mexico. Retrieved June 14, 2012, from https://www.cia.gov/library/publications/the-world-factbook/geos/mx.html

World Health Organization Regional Office for Europe (WHO Europe). (2005). *Air quality guidelines: Global Update 2005*. Copenhagen, Denmark. WHO Europe.

World Bank. (2006). *Ecosistema urbano y salud de los habitantes de la zona metropolitana del valle de México* [Urban ecosystem and health of the inhabitants of the metropolitan area of Mexico Valley]. Washington, DC: World Bank.

Berkshire's authors and editors welcome questions, comments, and corrections. Send your emails about the *Berkshire Encyclopedia of Sustainability* in general or this volume in particular to: sustainability.updates@berkshirepublishing.com

Mining (Andes)

There has been a dramatic expansion of mining in the Andes since the 1990s. Governments with different political ideologies have promoted mining as a way to increase economic growth and alleviate poverty, but the industry puts pressure on land and water resources, undermines traditional livelihoods, and creates environmental and health risks. The growth of mining has led to conflicts with affected populations and to ongoing debate regarding the policies needed to promote more equitable and sustainable extraction.

The world's longest continental mountain range, the Andes runs through seven countries—Argentina, Bolivia, Chile, Colombia, Ecuador, Peru, and Venezuela—along the western coast of South America. Mining, or the process of extracting minerals and other valuable materials from the Earth, has a long history in many parts of the region (Dore 2000). During the colonial period, for instance, the mines of Potosí in Upper Peru (present-day Bolivia) were a rich source of silver for the Spanish. From the mid-1800s to the 1920s, the Atacama Desert in the central Andes was mined intensively for sodium nitrate, which was used in Europe and the United States as fertilizer and in the production of explosives. During the 1900s, industrial copper production expanded in Chile and Peru, while Bolivia was one of the world's major tin producers.

Mining is one of the principal industries that links Andean societies with the global economy. It has driven regional economic growth and provided revenue for Andean governments. At the same time, it has been associated with many social and ecological problems, including inhumane labor conditions, extreme levels of material inequality, ecological destruction, and long-term human health impacts. The smelter town of La Oroya, Peru, is a stark illustration of the effects of mining: having processed ores mined from Peru's central highlands for nearly a century, the town was recently identified as one of the ten most polluted places in the world, with average blood lead levels among children three times as high as World Health Organization limits (Blacksmith Institute 2007). Mining investment in the Andes has intensified since 1990, and mining activities have multiplied. This has led to conflicts with local affected populations and to new efforts to promote more equitable and sustainable forms of mineral development. Debate continues, however, regarding what sustainable mining in the Andes would entail and the mechanisms through which it might be achieved.

Boom Times: Growth and Conflict

Three main factors lie behind the recent growth of mining in the Andes: (1) increased demand for minerals on global markets, especially from rapidly industrializing countries like Brazil, China, and India; (2) advances in extraction and processing technologies that have made previously uneconomical mineral deposits profitable to exploit; and (3) government policies that have facilitated foreign mineral investment and led to a new round of privatization and transnationalization of Andean mining sectors (this following a period of greater state involvement). A geographical expansion of mineral development activities has occurred in countries with long-standing mining traditions, like Chile and Peru, as well as in countries without such traditions, for example, Colombia and Ecuador. Mining takes diverse forms in the Andes, and some areas have seen a growth in small- and medium-scale operations. Colombia and Peru, for example, have seen a jump in small-scale gold production from alluvial deposits. Much new investment, however, has been directed toward the large-scale mining sector. The British geographer Gavin Bridge (2004) reported that twelve of the world's top twenty-five mine investments by value made between 1990 and 2001 were located in Andean countries, the largest being the US$2.35 billion Antamina polymetallic mine in Peru's Ancash region. These enormous investments have resulted in the development of numerous capital-intensive open-pit operations, which are often capable of processing tens of thousands of tonnes of ore per day from widely dispersed, low-grade mineral deposits.

In countries where recent mining investment has been concentrated, industry growth has led to surging production. In Chile, for example, copper production rose from 2.2 million tonnes in 1994 to 5.4 million tonnes in 2009 (which accounted for 34 percent of that year's total world mine production of copper). Notably, 20 percent of Chilean copper production in 2009 came from just one operation, the Escondida mine. Located in Chile's Atacama Desert, Escondida is the world's largest single producer of copper. As a result of these production increases, the importance of mining to these countries' economies has been consolidated. In 2007, for instance, Peruvian mining exports, which totaled US$17.2 billion, accounted for 61.8 percent of Peru's total exports, and the mining sector contributed 49 percent of all revenue received by the treasury (MINEM 2011; SNMPE 2011).

The growth of mining has triggered social, ecological, and territorial conflicts (Bebbington 2009). In many parts of the Andes, areas targeted for mining investment have become contested zones, with struggles revolving around the impacts of mining on land and water resources, the rights of affected people to participate in mining decisions, and the distribution of mining's economic benefits. It has become increasingly common for the proposed construction of a new mine (or the proposed expansion of an existing operation) to elicit opposition from potentially affected groups who feel their health and livelihood may be threatened. At times, antimining activism during the early stages of mine development has led to the suspension of projects, as has occurred in Esquel, Argentina (Urkidi and Walter 2011); Cotacachi, Ecuador (Bebbington et al. 2008b); and Tambogrande, Peru (Muradian, Martínez-Alier, and Correa 2003). In early 2012, the future of the planned US$4.8 billion Minas Conga gold mine in Peru's Cajamarca region was uncertain due to broad social opposition revolving around the potential impacts of the operation on regional water supplies (Poulden 2012).

Sustainable Mining?

Recent mining trends in the Andes have various implications for sustainability. As suggested by adherents to the "resource curse" hypothesis, the concentration of economic activity in the mining sector may leave Andean governments and economies vulnerable to fluctuations in global commodity prices and also undermine democratic governance, including by encouraging corruption (Bebbington et al. 2008a). In addition, while huge mining operations may be highly lucrative, they tend to offer relatively few employment opportunities for local people, due to their particular labor and input requirements. Because these large-scale mining enterprises operate outside the local social, community, and economic structure, they are often limited in their capacity to contribute to broad-based and sustainable socioeconomic development at the local and regional levels. Given that much mining in the Andes takes place in relatively poor and historically marginalized areas, such sustainable development is especially critical. Furthermore, the trend toward open-pit mining dramatically increases the spatial and environmental footprints of mining operations due to the greater quantity of resources required (land, water, and energy) as well as the higher volumes of wastes generated. To make way for the large open-pit mines, local people are often displaced, in the process losing their traditional land-based livelihood practices, such as farming and ranching (Szablowski 2002). Moreover, the tendency for mines to be located in the upper reaches of watersheds intensifies the potential for mining expansion to degrade rural and urban water supplies (Bebbington and Bury 2009). Finally, new mineral processing techniques often entail numerous ecological and human health risks, including risks related to the use of large quantities of toxic chemicals, such as cyanide in the case of heap-leach gold mining.

In the context of these trends, the industry has made efforts to transform mining to make it more socially and environmentally sustainable. While the scope and nature of these efforts varies among mining firms (including within the same country), they often involve several emphases. One is eco-efficiency, or using cleaner and more environmentally efficient production and waste-management techniques. To reduce its carbon footprint, for instance, Barrick Gold Corporation recently built a wind farm at its Veladero mine in Argentina that provides up to 20 percent of the mine's electricity needs. Another emphasis is community-level social development programs. These may be undertaken in conjunction with civil society organizations and/or local and regional governments; they typically focus on populations in the vicinity of mine operations (known as "host" communities). A third emphasis is mine-site rehabilitation, usually designed to stabilize the mine site physically and chemically to allow it to be used in a different way after the mine is closed.

While mining firms often point to these efforts as evidence of their proactive dedication to the principles of sustainability, improvements in social and environmental performance are typically the result of a complex mix of pressures from local populations, activist networks, nongovernmental organizations, and international financial institutions. There has also been a general trend toward more stringent state-based environmental regulations for mining, though critics note that governments are often reluctant to enforce such regulations given the economic importance of mining (Bebbington 2009).

Ongoing Debates

It is notable that, overall, corporate strategies tend to approach the mining–sustainability relationship as a techno-engineering or managerial issue. In policy and academic circles, broader debate is taking place on the institutions that are needed to foster more just and sustainable mining. Indeed, the recent surge in mining-related conflicts has placed the mining–environment–development relationship squarely on the public agenda in many Andean countries (Bebbington 2009). In upcoming years, these debates are likely to involve several pending issues. One is legislation that guarantees the rights of affected people to participate in mining decisions and oversight (including the right of free, prior, and informed consent). Another issue is land-use planning and the policies needed to reduce the likelihood that mining will conflict with important existing land uses and environmental services. This will involve an especially thorny political debate over who will decide what areas will be off-limits to mining and how the decisions will be made. A third pending issue is how to better collect and distribute revenue generated through mining in order to promote local and regional socioeconomic development (and the respective roles of states, corporations, and civil society in these development efforts). Related to this is the issue of how to guarantee greater transparency from governments and corporations regarding the collection and use of taxes on mining operations.

Debates on these issues will be shaped by a number of dynamics. One is the election of left-leaning politicians and governments in Andean countries, such as Evo Morales in Bolivia and Rafael Correa in Ecuador. The evidence suggests that these administrations will continue to pursue development strategies based on mining and other extractive industries, using some of the income generated to support progressive social programs (Gudynas 2009; Kaup 2010). Some social movements that broadly share these administrations' political goals are nonetheless critical of mining expansion. Such movements have been important in pressuring the industry to reform its social and environmental practices, and the way they relate to the left-leaning administrations will impact the future of mining–sustainability debates in these countries.

Another significant dynamic is a shift in the source of mining investment, in particular a growth of investment from emerging economies like China. In Chile, for instance, the state mining company Codelco formed a joint venture with a Chinese firm to develop new mining properties. In Peru, Chinese companies plan to invest more than US$7.4 billion in mining ventures between 2009 and 2014 (Sanborn and Torres 2009). Chinese firms often differ from other transnational mining firms in important ways, such as ownership structure, forms of organization and decision making, and sources of financing. Because the growth of Chinese investment is a relatively new phenomenon, it is unclear how these firms will relate to governments, civil society, and communities in the Andes around sustainability issues.

In sum, trends suggest that Andean countries will continue to be important targets for international mining investment in upcoming years. It remains uncertain, however, whether frameworks can be established to reduce conflicts around the ongoing expansion of mining and make it more compatible with the goals of social justice and environmental sustainability.

Matthew D. HIMLEY
Illinois State University

See also Andes Mountains; Appalachian Mountains; Amazonia; Labor; Mining (Australia); Multilateral Environmental Agreements (MEAs); Organization of American States (OAS); Rocky Mountains; Social Movements (Latin America)

Further Reading

Bebbington, Anthony J. (2009). The new extraction: Rewriting the political ecology of the Andes? *NACLA Report on the Americas, 42*(5), 12–20.

Bebbington, Anthony J., & Bury, Jeffrey T. (2009). Institutional challenges for mining and sustainability in Peru. *Proceedings of the National Academy of Sciences, 106*(41), 17296–17301.

Bebbington, Anthony J.; Hinojosa, Leonith; Humphreys Bebbington, Denise; Burneo, Maria Luisa; & Warnaars, Ximena. (2008a). Contention and ambiguity: Mining and the possibilities of development. *Development and Change, 39*(6), 887–914.

Bebbington, Anthony J., et al. (2008b). Mining and social movements: Struggles over livelihood and rural territorial development in the Andes. *World Development, 36*(12), 2888–2905.

Blacksmith Institute. (2007). *The world's worst polluted places: The top ten of the dirty thirty.* New York: Blacksmith Institute.

Bridge, Gavin. (2004). Mapping the bonanza: Geographies of mining investment in an era of neoliberal reform. *The Professional Geographer, 56*(3), 406–421.

Dore, Elizabeth. (2000). Environment and society: Long-term trends in Latin American mining. *Environment and History, 6*(1), 1–29.

Gudynas, Eduardo. (2009). *Diez tesis urgentes sobre el nuevo extractivismo: Contextos y demandas bajo el progresismo sudamericano actual* [Ten urgent theses regarding the new extractivism: Contexts and demands under the current South American progressivism]. In CAAP & CLAES (Eds.), *Extractivismo, política y sociedad* [Extractivism, politics and society] (pp. 187–225). Quito, Ecuador: Centro Andino de Acción Popular (CAAP) & Centro Latino Americano de Ecología Social (CLAES).

Kaup, Brent Z. (2010). A neoliberal nationalization? The constraints on natural-gas-led development in Bolivia. *Latin American Perspectives, 37*(3), 123–138.

Ministerio de Energía y Minas (MINEM). (2011). *Perú 2010: Anuario minero* [Peru 2010: Annual mining report]. Lima, Peru: MINEM.

Muradian, Roldan; Martínez-Alier, Joan; & Correa, Humberto. (2003). International capital versus local population: The environmental conflict for the Tambogrande mining project, Peru. *Society and Natural Resources, 16*(9), 775–792.

Poulden, Gervase. (2012). Tainted gold: Thousands join protest against Peru's largest ever mining project. Retrieved February 4, 2012, from http://www.theecologist.org/News/news_analysis/1202914/tainted_gold_thousands_join_protest_against_perus_largest_ever_mining_project.html

Sanborn, Cynthia A., & Torres, C. Victor. (2009). *La economía china y las industrias extractivas: Desafíos para el Perú* [The Chinese economy and extractive industries: Challenges for Peru]. Lima, Peru: CooperAcción & Universidad del Pacífico.

Sociedad Nacional de Minería, Petróleo y Energía (SNMPE). (2011). *La tributación minera en el Perú: Contribución, carga tributaria y fundamentos conceptuales* [Mining taxation in Peru: Contribution, tax burden and conceptual foundations]. Lima, Peru: SNMPE.

Szablowski, David. (2002). Mining, displacement and the World Bank: A case analysis of Compania Minera Antamina's Operations in Peru. *Journal of Business Ethics, 39*(3), 247–273.

Urkidi, Leire, & Walter, Mariana. (2011). Dimensions of environmental justice in anti-gold mining movements in Latin America. *Geoforum, 42*(6), 683–695.

Share the *Encyclopedia of Sustainability*: Teachers are welcome to make up to ten (10) copies of no more than two (2) articles for distribution in a single course or program. For further permissions, please visit www.copyright.com or contact: info@berkshirepublishing.com

Mining (Australia)

Sustainably managed mining is based on three dynamic control factors—sociopolitical, techno-environmental, and techno-economic—that drive innovation and engineering toward cheaper and more efficient solutions. In Australia, high productivity and the ability to mine lower grades in harsher environments have led to an increase in mining waste as the commodity demand increases. More-stringent social and environmental protection measures, however, will advance responsible and efficient mining.

Minerals and metals make up an important part of the essential primary inputs, or base-level ingredients, for the continued existence of modern society. The processes of industrialization, economic development, and economic growth are thus inextricably bound to mining. Although mineral wealth is geographically predetermined, its benefits are spread across the world through international trade. Most mineral-rich countries sell their mineral products in the international arena and use the gains from trade to purchase other natural resources, manufactured goods, and services from the rest of the world.

Australia is particularly well endowed with mineral deposits. Metal mining is dominant in the west and south of the country, while coal mining is prevalent in the eastern part of the country. Australia is the world's primary producer of bauxite, the second largest producer of iron ore, lead, alumina, and manganese, and the third largest producer of gold, nickel, zinc, uranium, and brown coal. On the whole, the economically viable deposits are efficiently mined, giving rise to significant levels of employment, aligned manufacturing, and services. The Minerals Council of Australia asserts that for the period 2009–2010 the mining industry employed 187,200 people directly plus 599,680 in support industries, totaling approximately 7 percent of the labor force. Further, it exports most of its minerals and metals, which generates considerable foreign exchange. In 2011, the Minerals Council published that contribution of the mining industry to Australian export income was about $138 billion, or 54 percent of all exports (MCA 2011, 1). Australia is also well ahead of other countries in terms of mining technologies; for example, over 60 percent of the world's mines operate with Australian-based software (Australian Mining n.d.).

Mineral deposits are nonrenewable, in that once they have been mined, they cannot be re-created in economically feasible time. Although Earth processes continuously create anomalous concentrations of minerals, this takes millions of years. In addition, each mineral deposit is unique, with inherent attributes that make it economically viable or not. Some important attributes are the mineralogy or minerals that make up the rock, the depth under the Earth's surface of the deposit, the geological environment in which the deposit occurs, the geographical location of the deposit, and the grade of the deposit. Grade is the proportion of valuable to waste material contained in the deposit. To compound matters further, mineral deposits do not have uniform grade distributions.

The Joint Ore Reserves Committee of Australia developed guidelines to classify an economically viable mineral deposit (called a reserve) from a resource (which includes both the reserve and the uneconomical known deposits). Increased geological and engineering knowledge reduces uncertainty about the potentially viable mineral deposits.

Dynamic Control Factors

Three dynamic control factors—sociopolitical, techno-economic and techno-environmental—generate transitions from resource to reserve, and vice versa. The dynamic control factors reflect the impacts of the social and political environment, technological advances, and changes that the natural environmental have on the reserve/resource definition. All relate directly to managing the mining industry in a sustainable and responsible manner.

Sociopolitical Dynamic Control Factors

The majority of writing, codes, and declarations on sustainable mining deal with the sociopolitical dynamic control factors. Foremost among these is the Mining Minerals and Sustainable Development Project (MMSD), which is described below. Second, Aboriginal land rights are entrenched in the Australian system of laws and are meant to protect the (usually marginalized) indigenous people. Third, mining royalty systems in Australia are also used in the political arena as a means to redistribute mineral wealth. Fourth, fly-in/fly-out (FIFO) workforces remain contentious sociopolitical issues.

In response to several high-profile global environmental and sustainable development initiatives, the mining industry took up the challenge in 1999 to develop its own particular framework on sustainable development. This was conducted under the auspices of the Global Mining Initiative, which commissioned the MMSD. Australia was one of four regional partners in the independent study, and its MMSD report, *Facing the Future*, was published in 2002. It calls for a socially inclusive approach to mining activities, fairer distribution of costs and benefits, and mindfulness of the rights and well-being of indigenous communities. It also provides guidelines for seven critical areas relating to how the mining industry can contribute to Australia's transition to sustainable development. Although the guidelines remain voluntary, they provide a blueprint for individual mining companies and industry bodies to gain a social license to operate. Most industry organizations, such as the Mineral Council of Australia, adhere to the guidelines. No consensus, however, yet exists on the application, design, and measurement of operational rules to achieve the critical standards.

The rights of indigenous Australians were entrenched during 1992 when the Australian High Court, in the famous *Mabo* case (*Mabo v. Queensland* 1992), ruled that Aboriginal people have rights to land, called Native Title. The ruling led to the passing of the Native Title Act 1993, which gave Aboriginal people the right to negotiate interests on land over which they had been awarded Native Title. The Native Title Amendment Act 1996 replaced the right to negotiate with the right to be consulted on the granting of mining leases. Although there is still much room for improvement, respect for Aboriginal community values and their cultural attachment to the land increasingly has been shown by mining companies in Australia, often to the benefit of both parties. Contention still exists regarding the application of the act, the long delays to complete mining lease negotiations, and the actual establishment of historical cultural value on the lands.

Mining-specific taxes and royalties are charges levied by state and federal governments under the assumption that excess profits, or rents, are made in the process of mining. Also, because Australia is fiscally decentralized into three tiers of government—federal, state, and local—the collection of mining taxes remains a politically contested domain. Theoretically, the federal government should concern itself only with issues of overarching national importance; for example, defense, foreign relations, macroeconomic management, and redistribution of wealth. State governments should be concerned only with issues confined to their borders, and local governments should deal only with municipal issues. In this light, the state governments purport that royalties from mining should accrue to them, since mining is geographically fixed. Further, mineral-rich states often require greater than normal infrastructure building. The federal government, however, argues that additional taxes, or royalties, accruing from mining activities should benefit the entire country. Both are correct, but the outcome of the debate remains undetermined. Most mining companies are indifferent about who charges the tax as long as the system is predictable. Mining projects are long-term investments, and unpredictable factors add undesirable risk.

The FIFO workforces are people who live in one place, such as a city, and travel long distances to their workplaces, such as a mine site. The advantages of a FIFO workforce, particularly with short-duration mining projects ranging between five and ten years, is that no unsustainable townships are built. The disadvantages are more numerous. Fly-in/fly-out workers experience more social and physiological displacement than those who return home every day. Existing settlements near a mine site with FIFO workers seldom gain from the benefits of mining, even though it occurs in their immediate vicinity. The debate on FIFO workforces is still strong in the Australian sociopolitical environment; however, there is a loose consensus that each mine site should be judged on its particular merits, and that generalizations can be more harmful than helpful.

Techno-Economic Dynamic Control Factors

The techno-economic factors of mining are expressed as advances in technologies that come about by changes in prices. Price drivers can be separated into output prices and input prices. The output prices, or prices of the commodities themselves, have an impact on revenues. Conversely, input prices, such as wages and fuel prices, control costs. Declining output prices or increasing input prices creates incentives for technological and engineering advances that lead to more efficient production methods and, consequently, lower costs.

Australia has little influence on commodity prices, which are determined by the interaction of world demand and supply. The historic consequences that output prices have had on mining are complicated but can be reasonably understood through three effects. First, two economists, Raúl Prebish (1950) and Hans Singer (1950), proposed that the prices of primary commodities, which include all mining outputs, have increased less quickly relative to prices of manufactured goods. This hypothesis has been substantiated through many studies; see, for example, the 2008 United Nations *Trade and Development Report*. Second, rich high-grade deposits that are easy to access and fall into known geological sequences are mined first. Generally, the grade and quality of remaining deposits declines over time. Third, decreasing relative prices have been more than offset by technological advances in mining, but at the cost of an exponentially increasing generation of mining wastes and energy use along with higher environmental degradation and social impacts.

The Australian mining industry usually separates input prices into the price of labor, the price of capital machinery, and the price of fuels including explosives. Similar to the situation with output or commodity prices, the Australian mining industry has little control over fuel and machinery prices, which are determined in the world market. The price of labor, however, can be controlled. Compared to other mining-intensive economies, Australia is relatively underpopulated and has what is called a labor-scarce economy. As a consequence, the price of labor relative to the price of machinery is high, resulting in what is called a capital-intensive industry. High labor costs create strong incentives for technological advance, which translates into the utilization of more machinery in an attempt to capture the decreasing per-unit costs as output expands, or returns-to-scale. The returns-to-scale also result in the generation of increasing amounts of energy used and waste produced.

The compounding waste-generating effects from decreasing relative commodity prices and high wages concern the mining industry, individual mining companies, government, and civil society in Australia. In response, the concept of mine environmental management, as a continuous process implemented through the entire life of the mine, has become almost synonymous with Australian mining. Mine environmental management demands an increasingly efficient mine design and feasibility processes along with better and safer mining practices. The safe treatment of wastes and the more efficient use of energy are synonymous with good mining engineering and minerals processing. These efficiency-enhancing processes, or techno-environmental dynamic control factors, have additional drivers and incentive structures.

Techno-Environmental Dynamic Control Factors

In Australia, the techno-environmental control factors are those incentives and drivers that promote a precautionary environmental risk management process in engineering design. Although regulations differ from state to state, they essentially provide similar guidelines. Important among them are protection of vulnerable ecosystems, use of environmental bonds, and adherence to specific aspects of waste management. In a similar vein, the proposed carbon tax can be considered a driver toward more efficient energy use. The carbon tax is based on a charge per unit of equivalent carbon emissions, in effect increasing the cost of atmospheric polluting activities. Before mining can commence, a redeemable environmental bond and an environmental risk management plan, based on an environmental impact study, must be ratified by the environmental protection authority of the state in which mining will take place.

Mining activities in Australia are subject to strict environmental regulations made to protect valuable ecosystems and to ensure that impacts are minimized or mitigated. Most of the regulations are not specific to mining; however, issues such as mine water usage and disposal, acid mine drainage, and the various kinds of mineral processing discharges are carefully controlled by environmental authorities. The monitoring is mainly undertaken by the mines themselves but is subject to government oversight.

Environmental bonds are an important incentive for mining companies to minimize their environmental impact, but only if they are set at a reasonably high level. The bond is a sum of money held aside at the start of a mining project and redeemable only after the satisfactory rehabilitation of the mine after it has closed. If the bond is set too high, mining might not occur at all, and the benefits are lost. But it has to be high enough to create an incentive for the mining company to spend money on rehabilitation. The value of the bond also depends on the type of mineral or metal to be extracted, the type of mining, and the environmental footprint arising from mining activities. In response to the environmental bond, and other regulations, Australian mining companies have discovered that a continuous process of environmental monitoring and mitigation results in lower overall costs than simply cleaning up after mining activities have finished. The incentive has worked to the extent that mine environmental management is becoming integral to day-to-day operations, not only in the long-term planning and feasibility stage.

One important innovation that has arisen in the Australian mining industry, particularly among the large mining companies, is the weak sustainability option. This is applied to an economic definition of sustainability, namely, that net economic benefits should be maximized while sustaining the capital stock over time. The weak sustainability option proposes that different types of capital are substitutable. For example, natural capital in the form of a mineral deposit can be substituted for other types of capital, such as ecological natural capital, human capital, or physical infrastructure like roads. Although mining makes a substantial contribution to human and physical or built capital, Australian mining companies are committed to sustaining natural capital by offering environmental capital swaps. An environmental capital swap might occur when the ecological footprint of current mining is partly mitigated by the mine company rehabilitating environmentally degraded land elsewhere. Usually the rehabilitated land is larger than the footprint of the working mine. So far, swaps have been mainly voluntary and have not released the mine from its other obligations to minimize environmental risk from its operations.

The techno-economic and techno-environmental dynamic control factors both involve technical solutions, at least from a weak sustainability point of view, through the application of best-practice engineering. Mitigating the sociopolitical dynamic control factors, however, is what gives the mine its social license to operate and forms the third leg of the sustainable development tripod. Managing Australian mining in a sustainable way thus requires stable economic incentive structures, best practices and innovative engineering solutions, a continuous process of improving the well-being of communities affected by mining, and the fair redistribution of excess mining profits.

Future Outlook

The three dynamic control factors will continue to affect the Australian mining industry in different and sometimes conflicting ways. On the techno-economic side, the increased demand for mineral and mineral products will drive investment into mining-related activities; most importantly, exploration and engineering innovations. For example, advances in mining and metallurgical technology enable the exploitation of deposits in hasher environments, in deeper locations, and with lower grades. The sociopolitical outlook in the form of a carbon tax, a federal government's mineral resource rent tax, and more stringent environmental regulations, should provide further incentives to lower costs through efficient and effective engineering solutions.

The big challenge will be how to handle an increasing volume of mining waste and its associated environmental hazards. In response to such techno-environmental problems, the treatment and containment of mining wastes are gaining in importance in Australia and will continue to play an increasingly vital role in the industry. Finally, a law reform process on Native Title for Aboriginal people is likely, with a positive outcome expected for both mining companies and the Aboriginal people.

Erkan TOPAL and Diarmid MATHER
Western Australian School of Mines, Curtin University

See also Andes Mountains; Appalachian Mountains; Australia; Labor; Mining (Andes); Rocky Mountains

Further Reading

The Australasian Joint Ore Reserves Committee. (2004). Homepage. Retrieved January 20, 2012, from http://www.jorc.org/

Australian Government, Bureau of Resources and Energy Economics. (2012). Resources data. Retrieved January 20, 2012, from http://www.bree.gov.au/data/resources/2011-resources.html

Australian Government, Department of Resources, Energy and Tourism. (2011). Leading practice sustainable development program handbooks. Retrieved January 20, 2012, from http://www.ret.gov.au/resources/resources_programs/lpsdpmining/handbooks/Pages/default.aspx

Australian Government, Geoscience Australia. (2012). Australian atlas of mineral resources, mines & processing centres. Retrieved January 20, 2012, from http://www.australianminesatlas.gov.au/

Australian Mining. (n.d.). This is our story. Retrieved March 21, 2012, from http://www.thisisourstory.com.au/our-contribution.aspx

International Institute for Sustainable Development. (2002a). *Breaking new ground: Mining, mineral and sustainable development.* Retrieved January 20, 2012, from http://www.iied.org/sustainable-markets/key-issues/business-and-sustainable-development/mmsd-final-report

International Institute for Sustainable Development. (2002b). *Facing the future.* Retrieved January 20, 2012, from http://pubs.iied.org/G02337.html

Minerals Council of Australia (MCA). (2011). 2011–2012 pre-budget submission. Retrieved January 20, 2012, from http://www.mineralscouncil.com.au/file_upload/files/submissions/MCA_Pre%20Budget_FINAL.pdf

Mudd, Gavin M. (2009, April). *The sustainability of mining in Australia: Key production trends and their environmental implications for the future* (Rev. ed.). Melbourne, Australia: Department of Civil Engineering, Monash University and Mineral Policy Institute.

Prebisch, Raúl. (1950). *The economic development of Latin America and its principal problems.* Lake Success, NY: United Nations Economic Commission for Latin America.

Singer, Hans W. (1950, May). The distribution of gains between investing and borrowing countries. *American Economic Review, 40*(2), 473–485.

United Nations (UN). (2008). *Trade and development report: Commodity prices, capital flows and the financing of investment.* New York: UN. Retrieved January 20, 2012, from http://www.unctad.org/en/docs/tdr2008_en.pdf

Mabo and Others v. Queensland (No. 2) (1992) 175 CLR 1 F.C. 91/014. Retrieved June 20, 2012, from http://foundingdocs.gov.au/item-did-33.html

Mississippi and Missouri Rivers

The Mississippi and Missouri rivers have been economically important for centuries, but the commercial benefits have come with environmental costs, including floods, dead zones, and pollution. Efforts to restore the river system to a more natural state have evolved into a twenty-first-century plan to transform the region into a biomass corridor, which will encourage preservation as it diminishes impacts from fossil fuels.

Draining two-thirds of the continental United States, the system of the Mississippi (3,782 kilometers) and Missouri rivers (3,967 kilometers) is one of the longest waterways in the world. It is also among the most transformed by human engineering.

Centuries before the arrival of European settlers, these rivers (which come together at the present site of St. Louis, Missouri) formed the basis of a vast trade network that supported some of the most technologically advanced civilizations in North America. Later, French colonists exploited and modified this network to organize an extensive trade in fur during the eighteenth century. Following the transfer of political authority to the United States in 1803, the Lewis and Clark expedition of the next year, and the advent of steam power in the 1810s, river traffic increased considerably. The Missouri became the great highway to the West, charting a path for European settlement and Native American subjugation. A flourishing trade in lead, flour, and lumber spurred the growth of towns up and down the Mississippi, most of which were located on high bluffs that offered protection from rising waters. Colorfully portrayed by writers such as Mark Twain and artists such as Karl Bodmer, these rivers became central to the popular imagery and mythology of the nineteenth-century West.

Environmental Issues

The environmental impact of steamboat traffic, the expansion of commercial agriculture, and urbanization presented western settlers with a host of new problems. The felling of forests to fire steamboat boilers destabilized riverbanks and contributed to unpredictable channel migration. Runoff from plowed fields added considerably to the sediment load in the rivers and facilitated the formation of dangerous sandbars. Floods became more menacing, and towns expanded into low-lying land. Meanwhile, direct discharge of industrial and domestic waste damaged the health of downstream users.

It was not until the twentieth century that these problems were attacked systematically. Floods on the Mississippi in 1927 and the Missouri in the 1940s provided the political impetus for federal involvement in river management. Under the principles of multiple-use planning that had been established during the Progressive Era (1890s–1920s), river channels were straightened and deepened, levees were raised, and water was impounded in reservoirs for irrigation and the generation of electricity. These large-scale modifications brought economic benefits but imposed heavy environmental and social costs. Fish, wildlife, and human habitats were destroyed; Native American tribes along the Missouri River lost thousands of acres of land to dam and reservoir construction. Embankments and walls squeezed higher volumes of water through narrower channels and increased the risk of inundation for downstream communities that were unable to procure federal flood-protection funds.

In the wake of the post–World War II environmental movement, there have been attempts to restore the rivers to their natural condition, including several

Native American–European Trade on the Missouri

Gene Weltfish (1902–1980) was an anthropologist specializing in studies of the Pawnee Nation. In her book The Lost Universe *she provides a glimpse of life along the Missouri River during the eighteenth and nineteenth centuries.*

In the 1700s when the trade and travel records were written, the Missouri River was a main artery of European–Indian trade. Commercial companies centered in St. Louis maintained regular contact with trade centers up the river, and in the 1800s steamboats plied their way upstream with goods and guns to exchange for furs. Trade centers for exchange were an ancient tradition of American Indian life, and now they eagerly made their way to the trade centers of the European where new goods and materials could be gotten. But the price was dear. For besides the new goods, there came new and fatal diseases—measles, smallpox, cholera, and a variety of fevers—wiping out hundreds and even thousands of people at one blow. Whole tribes that had lived in the region for hundreds of years were wiped out or left in such a fragmentary condition that they joined with other tribes and lost the knowledge of their past identity.

The Pawnees who lived outside the mainstream of commercial traffic were less affected than the others by this holocaust. They lived along the outlying tributaries of the Missouri—the Loup, the Platte, and the Republican—that flow eastward across the present State of Nebraska and join the Missouri at their eastern ends.

Source: Weltfish, Gene. *The Lost Universe with a Closing Chapter on "The Universe Regained."* New York: Basic Books, 1965, p. 3.

---

wetland-preservation projects and a plan to reintroduce seasonal fluctuations in flow to the Missouri River. Stricter pollution regulations have resulted in cleaner effluents from industries and cities, although pesticide and herbicide runoff from farms continues to raise health concerns. This nutrient runoff has also resulted in eutrophication (changes in a body of water resulting from nitrogen and phosphorus input) in the Gulf of Mexico, creating a dead zone of over 17,000 square kilometers in size (EPA 2011), an increase of approximately 7,000 square kilometers since 2008 (Green Nature 2009).

On 2 July 2011, an ExxonMobil pipeline burst under the Yellowstone River, a tributary to the Missouri whose headwaters are in the Absaroka Mountains south of Yellowstone National Park; it is the largest undammed river in the Lower 48 states. Approximately 1,500 barrels of oil spilled into the river, causing a 40-kilometer plume along the riverbank and prompting the evacuation of residents due to dangerous fumes and the possibility of explosions. The cost to clean up the spill was around $135 million, and flood conditions complicated cleanup efforts. Only ten barrels of oil were recovered. Even with the use of booms and absorbent materials, much of the plume was dissipated in the river and washed downstream (*The Guardian* 2011; *The Huffington Post* 2012).

Conservation organizations have jumped into the effort to address environmental concerns surrounding the state of these rivers. The Audubon Society has partnered with several other nongovernmental organizations in an attempt to tackle a wide variety of problems, including the disappearance of wetlands (Audubon 2012). The Missouri River Recovery Program has devoted itself to ecosystem recovery and development of sustainable practices along the banks of the Missouri river (MRRP n.d.).

Future Plans

Future plans for these rivers go beyond conservation and preservation. The Mississippi/Missouri River Advanced Biomass/Biofuel Consortium (MRABC) plans to transform the region into a biofuel-producing source, referred to as a biomass corridor. The switchgrass that grows abundantly along the banks of the rivers is a prime source for cultivating biofuel (Burden 2012). Changing the way this region is valued (for biofuel and for its innate natural beauty, rather than simply as a transport system) simultaneously will encourage preservation of the land for its biofuel and other resources while diminishing impacts from fossil fuels, such as air pollution and oil spills.

Andrew HURLEY
University of Missouri, St. Louis

See also Amazon River; Columbia River; Great Lakes and Saint Lawrence River; Mackenzie River; Murray-Darling River Basin; New Orleans, United States; Rocky Mountains; United States; Water Use and Rights; Yellowstone To Yukon Conservation Initiative (Y2Y)

This article was adapted by the editors from Andrew Hurley's article "Mississippi and Missouri Rivers" in Shepard Krech III, J. R. McNeill, and Carolyn Merchant (Eds.), Encyclopedia of *World Environmental History*, pp. 855–856. Great Barrington, MA: Berkshire Publishing (2003).

FURTHER READING

Audubon. (2012). Mississippi River initiative. Retrieved March 7, 2012, from http://conservation.audubon.org/mississippi-river-initiative

Burden, Mike. (2012, January 13). Fueling the future: The center for agroforestry helps a biobased economy take root in the Midwest. *CAFNRnews*. Retrieved April 5, 2012, from http://cafnrnews.com/2012/01/fueling-the-future/

Colten, Craig. (2002). Reintroducing nature to the city: Wetlands in New Orleans. *Environmental History*, 7(2), 226–246.

Colten, Craig. (Ed.). (2000). *Transforming New Orleans and its environs*. Pittsburgh, PA: University of Pittsburgh Press.

Green Nature. (2009). Mississippi River pollution. Retrieved March 7, 2012, from http://greennature.com/article620.html

The Guardian. (2011). Yellowstone river suffers oil spill. Retrieved March 8, 2012, from http://www.guardian.co.uk/environment/2011/jul/03/yellowstone-river-suffers-oil-spill

The Huffington Post. (2012). Exxon: Yellowstone oil spill involved more barrels than estimated. Retrieved March 8, 2012, from http://www.huffingtonpost.com/2012/01/19/exxon-yellowstone-oil-spill_n_1216830.html

Kelman, Ari. (2003). *A river and its city: An environmental history of New Orleans*. Berkeley: University of California Press.

Missouri River Recovery Program (MRRP). (n.d.). Homepage. Retrieved March 7, 2012, from http://www.moriverrecovery.org/mrrp/f?p=136:1:3721947681049289::NO:::

Scarpino, Phillip V. (1985). *Great river: An environmental history of the upper Mississippi River, 1890–1950*. Columbia: University of Missouri Press.

Thorson, John E. (1994). *River of promise, river of peril: The politics of managing the Missouri River*. Lawrence: University Press of Kansas.

United States Environmental Protection Agency (EPA). (2011). Hypoxia in the news. Retrieved March 7, 2012, from http://water.epa.gov/type/watersheds/named/msbasin/gulfnews.cfm

Berkshire's authors and editors welcome questions, comments, and corrections. Send your emails about the *Berkshire Encyclopedia of Sustainability* in general or this volume in particular to: sustainability.updates@berkshirepublishing.com

Mobility

Urban mobility, the way public and private transportation moves through a city, helps build dynamic and efficient urban areas. Social and economic factors and technological processes contribute to sustainable urban mobility patterns. To reach higher mobility, cities need to consider transportation alternatives, motorized and non-motorized modes of transportation, transportation integration, and also pursue a transit-oriented development pattern. Urban planning plays a major role in developing sustainable urban mobility.

Although *mobility* has a broad definition, one aspect of mobility in the context of cities is the urban dynamic supported by individual and public transportation. Specifically, mobility relates to the circulation of people and goods within the urban territory. Urban mobility is characterized by various forms of transportation in the context of regional cultural traditions and socioeconomic developments throughout the world.

In the Americas and Oceania, there are many fine examples of improved mobility through the implementation of advanced transportation systems that have at the same time reduced automobile dependence. These systems include the New York subway system (New York, United States), the Chicago "L" train system (Chicago, United States); and the Curitiba Bus Rapid Transit (BRT) system (Curitiba, Brazil). Auckland, New Zealand, and the Australian cities of Brisbane, Adelaide, Perth, Melbourne, and Sydney have also experienced great improvement in their mobility patterns through the prioritization of public transportation.

The sustainability of urban mobility rests on the relationship between the city's physical structure, the available natural resources, and transportation. The more environmentally friendly and efficient transportation is utilized, the less urban land and natural and material resources are consumed to accomplish daily tasks. Simply put, implementing sustainable transportation systems directly builds better cities.

Infrastructure and Networks

The availability of a variety of transportation alternatives and their related infrastructures obviously contributes to increased urban mobility. These transportation modes and infrastructures can include, but are not limited to, automobiles and road networks; buses and bus routes; bicycles and bikeways; pedestrians, sidewalks, and public spaces; and subways and railroad networks.

Transportation facilities such as stations, terminals, stops, and integration hubs are all components of the public transportation system, and their presence, quality, and number help to increase urban mobility. Amenities such as benches, trash bins, signs, flower beds, drinking fountains, and so on bring higher quality to sidewalks, public spaces, and transportation facilities, encouraging people to use them and thus contributing to increased urban mobility.

Integration

Integration is the key to sustainable mobility. The simple availability of different transportation modes cannot guarantee the sustainability of the urban mobility system. To be sustainable, transportation modes and their related infrastructures must be interconnected; that is, they must be integrated with one another. The more integrated the transportation modes, the more efficient and sustainable the urban mobility system. For instance, bus routes should be integrated with subway systems. Subway systems should be integrated with bikeways. These bikeways should then be integrated with sidewalks and public spaces, and so on, with all of these structures operating as part of a whole transportation network.

The transportation planner and scholar Michael J. Bruton (1970) suggests that integration should be planned to happen simultaneously at two levels, the physical and the operational.

- On the *physical* level, transportation facilities are interconnected, allowing for a continuous flow of users. For instance, a bus stop and a subway entrance are placed as close together as possible so that passengers do not have far to walk. Integrating more transportation modes results in a more advanced system with higher urban mobility.
- On the *operational* level, coordinated operations such as scheduling, ticketing, fare collection, embarking and disembarking, and information systems that allow passengers a clear and smooth transition between modes are implemented.

Finally, the integration of nonmotorized transportation modes, such as bicycles and pedestrians, with collective modes, such as mass transit, strengthens urban sustainability and environmental friendliness. Modern and dynamic cities should pursue this kind of transportation integration.

Urban Traffic Congestion

In large cities and important urban hubs, a balance between individual and collective transportation modes will reduce urban congestion and car dependency by encouraging people to use mass transit. Traffic congestion is a gigantic problem in large cities throughout the world. Congestion wastes time, resources, and energy. This wastefulness directly affects the economy as well as the health of the cities' inhabitants and the environment. Mass transit and careful urban planning are the best alternative for large cities to reduce daily traffic problems and conserve resources.

Transit-Oriented Development (TOD)

Effective urban planning should achieve a balance between individual and collective transportation while prioritizing mass transit. Transit-oriented development (TOD) is one possible approach to moving in such a direction. A TOD is a coordinated and planned effort to promote mixed-use development surrounding a transit stop. This mix of uses includes, but is not limited to, housing, parks, businesses, government offices, and civic facilities. The type of mass transit can take a variety of forms: subway, light rail, bus rapid transit, and other forms.

Cities and metropolitan areas throughout the Americas and Oceania such as Portland, Oregon; Denver, Colorado; the San Francisco Bay area in California; Vancouver, Toronto, and Calgary, Canada; Melbourne, Australia; and Guatemala City, Guatemala, among others, have adopted the TOD development approach.

Due to the commitment to collective transportation, these cities are considered more efficient and sustainable than others of comparable size, meaning population, occupied area, and economic development. Their effectiveness can be seen in reduced traffic congestion and in the preservation of natural resources like fuel, urban land, and urban infrastructure, meaning mainly the road network and underground systems as drainage, water supply, and sewage collecting.

Sustainable Transportation

For urban mobility purposes and within the context of a sustainable and environmentally friendly city, urban planners must address sustainable transportation—more efficient and less harmful modes of transporting passengers and goods. Load capacity and resource consumption both factor into sustainability measures. Improvements in engine technology through continuous research will reduce resource consumption and increase load capacity and be critical in future transportation improvements. Such technologies include hybrid, electric, hydrogen cell, and solar-power engines and are collectively known as zero- and low-emission vehicles.

Continuously rising gasoline prices have stimulated research into more efficient vehicles, which has contributed new possibilities for more sustainable urban transportation. Sustainable transportation will only be achieved, however, with more efficient, higher capacity transportation modes. The balance between costs to provide the transportation and savings of time, energy, and resources will dictate how sustainable transportation will be, and will determine the nature of modern, more efficient cities.

Nonmotorized Transportation

Nonmotorized transportation, consisting of pedestrians and bicyclists, complements motorized urban transportation's main axes. Two very important factors allow for the linkage between nonmotorized and motorized transportation: the availability of resources and infrastructure for nonmotorized transportation such as sidewalks, bikeways, and high quality public spaces. Integrating these motorized and nonmotorized modes benefits both forms of transportation. Cities can achieve efficient transportation alternatives by integrating nonmotorized transportation modes with mass transit. To do this, urban planning must move in the direction of a less car-dependent future with an environmentally friendly design.

Walkability

Walkability describes how easy it is for pedestrians to move around a location. It is essentially a walking index that measures how open and closed public spaces allow pedestrians a safe and comfortable walking experience. Initially developed by the Canadian politician and environment activist Chris Bradshaw (1993), walkability has evolved into a measure of the urban quality of life. It helps gauge pathways, sidewalks, and public spaces, encouraging urban authorities to improve conditions and giving them guidelines to do so. The more walkable the place, the healthier and more environmentally friendly it will be.

The professor of urban planning and design Evandro C. Santos (2006a) adapted the walkability index into two basic complementary aspects, safety and comfort. In order to rate highly, walkable areas should score well in both physical characteristics and design. According to the *American Association of State Highway and Transportation Officials* (2004), there are several factors to evaluate:

- *Width.* A minimum of 1.5 meters of free path is suggested, but depending on pedestrian flow, the width may be higher. A practical approach might be enough width for two wheelchairs to pass each other or for two pedestrians carrying umbrellas to pass each other without touching umbrellas.
- *Pavement conditions.* Nonslip, even, and well-maintained pavement is required.
- *Grading.* No more than 2 percent transversal grading, and no more than 15 percent longitudinal grading is permitted; otherwise, a handrail is recommended.
- *Street lighting.* May reduce possibility of danger after dark.
- *Crossings and curb ramps.* Clearly marked, they allow smooth and safe connections between edges for mobility-impaired pedestrians like wheelchair users and the elderly. Features such as tactile pavement (a stripe with tiles in a different texture and color) and sound signals can be placed in the free path, close to curb ramps, and at street intersections, allowing blind people to cross safely.
- *Trees.* These guarantee shade while purifying the air and bringing beauty to the landscape.
- *Street furniture.* Items such as trash bins, benches, drinking fountains, and signs provide convenience and comfort to pedestrians.
- *Absence of hurdles.* The absence of hurdles on the paths provides for safe walking, especially for the elderly and vision-impaired pedestrians.

Bikeways

Bicycles are nonmotorized transportation, and as urban vehicles, they should respect traffic laws. At the same time, because they are fragile when compared with automobiles, trucks, and buses, bicycles should be protected to some extent from the general traffic by designated bike lanes or bikeways.

According to the American Association of State Highway and Transportation Officials (1999), bike lanes are clearly marked, inground strips that identify the path for bicycles amid general traffic, and should be ideally 3 meters wide in order to provide safe circulation. Bikeways are dedicated pathways that can run adjacent to a street or on a completely different track. Bikeways also should be 3 meters wide, and both bike lanes and bikeways should be integrated with the regular and nonmotorized transportation network. Depending on bicycle flow, the minimum width for bike lanes and bikeways might be larger.

Urban Planning

Urban planning is the tool that allows cities to grow and develop socially, economically, and environmentally. Through zoning and control of land use, urban planning determines the directions and characteristics for such growth and development.

The big issue in urban planning, affecting millions of people worldwide, especially in large cities and very prominently in North America, is the suburbanization phenomenon. The expansion of city boundaries into less expensive land on the outskirts compromises city development by creating distant suburbs and urban sprawl. This growth forces residents to undertake long commutes to accomplish daily tasks. Urban sprawl has enormous negative impacts on infrastructure costs, the environment, and social development. It is seen as a side effect of urban planning, since what is decided in cities affects what happens on their outskirts, or as a complete lack of urban planning.

In terms of mobility and sustainability, urban planning should be concerned about cities' movement toward a balanced environment. This balance between private and collective modes of transportation and the movement of goods and their distribution must be maintained. In order to be sustainable in terms of mobility, cities should be compact, walkable, integrated, and livable.

Approaches to urban planning such as New Urbanism (Katz 1994) advocate livable, sustainable communities and promote the creation and restoration of diverse, walkable, compact, vibrant, mixed-use communities. Such communities have the same components as conventional developments, but are assembled in a more integrated fashion to form self-contained communities.

Zoning and ordinances should prioritize mass transit and public transportation. They should also govern and manage street parking and parking lots. Allowing higher density building along transit corridors, as happens with TOD, supports sustainability. TOD, for example, has been shown to reduce costs to infrastructure while promoting vibrant neighborhoods and fighting urban sprawl (Katz 1994).

Regional Considerations and Future Outlook

Urban mobility is universal, but each city has a particular way to deal with mobility components. Each city will arrange and manage the components to serve its needs and according to its own conditions, preferences, and possibilities that are based on individual cultural, technological, economic, and historical factors. For example, while in the Americas, the United States has developed a powerful automobile industry and related urban infrastructure making automobiles affordable and popular, in Oceania, countries like Australia and New Zealand have experienced great improvement on the mobility patterns by investing in collective and nonmotorized transportation.

Due to limited fossil fuel resources and rising gasoline prices, there is a worldwide trend to research and develop technology focused on renewable and clean energy sources to propel transportation. Such technological developments will create new possibilities for urban mobility.

Evandro C. SANTOS
Jackson State University

See also Amazonia; Architecture; Auckland, New Zealand; Curitiba, Brazil; Guatemala City; New York City, United States; Perth, Australia; Public Transportation; Sydney, Australia; Urbanization

FURTHER READING

American Association of State Highway and Transportation Officials (AASHTO). (1999). *Guide for the development of bicycle facilities* (3rd ed.). Washington, DC: AASHTO.

American Association of State Highway and Transportation Officials (AASHTO). (2004). *Guide for the planning, design, and operation of pedestrian facilities.* Washington DC: AASHTO.

American Public Transportation Association. (2011). Transit oriented development: Reports and publications. Retrieved July 12, 2011, from http://fta.dot.gov/about/library.html

Bradshaw, Chris. (1993, October 1). Creating—and using—a rating system for neighborhood walkability: Towards an agenda for "local heroes" (paper, 14th International Pedestrian Conference). Boulder, CO. Retrieved April 24, 2012, from http://www.cooperativeindividualism.org/bradshaw-chris_creating-and-using-a-rating-system-for-neighborhood-walkability-1993.html

Bruton, Michael J. (1975). *Introduction to transportation planning.* London: Hutchinson & Co. Ltd.

Goodwill, Julie, & Hendricks, Sara J. (2002). Building transit oriented development in established communities. *Journal of Public Transportation (Center for Urban Transportation Research at the University of South Florida).* Retrieved August 11, 2011, from http://www.nctr.usf.edu/jpt/journal.htm

Katz, Peter. (1994). *The new urbanism: Toward an architecture of community.* New York: McGraw-Hill.

Melbourne City Council. (1985). *Streets for people: A pedestrian strategy for the Central Activities District of Melbourne.* Melbourne, Australia: Melbourne City Council, City Strategic Planning Division, Technical Services Department.

Santos, Evandro C. (2006a). Survey on the urban bikeability index: A diagnosis and lecture of urban conditions for the development of bikeroutes and bikelanes in Montevideo, Uruguay (paper, 1st Seminario de la Bicicleta Urbana: Ciudad en Dos Ruedas, UNESCO & Goethe Institut of Montevideo). Montevideo, Uruguay.

Santos, Evandro C. (2006b). Diagnosis of walkability's index of main Brazilian southern cities (Curitiba, Porto Alegre, Blumenau, Londrina, Maringa, Foz do Iguacu, Cascavel) (Vols. 1–7) [Multimedia CD-ROM]. Curitiba, Brazil: Brazilian Association of Portland Cement—South region (ABCP-Sul).

Stevens, Quentin. (2007). *The ludic city: exploring the potential of public places.* New York: Routledge

United States Department of Transportation, Federal Transit Administration. (n.d.). Research, technical assistance & training—technology. Retrieved August 15, 2011, from http://fta.dot.gov/about/12351_technology.html

Wright, Charlie L. (1992). *Fast wheels, slow traffic: Urban transport choices.* Philadelphia: Temple University Press.

Share the *Encyclopedia of Sustainability*: Teachers are welcome to make up to ten (10) copies of no more than two (2) articles for distribution in a single course or program. For further permissions, please visit www.copyright.com or contact: info@berkshirepublishing.com

Multilateral Environmental Agreements (MEAs)

The adoption of multilateral environmental agreements (MEAs) during the last several decades constitutes a noteworthy step toward the protection of the environment. One of the most prominent MEAs worldwide is the Convention on Biological Diversity (CBD). Australia, Brazil, and Canada, regions with huge biodiversity significance, have implemented some of the most important biodiversity strategies, action plans, and legislation to honor their obligations to the CBD.

The adoption of multilateral environmental agreements (MEAs) during the last decades constitutes a noteworthy step toward the protection of the environment (Andresen and Hey 2005). MEAs are agreements between states that may take the form of "soft" law, setting out nonlegally binding principles parties will respect when considering actions that affect a particular environmental issue. "Hard" laws specify legally binding actions states need to take to work toward an environmental objective (Ministry of the Environment 2012). Numerous countries, in a series of global conferences, have adopted about twenty-six MEAs of a functional nature at the global level and numerous others at the regional level, constituting a key characteristic of the existing environmental governance system. These MEAs directly or indirectly affect various world regions, including Oceania and the Americas. (See table 1 on the next page.)

One of the most prominent MEAs constituting a landmark of global environmental governance is the Convention on Biological Diversity (CBD) (Muñoz, Thrasher, and Najam 2009). Signatory parties in Oceania and the Americas have honored their obligations through biodiversity strategies, action plans, and legislation. Controversies and challenges remain, however. One of the main concerns associated with MEAs as institutions of environmental governance is their lax implementation (Minang and McCall 2008). Australia, Brazil, and Canada, all regions with huge biodiversity significance, have each implemented efforts toward CBD compliance.

Convention on Biological Diversity

The Convention on Biological Diversity (CBD) opened for signature on 5 June 1992 at the United Nations Conference on Environment and Development and entered into force on 29 December 1993. CBD aims to foster the sustainable use of the components of biological diversity and ensure the equitable and fair sharing of the benefits arising from the utilization of genetic resources. In this regard, CBD recognizes the sovereign right of states to use their own resources pursuant to their own environmental policies and the responsibility to ensure that activities within their jurisdiction or control do not damage the environment of other states or of areas beyond the limits of national jurisdiction. The signatory parties are obliged to inventory and monitor biodiversity, incorporate concepts of conservation and sustainable development into national strategies and economic development, and preserve indigenous conservation practices (Andresen and Hey 2005, 161). The principal instruments for implementing the CBD at the national level are national biodiversity strategies and action plans (NBSAPs). As of 2012, 173 parties have developed NBSAPs in line with article 6 of the CBD. Next to NBSAPs, voluntary initiatives and market-based instruments, such as certification, also assist the fostering of CBD objectives.

TABLE 1. Multilateral Environmental Agreements

Atmosphere	Biodiversity	Chemicals and Wastes	Land	Oceans, Sea, and Water
United Nations Convention on Climate Change (UNFCCC) Vienna Convention for the Protection of the Ozone Layer	Convention on Biological Diversity (CBD) Convention on International Trade in Endangered Species (CITES) Bonn Convention on Migratory Species (CMS) Cartagena Protocol on Biosafety Marine Mammal Action Plan (MMAP) United Nations Forum on Forests (UNFF)	Montreal Protocol on Substances That Deplete the Ozone Layer Multilateral Fund for the Implementation of the Montreal Protocol Basel Convention on the Control of Transboundary Movements of Hazardous Wastes and Their Disposal Rotterdam Convention on the Prior Informed Consent Procedure for Certain Hazardous Chemicals and Pesticides in International Trade Stockholm Convention on Persistent Organic Pollutants	United Nations Convention to Combat Desertification (UNCCD)	Barcelona Convention for the Protection of the Marine Environment and the Coastal Region of the Mediterranean Abidjan Convention for Co-operation in the Protection and Development of the Marine and Coastal Environment of the West and Central African Region East Asian Seas Action Plan Cartagena Convention for the Protection and Development of the Marine Environment of the Wider Caribbean Region Nairobi Convention for the Protection, Management and Development of the Marine and Coastal Environment of the Eastern Africa Region North-West Pacific Action Plan (NOWPAP) Guatemala Convention for the North-East Pacific Helsinki Convention on the Protection of the Marine Environment of the Baltic Sea Area OSPAR Convention for the Protection of the Marine Environment of the North-East Atlantic (Oslo and Paris conventions) Arctic Council for the Protection of the Arctic Marine Environment United Nations Convention on the Law of the Sea (UNCLOS) Global Programme of Action for the Protection of the Marine Environment from Land-based Activities

Source: Compiled from InforMEA (n.d.).

Australia

Australia is, next to the United States of America, the only other country classified as developed among the seventeen most megadiverse countries of the world, which are a group of countries hosting the richest biodiversity on Earth (Conservation International 2011). The Australian government reports that major threats to Australia's biodiversity are habitat loss, degradation and fragmentation, invasive species and diseases, unsustainable use and management of natural resources, marine and coastal pollution including from land-based sources and vessels, changes to the aquatic environment and water flows, changing fire regimes, and climate change.

The National Strategy for the Conservation of Australia's Biological Diversity is the guiding framework for conserving biodiversity over the coming decades. According to the Australian Department of Sustainability, Environment, Water, Population and Communities, this strategy functions as a policy umbrella over other, more specific national frameworks covering water, weeds, pest animals, and national reserves. The strategy contains ten interim national targets for implementation in the first five-year period and three priorities for action, which include engaging all Australians in biodiversity conservation, building ecosystem resilience in a changing climate, and getting measurable results. Subpriorities, outcomes, measurable targets, and actions support each of these priorities.

The Environment Protection and Biodiversity Conservation Act 1999 (EPBC Act) gives the Australian government legal responsibilities for biodiversity conservation. The EPBC Act is the country's key piece of environmental legislation. The EPBC Act provides a legal framework to protect and manage impact on matters of national environmental significance defined in the act as listed threatened species and ecological communities, migratory species protected under international agreements, Ramsar wetlands of international importance, the commonwealth marine environment, world heritage properties, national heritage places, the Great Barrier Reef Marine Park Act, and nuclear actions.

Next to legal instruments for the protection of biodiversity, the Australian government also supports softer instruments in the form of voluntary programs that target behavioral changes of key stakeholders. Caring for Our Country is one of the most prominent programs. It targets specifically sustainable farm practices and landscape use. The government has reportedly invested $2 billion in its successful operation. The funding supports a range of stakeholders that aim to shift to more biodiversity-supporting practices, including regional natural resource management groups; local, state, and territory governments; indigenous groups; industry bodies; land managers; farmers, land-care groups; and communities who implement projects related to biodiversity conservation (Caring for Our Country 2012).

Brazil

Brazil, one of the world's seventeen megadiverse countries, incorporates 70 percent of the Earth's cataloged animal and plant species. Brazil hosts an estimated 15–20 percent of the Earth's biological diversity and the greatest number of endemic species on a global scale (CBD n.d.a). The major threats to biodiversity, according to the Brazilian government, are the fragmentation and loss of habitats, introduction of alien species and exotic illnesses, overexploitation of plants and animals, use of hybrids and monoculture in agro-industry and reforestation programs, pollution, and climate change.

A series of macrodocuments and initiatives developed for CBD implementation constitutes the Brazilian National Biodiversity Strategy and Action Plan. Its implementation is supported by a National Biodiversity Policy and the National Biodiversity Targets for 2010, defined by the National Biodiversity Commission (in Portuguese, Comissão Nacional de Biodiversidade, or CONABIO) in 2006 (Brazil's Ministry of the Environment 2010, 108). In addition, Brazil implements a number of projects intended to contribute to the achievement of CBD objectives. The most important ones are the PROBIO projects (I and II), designed specifically to address CBD implementation. PROBIO I (Project on the Conservation and Sustainable Use of Brazilian Biodiversity) aimed to identify priority actions, promote public–private partnerships, and generate and disseminate biodiversity knowledge and information. PROBIO II (National Biodiversity Mainstreaming Project) intends to transform the production, consumption, and land occupation models, starting with the agricultural, science, fisheries, forest, and health sectors, on the basis of public-private partnerships.

The National Cadastre of Protected Areas (Cadastro Nacional de Unidades de Conservação [CNUC]), created in 2006, is the official database on Brazilian protected areas. The Ministry of the Environment, with the collaboration of the federal, state and municipal environmental agencies, manages CNUC (Brazil's Ministry of the Environment 2010). Brazil set the goal in 2006 to protect at least 30 percent of the Amazon and 10 percent of its other biomes in protected areas, including those situated in the coastal and marine zone, such as mangroves. Until August 2010, Brazil had 1,963 protected areas within its territory, covering a total area of 1,539,416 square kilometers (Brazil's Ministry of the Environment 2010, 140). To achieve its stated objective, however, Brazil needs to create an additional 207,170 square kilometers of continental protected areas and 299,871 square kilometers of marine protected areas.

The Brazilian government endorses forest certification as an instrument to control illegal logging and conserve biodiversity. Certification is a market-based, voluntary instrument that assists in the implementation of CBD objectives when including a specific biodiversity protection and enhancement focus. The Forest Stewardship Council (FSC) organizes forest certification in Brazil. FSC is an independent nonprofit organization encouraging sustainable forestry management and supported by Brazilian conservation organizations such as the Instituto do Homem e Meio Ambiente da Amazônia (IMAZON; Amazon Institute of People and the Environment), the Instituto Socioambiental (ISA; Socio-Environmental

Institute), and the Amazon Institute of Environmental Studies (IPAM) (Fearnside 2003). According to Brazil's Fourth National Report to the CBD, the FSC had certified by 2007 more than 50,000 square kilometers of Brazilian forests for timber and nontimber products from planted and native forests (Guia de compras de produtos certificados FSC n.d.).

A presidential decree of 18 March 1999 created Bioamazonia, another voluntary program aiming at the preservation of genetic resources in the Amazon by harnessing market forces (Peña-Neira, Dieperink, and Addink 2002). Contrary to certification efforts, however, this initiative was not as successful as other programs. Bioamazonia's rationale was to preserve biodiversity through contracting pharmaceutical companies that, under the CBD, no longer had the right to collect valuable genetic material from Brazilian wild plants without obtaining consent for access and without sharing benefits (Schroeder and Pogge 2009). Despite initial enthusiasm, the contract Bioamazonia signed with the Swiss pharmaceutical company Novartis jeopardized the project. The contract for the exclusive access to genetic material in the Amazon created a scandal and civil society outrage regarding indigenous peoples' rights. Novartis withdrew, and the scandal cast Bioamazonia's future in doubt (Fearnside 2003).

Canada

Canada is one of the largest countries on the planet in area and contains almost 20 percent of the world's wilderness, 20 percent of its freshwater, 24 percent of its wetlands, and 10 percent of its forests. Canada has a wide variety of ecosystems, including arctic ecosystems that cover one-quarter of the country's land mass, and great species diversity, with over seventy thousand described species (CBD n.d.b). The most common threats to biodiversity according to the Canadian government are habitat loss, invasive species, pollution, population growth, overconsumption or unsustainable resource use, and climate change.

Federal, provincial, and territorial governments under the auspices of the Canadian Council of Ministers of the Environment jointly developed the Canadian Biodiversity Strategy. Although ecologists considered the strategy comprehensive in its coverage, it did not identify measurable targets against which Canada could report progress. The government developed a Biodiversity Outcomes Framework for Canada in 2006, which identified a number of desirable outcomes, specifically healthy and diverse ecosystems, viable populations of species, genetic resources and adaptive potential, and sustainable use of biological resources. It created an "assess, plan, do, track," adaptive management approach aimed at effective planning and decision making and continuous learning and improvement (Ecosystems and Biodiversity Priorities Division, Environment Canada 2009).

Canada has several systems of protected areas that various levels of government develop and manage. Canada's total terrestrial protected areas cover 933,930 square kilometers. The number of protected areas has increased steadily since 1992. The percentage of land covered by protected areas is 9.4 percent as of June 2009. Canada's terrestrial protected areas network covers more than 4,850 protected areas, including some very old parks (Ecosystems and Biodiversity Priorities Division, Environment Canada 2009, 4). Approximately 45,280 square kilometers (0.64 percent) of Canada's oceans are protected. Canada's Great Lakes contain 20 percent of the world's accessible surface freshwater. Although only 0.54 percent of the Great Lakes system is protected, the largest freshwater protected area in the world, Lake Superior National Marine Conservation Area, is in the Canadian part of the Great Lakes. Canada's governments and other key national nongovernment interests are developing a national framework for action on protected areas to facilitate a coordinated approach to protected area planning.

Article 8j of the CBD requires governments to include indigenous and local communities in the designation and management of protected areas. In Canada 12 percent of national, provincial, and territorial parks overlap indigenous lands. Indigenous lands cover 40 percent of the Canadian landscape (Leroux, Schmiegelow, and Nagy 2006). According to Canada's Fourth National Report to the CBD, the government has developed a number of federal strategies, acts, and programs concerning biodiversity through consideration of or in collaboration with indigenous (aboriginal) peoples. Examples include the Canadian Boreal Initiative, the Aboriginal Fisheries Strategy, and the National Aboriginal Council on Species at Risk, as well as initiatives concerning the conservation and use of traditional knowledge, such as the Northwest Territories' Policy on Traditional Knowledge, the Nunavut Inuit Land Use and Ecological Knowledge Database, and the Inuit Knowledge of Bowhead Study.

Outlook

Australia, Brazil, and Canada have all taken important steps toward the protection of biodiversity. They have used a plurality of instruments including national action plans, voluntary initiatives, and market-based approaches such as certification. Given the complexity of biodiversity concerns, multiple instruments that complement each other at the national and subnational levels have the potential to enhance implementation.

There are challenges to successful implementation, however. The first challenge relates to the voluntary nature of many of the initiatives. Voluntary initiatives may overcome some of the concerns associated with the rigidity of governmental regulation but may fail to attract participation of the relevant actors in the absence of appropriate incentives. A second challenge is the development of instruments that stakeholders perceive as threatening to core national objectives. Brazil's Bioamazonia, for instance, involved corporations that some perceived as a threat to indigenous and national economic interests. Finally, a third challenge is the coordination of policies and initiatives at all different levels of governance in order to conserve and enhance biodiversity nationally, regionally, and globally.

Despite these challenges, MEAs will continue to play a significant role in global environmental governance by providing the legal and institutional context within which state and inter-states action can develop in a cooperative and consistent manner to address the various environmental crises of our time.

Agni KALFAGIANNI
VU University Amsterdam

See also Ecotourism (the Americas); Forest Management; Marine Preserves; North American Free Trade Agreement (NAFTA); Organization of American States (OAS); Parks and Protected Areas; Rio Earth Summit (UN Conference on Environment and Development); Yellowstone to Yukon Conservation Initiative (Y2Y)

Further Reading

Andresen, Steinar, & Hey, Ellen. (Guest Eds.). (2005). Special issue: International environmental agreements. *Politics, Law and Economics, 5*(3), 211–376.

Australian Government. (2009, March). Australia's fourth national report to the United Nations Convention on Biological Diversity. Retrieved November 11, 2011, from http://www.cbd.int/doc/world/au/au-nr-04-en.pdf

Australian Government, Department of Sustainability, Environment, Water, Population, and Communities. (2011). Australia's Biodiversity Conservation Strategy 2010–2030. Retrieved November 11, 2011, from http://www.cbd.int/doc/world/au/au-nbsap-v2-en.pdf

Brazil's Ministry of the Environment. (2010, October). Fourth national report to the Convention on Biological Diversity. Retrieved November 11, 2011, from http://www.cbd.int/doc/world/br/br-nr-04-en.pdf

Caring for Our Country. (2012). Homepage. Retrieved April 19, 2012, from http://www.nrm.gov.au

Chasek, Pamela S.; Downie, David L.; & Brown, Janet Welsh. (2006). *Global environmental politics* (4th ed.). Boulder, CO: Westview Press.

Cock, Matthew J. W., et al. (2010). Do new access and benefit sharing procedures under the Convention on Biological Diversity threaten the future of biological control? *BioControl, 55*(2), 199–218.

Convention on Biological Diversity (CBD). (n.d.a). Country profile: Brazil. Retrieved April 10, 2012, from http://www.cbd.int/countries/?country=br

Convention on Biological Diversity (CBD). (n.d.b). Country profile: Canada. Retrieved April 8, 2012, from http://www.cbd.int/countries/profile.shtml?country=ca#status

Conservation International. (2011). Homepage. Retrieved November 11, 2011, from http://www.conservation.org/Pages/default.aspx

Ecosystems and Biodiversity Priorities Division, Environment Canada. (2009). Canada's fourth national report to the United Nations Convention on Biological Diversity. Retrieved April 19, 2012, from http://www.cbd.int/doc/world/ca/ca-nr-04-en.pdf

Fearnside, Philip M. (2003). Conservation policy in Brazilian Amazonia: Understanding the dilemmas. *World Development, 31*(5), 757–779.

Guia de Compras de Produtos Certificados FSC. (n.d.). Retrieved April 19, 2012, from http://www.fsc.org.br/arquivos/Completo_PV.pdf

InforMEA. (n.d.). MEA explorer. Retrieved July 5, 2012, from http://informea.org/

Kanie, Norichika. (2007). Governance with multilateral environmental agreements: A healthy or ill-equipped fragmentation? In Walter Hoffmann & Lydia Swart (Eds.), *Global environmental governance* (pp. 67–86). New York: Center for UN Reform Education.

Leroux, Shawn J.; Schmiegelow, Fiona K. A.; & Nagy, John A. (2006). Potential spatial overlap of heritage sites and protected areas in a boreal region of northern Canada. *Conservation Biology, 21*(2), 376–386.

Minang, Peter A., & McCall, Michael K. (2008). Multilevel governance conditions for implementing multilateral environmental agreements: The case of CDM forestry readiness in Cameroon. *Energy & Environment, 19*(6), 845–860.

Ministry of the Environment, Government of New Zealand. (2012). Multilateral environmental agreements. Retrieved April 8, 2012, from http://www.mfe.govt.nz/laws/meas/

Muñoz, Miquel; Thrasher, Rachel; & Najam, Adil. (2009). Measuring the negotiation burden of multilateral environmental agreements. *Global Environmental Politics, 9*(4), 1–13.

Peña-Neira, Sergio; Dieperink, C.; & Addink, H. (2002, April 19). Equitability sharing benefits from the utilization of natural genetic resources: The Brazilian interpretation of the Convention on Biological Diversity (Paper presented at the 6th Conference of the Parties of the Convention on Biological Diversity). The Hague, The Netherlands.

Schroeder, Doris, & Pogge, Thomas. (2009). Justice and the Convention on Biological Diversity. *Ethics & International Affairs, 23*(3), 267–280.

Secretariat of the Convention on Biological Diversity. (2010). Global biodiversity outlook 3. Retrieved November 11, 2011, from http://www.cbd.int/doc/publications/gbo/gbo3-final-en.pdf

Soberón Jorge, & Peterson, A. Townsend. (2009). Monitoring biodiversity loss with primary species-occurrence data: Toward national-level indicators for the 2010 target of the Convention on Biological Diversity. *AMBIO: A Journal of the Human Environment, 38*(1), 29–34.

Murray-Darling River Basin

The Murray-Darling river basin is Australia's largest river basin. It accounts for more than 40 percent of Australia's gross value of agricultural production and about 65 percent of all irrigation, but water extraction from the basin's river systems has led to significant ecological damage. Commonwealth and state governments have established several regulatory agencies to try to balance agricultural and environmental needs.

The Murray River is Australia's second-longest river (2,530 kilometers). Together with the Darling (2,740 kilometers) and Murrumbidgee (1,690 kilometers) rivers, the Murray drains the Murray-Darling basin, which covers 1,061,469 square kilometers, 14 percent of Australia's total area. The basin extends over the states of New South Wales, Victoria, Queensland, South Australia, and the Australian Capital Territory.

The Murray-Darling basin is of immense cultural, economic, and environmental significance. Although most of the inland basin is flat and low-lying and receives relatively little direct rainfall, it accounts for around 40 percent of Australia's gross value of agricultural production. About 65 percent of all irrigation in Australia takes place in the basin, with important crops including cotton, rice, citrus fruits, and grapes. Dryland farming in the basin includes wheat, sheep, and beef production (MDBA 2010).

Differences in climate, geology, and soils over the very large area of the basin have led to substantial variation in water flows. Cyclonic rainfall in Queensland and northern New South Wales cause regular, major flooding. Conversely, episodic drought is also a characteristic of the basin. Lower than average flows may be seasonal or extend over a number of years. (One recent drought lasted from 1999 through 2008.) The total water flow in the Murray-Darling basin from 1885 to the present has averaged approximately 24,000 gigaliters per year. This is the lowest rate of any of the world's major river systems. Extracting water from the Murray River upstream has reduced average annual water flow at the river's mouth by 61 percent (SEWPaC 2011). No water at all reaches the mouth of the river 40 percent of the time, compared to 1 percent before people began to develop the river's water for agricultural, industrial, and urban uses. Climate change is forecast to place further pressure on the basin's water system (SEWPaC 2011).

History

At the time Europeans began to settle in Australia in 1788, approximately 28 percent of Australia's mammal species, 48 percent of its bird species, and 19 percent of its reptile species were found in the basin (SEWPaC 2011). The basin still contains more than thirty thousand wetlands, including sixteen wetlands of international significance for migratory birds. As a result of human impact, however, at least thirty-five bird species and sixteen mammal species that live in the basin are classified as endangered. Twenty mammal species have become extinct in the basin since 1900, and the Murray cod (*Maccullochella peelii*), Australia's largest exclusively freshwater fish and one of the largest in the world, is in severe decline as a result of fluctuating water levels, habitat degradation, and overfishing. In 2003, 80 percent of the remaining River Red Gums (*Eucalyptus camaldulensis*) on the Murray River floodplain in South Australia were stressed to some degree due to the combination of human activity and drought, and 20–30 percent of those were severely stressed (SEWPaC 2011).

The river system has a very long history of human activity and use: gravesites at Roonka and Big Bend in South Australia demonstrate that Aboriginal communities lived there continuously for at least thirty-five thousand years. During the early stages of European settlement, the river was discovered by explorers Hamilton Hume and William Hovell in 1824. Although it was originally named the Hume River, in 1830 Captain Charles Sturt renamed it the Murray after Sir George Murray, British secretary of state for the colonies. The publication in London in 1833 of Sturt's account of his river explorations indirectly led to the establishment of the colony of South Australia.

In 1852, the first paddle steamer from South Australia reached Echuca in Victoria. The Murray was of such economic importance as a transportation route that in 1863 authorities in New South Wales, Victoria, and South Australia held a conference about improving the navigability of the river. Despite further meetings and the development of irrigation plans beginning in the 1880s, however, it was not until the severe drought of 1895 to 1902 and the creation of the Commonwealth of Australia in 1901 that the newly formed states were able to reach limited consensus on river regulation.

Management

The River Murray Waters Agreement, providing for the construction of water storage dams and reservoirs, weirs, and locks and agreed shares of water usage, was signed in 1915 by the commonwealth government of Australia and the state governments of New South Wales, Victoria, and South Australia. In 1917, the River Murray Commission was established to implement the agreement. The commission was at first primarily concerned with water quantity. By the late 1960s, however, its powers spread to quality issues as a result of increased water salinity.

The agreement was amended in 1982 and 1984 to take account of environmental issues. These amendments, however, did not solve the existing management problems. Salinity and species and wetland loss continued to worsen. As a result, new institutional arrangements were agreed to by the commonwealth and the three states in 1987, and in 1992 the Murray-Darling Basin Agreement replaced the previous River Murray Waters Agreement. Queensland became a signatory in 1996.

The 1992 agreement established a commission, a ministerial council, and a community advisory committee to coordinate the equitable, efficient, and sustainable use of the water, land, and other environmental resources of the Murray-Darling basin. According to the commission, the public–private initiative was the largest integrated water catchment management program in the world. In 1997, the Murray-Darling Basin Ministerial Council introduced the Murray-Darling cap, which limits water diversions in the basin to 1993 levels, with the goal of ensuring the long-term environmental health of the river.

In 2007, the Murray-Darling Basin Authority was given the principal responsibility under the national Water Act to manage the basin as part of the National Water Plan for Water Security. The Water Act authorized the National Water Commission to audit the effectiveness of implementation of the Murray-Darling Basin Plan and associated water resource plans. The commission was established by the National Water Initiative (NWI), which was an intergovernmental agreement between the commonwealth and the states to achieve a national market, regulatory, and planning system for managing water resources. Under the initiative, each state and territory government is required to develop an NWI implementation plan, and the commission provides a biennial assessment of progress on the initiative. The commission's assessment is then used in the development of water policy.

Outlook

The Murray-Darling Basin Authority is charged with planning and managing the water resources of the basin in an integrated and sustainable manner. In 2010, the authority released its first draft plan to secure the long-term environmental health of the basin. (The intergovernmental Murray-Darling Basin Ministerial Council acts in an advisory role in the preparation of the basin plan.) The 2010 proposals included cutting existing water allocations for irrigation and increasing river water flows to help maintain or restore river ecology. The plan has led to substantial and heated debate among agricultural, business, and conservation groups as well as different state governments over the relative balance between economic and environmental needs for water. Response to the draft plan led to the release of a second draft late in 2011. The basin plan implementation was scheduled to start in 2012, although public consultation processes and the development of relevant responses may extend that timeline. Aspects of the plan, such as water trading rules, take effect from the date of final release of the plan, while other aspects begin only when new state water resources plans are implemented. Despite the initiative, the Murray's environmental problems continue to worsen as water usage outstrips availability, and it seems likely that in the future the Murray will fail to reach the sea unless water usage can be lowered.

C. Michael Hall
University of Canterbury

See also Amazon River; Australia; Columbia River; Great Lakes and Saint Lawrence River; Mackenzie River; Mississippi and Missouri Rivers; New Zealand; Oceania; Perth, Australia; Phoenix, United States; Sydney, Australia; Water Use and Rights

FURTHER READING

Connell, Daniel (2007). *Water politics in the Murray-Darling Basin*. Annandale, Australia: Federation Press.

Department of Sustainability, Environment, Water, Population and Communities (SEWPaC). (2011). Murray-Darling Basin. Retrieved October 10, 2011, from http://www.environment.gov.au/water/locations/murray-darling-basin/index.html

Murray-Darling Basin Authority (MDBA). (2010). *Managing the Murray-Darling Basin's water resources*. Canberra, Australia: Murray-Darling Basin Authority.

Murray-Darling Basin Authority (MDBA). (2011). About us. Retrieved October 10, 2011, from http://www.mdba.gov.au/

National Water Commission. (2011). Homepage. Retrieved January 31, 2012, from http://www.nwc.gov.au/

Pigram, John J. (2007). *Australia's water resources: From use to management*. Collingwood, Australia: CSIRO Publishing.

Powell, Joseph M. (1993). *The emergence of bioregionalism in the Murray-Darling Basin*. Canberra, Australia: Murray-Darling Basin Commission.

Sinclair, Paul (2001). *The Murray: A river and its people*. Carlton, Australia: Melbourne University Press.

Weir, Jessica K. (2009). *Murray River country: An ecological dialogue with traditional owners*. Canberra, Australia: Aboriginal Studies Press.

Berkshire's authors and editors welcome questions, comments, and corrections. Send your emails about the *Berkshire Encyclopedia of Sustainability* in general or this volume in particular to: sustainability.updates@berkshirepublishing.com

N

New Orleans, United States

344,000 est. pop. 2010 (contested)

The city of New Orleans, Louisiana, depends upon water, yet the water surrounding it threatens its continued existence. After generations of intense human manipulation of water and other natural resources in and near New Orleans, the disasters the city and region suffered in recent years are sadly predictable, a situation exacerbated by the region's shocking income inequality. Although New Orleans was the third largest US city by population in 1840, in the aftermath of Hurricane Katrina it no longer ranks among the top 50 most populous cities in the country. The long-term sustainability of the city is highly uncertain without aggressive action.

New Orleans, Louisiana, is a city whose fortunes are, and always have been, determined to a disproportionate degree by one environmental resource—water—whether fresh water from the Mississippi River or salt water from the Gulf of Mexico. Situated about 160 kilometers upriver from the point where the Mississippi River feeds into the Gulf of Mexico, the strategic siting of New Orleans in 1699 by the French explorer Jean-Baptiste Le Moyne de Bienville sought to maximize the French Crown's trade advantages. Its location provided New Orleans strategic control of the river, not just of the gulf. The site Bienville selected was also high ground, wedged between the river and the large brackish-water estuary known as Lake Ponchartrain. The lake itself covers more than 960 square kilometers. The city of New Orleans's location, therefore, gave its governors control over that natural resource, with resulting access routes both upriver and inland to the west (Campanella 2008).

Location, Location, Location

For good and for ill, the Mississippi River shapes the city's life and identity. The Mississippi River made the city a strategic prize for waves of adventurers and nation-states, including a succession of French, Spanish, and ultimately, US overlords. The Mississippi River also allowed New Orleans to become a major port—the principal southern US port of call for trade from Latin America and Europe for much of the eighteenth and nineteenth centuries. This fact helps explain the city's unusually rich ethnic and cultural diversity, as well as its famed tolerance for eccentricity and sometimes excess, despite its location in a socially and politically conservative region.

The Mississippi River, with its generous deposits of silt and mud, also made the region around New Orleans an exceptionally productive agricultural one; it spawned a strong plantation culture, one dependent on African-descended slave labor. Paradoxically, the Mississippi River repeatedly threatens the continued vitality of New Orleans during the late summer and early fall hurricane season, when warm waters push in from the Gulf of Mexico, raising water levels, breaking levees, and inundating the city, much of which lies below sea level. The city also is vulnerable during spring floods, when the river swells upstream, menacing the region's existence from the other direction.

Recent examples of such catastrophic flooding are not new phenomena. In 2005, a pair of Category 3 (on a scale of 5, with 5 being the most severe) storms—Katrina and Rita—devastated the city, with a combined loss of nearly two thousand lives, to say nothing of property damage estimated at US$120 billion (Knabb, Brown, and Rhome 2005, 13; 2006, 8). Again, it should be stressed that damage in New Orleans from tropical storms coming in from the gulf in the late summer and early fall is not a new phenomenon. Storms destroyed early structures in one of the city's earliest periods of settlement, in 1722, and again between 1776 and 1781 and between 1865 and 1871; the city itself was spared during the catastrophic 1927 flood only because some upstream levees were dynamited (Campanella 2008). In 2011, heavy spring rains again threatened portions of the city and the now heavily urbanized region (Finn 2011). Throughout the city's history, moreover, leaks in the flood protection system have caused various degrees of damage to the city. What seems to be changing is that the number and intensity of storms—and associated human and economic damage—appears to be increasing.

New Orleans thus presents unusual challenges for those interested in sustainable development. On the one hand, it sits where it does exactly to derive maximum advantage from the abundant natural resources that surround it—not just agriculture and marine resources, but also the petroleum deposits that still remain centrally important to the region's economy (Scott 2011, iv). This location also positions the city and region to distribute those resources inland in the United States and overseas. In some sense, then, New Orleans is located to maximize its potential for sustainable development; fulfilling this potential, however, requires that human manipulation of natural resources not be so overbearing and driven by short-term, profit-maximizing interests that it eclipses the possibility of living, if not exactly in harmony with nature, at least in a tolerable balance with it.

On the other hand, however, since the city's founding, New Orleans and its surrounding landscape have become one of the most manipulated in the continental United States (Campanella 2008). The rapacious extent of that manipulation risks leaving the city and its environs in a completely unsustainable state (Davis 2009). This lack of sustainability can be seen regarding both water management and petroleum-related activities.

Hurricanes Katrina and Rita served as wake-up calls to New Orleans because they revealed to most analysts that the human and environmental disasters the storms caused were the product of avoidable human error. In particular, the region's anthropogenic development (how humans impacted the environment) worked against natural forces rather than in concert with them, by, for example, maintaining wetlands to serve their myriad environmental service functions, including their role as storm buffers. The deaths attributed to the hurricanes, moreover, both directly and indirectly demonstrated a failure to acknowledge the probability and extent of severe weather damage, with faulty government-supervised construction of water management and storm protection facilities, notably the New Orleans levee system. In fact, at least one expert foresaw the grave repercussions that could befall the city after a storm because of faulty planning and preparation (Fischetti 2009). All of these conditions suggest a need to reconsider what it truly means to live among natural resources that simply cannot be tamed to fit human desires. The region's extreme income inequality means that the people most seriously affected by these disasters are poor, largely racial and ethnic minority residents of the city and region (Dyson 2006).

Similar concerns exist about the safety of the region's intense extractive resource activity. The 130-kilometer stretch from New Orleans to the state capital of Baton Rouge has long been known as "Cancer Alley" by the environmental justice activists who decry the proximity of residential communities, many of them low income and predominantly African American, to refining activities along the Gulf Coast (Cole and Foster 2001, 78). Oil drilling nevertheless remains an important part of the Louisiana economy, producing an estimated US$77.3 billion in sales for Louisiana firms; the petroleum industry alone was responsible for 310,217 jobs in the state in 2009, concentrated in New Orleans and its periphery (Scott 2011, iv). More recently, however, environmental health concerns have expanded well beyond the location of the coastal refineries to the deep-sea exploration in the gulf. The summer 2010 British-Petroleum (BP) deep-sea oil leak became the worst such disaster in history when 4.9 billion barrels of crude oil leaked into the Gulf of Mexico (Achenbach and Fahrenthold 2010). This disaster, in turn, reverberated for the economy of New Orleans and the region, most prominently raising concerns about gulf fisheries important to the city and region that generated US$2.4 billion annually for Louisiana (Bigg, Gorman, and Fletcher 2010).

In terms of sustainability, the relentless focus on natural resources produces negative economic externalities (unintended consequences) that might be corrected with more robust social, economic, and environmental planning. For example, tourism is a mainstay of hundreds of smaller- and medium-sized enterprises in New Orleans and its environs. Six years after hurricanes Katrina and Rita, though, the total number of visitors to the city was only about two-thirds of the number before the storms (although the total dollar amount tourists spent was, admittedly, much higher) (New Orleans Convention and Visitors Bureau 2012).

Population Fluctuations

Its advantageous location also allowed New Orleans to draw a large population. Although New Orleans was in 1840 the third largest US city by population (about a third of the size of New York and slightly smaller than Baltimore, Maryland), by 2010 the US Census estimated a mere 344,000 people living in the city, meaning that New Orleans was no longer even in the top 50 most populous US cities (Campanella 2010; US Census 2012b). The 2010 census estimate is disputed, however, as a close population figure is difficult to determine in the wake of Hurricane Katrina. The hurricane destroyed many city records, and information such as population numbers have only just begun to be reconstructed, making current census estimates difficult to determine. Although data dating from 1990 show the population steadily shrinking, the 2010 census showed a striking decline of almost 30 percent since the previous census of 2000, a steep drop attributed to the aftermath of Katrina.

Some argue that the census failed to take into account those people who moved back into abandoned houses, or people staying with various family members for short periods of time while waiting for housing to become available, which means it will still be some time before accurate estimates can be made. (Robertson 2011).

Toward Sustainability

Recent evidence of human failures having a direct and devastating consequence on the lives and livelihoods of New Orleans and its region thus raises the question about the city's and the region's future sustainability. A preliminary response about New Orleans's future sustainability is a positive one, depending on the future success of new ways of doing business and working with natural forces. This situation can be understood first by looking at the specific ways New Orleans has focused on its sustainability policies since Hurricane Katrina and then at the broader efforts to regulate water management and storm protection more effectively, and to do the same for extractive industries. The available data also suggest, however, a need to take a more holistic look at the city's and the region's potential—evaluating with a hard eye the benefits of tourism- and leisure-focused business development against extractive development as

parallel paths to the city's and the region's future sustainable development.

New Orleans since Hurricane Katrina has generated a flurry of innovative ideas in favor of sustainability, especially by government actors and members of civil society. First, in the immediate aftermath of the storms, the New Orleans City Council enacted in 2008 the GreeNOLA plan, which aimed to make the city more forested, more walkable, and more sustainable. These features subsequently became part of a land-use planning Master Plan. Remarkably, New Orleans never before had approved a land-use Master Plan, but in August 2010, the city council did so. The document is impressive on paper because it does what many such plans fail to do, namely, to integrate land use and environmental planning. The Master Plan's green agenda is ambitious: it aims, for example, to promote the development of green jobs, such as those in alternative energy, to make the city both more walkable and more dependent on public transportation and to work toward the use of a sustainable building code for new construction and renovations.

Importantly, too, the Master Plan acknowledged that nature should be an ally and not an enemy the city should defend against, however imperfectly. With respect to water, for example, the Master Plan "advocates learning to live with water rather than fight it" (Sousa and Crawford 2012, 392 and 396).

In addition to these government initiatives, post-Katrina New Orleans saw a blossoming of civil society organizations that sought both to connect with and contribute to official actions and also to develop environmentally sustainable initiatives themselves. Some of these efforts were born of opportunity and necessity, such as the now-famous trash removal services offered by New Orleans native Sidney D. Torres IV after the storms. Torres's SDT Waste & Debris Services introduced a new level of efficiency and civic pride into previously listless efforts (Jervis 2010). Other efforts included everything from recycling Christmas trees for bayou and wetland reconstruction to increased development of green bike paths and waterways winding through the city.

Similarly, the years immediately after the storms saw focus on the adoption of new energy efficiency measures, with incentives for citizens who installed reduced-carbon technologies. The city undertook to approve green building codes, and a range of new urban development projects feature sustainable building. The most celebrated of these projects is the US actor Brad Pitt's Make It Right Foundation, which, by the end of 2012, aims to have more than thirty sustainable, affordable homes for working-class families displaced from the Lower Ninth Ward, the area most devastated by Hurricane Katrina. Other such efforts are peppered across the city, as environmental and sustainability entrepreneurs seek to turn the city into a laboratory following the spectacle of human failure that caused the storm. Important participants in such efforts also include, for example, the New Orleans Recovery School District and the public library system, which aim to reconstruct to LEED Silver levels (LEED stands for Leadership in Energy and Environmental Design and is a multitiered, voluntary certification program the US Building Council oversees). This development is significant in a city and region not known for such environmental consciousness. These developments arguably represent a new, burgeoning environmental sensitivity in the region (Sousa and Crawford 2012, 392 and 396).

Despite the promise of the above and similar efforts, however, there is cause for worry. Many of these efforts, although welcome and long overdue, only begin to touch on New Orleans's sustainability challenges. For example, efforts to reintroduce solid waste recycling throughout the city remain stymied, even several years after the storms. Public transportation, too, continues to be erratic and of poor quality overall, despite much rhetoric pointing toward a consensus on the need and importance of an integrated and dependable network, to say nothing of the need for more walkways and bike trails.

These concerns are equally serious regarding the water management and extractive resource industry issues that challenge the city and the region. Since hurricanes Katrina and Rita, the task of rebuilding the 560 kilometers of levees making up the New Orleans system is nearly complete at a cost of more than US$15 billion. Public mistrust of the levee system persists, however, and many experts contend that even this fortified system remains inadequate to protect the city from storms of increasing strength (Finn 2011). Similarly, deep-sea drilling in the Gulf of Mexico resumed six months after the BP oil leak disaster (Baker 2010). The jury remains out about whether the federal Minerals and Management Agency, the Environmental Protection Agency, and the other entities responsible for regulating these activities will go ahead with a truly sustainable agenda in mind (Center for Progressive Reform 2005). The risk is high that such disasters could be repeated unless the city takes more vigorous efforts to reform extractive practices (*New York Times* 2012). This reform would likely further damage the weakened tourism and leisure sector, with negative environmental, social, and economic effects throughout the city and the region.

Outlook

If New Orleans and the region for which it is the anchor are to sustain themselves through the twenty-first century, it seems very clear that much more needs to be done, and quickly. Continued major disasters on the scale of hurricanes Katrina and Rita or the 2010 BP oil spill likely could lead to the demise of a once great and original city. If the city can focus on sustainability and build on its successes in living in concert with its watery surroundings, though, the city and its residents would ensure a future for New Orleans.

Colin CRAWFORD
Tulane University Law School

See also Caribbean; Detroit, United States; Las Vegas, United States; Mississippi and Missouri Rivers; Mobility; New York City, United States; Phoenix, United States; Public Transportation; Travel and Tourism Industry; United States; Water Use and Rights

FURTHER READING

Achenbach, Joel, & Fahrenthold, David A. (2010, August 3). Oil spill dumped 4.9 million barrels into Gulf of Mexico, latest measure shows. *Washington Post*. Retrieved June 4, 2012, from http://www.washingtonpost.com/wp-dyn/content/article/2010/08/02/AR2010080204695.html

Baker, Peter. (2010, October 12). White House is lifting ban on deepwater drilling. Retrieved March 30, 2012, from http://thecaucus.blogs.nytimes.com/2010/10/12/white-house-to-lift-ban-on-deep-water-drilling/

Bigg, Matthew; Gorman, Steve; & Fletcher, Pascal. (2010, May 30). Factbox: Gulf oil spill impacts fisheries, wildlife, tourism. *Reuters News Service*. Retrieved March 30, 2012 from http://www.reuters.com/article/2010/05/30/us-oil-rig-impact-factbox-idUSTRE64T23R20100530

Campanella, Richard. (2008). *Bienville's dilemma: A historical geography of New Orleans*. Lafayette: Center for Louisiana Studies, University of Louisiana.

Campanella, Richard. (2010). *Lincoln in New Orleans: The 1828–1831 flatboat voyages and their place in history*. Lafayette: Center for Louisiana Studies, University of Louisiana.

Center for Progressive Reform. (2005, September). An unnatural disaster: The aftermath of Hurricane Katrina. Retrieved April 4, 2012, from http://www.progressivereform.org/articles/Unnatural_Disaster_512.pdf

Cole, Luke, & Foster, Sheila. (2001). *From the ground up: Environmental racism and the rise of the environmental justice movement*. New York: New York University Press.

Davis, Mark. (2009, February 16). Not by accident. Retrieved April 5, 2012, from http://prospect.org/article/not-accident

Dyson, Michael Eric. (2006). *Come hell or high water: Hurricane Katrina and the color of disaster*. New York: Perseus Books Group.

Finn, Kathy. (2011, September 4). New Orleans' post-Katrina flood defenses pass big test. Retrieved March 30, 2012, from http://www.reuters.com/article/2011/09/04/us-storme-usa-gulf-floodgates-idUSTRE78325U20110904

Fischetti, Mark. (2008, September 5). Drowning New Orleans. Retrieved March 30, 2012, from http://www.scientificamerican.com/article.cfm?id=drowning-new-orleans-hurricane-prediction

Hoch, Maureen. (2010, August 2). New estimate puts Gulf oil leak at 205 million gallons. Retrieved March 30, 2012, from http://www.pbs.org/newshour/rundown/2010/08/new-estimate-puts-oil-leak-at-49-million-barrels.html

Houck, Oliver. (2010). *Down on the Batture*. Jackson: University of Mississippi Press.

Jervis, Rick. (2010, February 14). Katrina, Mardi Gras, Super Bowl made him trash king. Retrieved April 5, 2012, from http://www.usatoday.com/news/nation/2010-02-14-mardi-gras-trashman_N.htm

Knabb, Richard; Brown, Daniel; & Rhome, Jamie. (2005, December 20). Tropical cyclone report: Hurricane Katrina. Miami, FL: National Hurricane Center. Retrieved March 30, 2012, from http://www.nhc.noaa.gov/pdf/TCR-AL122005_Katrina.pdf

Knabb, Richard; Brown, Daniel; & Rhome, Jamie. (2006, March 17). Tropical cyclone report: Hurricane Rita. Miami, FL: National Hurricane Center. Retrieved March 30, 2012, from http://www.nhc.noaa.gov/pdf/TCR-AL182005_Rita.pdf

New Orleans Convention and Visitors Bureau. (2012, March/April). New Orleans receives 8.75 million visitors in 2011.

New York Times. (2012, April 18). The big spill: Two years later: much remains to be done to restore the Gulf of Mexico and make deep-sea drilling safer, p. A24.

Schwartz, John. (2010, August 23). *New Orleans levees nearly ready, but mistrusted*. Retrieved March 30, 2012, from http://www.nytimes.com/2010/08/24/us/24levee.html

Scott, Loren C. (2011, August). The energy sector: Still a giant economic engine for the Louisiana economy. Baton Rouge, LA: Mid-Continent Oil and Gas Association. Retrieved March 30, 2012, from http://www.lmoga.com/assets/Economic_Impact_Study_2011.pdf

Sousa, Brandon, & Crawford, Colin. (2012). Greening New Orleans city government after Katrina. In Keith Hirokawa & Patricia Salkin (Eds.), *Greening local government: Legal strategies for promoting sustainability, efficiency and fiscal savings* (pp. 385–412). Chicago: American Bar Association Press.

United States (US) Census Bureau. (2012a). State and county quick facts: New Orleans (city) Louisiana. Retrieved June 5, 2012, from http://quickfacts.census.gov/qfd/states/22/2255000.html

United States (US) Census Bureau. (2012b). Interactive population map. Retrieved June 19, 2012, from http://2010.census.gov/2010census/popmap/

New York City, United States

8.24 million est. pop. 2011

New York City has historically been the most important city in the United States, a center of culture and commerce. Often the leader in municipal policy, since 2000 New York City has implemented a strategy to make it one of the most sustainably oriented cities in the country. At the same time, however, New York faces significant challenges, including aging infrastructure, poverty, and unemployment.

New York City, founded in a beautiful and ecologically rich harbor, has developed in stages from a commodity-trading center to an industrial powerhouse, to a global financial center, and to a hub of high- and biotech research on sustainability-related issues. Although the city faces immense challenges common to many urban centers, such as poverty, unemployment, water and waste management, and the upgrading or replacement of outdated infrastructure, New York City's endeavors toward sustainable city planning and administration remain in character with its role as a leader and innovator.

Physical Geography and Natural Setting

The beauty of New York City is, in part, due to its geography. The city is located on the Hudson River estuary, which provides a protected deepwater harbor and rich biodiversity. The Hudson River, a glacially carved valley, allows ocean water at high tide to travel more than 150 kilometers upstream (to the state capital of Albany), creating a unique environmental combination of saltwater marshes, coastal islands, and beaches sitting next to temperate forests of chestnuts, hemlocks, oaks, and tulip trees. In previous eras, resources included massive oyster beds and coral reefs. New York is located along migratory routes for more than 150 bird species, 9 fish species, and monarch butterflies. Despite intensive development, an estimated 330 different species of birds, 30 mammals, 32 reptiles and amphibians, and more than 200 kinds of fish inhabit the city. Adding invertebrates to that list, biodiversity within the city includes more than 10,000 different species (Mittelbach and Crewdson 1997).

To protect its natural heritage and provide recreation opportunities, the city manages approximately 1,700 parks totaling more than 11,000 hectares of parkland and 2,400 hectares of wild forests. Success is evident. Within the concrete confines of the city reside large mammals including beaver, raccoons, white-tailed deer, and turkeys; a large breeding population of egrets, herons, and other wading birds on a number of small islands in the harbor; peregrine falcons nesting in church towers; and coyotes, which sometimes wander into the city. Beginning in 1991, a now-famous red-tailed hawk, Pale Male, lived above a Fifth Avenue apartment window and had multiple successful offspring, which themselves attempted to raise families around the city.

Population Growth

European colonists were originally drawn to the site of New York by the natural harbor and rich biodiversity. When Henry Hudson first explored the coast and met with local Lennapes, members of the Algonquin people, their deerskin clothing and beaver belts immediately attracted his attention. The Dutch settled Manhattan Island in 1624 with the primary objective of furnishing beaver and other skins to Europe.

The Dutch settlement of New Amsterdam flourished under Peter Stuyvesant, until, in 1664, the British took over and renamed it New York. After the Revolutionary War, the city was rebuilt and developed very rapidly. By 1812, New York was the nation's most important port and center for commerce. According to US Census Bureau figures, by 1900, it was the nation's largest urban center, with 3.4 million people; by 1930, there were 6.9 million New Yorkers, and by 1950, approximately 7.9 million people lived in the city. It would then take another fifty years for the population of the city to exceed 8 million. In 2011, there were approximately 8.24 million New Yorkers, and the city continues to grow (New York City, Department of City Planning 2012).

Economy and Society

Several important factors helped to frame the economic and social development of New York. One of the most important has been the city's position as an important port that provided the basis for growing commercial activity. Colonial-era fur trade gave way to trade of timber, tobacco, wine, rice, and, sadly, slaves. Shortly after the Revolutionary War, the city regularized shipping schedules, which increased business dramatically. (From 1785 to 1790, the city also served as the US capital.) During the nineteenth century, 60 percent of the country's imports came through New York's harbor. By 1930, New York was the world's busiest port, with approximately one ship arriving or departing every ten minutes. At midcentury, the adoption of containerization required large tracts of land. Given limited space in the city, the port facilities moved to New Jersey, expanding the Port of New York to include its neighboring state, but shifting employment across the river, too. Each year more than 12,000 ships enter or leave New York Harbor (Ascher 2005) and water freight still accounts for approximately 12 percent by weight of all goods coming into the New York City region (US DOT 2010). While the city retains many important port functions, much of the shoreline is now reserved for other uses.

In the twenty-first century, trade flows directly into the city are based largely on trucking. Approximately 79 percent of freight travels by truck over the 32,000 kilometers of streets and highways and across the twenty bridges and tunnels that connect the borough of Manhattan to other parts of the region (Ascher 2005; US DOT 2010). The regional airports handle about 2.6 million tons of air cargo annually, worth more than $140 billion (Ascher 2005). Together, Kennedy, Newark, and LaGuardia airports account for roughly 25 percent of the nation's air imports and 17 percent of its exports (US DOT 2010).

Another important factor in the city's economic growth has been the regulation of land development. The first planning decision entailed a large-scale grid for city streets. In 1811, a plan to accommodate north–south traffic through twelve straight, parallel, numbered avenues and approximately 155 cross streets created the gridiron pattern that the city is known for. The standardization of plots facilitated real estate development and regularized the growth of the city.

A second planning decision effected in 1898 consolidated the island of Manhattan and Brooklyn (then an independent city, it was joined to the island in 1883 by the Brooklyn Bridge), with sections of outlying counties to form the single five-borough municipality now known as New York City. (The boroughs are Manhattan, Brooklyn, Bronx, Queens, and Staten Island.) The creation of Greater New York (its original, official name) tripled the city's area and nearly doubled its population overnight. At that time, the city grew to twice the population of Chicago, its closest US rival, and became larger than any city in Europe except London.

After the Civil War, the country industrialized rapidly. New York City's capital, labor, proximity to markets, port facilities, and rail links all contributed to making it a manufacturing center. Industrial production specialized in clothing, printed materials, textiles, leather goods, and tobacco products.

The growing number of low-wage factories led to a rise in immigration to New York. In 1900, the city's factory workers accounted for 11 percent of the national total (Drennan and Matson 1995). The influx of immigrants was an important component in industrial success and the basis of the future cosmopolitan cultural milieu of the city. Even at that early date, however, immigration presented challenges. During one day at the height of the immigrant wave in 1907, for example, more than 11,000 people queued up on Ellis Island for entry, and during that year over 1.28 million people came into New York (Burns, Sanders and Ades 1999; Trager 2003). Many immigrants looking for factory work were poor, and their numbers presented challenges for the city. For example, in terms of health alone, the use of hospital services increased by 85 percent between 1890 and 1905 (Opdycke and Rosner 1995) and the mortality rate was five times higher than it is now (Ellis 1966). By 1910, 2.2 billion liters per day of untreated waste was being discharged from New York City sewers, and as such, people caught typhoid fever merely from handling oyster and clamshells (Waldman 1999).

New York City's economy remained fairly diversified (and remains so in the early twenty-first century). In addition to being a manufacturing center and the country's leading port, the city was a leader in commerce, finance, and business services. These important functions attracted the headquarters of many major corporations, and the city grew to house the nation's elite.

As a consequence, turn-of-the-century New York was a mixture of ethnicities, incomes, technologies, land uses, and transportation modes. The chaos threatened to choke the city. The construction of the forty-two-story Equitable Building in Lower Manhattan, which literally prevented sunlight from reaching a three-hectare area and affected real estate in the neighborhood, promoted the implementation of a comprehensive zoning law, promulgated in 1916. The first of its type in the United States, the 1916 Zoning Resolution designated land uses (e.g., residential and commercial) as well as height and setback requirements for buildings. While the law did establish order in infrastructure for a time, an unfortunate side effect included the segregation of high- and low-income populations.

All this planning would have been for naught if the city and New York State had not invested in economic and social infrastructure. One project that catapulted the city to economic heights was the Erie Canal. When it opened in 1825, it linked the Hudson River to Lake Erie, and provided a transportation link between the Great Lakes region and the city. The canal opened up the agricultural and commodities production of the Midwest to New York businesses, lowered transportation costs, and sped delivery. In a few years, the value of freight transported along the canal reached $15 million, twice the amount that reached New Orleans (Burrows and Wallace 1999).

Other important investments included the water supply system that in the twenty-first century brings 5 billion liters of water a day into the city from as far away as 200 kilometers and a sanitation system that includes fourteen treatment plants (Galusha 1999). Just as important as infrastructure projects was legislation that promoted better housing, promoted child welfare and women's rights, and restricted the abuses of factory owners. Many of the national social-welfare programs that appeared in the 1930s were conceived and tested in New York.

Throughout the nineteenth and early twentieth centuries, New York City was able to hold onto its preeminent position through the efforts of one of the most powerful planning bureaucrats in the history of the nation, Robert Moses. Moses helped to bring federal dollars to the city and with them built massive public housing projects, transportation infrastructure, additional parks and recreation facilities, and two world's fairs, altogether costing $27 billion (Jackson 1993).

During the 1960s, poverty and its link to race became important city issues. The rising consciousness about social injustices and the civil rights movement were underpinned by losses in manufacturing employment. Starting at the end of the decade, the city underwent a painful adjustment period, plagued by strikes, shifting populations, loss of its tax base, congestion, aging physical plants, crime, and rising costs of land and labor. In 1950, approximately 1 million people were employed in manufacturing in the city. By 1990, there were fewer than 340,000 manufacturing jobs.

From 1970 to 1990, the city lost population (Kantrowitz 1995). During the 1970s, the city almost went bankrupt, as it couldn't meet its bond obligations. Even skilled mayors such as Ed Koch could not overcome municipal corruption. With an increasingly polarized income distribution, the city took on a dual character: one city for the rich and another for the poor. By 1990, the city hit a nadir; *Time* magazine published a cover story titled "The Rotting of the Big Apple."

Underneath the economic restructuring and shifting social conditions, however, was the future economic success of the city—the rise in the business service sector. As New York lost blue-collar jobs in manufacturing, it became increasingly important as a center of white-collar finance, real estate, accounting, and legal business services. New York became one of the most powerful centers of the new global economy. During the 1990s and throughout the early twenty-first century, New York City's economy expanded as it maintained its position on top of the global city hierarchy. With Mayor Rudolph Giuliani's focus on crime during his two terms in office (1994–2001), the city was cleaned up, and business as well as the quality of life for most New Yorkers improved.

Despite the slump on Wall Street following the financial downturn that began in 2008, New York City's economy continues to grow. While it remains a center for national and international finance, there are signs of another transition. Finance employment is decreasing, while industries such as publishing, clothing, high-tech and "new media" industries, television and film production, and tourism are growing.

Sustainability

Michael Bloomberg, who began his tenure as mayor in 2001 and remains in his post as of 2012, made sustainability and quality of life an important part of his political platform. During his administration, the city developed and began to implement its first sustainability plan. This far-reaching plan, which has been updated, covers land (housing, open space, brownfield sites [unused commercial or industrial sites available for redevelopment], parks, and greenery), water (water quality and sanitation), transportation (congestion and maintenance), energy (provision, efficiency, and distribution), air quality, and climate change. Mayor Bloomberg positioned New York as one of the preeminent cities in climate-change research and policy. The city has been moving forward by attempting to implement congestion pricing, greening the taxi service, implementing bus rapid transit, rezoning for transit-oriented development, financing green infrastructure, finding new energy sources, and putting into effect a host of energy-efficiency strategies. In the meantime, Times Square has been revitalized. The city has developed bicycle lanes and pedestrian areas in midtown; as of 2011, New York City had 1,100 kilometers of dedicated bike lanes and a target of 2,900 kilometers by 2030, according to Mayor Bloomberg's office (*Daily News* 2011). New parks have been located along riverfronts—notably, the Hudson River Park and the acclaimed High Line, a reclaimed elevated train track very popular with tourists and pedestrian commuters. Improved leisure and recreational facilities are making life for New Yorkers more pleasant. The city remains committed to reducing its greenhouse gas (GHG) emissions 30 percent by 2030, having already reduced citywide GHG emissions by 13 percent below 2005 levels since 2007 (Bloomberg 2011). Brooklyn in particular has emerged as a center for the production of craft goods such as bread, beer, whiskey, and pickles; the economics journalist Adam Davidson has called the borough "ground zero of the artisanal-food universe" (Davidson 2012).

Despite these and other successes, challenges remain. For example, the city is battling to control combined sewer overflow, where approximately 102 billion liters of raw sewage still run into the estuary annually; recycling rates are relatively low; and solid waste treatment currently transports waste outside the city (Bloomberg 2011; Seggos and Plumb 2006). Estimates suggest that the city needs over $90 billion for addressing its infrastructure needs (Hevesi 1998). New York also still struggles with large differences in socioeconomic status among its citizens. Although the city is home to some of the wealthiest residents in the world, unemployment exceeds 9 percent, and the poverty rate is more than 20 percent (Bloomberg 2010; DiNapoli 2010; Massey 2011).

Peter J. MARCOTULLIO
Hunter College, City University of New York

See also Appalachian Mountains; Detroit, United States; Energy Efficiency; Las Vegas, United States; Mobility; New Orleans, United States; Phoenix, United States; Public Transportation; Sanitation; Toronto, Canada; United States; Urbanization; Water Use and Rights

FURTHER READING

Abu-Lughod, Janet L. (1999). *New York, Chicago, Los Angeles: America's global cities*. Minneapolis: University of Minnesota Press.

Ascher, Kate. (2005). *The works: Anatomy of a city*. New York: Penguin.

Bloomberg, Michael R. (2010). *The CEO poverty measure: 2005–2008*. New York: NYC Center for Economic Opportunity.

Bloomberg, Michael R. (2011). *PlaNYC: A greener, greater New York*. New York: Office of the Mayor.

Burns, Ric; Sanders, James; & Ades, Lisa. (1999). *New York: An illustrated history*. New York: Alfred A. Knopf.

Burrows, Edwin G., & Wallace, Mike. (1999). *Gotham: A history of New York City to 1898*. New York: Oxford University Press.

Daily News. (2011, 4 October). New York City embraces bicycle culture by adding bike lanes, planning ambitious bike-sharing program. Retrieved June 19, 2012, from http://articles.nydailynews.com/2011-10-04/news/30261667_1_bike-lanes-bike-sharing-janette-sadik-khan

Davidson, Adam. (2012, February 15). Don't mock the artisanal-pickle makers. *New York Times Magazine*. Retrieved June 19, 2012, from http://www.nytimes.com/2012/02/19/magazine/adam-davidson-craft-business.html?_r=4&adxnnl=1&adxnnlx=1329336006-V7ZklU/RioSXk1hVeVlWXw

Day, Leslie. (2007). *Field guide to the natural world of New York City*. Baltimore: John Hopkins University Press.

DiNapoli, Thomas P. (2010). *Economic trends in New York State*. New York: Office of the State Comptroller, New York City Public Information office.

Drennan, Matthew, & Matson, Cathy. (1995). Economy. In Kenneth T. Jackson (Ed.), *The encyclopedia of New York City* (pp. 358–363). New Haven, CT: Yale University Press.

Ellis, Edward Robb. (1966). *The epic of New York City: A narrative history*. New York: Old Town Books.

Galusha, Diane. (1999). *Liquid assets: A history of New York City's water system*. New York: Purple Mountain Press.

Hevesi, Alan C. (1998). *Dilemma in the millennium: Capital needs of the world's capital city*. New York: City of New York, Office of the Comptroller.

Jackson, Kenneth J. (Ed.). (1993). *The great metropolis: Poverty and progress in New York City*. New York: American Heritage.

Jackson, Kenneth J. (Ed.). (1995). *The encyclopedia of New York City*. New Haven, CT: Yale University Press & the New York Historical Society.

Kantrowitz, Nathan. (1995). Population. In Kenneth T. Jackson (Ed.), *The encyclopedia of New York City* (pp. 920–923). New Haven, CT: Yale University Press.

Massey, Daniel. (2011, September 22). City's poverty rate jumps past 20%. *Crain's New York Business*. Retrieved May 8, 2012, from http://www.crainsnewyork.com/article/20110922/ECONOMY/110929962

McCully, Betsy. (2007). *City at the water's edge: A natural history of New York*. New Brunswick, NJ: Rutgers University Press.

Mittelbach, Margaret, & Crewdson, Michael. (1997). *Wild New York: A guide to the wildlife, wild places and natural phenomena of New York City*. New York: Crown Publishers.

New York City, Department of City Planning. (2012). Current estimates of New York City's population for July 2011. Retrieved May 8, 2012, from http://www.nyc.gov/html/dcp/html/census/popcur.shtml

NYC Bike Maps. (2012). New York City's bike paths, bike lanes & greenways. Retrieved June 19, 2012, from http://www.nycbikemaps.com/

Opkycke, Sandra, & Rosner, David. (1995). Hospitals. In Kenneth T. Jackson (Ed.), *The encyclopedia of New York City* (pp. 560–563). New Haven, CT: Yale University Press.

Rosenzweig, Cynthia, & Solecki, William D. (Eds.). (2001). Climate change and a global city: The potential consequences of climate variability and change: Metro East Coast. Report for the US Global Change Research Program: National assessment of potential consequences of climate variability and change for the United States. New York: Earth Institute, Columbia University.

Sanderson, Eric W. (2009). *Mannahatta: A natural history of New York City*. New York: Harry H. Abrams.

Sassen, Saskia. (1991). *The global city: New York, London, Tokyo*. Princeton, NJ: Princeton University Press.

Seggos, Basil, & Plumb, Mike. (2006). *Sustainable raindrops: Cleaning New York Harbor by greening the urban landscape*. Tarrytown, NY: Riverkeeper.

Trager, James. (2003). The New York chronology: The ultimate compendium of events, people, and anecdotes from the Dutch to the present. New York: Harper-Collins.

United States Department of Transportation (US DOT). (2010). FAF³ network database and flow assignment: 2007 and 2040 data file: Version 3. Washington, DC: Federal Highway Administration.

Waldman, John. (1999). Heartbeats in the muck: A dramatic look at the history, sea life and environment of New York Harbor. New York: The Lyons Press.

Berkshire's authors and editors welcome questions, comments, and corrections. Send your emails about the *Berkshire Encyclopedia of Sustainability* in general or this volume in particular to: sustainability.updates@berkshirepublishing.com

New Zealand

4.3 million est. pop. 2012

New Zealand, a land of vast forests and mountains, is renowned for its natural beauty. Human contact is recent but has drastically altered the landscape and affected the biodiversity of animal and plant life. Colonization, biological invasions, habitat loss, and environmental hazards are part of its environmental history. Concerns over these issues have led to initiatives such as the Resource Management Act, which attempts to regulate the sustainable use of resources.

New Zealand, also known by the Māori word Aotearoa, popularly translated as "long white cloud," comprises three main islands: the most densely populated North Island (Te Ika-a-Māui), the more sparsely populated and rugged South Island (Te Wai Pounamu), and Stewart Island (Rakiura), located off the southern coast of the South Island. The country, approximately the size of the US state of Colorado, has an estimated 2012 population of 4.3 million people (US CIA 2012). It is located roughly 1,600 kilometers southeast of Australia and would stretch from New York to Florida if superimposed over the East Coast of the United States.

Aotearoa/New Zealand holds a special place in environmental history for at least two reasons. First, it is a fragment of the ancient supercontinent of Gondwana, cast adrift before the advent of mammals. The Australian ecologist Tim Flannery (2004) calls it "a completely different experiment in evolution to the rest of the world," showing how things might have looked had the birds been left "to inherit the globe." The birds inhabited a landscape of extremes, one that is geologically vigorous and mountainous from its location astride two of the world's great tectonic plates (the Indo-Australian to the west and the Pacific to the east). It also had extensive wetlands, coastlines, and offshore islands. It was 80 percent clothed in forest, ranging from the subtropical to subalpine, at the time of first human contact. Such recent contact—within the last thousand years—is the second reason for New Zealand's distinct environmental history, as successive waves of human immigrants have moved into this unusual biotic setting and produced dramatic impacts.

The impacts are so dramatic, in fact, that the geographer Kenneth Cumberland alleged in 1941 that the landscape transformation from forest to grassland farm had occurred in little more than a century in New Zealand, compared to 400 years in North America and two millennia in Europe. Cumberland published his essay 101 years after the signing of the Treaty of Waitangi between representatives of the British Crown and tribal leaders of the Māori, New Zealand's indigenous people. The essay, therefore, was largely a celebration of European settler environmental "progress," although Cumberland was aware of its costs; three years later he published the first comprehensive account of the extent of soil erosion on deforested lands. He did perhaps underestimate, however, the extent of the pre-European landscape consequences of the Māori, whose forest burn-offs and hunting activities led to the extinction of more than thirty species of native birds, including those of the famous flightless moa, which could be larger than a modern ostrich.

Environmental impacts nonetheless have been more intense since European arrival. Europeans first sighted the "large land, uplifted high" in 1642, and the British explorer Captain James Cook began the process of introducing Northern Hemisphere flora and fauna on his first visit in 1769. New Zealand's incorporation into an international division of labor as Britain's "southern farm" after the 1850s initiated the development of tidy geometries of farming, followed by exotic forestry in the early twentieth century. Its native forests now cover less than a quarter of the land area, and 85 percent of the wetlands have been drained (compared to less than half in the United States). Just over half of New Zealand is covered in grass, most of it imported pastures from Britain, compared to a global average of 37 percent (Pawson and Brooking 2002). Much of the remainder, mountains and some native forests, is held in the national conservation estate, the designation reflecting its negligible value for productive purposes, but high worth as part of the "clean, green" national brand.

A relatively small population (fewer than 1 million before 1910 and just more than 4 million in 2012) carried out this extraordinary transformation, much of it caught on canvas and by camera and written about at length in a huge online archive (access details for which given at the end of this entry: Statistics New Zealand n.d.; National Library of New Zealand n.d.). Little wonder that the transformation has attracted the gaze of overseas scholars since at least the 1940s. The Canadian geographer Andrew Hill Clark spent a wartime visit researching the acclimatization of exotic species in the South Island, subsequently publishing *The Invasion of New Zealand by People, Plants and Animals* (1949). The US historian Alfred W. Crosby elaborated this theme; he used New Zealand as a prominent case study in his volume *Ecological Imperialism* (1986). Other US environmental historians, such as Stephen Pyne, John McNeill, and Thomas Dunlap, have worked on or in the country. In 1999, the US historian William Cronon wrote a foreword to a new edition of the farmer and conservationist Herbert Guthrie-Smith's *Tutira, the Story of a New Zealand Sheep Station*. This work is a classic in environmental history, to which Cronon attributed his own early interest in the field.

Guthrie-Smith's book, first published in 1921, is the story of how his own land reclamation activities affected the ecology on his run, or large sheep farm, in Hawke's Bay, in the east of the North Island. It is widely quoted as an example of the unintended consequences of European impacts realized in settler lands, with loss of habitat leading to the decline of native bird populations and land disturbance hastening the spread of exotic weeds as well as erosion (Wynn 1997). Since the late twentieth century, New Zealand geographers, ecologists, and historians have written thematic environmental histories. Archaeologists and anthropologists have contributed to lively discussions on pre-European Polynesian impacts.

The *New Zealand Historical Atlas* (McKinnon 1997), drawing on these disciplines, took the understanding of environmental change to a new level. It uses dramatic representations of Māori construction and use of territory, alongside archaeologists' maps of the traces of such activity in the landscape. Thereafter, it portrays the dispossession of Māori from their lands by Pakeha (European) methods of colonization, illustrates the progressive outcomes of this colonization, and maps some of the environmental hazards that ensued. This project was one of the prompts for an interdisciplinary exploration of the main themes of New Zealand's environmental history, in the form of a book of essays organized chronologically and thematically (Pawson and Brooking 2002; 2013). This book and the *Atlas* are the most comprehensive single-coverage treatments available. Little, however, has been written specifically on New Zealand's marine environmental histories, despite New Zealand laying claim to the world's fifth-largest marine area (Johnson and Haworth 2004).

Māori Impacts

Recent scholarship confirms that Māori changed the environment in more substantive ways than often has been realized, particularly because of an earlier tendency to romanticize the relationship between indigenous peoples and environments. Migrants began arriving from the Polynesian islands in the Pacific starting in the early 1200s, according to the evidence of the latest dating techniques, although considerable debate continues over the exact timing. They found the new land lacking in familiar staples and too cold for many of their tropical crops. Consequently, like new colonists everywhere, they used the richest, most accessible resources with pitiless energetic efficiency. Widespread vertebrate extinctions and deforestation occurred until environmental learning brought about adaptive change, at different rates in different parts of New Zealand. How Māori affected the marine environment is sketched in various reports of the Waitangi Tribunal, an official body established in 1975 to research Māori grievances under the Treaty of Waitangi and make recommendations for redress to government. Captain Cook and Joseph Banks, the British naturalist and botanist who accompanied Cook on his voyage, both expressed surprise at the number and size of Māori fishing nets. Freshwater eels were an important food source, and eel weirs (enclosures set in a waterway) sometimes encompassed entire streams (Johnson and Haworth 2004). In the interests of long-term survival, Māori family (*hapu*) and tribal (*iwi*) units developed rules of guardianship (*kaitiakitanga*) to natural resources within well-defined but frequently disputed territories.

European Colonization

Such disputes intensified once regular European incursions began in the 1790s, after the British annexation of New South Wales. Māori were keen traders, and competition for tradable commodities, such as flax, sold in exchange for muskets and agricultural goods, destabilized social organization and its territoriality. At the same time, European diseases began to wreak a terrible toll, as Crosby's *Ecological Imperialism* makes clear. The stories of the consequences of European colonization depend on who is telling them, Māori or Pakeha, and whose perspectives among Māori or Pakeha are given voice. This has been the case ever since the signing of the Treaty of Waitangi, which was written in both Māori and several English-language versions. To Māori it guaranteed *rangatiratanga,* or chieftainship, over lands they wished to keep; to Europeans it was the instrument of British sovereignty and the imposition of individual rights to land held under title from the Crown (Kawharu 1989).

European appropriation of New Zealand's resources was focused at first on coastal regions, with Auckland in the north being a major trading center. Land settlement, initially organized most often by British-based colonizing companies, proceeded most rapidly in the South Island, from the late 1840s, because of the extensive areas of less rugged, less forested land and the small Māori populations. In the North Island, competition for and between Māori owners and Pakeha led to war, in the 1840s and subsequently in the 1860s, before the Crown imposed widespread confiscations. As Māori lands shrank in extent, so too, depleted by disease and disease-induced infertility, did the Māori population. It reached its nadir in the 1890s, the very decade in which Pakeha acquisitions of tribal lands reached their peak (Brooking 1996). At this point, even sympathetic Europeans felt that Māori demise was inevitable, just as it was thought—in keeping with prevalent Darwinian thinking—that the native flora and fauna was retreating before the onslaught of inherently superior Northern Hemisphere species.

This onslaught was, however, the product of an energetic colonizing process, backed by laws that mandated treating land as a commodity and facilitated exploitation of resources (Pawson and Brooking 2002). Individual colonists experimented widely in determining what would and would not grow where, but much also was carried out with little knowledge of the particularities of specific places. Settlers fired South Island, high-country tussock lands (composed of the compacted tufts of grass or sedgelike species) to provide sheep pasture, leading to pest invasions and the collapse of stocking capacity in some places as early as the 1870s, although Robert Peden (2011) argues that this firing was less indiscriminate than often supposed. Huge areas of swampland in both islands, powerhouses of indigenous ecologies and rich reservoirs of food for Māori, were demonized as "waste" and converted into what the New Zealand ecologist Geoff Park (1995) calls "imperial landscapes," in which the "linear logic" of modernity met and seemed to beat "the chaos of nature." Settlers cut over and burned off much of the North Island's *bush*, as Europeans termed the island's seemingly impenetrable forest, between the 1860s and 1900.

An earlier, and then parallel, onslaught took place at sea. Sealing and whaling had developed quickly: from 1806 to 1807, one Sydney trader alone reputedly shipped 200,000 New Zealand–sourced sealskins. Sealing extended to the sub–Antarctic Islands, but by the 1820s, the seal boom was over and the rush for whale oil to service the Industrial Revolution replaced it. English and US whalers flooded into the South Pacific, many basing themselves in the Bay of Islands, and shore stations spread around the South Island and lower North Island, until exhaustion of the resource by the mid-1840s. The boom-and-bust experience in fisheries was to continue with other species for more than a century, really changing only in the late 1980s with the advent of the Quota Management System (QMS).

Conservation

During colonization, concern quickly developed over the destruction of resources. The New Zealand Forests Act of 1874, informed by the book *Man and Nature* (1864), written by the US conservationist George Perkins Marsh, has been labeled one of the earliest conservation measures in the British Empire (Wynn 1979). Although ineffectual, it attempted to regulate timber use and stave off a "timber famine" in a country dependent on wood for all sorts of purposes. One of the insights of research since the late twentieth century is that this initiative was not isolated. Fisheries protection legislation was passed in the 1870s and 1880s, and by the 1890s, urban-based conservation bodies succeeded in establishing island bird sanctuaries and scenic reserves. Extensive areas of alpine lands were protected in national parks by the 1920s; the first such park, Tongariro in the volcanic center of the North Island, has its roots in the 1880s. Mountains became an important symbolic resource, featuring prominently on the first national issue of pictorial postage stamps in 1898. Motives and meanings often were mixed, however. Such moves reflected pride in "possession" of spectacular scenery and its value for tourism as often as they did any interest in conserving scenery or habitat.

The Twentieth Century

Environmental transformation intensified in the twentieth century. The remaking of South Island native grasslands into "English" pastures was paralleled through the North Island as the bush was removed (Brooking and Pawson 2011). A "grasslands revolution" based on improved seed and use of fertilizer underpinned massive expansion of livestock numbers from 1920. Superphosphate (made by mixing sulfuric acid with concentrated bird droppings from the Pacific Island of Nauru) revived soil fertility that flagged after the initial clearance of bush. Airplane delivery of fertilizer after 1949 underwrote soaring sheep numbers, which peaked at 70 million in 1980. Prosperity encouraged a belief in the capacity of applied science to solve all problems cheaply and expeditiously, which the growing incidence of environmental hazards, such as soil erosion, did little to dent. This blind faith was reinforced in part by the state's ongoing investment in programs of *wise use* of resources. These set out to manage in particular soil and water issues, alongside reforestation using fast-growing Californian *Pinus radiata* (Roche 1990, 1994). At the same time, urban areas, in which a majority of people have lived since 1911, have had to be insulated by an increasingly elaborate infrastructure of flood and earthquake proofing, to protect investment in and the amenity values of what has long been a predominantly suburban nation (Pawson 2000). The Christchurch earthquakes of 2010–2012 have shown how false the sense of insulation from an unstable land has been (Pawson 2011). (A series of quakes started in September of 2010 with a magnitude 7.1 event, and culminated in a devastating magnitude-6.8 earthquake, in February of 2011, that killed 185 people; Christchurch has been plagued by over ten thousand aftershocks since the first shock.)

In fisheries, the last thirty years of the twentieth century saw a massive change, in part due to the rapid growth in marine recreation and tourism associated with coastal urbanization. Concurrently, in response to demands effectively to nationalize offshore fisheries, New Zealand declared a 12-nautical-mile Territorial Sea and a 200-nautical-mile Exclusive Economic Zone (EEZ). In the 1980s, in order to manage fish stocks more sustainably, the QMS and associated Individual Transferable Quota (ITQ) were introduced. These regulations essentially privatized the right to harvest fish commercially within a scientifically determined total allowable catch, but led to a backlash from Māori who perceived the limits as an illegal confiscation of their rights to fish and trade. The resulting negotiations led to Māori again becoming major players in commercial fisheries through ownership of one of the largest companies and provisions for greater control over the regulations governing traditional fisheries. Debate continues, however, over who owns the foreshore and seabed: Māori or the government.

The 1970s also saw the passage of the Marine Reserves Act 1975 and the Marine Mammals Protection Act 1978, enabling the establishment of the first no-take marine protected areas and marine mammal sanctuaries. Such reserves remain contentious, but by 2000, fifteen marine reserves and two marine mammal sanctuaries had been established. Internationally, New Zealand had shifted from being a commercial whaler member of the International Whaling Commission to being an advocate for the protection of whales. These moves in the marine area were paralleled by initiatives to extend the conservation estate on land, bringing in more representative landscapes with the addition of areas of native forest. This followed the end of logging on state land in the 1980s and 1990s due to public pressure and the loss of commercial interest in working increasingly remote resources.

Contemporary Issues

Contemporary New Zealand environmental histories focus on four main themes. The first is the extent to which processes of colonization and modernization persist as the driving forces of agriculture and forestry. Diversification of land use is now widespread, given what was for long the decline in terms of trade for basic commodities such as wool and sheep meat (although there was some recovery in prices with the global commodity boom in the first decade of the twenty-first century) and the need to find a wider range of markets for a broader range of products. Diversification often leads to intensification: for instance, the conversion of land for dairying, with its accompanying demands for irrigation water and growing production of solid wastes and gaseous emissions. Debate over how to control the environmental impacts of dairying persists.

The second theme concerns the continued prominence of conservation initiatives. Since the 1980s, the national conservation estate has expanded considerably to include large areas of native forests, although the loss of commercial value in these forests has facilitated the success of urban-based environmentalist campaigning to this end as more readily worked plantations come onstream. The estate is of inestimable value for branding the country as "clean and green" in promotion of the tourist industry, which sits second to dairying as the largest source of foreign exchange earnings.

Third, Māori resource claims arising from perceived breaches of the Treaty of Waitangi have become numerous. The body charged with examining such claims, the Waitangi Tribunal, has commissioned extensive research into each case it has heard since the 1970s. Its reports are a record of the ways in which iwi and hapu, growing in size and confidence, have maintained ties to territory, even where land has long since been lost and landscapes remade (Kawharu 1989). These reports, all available online, are testimony to the many voices and multiple perspectives that construct environmental histories, and they place a radically different perspective on standard accounts of environmental transformation. In turn, there is a parallel realization that Pakeha relations to land in postcolonial New Zealand are more layered than usually represented (Dominy 2001).

The fourth theme focuses on the ongoing tensions between the neoliberalism experiment begun in the 1980s and the desire to protect New Zealand's environmental heritage. New Zealand has been a leader in the adoption of the language of sustainability, initially in fisheries and subsequently in the form of the Resource Management Act 1991 (RMA), although whether this has fundamentally shifted the bias of law away from exploitation is subject to much debate. The RMA focuses on the containment of adverse effects of specific development initiatives and has proved less successful as a framework for regulating emerging issues such as water use in dairying or the control of greenhouse gas emissions, half of which in New Zealand's case are attributable to agriculture.

Outlook

The New Zealand economy remains vulnerable to exporting commodities and international tourism markets. Its fortuitously large conservation estate and its frequent innovation in environmental regulation and attempts to save endangered species tend to cloud the underlying ongoing destruction of its environment through intensified land use and increasing ease of international movement of pest species. The introduction and rapid spread of waterborne pests, such as didymo (*Didymosphenia geminate*) and giardia (*Giardia lamblia*), are part of a process of ongoing environmental degradation that began with the arrival of humans one thousand years ago and, despite best efforts, continues to worsen. The commodity boom of recent years has merely continued a long-run process of the opening of new resource frontiers, notably in dairying but also in mining and fishing. Ongoing conservation efforts, sanctuaries, and reserves may help protect New Zealand's environmental heritage, which is also attractive to its tourism interests, although there will always be much work to be done.

Tom BROOKING
University of Otago

Eric PAWSON
University of Canterbury

Hamish G. RENNIE
Lincoln University

See also Auckland, New Zealand; Australia; Forest Management; Oceania; Pacific Island Environmental Philosophy; Parks and Protected Areas; Small Island States; Travel and Tourism Industry

The editors are grateful to Eric Pawson and Hamish Rennie for their work updating and adapting this article. The original article is from Tom Brooking and Eric Pawson's article "New Zealand" in Shepard Krech III, J. R. McNeill, and Carolyn Merchant (Eds.), the *Encyclopedia of World Environmental History*, pp. 895–898. Great Barrington, MA: Berkshire Publishing (2003).

Further Reading

Brooking, Tom. (1996). *Lands for the people? The Highland clearances and the colonisation of New Zealand. A biography of John McKenzie.* Dunedin, New Zealand: Otago University Press.

Brooking, Tom, & Pawson, Eric. (2011). *Seeds of empire. The environmental transformation of New Zealand.* London: I. B. Tauris.

Cumberland, Kenneth B. (1941). A century's change: Natural to cultural vegetation in New Zealand. *Geographical Review, 31*(4), 529–554.

Dominy, Michèle D. (2001). *Calling the station home: Place and identity in New Zealand's high country.* Lanham, MD: Rowman & Littlefield.

Flannery, Tim F. (2004). *The future eaters: An ecological history of the Australasian lands and people.* Chatsworth, Australia: Reed Books.

Guthrie-Smith, Herbert. (1999). *Tutira. The story of a New Zealand sheep station.* Auckland, New Zealand: Random House (originally published 1921).

Johnson, David, & Haworth, Jenny. (2004). *Hooked: The story of the New Zealand fishing industry.* Christchurch, New Zealand: Hazard Press.

Kawharu, I. H. (Ed.). (1989). *Waitangi: Māori and Pakeha perspectives of the Treaty of Waitangi.* Auckland, New Zealand: Oxford University Press.

McKinnon, Malcolm. (Ed.). (1997). *The New Zealand historical atlas.* Auckland, New Zealand: David Bateman.

National Library of New Zealand. (n.d.a). Homepage. Retrieved June 13, 2012, from http://beta.natlib.govt.nz

National Library of New Zealand. (n.d.b). AtoJs online. Retrieved June 13, 2012, from http://beta.natlib.govt.nz/collections/atojs-online

Park, Geoff. (1995). *Nga Uru Ora / The groves of life: Ecology and history in a New Zealand landscape.* Wellington, New Zealand: Victoria University Press.

Pawson, Eric. (2000). Confronting nature. In John Cookson & Graeme Dunstall (Eds.), *Southern capital: Christchurch: Towards a city biography* (pp. 60–84). Christchurch, New Zealand: Canterbury University Press.

Pawson, Eric. (2011). Environmental hazards and natural disasters. *New Zealand Geographer, 67*(3), 143–147.

Pawson, Eric, & Brooking, Tom. (Eds.). (2002). *Environmental histories of New Zealand.* Melbourne, Australia: Oxford University Press (2nd ed., Dunedin, New Zealand: Otago University Press, 2013 [in press]).

Peden, Robert. (2011). *Making sheep country: Mt Peel Station and the transformation of the tussock lands.* Auckland, New Zealand: Auckland University Press.

Roche, Michael M. (1990). *History of forestry.* Wellington, New Zealand: New Zealand Forestry Corporation in association with GP Books.

Roche, Michael M. (1994). *Land and water. Water and soil conservation and central government in New Zealand, 1941–1988.* Wellington, New Zealand: Department of Internal Affairs.

Statistics New Zealand. (n.d.). Digital yearbook collection. Retrieved June 13, 2012, from www.stats.govt.nz/yearbooks

Te Ara. The Encyclopedia of New Zealand. (n.d.). Homepage. Retrieved June 13, 2012, from www.teara.govt.nz/

United States Central Intelligence Agency (US CIA). (2012). *The world factbook: New Zealand.* Retrieved June 8, 2012, from https://www.cia.gov/library/publications/the-world-factbook/geos/nz.html

University of Otago. (n.d.). Hocken snapshot. Retrieved June 13, 2012, from http://hockensnapshop.ac.nz

Waitangi Tribunal. (2012). Reports. Retrieved June 13, 2012, from www.waitangi-tribunal.govt.nz/reports/

Wynn, Graeme. (1979). Pioneers, politicians and the conservation of forests in early New Zealand. *Journal of Historical Geography, 5*(2), 171–188.

Wynn, Graeme. (1997). Remapping Tutira: Contours in the environmental history of New Zealand. *Journal of Historical Geography, 23*(4), 418–446.

Share the *Encyclopedia of Sustainability*: Teachers are welcome to make up to ten (10) copies of no more than two (2) articles for distribution in a single course or program. For further permissions, please visit www.copyright.com or contact: info@berkshirepublishing.com

North American Free Trade Agreement (NAFTA)

The North American Free Trade Agreement (NAFTA) is a treaty between Canada, Mexico, and the United States that eliminated or reduced many barriers to trade and investment between them. In response to criticisms that NAFTA would undermine labor and environmental protections, the parties negotiated supplemental agreements. The environmental side agreements have produced some tangible benefits but have not resolved all criticisms.

The North American Free Trade Agreement (NAFTA) is a free trade agreement between Canada, Mexico, and the United States, which entered into force in 1994. Proponents of NAFTA and other trade agreements argue that they promote economic growth, but critics allege that they do not foster *sustainable* growth. In response to such criticisms, the North American countries reached supplemental agreements aimed at improving environmental protection.

Background

A common view among economists is that reducing barriers to international trade and investment can increase the prosperity of all of the countries involved. Because countries are often unwilling to reduce their own barriers to imported goods except in exchange for reciprocal reductions by their trading partners, they have entered into international trade agreements that restrict the member states' ability to impose trade barriers. In 1947, twenty-three countries signed the General Agreement on Tariffs and Trade (GATT), a multilateral treaty that committed them to reduce tariffs and other barriers to trade in goods. The GATT parties engaged in several rounds of subsequent negotiations, including the Uruguay Round, which culminated in 1994 with the establishment of the World Trade Organization (WTO) and the adoption of a group of multilateral agreements that further lowered barriers on trade in goods and extended international disciplines to new areas, including trade in services and trade in intellectual property. As of 2012, the number of WTO members had grown to more than 150.

Countries have also negotiated bilateral and regional free trade agreements (FTAs) that reduce barriers to trade beyond the requirements of the WTO agreements. NAFTA, which was negotiated in 1991–1992, is one of the most important of these FTAs. In addition to lowering barriers to trade in goods and services, NAFTA addresses topics beyond those covered by the WTO agreements, including cross-border services.

The negotiation of NAFTA was controversial, particularly within the United States, because of concerns that it would harm labor and the environment. In the 1992 presidential election, Republican incumbent George H. W. Bush defended the agreement, Independent Ross Perot attacked it, and Democrat Bill Clinton took a middle position, stating that he would support the agreement only with additional protections for labor and the environment. After Clinton took office in January 1993, the NAFTA parties negotiated side agreements on labor and the environment, which entered into force together with NAFTA on 1 January 1994.

Lowering Barriers to Trade and Investment

NAFTA has generally phased out tariffs on trade in goods between the three North American countries. It also imposes general requirements, including that the parties not discriminate against foreign goods in favor of goods of national origin. It limits restrictions on cross-border provision of services beyond WTO requirements, although many restrictions remain. It also prohibits certain measures against foreign investors, including discrimination and expropriation.

Since NAFTA entered into force, trade and investment among the three North American countries has greatly increased, but it is difficult to determine how much of the increase is due to NAFTA. As the US economists Gary Clyde Hufbauer and Jeffrey Schott state, the agreement is "only one component of the rich complex of economic relations among the three countries," and its effects are "difficult to disentangle from … other events in the North American and global economies," such as the Mexican peso crisis in the mid-1990s, the high-tech boom in the United States later in the 1990s, and the global downturn that began in 2008. Nevertheless, they conclude that "the available evidence points to a strong positive impact" (Hufbauer and Schott 2005, 2, 19).

Environmental Criticisms

From the beginning of the negotiation of NAFTA, critics argued that it would harm the environment in several ways (Markell and Knox 2003, 3–7). First, they expressed concerns that increased cross-border trade between Mexico and the United States would overwhelm water, wastewater, and solid waste treatment facilities along the border. They pointed to evidence that rapid economic growth in northern Mexico—spurred by the Mexican *maquiladora* program, which encouraged foreign investment in a zone along the border for factories making goods for export to the United States—had already degraded the local environment and caused pollution of shared water resources, including the Rio Grande (known as Rio Bravo del Norte in Mexico).

Second, they argued that lowering barriers to cross-border investment would lead US and Canadian companies to move to Mexico to take advantage of its relatively lax environmental laws. To keep local companies from leaving in search of pollution havens, the Canadian and US governments would feel pressure to lower their own environmental standards, causing a "race to the bottom."

Third, environmental critics feared that the NAFTA system of dispute resolution, which allows governments to bring claims against one another for failing to comply with its trade disciplines, would be used to undermine US environmental laws. In response to a complaint by Mexico under GATT, an arbitral tribunal had stated in 1991 that a US law restricting imports of tuna caught in a manner that harmed dolphins violated GATT. The panel reasoning implicated other laws restricting imports for environmental reasons, and environmentalists wanted to ensure that NAFTA would not result in similar decisions.

Environmental Side Agreements

The NAFTA parties responded to some of these criticisms in the text of NAFTA itself. For example, the agreement states that each of its parties "should not" relax its environmental or health laws to encourage foreign investment (NAFTA 1992, art. 1114). This language was too weak to satisfy critics, however. The Clinton administration therefore proposed two new environmental agreements, which were negotiated and signed in 1993. One bilateral agreement between the United States and Mexico is directed at their border environment; the other agreement, between all three NAFTA parties, addresses the concerns over pollution havens and a race to the bottom.

The agreement between Mexico and the United States created two institutions, the Border Environment Cooperation Commission (BECC) and the North American Development Bank (NADB), and gives them a mandate to support environmental infrastructure, including water supply, wastewater, and solid waste facilities. The NADB, an international bank funded by the two governments, provides grants and loans for projects in the border region that are certified by the BECC as meeting certain environmental and financial requirements (Agreement Establishing BECC/NADB 1993).

The BECC began receiving applications for assistance and certification in 1995. As of September 2011, the BECC had certified 185 projects (100 in Mexico and 85 in the United States), and the NADB had committed more than US$1.3 billion to support their implementation (BECC and NADB 2011, 14, 18). Much of this support went to traditional infrastructure projects. For example, the NADB supported the first wastewater treatment plant in Matamoros, Tamaulipas, a town of more than 400,000 on the Rio Grande. The institutions also promote sustainable development more generally, including by assisting pilot projects aimed at energy efficiency and renewable energy, such as biodiesel production in El Paso, Texas, methane capture at a large dairy farm in Chihuahua, Mexico, and residential solar panels in Baja, California (NADB 2009, 12, 14).

The trilateral agreement, the North American Agreement for Environmental Cooperation (NAAEC), is directed primarily at the pollution haven concern. During the NAFTA negotiation, it became clear that Mexico's environmental laws were, on their face, comparable to those of Canada and the United States (Magraw 1995, 583, 615). NAFTA critics shifted their focus to the poor enforcement of those laws, which they said would induce companies to move south in search of lower compliance costs.

To respond to these concerns, the NAAEC requires its parties to "effectively enforce" their environmental laws (NAAEC 1993, art. 5(1)), and it provides for cooperation among the parties to promote effective enforcement. The NAAEC establishes an international organization, the Commission for Environmental Cooperation (CEC), with a governing council composed of the parties' three environmental ministers. The NAAEC enjoins the council to encourage effective enforcement of, and compliance with, domestic environmental laws (NAAEC 1993, art. 10(4)). To increase pressure on the parties, the NAAEC also establishes a procedure through which individuals and organizations may file complaints with the CEC Secretariat alleging that a NAAEC party is failing to effectively enforce its environmental law. If a submission meets certain requirements, it may lead to an investigative report (NAAEC 1993, arts. 14, 15). Finally, any NAAEC party may accuse another of engaging in a persistent pattern of failure to effectively enforce its environmental law. The council may convene an arbitral panel to hear the complaint and, under certain circumstances, the panel has the authority to establish an action plan to remedy the problem and to impose fines on a recalcitrant party. If the party does not pay, the other party may suspend NAFTA benefits (NAAEC 1993, part V).

The effectiveness of these mechanisms has been debated. Studies have cast doubt on the idea that companies shift their operations in search of pollution havens. The marginal costs of abating pollution in developed countries do not appear to be high enough to cause corporations to search for lower costs in countries with lower environmental standards (CEC 2002, 13; Gallagher 2004, 25–33; Nordström and Vaughan 1999, 37). In any event, the intergovernmental dispute resolution procedure has never been triggered.

Increasing the effective enforcement of environmental laws may have other benefits, however, including the promotion of sustainable development generally. There are indications that the CEC has had some positive effect in this respect. The submissions procedure, for example, has attracted a steady stream of complaints about nonenforcement, especially in Mexico, and has resulted in a number of investigative reports, some of which seem to have resulted in concrete improvements (Graubart 2008). More generally, the CEC has coordinated cooperative programs that have helped to phase out the use of toxic substances, such as the pesticides chlordane and DDT, in Mexico, and to institute a national system to track pollutant releases and transfers (Markell and Knox 2003, 30–33). The CEC also provides avenues for public participation, including a joint public advisory committee composed of fifteen citizens of the NAFTA countries. Moreover, the CEC has held a series of symposia that have clarified many aspects of the relationship between trade and environment in North America. Nevertheless, the CEC is hampered by its small annual budget, which is less than US$10 million.

The NAAEC does little to address the third environmental criticism of NAFTA: the concern that environmental laws could be challenged as inconsistent with trade agreements. This fear may have shifted since NAFTA entered into force. Environmental laws may seem less susceptible to challenge as inconsistent with trade requirements, since WTO decisions have dismissed some such arguments and no such challenges have been brought under NAFTA. At the same time, concerns have arisen that NAFTA tribunals may hold that environmental laws conflict with provisions protecting foreign investment. Chapter 11 of NAFTA allows investors claiming that their rights have been violated—by expropriation, for example—to take the governments to international arbitration. Many of the cases brought under Chapter 11 have argued that environmental regulations have effectively expropriated foreign investments, giving rise to concerns that environmental and other social regulations are at risk (Wood and Clarkson 2009).

NAFTA as a Model

The approach taken by NAFTA and the NAAEC to trade and the environment has been a model for subsequent bilateral and regional FTAs entered into by the United States. Since NAFTA came into force, the United States has negotiated twelve FTAs, all of which repeat many of the NAFTA/NAAEC provisions (Knox 2010). The post-NAFTA agreements are weaker than NAFTA in some respects. Although they all provide for intergovernmental environmental cooperation, none creates a new international organization like the CEC with a set annual budget, a dedicated secretariat, and a public advisory committee; and only four (bilateral FTAs with Colombia, Panama, and Peru, and a regional agreement with the Dominican Republic and several Central American countries) establish independent monitoring mechanisms like the CEC citizen submissions procedure. The effect of these agreements on sustainability, like that of NAFTA, will continue to be controversial.

John H. KNOX
Wake Forest University

See also Canada; Fair Trade; Great Lakes and Saint Lawrence River; Labor; Mexico; Multilateral Environmental Agreements (MEAs); Organization of American States (OAS); United States

FURTHER READING

Agreement Between the Government of the United States of America and the Government of the United Mexican States Concerning the Establishment of a Border Environment Cooperation Commission and a North American Development Bank (Agreement Establishing BECC/NADB). (1993). 32 *International Legal Materials* 1545.

Audley, John J. (1997). *Green politics and global trade: NAFTA and the future of environmental politics*. Washington, DC: Georgetown University Press.

Border Environment Cooperation Commission (BECC) & North American Development Bank (NADB). (2011). Quarterly status report (BECC/NADB Joint Report). San Antonio, TX: BECC & NADB.

Commission for Environmental Cooperation (CEC). (2002). *Free trade and the environment: The picture becomes clearer*. Austin: University of Texas.

Gallagher, Kevin. (2004). *Free trade and the environment: Mexico, NAFTA, and beyond*. Stanford, CA: Stanford Law and Politics.

Graubart, Jonathan. (2008). *Legalizing transnational activism: The struggle to gain social change from NAFTA's citizen petitions*. University Park: The Pennsylvania State University Press.

Hogenboom, Barbara. (1998). *Mexico and the NAFTA environment debate: The transnational politics of economic integration*. Dublin, Ireland: International Books.

Hufbauer, Gary Clyde, & Schott, Jeffrey J. (2005). *NAFTA revisited: Achievements and challenges*. Washington, DC: Institute for International Economics.

Johnson, Pierre Marc, & Beaulieu, André. (1996). *The environment and NAFTA: Understanding and implementing the new continental law*. Washington, DC: Island Press.

Kirton, John J., & Maclaren, Virginia W. (Eds.). (2002). *Linking trade, environment, and social cohesion, NAFTA experiences, global challenges*. London: Ashgate Publishing.

Knox, John H. (2004). The judicial resolution of conflicts between trade and the environment. *Harvard Environmental Law Review, 28*, 1–78.

Knox, John H. (2010). The neglected lessons of the NAFTA environmental regime. *Wake Forest Law Review, 45*(2), 101–134.

Magraw, Daniel. (Ed.). (1995). *NAFTA & the environment: Substances and process*. Chicago: American Bar Association.

Markell, David L., & Knox, John H. (Eds.). (2003). *Greening NAFTA: The North American Commission for Environmental Cooperation*. Stanford, CA: Stanford Law and Politics.

Mayer, Frederick. (1998). *Interpreting NAFTA: The science and art of political analysis*. New York: Columbia University Press.

Nordström, Håkan, & Vaughan, Scott. (1999). Trade and environment. Retrieved March 2, 2012, from http://www.wto.org/english/news_e/pres99_e/environment.pdf

North American Agreement on Environmental Cooperation (NAAEC). (1993). 32 *International Legal Materials* 1480.

North American Development Bank (NADB). (2009). Annual report 2008. Retrieved March 2, 2012, from http://www.nadb.org/pdf/publications/2008AnnualReport.pdf

North American Free Trade Agreement (NAFTA). (1992). 32 *International Legal Materials* 642.

Wold, Chris. (2008). Evaluating the NAFTA and commission for environmental cooperation: Lessons for integrating trade and environment in free trade agreements. *St. Louis University Public Law Review, 28*, 201–252.

Wood, Stepan, & Clarkson, Stephen. (2009, November 5). NAFTA Chapter 11 as Supraconstitution (CLPE research paper 43/2009). Retrieved March 2, 2012, from http://ssrn.com/abstract=1500564

Berkshire's authors and editors welcome questions, comments, and corrections. Send your emails about the *Berkshire Encyclopedia of Sustainability* in general or this volume in particular to: sustainability.updates@berkshirepublishing.com

Northwest Passage

The Northwest Passage is the bundle of maritime paths through the Canadian Arctic archipelago connecting the North Atlantic and North Pacific oceans. Northern Canadian indigenous peoples derive economic, social, and cultural benefit from lifestyles predicated upon this unique ice-filled marine environment. Their livelihoods and cultures are now threatened by rapid climatic change and potential environmental degradation resulting from increasing traffic in the passage's waters.

The Northwest Passage is the marine route between the North Atlantic and North Pacific oceans that threads through the more than thirty-six-thousand islands of the Canadian Arctic archipelago. It is located in the Canadian territories of Nunavut and the Northwest Territories. From the fifteenth century, European merchants sought the passage as a shorter route to Asian markets. A sledge party from the British ship HMS *Investigator* confirmed the passage's existence in 1850, and the Norwegian explorer Roald Amundsen accomplished the first marine transit between 1903 and 1906.

Climatic conditions there are now altering rapidly, threatening the sustainability of northern indigenous peoples' preferred lifestyles and livelihoods. With the increased melting of sea ice during the summer, the passage is becoming more easily traversable than ever before. Companies involved in resource extraction and shipping have been attracted to this easier passage because it offers potential savings in time and money. The passage provides a shorter route between Asian countries on the Pacific Rim and the Eastern Seaboard of the United States than others in current use, including the Panama Canal. The steady increase of marine traffic in the passage will likely result in environmental disturbances and pollution if Canada does not enforce strict marine regulatory systems.

Geography

Strictly speaking, the Northwest Passage is a collection of passages. In the past, ships have been able to use any one of seven routes through the archipelago, but they commonly take two routes, one northern and one southern. In all cases, ships enter from the Labrador Sea in the east and exit in the west into the Beaufort Sea, passing through the Chukchi Sea, the Bering Strait, and the Bering Sea en route to the Pacific Ocean. The northern route proceeds east–west through Davis Strait, Lancaster Sound, Barrow Strait, Viscount Melville Sound, and finally M'Clure Strait (or alternatively Prince of Wales Strait). It is the shortest route and the one most suitable for deep draft navigation, but thick, old sea ice often chokes the route near M'Clure Strait. About 90 percent of vessels choose the comparatively ice-free southern route, which also proceeds through Davis Strait, Lancaster Sound, and Barrow Strait. It then winds south through Peel Sound, Franklin Strait, and Victoria Strait, and follows the continental coastline closely westward through Queen Maud Gulf, Coronation Gulf, and the Amundsen Sea. This route is suitable only for vessels with a draft (the depth of water a ship draws when loaded) of less than 10 meters.

There had been only 135 full transoceanic transits of the passage to the end of 2009, and 95 of those had occurred since 1990 (Headland 2010). Traffic through the passage is steadily rising. The Canadian Coast Guard recorded 15 complete and 2 partial transits of the passage in 2008, 20 complete and 4 partial transits in 2009, 18 complete and 21 partial transits in 2010, and 23 complete and 17 partial transits in 2011 (personal communication with author, 8 February 2012). The operational season of the passage is short, running between late July and mid-October, depending on the route and year. Rapid and unprecedented environmental change in the Arctic is likely to extend this season, however, and admit greater activity in the passage's waters in the future.

Climate Change

Rising levels of human-produced greenhouse gases in the planet's atmosphere have rendered the Arctic one of the global regions most vulnerable to climatic change. Surface air temperatures there are warming at twice the average global rate. The Arctic Ocean is warming as well, and the amount and extent of sea ice there, including in the Northwest Passage, has declined 11–12 percent per decade since 1979. The summers from 2007 to 2011 have produced the five lowest minimum extents of sea ice in the Arctic Ocean since satellite records began, and the decade from 2002 to 2011 has produced nine of the ten lowest minimum extents (Richter-Menge, Jeffries, and Overland 2011). This decline has global environmental ramifications. Arctic sea ice has a high albedo, meaning that it reflects most of the sun's heat and light back into space. This reflection plays an integral role in maintaining the Northern Hemisphere's cooler temperatures. With increasing amounts of sea ice melting, a process known as *Arctic amplification* comes into play. As the amount of open water in the Arctic Ocean increases, the water absorbs more solar energy, and the ice reflects less. The Arctic Ocean then releases that heat into the atmosphere in the autumn, causing both Arctic and global temperatures to rise.

Regional Societies and Economies

Climatic and environmental changes are greatly affecting the inhabitants of the twenty-three small coastal communities in the Canadian Arctic that line the passage. These settlements are predominantly populated by Inuit (central and eastern Arctic) and Inuvialuit (western Arctic) northern indigenous peoples, and are usually between five hundred and five thousand people in size. The colonial policies of the Canadian government created most communities in the post–World War II period by pressuring seminomadic hunting groups to move into fixed, centralized settlements.

A mixed economy consisting of both waged employment and subsistence harvesting characterizes Canadian Arctic communities. Hunting, fishing, and trapping continue to be crucial to Inuit and Inuvialuit economic and social life. In Ulukhaktok, on the west coast of Victoria Island, 76 percent of community members engage in hunting and fishing (Andrachuk and Pearce 2010). These activities are an important means of food security in a region where imported food is often both of low nutritional value and prohibitively expensive. The consumption of "country" or wild food ranges from 106 to 440 grams per day in Nunavut, and comprises 6–40 percent of a person's daily energy intake (Anisimov 2007).

Some anxiety surrounds country food consumption, however. Such meat often contains levels of persistent organic pollutants (POPs), heavy metals, petroleum hydrocarbons, or radionuclides above those scientists consider technically safe for human consumption. The bioaccumulation of these substances in Arctic marine and terrestrial ecosystems threatens humans because of the process of biomagnification, where the concentration of such substances increases as it proceeds up a food chain. POPs concentrate more readily in the blubber of animals such as seals, and Inuit have traditionally prized this blubber as a source of valuable nutrients. The continued inclusion of seal fat and other country foods in northern indigenous diets exposes humans, who are high in Arctic food webs, to accordingly high doses of various environmental contaminants.

Marine species hunted vary by community location but may include ringed seals (*Pusa hispida*), bearded seals (*Erignathus barbatus*), harp seals (*Pagophilus groenlandicus*), beluga whales (*Delphinapterus leucas*), bowhead whales (*Balaena mysticetus*), narwhal (*Monodon monoceros*), walruses (*Odobenus rosmarus*), and polar bears (*Ursus maritimus*). Inuit fish for Arctic cod (*Arctogadus glacialis*), Arctic cisco (*Coregonus autumnalis*), Arctic char (*Salvelinus alpinus*), Pacific herring (*Clupea pallasii*), and other species, either individually or on a small-scale communal basis. Inuit are also involved in commercial Greenland halibut (*Reinhardtius hippoglossoides*) and shrimp fisheries in Davis Strait and Baffin Bay. The Nunavut Land Claims Agreement and the Inuvialuit Final Agreement grant Inuit and Inuvialuit peoples, along with representatives from territorial and federal governmental agencies, the right to participate in the co-management of natural maritime resources. Wildlife co-management boards in Nunavut and the Northwest Territories define, maintain, and adjust regulations for the lawful harvesting of individual species.

Community Impacts

Inuit hunters and elders possess sophisticated knowledge about local and regional marine environments, acquired from observing and interacting with coastal shorelines, sea ice, and water over many years. Since 2000, Inuit across the Canadian Arctic have noted consistent environmental changes that reflect the scientific consensus that a major environmental transformation is under way in the Arctic Ocean. A principal characteristic of the emerging regime is less sea ice, a change to which Inuit are acutely sensitive. Sea ice acts as a platform for hunting marine animals, an environment that sustains those animals and traditional sociocultural practices built atop harvesting, and a means of travel between communities in the winter months.

Sea ice now breaks up earlier in the year and forms later in the year. For the community of Igloolik, situated on a small island in Cumberland Sound, the latter change has been drastic. Before 1970, the sea ice used to begin freezing in late September or early October, but now it forms in November. Residents of Igloolik also used to be able to safely cross Fury and Hecla Strait, to reach Baffin Island, before Christmas. Now this ice crossing is not safe until late January or early February (Laidler et al. 2010). Sea ice also generally takes much longer to form properly in the autumn than it did before 1970. Once it forms, the ice is thinner than it used to be, and therefore less stable for travelers and hunters. The weather has not only warmed overall but has also become less predictable, with mercurial and unexpected winds, increased amounts of precipitation, and more frequent extreme weather events (Ford et al. 2010; Laidler et al. 2010).

These environmental changes have created newly hazardous conditions for both animals and people. Many Arctic marine mammals, including seals, walruses, polar bears, and whales, depend upon sea ice as a platform upon which to feed, breed, or rest, or as a source of food. The plight of ringed seals is particularly important, as they are abundant throughout the passage and provide a principal source of food for Inuit throughout the year. These seals need stable, shore-fast ice for giving birth to seal pups, shedding their hair in springtime, and resting. They feed there on ice amphipods, which are tiny crustaceans less than 50 millimeters long, and Arctic cod, both found at the floe edge. With sea ice breaking up earlier in the spring, pups have less time to develop out of the water and thus suffer higher mortality rates. Older seals that Inuit catch are smaller, providing less food, and have less healthy pelts, which are harder to sell for cash.

Reductions in the thickness, extent, and longevity of sea ice constrain access to hunting grounds and other communities, increase the danger of traveling on sea ice, and force the development of new, safer trails, which are often longer and run over more difficult territory to travel. Common Inuit adaptations to these new environmental and climatic conditions include harvesting different sources of country food when more usual sources are scarcer, relying on extended family and community networks of sharing to obtain country food in times of scarcity, altering the timing and modes of travel and harvesting, and taking extra precautions when hunting or traveling away from communities (Andrachuk and Pearce 2010; Ford et al. 2010).

Geophysical changes include the thawing of permafrost (a permanently frozen layer of land), accelerated coastal erosion, and more active slope processes (erosion). Combined with rising sea levels that bring larger waves and more frequent storm surges to low-lying coastal regions, these changes threaten the integrity of Inuit cultural sites and the infrastructure and longevity of some settlements. In the western Arctic settlement of Tuktoyaktuk, the government has enacted shoreline protection measures since the mid-1970s. Residents have lost significant amounts of property in the last five years, however, and have had to relocate farther inland. In the summer of 2009, the village of Pangnirtung, on the southeast coast of Baffin Island, lost two bridges to flash flooding and erosion.

Tourism and Shipping

Marine traffic in the Northwest Passage continues to increase. Cruise tourism in the Canadian Arctic has grown rapidly in popularity since 2006. The number of cruise vessels doubled from eleven to twenty-two between 2005 and 2006. Of the C$4.4 million garnered from tourism in Nunavut in 2007, C$2.1 million came from that sector (Stewart et al. 2010). Smaller vessels are generally used for tourist cruises in Nunavut. They make stops ashore at places renowned for local wildlife gatherings and at communities, where tourists learn about Arctic indigenous culture (Maher 2010). Despite the extensive fossil fuel consumption and carbon emissions associated with these long-haul journeys originating in southern North America or Europe, some regard cruise tourism as a more sustainable activity upon which to base long-term regional economic development than either subsistence hunting or nonrenewable resource extraction. Tourists hire guides for hunting and fishing trips, purchase indigenous arts and handicrafts, and frequent local hotels and restaurants, providing an important source of economic revenue for small Arctic communities.

Experts predict destinational shipping in the Canadian Arctic will expand into the 2020s (Arctic Council 2009). There may be more sealifts to Arctic communities, which ship dry foods, fuel, building materials, and other items north from southern Canada. More shipping in conjunction with active and anticipated sites of nonrenewable resource extraction is also likely. The Canadian government sold long-term leases for oil and gas exploration in the Canadian segment of the Beaufort Sea in 2008. Baffinland Iron Mines Corporation is in the process of obtaining permission to construct an 18 million tonne–per annum iron ore mine at Mary River on north Baffin Island. Once operational, this mine will ship iron ore to Europe for a projected minimum of twenty-five years.

Shipping companies have widely touted the Northwest Passage as a preferable, shorter transoceanic shipping route compared to the Panama Canal. A ship using the Northwest Passage for a transit between Shanghai and New Jersey, for example, would save 7,000 kilometers of travel. Experts agree, however, that transoceanic container and cargo traffic is not expected to increase significantly in the short term because ice conditions in the archipelago vary highly, both between the western and eastern Canadian Arctic in the same year and from year to year. It is difficult for shipping companies to predict conditions well enough to construct economically viable shipping timetables. Other reasons for the reluctance include the high cost of marine insurance for shippers in ice-laden waters, the lack of infrastructure for commercial shipping in the Northwest Passage, and the notoriously inaccurate marine charts of the archipelago, which put ships at increased risk of collisions or groundings.

Environmental Challenges, Policies, and Regulations

Even a small anticipated increase in levels of shipping through the passage could have substantial environmental consequences. The main shipping routes in Davis Strait, Lancaster Sound, and the Beaufort Sea shadow the migration routes of large populations of narwhal, beluga, and bowhead whales. Between 80 and 90 percent of the planet's narwhal population travels through Lancaster Sound each spring. By emitting noises and disrupting migration routes and meeting areas, ships stress these mammals. In December 2010, the Canadian government protected Lancaster Sound, which is one of the passage's most ecologically productive and sensitive areas, by declaring it a national marine conservation area. It will remain out of bounds to future oil and gas exploration (Parks Canada 2010).

Ships can bring alien microbes, fungi, plants, and animals into the Arctic, and can release such organisms into the marine environment through discharges such as ballast water, with unpredictable ramifications for regional ecosystems. There is also the potential for ships to accidentally discharge oil or toxic chemicals into the passage's waters, which would have serious short- and long-term health effects on marine mammals and migratory birds. In 1970, the Canadian government passed the Arctic Waters Pollution Prevention Act (AWPPA), which sets out extensive regulations to protect the Canadian Arctic marine environment. AWPPA prohibits the discharge of fluids or solid wastes from ships into Arctic waters except in emergency situations. It sets certain design requirements for ships transiting Canadian Arctic waters, and prescribes sixteen shipping safety control zones, giving the dates from which fourteen different classes of ships can enter and leave arctic waters safely. All vessels above 100 tonnes traversing Canadian Arctic waters are subject to these regulations (Transport Canada 2010a and 2010b).

This stringent federal regime of environmental monitoring and protection may not remain in place, however, if other countries challenge the passage's status under international law. The Canadian government claims that the passage constitutes internal waters and is subject to national laws. Other countries, including the United States and members of the European Union, assert that the passage is an international strait that connects two bodies of the high seas. In the latter case, under the right of transit passage, Canada would be able to enforce international environmental regulations only for shipping in Arctic waters, as prescribed by the International Convention for the Prevention of Pollution from Ships, 1973 as Modified by the Protocol of 1978 Relating Thereto (MARPOL 73/78). MARPOL's standards are less strict than those of AWPPA. Annex 1 of the former allows the release of oily ballast and oily bilgewater into Arctic marine environments, although AWPPA has a zero-tolerance policy for such discharges.

Outlook

The Northwest Passage will continue to undergo climatic and environmental changes, to which animals and people living in the region will have to adapt. Terrestrial and marine temperatures will increase, extending the summer shipping season. Ice in the Arctic Ocean is melting at a rate faster than that predicted by any of the model climatic projections in the Intergovernmental Panel on Climate Change's 2007 report (Solomon et al. 2007). The southern passage route has been nearly ice-free for a period of time during each summer since 2007, and the northern passage experienced similar periodic low-ice conditions in the summers of 2007, 2010, and 2011. Experts agree that climatic change may also bring about conditions in which the northern passage becomes more choked with ice, however. Scientists expect that as younger ice melts more rapidly in the summertime, the winds and currents of the Beaufort Gyre are expected to draw more multiyear ice south from the Arctic Ocean into M'Clure Strait, making it more, not less, difficult to navigate. Canada nevertheless expects certain kinds of destinational shipping and cruise tourism to increase. Such activities may have serious environmental consequences, despite the strictures of Canadian regulatory regimes.

Christina ADCOCK
University of British Columbia

See also Canada; Central America; Ecotourism (the Americas); Mackenzie River; Marine Ecosystems Health; Marine Preserves; Mobility; Multilateral Environmental Agreements (MEAs); North American Free Trade Agreement (NAFTA); Parks and Protected Areas; Small Island States; Travel and Tourism Industry; United States; Yellowstone to Yukon Conservation Initiative (Y2Y)

FURTHER READING

Andrachuk, Mark, & Pearce, Tristan. (2010). Vulnerability and adaptation in two communities in the Inuvialuit Settlement Region. In Grete K. Hovelsrud & Barry Smit (Eds.), *Community adaptation and vulnerability in Arctic regions* (pp. 63–81). New York: Springer.

Anisimov, Oleg A., et al. (2007). Polar Regions (Arctic and Antarctic). In Martin L. Parry, Osvaldo F. Canziani, Jean P. Palutikof, Paul J. van der Linden & Clair E. Hanson (Eds.), *Climate change 2007: Impacts, adaptation and vulnerability. Contribution of Working Group II to the Fourth Assessment Report of the Intergovernmental Panel on Climate Change* (pp. 653–685). Cambridge, UK: Cambridge University Press.

Arctic Council. (2009). *Arctic marine shipping assessment 2009 report*. Akureyri, Iceland: Protection of the Arctic Marine Environment (PAME) Working Group.

Berton, Pierre. (1988). *The Arctic grail: The quest for the Northwest Passage and the North Pole, 1818–1909*. Toronto: McClelland & Stewart.

Byers, Michael. (2009). *Who owns the Arctic? Understanding sovereignty disputes in the North*. Vancouver, Canada: Douglas & MacIntyre.

Ford, James D.; Pearce, Tristan; Duerden, Frank; Furgal, Chris; & Smit, Barry. (2010). Climate change policy responses for Canada's Inuit population: The importance of and opportunities for adaptation. *Global Environmental Change, 20*(1), 177–191.

Ford, James D., & Smit, Barry. (2004). A framework for assessing the vulnerability of communities in the Canadian Arctic to risks associated with climate change. *Arctic, 57*(4), 389–400.

Griffiths, Franklyn. (Ed.). (1987). *Politics of the Northwest Passage*. Montreal: McGill-Queen's University Press.

Hassol, Susan J. (2004). *Impacts of a warming Arctic: Arctic climate impact assessment*. Cambridge, UK: Cambridge University Press.

Headland, Robert. (2010). Ten decades of transits of the Northwest Passage. *Polar Geography, 33*(1–2), 1–13.

Laidler, Gita J.; Elee, Pootoogoo; Ikummaq, Theo; Joamie, Eric; & Aporta, Claudio. (2010). Mapping Inuit sea ice knowledge, use, and change in Nunavut, Canada (Cape Dorset, Igloolik, Pangnirtung). In Igor Krupnik, Claudio Aporta, Shari Gearheard & Gita J. Laidler (Eds.), *SIKU: Knowing our ice: Documenting Inuit sea ice knowledge and use* (pp. 45–80). New York: Springer.

Maher, Patrick T. (2010). Cruise tourist experiences and management implications for Auyuittuq, Sirmilik and Quttinirpaaq National Parks, Nunavut, Canada. In C. Michael Hall & Jarkko Saarinen (Eds.), *Tourism and change in Polar Regions: Climate, environments and experiences* (pp. 119–134). London: Routledge.

Nickels, Scot; Furgal, Chris; Buell, Mark; & Moquin, Heather. (2005). *Unikkaaqatigiit: Putting the human face on climate change*. Ottawa, Canada: Inuit Tapiriit Kanatami, Nasivvik Centre for Inuit Health and Changing Environments, and National Aboriginal Health Organization.

Parks Canada. (2010). Government of Canada presents boundary proposal for Lancaster Sound National Marine Conservation Area. Retrieved March 1, 2012, from http://www.pc.gc.ca/apps/cp-nr/release_e.asp?id=1679&andor1=nr

The Pew Environment Group. (2010a). Baffin Bay & Davis Strait. Retrieved February 21, 2012, from http://oceansnorth.org/baffin-bay-davis-strait

The Pew Environment Group. (2010b). Lancaster Sound. Retrieved February 21, 2012, from http://oceansnorth.org/lancaster-sound

Richter-Menge, Jackie; Jeffries, Martin O.; & Overland, James E. (Eds.). (2011). Arctic report card: Update for 2011. Retrieved May 8, 2012, from http://www.arctic.noaa.gov/reportcard/

Solomon, Susan, et al. (Eds.). (2007). *Climate change 2007: The physical science basis. Contribution of Working Group I to the Fourth Assessment Report of the Intergovernmental Panel on Climate Change*. Cambridge, UK: Cambridge University Press.

Stewart, Emma J.; Howell, Stephen E. L.; Draper, Dianne; Yackel, John; & Tivy, Adrienne. (2010). Cruise tourism in Arctic Canada: Navigating a warming climate. In C. Michael Hall & Jarkko Saarinen (Eds.), *Tourism and change in Polar Regions: Climate, environments and experiences* (pp. 71–88). London: Routledge.

Transport Canada. (2010a). Arctic Waters Pollution Prevention Act (AWPPA). Retrieved March 1, 2012, from http://www.tc.gc.ca/eng/marinesafety/debs-arctic-acts-regulations-awppa-494.htm

Transport Canada. (2010b). Arctic Shipping Pollution Prevention Regulations (ASPPR). Retrieved March 1, 2012, from http://www.tc.gc.ca/eng/marinesafety/debs-arctic-acts-regulations-asppr-421.htm

Williams, Glyn. (2009). *Arctic labyrinth: The quest for the Northwest Passage*. London: Penguin.

O

Oceania

The tens of thousands of islands in the Pacific Ocean that make up Oceania have been affected by resource exploitation by traders, planters, and, more recently, fishers and transnational corporations, as well as pollution from mining, irresponsible forestry, and nuclear testing. World War II brought effects from the war itself and also vastly increased the introduction of disruptive biota and pathogens. As the Earth's oceans respond to global climate change, Oceania is especially vulnerable.

A region of little land and much sea, Oceania covers 45 percent of the Earth's surface but contains only 0.01 percent of its total land area and human population. Oceania includes between twenty thousand and thirty thousand islands in the Pacific, plus the larger land masses of Australia, Papua New Guinea, and New Zealand. Its diverse environments range from, in the southwest, large, high forested islands with a more continental geology to, in the north and central regions, small coral atolls where freshwater and trees are scarce. Within the North and South Pacific are also high volcanic islands, such as tropical Tahiti and the Hawaiian Islands. Oceania has been classified into three geographic regions—Melanesia, Micronesia, and Polynesia—that generally reflect this geological diversity as well as some cultural similarities within each region. Tahiti and the Hawaiian Islands sustained significant indigenous populations long before contact with Europeans, as did New Zealand and Easter Island (Rapanui) on the cooler temperate fringes. This article picks up the environmental history of Oceania beginning in the sixteenth century when European explorers began to arrive.

Resource Reconnaissance

Starting with Portuguese explorer Ferdinand Magellan in 1520 and ending with the last of three voyages of the Englishman James Cook from 1776 to 1780, a number of European explorers crisscrossed the Pacific searching variously for gold, trade, the Great South Land, and new knowledge. Cook's discoveries resulted in the British settlement of Australia (1788) and later New Zealand (1840) and a huge corpus of knowledge about the Pacific's resources.

Early Exploitation

Oceania's potential soon attracted European and North American entrepreneurs. From the late eighteenth century, the newcomers' activities drew Oceania into the global economy. There were two trade loops that dominated the Pacific Islands from the 1780s until the 1860s. The first linked Europe, North America (and later Australia and New Zealand), and China. Beginning in 1785 seal, beaver, and otter on the northwest US coast attracted British, US, and Russian traders, who sought furs to trade with China for tea. The Hawaiian Islands became a refreshment center on the passage to China and for overwintering, involving the Hawaiian people in food production for the ships; in addition, Hawaii was involved in supplying the new gold rush settlements in California in the mid-nineteenth century (before rail links from the eastern United States were completed). The search for seal furs also reached the Pacific coast of Peru, the South Island of New Zealand and its small offshore islands, as well as Tasmania. By 1830, however, seal numbers had fallen so much that the trade became unviable. Other commodities to trade with China were sought from the Pacific Islands—*bêche-de-mer* (sea cucumbers) until about 1850 from tropic lagoons around Belau and Fiji, and sandalwood from Fiji, the Marquesas, and Hawaii. By the 1820s, these sources were depleted, but there followed the discovery of substantial stands in the New Hebrides and New Caledonia. By 1860 little sandalwood remained to harvest.

The second trade nexus had a similar outcome. The exhaustion of whale stocks in the Atlantic led whalers from England and the east coast of the United States into the Pacific from 1788 seeking whale oil for lubrication and lighting. First the sperm whale and then the right whale were hunted by hundreds of ships a year until the 1860s when catches declined, followed by the loss of much of the US whaling fleet in the Civil War and in the northern ice during in the early winter in 1871. The growing popularity of kerosene also made whaling increasingly unprofitable.

Ecological Shadowlands

The 1860s saw most islands of Oceania drawn into the economic orbit of Europe, North America, and the British colonies of Australia and New Zealand. These linkages cast an ecological shadow over the islands as they drained and almost destroyed parts of the resource web in numerous locations. For example, whalers had found that Pacific Islanders produced coconut oil for cosmetic purposes and that there was a growing market for the oil in Europe. Traders collected the oil in the 1840s and 1850s but depended on the inclinations of the islanders regarding the quantity and quality of the product. German traders in Micronesia and Samoa in the late 1860s discovered that pressing the dried coconut kernel under factory conditions produced a superior product, and, in order to ensure a regular supply, Europeans began to seek land for plantation agriculture. At the same time, the US Civil War stimulated demand for cotton. Planters sought land for growing cotton in Fiji, Samoa, Tahiti, New Hebrides, and the British colony of Queensland, Australia. Although the Pacific cotton boom faded with the end of the Civil War, plantation agriculture focused on sugar and copra (coconut) was common on the larger islands by the 1890s and the first decade of the twentieth century. Planting everywhere resulted in increased forest clearance and swamp drainage, altering coastal and lowland ecology.

From the 1870s and into the 1890s, desiring to regulate conflicts with the indigenous people over land and labor, guarantee European property, and prevent friction among themselves, European powers and the United States proceeded to annex most of the Pacific Islands. Colonial governments set up there had few conservation regulations and often were more concerned with international politics than protection. With land access secured, Europeans now needed labor to clear the forest and plant and harvest their crops. About 250,000 Pacific Islanders (with 186,000 Asians) were taken to workplaces outside their home islands before World War I. These islanders initially suffered high mortality from foreign microorganisms, though gradually populations became more resistant.

Diseases previously unknown in the Pacific Islands and for which the indigenous population had no immune defense had entered the region on the first European ships, and island populations suffered dramatic declines of up to 80 and even 90 percent from diseases such as measles, smallpox, and venereal afflictions. Though all populations declined to varying degrees, those most affected were on islands where large areas of land had been decimated, destroying their resource base and thus undermining their resistance to introduced illness. Decline or forced removal of population by colonial governments led to the decay of horticultural and aquacultural systems put in place by the indigenous peoples, sometimes allowing the original fauna and flora, from before human settlement, to recover. More commonly, however, niches opened for introduced weed species, such as the guava, and introduced domesticated animals, such as cattle, goats, dogs, and cats, as well as the European rat and, in New Zealand, rabbits. These destroyed both habitat and the young of native species, causing many extirpations and even extinctions at a rate far greater than the first indigenous settlers, who had done their own major alterations to Oceania's flora and fauna. In temperate New Zealand, European settlers felled and burned forests for pastoral uses on a massive scale, changing the ecology of millions of acres. The way that remaining virgin lands were managed also changed with the incoming technology; for example, with machetes and steel axes, land could be cleared more easily. Capitalism and colonial taxation systems led not only to commercial plantations but also to small-scale crop production by Pacific Islanders. Incoming ideology also played a part in change, as Christianity ousted many traditional methods of population limitation; in some places, this probably assisted the gradual recovery of population numbers noted during 1880–1920. Also, Christian practices included contributing to church upkeep, which reinforced the need to produce cash crops.

Several tropical lagoons were home to pearl shell. European traders sought the shell and pearls, relying on local divers. Once the diving helmet became available in the 1870s, Europeans, having capital to invest, gained access to shell at deeper levels along with considerable control of the industry. Local people resisted this, but colonial laws tended to favor open access. With the availability of inexpensive flippers, snorkels, and masks in the 1950s, local people often depleted the resource themselves (a common pattern when new technology first enters island societies). To revive the industry in the twentieth century some governments, such as the Japanese in Balau during the 1930s with pioneering pearl farming, encouraged farming the shell, with some success, though in some cases mollusk disease has posed problems.

Although the advent of the steamship in the 1880s enhanced access for relatively small suppliers to large consumers in the distant metropolises, economies of scale along with the vagaries of weather often meant that it was commercially marginal to use scattered islands as plantation sites. This was all the more so as the world market experienced periodic gluts of vegetable oils in the 1920s and collapsed in the Great Depression of the1930s. On the larger archipelagoes, the Fiji sugar industry continued strong, and in Hawaii both sugar and pineapple production were buoyed up by integrated companies that invested in improving varieties and equipment and maintaining the fertility of the soil, mainly with chemical fertilizers. The expansion of commercial agriculture and especially pastoralism in Australia and New Zealand saw the smaller and even the tiniest islands of the Pacific fall within the ecological shadows of these metropolitan areas. Australia and New Zealand from the middle to the late nineteenth century sent their wool to Britain; following the introduction of refrigerated shipping in the 1880s, their exports included sheep and cattle meat. In both countries, phosphorous- and sulfur-poor soils hindered both agriculture and pastoral development, and led to the search for fertilizers.

Uninhabited guano islands such as Laysan soon lost their guano to collectors to sell as fertilizers, but others proved a source for the raw material for superphosphate, a source of phosphorus and sulfur. Makatea in the Society Islands and Angaur in the Carolines were mined from the 1900s. Japan controlled Angaur after 1914 and used its phosphates to fertilize crops at home and within Micronesia once it gained this territory as a mandate of the League of Nations. Over ninety-eight thousand Japanese migrants grew mainly sugarcane, clearing and planting entire islands, such as Saipan. Tiny Nauru became a British Empire mandate and was mined, along with nearby Ocean (Banaba) Island, part of the British Protectorate of the Gilbert and Ellice Islands. The British Phosphate commission sold Nauru phosphate, mainly to Australia and New Zealand, at cost, far below the price for Makatea phosphate, for example. The British relocated the Banabans in 1947 to a Fiji island. By the 1960s, the Nauruan people were left with an island of coral pinnacles and little useful vegetation.

World War II in the Pacific

Japan entered World War II in 1941 and dominated the western Pacific as far as Guadalcanal during 1942 and early 1943. The war ushered in Oceania's greatest human invasion, considering the scope of events occurring over the brief span of four years. The war introduced the airplane as a means of rapid communication, but also a means of rapidly spreading potential pests and pathogens. Japanese and Allied forces bombarded islands, and, despite later demolition operations, unexploded munitions remain a danger. In some areas, such as north of Guadalcanal, the sea floor is littered with wrecked battleships now leaking oil, and there are fears that dumped chemicals, such as mustard gas, are deteriorating in Micronesian and Melanesian swamps. Throughout the Pacific, thousands of tons of coral were crushed to make airfields and to clear channels for large ships, changing the lagoon environments. Construction often destroyed taro pits, the subsistence base of many atoll dwellers.

Alien biota followed the troops. To supplement their diet, the Japanese introduced the destructive Great African snail (*Achatina*) to northern New Guinea, and it spread rapidly. Shipments of equipment from Manus after the war introduced to Guam the brown tree snake (*Boiga irregularis*), which has undermined the basis for a mixed tropical forest by killing the bird and bat life, the seed carriers; the snake is also a pest to human beings. The US army introduced the cattle tick (*Boophilus microplus*) to New Caledonia. Many weed species radiated out from wartime airfields, island-hopping in the cuffs of military trousers. Air transport and the rapid movement of warships meant insect transfer was more likely, so colonial health authorities were extra vigilant. The feared extension of the malarial mosquito,

Anopheles, beyond Buxton's line (170° east longitude and 20° south latitude, east and south of which malaria had not existed) did not occur, though infected soldiers, returning to north Queensland where the vector was endemic, induced malaria epidemics in local military and civilian populations in 1942.

Rear areas became suppliers of fresh food. Islands such as Fiji, New Caledonia, and New Zealand found their herds and soils depleted by wartime demand. This also meant greater mechanization of the agricultural sector and more land under cultivation. In the battle areas of coastal New Guinea and the western Solomons there was population decline, mainly due to disturbed conditions, malnutrition, and dysentery. Behind the front, the birth rate rose in many areas as US troops fathered hundreds of children by women in the Cooks, the Samoan Islands, Bora Bora, and Tonga, though fewer, it seems, in Fiji.

Nuclear Testing and Decolonization

Oceania's remoteness—from the perspective of the United States, Britain, and France—made it an ideal atomic testing ground. From the first US atmospheric test on Bikini in 1946 to the last underground nuclear detonation by the French on Mururoa in 1996, the islands and the people have absorbed unmeasured quantities of radioactivity. Some islands are uninhabitable. Long-term outcomes are unknown. Nonetheless, the Bikinians briefly revisit their island and replant in the hope of a tourist boom of divers wanting to see the wrecks of derelict warships or sharks in the maritime sanctuary.

Elsewhere life generally returned to the old pattern, though seeing how the US visitors had utilized local supplies of timber and coral, some indigenous peoples discerned that their lightly used resources had potential for making money. The United Nations' emphasis on decolonization prompted more systematic surveys of resources, such as minerals, forests, and soil, throughout the colonial Pacific from the late 1940s through the 1970s. Although some colonial governments attempted to set up sustainable regimes in forestry, this sector as well as mining have been associated with vast ecological changes in the Melanesian islands since the 1980s, where resources are exploited by transnational companies that contribute much to the coffers of governments, but little to environmental management. In Papua New Guinea, for example, the tailings from copper mining at Ok Tedi have inundated the lowlands with heavy metals, destroying the vegetation and thus a habitat that is home to thirty thousand people. Mining continues apace elsewhere with nominal or no institutional controls on long-term effects on the ecology of land and coastal waters. Forests in the Solomons have been logged unsustainably since the 1980s and may be exhausted in the near future. Both the mining and forestry industries, along with use of imported fertilizers by cash-crop growers, create deleterious runoff, posing a threat to the vital inshore fishery and its reef-lagoon ecology that provides the bulk of fresh protein to coastal dwellers.

Sustainability Issues

Oceania's resource base is under pressure. Population growth is 2.7 percent annually in some areas. Migration to metropolitan areas has helped, but population increase, especially on atolls, has pushed these islands beyond their carrying capacity in terms of demands for freshwater and food. People in search of living space have sometimes infilled and built on natural swamplands, which had acted as sponges at high tides. Pollution and sanitation are increasing problems in urban and peri-urban centers on atolls as well as on high islands.

Natural forces have always shaped Oceania. The rising sea level due to climate change is one such example. This is an increasing concern as low-lying islands and atolls become flooded and eroded, and gardens and the freshwater lens (the layer of fresh groundwater that floats on top of denser saltwater) become salinated. Coral reefs, a major food-source habitat for lagoon people, are dying in some places because water temperatures are rising. When El Niño occurs, the ocean warms up, rainfall is reduced in the western Pacific, and heavy rain is induced in the central Pacific near the equator—and El Niño is occurring more frequently. Although adaptable, coral reef ecology is also vulnerable to increasing levels in the sea of anthropogenic (human-caused) carbon dioxide because it increases the water's acidity and interferes with calcification. Populations of islands—and in the cases of Kiribati and Tuvalu, entire countries—may have to migrate or perish. Probable destination countries, especially Australia and New Zealand, as yet prefer to fund island states threatened by rising seas for strategies of adaptation and management, such as more large water storage tanks for rain and extensive coastal mangrove planting to combat erosion.

Since the 1980s, agencies of the Pacific Islands Forum, a regional organization of Pacific countries, have been working to ameliorate these environmental problems. In 1987 they gained some financial returns for the region from the tuna fishery through license fees to outsiders to fish within each country's exclusive economic zone (EEZ); unfortunately this has not been matched with conservation of the resource by foreign fishers. The forum countries negotiated a ban on drift net fishing in 1989.

Globalization and increasingly efficient technology have put huge demands on fishery, particularly tuna, in the early years of the twentieth-first century. Add to that the difficulties of policing such vast areas of ocean and its survival is under threat. The creation of huge regional maritime reserves may help, but this will require transnational resolve and alternate means of income for several small island states. New Zealand's quota system for its own fisheries, introduced in 1986, has won praise for its conservation value. Another regional conservation success has been a virtual ban on whaling. Japan, however, still attempts annually to take more than nine hundred minke whales from the Southern Ocean, supposedly for scientific research. Its whalers meet lively opposition each year from conservationists' vessels.

Within islands, consciousness of the need for more active conservation seems to be emerging in some quarters, and the use of sustainable solar-powered energy is becoming more common, especially on smaller islands. In regard to major resources, however, communities commonly prefer to see resource exploitation, no matter the environmental outcomes, as "rent" for extraction and make little or no use of the resource by any domestic processing industries that could better support their increasing populations. Reliance on traditional environmental knowledge to translate to a generalized conservation ethic is not effective; while of value to small communities, it cannot co-exist with an active cash economy or address more regional concerns unless it is firmly backed by government action. Conservation groups succeed only when they secure mutual benefit coalitions with resource holders. Donor countries now include environmental impact assessments in aid packages. In western Melanesia, for example, despite decades of legislation, commissions of inquiry, and pressure from the World Bank and donor countries, unsustainable and illegal logging continues in much of the area because of understaffing of official bodies, corruption, and bribery.

Oceania faces many of the same sustainability issues as other areas of the world, including recovery from overharvesting of resources, management of existing resources in sensitive ecological environments, effects of global climate change, and the need for government initiative in policy making. What makes the problems especially complex is the range of this vast region, which encompasses tens of thousands of microenvironments on its widely dispersed islands.

Judith A. BENNETT
University of Otago

See also Auckland, New Zealand; Australia; Forest Management; Marine Ecosystems Health; Marine Preserves; Mining (Australia); Murray-Darling River Basin; New Zealand; Pacific Island Environmental Philosophy; Perth, Australia; Sanitation; Small Island States; Sydney, Australia; Water Use and Rights

FURTHER READING

Baker, John Victor T. (1965). *The New Zealand people at war: War economy*. Wellington, New Zealand: Department of Internal Affairs.

Beaglehole, John C. (1934). *The exploration of the Pacific*. London: A. & C. Black.

Bennett, Judith A. (2000). *Pacific forest: A history of resource control and conflict in Solomon Islands, c. 1800–1997*. Cambridge, UK: White Horse Press.

Bennett, Judith A. (2001). War, emergency and environment: Fiji, 1939–1946. *Environment and History, 7*, 255–287.

Bennett, Judith. A. (2009). *Natives and exotics: World War II and environment in the Southern Pacific*. Honolulu: University of Hawaii Press.

Brewer, David T., et al. (2007). Impacts of gold mine waste disposal on deepwater fish in a pristine tropical marine system. *Marine Pollution Bulletin, 54*(3), 309–321.

Campbell, Ian C. (1989). *A history of the Pacific Islands*. Christchurch, New Zealand: University of Canterbury Press.

Daws, Gavan. (1968). *Shoal of time: A history of the Hawaiian Islands*. New York: Macmillan.

Denoon, Donald; Firth, Stewart; Linnekin, Jocelyn; Meleisea, Malama; & Nero, Karen. (1997). *The Cambridge history of the Pacific Islanders*. Cambridge, UK: Cambridge University Press.

Fabricius, Katharina E., et al. (2011). Losers and winners in coral reefs acclimatized to elevated carbon dioxide concentrations. *Nature Climate Change, 1*(3), 165–169.

Hunt, Colin. (2003). Economic globalisation impacts on Pacific marine resources. *Marine Policy, 27*(1), 79–85.

Johnston, Alex. (2011, October 4). Despite criticism, Japan whaling to continue this season. *Epoch Times*. Retrieved February 3, 2012, from http://www.theepochtimes.com/n2/world/despite-criticism-japan-whaling-to-continue-this-season-62404.html

Kunitz, Stephen. (1994). *Disease and social diversity: The European impact on the health of non-Europeans*. Oxford, UK: Oxford University Press.

Macintyre, Martha, & Simon, Foale. (2004). Politicized ecology: Local responses to mining in Papua New Guinea. *Oceania, 74*(3), 231–251.

MacNeill, Jim; Winsemius, Pieter; & Taizo, Yakushiji. (1991). *Beyond independence: The meshing of the world's economy and the Earth's ecology*. New York: Oxford University Press.

McNeill, John R. (1994). Of rats and men: A synoptic environmental history of the island Pacific. *Journal of World History, 5*(2), 299–349.

Marchal, Paul; Lallemand, Philippe; Stokes, Kevin; & Thebaud, Olivier. (2009). A comparative review of the fisheries resource management systems in New Zealand and in the European Union. *Aquatic Living Resources, 22*(4), 463–481.

Moore, Clive; Leckie, Jacqueline; & Munro, Doug. (Eds.). (1990). *Labour in the South Pacific*. Townsville, Australia: James Cook University.

Nunn, Patrick D. (1999). *Environmental change in the Pacific Basin*. Chichester, UK: Wiley.

Ovetz, Robert. (2006). Overfishing threatens tuna stocks. Retrieved February 3, 2012, from http://archives.pireport.org/archive/2006/April/04-11-com.htm

Peattie, Mark R. (1988). *Nanyo: The rise and fall of the Japanese in Micronesia, 1885–1945.* Honolulu: University of Hawaii Press.

Rallu, Jean-Louis. (1991). Population of the French overseas territories in the Pacific: Past, present and projected. *Journal of Pacific History, 26,* 169–186.

Rapaport, Moshe. (1995). Oysterlust: Islanders, entrepreneurs, and colonial policy over Tuamotu lagoons. *Journal of Pacific History, 30*(1), 39–52.

Spate, Oskar H. K. (1988). *The Pacific since Magellan: Volume 3. Paradise found and lost.* Sydney: Australian National University Press.

Spennemann, Dirk. (1998). Japanese poaching and the enforcement of German colonial sovereignty in the Marshall Islands. *Journal of Pacific History, 33*(1), 51–67.

Storey, Donovan, & Hunter, Shawn. (2010). Kiribati: An environmental "perfect storm." *Australian Geographer, 41*(2), 167–181.

Yamano, Hiroya, et al. (2007). Atoll island vulnerability to flooding and inundation revealed by historical reconstruction: Fongafale Islet, Funafuti Atoll, Tuvalu. *Global and Planetary Change, 57*(3–4), 407–416.

Organization of American States (OAS)

Although the Organization of American States (OAS) has had limited effectiveness in its original goals of regional cooperation, the institution has responded to changes in the global order over time. Recent initiatives have shifted the emphasis from regional security and mutual defense to promoting economic and environmental sustainability through agricultural collaboration, climate change research, and regional sustainable development projects.

What later became the Organization of American States (OAS)—"the oldest international organization of a regional character"—was a product of US policy in Latin America in the late nineteenth century (Stoetzer 1993). It evolved out of the Monroe Doctrine and its corollaries, which many contend named the Western Hemisphere as the exclusive sphere of US influence. This pan-American movement began as a series of inter-American conferences designed to facilitate regional cooperation in peace and dispute resolution, as well as trade (Stoetzer 1993).

The OAS, as it exists today, is based on its charter, signed by twenty-one American nations in 1948 and amended by protocols in 1967, 1985, 1992, and 1993. The organization's express purpose is to "achieve an order of peace and justice, to promote . . . solidarity, to strengthen [regional] collaboration, and to defend [the members'] sovereignty, . . . territorial integrity, and . . . independence" (OAS 1993). These general principles have been born out in recent years to promote economic and environmental sustainability through agricultural collaboration, climate change research, and regional sustainable development projects.

Inter-American relations have been characterized historically by alternating periods of increased US intervention in Latin America and efforts to moderate that intervention; from the quasi-imperial intervention of the early twentieth century to the Good Neighbor policies of the 1930s and back again (in response to the global threat of communism). The OAS has been criticized by those who see it as an instrument of US policy in the region rather than as an institution of true regional cooperation. Over time, the OAS has responded to changes in the global political and economic order, shifting its emphasis from regional security and mutual defense to goals in social, economic, and environmental development.

Agricultural Cooperation

The Inter-American Institute for Cooperation in Agriculture (IICA) (previously called the Inter-American Institute for Agricultural Sciences) is one of three principle OAS initiatives aimed at sustainable development. Originally established to promote regional agricultural cooperation, in the 1980s the IICA began to modernize agricultural techniques and stimulate intraregional agricultural trade when much of the region's economic growth had stalled.

The IICA shifted focus in 2001, "to promote the sustainable improvement of agriculture and rural life . . . in the Americas" (IICA 2011). Farms throughout the Americas face the dual challenge of a constantly increasing demand for food and environmental degradation from traditional yield-increasing production methods. As an intergovernmental institution, the IICA has limited ability to intervene directly in agricultural policy. In its regional role, however, it assists national governments in developing agricultural policies that enhance sustainability and increase the competitiveness of agricultural exports to global markets.

Climate Change

On the heels of the Rio Earth Summit in 1992, several OAS member states established the Inter-American Institute for Global Change Research (IAI). Although only eighteen countries joined in the initiative, the institute actively engages researchers from all over the region to answer questions about biodiversity, water and food scarcity, and sustainable ecosystems in the Americas (IAI 2011a). The IAI is primarily a scientific body that submits proposals and recommendations for action and encourages researchers across the continent to collaborate. The IAI also works in governance, attempting to build national capacity for facing climate change through education, technical workshops, training institutes, and seminars for students from all over the Americas. In 2010–2011, the IAI sponsored training in land-use change analysis, water and food security, the impact of climate on health, and the use of seasonal climate predictions, as well as urban responses to climate change (IAI 2011b).

Sustainable Development

Perhaps the broadest sustainability-based initiative of the OAS is the Executive Secretariat for Integral Development, whose Department of Sustainable Development (DSD) designs and implements projects in the region that "integrate environmental priorities with poverty alleviation, and socioeconomic development goals" (OAS 2011). From its beginnings as the Department of Regional Development and Environment, the DSD has evolved into one of the most active arms of the OAS, supporting projects in water management, land use, renewable energy, and other areas of environmental concern. As a result of DSD initiatives in the Bermejo River basin, for example, Argentina and Bolivia have extended water channels both for drinking and irrigation, local people have been trained in water and soil management, and "sustainable and cost-effective sanitation strategies have been successfully implemented" (OAS 2006).

Modern Controversy

Although the OAS has been criticized historically as a tool of the United States in the region, the US House Foreign Affairs committee passed an amendment in July 2011 that cut the entire annual US contribution to the organization. The proponents of this legislation claim that the OAS "has become a tool of Cuba, Venezuela and other leftist regimes" (Oppenheimer 2011). Ironically, those same regimes accuse the OAS of promoting US interests in the region. Venezuela and others have established competing blocs, such as the Union of South American Nations (UNASUR) and the Bolivarian Alliance for the Americas (ALBA). Both attempt to be a uniquely Southern response to the same issues of peace, security, and trade, among others.

What the Future Holds

The OAS has had limited effectiveness in reaching its goals. Still, the institution has survived longer than any other existing regional organization, maintaining institutional continuity in the face of regime changes, world wars, and civil strife. The OAS has changed direction, as have many regional organizations around the world, away from political and military security and toward sustainable economic and environmental development. As the organization focuses more on sustainability issues of common concern, it may be more effective in its new aims than it ever was in its original purposes.

Rachel Denae THRASHER
Pardee Center for the Study of the Longer-Range Future, Boston University

See also Agriculture, Tropical (the Americas); Amazonia; Brazil; Canada; Central America; Forest Management; Mexico; Multilateral Environmental Agreements (MEAs); North American Free Trade Agreement (NAFTA); Rio Earth Summit (UN Conference on Environment and Development); Southern Cone; United States

FURTHER READING

Bloom, Barbara Lee. (2008). *The Organization of American States*. New York: Chelsea House.

Inter-American Institute for Cooperation on Agriculture (IICA). (2010). Promoting competitive and sustainable agriculture in the Americas: 2010–2014 medium-term plan. Retrieved August 6, 2011, from http://www.iica.int/Esp/dg/Documentos%20Institucionales/PMP_2010_2014_ingles.pdf

Inter-American Institute for Cooperation on Agriculture (IICA). (2011). History of IICA. Retrieved July 27, 2011, from http://www.iica.int/Eng/infoinstitucional/Pages/Brief%20history%20of%20IICA.aspx

Inter-American Institute for Global Change Research (IAI). (2011a). Current project summaries. Retrieved July 27, 2011, from http://www.iai.int/index.php?option=com_content&view=article&id=79&Itemid=70

Inter-American Institute for Global Change Research (IAI). (2011b). Capacity building. Retrieved August 19, 2011, from http://www.iai.int/index.php?option=com_content&view=article&id=29&Itemid=77

Monroe, James. (1823). Message of President James Monroe at the commencement of the first session of the 18th Congress (the

Monroe Doctrine). Retrieved July 13, 2011, from http://www.ourdocuments.gov/doc.php?flash=true&doc=23

Oppenheimer, Andres. (2011). OAS is a basket-case, but a needed one. Retrieved July 27, 2011, from http://www.modbee.com/2011/07/27/1791393/andres-oppenheimer-oas-is-a-basket.html

Organization of American States (OAS). (1993). Charter of the Organization of American States. Retrieved July 13, 2011, from http://www.oas.org/dil/treaties_A-41_Charter_of_the_Organization_of_American_States.htm#ch1

Organization of American States (OAS), Department of Sustainable Development (DSD). (2006). Project highlights from the field. *Sustainable Development Newsletter, 1*(1). Retrieved July 27, 2011, from http://www.oas.org/dsd/Working%20Documents/english/Newsletterfinalvol1no1.pdf

Organization of American States (OAS), Department of Sustainable Development (DSD). (2011). Mission. Retrieved March 2, 2012, from http://www.oas.org/en/sedi/dsd/mission.asp

Stoetzer, O. Carlos. (1993). *The Organization of American States*. Westport, CT: Praeger Publishers.

P

Pacific Island Environmental Philosophy

The Pacific Islands constitute a vast region, with thousands of islands distributed across millions of square kilometers of ocean. While it would be a monumental task to describe traditional and modern resource management and environmental philosophy throughout the islands, that of Pohnpei—the highest and one of the largest islands in Micronesia—can serve as a good representative model.

The Pacific Islands cover an enormous region: an estimated twenty thousand to thirty thousand islands are spread across an area of ocean constituting over one-third of the Earth's surface but holding less than 0.1 percent of the world's population. They may be classified as terrestrial islands, high volcanic islands, and low coral atolls. As the ocean level continues to rise due to climate change, low coral atolls will continue to become submerged, and the coastlines of the high islands will transform. The variability in climates, geology, geomorphology, cultures, and biota among the islands makes it difficult to generalize about "typical" traditional and modern resource use and environmental philosophy. The Micronesian island of Pohnpei, however, provides a good model.

Pohnpei was settled by ancient navigators from the east and southeast in the first to second centuries CE. Pohnpeian environmental philosophy has been in practice for many generations, and its sustainable ecological practices are in accord with the science of ecological sustainability (Manner 2008; Raynor and Kostka 2003). Pohnpeian philosophy is contained in oral traditions and various practices expressed in cultural rituals, social mores, habits, attitudes, beliefs, and thoughts. Environmental philosophy is an important aspect of Pohnpeian cultural philosophy, to the extent that to study Pohnpeian cultural philosophy is in large part to examine its environmental philosophy. The peoples of the Pacific in general, and the peoples of Micronesia in particular, construct a worldview or philosophy based on their experience of living on a metaphorical edge between conflict and harmony with the environment that results from living on the physical edge of the ocean-island realm below and the sky-world above. In a context of rapid and ongoing social, political, and economic change, it is safe to say that a majority of native-born people in Micronesia practice a traditional way of life in that they continue to speak their native languages (although these languages are in danger of extinction), and they continue to preserve cultural values and artifacts.

Pohnpei (previously spelled *Ponape*) is located on the eastern side of the Caroline Island chain at latitude 6°54' N and longitude 158°14' E. It is located about halfway between Honolulu and Manila, 666 kilometers north of the equator and 277 kilometers west of the International Date Line. After Guam, Pohnpei is the second largest island in Micronesia and the tallest island in the region at 791 meters above sea level. The island is the eroded remnant of a large shield volcano that formed due to hot spot activity approximately 3–8 million years before present. Its form is that of a jagged, indented circle (Ashby 1993, 3, 5). Pohnpei is one of the wettest places in the world, receiving nearly 1,016 centimeters of rainfall a year at its interior and about 480 centimeters per year in the island's capital, Kolonia. The temperature fluctuates between about 22°C and 30°C, and the humidity is relatively high, between 80 and 90 percent. Tropical depressions often form near Pohnpei and become typhoons as they move to the west or north. The island is almost surrounded by an external barrier reef about 2 miles offshore that provides a natural fishery. The capital of the Federated States of Micronesia (FSM) is located in Palikir, Pohnpei. The FSM is comprised of four states: Pohnpei, Kosrae toward the east; Chuuk (formerly Truk) toward the west, and Yap farther west.

Permaculture and Philosophy at the "Edge"

The environmental and ecological philosophy known as permaculture contains the concept of "living on the edge" (Sellmann 2002a). Permaculture is based on the notion of sustainable agriculture (permanent agriculture), and has been transforming and expanding to become a model and a philosophy for "permanent culture." In permaculture theory the concept of the edge denotes the environmental power that creates productive energy and unique opportunities for human life on the edge—that is, at the zone of contact between ecological niches (Hena and Anschuetz 2000; Mollison 1988). The Native American permaculture advocate Louie Hena and anthropologist and archaeologist Kurt F. Anschuetz describe the concept of the edge in permaculture:

> Edge is a key idea used in this discipline to convey how interfaces between unlike niches enhance the concentration of productive energy through the interaction of diverse but complementary parts. Such interactions are essential for creating and sustaining the healthy functioning of a system. (Hena and Anschuetz 2000, 38)

Generally speaking Micronesian islands are vibrant and productive places because they maintain dynamic energy on the edge of the ocean and the island, and the edge of the atmosphere and the mountaintop. As climate change continues to melt glaciers and the polar ice packs, which causes the ocean level to rise, the low-lying atolls will continue to be submerged. In areas like the northern province of Torba in Vanuatu, climate change refugees have already been relocated due to rising sea levels and increased vulnerability to natural disasters. Rising sea levels also threaten state sovereignty (Pacific SIDS 2009). Rising ocean levels will naturally change the shape and beaches of the high islands, moving the beach inland and making the islands smaller. The barrier reef around Pohnpei will be submerged at some point, and the natural fishery that it provided will be transformed. Climate change and the rise of the ocean level will create new challenges for people living on the edge of the Pacific Islands.

Beach Philosophy

The first edge a person encounters when living on an island is the edge that exists between the ocean and the island itself. The reef and beach provide a dynamic and productive ecosystem for island life. Just behind the beach, the island forest or jungle takes root. There the trees provide shelter for other plants, crops, and humans, who find refuge from the sun and elements. Island cultures typically distinguish between the ocean side or beach and the inland or mountainside area and their respective concomitant experiences. Usually the people who live along the beach are responsible for harvesting resources from the ocean. The inland villages are responsible for harvesting the resources of the land, forest, or jungle. This is especially the case with Pohnpei (Petersen 2009).

The island of Pohnpei has traditionally been, and still is, divided into five sections that extend from the mountainous interior to the coastal reef areas. Pohnpei is surrounded by an average of 3 kilometers of outer barrier reef, with a fringing barrier reef enclosing an area of 181 square kilometers (Balick 2009). The traditional methods of fishing are keyed to subsistence purposes. Those methods dictate who may fish, when to fish, and what species of fish may be caught for consumption and for other traditional functions. With the commercialization of fishing, however, many people have become fishermen. This modern practice not only removes people from their traditional economic system of reciprocity to a moneymaking fishing practice, it also conflicts with the island's indigenous and traditional conservation methods. Traditionally, when to fish and the species of fish to catch for ritual offerings is dependent on the kinds of fruits that are readily available for harvest, because the fish will be the protein supply to complement certain maturing fruits for consumption. For instance, the "early" breadfruit season, called *ketingin engek,* brings fruit that matures a couple of months before the regular annual breadfruit season, called *rahk,* the "season of plenty," and provides carbohydrates for the rabbit fish season, a supply of protein for traditional offering and nourishment known in Pohnpeian as *mwomwidahr.* During the early stage of any breadfruit season, it is prohibited to eat roasted crab with breadfruit, because it is believed that this can cause that particular breadfruit season to be ruined, thus creating famine.

Mountain Philosophy

All high islands—that is, those that are not low-lying atolls—have some elevation. The island mountain ecosystem is a vibrant place where the wind, rain, trees, and the slopes of the mountain create fertile niches for plant and animal life. The mountain valleys provide richly fertile habitats where crops and people can thrive. Because Pohnpei is the tallest island in Micronesia, it would have been relatively easy for ancient navigators to discover, in part because its height would make it visible from a distance, and also because it would attract birds, turtles, and other sea life, which the ancient navigators would have sighted and followed. Clouds also form on its peak, making it more noticeable to the trained navigator's eye. On Pohnpei, one of the wettest places on the planet, the abundant rainfall and sunlight keep the plants, fruits, and tubers growing constantly. The traditional practice of food and plant cultivation on Pohnpei, known as *sapwasapw en Pohnpei* ("the traditional farming of Pohnpei"), is a type of agroforestry, allowing cultivation of multiple food crops in a given land area. Such crops include but are not limited to fruit-bearing plants such as breadfruit and banana and root crop cultivars such as yam and dry-land taro. Subsistence farming, being the basic source of the peoples' livelihood, promotes not only healthy living practices by way of appropriate nutritional eating habits, but also requires extensive hours of physical activities, which gives the impression that Pohnpeians live to work.

Such farming techniques existed long before modern agriculture came to name it agroforestry (Manner 2008). The growing of crops served the fundamental human physical need for nourishment. The efforts involved in planting, nourishing, and propagating crops like *sakau* and yam, for example, are so intensive, requiring patience, perseverance, and dedication, that such crops both reflect and determine one's manhood. Competitive rituals culminate in recognizing the maturation of boys into adult men, based on their success in growing the largest yam or the strongest sakau. It is these things that make land (*sahpw*) one of the most valued possessions in Pohnpei.

Sakau (*Sakau en Pohnpei*), a sacred plant, scientifically known as *Piper methysticum*, is more commonly known by its Polynesian name, *kava*; it is also known in Pohnpeian as *tuhken saledek, wahu, popohl, oh meleilei*, which translate into English as the plant of relaxation, respect, peace, and harmony. Sakau is so important and so integrated into the cultural practices of Pohnpei that it is a medium through which respect or honor are communicated, practiced, and therefore learned. Sakau can be grown anywhere from the lowland region, known in Pohnpeian as *nansapw*, to the inner forest or high regions, called *nanwel*. Sakau grows best in the interior regions of Pohnpei, where frequent rainfall, tall trees, thick mosses, and other soil conditions provide the ideal environment for it (Merlin and Raynor 2005).

Pohnpeian Cosmology—Ocean Experience

The geographic term *Micronesia* refers to the islands located in a large expanse of the western Pacific, covering an area larger than the continental United States, but altogether having a landmass of little more than the tiny state of Rhode Island. There are two distinct island types in Micronesia that greatly impact the lifestyles and cultures. High islands are volcanoes, either active or dormant, surrounded by coral reefs. Low islands or atolls represent emergent coral reefs that have formed around the perimeters of ancient volcanoes worn down by erosion, their summits now lying beneath the surface of the ocean. The cultures of Micronesia are various. Despite their relative isolation, the ancient canoe navigators had long ago connected the atolls and islands, as ship and airplane navigators connect them today (Petersen 2009).

Generally speaking there are three major cultural areas in Micronesia that overlap. In western Micronesia, the arch of islands extending from just north of Indonesia to south of Japan—the Palau-Yap-Mariana islands—share important material goods and spiritual values. Through the spiritual (magical) power and natural resources of Yap, the first cultural group shares values and trade goods eastward through the Caroline atolls with the second cultural area. Yap had a complex social-political organization that included spiritual leaders who were believed to be able to control the forces of nature, especially being able to summon storms or divert them. Traders from the atolls went to Yap for soil, plants, animals, and to pay tribute to maintain good relations with the leaders to divert storms away from their home islands (Osborne 1961). The second area comprises the Chuuk-Pohnpei-Kosrae cultural complex. The long-standing knowledge of the migration out of Kosrae westward to Pohnpei and from Pohnpei farther westward to Chuuk lagoon and into the Caroline atolls is confirmed by modern research. The Chuuk-Pohnpei-Kosrae culture complex maintains relations with the third cultural area, the Gilbert-Marshall cultural area. (For more on these cultural areas, see Alkire 1977; Oliver 1989, vol. 2, chap. 18; and Osborne 1961). Although there is no unifying essence, thread, or definition, it is inevitable that the generalization "Micronesian cultures" is employed as a convenient teaching tool, a shorthand expression.

Micronesian Philosophy

The natural environment of an island is manifested between two ecological edges, namely between land and ocean and between land and sky. The various philosophies of Micronesia in general and of Pohnpei in particular are first and foremost environmental philosophies. They are not philosophies that speculate about the nature of abstract, eternal substances or ideas, but rather they, like many of the world's ancient cultural philosophies, developed out of human experiences with the forces of nature. Micronesian and Pohnpeian environmental experience focuses on people living with the forces of nature (fire, air, earth, water, wind, sun, moon, stars, mountains, beaches, rivers, reefs, the ocean and its currents) and on people living with and making use of animals (dolphins, turtles, fish, birds, rodents, bats, etc.) and plants (fruits, tubers, the coconut, herbs, medical herbs, trees, shrubs, etc.). The coconut deserves special note because the human migration into and around the Pacific most likely could not have occurred without it. Coconut contains a high amount of nutritional fat and protein that is readily available even during a drought or famine. Coconut fiber was the main source for producing twine and rope needed to build protective shelters and for building outrigger canoes. The coconut's buoyancy, in sufficient number, can also keep a person afloat. The philosophical tendency is to place emphasis on the particular person, plant, animal, or object instead of the generalization or the universal. The particular has precedence and as such a type of equality by parity or ratio equality comes to dominate thinking, such that few things are considered insignificant.

In essence Pohnpei exists as a result of peculiar circumstances, such as the past and present migration to the island of different peoples with different values, traditions, and legends, some of which are specific to each of the chiefdoms and their regions. All the peculiarities of the different values, traditions, and legends taken together make up the traditional norm that helps to resolve conflicts, without which life would be very difficult, if not chaotic, due to various internal (namely family, clan and district) and external (namely interdistrict, Federate States of Micronesia national, and international social, political and economic) forces exerting themselves. A good example would be the obvious differences that exist in the sakau rituals among the five chiefdoms of Madolenihmw, Uh, Kitti, Sokehs, and Nett. Interestingly, sakau rituals in Madolenihmw and Uh municipalities are somewhat similar, but they are very much distinct from sakau ceremonies in Kitti, Sokehs, and Nett municipalities, which share somewhat related, but different, sakau ceremonies. Different municipalities use different ending rhythms for their sakau ceremonies, such as a sudden stop, or a repeated rhythm. Sakau ceremonies also have a strict cultural code about the order in which the highest ranking chiefs and their wives are served during sakau drinking.

The subsistence lifestyle, as affluent as it was and still is, keeps people in contact with the natural environment. Micronesians, and Pohnpeians specifically, thus describe their world in dynamic terms. The environment is changing, and impermanence is the constant. Their world is hylozoistic—that is, it is seen as a world that is itself a living, growing, and dying creature. The living character of the world is evidenced on the volcanic islands in the form of the volcano goddess or god. On the low-lying atolls, it is clear that the top of the island consists of what was living coral; the atoll appears to have grown out of the ocean. Various myths and legends from Micronesia, namely from the Mariana chain and Palau, describe the islands as the remains of a primordial person or giant; other narratives, from Chuuk and the Marshall Islands, describe how cultural heroes fish the islands out of the sea, or they build the island on top of a submerged reef, as is the case with Pohnpei (Lessa and Dobbin 1987; Poignant 1967). The hylozoistic world is replete with creative energy, life power, spirit power, and ancestor spirits.

Micronesians have their respective words that denote something similar to the Polynesian concept of *mana*—the life force or power that permeates the universe and links living people to their ancestors and the land. The Chamorros of the Mariana island chain call it *aniti*. In Yap, the power is called *kael* (pronounced "kai"). In Pohnpei and Chuuk, it is called *manaman*. These terms denote the creative, life-sustaining power of nature. The life force consists of a balance of two opposing yet interrelated energies, such as male/female, light/dark, right/left, and life/death. The interaction or interpenetration of the two forces gives birth to the creatures, plants, and other things of the world. Persons, creatures, plants, and objects are arranged in a hierarchical order, granting them superior or inferior positions depending on the amount of life power perceived to be dwelling in them. In human society the life power dictates the social, economic, and political power and the position of the upper caste (chiefs, navigators, warriors) over the commoners.

Micronesian environmental philosophy is derived from peoples' experience of both living in harmony with and living in conflict with the forces of nature. Ideally the totems, the taboos, the medicine woman's and medicine man's skills are understood to maintain a balance among the forces of nature, and between those forces and the people. For any number of perceived reasons (broken taboos, the lack of skill of a medicine man or woman, for example) or for no apparent reason at all, Micronesians find themselves trying to live while they perceive that a force of nature, a spirit, or an ancestor is threatening them. Perhaps they need fish but do not catch any; they seek a certain current, wind, or star for navigation but cannot find it; their crops need rain but drought persists; or they are threatened by storms, typhoons, waves, relentless wind and rain, thunder, and lightning. Trying to balance between harmony and conflict with the natural environment, Micronesians shape their lives and their various worldviews.

The Micronesian cosmology is value laden. There are no bare "facts." Things always have value built into them. Ideally the people want to live in harmony with the forces of nature, to enjoy eating and cohabitating at leisure, and yet they may find themselves struggling to stay alive—starving without fish or fruit, drowning in the ocean, being blown off course, or adrift without a breeze. When the forces of nature are in balance with each other and when humans abide by the taboos, then harmony prevails. When the forces of nature are out of balance or when human needs or desires are out of balance with the forces of nature, then conflict is apt to arise.

Micronesian and Pohnpeian environmental philosophy contains an environmental ethic. Living on the edge between harmony and conflict, a person can move in either direction toward one or the other. The ethnocentric perspective that promotes balance and harmony within the forces of nature and within human interactions with nature might be called the ideal Micronesian environmental ethic. There is also, however, what can be called the practical or anthropocentric Micronesian environmental ethic that is exhibited when people find the forces of nature or the human interactions with nature to be out of sorts such that imbalance and conflict arise. This practical or anthropocentric ethic pits humans against the forces of nature. It may well explain why some contemporary Micronesians embrace an anthropocentric view of nature and the self-interest benefits of capitalism. When environmentally minded scientists or ecotourists discover that Micronesian property holders want to build huge hotels, oil refineries, or a fishing industry despite the environmental degradation that will result, they may be mystified because they naively think that the only local cultural value is harmony with nature. The experience of conflict, however, gives credence to another value, namely one of domination and exploitation. Micronesians living on the edge between harmony and conflict with nature are currently shaping and reshaping the cultural ocean and landscape.

Parity and the Existential Commitment

The current environmental crisis that is threatening communities and the world at large seems to challenge us to rethink our place in the world and our relationship with it. What is needed is a worldview in which self-interest and other-interest are mutually determined and coterminous. The organismic and environmental elements in Micronesian and Pohnpeian philosophy, coupled with the modern concepts of human dignity and justice as fair play, could provide such a worldview. The concept of parity expands the horizons of justice to include nonhuman animals and the environment. Parity does not mean identical sameness; it means that each particular contributes its uniqueness, though the particulars are not quantitatively equivalent. Nor does parity mean equal opportunity; some people will naturally take advantage of opportunities more skillfully than others, and they should be leaders and rulers. Parity provides an existential perspective from which equal consideration of interests could be reconceived and defended. Humans will exploit natural resources and other animals. In the interest of the environment and for the protection of others both human and nonhuman, people must treat other creatures and the environment with fairness and justice.

This concept of existential parity generates a moral corollary—what can be called the existential commitment (Sellmann 2002b). The existential commitment is the moral attitude and practice of responsibility for, and obligation to show concern and provide care for, the lives of others. The ontological and cosmological understanding of the interrelatedness of particulars leads people to acknowledge their moral obligation to promote the interests of another. From the perspective of existential parity, the value of others must be understood as having significance for oneself. This parity, as a fundamental characteristic of existing in a world of interrelationships, extends beyond human society to entail other animals and the environment. The existential commitment is a demographic reality in Pohnpei founded on the philosophy known by the simple Pohnpeian expression *tiahk en sahpw*, translated into English as "the custom of the land," which has always defined life on Pohnpei. It is the existential commitment that designates traditional fishermen for the Nahnmwariki, the traditional chiefs of Pohnpei, a cultural practice that selects only a few people to fish, thus promoting social reciprocity and environmental protection. Pohnpeian environmental philosophy provides a worldview and a way of life that can be coupled with democratic concepts and practices to create and maintain social and ecological harmony as humanity attempts to live on the edge of planet Earth.

James D. SELLMANN
University of Guam

Robert ANDREAS
College of Micronesia

See also Ecovillages; Marine Ecosystems Health; Oceania; Small Island States; Travel and Tourism Industry; Water Use and Rights

FURTHER READING

Alkire, William H. (1977). *An introduction to the peoples and cultures of Micronesia* (2nd ed., abridged.). Menlo Park, CA: Cummings Publishing.
Ashby, Gene. (1993). *A guide to Pohnpei: An island argosy*. Eugene, OR: Rainy Day Press.
Athens, J. Stephen. (1980). Pottery from Nan Madol, Ponape, Eastern Caroline Islands. *Journal of the Polynesian Society, 89*, 95–99.
Athens, J. Stephen. (1981). A stone adze from Ponape, Eastern Caroline Islands. *Asian Perspectives, 24*, 43–46.
Ayres, William S. (1983). Archaeology at Nan Madol, Ponape. *Bulletin of the Indo-Pacific Prehistory Association, 4*, 135–142.
Ayres, William S. (1990). Pohnpei's position in Eastern Micronesian prehistory. *Micronesica, Supplement 2*, 187–212.
Balick, Michael J. (Ed.). (2009). *Ethnobotany of Pohnpei: Plants, people, and island culture*. Honolulu: University of Hawai'i Press.
Hena, Louie, & Anschuetz, Kurt F. (2000). Living on the edge: Combining traditional Pueblo knowledge, permaculture, and archeology. In Ronald M. Greenberg (Ed.), *Beyond compliance: Tribes of the southwest. Cultural Resource Management, 23*(9), 37–41.
Lessa, William A., & Dobbin, Jay. (1987). Micronesian religions: An overview. In Mircea Eliade (Ed.), *The encyclopedia of religion: Vol. 9* (pp. 498–505). New York: Macmillan Press.
Luomala, Katharine, & Rynkiewich, Michael. (1987). Micronesian religions: Mythic themes. In Mircea Eliade (Ed.), *The encyclopedia of religion: Vol. 2* (pp. 717–722). New York: Macmillan Press.
Manner, Harley. (2008). Directions for long-term research in traditional agricultural systems of Micronesia and the Pacific Islands. *Micronesica, 40*(1/2), 63–86.
Merlin, Mark, & Raynor, William. (2005). Kava cultivation, native species conservation, and integrated watershed resource management on Pohnpei Island. *Pacific Science, 59*(2), 241–260.
Mollison, Bill. (1988). *Permaculture: A designer's manual*. Tyalgum, Australia: Tagari Publications.
Oliver, Douglas L. (1989). *Oceania: The native cultures of Australia and the Pacific Islands*. Honolulu: University of Hawai'i Press.
Osborne, Douglas. (1961). Archaeology in Micronesia: Background, Palau studies and suggestions for the future. *Asian Perspectives: Bulletin of the Far-Eastern Prehistory Association, 2*, 156–163.
Pacific Small Island Developing States (SIDS). (2009). Views on the possible security implications of climate change to be included in the report of the secretary-general to the 64th session of the United Nations General Assembly. Retrieved May 8, 2012, from http://www.un.org/esa/dsd/resources/res_pdfs/ga-64/cc-inputs/PSIDS_CCIS.pdf
Petersen, Glenn. (2009). *Traditional Micronesian societies: Adaptation, integration, and political organization*. Honolulu: University of Hawai'i Press.
Poignant, Roslyn. (1967). *Oceanic mythology*. London: Paul Hamlyn.
Raynor, Bill, & Kostka, Mark. (2003). Back to the future: Using traditional knowledge to strengthen biodiversity conservation in Pohnpei, Federated States of Micronesia. *A Journal of Plants, People, and Applied Research, Ethnobotany Research & Applications, 1*, 55–63. Retrieved November 16, 2011, from: http://www.ethnobotanyjournal.org/vol1/i1547-3465-01-055.pdf
Sellmann, James D. (2002a). Living on the edge in Micronesian ecological philosophy. *International Research in Geographical and Environmental Education, 11*(1), 54–57. doi: 10.1080/10382040208667464
Sellmann, James D. (2002b). *Timing and rulership in Master Lü's spring and autumn annals*. Albany: State University of New York Press.

Berkshire's authors and editors welcome questions, comments, and corrections. Send your emails about the *Berkshire Encyclopedia of Sustainability* in general or this volume in particular to: sustainability.updates@berkshirepublishing.com

Parks and Protected Areas

Parks and protected areas have been the foremost mechanism for the conservation of nature in the Americas and Oceania. Parks exist on every continent. National governments largely manage them, although there are private, regional, state, and local parks as well. Protected areas constitute one way humans can mitigate their presence on the land by recognizing the need for spaces with small or negligible human footprints.

The Americas and Oceania have been formative areas for the creation of parks and nature protection areas. It is not a coincidence that the world's earliest national parks were created in the Americas and Australia. These regions share the distinction of hosting extensive wild areas that lack dense settlement and have beautiful scenery. These emerging settler-society nations became conscientious of their landscapes during the process of nation building. Each region has defined parks and protected areas in similar yet distinct ways. Nations have classified types of protection and allowable uses within them. Uses have included scientific research, recreation and enjoyment of scenery, and sustainable harvesting of forest products. The size of parks trends toward larger parks distant from important cities, and the contents vary with ecosystems. Controversies include resident peoples living within protected areas, illegal extraction and mining, competition for rural livelihoods, and climate change.

Definition

People in the Americas and Oceania have used and put aside swaths of nature for public enjoyment for hundreds if not thousands of years. Chapultepec Park in Mexico City is perhaps the oldest continuous nature park in the Western Hemisphere. Aztec emperors in the fifteenth century used it as a zoo, it became a public space in Spanish colonial times, and today it is an urban oasis housing museums. Definitions of parks and reserves have changed over time to accommodate shifting social priorities. Societies have conserved nature nearly any time groups felt scarcity and also articulated scenic, recreational, or scientific values. Although people use the term *conservation* across space and in various contexts, the social concept of what it means to different groups of people is not static.

The International Union for Conservation of Nature (IUCN) (founded as the International Union for the Protection of Nature in 1948) maintains a globally recognized set of criteria comparing protected areas. They currently describe a protected area as "a clearly defined geographical space, recognized, dedicated and managed, through legal or other effective means, to achieve the long term conservation of nature with associated ecosystem services and cultural values" (IUCN 2011b). Each nation determines its own definitions for parks and reserves, although the IUCN and other global entities, including the United Nations Educational, Scientific, and Cultural Organization (UNESCO) World Heritage Site designations provide guidelines for international recognition. Protected areas include national, state, and local parks, wildlife reserves and sanctuaries, forest and wetland reserves, conservation areas, natural and national monuments, biosphere reserves, and other similar designations. This heterogeneity results in a large portfolio of areas including seemingly contradictory spaces. In the United States, for instance, protected areas include monuments, such as the Gateway Arch in St. Louis, Missouri, that have particular cultural meanings and many visitors, and swaths of wilderness, such as the Arctic Wildlife

Refuge in Alaska, that rarely host visitors but maintain a weighty position in the popular imagination.

The range of national classifications for parks and reserves spans greatly. The United States manages a large taxonomy (classification system) of conservation areas; the National Park Service alone has at least fifteen designations for landscape protection, and other federal land management agencies also have nature reserves and wilderness areas. Brazil calls its broad portfolio of protected areas *conservation units,* which are more socially oriented. Brazil has provided innovative designations for indigenous reserves to protect native peoples from contact with the modern world and also maintains extractive reserves facilitating the lower impact activities of traditional peoples, including rubber harvesting. There are a variety of international classifications for parks and reserves. The IUCN standards for protected areas today are as follows in order of strictest protection to least strict: (1a) strict nature reserve, (1b) wilderness area, (2) national park, (3) natural monument or feature, (4) habitat/species management area, (5) protected landscape/seascape, and (6) protected area with sustainable use of natural resources (IUCN 2011a).

National parks are among the most widely recognized designations for protecting nature. Yellowstone National Park in the US states of Wyoming, Montana, and Idaho is largely recognized as the world's first national park (1872) although the government publicly protected earlier parks (Yosemite in California and Hot Springs in Arkansas). Australia (Royal National Park in New South Wales, 1879) and New Zealand (Tongariro, 1887) created national parks shortly after the United States did. Argentina created South America's first park with the National Park of the South (Parque Nacional del Sur, later called Nahuel Huapi National Park) in 1903. Canadians boasted the first federal agency dedicated to protecting parks, Parks Canada (Tyrell 2012). Numerous state and regional parks and reserves also exist and complement or predate these reserves.

The nation-state has played a pivotal role in shaping parks and protected areas. Widespread conservation began at the national level in the nineteenth century and has increased its pace over time. Nations have had more success creating parks and reserves than have transnational bodies. Many nations have parks along national borders, such as Glacier National Park in the United States, which is adjacent to Canada's Waterton Lakes National Park. Parks have played a role in marking national and collective identity on the landscape, although this role has been distinct in different nations. Parks reflect the relationship between societies and the natural landscapes they inhabit and the values, ideas, and concerns of any given society.

In the past one hundred years, conservation areas have undergone a rapid shift in intention and scale. They have become publicly supported (both morally and financially) reserves with federal budgets. They have expanded globally from an area equivalent to the size of the United Kingdom to an area equivalent to all of South America. Many of these shifts have come since the end of World War II, the design of international governance institutions like the United Nations, and the rise of conservation biology as a discipline. National parks exist in more than one hundred nations around the world. South American nations protect the highest number of large reserves, with eighty-three more than 1 million hectares in size. The next highest is North America, with sixty-nine, and North Eurasia, with thirty-three. South American nations also retain the highest percentage of reserves with people living inside, by some estimates 85 percent (Amend and Amend 1992). Marine protection areas have increased in the last decade. Much of the added size of the increase in protected areas comes from tropical nations like Brazil.

Size and Scope

Parks in the Americas and Oceania protect a large and diverse range of ecosystems. The Americas alone have more than 34,000 parks classified by the IUCN, with 7 percent of those marine parks. There are 3,535 parks and reserves that meet the IUCN designation as strict nature reserves or wilderness areas (1a and 1b). All but 93 of these are terrestrial parks. The totals include regional and state reserves. The nations with the greatest number and area protected include Brazil, with more than 26 percent of its territory protected (2,238,962 square kilometers protected out of 8,531,276 square kilometers) and 4.4 percent of its marine area protected. Costa Rica protects nearly 19 percent of its terrestrial land (9,755 of 51,634 square kilometers) and 1.4 percent of its marine area. In North America, the United States protects 12.87 percent of its terrestrial area (1,205,919 of 9,372,163 square kilometers) and 12.19 percent of its marine area. Oceania has more than 11,400 classified parks, and nearly 9 percent are marine reserves. These include 3,002 of the highest category, with 227 of those designated marine reserves. Australia protects 9.5 percent of its terrestrial territory (730,636 of 7,721,798 square kilometers) and nearly 12 percent of its marine area. The range of protection varies greatly; and although some countries protect a considerable amount of their territory, the relative size of the protected areas is comparatively small (IUCN and UNEP-WCMC 2010).

The parks' contents include the largest remaining tropical rain forests (Amazonian South America), the last tidewater glaciers (Chile and the United States' Alaska), and the world's driest deserts, including the Atacama of Pacific South America, and many thousands of endemic avian (bird) species in New Zealand. The Americas and Oceania have a range of reserve sizes that protect everything from butterflies to wolves and whales.

Parks and Society

Conservation has been used globally as a general concept promoting a spectrum of values with at least three distinct orientations toward nature protection. Some scientists and policy makers, including the US conservationist Aldo Leopold (1887–1948), have used conservation to advocate nature's right to exist through the promotion of a wilderness ethic. Other advocates, including the Mexican engineer Miguel Ángel de Quevedo (1862–1946) and the Argentine explorer Francisco P. Moreno (1852–1919), have promoted conservation as a mechanism for advancing utilitarian knowledge about landscapes where humans have minimal presence by using conservation areas to further scientific study and promote education through tourism. Still other conservationists, like the US forester Gifford Pinchot (1865–1946), have explained nature protection as a means of utilitarian rational planning that will ensure a stable national future by saving resources to later exploit. Classically, historians have seen a dispute between Pinchot's conservation and the naturalist John Muir's (1838–1914) work arguing for more careful preservation of landscapes, including the redwood forests of California. More recent studies emphasize the role of the US president Theodore Roosevelt (1858–1919) in putting into place a vast program of conservation that mitigated the differences between conservationists and preservationists (Brinkley 2009, 21). Various dimensions and mixtures of these rationales for broad conservation appear independently in nearly all nations that today have parks.

The rise of parks is neither random nor serendipitous. The spread of industrial capitalism and an increasingly interconnected global economic system amplified the exploitation of natural resources, shaped the development of scientific knowledge, and triggered reactionary reflection on the value of areas where nonhuman nature dominates. The cultural perceptions that supported the rise in protected areas, the science to recommend such land tenure and occupation changes, and the political will to declare territory safeguarded for national—and later global—patrimony mark a significant shift in social values despite the important contestations and critiques of conservation in practice. This expansion in the moral appropriateness of nature conservation went hand in hand with a concomitant push for development and modernization, a collective consumption of resources that far outstrips any previous historical era, and an improvement in lifespan that transformed the human species on the planet from a mere biological agent to a collective geological force.

Conservation is a mature concept. Historians can trace its intellectual roots to times when a society felt pressures of scarcity. Ideas about conservation's place in the public sphere and relation to a general sense that particular resources—marine, forest, faunal—contribute to healthier and more modern societies present much more recent dynamics. Scholars are only beginning to understand how geographically distinct societies create social values. Nationally led frontier expeditions, domestic natural history societies, and the proliferation of publications explaining these expeditions and their findings certainly contributed to the waxing and waning of concerns about the fragility of nature within countries in ways that were not contemporaneous with those of other countries. Brazilian scholars have called these disjointed episodes *generations* and lament the disregard of new generations for the old (Franco and Drummond 2008). More research should be done to better understand the processes through which social values contribute to landscape conservation.

Purposes

Parks generally promote a mixture of recreational (including scenic), scientific, and moral reasons for existence in different components. Tourism, including ecotourism, provided early motivation for national parks and a clear rationale for displacing extractive economic activity (such as mining or logging) with consumptive forms (tourism) in areas slated for parks. This rationale proved the primary reason for creating parks in the Americas in the late nineteenth and early twentieth centuries. Scientific research rose as a reason for large-scale reserves and especially biosphere reserves to accommodate the growing need to conduct scientific research in areas with little impact from humans. A variety of early and recent supporters argued for the social and moral value of parks for humanity. Supporters of wilderness and defenders of nonhuman nature have maintained that intact ecosystems have a right to exist beyond their economic value.

Recreation

Many early parks started as human populations moved from the countryside into the cities during the process of industrialization. Some people came to view cities as unhealthy, and the rise of leisure time led to excursions in nature as an antidote to the congestion of urban residence. Parks like the Adirondacks or Niagara Falls in the eastern United States, Desierto de los Leones outside Mexico City, or Tijuca National Park near Rio de Janeiro, Brazil, served these recreational needs. Tourism came to be a reason for creating parks, and it continues to this day to be a leading economic justification for the creation of parks. Conservationists view Costa Rica's parks as promoting ecotourism, or tourism with a socially responsible bent. Whether or not the revenues from conventional tourism or ecotourism offset the losses in extractive revenue varies greatly by park and nation. Well-managed or popular parks, like Yellowstone or Machu Picchu (in Peru), can be incredibly lucrative for host countries. Common recreational activities within parks include hiking, camping, bird watching, kayaking, rafting, rock climbing, bicycling, horseback riding, and touring, among other activities specific to each locale. These activities often provide job opportunities for local or expert guides. In some places, the promotion of tourism has been overly successful and led to overuse. Park managers have needed to weigh the constant use of resources in the parks (such as trails or water) with their conservation goals. For instance, use of the Inca Trail en route to Machu Picchu has been restricted as have numbers of climbers allowed on the mountain Huayna Picchu in the park to reduce the subsidence of the trail and archaeological site. One effective way the social carrying capacity of parks has been managed is by enforcing permits for use and daily or yearly quotas.

Scientific Rationale

Another important justification for keeping certain natural areas reserved from development is the need to conduct scientific studies on areas relatively undisturbed by humans. Although most, but certainly not all, places have experienced human impact of some scale at one point or another, many of the lands within parks, especially those in the Amazonian and Patagonian regions of South America, the arctic northern areas of North America and Antarctica, and the central deserts of Australia, have been minimally disturbed in the last one hundred to two hundred years. This lack of human impact allows these regions to be virtual laboratories for research on the energy flows and interactions among species in given ecosystems. Scientists and their organizations began to design and promote sites for repeated scientific experiments (largely tropical biological research stations) and the parallel conservation of the lands around these stations. Many scientific field stations, such as Cocha Cashu Biological Station in Peru's Manú National Park or La Selva Biological Station in Costa Rica's Cordillera Volcánica Central Biosphere Reserve, have hosted decades of ecosystem-level projects on soils, forestry, and evolutionary biology.

From at least the travels of the German naturalist Alexander von Humboldt (1769–1859) and the British evolutionary biologist Charles Darwin (1819–1882) forward, scientists have recognized the transcendent importance and peculiarities of South American ecosystems and the role of humans within them. Research within parks and protected areas has furthered important understandings of the functions of nature. Two concepts that arose to shape conservation in the area include the theory of island biogeography, which postulated in part that large contiguous spaces have more value for natural processes, and biodiversity, a term that accounts for the amount of variation of life in a given area. These concepts achieved widespread use as a way of expressing concern for nature conservation. In temperate North America, the reintroduction of wolves in conservation areas has helped transform knowledge of the role of top predators in ecosystems and the resulting trophic cascades that occur when such species are removed. Scientists have debated the need for a single large reserve or several small reserves to protect species diversity and retain intact ecosystems. In the tropics, scientists like the US conservation biologists John Terborgh and Michael Soulé tell us that conservation is the leading mechanism for avoiding species extinctions. Scientific research on ecosystems and species interactions depends on large areas devoid of large scale human impacts.

Moral Defense

Justifications for protecting wild spaces have been made by individuals in nearly all societies on the grounds that humans have the capacity and obligation to allow species other than their own to prosper. US activists, including

Robert Sterling Yard (1861–1945) and Bob Marshall (1901–1939), advocated a kind of preservation free of roads that came to be known as wilderness, and the US ecologist Aldo Leopold saw a need for an ethical sensibility of human approaches to the land, a precursor to more recent articulations of sustainability (Sutter 2004). The Norwegian philosopher Arne Naess (1912–2009) helped articulate the contemporary philosophy of deep ecology, which recognizes the inherent worth of other beings. His ideas have influenced many private conservation areas, including Parque Pumalín in southern Chile. Peter Singer (b. 1946), an Australian philosopher, has made the case for animal protection using bioethics, although he does not extend it to nature conservation per se. Although there is no single moral stance, ethical considerations about the human place in nature have undergirded the establishment of parks and protected areas in most societies.

Controversies

Despite the widespread and general popularity of parks worldwide, certain controversies highlight the interplay between people and the environment. Many scholars of conservation have critiqued the exclusionary role parks have played in societies as diverse as the United States, South Asia, and sub-Saharan Africa. These authors contend that native and local peoples were unjustly pushed out of areas deemed scientifically valuable and that wilderness was thus "created" (Neumann 1998; Spence 2000). It is important not to overgeneralize the occurrences of eviction. Perhaps surprisingly, there is little social science literature on historical conservation in Latin America. What literature there is does not reach this same conclusion about exclusion (Simonian 1995; Franco and Drummond 2009; Wakild 2011). Social scientists and planners should consider debates over residents in parks in two ways: relationships between livelihood and sovereignty and concerns about population growth. Other controversies include debates over the compatibility of certain scales of use with larger scale protection within the management of landscapes and their contents.

Livelihood and Sovereignty

Much recent social science literature critiques the role of parks in dispossessing native residents of their territories. This occurred, for example, when the US army prevented the Blackfeet peoples from hunting in Yellowstone in the late nineteenth century. In this case, the growing national state wrested territory, and with it livelihoods and security, from already marginalized peoples, thus persecuting a minority of people for supposed benefits to the majority down the line. This sort of eviction in the name of conservation was not rare. Governments in other areas, however, have allowed native peoples to remain on the land. Peru's Manú National Park, for instance, retains separate sections explicitly to protect native peoples that remain uncontacted by modern society. In Mexico during the 1930s, the federal government and local residents negotiated over parks so that locals received preference in jobs associated with the parks. In 1985 the Australian government returned ownership of Uluru-Kata Tjuta National Park to local Aborigines. A spectrum of negotiation and respect for previous inhabitants thus has occurred throughout the region. One reason that there has been less conflict over evictions in parks in the Americas than in Africa or South Asia is the smaller size of human populations in the areas. Fewer ruminants (animals such as cattle and sheep) and large biomass animals in these parks provide food to populations, thus reducing conflicts. These nations have also been more socially aware of the risks of eviction. The vast majority of protected areas outside the United States thus have residents of one form or another.

Competing Populations and Population Growth

Because parks in Latin America host human populations, managing the land tenure and population growth of these communities is a constant issue. Managers must consider preexisting populations of native peoples, mixed-race rural dwellers (sometimes called traditional peoples), and immigrants and settlers, as well as tourists and scientists, and weigh the varying needs and desires of these social groups within and around the parks. The size of these groups also changes over time. The Matsigenka population within Peru's Manú National Park, for instance, has a long-standing mutual relationship with the scientific research station nearby. The Matsigenka have recently transitioned from mostly semisedentary groups to more permanent settlement, however, with a school and other fixed structures. The park population went from 1,645 in 2003 to 2,203 in 2011, with a growth rate of 4.7 percent in seven years. As this population clears land for farming, the effects on the research station and larger park ecosystems will increase. How to manage the sovereignty of the indigenous groups while still maintaining the integrity of the park remains an important controversy.

Compatibility of Use and Protection

Scholars continue to debate the compatibility of human and nonhuman nature in wild spaces. Some twenty-first-century research has shown that the complex matrices of agriculture and wild nature result in the creation of new species (Perfecto, Vandermeer, and Wright 2009). This *nature's matrix* is particularly relevant to heavily inhabited areas of Central America where, for example, small-scale coffee farming alongside open forests results in important corridors for migratory birds. Rather than set aside land in strict parks, some advocates call for mechanisms that support hybrid landscapes as a means of protecting nature and rural peoples' livelihoods. The rapidity with which humans have transformed the landscape since the early twentieth century gives cause to retain certain areas with minimal human influence, however. In addition, research on trophic cascades, the tumbling changes that occur in landscapes where key species are removed, demonstrates that hunting can be among the most destructive forces in changing not just animal populations but the entire forest where they reside (Estes et al. 2011). Scientists, international conservation organizations, federal governments, and local residents continue to debate the mixture of restrictions and permissions on use and preservation that are appropriate for each protected area.

Outlook

Parks and reserves cover an impressive amount of territory, and countries continue to create them in substantial numbers. This results in large swaths of land without substantial human presence that are important for scientific, recreational, and moral reasons. It is difficult to measure the direct effect parks have had on stalling deforestation or preventing land conversion. Although significant portions of national territory have been set aside, illegal activities may continue within because of a lack of enforcement. Assessments of Costa Rican conservation in the 1990s revealed that conservation in parks led to an increase of deforestation outside of parks, leaving islands of forests in a sea of destruction (Vandermeer and Perfecto 1995). Although societies favorably support most parks, many threats continue to compromise parks' effectiveness. The largest of these remain extractive industries, licit and illicit, that encroach upon park territory. These industries include logging, especially for lucrative woods like mahogany; mining, especially as the price of gold soars; and cattle ranching and clearing land for soybeans and other products. As demand for these products increases internationally, the pressure on parks increases as well. Many parks are constantly underfunded by national governments. Some suffer too much popularity while others are neglected by not enough use. Governments' refusal to deal with obvious problems, like population growth or road construction, will compromise many parks. Climate change will likely compromise the effectiveness of parks. Rising temperatures force species to migrate beyond the preexisting park boundaries. Parks and protected areas will continue to provide popular configurations of natural spaces without substantial human footprints.

Emily WAKILD
Boise State University

See also Agriculture, Tropical (the Americas); Amazon River; Amazonia; Andes Mountains; Appalachian Mountains; Australia; Brazil; Canada; Caribbean; Central America; Ecotourism (the Americas); Forest Management; Great Lakes and Saint Lawrence River; Mackenzie River; Marine Preserves; Mining (Andes); Mining (Australia); Mississippi and Missouri Rivers; New Zealand; Oceania; Rocky Mountains; Southern Cone; Travel and Tourism Industry; United States; Yellowstone to Yukon Conservation Initiative (Y2Y)

Further Reading

Adams, William M. (2004). *Against extinction: The story of conservation*. London: Earthscan.

Ali, Saleem H. (2007). *Peace parks: Conservation and conflict resolution*. Cambridge, MA: MIT Press.

Amend, Stephan, & Amend, Thora. (Eds.). (1992). *¿Espacios sin habitantes? Parques nacionales de América del Sur* [National parks without people? The South American experience]. Caracas, Venezuela: International Union for Conservation of Nature & Nueva Sociedad.

Brinkley, Douglas. (2009). *The wilderness warrior: Theodore Roosevelt and the crusade for America*. New York: Harper Collins.

Bustillo, Ezequiel. (1972). *Huellas de un largo quehacer: Discursos, conferencias, artículos y publicaciones diversas* [Footprints of a long journey: Essays, conferences, articles and diverse publications]. Buenos Aires: Ediciones Depalma.

Carruthers, Jane. (1995). *The Kruger National Park: A social and political history*. Pietermaritzburg, South Africa: University of Natal Press.

Chakrabarty, Dipesh. (2009). Climate of history: Four theses. *Critical Inquiry, 35*(2), 197–222.

Christen, Catherine A. (2002). At home in the field: Smithsonian tropical science field stations in the US Panama Canal Zone and the Republic of Panama. *The Americas, 58*(4), 537–575.

Dasmann, Raymond F. (1968). *A different kind of country*. New York: Macmillan.

Dudley, Nigel. (2008). *Guidelines for applying protected area management categories*. Gland, Switzerland: International Union for Conservation of Nature.

Elliott, Hugh. (1974). *Second world conference on national parks*. Gland, Switzerland: International Union for Conservation of Nature.

Estes, James A., et al. (2011, July 15). Trophic downgrading of planet Earth. *Science, 333*(6040), 301–306.

Evans, Sterling. (1999). *The green republic: A conservation history of Costa Rica*. Austin: University of Texas Press.

Franco, José Luiz de Andrade, & Drummond, José Augusto. (2008). Wilderness and the Brazilian mind (I): Nation and nature in Brazil from the 1920s to the 1940s. *Environmental History, 13*(4), 724–750.

Franco, José Luiz de Andrade, & Drummond, José Augusto. (2009). Wilderness and the Brazilian mind (II): The First Brazilian Conference on Nature Protection (Rio de Janeiro, 1934). *Environmental History, 14*(1), 82–102.

Grusin, Richard. (2004). *Culture, technology and the creation of America's national parks.* New York: Cambridge University Press.

Guha, Ramachandra. (1989). Radical American environmentalism and wilderness preservation: A third world critique. *Environmental Ethics, 11*(1), 71–83.

Harmon, David. (1987). Cultural diversity, human subsistence, and the national park ideal. *Environmental Ethics, 9*(2), 147–158.

Hays, Samuel. (1959). *Conservation and the gospel of efficiency: The progressive conservation movement, 1890–1920.* Cambridge, MA: Harvard University Press.

International Union for Conservation of Nature (IUCN). (2006). List of world's protected areas. Morges, Switzerland: IUCN.

International Union for Conservation of Nature (IUCN). (2011a) Guidelines for applying the IUCN protected area management categories to marine protected areas. Retrieved March 3, 2012, from www.iucn.org/dbtw-wpd/edocs/PAPS-016.pdf

International Union for Conservation of Nature (IUCN). (2011b). Homepage. Retrieved March 3, 2012, from http://www.iucn.org/about/work/programmes/pa/pa_what/

International Union for Conservation of Nature (IUCN), & United Nations Environment Programme World Conservation Monitoring Center (UNEP-WCMC). (2010). World database of protected areas (WDPA). Retrieved March 19, 2012, from www.protectedplanet.net

MacArthur, Robert H., & Wilson, Edward O. (1967). *The theory of island biogeography.* Princeton, NJ: Princeton University Press.

Meine, Curt; Soulé, Michael; & Noss, Reed F. (2006). A mission driven discipline: The growth of conservation biology. *Conservation Biology, 20*(3), 331–351.

Miller, Shawn William. (2007). *An environmental history of Latin America.* New York: Cambridge University Press.

Neumann, Roderick. (1998) *Imposing wilderness: Struggles over livelihood and nature preservation in Africa.* Berkeley: University of California Press.

Protected Planet Database. (2011). Homepage. Retrieved October 27, 2011, from www.protectedplanet.net

Perfecto, Ivette; Vandermeer, John; & Wright, Angus. (2009). *Nature's matrix: Linking agriculture, conservation, and food sovereignty.* London: Earthscan.

Soulé, Michael E., & Terborgh, John. (1999). *Continental conservation: Scientific foundations of regional reserve networks.* Washington, DC: Island Press.

Spence, Mark David. (2000). *Dispossessing the wilderness: Indian removal and the making of the national parks.* New York: Oxford University Press.

Simonian, Lane. (1995). *Defending the land of the jaguar: A conservation history of Mexico.* Austin: University of Texas Press.

Sutter, Paul S. (2004). *Driven wild: How the fight against automobiles launched the modern wilderness movement.* Seattle: University of Washington Press.

Tyrrell, Ian. (2012). America's national parks: The transnational creation of national space in the Progressive Era. *Journal of American Studies, 46*(1), 1–21. Retrieved March 19, 2012, from http://journals.cambridge.org/action/displayCustomArticles?jid=AMS&articleListId=1641

United Nations Educational, Scientific and Cultural Organization (UNESCO) World Heritage. (2011). Manú National Park. Retrieved March 3, 2012, from http://whc.unesco.org/en/list/402

Vandermeer, John H., & Perfecto, Ivette. (1995). *Breakfast of biodiversity: The political ecology of rain forest destruction.* Oakland, CA: Food First Books.

Wakild, Emily. (2011). *Revolutionary parks: Conservation, social justice, and Mexico's national parks, 1910–1940.* Tucson: University of Arizona Press.

Share the *Encyclopedia of Sustainability*: Teachers are welcome to make up to ten (10) copies of no more than two (2) articles for distribution in a single course or program. For further permissions, please visit www.copyright.com or contact: info@berkshirepublishing.com

Perth, Australia

1.7 million est. pop. 2011

Perth, Western Australia, is the capital of one of the world's largest political units, covering 2,525,000 square kilometers, or approximately one-third of the Australian continent. Renowned for its earlier isolation, Perth has grown from a struggling colonial outpost into a modern metropolis and hub of the state's mining operations in less than two hundred years. Future growth seems assured, with a greater emphasis upon sustainable practice.

Perth, the state capital of Western Australia situated on the Swan River, is often described as the most isolated capital city in the world. It is located 2,138 kilometers (km) from Adelaide, the nearest Australian state capital, and is somewhat closer to Jakarta, the capital of Indonesia (3,002 km), than to Australia's federal capital, Canberra (3,106 km). As an extreme example of urban primacy, in 2011, Perth held three-quarters of Western Australia's 2.2 million people on just 0.2 percent (5,386 km^2) of the state's area. While early progress was slow and settlement relatively unconstrained, since 1980 continuing population growth and low density development have coincided with a period of reduced regional rainfall. This situation has raised questions about the city's future size, shape, and sustainability, a discussion that has taken on greater urgency amid an ongoing national debate regarding climate change and appropriate policy responses.

History

European settlement dates from 1829, when the British government extended its control over the western part of the continent through the establishment of the first nonconvict colony in Australia. Three initial town sites were set up—Perth the capital, Fremantle the port, and Guildford the agricultural center, early foundations that have given rise to a multicentric urban region. At first, however, the new Swan River Colony was slow to develop on an inhospitable and alien coastal sandplain populated by indigenous inhabitants who were dispossessed by occupation rather than treaty. The first European settlers who purchased or were granted land looked upon the Aborigines (indigenous people) with both apprehension and distaste, at best tolerated (as long as they didn't cause trouble) and at worst as trespassers. Perth, today, still contains less than 5 percent of Australia's indigenous population.

The fledgling colony, beset by environmental and organizational problems, did not match settlers' expectations, and the small number of annual arrivals was augmented by the belated introduction of convicts from Britain. This transfer took place from 1850 to 1868 and stimulated increased economic activity through ambitious public works programs. Yet by 1881, the population of Perth was still only 5,044, and that of Fremantle was 3,641 (Gentilli 1979, 339). Not until the 1890s, when significant amounts of gold were discovered near Kalgoorlie, 400 kilometers east of Perth, was the success of Western Australia finally established. By 1901, Perth had reached a population of 36,274 and Fremantle, 20,444, the latter confirmed as the major port along Australia's western seaboard. At this time, renewed public building construction gave the city a degree of architectural grandeur, in keeping with increased civic confidence arising from newly found wealth. Rather ironically, much of this legacy was replaced by high-rise office buildings during the next boom period, which began during the 1960s.

Urban Growth

The early twentieth century saw a string of residential suburbs, socially differentiated on the basis of house type, building materials, and tenancy status, as urbanization was consolidated along the Fremantle-Perth-Guildford railway axis. Perth's subsequent preoccupation with single-story, owner-occupied homes was established at this time, and was extended through public streetcars and bus routes. From the late 1940s, this low-density pattern spread as additional suburbs were added north and south of the Swan River, resulting in increased car traffic. In the second half of the twentieth century, accelerated population growth associated with rapid economic development caused by a succession of mineral booms took the Perth metropolitan area population from 303,000 in 1947 to 1.3 million in 2001 (Gentilli 1979, 315; Weller 2009, 52). Historically, the number of local governments increased along with growth in population and area. Some consolidation was achieved under the banner of the "Greater Perth" movement in the early twentieth century, but the legacy of fragmentation, with more than thirty separate bodies, prevented the creation of any powerful and effective local government authority. Melbourne, by comparison, has a similar number of local government areas, but for a much larger metropolitan population of some 4 million. Recently, plans for a reduction in the number of local councils have been suggested.

Fractured governance at the local level was countered by the Town Planning and Development Act 1928, the first in Australia, which created the Metropolitan Town Planning Commission. Following the Great Depression and World War II, the revival of metropolitan planning gave rise to the Stephenson-Hepburn Plan for the Metropolitan Region, Perth and Fremantle Western Australia 1955. This plan favored the establishment of "identifiable and self-contained communities," but it was quickly outdated through an increasing decentralization of not only residential, but also commercial and industrial land uses, facilitated by an unprecedented growth in private car ownership. A new vision, the Corridor Plan for Perth 1970, sought to contain expansion within designated corridors of urban communities separated by open space, including areas of national parks, agricultural, institutional, and special land uses. Employment hubs were to be developed in subregional centers to reduce the dominance of the Perth Central Area. Released just before the first oil crisis, this planning approach represents the extreme of low density, private car–oriented Perth. Subsequent thinking, notably Metroplan 1990, stressed the need for greater urban consolidation through increased housing densities in the inner city, and regional centers near public transportation hubs. The Western Australian Planning Commission's *Network City*, released in 2004, extended these principles with the added components of "sustainability, liveability and environmental responsibility" (WAPC 2004).

Perth's rapid development, particularly since Western Australia's mineral boom of the 1960s, belies earlier notions of isolation as more effective domestic and international communications have overcome the "tyranny of distance." In 2006, one-third of Perth's population was born overseas, and more flexible federal immigration policies have brought increasing numbers of migrants from outside traditional Anglo-Celtic source regions. Some of this increasing ethnic and cultural diversity has manifested itself in increased social polarization: attractive natural features of river, coast, and hills are prime residential locations, while poorer households in the outer southeastern and southwestern corridors, often without easy vehicle access, are the greatest casualties. Perth is one of the world's most car-dependent cities; only 10 percent of residents travel to work by public transportation. Increasingly, households with annual incomes in the lowest 40 percent are struggling to attain the suburban ideal of detached-home ownership on a "quarter acre block (lot)." Today's lot sizes have been substantially reduced, and the search for affordability has resulted in people moving farther from workplaces, excessively lengthening commute times and contributing to social isolation for outer suburban dwellers lacking mobility.

Excluding nonurban land uses such as parks, forest reserves, recreational land, and watershed preserves, the 2006 population density of the Greater Perth region was calculated at 1,090 people per square kilometer, a figure more than twice that of Canberra (428), somewhat more than Adelaide (659), and similar to Brisbane (918). Population densities were considerably higher in the two major Australian cities of Melbourne (1,566) and Sydney (2,058). International population density comparisons place Perth alongside newer car-oriented metropolitan areas such as Houston (1,505) and Phoenix (1,188), but well below many older Eastern Seaboard cities in North America. Urban counterparts in Europe are often considerably denser (London 4,978), higher still in developed Asia (Tokyo 6,027), and much, much higher in the developing world (Mumbai 20,694).

Outlook

The combination of low-density development, high standards of living, and a culture of mass consumption led the Australian Conservation Foundation to place Perth last out of the twenty largest Australian cities on the 2010 Sustainable Cities Index. Perth fared worst in ecological footprint (estimated as 7.66 hectares per person per year), water consumption (268 kiloliters per property per year) and transportation (640.9 private passenger vehicles per 1000 people). Rated less harshly but still matters of concern are air quality, with worries over photochemical smog and particulate haze, loss of habitats including wetlands, and increased eutrophication (concentration of polluting nutrients) in the Swan and Canning rivers, together with the amount of solid waste being disposed of in metropolitan landfills. The prospect that climate change will adversely affect Perth's water supplies has prompted the state government to commission two saltwater desalinization plants, destined to provide half of metropolitan water supply needs by late 2012.

Such concerns notwithstanding, Perth invariably scores highly on the recurring lists of "most livable world cities," vying with Melbourne and Sydney in Australia as most favored places to live. Until now, the price of such affluence, in both environmental and social terms, has not been taken into account, but this may soon change. Recently, two publications—the Western Australian government's *Directions 2031* and the more speculative *Boom Town 2050*—have pondered the future for the Perth metropolitan population, which is predicted to increase to at least 2.2 million by 2031, and potentially 4 million by 2051. Substantial urban infill and increased residential densities are likely to transform the character of this most livable city as its citizens adapt to pressing environmental constraints by adopting a much reduced ecological footprint.

Brian J. SHAW
The University of Western Australia

See also Auckland, New Zealand; Australia; Las Vegas, United States; Lima, Peru; Mobility; Parks and Protected Areas; Phoenix, United States; Public Transportation; Sydney, Australia; Urbanization; Water Use and Rights

FURTHER READING

Appleyard, Reginald Thomas, & Manford, Toby. (1979). *The beginning: European discovery and early settlement of Swan River, Western Australia*. Crawley: University of Western Australia Press.

Australian Conservation Foundation. (2010). *Sustainable cities index*. Retrieved January 17, 2012, from http://www.acfonline.org.au/default.asp?section_id=360

Australian Government, Department of Infrastructure and Transport, Major Cities Unit (2011). *State of Australian cities 2011*. Canberra, Australia: Department of Infrastructure and Transport, Major Cities Unit.

Gentilli, Joseph. (Ed.). (1979). *Western landscapes*. Crawley: University of Western Australia Press.

Gregory, Jenny. (2003). *City of light: A history of Perth since the 1950s*. Perth, Australia: City of Perth.

Kennewell, Catherine, & Shaw, Brian J. (2008). City profile: Perth, Western Australia. *Cities*, 25(4), 243–255.

Seddon, George. (1973). *Sense of place: A response to an environment. The Swan Coastal Plain, Western Australia*. Crawley: University of Western Australia Press.

Stannage, Charles Thomas. (1979). *The people of Perth: A social history of Western Australia's capital city*. Perth, Australia: Perth City Council.

Weller, Richard. (2009). *Boomtown 2050*. Crawley: University of Western Australia Publishing.

Western Australia Planning Commission (WAPC). (2004). *Network city*. Perth, Australia: WAPC.

Western Australia Planning Commission (WAPC). (2009). *Directions 2031: Draft spatial framework for Perth and Peel*. Perth, Australia: WAPC.

Berkshire's authors and editors welcome questions, comments, and corrections. Send your emails about the *Berkshire Encyclopedia of Sustainability* in general or this volume in particular to: sustainability.updates@berkshirepublishing.com

Phoenix, United States

4 million est. pop. 2012

More than 4 million people live in the metropolitan area of Phoenix, Arizona. This "oasis city" in the Sonoran Desert has a past that is inextricably tied to water and a boom-bust economy based on growth and development. Moving Phoenix toward a more sustainable future will involve solutions at the water-energy nexus, a focus on economic diversification, and a readiness to address a legacy of social inequities.

The Phoenix metropolitan area—the Salt River Valley—has been home to humans for thousands of years, notably since the Hohokam people began an agricultural society roughly 2,500 years ago. Within several centuries, the Hohokam developed a network of nearly 1,600 kilometers of canals to irrigate roughly 10,000 square kilometers of fields. The Salt River Valley sustained this advanced society of up to 40,000 people until a combination of prolonged drought and massive floods led to its collapse by the mid-1400s CE (Abbott 2003). In the centuries that followed, Spanish settlers did not venture north of the Tucson region, so the next major settlement in the valley did not take hold until the mid-1800s, when European settlers established what is now Phoenix and named it as a place that would rise, phoenix-like, from the ashes of the previous civilization.

When Phoenix officially incorporated as a city in 1881, it had about 2,500 inhabitants. By 1900, that population had doubled. Phoenix has since grown to be the nation's sixth-largest city, and its metropolitan area was home to more than 4 million residents by 2010 (US Census Bureau 2008; US Census Bureau 2010).

Twentieth-Century Phoenix

The modern history of Phoenix began, as with the Hohokam, as a largely agrarian venture. Early Salt River Valley farmers reconstituted many of the Hohokam irrigation canals to water their crops. Much of the modern-day urban canal system in Phoenix still mirrors these ancient canals. By World War I, the valley had become a major producer of cotton, and this commodity remains an agricultural mainstay.

Water is a critical resource for any city, but even more so for Phoenix because it is located in the hot, dry Sonoran Desert. In order to ensure consistent water supplies for irrigation while also controlling for destructive flooding, the federal government constructed seven dams on both the Salt River and adjacent Verde River upstream of Phoenix. The last of these reservoirs was in place by the late 1930s, and since then the once-perennial Salt River has flowed through Phoenix as a true river only during extreme flow events caused by rainfall and/or snowmelt and dam releases. To date, the network of dams, reservoirs, and associated supply canals has sustained both agriculture and growth in the Phoenix metropolitan area, but 100 percent of the water generated by the 27,190-square-kilometer Salt–Verde watershed is now sequestered for human use (Gammage et al. 2011).

The national challenges of World War II proved to be an economic boon for Phoenix. Both the military-industrial complex and the military itself moved into the valley in the early 1940s, bringing jobs, housing growth, and the beginning of a population boom that has scarcely slowed since. The federal defense investment in Phoenix and in the Southwest in general continued through the Cold War and remains a considerable economic force

(Markusen et al. 1991). By the turn of the twenty-first century, several large high-tech industries had made the valley their home, the health care industry was a significant employer in the area, and Phoenix Sky Harbor International Airport and associated businesses were important economic players. None of this made for a diverse or resilient economy, though.

Since the 1960s, a significant driver of the valley's economic machine has been the development and construction industry. To accommodate a population that grew from fewer than 150,000 people in 1950 to more than 4 million by 2010 (the time of the latest US census), many homes, schools, hospitals, strip malls, roads, and parking lots had to be built. The Phoenix metropolitan area has become the epitome of suburban sprawl and its associated automobile-dependent and auto-centric lifestyles. Water supply was once again a factor in this explosive growth. A federal agreement in 1968 reaffirmed Arizona's partial distribution of Colorado River water set forth in the 1922 Colorado River Compact (Donahue and Rose 1998), and in the 1980s the federally funded $4.4 billion Central Arizona Project (CAP) was constructed. The signature feature of CAP is a 540-kilometer canal built through the desert to move water 381 meters uphill from Lake Mead to the Phoenix metropolitan area then another 305 meters to regions as far south as Tucson. Once completed in 1993, the CAP canal system allowed for 30 percent of the approximately one thousand liters per day of water Phoenix residents consume (on average) to come from the distant Colorado River. Of the remaining 70 percent, the Salt–Verde watershed supplies approximately 50 percent, and local groundwater sources provide approximately 20 percent. This seemingly sustainable water supply has allowed Phoenix to maintain its oasis character of irrigated, green, vegetated urban landscapes and cityscapes.

Water alone cannot sustain a regional economy, however. The collapse of the financial markets and the deflation of the real estate bubble, beginning in 2006, brought growth in the valley to a standstill. Because the Phoenix economy was so dependent on construction-related industries, the region fared far worse during the recession of 2007–2011 than most other regions of the United States. Average home values in the Phoenix metropolitan area in 2011 were less than half of what they had been in 2006–2007 (Curry 2010). Unemployment was well above the national average throughout the recession. The dramatic pause in growth gives Phoenix a chance to rethink, reinvent, and retool itself based on more sustainable principles—another opportunity to rise from the ashes.

The growing field of environmental justice has produced normative retrospectives that provide "lessons learned from the past" about inequities in both cities and societies (Boone 2010). The history of environmental injustice and social inequity in Phoenix is as old as the city itself. The Salt River and the main east-west rail corridor just north of the river, both just south of the downtown center, have always been the center of heavy industry in Phoenix. Among the notoriously dirty activities located there—including asphalt and concrete production, and sand and gravel mines—are businesses that collect and manage hazardous waste imported from the entire Southwest (Ross 2011). Much of the Salt River industrial corridor is thus made up of brownfields.

Immediately adjacent to this corridor is the community of South Phoenix, which has long been composed primarily of Mexican Hispanic and African American residents (Bolin, Grineski, and Collins 2005). For more than a hundred years, "other side of the tracks" policies have isolated South Phoenix from the more affluent white residents who live north of the downtown center. Numerous studies have shown that South Phoenix residents are more vulnerable to toxin-related health issues than anyone else living in the Phoenix metropolitan area (Bolin, Grineski, and Collins 2005). Growing awareness of the implications of this environmental injustice legacy is affecting decisions about the future of Phoenix as people come to understand that repairing social inequities must be a central component of building a more sustainable future in the region.

Sustainability Challenges and the Future

An irrigation-dependent oasis city of 4 million people located in the Sonoran Desert, where average rainfall is about 20 centimeters a year, faces enormous sustainability challenges. Several authors and researchers have concluded this (e.g., Ross 2011), and archaeologists and anthropologists have documented many examples where past civilizations have collapsed because their growth and complexity exceeded the resource base that supported them (Redman 1999; Diamond 2004; Heinberg and Lerch 2010). Sustainability challenges involve how Phoenix manages water, energy, development, and social inequities.

In Phoenix, water and energy form a nexus. Management of the Salt–Verde watershed and the CAP system sequester and move water long distances to the city while also providing hydroelectric power. Much of this water is used to irrigate landscapes that cool the urban environment, reducing the need for air conditioning. Projections for growth in the Salt River Valley are based on future water use trade-offs among agriculture, lifestyle, and growth (Gammage et al. 2011). The environment notably is not part of this tripartite of trade-offs—as evidenced by the fact that Phoenix currently sequesters 100 percent of the runoff from the Salt–Verde watershed. A key concept of the trade-off model is that agriculture, which uses considerably more water per acre than development and consumes about half of all water used in the Phoenix metropolitan area, can be "retired to create water" for urban growth. In other words, water can be saved by developing on agricultural land. Water conservation can be greatly improved in both sectors, though, including drip irrigation of crops and no-irrigation native plant xeriscaping (landscaping with slow-growing, drought-tolerant plants) of urban spaces. Encouraging these technologies will make the water future more sustainable while also allowing a reallocation of some water resources back to natural systems.

Energy use in Phoenix is dominated by electricity—roughly half of which comes from aging coal-fired plants—and transportation, which is driven by the sprawling auto-centric development patterns of the past. In a city that averages more than 330 sunny days per year, the most obvious sustainable energy source is solar. With the proper leadership, the Phoenix valley could become a global center of solar innovation, development, and application—which would also help diversify the region's economy. Sustainable solutions to the transportation-energy dilemma may require more transformative solutions. These plans might include a reconceptualization of future growth and development focused on mass transit—such as the successful light rail system that now connects north Phoenix to downtown, Sky Harbor Airport, and the neighboring cities of Tempe and Mesa—and strategic urban infill development. The key may be a redirecting of governmental investments in "sprawl subsidizing" roads to expansion of mass transit and walkable and bicycle-friendly urban environments.

The final element of any sustainable future is social equity. Phoenix has environmental injustice legacies that present considerable equity challenges. A history of lax environmental regulation that has favored business over the health of vulnerable residents, along with recent developments such as the SB 1070 immigration law enacted in 2010, suggests that these challenges may be formidable (Ross 2011). A sustainable future Phoenix, however, must be a city that provides diverse economic opportunities and a safe living space for all residents, as well as urban landscapes that are compatible with both the environmental constraints of the region and an uncertain climatic future.

Sustainability is not about the present state of a city, system, or society, nor is sustainability about a rigid future utopian end point. Sustainability is a process, and in a constantly changing world this process must be flexible, nimble, and adaptive. Phoenix has numerous opportunities to progress in a more sustainable direction.

Daniel L. CHILDERS
Arizona State University

See also Detroit, United States; Las Vegas, United States; Lima, Peru; Mobility; New Orleans, United States; Perth, Australia; Public Transportation; United States; Water Use and Rights

FURTHER READING

Abbott, David. (2003). *Centuries of decline during the Hohokam Classic Period at Pueblo Grande*. Tucson: University of Arizona Press.

Bolin, Bob; Grineski, Sara; & Collins, Timothy. (2005). The geography of despair: Environmental racism and the making of South Phoenix. *Human Ecology Review, 12*(2), 156–168.

Boone, Christopher. (2010). Environmental justice, sustainability, and vulnerability. *International Journal of Urban Sustainable Development, 2*(1–2), 135–140.

Curry, Sheree R. (2010, December 3). Phoenix home prices attract 20-somethings. Retrieved May 3, 2012, from http://wpcarey.asu.edu/finance/news-events/upload/Guntermann-Phoenix-Home-Prices-Attract-20-Somethings-12-3-10.pdf

Diamond, Jared. (2004). *Collapse: How societies choose to fail or succeed.* New York: Viking Press.

Donahue, John, & Rose, Barbara. (1998). *Water, culture, and power: Local struggles in a global context.* Washington, DC: Island Press.

Gammage, Grady; Stigler, Monica; Daugherty, David; Clark-Johnson, Susan; & Hart, William. (2011). *Watering the Sun Corridor: Managing choices in Arizona's megapolitan area.* Tempe: Arizona State University, Morrison Institute for Public Policy.

Heinberg, Richard, & Lerch, Daniel. (2010). *The post carbon reader: Managing the 21st century's sustainability crisis.* Healdsburg, CA: Watershed Media.

Markusen, Ann; Hall, Peter; Campbell, Scott; & Dietrick, Sabina. (1991). *The rise of the gunbelt: The military remapping of industrial America.* New York: Oxford University Press.

Redman, Charles. (1999). *Human impact on ancient environments.* Tucson: University of Arizona Press.

Ross, Andrew. (2011). *Bird on fire: Lessons from the world's least sustainable city.* New York: Oxford University Press.

United States (US) Census Bureau. (2008). Newsroom: Profile America: Facts for features. Retrieved May 3, 2012, from http://www.census.gov/newsroom/releases/archives/facts_for_features_special_editions/cb08-ffse01.html

United States (US) Census Bureau. (2010). State & county quick facts: Phoenix (city) Arizona. Retrieved May 3, 2012, from http://quickfacts.census.gov/qfd/states/04/0455000.html

Public Transportation

Public transportation is an essential service for sustainable development in cities. Reliable water-, wheel-, or rail-based systems alleviate some of the challenges that face large cities as they grow. Urban and transportation planners can work together to create functional, well-designed cities. In general, a less automobile-dependent public transportation system creates a more livable and sustainable city and region. Public transportation is the key for any city's development regardless of historical, cultural, social, and economic contexts.

Public transportation is essential to sustainable city development. It can be said to be the heart of a city. A healthy heart beats regularly, carrying the right amount of blood through the arteries in order for the body to function well in different circumstances. Similarly, public transportation regularly carries passengers throughout the city using the available infrastructure and facilities. This flow should happen with the lowest possible environmental impact and cost. In the context of the Americas and Oceania, many cities, including those in the United States, Canada, Brazil, Australia, and New Zealand, have developed successful underground, surface, and elevated public transportation systems.

Definitions

Urban public transportation can be privately or publicly owned and managed. In practice, many systems make use of public–private partnerships for owning the fleet and managing the service.

According to the civil engineering professors Constantinos Papacostas and Panos Prevedouros, public transportation should be understood as a system with parts, components, and specific ways to function effectively according to a preestablished goal (Papacostas and Prevedouros 1993). The overall goal is to transport the maximum number of passengers possible quickly, safely, comfortably, and at the lowest possible cost. Public transportation's main components are vehicles (buses, trains, trolleys, boats, etc.), infrastructure, and facilities (road networks, canals, stations, terminals, stops, etc.), rules (laws, regulations, management, and control), and passengers.

Public transportation has two major environments: transportation means and transportation modes. There are three basic categories of transportation means: private (for example, automobiles and motorcycles), semipublic (for example, taxis and carpools), and public (buses, trains, and subways). Transportation modes are the vehicles used to carry out the transportation task. Transportation modes include cars, motorcycles, trains, bicycles, trucks, buses, and so on. Each mode can be subdivided into many different models and types according to transportation planning goals and needs, cultural circumstances, and technological developments.

Public transportation has a major role in city development. Without an effective public transportation system, a city stands still. Transportation modes might vary by time and place, but the need for mobility and accessibility for basic daily tasks, moving goods, commuting to and from work, shopping, and socializing is the same. In Japan, for instance, most city dwellers can successfully accomplish their transportation tasks without driving private automobiles, relying instead on an effective network of buses, subways, and trains. For short trips, ordinary one-speed bikes are the preferred mode for everyone including students, homemakers, and workers commuting to local train stations. These transportation modes are part of a sustainable, efficient, and readily available public transportation system.

The construction of any public transportation system in the world, from the simplest to the most complex, goes through essential phases.

1. Planning—Local conditions and characteristics, needs, available resources, and other major components for the future system are investigated, and what to build, where, how, when, and at what price are decided. Urban planning, transportation planning, urban design, and environmental planning should work together for this phase.
2. Implementation—The plan comes to fruition, and resources go into building the planned system.
3. Operation—The system is put into action under certain rules and regulations and according to its predefined goal.
4. Management and maintenance—The system is monitored, and plans are laid for developments for the whole system, as well as the security and safety of passengers.

Historical Background

There are three different historical periods in the development of public transportation based on different stages of technology and conceptualization: before the Industrial Revolution, the Industrial Revolution, and the modern era. Cities evolved to accommodate new modes, systems, and vehicles simultaneously with developments in the technology surrounding public transportation.

Since ancient times, humans have recognized the benefits and advantages of collective transportation, beginning with carriages and wagons propelled by horses, oxen, and other draft animals. Before the development of public transportation networks, cities had to be dense and compact because it was difficult for people to get around in them. Even before the Industrial Revolution, however, the development of railways brought greater efficiency to passenger transportation. (The inspiration for rail transportation was apparently dumpsters in coal and gold mines.) Demonstrations of underground rail transportation took place in important world cities like London, in 1863, and New York, in 1869.

Rail systems allowed cities to expand their territories, and city structure began to change from compact and dense cities to sprawling urban areas. Changes in city design contributed to improved quality of life and healthier environments. The new urban design, along with the discovery of vaccines, reduced the incidence of diseases like cholera, yellow fever, black plague, and many others. This new city design, with improvements in water supply, drainage, and sewer systems, was known in Europe as sanitary urbanism.

During the late eighteenth and early nineteenth centuries, the Industrial Revolution, with an array of inventions and technological developments, greatly contributed to better public transportation efficiency. The evolution started in Europe, but it spread quickly to the Americas and Oceania. Later developments in transportation were built on this foundation. Steam-propelled engines, electricity, and Otto cycle (fuel-powered) engines were responsible for transformations in public transportation and city organization and growth. Harnessing electricity for transportation purposes in the early years of the twentieth century was a very important step in mass transportation development. Rail systems and electrically propelled vehicles made underground rapid transit possible in many important cities worldwide.

Subways

From slow, steam-propelled vehicles and modest lines to fast, modern electric trains and vast networks, underground transportation changed radically over time. Responsible for daily commutes in important cities around the world, underground transportation is considered to be a "heavy" mass transit system due to the large number of passengers transported. Underground transportation is known by a variety of names: *underground* or *tube* in the United Kingdom or *subway* in the United States. These systems have changed cities' structures, expanding urban boundaries while carrying hundreds of millions of passengers worldwide. In the context of the Americas and Oceania, there are subway systems in many major cities including New York, Chicago, and San Francisco in the United States; Montreal, Canada; Auckland, New Zealand; and Sydney, Australia.

One story about the original inspiration for subways is that even before the Industrial Revolution, some of the heaviest public transportation routes in London were dug down below street level and regraded, separating them from sidewalks to protect pedestrians from direct contact with vehicles and the traffic noise, dust, and smell of horses and carriages. The idea worked, and public authorities went on to completely excavate the routes.

Surface Systems

Surface public transportation systems are the most common because of their simplicity and low cost compared with underground systems. Almost every city in the world has a surface public transportation system. They range from small and simply operated systems to very complex and integrated modern systems and networks.

Trains and streetcars are the most common passenger vehicles for rail transportation at the surface level.

Because it is able to transport large numbers of commuters, mass rail transit is often used to extend metropolitan boundaries for long-range trips. Streetcars and small trains, like light rail transit, often access city centers and adjoining areas for short- and medium-range trips. Cable cars are a type of rail transportation powered by underground cables. The cable cars in San Francisco, California, are a world-famous example of this type of system. New Orleans, Louisiana, boasts the oldest continuously operated streetcar system in the world.

Bus Rapid Transit (BRT)

Bus rapid transit (BRT) is a tire-based, surface public transportation system. It makes use of high-capacity vehicles and operates in a similar way to subways. BRT is used where it is too expensive or too technologically complex to build subways.

As a mass transit system, BRT usually provides dedicated bus lanes, express routes, upper level stops and platforms allowing for rapid embarking and disembarking, fewer stops along routes, and an advanced information system that makes it easier for passengers to identify routes, lines, itineraries, and destinations. BRT systems are usually integrated with feeder systems such as subways, regular buses lines, and nonmotorized transportation modes. Integration makes connections to sidewalks, bikeways, parking lots, and taxi hubs highly accessible. BRT systems are intended to work in corridors accessing central urban sites and suburbs and metropolitan areas.

Due to the advances in technology, many BRT systems around the world use modern, efficient vehicles and facilities, as well as intelligent transportation systems (ITSs) for operations. ITSs are computerized systems for scheduling, routing, programming, and controlling transit operations.

Curitiba, Brazil, operates one the most successful BRT systems in the world. Many cities worldwide are currently developing modern, cheap, and efficient BRT systems (Santos 2011). These cities include Bogotá, Colombia (Transmilenio project); Santiago, Chile (Transantiago project); and Los Angeles, United States (Orange Line—San Fernando corridor). Boston, Las Vegas, Miami, and Seattle, in the United States, and Ottawa and Vancouver, in Canada, are developing BRT systems as part of, or as complementary to, larger public transportation systems. Brisbane, Adelaide, Perth, Melbourne, and Sydney, in Australia, and Auckland, in New Zealand, are considering BRT.

Rail Systems

Several types of surface rail transportation systems exist in cities worldwide. The different ways they are implemented and developed are related to social, economic, cultural, and technological factors.

Light Rail Transit (LRT) Systems based on electric rails are common in US cities. They make use of high-occupancy vehicles but cannot carry as many passengers as subway or suburban "heavy" train systems due to specific characteristics and requirements. In Canada, one such system is Edmonton (Alberta) Light Rail Transit. In the United States, Baltimore, San Diego, and Dallas all have efficient, modern systems. Tram and light rail transit systems are in place in Adelaide, Ballarat, Bendigo, Melbourne, Perth, and Sydney, in Australia, and Christchurch, in New Zealand.

Elevated Rail Transit (ERT) The City Center Tram–Las Vegas monorail, in Las Vegas, and the Chicago "L" trains are examples of elevated rail systems in the United States. The elevated rail system in Sydney, Australia, was part of the sustainable development program for the 2000 Olympic Games.

Suburban Rail Suburban rail is a "heavy" rail transit system, often known as commuter rail. This system is present mainly in large urban centers and metropolitan areas. Examples of effective suburban rail systems are City Rail in Sydney, Newcastle, and Wollongong (the largest metropolitan network in Australia), and New Zealand commuter rail systems in Auckland and Wellington.

Automated Guided Vehicles (AGV) Automated guided vehicles can be rail or wheel based. The technology involved is sophisticated, and as a result, AGVs are not as common as other types of mass transit. The O-Bahn Busway route in Adelaide, Australia (a bus-based system), is the best example and one of the most famous of this type of system.

Water-Based Systems

Boats, including ferries, are common public transportation vehicles in many countries. They have transported people and goods between and within cities since ancient times. In countries with abundant rivers and lakes, boats are part of the tradition, culture, and infrastructure of public transportation. The Mississippi River in the United States, Lake Titicaca in Peru, and the Amazonian rivers in Brazil are all important water transportation corridors. Some coastal cities have also developed efficient water-based public transportation systems. On fresh- and salt water, boats are part of day-to-day life in many cities worldwide. In general, water-based public transportation is complementary to and integrated with land-based systems.

A large number of cities are known as river towns, cities whose life is dependent on the river. The river is both a water supply and a means of transport for individuals and businesses. New York City, for example, is strongly connected with the Hudson River for transportation of goods and passengers. Due to the many islands and extensive coastline of Oceania, many countries there, especially Australia and New Zealand, have developed efficient water-based public transportation systems. Ferries and water taxis are an important transportation feature of Sydney, Australia, and Auckland and Wellington, New Zealand.

Sustainable Public Transportation

The urban daily transportation task, especially in large cities and important urban hubs, has to balance individual and collective needs. This balance reduces urban congestion and car dependency by encouraging people to use public transportation. City planning must strive to achieve the balance through a coalition between urban design and public transportation planning. In the Americas and Oceania, Curitiba, Brazil; Portland, Denver, and San Francisco, in the United States; Vancouver, Toronto, and Calgary, in Canada; Melbourne, Australia; and Guatemala City, Guatemala, are a few examples of such development. Due to their commitment to public transportation, these cities are considered more efficient and sustainable than other cities. They have managed to reduce traffic congestion and conserve natural resources.

In sustainable public transportation, the greatest number of passengers is transported with the expenditure of the least amount of resources. In a sustainable and environmentally friendly city context, sustainable public transportation is based on certain key features: integration with nonmotorized transportation, technologically advanced vehicles and engines, and prioritization of collective over individual transportation.

Sustainable transportation also includes more efficient and less environmentally impactful transportation of goods. Maximizing load capacity and minimizing resource consumption make the movement of goods both more efficient and less environmentally damaging. This goal, along with rising gasoline prices, drives research into engine technology. Such research has created hybrid and electrically powered vehicles, hydrogen cells, and solar-powered vehicles (collectively known as zero- or low-emission vehicles). Advances in sustainable transportation improve the quality of urban life by preserving open space and conserving resources. Sustainability thus becomes part of a modern and more efficient city.

Urban Planning

Urban planning provides for well-thought-out development of cities. In terms of public transportation and sustainability, cities should strive toward balance between private and public transportation. Since automobiles are the primary means of transportation in many cities, zoning and ordinances should prioritize mass transit and public transportation. Public and private street use and parking lots should be regulated to maximize public space for social and leisure activities. Planned cities that prioritize public transportation more successfully meet the challenges of urban growth by lessening traffic congestion, lowering air pollution, reducing noise pollution, preserving infrastructure and resources, and saving time.

An alliance between transportation planning and urban planning will provide the best outcome for public transportation system efficiency and sustainability (Bruton 1970). This partnership is essential in making accurate estimates for land use, population growth, and economic development. The success of a public transportation system created through the integration of good urban planning practices can clearly be seen in Curitiba, Brazil.

Regional Considerations and Outlook

Public transportation systems vary considerably from place to place and through time. In spite of regional characteristics, though, public transportation systems are composed of vehicles, infrastructure, regulations, and passengers. The goal should be universal: to make passenger transportation as efficient, safe, and sustainable as possible. Vehicles vary in terms of type, model, capacity, and operation. Infrastructure and facilities also vary according to particular vehicle characteristics. Regulations, laws, and rules, including zoning, ordinances, and building codes, vary from simple to highly complex.

Cities use the available natural resources as a basis for public transportation development. For instance, when water is an abundant resource, public transportation tends to be based on water, often in combination with land transportation. When the landscape is hilly, appropriate vehicles, like cable cars in San Francisco, California, and Wellington, New Zealand, make public transportation more efficient. Local traditions and culture are often incorporated, giving a unique identity to each city's transportation choices. Regional and national architecture feature prominently in facilities and amenities such as bus stations and terminals, as well as in the choice of vehicles.

Public transportation has a large environmental impact, because it consumes large amounts of natural resources for energy and fuel. In the future, clean energy and low-emission vehicles will play an important role. Hydrogen-cell, solar-powered, biofuel-propelled, and zero-emission vehicles are all in production. Advances in technology are helping to turn public transportation systems into more efficient and environmentally friendly operations. Urban planning also plays a very important role—helping cities grow more rationally and efficiently. Adopting transit-oriented development (development based on access to public transportation) makes cities more livable and public transportation more sustainable.

Evandro C. SANTOS
Jackson State University

See also Architecture; Auckland, New Zealand; Australia; Bogotá, Colombia; Brazil; Canada; Curitiba, Brazil; Detroit, United States; Guatemala City; Mississippi and Missouri Rivers; Mobility; New York City, United States; New Zealand; Oceania; Perth, Australia; Sanitation; Sydney, Australia; Toronto, Canada; Travel and Tourism Industry; United States; Urbanization; Vancouver, Canada

FURTHER READING

American Association of State Highway and Transportation Officials (AASHTO). (2004). *Guide for high-occupancy vehicle facilities.* Washington, DC: AASHTO.

American Public Transportation Association. (2011). Transit oriented development—Reports and publications. Retrieved July 12, 2011, from http://www.fta.dot.gov/publications/about_FTA_11008.html

Bruton, Michael. (1970). *Introduction to transportation planning.* London: Hutchinson & Co.

Calthorpe, Peter. (1994). The region. In P. Katz (Ed.), *The New Urbanism: Toward an architecture of community* (pp. xi–xvi). New York: McGraw-Hill.

NYCSubway. (n.d.). NYC subway history. Retrieved August 15, 2011, from http://www.nycsubway.org

Papacostas, Constantinos S., & Prevedouros, Panos D. (1993). *Transportation engineering and planning* (2nd ed.). Upper Saddle River, NJ: Prentice Hall.

Powell, Kenneth. (2000). *City transformed: Urban architecture at the beginning of the 21st century.* London: Laurence King.

San Francisco Cable Car. (2011). Homepage. Retrieved August 23, 2011, from http://www.sfcablecar.com

Santos, Evandro C. (2009). Curitiba, Brazil: Systems planning pioneer. In Gary Hack, Eugénie Birch, Paul Sedway & Mitchell Silver (Eds.), *Local planning: Contemporary principles and practice* (pp. 385–387). Washington, DC: International City/County Management Association (ICMA) Press.

Santos, Evandro. C. (2011). *Curitiba, Brazil: Pioneering in developing bus rapid transit and urban planning solutions.* Saarbrücken, Germany: LAP Lambert Academic Publishing.

Wellington, New Zealand. (2011). Wellington cable car. Retrieved August 23, 2011, from http://www.wellingtonnz.com/sights_activities/wellington_cable_car

Williams, Hywel. (2011). Underground history. Retrieved August 15, 2011, from http://underground-history.co.uk/front.php

Wright, Charlie L. (1992). *Fast wheels, slow traffic: Urban transport choices.* Philadelphia: Temple University Press.

Wright, Lloyd. (2005). *Car-free development.* Eschborn, Germany: Deutsche Gesellschaft fur Technische Zusammenarbeit.

 Berkshire's authors and editors welcome questions, comments, and corrections. Send your emails about the *Berkshire Encyclopedia of Sustainability* in general or this volume in particular to: sustainability.updates@berkshirepublishing.com

R

Rio de Janeiro, Brazil

6.3 million est. pop. 2010

Rio de Janeiro sprawls across a huge area bordered by the Atlantic Ocean, mountain ranges, and one of the world's great natural harbors. While Rio displays many of the growing pains and environmental threats typical of megacities, Brazil's emergence as a global economic player offers opportunities—aided by hosting the Rio ECO 92 Earth Summit—for its second-largest city to resolve some of its greatest sustainability challenges. Rio de Janeiro hosted the twentieth anniversary of the original Earth Summit in June 2012, called "Rio+20."

Rio de Janeiro was the center stage for environmental issues and development in June 2012. The twentieth anniversary of the Rio Earth Summit (Rio+20) was planned to assess progress of programs put into place during the original Earth Summit of 1992 and address the challenges and changes that sustainable environmental development faces in coming decades. (See the sidebar in the article on the Rio Earth Summit on page 260.)

Rio de Janeiro—literally "River of January"—is so named because Portuguese explorers entered what is now called the Bay of Guanabara on 1 January 1502, thinking it a giant river. The striking physical setting is dominated by water (both salt and fresh) and forest resources. The Bay of Guanabara is one of the world's great natural harbors. At approximately 400 square kilometers, it has an average depth of 7.6 meters (IADB n.d., 1), which allows it to accommodate large ocean tankers. The greater metropolitan area of Rio de Janeiro also comprises other idyllic natural harbors, including the heavily industrialized and polluted Bay of Sepetiba to the southwest of the city center, a deepwater harbor of more than 300 square kilometers. To the city's south and along the southern coastline sit some of the world's most famous beaches, including Ipanema and Copacabana, although there are dozens of others, many of which have become major tourist draws since the twentieth century.

What is more, this megacity sits in the middle of the Atlantic Rainforest, the second largest tropical forest system in continental South America, after the Amazon Rainforest. The Atlantic Rainforest, a largely coastal system now but 7 percent of its original size when first encountered by European explorers, once stretched from northern Argentina to eastern Venezuela. The Atlantic Rainforest could not be more different from its Amazonian cousin. The terrain is rocky and hilly and the forests are less dense. The Atlantic Rainforest also boasts a much higher biodiversity index than the Amazon Rainforest and is rich in, for example, bromeliads, orchids, and flowering plants, as well as fauna, including a wide diversity of primates, felines, amphibians, reptiles, birds, and fish.

Although tropical, Rio's coastal climate is agreeable, regularly under 30°C, even in the year's hottest months (November–February). Winter temperatures tend to remain in the low 20s°C. Rainfall is heaviest from December to April, averaging around 12.7 centimeters per month (Weather Channel 2012). In sum, the unique physical location of the city has made it, as one says in Portuguese, the nation's "postcard" (*cartão postal*)—its principal image abroad.

Despite the fact that the riches of the Atlantic Rainforest have been seriously depleted, Rio's natural tourist attractions remain a powerful draw. Rio is the major point of departure for some of Brazil's most celebrated beach and mountain resorts, many of them concentrated in the greater metropolitan area. Rio tops the charts as the main tourist destination in the Southern Hemisphere. Annually, Rio receives 2.82 million tourists, a figure projected to increase by 10–15 percent between 2015 and 2016 because of the Olympic Games (Rio 2016 Now 2010). The announcement that the 2014 World Cup will be held in Brazil—with many games and the all-important finals to be played in Rio—as well as the successful bid for the 2016 Olympic Games have helped reinforce recognition of the city's potential as a tourist center. This fact entails a menace to the physical environment but, if managed intelligently, could bring with it an expansion of dedicated environmental protection.

Rio's and Brazil's governments might successfully exploit the city's image in aims of sustainable development, if they so desire, particularly given the city's strong tourist appeal. To be sure, there is strong interest among sectors of the Carioca (as residents of Rio are known locally) to do just this, and there has been for some time. It was, after all, the celebrated Brazilian composer and writer Antônio "Tom" Jobim (the co-author of "The Girl from Ipanema" and other bossa nova hits) who, with a group of friends, successfully lobbied for the United Nations to hold its first major conference on the environment and development in a city in the global South, in 1992. Since then, the UN's Rio Declaration on the Environment and Development and other documents issued at that event have become international reference points for the definition of the term *sustainable development*. Another UN conference, Rio+20, was slated for the time of publication of this encyclopedia (June 2012). Whether the city that gave its name to the key principles of sustainable development will be faithful to their fulfillment, however, remains in question.

Complicating the drive for the city's sustainable future is the fact that Rio is a major commercial and industrial center. The area in and around the city is a major maritime hub for petroleum production, foremost for the extensive Campos Basin, an offshore oil field of more than 40,000 hectares. Petroleum exploration in and around Rio shows no signs of stopping, especially after the 2007 discovery of the deep-sea Tupi oil basin, an area of 105,000 hectares off Rio de Janeiro's southern coast (EIA 2012). Former president Luiz Inaçio "Lula" da Silva gave witness to the immensity of the find when he referred to the Tupi discovery as the source of Brazil's future prosperity as he prepared to leave office in 2010. Early auctions on the Tupi oil fields, as well as national negotiations about the division of royalties, occurred as the world's largest deep-sea oil spill, the British Petroleum disaster in the Gulf of Mexico, unfolded. Lula disregarded the risks demonstrated by the Gulf of Mexico deepwater exploration example, as has his successor, President Dilma Rousseff, who insists that the deep-sea riches are Brazil's "passport to the future" (Gall 2011). For many this raised a worry that the rush to begin drilling will lead to future comparable disasters off Rio's coast—with spills in 2011 and 2012 confirming their fears.

Although São Paulo began to displace Rio's economic and industrial dominance around the turn to the twenty-first century (Helena and Alves 2004), Rio de Janeiro remains Brazil's second city in terms of economic activity and home to two of Brazil's most important global enterprises, namely, the mining multinational company VALE (formerly the Companhia do Vale do Rio Doce) and the private-public oil company Petrobras, among thousands of others. The economic dominance of these and other entities, however, often occludes sound environmental planning, as the contamination by petroleum and other industrial enterprises of the Guanabara and Sepetiba bays attests.

Rio also remains home to the O Globo media empire, one of the nation's largest news and entertainment providers. With this and other important media enterprises, the city manages to maintain a disproportionate influence over the nation's cultural life, a fact that could help make the it a leader in public education aimed at sustainable development. This is particularly true in the years up to and beyond Brazil's hosting of the 2014 World Cup and Rio's status as the 2016 Olympics host site, when the city will most feel the strain of its international ambitions and commitments.

History and Current Sustainability Challenges

To understand the challenges of sustainable development in Rio de Janeiro, it is essential to understand competing tensions for use of its land. Is it a tourist paradise, the chic entry point to tropical South America, or a major commercial and industrial center? Always lurking in the background of any discussion of sustainable development in Rio is the striking fact of the city's social and economic inequality, a fact that dominates any attempt to use land and resources sensibly. Although in 2011 Brazil surpassed Great Britain as the world's sixth largest economy, it still remains one of the most unbalanced countries in the world in terms of social and economic equality (Riley 2012). For example, Brazil's Gini coefficient (a commonly used measure of social inequality) is one of the world's highest, at 51.9 (CIA 2012).

For reasons both of history and geography, the jarring contrasts between rich and poor are especially evident in Rio de Janeiro. Although not Brazil's first capital (that honor is reserved for Salvador, Bahia), Rio was the continent-sized country's political, cultural, and economic capital longer than any other (Skidmore 1999). Until 1822, Brazil remained a colony of Portugal, populated mainly by a small elite of mostly European male settlers, commanding the services of indigenous and Afro-descendant peoples, most of whom were enslaved. This set in motion the historical inequality that has since plagued the country's development. As the diplomat and historian Sérgio Buarque de Holanda (1995, 52) explained, the Portuguese in Brazil mostly "wanted to extract from the soil excessive benefits without great sacrifices. Or, as the oldest of our historians once said, 'they wanted to make use of the land, not as lords, but as usufructuaries,' only to enjoy the land and leave it destroyed." This situation changed only somewhat in January 1808, when the Portuguese Crown, fleeing Napoleon Bonaparte's march on Lisbon, fled to Brazil and reestablished itself in Rio, bringing with him a court estimated at between 10,000 and 15,000 people, increasing the city's population by 30 percent between 1808 and 1822 (Gomes 2008, 166). This sudden burden on the resources began an irregular growth and strain on the area's natural sources that continues to this day.

During this period the patterns of land use that continue to the present began, with devastating environmental effects. Specifically, a relatively small elite controlled bountiful natural resources for its own benefit, leaving a poor majority with little access to managed resources or public services and creating a dynamic of serious environmental consequence. By the early 1800s, for example, the Atlantic Rainforest around Rio had been replaced with coffee plantations. This development quickly threatened clean water supplies because the tropical forest canopy retained water in a way the monoculture coffee plantations (full of squat, regularly planted shrubs) could not do, and erosion from the loss of the forest cover further degraded water resources. As a result, the scientifically minded emperor, Pedro II, ordered the reforestation of the hills around Rio (Dean 1995, 225). The incident reflects the push and pull of environmental waste and protection that have long characterized Rio's history.

The abolition of slavery in 1888 further strained Rio's forests and water resources (Dean 1995). The moment of abolition was one in which Brazilian history and Rio's geography combined to set in motion a long-term threat to the city's sustainable development. Suddenly free, largely illiterate, completely uneducated, and with no home to go to, many of the freed slaves settled in the Atlantic Rainforest hills peppered throughout the city, forming a kind of shantytown, or *favela*, that became a notorious aspect of Rio's landscape. From an environmental perspective, their location could not be less propitious, since they occupy once-verdant hillsides of the Atlantic Rainforest, resulting in biodiversity loss, reduced freshwater, uncontrolled sewage release and trash deposits, and erosion associated with construction and deforestation. As a result, the *favelas* continue to pose a major sustainability challenge. The situation worsened in the period of Brazilian industrialization since the end of the Second World War. In 1950, the population of the then-national capital State of Rio de Janeiro was 2.3 million with most people concentrated in and around the city (IBGE 1955, 1). In 2010, the population of the Rio de Janeiro metropolitan area was 6.3 million (IBGE 2010a). Poor immigrants with little access to public services make up most of this population increase. They live in dense settlements off the infrastructure grid, generating a host of environmental externalities that might have been avoided with better planning and more equitable social policies, such as the destruction of "rivers, streams, lakes, mangrove swamps and beaches" as they "increasingly become the channels or depositories for domestic sewage" from informal urban settlements (Carvalho and Rossbach 2010). Making matters worse, regionally coordinated land use policies incorporating environmental management and protection concerns remain more aspiration than reality (Fernandes 2011).

The more than a thousand estimated *favelas* with nearly a half a million people living in "informal agglomerations" that now characterize the city vary widely in their degree of poverty and service deprivation (IBGE 2010b; *The Telegraph* 2011). They often lack municipal water and wastewater service provision, not to mention paved road access, trash pickup, and other public utilities. Moreover, the press of new immigrants for accommodation means that, absent active state intervention to provide housing, many people push farther into protected Atlantic Rainforest to build their precarious dwellings.

These realities have extreme negative consequences for the natural environment, since heavy rainfall has for generations sent untreated wastewater, unfiltered stormwater runoff, and assorted trash straight into the city's freshwater and saltwater resources. More recently, drug-trafficking gangs have occupied many *favelas* and rendered them inaccessible to state actors, making any attempt to reduce their environmental footprint by integrating them into city services even more difficult. The strength and frequency of winter rains have led to increasing landslides and accompanying loss of life. Recent efforts by the government to "pacify" the *favelas* to make them suitable for entry by state actors may bode well for service integration and reduce the negative environmental externalities they cause, although the efforts are controversial in other ways (UNHCR 2010). "Pacification" involves a scheduled military occupation of a crime-ridden *favela*, followed by infrastructural and other social improvements.

Along with the transfer of the Portuguese Crown's physical home, the monarchy also opened up Brazil to foreign commerce and laid the way for the country's commercial and industrial development in the 1800s. The environmental footprint of these activities was nowhere stronger than in Rio de Janeiro, the center of these efforts, once again setting in place a tension between development and the protection of Rio's physical environment that continues to this day. The years of the monarchy saw expanded commercial exploitation of Rio's resources, including the Bay of Guanabara and the development of a major port and shipping center. For centuries Rio de Janeiro thus was Brazil's economic base. In the generations following independence, the city became a magnet for mostly European and later internal Brazilian migrants seeking opportunity—a flood that continues, with most of those migrants arriving with few skills and receiving few to no government services. Again, this places an enormous strain upon the natural environment as the new arrivals compete for limited services in a resource-rich but fragile landscape.

Sustainability Challenges

Questions of social and economic inequality continue to interfere with the capacity of Rio de Janeiro to solve most major sustainability challenges. This can be seen with respect to four major issues, all of them deeply linked to infrastructure provision, namely, public transportation, clean water delivery, sewage management and disposal, and the consequences of urban sprawl on habitat destruction and resource degradation.

Water quality and sewage management are intricately related. For the reasons of human and industrial contamination described above, generations in the making, the Bay of Guanabara and other water resources had by the late 1980s become seriously polluted, causing public and environmental harms on a wide scale. To help address this situation, in the early 1990s the Inter-American Development Bank (IADB) led a consortium of lenders in contributing nearly US$1 billion for an ambitious, multiyear effort to clean up Guanabara Bay and, in particular, to provide improvements in clean water and sanitation services for millions of people in the nearly dozen municipalities that constitute metropolitan Rio de Janeiro. It is estimated that the bay receives the effluent from roughly 11 million inhabitants (IADB n.d., 1). Some parts of this effort have enjoyed success. The IADB reports that sewage treatment in the metropolitan region between 1996 and 2006 went from 15 percent to 44 percent, and water delivery service went from 25 percent to 80 percent. In 2011, the IADB authorized an additional US$640 million to fund this ongoing effort. Despite the improvements since the 1990s, sewage treatment rates clearly need to be a continuing area of focus, for both public and environmental health.

Public transport is another infrastructure area requiring attention. Like many South American megacities, bus service is widely available but chaotic. The urban sprawl of recent decades further means that many of the metro area's poorest residents travel two to three hours each direction, per day, to get to work, taking two or three buses each way. Further, Brazil's economic expansion since the late 1990s has meant that more people have disposable income, and they are spending it disproportionately on vehicle purchases; 2012 estimates indicate that there are 2.2 million vehicles on Rio's roads, forming great gridlocks along the major road networks and worsening air quality. Suburban trains are old and crowded and so offer limited relief (DETRAN 2012). The in-town subway system (the Metrô), while clean, efficient, safe, and relatively affordable, remains limited in physical extension. Transportation infrastructure improvements related to the World Cup and the Olympics, including expansion of bikeways around the city and along the shoreline, promise to help ease congestion and efficiency. The Brazilian government has allocated 1.3 billion reais (although the singular is *real*, the plural is *reais*) (US$ 70.7 billion) for a thirty-six-month project to add a bus rapid-transit line and a light-rail transit line to the city (Around the Rings 2012). Some critics of the Olympic-related transportation upgrades, however, harshly criticized the government for focusing on more car-dependent, highway-oriented infrastructure than on greener alternatives (Barnes 2012).

Outlook

Metropolitan Rio grew exponentially between 1950 and 2010. For a city so rich in environmental resources, from the biodiverse Atlantic Rainforest in which it sits to the rivers, lakes, bays, and oceanfront that wrap around and inside it, this kind of growth can be worrisome only for those concerned about the city's long-term sustainability. The city's (and country's) extreme income and social inequalities drive poor migrants to seek space for housing in environmentally sensitive areas, encroaching evermore into irreplaceable environmental resources. Since the early twenty-first century, this sometimes has led concerns for the environment to be used as an excuse for combating urban "invasions" by the poor, including proposals, for example, to build walls around *favelas*. As a result, it is sometimes difficult to disentangle proposals for clearheaded environmental protection from class-based social struggles.

Civil society organizations devoted to environmental protection increasingly have worked to bridge this gap, connecting calls to repopulate abandoned areas of the city center with housing, for example, in order to reduce urban expansion. This and other developments have increased Carioca appreciation of their city's extraordinary and fragile environmental resources. Furthermore, as incomes grow, so does cautious optimism that more people will begin to demand a cleaner and better-managed environment in Rio de Janeiro. A place that stopped polluting its bays and waterways with human and industrial waste, that reduced transportation congestion and pollution with efficient and pleasant mass transit, and that integrated the asphalted city into its spectacular tropical rain forest setting offering environmental leisure opportunities to all of its citizens regardless of income would truly be *a cidade maravilhosa*—the marvelous city.

Colin CRAWFORD
Tulane University Law School

See also Bogotá, Colombia; Brazil; Curitiba, Brazil; Ecotourism (the Americas); Labor; Mobility; Organization of American States (OAS); Public Transportation; Rio Earth Summit (UN Conference on Environment and Development); Social Movements (Latin America); Travel and Tourism Industry

FURTHER READING

Around the Rings. (2012, March 23). Funding for crucial Rio 2016 transportation projects secured. Retrieved March 30, 2012, from http://www.aroundtherings.com/articles/view.aspx?id=39584

Barnes, Taylor. (2012, March 8). Rio's Olympic land grab. Retrieved March 30, 2012, from http://www.csmonitor.com/World/Americas/Latin-America-Monitor/2012/0308/Rio-s-Olympic-land-grab

Buarque de Holanda, Sérgio. (1995). *Raízes do Brasil* [Roots of Brazil]. São Paulo, Brazil: Companhia das Letras.

Carvalho, Celso Santos, & Rossbach, Anaclaudia. (Eds.). (2010). *The City Statute of Brazil: A commentary*. São Paulo, Brazil: Ministry of Cities; Cities Alliance. Retrieved May 25, 2012, from http://www.citiesalliance.org/sites/citiesalliance.org/files/CA_Images/CityStatuteofBrazil_Eng_ForewordandTOC.pdf

Dean, Warren. (1995). *With broadax and firebrand: The destruction of the Brazilian Atlantic Forest*. Berkeley & Los Angeles: University of California Press.

del Rio, Vicente, & Siembieda, William. (Eds.). (2009). *Contemporary urbanism in Brazil: Beyond Brasilia*. St. Petersburg: University Press of Florida.

Departamento Nacional de Trânsito (DETRAN) [National Department of Traffic]. (2012). Frota 2012: Frota de veículos, por tipo e com placa, segundo os Municípios da Federação [Fleet 2012: Fleet of vehicles by type and plate, according to the Federation of Municipalities]. Retrieved March 17, 2012, from http://www.denatran.gov.br/frota.htm

do Prado Valladares, Licia. (2008). *A invenção da favela: Do mito de origem a favela.com* [The invention of the slum: The myth of the origin of favela.com]. Rio de Janeiro: Editora Fundação Getulio Vargas (FGV).

Energy Information Administration (EIA). (2012, February 28). Country analysis briefs: Brazil. Retrieved March 17, 2012, from http://www.eia.gov/emeu/cabs/Brazil/pdf.pdf

Fausto, Boris. (1999). *A concise history of Brazil*. Cambridge, UK: Cambridge University Press.

Fernandes, Edésio. (2011). *Policy focus report: Regularization of informal land settlements in Latin America*. Cambridge, MA: Lincoln Institute of Land Policy.

Fernandes, Edésio, & Moraes Valença, Márcio. (Eds.). (2004). *Brasil urbano*. Rio de Janeiro: MAUAD Editora.

Galindo-Leal, Carlos, & de Gusmão Câmara, Isben. (Eds.). (2003). *The Atlantic Forest of South America: Biodiversity status, threats, and outlook*. Washington, DC: Island Press.

Gall, Norman. (2011, February 24). Deepest oil part I. Retrieved April 5, 2012, from http://www.brazilinfocus.com/samba/energy-a-enterprise/81-energy-a-enterprise/221-deepest-oil.html

Gomes, Laurentino. (2008). *1808*. São Paulo, Brazil: Planeta.

Helena, Maria, & Alves, Moreira. (2004). São Paulo: The political and socioeconomic transformations wrought by the New Labor Movement in the city and beyond. In Josef Gugler (Ed.), *World cities beyond the West: Global development and inequality* (pp. 303–305). Cambridge, UK: Cambridge University Press.

Instituto Brasileiro de Geografia e Estatística (IBGE) [Brazilian Institute of Geography and Statistics]. (1955). Estado do Rio de Janeiro: Censo Demográfico [State of Rio de Janeiro: Demographic Census]. Rio de Janeiro: IBGE. Retrieved March 30, 2012, from http://biblioteca.ibge.gov.br/visualizacao/monografias/GEBIS%20-%20RJ/CD1950/CD_1950_XXIII_t1_RJ.pdf

Instituto Brasileiro de Geografia e Estatística (IBGE) [Brazilian Institute of Geography and Statistics]. (2010a). Sinopse do censo demográfico 2010: Rio de Janeiro [Synopsis of the 2010 demographic census: Rio de Janeiro]. Retrieved March 17, 2012, from http://www.censo2010.ibge.gov.br/sinopse/index.php?uf=33&dados=1

Instituto Brasileiro de Geografia e Estatística (IBGE) [Brazilian Institute of Geography and Statistics]. (2010b). Tabela 1: Domicílios particulares ocupados e população residente em domicílios particulares ocupados, total e em aglomerados subnormais, e número de aglomerados subnormais, segundo as Grandes Regiões, as Unidades da Federação e os municípios: 2010 [Table 1: "Occupied private households," and "Resident population occupying private households" divided into "Total" and "Substandard conglomerates," organized by "Major Regions," "Units of the Federation," and "Municipalities:" 2010]. Retrieved March 17, 2012, from http://www.ibge.gov.br/home/estatistica/populacao/censo2010/aglomerados_subnormais/tabelas_pdf/tab1.pdf

Inter-American Development Bank (IADB). (n.d.). Environmental sanitation program for municípios in the Guanabara Bay area. Retrieved March 17, 2012, from http://idbdocs.iadb.org/wsdocs/getdocument.aspx?docnum=36524119

Perlman, Janice. (2010). *Favela: Four decades of living on the edge in Rio de Janeiro*. Oxford, UK: Oxford University Press.

Riley, Charles. (2012, March 7). Brazil's economy tops United Kingdom's. Retrieved March 17, 2012, from http://money.cnn.com/2012/03/07/news/economy/brazil-gdp-united-kingdom/index.htm

Rio+20. (2012). Homepage. Retrieved May 25, 2012, from http://www.uncsd2012.org/rio20/index.html

Rio+20, The Future We Want. (2012). Homepage. Retrieved May 25, 2012, from http://www.un.org/en/sustainablefuture/

Rio 2016 Now. (2010). Rio is the main tourist destination in the South Hemisphere. Retrieved March 17, 2012, from http://www.rio2016.org.br/en/rio-2016-now/rio-de-janeiro-is-the-main-tourist-destination-in-the-south-hemisphere

Skidmore, Thomas E. (1999). *Brazil: Five centuries of change*. Oxford, UK: Oxford University Press.

The Telegraph. (2011). Rio favelas: Key facts and figures. Retrieved March 17, 2012, from http://www.telegraph.co.uk/news/worldnews/southamerica/brazil/8882701/Rio-favelas-key-facts-and-figures.html

The United Nations High Commissioner for Refugees (UNHCR). (2010). State of the world's minorities and indigenous peoples 2010: Brazil. Retrieved March 17, 2012, from http://www.unhcr.org/refworld/country,,MRGI,,BRA,,4c33311ec,0.html

United States Central Intelligence Agency (US CIA). (2012). CIA world factbook: Distribution of family income Gini index. Retrieved March 18, 2012, from https://www.cia.gov/library/publications/the-world-factbook/fields/2172.html

Valladares, Licia do Prado. (2008) *A invenção da favela* (2a ed.) [The invention of the favela (2nd ed.)]. Rio de Janeiro: Editora Fundação Getulio Vargas (FGV).

Weather Channel. (2012). Monthly averages for Rio de Janeiro, Brazil. Retrieved March 17, 2012, from http://www.weather.com/weather/wxclimatology/monthly/graph/BRXX0201

Zaluar, Alba, & Alvito, Marcos. (2004). *Um século de favela* (4a ed.) [A century of shantytowns (4th ed.)]. Rio de Janeiro: Editora Fundação Getulio Vargas (FGV).

Rio Earth Summit (UN Conference on Environment and Development)

The Earth Summit in Rio de Janeiro in 1992 temporarily occupied center stage on the world political scene, pushing the twin issues of human development and environmental conservation to the fore. But its actual achievements are open to question, as is the very concept of sustainable development it helped to popularize, not least through initiatives around a plan of action known as Agenda 21.

The United Nations Conference on Environment and Development (UNCED) was held in the Brazilian city of Rio de Janeiro in 1992. Situated in an area of dramatic landscapes with famous beaches, Rio is one of the largest cities in the Americas. Its rapid growth, its inequalities, and the environmental problems of both the city and Brazil as a whole, notably deforestation in Amazonia, make it representative of the kind of environment in which a fast-increasing percentage of the world's population lives. (For a critical assessment, see Ransom 1992.)

The Earth Summit, as the UNCED became widely known, was, in some ways, a rerun of the "Only One Earth" Stockholm conference twenty years earlier, with some of the same faces. The switch to the Southern Hemisphere for a venue, however, reflected the changing face of world politics in which countries such as Brazil, India, and China had become a more significant force than in 1972. At the time, the 1992 Earth Summit was the largest gathering of world leaders in history. There were 108 heads of state and government, with representatives of 178 nations attending, a great many more than had been at Stockholm (Earth Summit 1997). Some 2,400 nongovernmental organizations were also represented. A great many journalists were present, and thousands of individuals attended fringe events under the umbrella of the global forum.

Like the 1987 Brundtland Report (also known as *Our Common Future*) from the World Commission on Environment and Development (WCED), the Earth Summit reflected and emphasized the concept of sustainable development, assuming that socioeconomic development and environmental conservation can go hand in hand. This was in marked contrast to the notion of limits to growth popularized in the early 1970s by publications like *A Blueprint for Survival* (*The Ecologist* 1972) and the report to the Club of Rome titled *Limits to Growth* (Meadows et al. 1972), which stressed constraints on all expansion.

The main outcomes of the Earth Summit can be divided into three general categories: formal treaties, general statements of principle, and ongoing processes. The most significant accord was the United Nations Framework Convention on Climate Change (UNFCCC), relating to the growing threat from the greenhouse effect. It led, in turn, to the Kyoto Protocol of 1997, which set out targets for reductions in greenhouse gas emissions by the main industrialized countries. Other agreements covered the protection of indigenous tribal peoples and their lands. The Convention on Biological Diversity sought to protect endangered species (like the Kyoto Protocol, it was not signed by the United States) (Sovereignty International 1998). There was a statement of principle concerning deforestation, as well as a broader Earth Charter that laid down general guidelines for environmental protection such as the polluter-pays and the precautionary principles (which state that if a policy is suspected of causing harm and there is no scientific consensus, the burden of proof that it is safe falls on those taking the action).

Action Program

The so-called Agenda 21 action plan embodied the main legacy of the summit in terms of an ongoing process. The relevant document was some seven hundred pages long.

A Commission on Sustainable Development (CSD) was set up after the Earth Summit to meet annually. Its main function was to monitor and report on the implementation of agreements at all levels. Within Agenda 21, nine sectors of society, known as CSD major groups, were seen as critical for the development and implementation of relevant policies for sustainable development: business, youth, farmers, indigenous people, local authorities, nongovernmental organizations (NGOs), the scientific community, women, and workers, including trade unions. (See Lucas, Ross, and Fuller 2003 regarding local government and what became widely known as Local Agenda 21.)

Linked to this initiative but focusing on specific matters were the 1994 Conference on Population and Development in Cairo, the 1995 World Summit for Social Development in Copenhagen, the 1995 World Conference on Women in Beijing, and the 1996 Conference on Human Settlements (known as Habitat II) in Istanbul. A follow-up World Conference on Sustainable Development was held in Johannesburg ten years later. Various NGOs (from what is often called civil society) are linked in the Stakeholder Forum (Stakeholder Forum n.d.).

Also part of ongoing activity following the Earth Summit was the Global Environment Facility (GEF). It had been given a trial run the year before under the auspices of the World Bank, the United Nations Development Programme (UNDP), and the United Nations Environment Programme (UNEP). After the Earth Summit, the fund was restructured to become the main source of multilateral lending to developing countries and countries in transition for global environmental projects. In its first decade, the GEF provided $4.2 billion for projects (GEF n.d.).

Evaluating the Earth Summit

There are, perhaps inevitably, considerable differences of opinion regarding the value of the Earth Summit and the processes it initiated. Those differing evaluations might be subdivided into three areas of argument: the effectiveness of the Earth Summit and its initiatives in and of themselves; the structures and mechanisms the summit endorsed; and, finally, underlying conceptual issues surrounding the linkage of "environment" with "development." There is, of course, a history of failed global conferences and international treaties, ones that were either ineffective because the measures they agreed on were inadequate and/or because they were ignored by certain governments and other socioeconomic forces (the League of Nations is one example of a failed international effort).

There have also been success stories, ranging from the 1911 Fur Seal Treaty to the 1987 Montreal Protocol on the protection of the ozone layer from depleting substances (Barrett 2005). The successes, however, tend to focus on either a specific species or a discrete part of environmental systems. In the case of the ozone layer, there was a general and undeniable threat, with severe human health costs likely, from a narrow range of identifiable chemicals, ones that could be replaced without great upheaval. The protection of whole habitats, like tropical forests, rather than certain species in them, is clearly a much more complex challenge, not least where other and powerful interests would have to be curtailed (ranching, mining, biofuel plantations, and so forth). Even international protection of species with much appeal to humans, like whales and tigers, has been very difficult.

Judgment of the Earth Summit should be put in the context of this rather troubled history of international negotiation. The summit's task was very difficult given the wide range of problems it sought to address. In some cases, the very existence of the problems has been controversial, especially the notion of anthropogenic climate change (climate change caused by human actions). Other problems have been minimized. For example, the economist Julian Simon argued that problems like deforestation and mineral depletion are not as bad as claimed or are part of ongoing global change that is simply the way of the world. Given that the causes, consequences, and solutions for all the matters addressed by the Earth Summit fall unevenly across the planet, there was even greater possibility for debilitating conflict and compromise.

Marginalization

The summit generated a lot of media interest and certainly helped to push environmental issues to the fore. Yet it is questionable how long that effect lasted. Over the following two decades, issues like terrorism and war dominated the global agenda, to be joined by pressing— and diverting—economic concerns in the wake of the global financial crisis that began in 2008. Early in the following decade, governments were prioritizing conventional economic growth (sometimes prefixed with the word *sustainable*, sometimes not). In 2011, the US president Barack Obama, for example, rejected tighter controls over "smog" on economic grounds (BBC News 2011c). Simultaneously, the British government was seeking to relax planning controls that protected the countryside from developers, a measure that conservationists like the Campaign to Protect Rural England (2011) and the National Trust (2011) strongly opposed. (It might be seen as an achievement of the Earth Summit that the government claimed that the changes were a means of delivering "sustainable development.")

Rio+20

"Rio+20" is short for the 2012 United Nations Conference on Sustainable Development, held in Rio de Janeiro, Brazil, in June of 2012—twenty years after the 1992 Earth Summit in Rio. Rio+20 was heralded as an opportunity to define "The Future We Want," the name of a UN campaign tied to the conference to engage people in Rio+20 by talking about their ideas for the future.

Many people around the world anticipated this to be the largest UN conference in history. More than a hundred world leaders joined thousands of participants from businesses, nongovernmental organizations (NGOs), and other groups around the globe. There were two official themes to the discussions: how to build a green economy to achieve sustainable development, thereby lifting people out of poverty, and how to improve international coordination for sustainable development. With "green economy" hardly a clearly defined term and international coordination an ever-elusive goal, many people in the past have been critical of these themes as being too broad to produce specific outcomes.

The political process to negotiate the text that comes out of Rio+20 was ongoing since at least 2011, although plans and discussions were afoot for many years. Leading up to the conference, a sprawling draft text included many nations' pet projects and many points about which there was much disagreement. Despite weeks of negotiations to prepare for Rio+20, the outcome draft lacked focus and clearly defined scope—a precarious place to be so close to the conference.

Many, however, are not dwelling on the likelihood that Rio+20 will produce a political outcome, but see it as a historic opportunity to have a global conversation about the pathways we can take to achieve a more sustainable future—defined by the United Nations as "a future with more jobs, more clean energy, greater security, and a decent standard of living for all." Hundreds of parallel events in Rio de Janeiro that were not part of the official conference took place, offering forums for anyone to exchange ideas, to make plans, and to share their work. Time will tell what the legacy of this latest conference (which took place during final preparation of this volume) will be: we hope it will be a positive one.

The Editors

Perhaps the clearest symbol of the way environmental issues had become marginalized again was in Brazil, the very country that had hosted the Earth Summit, where a giant dam, the Belo Monte in Amazonia, opposed by both tribal peoples and environmentalists, was given the go-ahead in 2011. Meanwhile, in the same country, the so-called Forest Code had been watered down, threatening further deforestation (BBC News 2011a and 2011b).

Critics might argue that the Earth Summit's agreements and statements of principle amount to too little, too late. The UNFCCC and subsequent Kyoto Protocol notwithstanding, greenhouse gases thus continue to be emitted in excessive quantities, while the balancing sinks (ecosystem absorption and storage of gases like carbon dioxide) continue to contract, with the consequence that adverse climate change remains a growing threat (IPCC 2011).

The weaknesses of the summit's accords are illustrated by the issue of forest protection. The relevant agreement was not legally binding, simply open for signature like the UNFCCC (the latter signed by 154 countries). Furthermore, many of the habitats the agreement sought to protect were in poorer countries. But politicians from such regions argue that their countries ought to be compensated in return for setting aside forests and other lands threatened by development. National sentiment in these countries often holds that rich countries that have already achieved a certain level of development are trying to deny economic growth to less developed parts of the world.

Other documents, like the Earth Charter, were adopted without a vote, something that might trigger doubt about the strength of any resulting commitment. Generally there was a lack of hard targets and timetables by which they were to be achieved: "most are generalizations which are hard to define or measure, and hardly any of them are backed up by adequate resources" (Grubb 1993). In many of the UNCED documents, phrases like "as far as possible" occur repeatedly, ones so open to differing interpretations that they arguably become rather meaningless.

Missing Links

It might be further argued that the Earth Summit focused upon symptoms, not root causes. It discussed deforestation rather than the timber trade and the pulp industry or the lifestyles they feed, for example. More generally, the summit did not address the resource-intensive living patterns of the world's more materially affluent social groups. Many observers thought that the US political leadership in particular took the stance that the dominant lifestyle in the United States—both in terms of its environmental costs and of the global inequities it aggravates—was not up for negotiation. Any proposals that threatened that way of life thus were thrown out or so watered down as to become useless as a result of US opposition (Luke 1999).

That said, unsustainable consumption patterns are not confined to the United States. Indeed a notable trend since 1992 has been the growth of the new middle class in what was once perceived as a generally poverty-stricken developing world (Naím 2008). There, new middle classes are growing quickly, with ominous implications for environmental conservation. This whole issue of consumerism was largely ignored, however, at the official Earth Summit. Instead, rather wishful thinking that the newly industrialized countries might become environmentally sustainable economies seems to have underpinned discussions, though events led by NGOs were rather more realistic.

Whatever the nature, desirability, and costs of affluence, overpopulation is arguably still the biggest and most urgent of all the pressures undermining social and environmental systems. At the time of the summit, global population was about 5,480 billion. Less than twenty years later, sometime in autumn 2011, that number had passed the 7 billion mark (US Census Bureau 2011). That huge—and ongoing—increase can only have intensified many of the problems that the summit addressed, as well as made solutions harder. Yet silence about it from almost all parts of the Earth Summit, official and unofficial, was notable. Thus, the Friends of the Earth Verdict on the Earth Summit (Friends of the Earth 2002) did not even mention the issue.

Similarly, the so-called rights of nonhuman species were not addressed in ways that some wildlife conservationists would want. In the tradition of Aldo Leopold and his land ethic, the US biologist David Ehrenfeld, for example, has stressed the so-called Noah principle, namely, that long-standing existence in nature carries with it the right to continued existence (Ehrenfeld 1981). Most debate about biodiversity at the Earth Summit, however, was about the loss of potential resources to satisfy human wants, not human responsibility to share the Earth with other forms of life. Yet what is sometimes called the resourcist approach accepts the logic of sacrificing more parts of the biosphere if the cost/benefit calculations deem it expedient (Foreman 2007; Livingston 2007).

At a conceptual level, the Earth Summit certainly helped to popularize the concept of sustainable development. But perhaps part of the reason for that popularity is the concept's very looseness. Its meaning can range from the conventional—more economic growth with some fine-tuning to remove the worst side effects—to something much more radical, including new definitions of what human life should be about. Yet the summit did open the door to those bigger questions about life and Earth.

More practically, the dominant perspective of the Earth Summit did not address very real tensions between human development, however defined, and the conservation of the rest of nature. Life expectancy, health, housing, and education might figure close to the top of most lists of human development criteria, yet all have ecological price tags. An increase in human longevity, for example, by itself increases population pressures. The construction of new homes will at some point eat into prime farmland, woodland, and other habitat, no matter how smartly planned. Hospitals consume considerable energy and material resources while generating considerable waste, some of it toxic. A single university can generate 72,000 tonnes of carbon dioxide each year (Berners-Lee 2010, 156).

Even in terms of symptoms, there were some notable gaps on the agenda of the Earth Summit. It did address climate change, but not energy resources per se, let alone other side effects of fossil fuel, nuclear, and alternative energy systems. Though there had been an oil shock in 1973, the concept of what is known as peak oil (the point at which extraction of petroleum begins to decline) did not loom large at the Rio summit. Related matters like energy efficiency and more sustainable energy choices were often buried in Agenda 21 rather than being given the importance that the economy's very lifeblood might deserve. Trends like urban sprawl similarly did not receive due attention. Even the ongoing threat to the world's whale population was one of a number of issues fudged or sidelined because of opposition from countries with a vested interest in their continuation or growth (McNeill 2000, 354).

Economics and the Environment

Within Agenda 21, notions such as free trade, comparative advantage, and global integration are taken as givens. The dominant view would appear to be the one popularized by writers like Paul Hawken, Amory and L. Hunter Lovins, and Jonathon Porritt, namely, that the market (capitalism) was the "only game in town" and could be made to work for, rather than against, people and planet, a position also represented by the World Business Council on Sustainable Development.

Yet many, especially those in the antiglobalization movement, see capitalism as part of the problem, not the solution. Indeed, structures like the GEF and an ongoing role for the World Bank were attacked by some critics for putting the fox in charge of the henhouse (Hildyard 1993, 22). Indeed such critics have argued that corporate interests managed to dominate the Earth Summit, effectively emasculating it or bending it to their own goals (Chatterjee and Finger 1994) as, critics allege, they have done across society in general (Hertz 2001; Korten 2001).

Perhaps the most contentious matter is whether human society has already grown too large, both in terms of human numbers and per capita consumption. Some argue that over the long term the Earth can sustain a human population of just 2 billion with lifestyles similar to those found in western Europe today (Pimentel et al. 1994; Pimentel et al. 2010). (For more information see also the Population Matters website). By contrast, many at the official summit seem to have believed that better management, economic incentives, technological innovation, and greater efficiency can facilitate more physical growth.

Wherever the truth lies, it might be agreed that there are limits to what any global summit might achieve in the context of today's political and economic framework. The last word, however, should perhaps be given to the UNCED Secretary-General Maurice F. Strong (1992), who, in his opening address to the UNCED, observed that "the Earth Summit is not an end in itself but a new beginning . . . first steps on a new pathway."

A twentieth-anniversary conference, Rio+20, took place in Rio in June 2012 during production of this volume. (See the sidebar on the Rio+20 conference on page 260.) A greater focus on the "greening" of the economy was planned. In the previous twenty years, Brazil had experienced considerable economic growth, but many social and environmental problems awaited resolution. Increased awareness of the interaction between human development and ecological sustainability, however, surely owes a great deal to the original 1992 Earth Summit and the ones that have followed not just in Rio but also in Copenhagen, Beijing, and Johannesburg.

Sandy IRVINE
City of Sunderland College, Emeritus

See also Agriculture, Tropical (the Americas); Amazonia; Australia; Brazil; Canada; Caribbean; Central America; Corporate Accountability; Ecovillages; Forest Management; Marine Preserves; Multilateral Environmental Agreements (MEAs); New Zealand; Oceania; Parks and Protected Areas; Rio de Janeiro, Brazil; Southern Cone; United States

FURTHER READING

Barrett, Scott. (2005). *Environment and statecraft: The strategy of environmental treaty-making.* Oxford, UK: Oxford University Press.

British Broadcasting Company (BBC) News. (2010, February 19). Indonesia's new middle class. Retrieved November 4, 2011, from http://news.bbc.co.uk/1/hi/world/asia-pacific/8524373.stm

British Broadcasting Company (BBC) News. (2011a, May 25). Brazil passes "retrograde" forest code. Retrieved November 4, 2011, from http://www.bbc.co.uk/news/science-environment-13544000

British Broadcasting Company (BBC) News. (2011b, June 1). Brazil grants building permit for Belo Monte Amazon dam. Retrieved November 4, 2011, from http://www.bbc.co.uk/news/world-latin-america-13614684

British Broadcasting Company (BBC) News. (2011c, September 3). Obama scraps tighter smog rules. Retrieved November 4, 2011, from http://www.bbc.co.uk/news/world-us-canada-14771354

Berners-Lee, Mike. (2010). *How bad are bananas: The carbon footprint of everything.* London: Profile Books.

Campaign to Protect Rural England. (2011, July 25). Radical planning shake-up threatens green fields. Retrieved November 4, 2011, from http://www.cpre.org.uk/media-centre/latest-news-releases/item/2392-radical-planning-shake-up-threatens-green-fields

Chatterjee, Pratap, & Finger, Matthias. (1994). *The Earth brokers: Power, politics and world development.* London: Routledge.

Coonan, Clifford. (2011, May 26). The "Chaoyang Chariot" has become the car of choice for rich citizens in China. *The Independent.* Retrieved November 4, 2011, from http://www.independent.co.uk/life-style/motoring/features/the-chaoyang-chariot-has-become-the-car-of-choice-for-rich-citizens-in-china-2288996.html

Earth Summit. (1997). UN conference on environment and development (1992). Retrieved May 9, 2012, from http://www.un.org/geninfo/bp/enviro.html

The Ecologist. (Eds.). (1972). *A blueprint for survival.* Harmondsworth, UK: Penguin.

Ehrenfeld, David W. (1981). *The arrogance of humanism.* New York: Oxford University Press.

Elliott, Lorraine. (2004). *Global politics of the environment* (2nd ed.). Basingstoke, UK: Palgrave Macmillan.

Financial Times. (2011.) Asia: The rise of the middle class. Retrieved November 4, 2011, from http://www.ft.com/cms/s/0/5841236e-183a-11e0-88c9-00144feab49a.html#axzz1XeqnSE5n

Foreman, David. (2007, March 1). Around the campfire with David Foreman: The arrogance of resourcism. Retrieved November 4, 2011, from http://www.rewilding.org/pdf/campfiremarch107.pdf

Friends of the Earth. (2002). Earth Summit: Frequently asked questions. Retrieved March 13, 2012, from http://www.foe.co.uk/resource/briefings/earth_summit_faq.pdf

Global Environment Facility (GEF). (n.d.) Homepage. Retrieved January 29, 2012, from http://www.thegef.org/gef/home

Goldsmith, Edward, & Mander, Jerry. (2001). *The case against the global economy.* London: Earthscan.

Grubb, Michael. (1993). *The Earth Summit agreements: A guide and assessment; An analysis of the Rio '92 UN Conference on Environment and Development.* London, Earthscan.

The Guardian. (2008, January 10). India gears up for mass motoring revolution with £1,260 car. Retrieved November 4, 2011, from http://www.guardian.co.uk/india/story/0,,2238983,00.html

Halpern, Shanna. (1992). *United Nations Conference on Environment and Development: Process and documentation.* Retrieved November 4, 2011, from http://www.ciesin.org/docs/008-585/unced-home.html

Hawken, Paul; Lovins, Amory; & Lovins, L. Hunter. (2005). *Natural capitalism: Creating the next industrial revolution.* London: Earthscan.

Hertz, Noreena. (2001). *The silent takeover.* London: Arrow.

Hildyard, Nicholas. (1993). Foxes in charge of chickens. In Wolfgang Sachs (Ed.), *Global ecology: A new arena of political conflict* (pp. 22–35). London: Zed.

Intergovernmental Panel on Climate Change (IPCC). (2011). Homepage. Retrieved November 4, 2011, from http://www.ipcc.ch/index.htm

Johannesburg Summit. (2002). Progress since the Earth Summit. Retrieved November 4, 2011, from http://www.johannesburgsummit.org/html/media_info/pressreleases_factsheets/wssd2_progress_rio.pdf

Korten, David. (2001). *When corporations rule the world.* Sterling, VA: Kumarian Press.

Livingston, John. (2007). *Fallacy of wildlife conservation.* Toronto, Canada: McLelland and Stewart.

Lucas, Karen; Ross, Andrew; & Fuller, Sara. (2003, May 27). *Local Agenda 21, community planning and neighbourhood renewal.* London: Joseph Rowntree Foundation. Retrieved November 4, 2011, from http://www.jrf.org.uk/publications/local-agenda-21-community-planning-and-neighbourhood-renewal

Luke, Tim. (1999, January 29). A rough road out of Rio. Retrieved November 4, 2011, from http://www.cddc.vt.edu/tim/tims/Tim599.htm

McCrummen, Stephanie. (2008, September 7). Africa's new middle class embraces consumerism. *Washington Post.* Retrieved November 4, 2011, from http://articles.sfgate.com/2008-09-07/news/17160965_1_cell-phone-industry-sub-saharan-kenya

McKinsey Global Institute. (2007, May 19). Next big spenders: India's middle class. Retrieved November 4, 2011, from http://www.mckinsey.com/mgi/mginews/bigspenders.asp

McNeill, John Robert. (2000). *Something new under the sun: An environmental history of the twentieth century.* London: Penguin.

Meadows, Donella H.; Meadows, Dennis L.; Randers, Jørgen; & Behrens, William W., III. (1972). *The limits to growth: A report for the Club of Rome's project on the predicament of mankind.* New York: Universe Books.

Naím, Moisés. (2008, February 19). Can the world afford a middle class? *Foreign Policy.* Retrieved November 4, 2011, from http://www.foreignpolicy.com/articles/2008/02/19/can_the_world_afford_a_middle_class

National Trust. (2011, October 19). Government reform threatens green spaces. Retrieved November 4, 2011, from http://www.nationaltrust.org.uk/main/w-chl/w-countryside_environment/w-planning-landing.htm

Pimentel, David; Harman, Rebecca; Pacenza, Matthew; Pecarsky, Jason; & Pimentel, Marcia. (1994). Natural resources and an optimum human population. *Population and Environment, 15,* 347–369.

Pimentel, David, et al. (2010). Will limited land, water, and energy control human population numbers in the future? Retrieved May 8, 2012, from http://www.populationmatters.org/documents/population_numbers.pdf

Population Matters. (2012). Homepage. Retrieved March 13, 2012, from http://populationmatters.org/

Ransom, David. (1992, April). Keynote: Green justice. *New Internationalist, 230.* Retrieved April 22, 2012, from http://www.newint.org/features/1992/04/05/keynote/

Simon, Julian. (1981). *The ultimate resource.* Princeton, NJ: Princeton University Press.

Sovereignty International. (1998). How the Convention on Biodiversity was defeated. Retrieved May 9, 2012, from http://sovereignty.net/p/land/biotreatystop.htm

Stakeholder Forum. (n.d.). Homepage. Retrieved January 29, 2012, from http://www.stakeholderforum.org/sf/

Strong, Maurice. (1992, June 3). Opening statement to the Rio summit. Retrieved April 23, 2012, from http://www.mauricestrong.net/index.php/speeches-remarks3/36-rio2

Susskind, Lawrence E. (1994). *Environmental diplomacy: Negotiating more effective global agreements.* New York: Oxford University Press.

United Nations (UN). (1992). Documents: Key conferences. Retrieved November 4, 2011, from http://www.un.org/esa/dsd/resources/res_docukeyconf_eartsumm.shtml

United Nations Development Programme (UNDP). (2011). Human development index. Retrieved November 4, 2011, from http://hdr.undp.org/en/statistics/hdi/

United Nations Department of Economic and Social Affairs (UN DESA), Population Division. (2011). Homepage. Retrieved November 4, 2011, from http://www.un.org/esa/population/unpop.htm

United Nations (UN) General Assembly. (2010). Resolution adopted by the General Assembly. Retrieved March 13, 2012, from http://www.un-documents.net/ares64-236.pdf

United States (US) Census Bureau. (2011). World population summary. Retrieved November 4, 2011, from http://www.census.gov/population/international/data/idb/worldpopinfo.php

Rocky Mountains

The Rocky Mountains are a vast, complex biome that has been shaped by a long history of natural and cultural forces. Over the past two centuries, however, the sheer extent and magnitude of human activities have begun to alter this ancient calculus, marking our species as one of the most important forces of environmental change in the region. As we move deeper into the second decade of the twenty-first century, any consideration of the region's future sustainability must take into account rapidly changing demographic, economic, social, and ecological trends.

The Rocky Mountains are the second longest mountain system in the world (only South America's Andes Mountains are longer). Commonly known as the Rockies, they are comprised of more than one hundred individually named ranges that form a vast mountain chain extending some 5,000 kilometers or 30 degrees of latitude from northwestern Canada across much of the interior American West to northern New Mexico. The Rockies vary in width from about 100 to 600 kilometers, and summits vary in elevation from about 1,800 to 4,399 meters, the latter being the elevation of Mount Elbert, Colorado, the range's highest point. They are bordered by the Great Plains on the east and by a series of high plateaus and extensive basins on the west. The crest line of the Rockies forms the Continental Divide, which acts as a watershed boundary separating the flow of rivers east to the Atlantic Ocean from those west to the Pacific Ocean, south to the Gulf of Mexico, and north to the Arctic Ocean. Interestingly, some geographic features contribute flow in multiple directions. For example, Triple Divide Peak in Montana's Glacier National Park is so named because precipitation that falls on the peak flows to the Pacific, the Atlantic, or the Hudson Bay, depending on which side of the mountain it falls. Many of North America's largest rivers, including the Yukon, Fraser, Columbia, Missouri, Colorado, Arkansas, and Rio Grande have their headwaters in the Rockies.

Across this extensive and diverse biome, high population growth rates, changing land use patterns, the desire for environmental amenities, and global climate change all pose inescapable challenges for the region's long-term sustainability prospects. Among the most fundamental considerations is population growth. Since 1950, the population of the Rocky Mountain states and provinces has increased nearly threefold, reaching a total of just more than 21 million in 2010/2011. Over the past decade alone, the Rocky Mountain states and provinces have been among the fastest growing regions of the United States and Canada, with annual population growth rates equaling or exceeding the national average in each case. The fastest growing state or province during this period was Utah, which increased its population by 23.8 percent between 2000 and 2010/2011 (US Census Bureau 2010; Statistics Canada 2011).

This boom in population has influenced land use patterns in a number of important ways. In particular, as the structure of the region's economy has shifted away from extractive industries (like mining and logging) and more toward service-based industries and nonlabor sources (like investment and retirement income), two new patterns of land use have emerged across the Rockies. First, the metropolitan fringes of large cities such as Calgary, Denver, and Salt Lake City have expanded rapidly, creating far larger and more sprawling urban and exurban areas along the foot of the Rocky Mountains. Second, a pattern of low-density development has been spreading across rural areas, often far removed from the larger cities. This pattern is particularly evident around resort towns like Crested Butte or Vail, Colorado, or near national parks like Glacier or Yellowstone, where second homes and nonworking ranches have been built on large parcels of land. Although each of these patterns influences regional environments in distinct ways, they also share certain similarities, such as the way they drive habitat fragmentation, threaten wildlife, alter wildfire regimes, and reshape regional hydrology (Baron 2002; Flores 2001; Wyckoff and Dilsaver 1995).

Tied up with these changing land use patterns and the region's population boom are social trends. The beauty, the perceived naturalness, and the wildness of the Rocky Mountain region have long attracted people, but recently this trend has accelerated. As US and Canadian societies have become more affluent and mobile and as the economic structure of the region has changed, more people have poured into the Rockies than ever before. With them have come all the accoutrements of modern life—roadways, infrastructure, and commercial establishments—that pose challenges to maintaining the very aesthetic and ecological characteristics that attracted people to the region in the first place (Baron 2002; Flores 2001; Wyckoff and Dilsaver 1995). Sustainable development in the Rockies, as in other corners of the globe, must involve not only ecological considerations but also a deeper understanding of the social trends that drive land use patterns and planning.

In addition to the challenges posed by changing demographic, economic, and social trends, the Rocky Mountain region also faces many issues linked to global climate change. Despite marked complexity and variability across the US and Canadian Rockies, overall historical climate trends suggest increases in annual and seasonal precipitation as well as increases in the mean minimum temperature over the past century. These changes already have begun to influence the region's hydrology, vegetation patterns, and wildlife in both linear and nonlinear ways. Although climate models remain the subject of intense debate, especially when applied at the regional level or to complex mountainous terrain, they do suggest that climate change will be part of the Rocky Mountain's future (Baron 2002). Studying the inherent complexity of climate change is a powerful reminder that working toward a sustainable future in the Rocky Mountains will not be simple and must involve a deep and meaningful consideration of both natural and cultural forces.

George VRTIS
Carleton College

See also Andes Mountains; Appalachian Mountains; Canada; Columbia River; Ecotourism (the Americas); Forest Management; Mackenzie River; Mississippi and Missouri Rivers; Parks and Protected Areas; Phoenix, United States; Rural Development (the Americas); Travel and Tourism Industry; United States; Yellowstone to Yukon Conservation Initiative (Y2Y)

FURTHER READING

Baron, Jill S. (Ed.). (2002). *Rocky Mountain futures: An ecological perspective.* Washington, DC: Island Press.

deBuys, William. (1985). *Enchantment and exploitation: The life and hard times of a New Mexico mountain range.* Albuquerque: University of New Mexico Press.

Flores, Dan. (2001). *The natural West: Environmental history in the Great Plains and Rocky Mountains.* Norman: University of Oklahoma Press.

Statistics Canada. (2011). 2011 census profile. Retrieved June 1, 2012, from http://www12.statcan.gc.ca/census-recensement/index-eng.cfm

United States (US) Census Bureau. (2010). United States census 2010: Guide to state and local census geography. Retrieved June 1, 2012, from http://2010.census.gov/2010census/

Wyckoff, William. (1999). *Creating Colorado: The making of a Western American landscape, 1860–1940.* New Haven, CT: Yale University Press.

Wyckoff, William, & Dilsaver, Lary M. (1995). *The mountainous West: Explorations in historical geography.* Lincoln: University of Nebraska Press.

Rural Development (the Americas)

Rural development refers to substantive improvements in life quality for residents of nonmetropolitan areas. Often rural development is understood as synonymous with economic growth when, in fact, it refers to equitable growth in addition to meaningful improvements in public and emotional health, social networks, empowerment, and the environment. A variety of theoretical approaches have been developed since the 1960s to explain why some places experience more development than others.

Rural development, and the assessment of its key economic and social considerations, is an important and widely debated phenomenon. There are historical, theoretical, and contextual distinctions between rural development in North America and Latin America. Often Mexico is identified as part of North America, but for organizational purposes here, Mexico will be included in the discussion of Latin America, while "North America" will refer to the United States and Canada. Rural tourism is used in promoting rural development in these areas, and social capital and community assets also play an important role in sustaining rural development.

Definition

Development is a term that means different things to different people. All too often, development is used as shorthand for economic growth. Policy makers and representatives of the global development industry generally have the promotion of economic growth as one of their primary objectives, and development therefore becomes a euphemism for strictly economic activities such as increasing commodity exports, improving household income levels, and alleviating poverty. The economist Herman Daly (1993, 268) questions this conflation of growth and development and offers a simple but important distinction. "When something grows, it gets bigger. When something develops it gets different." Development is not growth, although growth may constitute one aspect of development. Development, simply put, is improvement in the quality of life of individuals in a locality, which includes environmental concerns such as clean water and air as well as the equitable distribution of environmental burdens.

In the United States, there is also some question about what precisely constitutes rurality. Is a place determined to be rural by virtue of its culture, demography, economy, or some mix of these? Most often we define rurality in terms of population density. The US Census Bureau, for example, defines settlements as rural if they have fewer than 2,500 residents (USDA 2007). But the economic activities that predominate in a place, such as agriculture, and the agrarian culture of certain communities also commonly define rurality.

These questions regarding the definition of rural have become increasingly salient in recent years in the Americas. In Latin America, urban growth has driven metropolitan areas outward into previously rural zones at a rapid rate, changing the rural landscape. In the United States, as retirees and vacationers flock to the lakes and mountains of, among other regions, the Intermountain West, real estate development explodes, and the rural character of these places changes. Not only do such real estate booms transform local culture, but they also have contradictory impacts on the natural environment. On the one hand, the importance of natural amenities as a draw for visitors can lead to the protection and enhancement of these features of the landscape. On the other hand, real estate development can degrade the air and water quality and fracture ecosystems. Also in the United States, tourism and service industries are increasingly supplanting traditional rural industries such as mining and agriculture, and much of that investment capital in mining and agriculture is moving south into Latin America. So while the mining sector is shrinking in the United States, it is growing in Latin America, transforming agrarian communities into mining communities. In short, many rural places in the Americas, for different but related reasons, are undergoing cultural, economic, and demographic transformations that drive social scientists to question our old, simple typology of the terms *urban*, *suburban*, and *rural*.

Despite demographic trends that might suggest otherwise, rural underdevelopment is still a major issue that requires redress in the Americas. In Latin America, the majority of the population still lives in rural areas, whereas in the United States only about 20 percent of its citizens live in rural zones (World Bank 2008). On both continents, however, populations are rapidly urbanizing, and by 2020, Latin America is projected to be predominantly urban (World Bank 2008). Furthermore, since the 1990s, poverty has grown faster in urban settings than in rural settings in North and Latin America, reversing a long-standing trend (Brown and Swanson 2003; World Bank 2008). This change has more to do with unchecked urban growth than it does with substantive poverty alleviation in rural areas. Despite these trends however, rural residents on both continents still tend to have lower average incomes and lower educational attainment. Further, by virtue of the relative isolation of rural places, rural residents lack the access to the resources of upward mobility that their urban counterparts possess. Finally, since rural areas contain fragile ecosystems, biodiversity, and immense natural beauty, environmental protections in rural areas are particularly important.

In addition to economic growth and the satisfaction of basic needs (e.g., nutritious food in sufficient quantities, clean water, shelter, and basic material satiation), there are seven key criteria for evaluating rural development: (1) public health, (2) emotional ties to friends and family, and general emotional health, (3) civic strength, (4) empowerment, (5) educational attainment, (6) social equity, and (7) environmental sustainability.

For the purposes of this article, these criteria have been collapsed into three broad areas, which will be dealt with individually: economic, social, and environmental development. But first, for a theoretical understanding of development, it is important to briefly discuss the legacy of Latin American scholars.

Theories and Policies of Development in Latin America

Latin America has bequeathed us most of our theoretical interpretations of underdevelopment. Underdevelopment (sometimes referred to as uneven development) refers to the simple observation that some countries have lower development indicators than other countries—lower literacy and educational attainment rates, lower rates of maternal and child health, lower per capita incomes, and the like. Within one country, some communities often have lower development outcomes than other, similar communities. Explaining the simple fact of uneven development has proved a complex matter, and experts have introduced many theories since the 1950s to explain this phenomenon.

The earliest explanations for underdevelopment blamed environmental aspects of places for poor development performance. They argued that poor countries lacked the soil, climate, hydrological, mineral, and fuel resources to initiate the development process. In the 1950s, modernization theory emerged, which suggested that nation-states undergo a linear process from subsistence to industrial modernity, and that development was a matter of will and intelligence. In the late 1960s, scholars in Latin America began to develop a set of ideas known as dependency theory. These *dependentistas*, as they were called, were responding to the modernization theory's explanations for underdevelopment at the time, which blamed poor countries themselves for their poverty.

The Latin American *dependentistas* felt that these formulations did not capture their experiences and sought to formulate an alternative explanation. Dependency theory suggests that underdevelopment was a product of forces external to the nation-state—that the countries of Latin America were being kept poor by imperialist neighbors to the North rather than by simply having poor soil and lack of drive. World-systems analysis, emerging in the 1970s, suggested, like dependency theory, that dynamics external to the nation-state were principal causes of underdevelopment. World-systems analysis suggested that underdevelopment stemmed from the tendency in the world-system for disproportionate profits in the manufacture and marketing of commodities to accrue to the more advanced processing stages, rather than the extractive and early processing stages. Therefore, economies predicated on primary industries were prevented from industrializing and, in effect, were kept poor.

This set of ideas led these thinkers to suggest that the solution to underdevelopment in Latin America was to replace importing goods from other countries with domestic production. This policy approach became known as *import substitution industrialization* and was widely implemented in Latin America in the 1960s and 1970s. In many of the larger economies of Latin America such as Brazil, Argentina, and Mexico, this approach was generally effective at producing independence and industrialization. Across the board, however, it led to a great deal of borrowing and high levels of indebtedness, a major factor in the economic recession in Latin America in the 1980s, known as the "lost decade." Inflation during the late 1970s and early 1980s caused these loans to become more expensive. At the same time, falling prices for primary commodities made it more difficult for Latin American countries to repay these loans. These conditions set off a chain reaction throughout Latin America of epidemic unemployment, stagnant growth, and dropping real incomes. Rural communities in particular felt this economic crisis most sharply, and the rural development gains of the previous decade were lost.

At the same time, the United States was enduring a farm crisis for many of the same reasons. In the 1970s high commodity prices had encouraged US farmers to take on large amounts of debt to expand their acreage and update their agricultural technology, but high inflation and dropping commodity prices in the 1980s meant that when those debts came due, farmers were unable to pay. The 1980s saw a net population loss in US rural areas as a result.

In Latin America, the so-called lost decade led to the abandonment of import substitution industrialization and the adoption of policies derived from another theoretical approach to underdevelopment—the liberal economic approach. This idea suggests—in stark contrast to dependency and world-systems formulations—that more trade and more engagement with the world economy, rather than less, will improve development performance. According to the liberal approach—also referred to as neoliberalism or the Washington Consensus—governments must allow for unrestricted trade between their countries and other nations, encourage foreign direct investment, privatize any government-owned companies, limit social programs, and encourage decentralization. This set of policies was widely implemented with mixed success. In Latin America a growing middle class began to enjoy newfound affluence, but scores of rural peasants saw disproportionately modest gains or were left out altogether.

Starting around the year 2000, yet another transformation in development thinking and policy in Latin America has taken place. The uneven results of the neoliberal turn have led to a more recent turn toward stronger state intervention in the market economy, state-led planning for development, and expanded social programming. This change has been referred to as the "new developmental state."

Despite the variety of contradictory theories that have been mobilized to explain underdevelopment, economic growth and per capita income remain universally important.

Economic Considerations

Economic development is a key part of rural development more generally construed. Economic development is the expansion of opportunities for people to participate in the formal economy along with increasing returns to workers from economic production. There are three traditional sectors of the rural economy: agriculture, extractive industries, and tourism. The agricultural sector historically has dominated rural economies. These sectors vary in importance between North America and Latin America. The service sector, such as "big box" retail and restaurants, is also becoming increasingly important in many rural areas of North America.

In Latin America, agriculture is still the predominant economic activity in rural areas, and most agriculture is still smallholder agriculture. Smallholder agriculture is household-owned and -operated small-scale farming, primarily intended for subsistence and secondarily to sell surplus in local markets. Returns to peasant smallholder agriculture are minimal, and this sector does not offer a meaningful path out of poverty for peasants in Latin America.

In the 1980s, through government rural education programs—known as the Cooperative Extension Service—and initiatives of international development cooperation, peasant farmers in Latin America were encouraged to cultivate so-called nontraditional agricultural exports as an alternative to subsistence farming. The idea was that peasant farmers should use their agricultural know-how and land to produce export crops of higher value than the subsistence crops they traditionally cultivated. In particular, decorative flowers and high value vegetable crops, like broccoli and snow peas, were targeted. The results were uneven, and although this shift did result in high rates of short-term economic growth in some cases, over the longer term, the growth was not sustained. In the end the transition created opportunities for large landholders and agricultural elites to further consolidate their market power by capturing disproportionate shares of the nontraditional export markets (Barham et al. 1992).

In North America, over the past half century, however, the importance of agriculture in contributing to rural economic development has declined. In part, the globalization of agricultural commodity markets has driven prices down for these products. Also, in part, the mechanization of agriculture has made small-scale farming less competitive and has meant that industrial farming requires fewer workers and thus contributes less to job creation. This has meant that even as agricultural yields in the United States have increased, the number of farms and people farming has fallen precipitously. The number of farms in the United States dropped from 7 million in 1934 to 2 million in 2002 (Vias and Nelson 2006, 75–102). Because of the low price for agricultural goods and the high cost of labor, farming is not a profitable activity in the United States. Therefore, the federal government channels massive subsidies to farmers, without which most farmers would not stay in business.

The extractive industries—mining, logging, fishing, quarrying, and petroleum extraction—make up the second sector of the traditional rural economy. Again, this sector does not lend itself to equitable rural economic development. First, because extraction works only where there are resources to extract, not all rural areas can capitalize on this sector equally. Second, these extractions are often nonrenewable resources or resources that do not renew as quickly as they are drawn down, which means that eventually they will stop producing, so rural economies predicated on extraction will suffer. Economists refer to this dilemma as the boom-and-bust cycle. North America—both the United States and Canada—has historically been a world leader in mining. Since the 1990s, however, the amount of investment in mining in North America has diminished, while in Latin America mining has increased dramatically as a result. The growth of mining in Latin America has had mixed results, providing new employment opportunities to rural residents but also transforming their economies and landscapes and threatening the natural environment.

Rural parts of Latin America have witnessed a great deal of social conflict in recent years around the growth of the extractive industries. In Chile, Peru, Ecuador, southern Mexico, and much of Central America, social movements have arisen to oppose mining. In El Salvador and Costa Rica, governments have even gone so far as to effectively ban metal mining (Collins 2009; Reuters 2010).

As agriculture and mining have lessened in importance and productivity, rural communities have begun to look to varying forms of rural tourism to diversify their economies and improve their incomes. Rural tourisms, what the US ecotourism expert Martha Honey (2008) refers to as "experiential tourisms," have increased dramatically since the 1990s. Residents of urban areas increasingly seek rural environments as a means of leisure and a way of getting "back to nature." This interest presents an economic opportunity for certain rural areas. These rural tourisms include agricultural tourism (or agritourism), ecological tourism (or ecotourism), and culinary tourism. Agritourism—farm recreational experiences such as farm meals, corn mazes, and pumpkin picking—is most popular in rural parts of the United States. Similarly, culinary tourism—travel to experience culture and cuisine together—is growing in popularity in the United States as well. Wine tourism in California is a good example of this phenomenon.

Latin America has not witnessed significant growth in agritourism or culinary tourism, but ecotourism has grown considerably. Many of the world's most popular ecotourism destinations are in Latin America—places such as Costa Rica and the Galapagos Islands, for example. Ecotourism is rural tourism intended to address issues of rural underdevelopment and ecosystem degradation simultaneously. The International Ecotourism Society (TIES) defines ecotourism as: "responsible travel to natural areas that conserves the environment and improves the wellbeing of local people" (TIES 2012). Ecotourism has become a common term over the past two decades, which has caused large tourism operators and real estate developers to appropriate the term as a marketing tool for tourism that does not qualify. For these reasons, ecotourism researchers advocate third-party certification strategies, like those for organic food and fair trade products, to guarantee the legitimacy of ecotourism destinations (Honey 2008). Some scholars criticize ecotourism for having negative cultural impacts on host communities and privileging local elites over the general population (King and Stewart 1996).

In addition to agriculture, extraction, and tourism, remittance income has also become a pillar of the rural economy in certain parts of Latin America. A significant percentage of rural residents in Mexico and northern Central America (Guatemala, Honduras, and El Salvador) have emigrated to the United States, and to Canada to a lesser extent, in search of work. These immigrant workers regularly remit a percentage of their income back to their families and communities in their source countries. This process is referred to as *remittances,* and in some places remittances constitute the majority of income. Northern Mesoamerica sources a disproportionate number of immigrant workers from Latin America to the United States simply because of the push/pull of proximity and need. Furthermore, formal government programs, such as the US government's Bracero Program, which imported

Mexican agricultural guest workers from the 1940s until the 1960s, helped develop social networks that have continued to facilitate emigration, both legal and illegal, from Mexico through the first decade of the twenty-first century. In El Salvador, the introduction of the US dollar as the predominant official currency has facilitated greater numbers of emigrants to the United States, and as a result of US dependence on immigration, remittance income is now nearly 20 percent of the gross domestic product.

In sum, although traditional rural enterprises—agriculture and extractive industries—continue to expand yields, they employ fewer people, face diminishing profit margins, and contribute less to rural development in 2012 than in the past. Alternative economic development strategies such as niche agriculture or rural tourism can represent a meaningful path for communities with the right amenities. Rural residents should strive to diversify their economies so that they are not too dependent on just one industry and are therefore less vulnerable to the boom-and-bust cycle and the price fluctuations of primary commodity markets. Further, these communities should strive to put programs in place that distribute gains from economic development evenly. These processes are easier to put in place when a community possesses strong social ties and civic ideals. Additionally, rural tourism is largely dependent upon the availability of natural amenities in a locality, an environmental issue.

Social Considerations

Research on rural development indicates that economic development initiatives have the most broadly based and long-lasting impacts in communities with strong civic networks in place (Hunt 2000). Where social linkages are strong between individuals and associations in a locality, the gains to economic growth are distributed more evenly, which allows for more capital to circulate through the local economy, further promoting equitable development. Additionally, in civically active communities—communities where a wide swath of the population participates in community affairs—political institutions are more democratic and more effectively represent the interests of the community at large rather than the interests of a few powerful individuals (Putnam 1993). There are two general ways of conceptualizing the importance of social ties and civic activity for rural development—the concept of social capital and the asset-based approach to community development.

These ideas about civil society and its value for democracy and development come predominantly from the United States. Alexis de Tocqueville, a French aristocrat who traveled the United States in the early nineteenth century, was struck by the richness of civic life. His best known work, *Democracy in America*, documents the forms of civic life peculiar to the United States that he observed during his travels and their connection to equality and democracy. In the twentieth century, US philosophers such as John Dewey and, later, Jane Jacobs wrote prominently in this tradition regarding the robust forms of civic life in the United States and their bearing on the quality of life.

Social capital is the value embedded in social networks. It is made up of social obligations, expectations, and sanctions as well as norms of trust and reciprocity. The denser and more extensive the social networks in a locality, the better the prospects for rural development. This is the case for several reasons. First, social capital can generate financial and material returns to both individuals and whole communities. Individuals can benefit from the transmission of information regarding economic opportunities, and communities can benefit because strong social networks insulate places from the challenges of economic downturns. When commodity prices plunge or the factory leaves town, individuals with dense social networks can rely on one another to weather the storm. Second, high levels of social capital can reinforce collective identity, which can boost self-esteem and provide a basis for collective action on behalf of rural development. Third, social capital, because it promotes more involvement and engagement, can improve democratic institutions and promote equity.

Despite the fact that this intellectual tradition was codified in the US context, this set of ideas is applied effectively to Latin America. Mobilizing social capital is a particularly apt rural development strategy in Latin America because many of the primary destroyers of social capital are more pronounced in the developed countries. There may, therefore, be greater levels of social capital in rural parts of Latin America that simply require operationalization. Additionally, social capital is inexpensive. Unlike large-scale development projects that require substantial investments of financial capital, social capital, although it takes time to generate, requires no hardware for it to be actualized. In this sense it constitutes an ideal strategy for rural communities that are cash poor but possess rich social networks. Many rural communities in Latin America are embedded in transnational social networks that provide paths for emigration and job acquisition abroad. This is another key way in which social networks facilitate rural economic development.

Like social capital, the asset-based approach to community development suggests that local capacity and self-help are the most effective means to equitable and sustainable rural development. For decades the standard community development approach was outside technical assistance based on a needs assessment. Outside experts would conduct an inventory of deficiencies and problems to develop programs to address these needs. In the early 1990s, some researchers began to advocate an asset-based alternative to the needs assessment (Kretzmann and McKnight 1993). They argued that the focus on needs manufactured a culture of dependency on outside experts and a sense of inadequacy on the part of residents. Social service (e.g., literacy, nutrition) organizations made up of outside experts treated residents like clients, for example, whereas locally driven associations saw residents as citizens. They further argued that the needs-based approach overlooked the valuable local assets that could be effectively leveraged for community development. These assets, for researchers John Kretzmann and John McKnight (1993), focused on civic organizations (social capital), and the skills and capacities of locals (human capital).

In North America, the asset-based approach has generally been applied in urban areas, although it translates effectively to rural areas as well. The best known case of sustained asset-driven development in the United States is the Dudley Street Neighborhood Initiative in the Roxbury area of Boston, Massachusetts, which brought together diverse groups of residents, using participatory methods and savvy political engagement to achieve a dramatic transformation in the community, particularly with respect to the environment. Their first success was convincing the city to clean up illegal dump sites that created a public health hazard in their neighborhood (Medhoff and Sklar 1994).

Building on the work of Kretzmann and McKnight, but specifically with rural regions in mind, rural sociologists Cornelia Flora and Jan Flora (2004) elaborated the community capitals framework in which they identify seven types of community assets that are important for rural development: social capital, human capital, built capital (infrastructure), cultural capital, natural capital (natural amenities), financial capital, and political capital (power and influence). As the "stock" of one of these asset pools increases, it potentially flows between stocks of other community capitals, increasing stocks of other capitals as well. This process can create a beneficent upward spiral, enhancing community vitality in three key areas: economic development, environmental quality, and public health (Emery and Flora 2006).

In rural Latin America traditional natural resource management techniques such as polycropping (planting a variety of types of crops together), common-pool forest management, and gravity-flow irrigation systems persist and complement more modern, technological approaches to natural resource management. The persistence of traditional resource management techniques, particularly in rural areas with large indigenous populations such as southern Mexico, western Guatemala, the Andean region, and parts of Colombia, exemplifies the asset-based approach to sustainable rural development in Latin America.

In addition to the ideas of social capital and local assets, *grassroots development* is another common term that conforms to the self-help ideal of most rural development approaches. In the 1980s, there was a great deal of attention to the so-called grassroots approach to rural community development in Latin America—an approach in local beneficiaries, rather than outside experts, developed and carried out initiatives. The Inter-American Foundation (IAF), an institution funded by the US Congress that promotes grassroots development in Latin America, was a leader in publishing research and case studies on grassroots development throughout the 1980s. Shifting priorities and budget cuts, however, have meant that since 2000 the IAF focuses principally on funding proposals for local grassroots development. The IAF continues to publish its journal, *Grassroots Development,* but it is not as widely read today as it was in the 1980s and 1990s.

In addition to economic factors, then, important social factors contribute to sustainable rural development. These include high levels of public involvement on the part of residents, dense social networks, and a recognition and willingness to capitalize on the various social assets or community capitals present in a locality.

Environmental Considerations

A variety of environmental issues are crucial considerations in rural development. These include the variability of natural amenities between localities, the tensions between resource conservation and resource development, and solid waste disposal.

As discussed earlier, much of the success of tourism-led rural development is contingent upon the availability of natural amenities in rural places. Natural amenities include unique, nonreproducible aspects of localities such as rivers, lakes, mountains, forests, and climate, which draw in visitors or in-migrants. Culture, history, and tradition, while not strictly natural, are also important amenities. Most of the rural areas in the United States that have experienced population and economic growth since the 1990s have been high amenity regions. This means that not all rural localities are equal in terms of their ability to capitalize on tourism as a development strategy.

Although mineral and timber resources do not draw tourists and retirees like beautiful landscapes, these resources are an important source of rural development for many rural regions—often regions that have lower tourism potential. In such places, there are often tensions between efforts to exploit natural resources to promote rural development and efforts to protect the biophysical environment. In rural Latin America, where peasant agriculture is still quite common, this tension is particularly pronounced because peasant agriculturalists derive their livelihoods from the natural resources in their communities, yet many of these communities are in biodiverse and/or fragile ecosystems that should be conserved.

These tensions usually manifest themselves as conflicts between conservationists and locals regarding resource use, often referred to as the "people in parks" problem. In many of these biologically diverse areas, governments and conservation organizations have sought to declare protected areas to guard unique ecosystems, thus limiting local peoples' access to forest resources. In some cases rural peoples are prevented from harvesting timber and firewood, hunting, fishing, farming, and foraging for medicinal plants in areas to which they have historically had access. This creates significant social conflict and often results in "invasions" of parks and protected areas.

Much research has been devoted over the past two decades to addressing this issue (Terborgh et al. 2002). On the one hand, it is crucial to protect biodiverse, fragile, and unique ecosystems. On the other hand, impoverished and marginalized rural peoples should not be penalized with their livelihoods because of where they happen to live. One of the more recent solutions, which has had some success in Latin America, is called *payment for ecosystem services*. In effect, rural peoples are compensated, through cash transfers, for agreeing to give up access to parks and protected areas. The logic of this model is that the forest itself provides services such as carbon sequestration, water retention, erosion prevention, and the like, all of which have an economic value, and because the forest cannot spend the money it earns sequestering carbon, neighboring settlements should be compensated. The problem with this model, like many rural development approaches, is that it solves only short-term conflict. It does not address the root issues of the global population–resources mismatch and the added pressure on natural resources from multinational extractive companies. Further, it can create economic dependencies on the part of beneficiaries.

A third key environmental consideration in rural development, which is particularly pronounced in Latin America, regards managing and disposing of the additional solid waste and wastewater that accumulate during periods of high development. Responsibility for solid waste collection and treatment falls generally to the municipal government. In many countries of Latin America, however, collection is intermittent and incomplete, and treatment is minimal. Many rural hamlets are still inaccessible by motor vehicle, making waste collection impossible. Further, waste collection is an opt-in service that confers an additional fee, which many residents are unwilling or unable to pay. Therefore, informal dumping of solid waste in ravines or other clandestine locations is commonly practiced and widely accepted. This problem is exacerbated by the rugged, craggy, and highly eroded terrain that characterizes many rural areas of Latin America as well as the fact that potable water often comes directly from springs or rivers and receives little treatment. This means that clandestine dumps often contaminate already tenuous water sources and create public health problems.

Outlook

Rural development refers to any variety of processes that work toward the substantive improvement of life quality for residents of rural places. Rural development poses particular challenges compared to urban development. These challenges include the limited variety of economic activities available, which makes rural regions more vulnerable to economic downturns, the social isolation, the geographic distance from the resources and opportunities of the urban environment, and the lower returns to the primary industries that characterize rural regions. These factors can lead to underdevelopment of rural areas, in which incomes, educational levels, and public health indices are all lower, on average, than in cities.

The populist legacy of civic networks in the United States allows rural areas to rely on social networks and social capital effectively in the face of economic downturns. The shift away from agriculture and mining and toward the service sector in rural America, however, has meant a greater degree of differentiation between capitalists and wage workers. This separation occurs because service jobs are largely "bad" jobs in the sense that they do not provide many opportunities for advancement. Rural communities in the United States possess many underdeveloped social resources and assets, or community capitals, that can serve as the basis for rural revitalization, but that must be formalized and further developed. Natural amenities or natural capital are present in certain rural regions more than in others in the United States. The economist David McGranahan (1999) documents the extent to which amenities such as climate, varying topography, and proximity to surface water drive population growth in the United States. This phenomenon has taken place disproportionately in the western and southwestern regions of the country, while low amenity places are at a disadvantage in the new rural economy.

In Latin America, rural regions are still largely dependent on agriculture and also increasingly on investment in the extractive sectors, particularly metal mining, petroleum, and natural gas. The tourism and service industries are diminutive in Latin America compared with North America, although ecotourism is growing in certain amenity-rich localities. Additionally, since the 1990s, remittance income has become profoundly important. In Mesoamerica, this income comes from emigrants to the United States and Canada. In other parts of Latin America, south-south migration into middle-income countries or internal migration from rural to urban areas drives this trend. While emigration does signal substantial income growth for migrant source regions, it also confers a "brain drain" on the sending communities. Emigrants are disproportionately well educated and well capitalized, which allows them to emigrate. Their departure, however, means that their entrepreneurial contributions to local development are missing. In general, rural areas in Latin America are less stratified by income level than their North American counterparts. Therefore, gains to rural development accrue more evenly. Finally, social assets and resources receive less attention in Latin American rural development than they do in the United States. They nevertheless constitute a meaningful set of resources for development, and development practitioners in Latin America should capitalize on these assets.

Rural areas must continue to diversify their industry mix by encouraging (but not depending on) tourism, developing niche agricultural markets such as fair trade, organic, or biodynamic products, and developing small-scale industry to process and add value to agricultural products. Additionally, rural areas must focus on developing systems that distribute gains from economic growth evenly and on capitalizing on the rich social assets and social networks of their regions.

Michael L. DOUGHERTY
Illinois State University

See also Agriculture, Tropical (the Americas); Amazonia; Brazil; Canada; Caribbean; Central America; Ecotourism (the Americas); Fair Trade; Labor; Marine Preserves; Mining (Andes); North American Free Trade Agreement (NAFTA); Parks and Protected Areas; Sanitation; Small Island States; Southern Cone; Travel and Tourism Industry; United States

FURTHER READING

Barham, Bradford; Clark, Mary; Katz, Elizabeth; & Schurman, Rachel. (1992). Nontraditional agricultural exports in Latin America. *Latin American Research Review, 27*(2), 43–82.

Brown, David L., & Swanson, Louis E. (2003). *Challenges for rural America in the twenty-first century.* University Park, PA: Penn State Press.

Collins, Denis. (2009). The failure of a socially responsive gold mining MNC in El Salvador: Ramifications of NGO mistrust. *Journal of Business Ethics, 88*(2), 245–268.

Daly, Herman. (1993). Sustainable growth: An impossibility theorem. In Herman E. Daly & Kenneth N. Townsend (Eds.), *Valuing the Earth: Economics, ecology, ethics.* Cambridge, MA: MIT Press.

Emery, Mary, & Flora, Cornelia. (2006). Spiraling-up: Mapping community transformation with the community capitals framework. *Community Development. 37*(1), 19–35.

Flora, Cornelia Butler, & Flora, Jan. (2004). *Rural communities: Legacy and change* (2nd ed.). Boulder, CO: Westview Press.

Honey, Martha. (2008). *Ecotourism and sustainable development.* Washington, DC: Island Press.

Hunt, Robert W. (2000, November 18). Civic action and sustainable communities. Paper delivered to the Annual Meeting of the Association for Research on Nonprofit Organizations and Voluntary Action (ARNOVA). New Orleans, LA.

King, David A., & Stewart, William P. (1996). Ecotourism and commodification: Protecting people and places. *Biodiversity and Conservation, 5,* 293–305.

Kretzmann, John, & McKnight, John. (1993). Building communities from the inside out: A path toward finding and mobilizing a community's assets. Chicago: ACTA Publications.

McGranahan, David. (1999). Natural amenities drive rural population change (Agricultural economic report no. AER781). Washington, DC: USDA Economic Research Service.

Medhoff, Peter, & Sklar, Holly. (1994). *Streets of hope: The fall and rise of an urban neighborhood*. Cambridge, MA: South End Press.

Putnam, Robert. (1993). *Making democracy work: Civic traditions in modern Italy*. Princeton, NJ: Princeton University Press.

Reuters. (2010). Costa Rica lawmakers vote to ban open-pit mining. Retrieved on May 15, 2012, from http://af.reuters.com/article/metalsNews/idAFN0912629920101110

Terborgh, John; van Schaik, Carel; Davenport, Lisa; & Rao, Madhu. (2002). *Making parks work: Strategies for preserving tropical nature*. Washington, DC: Island Press.

The International Ecotourism Society (TIES). (2012). What is ecotourism? Retrieved April 4, 2012, from http://www.ecotourism.org/what-is-ecotourism

United States Department of Agriculture (USDA). (2007). Measuring rurality: What is rural? Washington, DC: USDA Economic Research Service. Retrieved February 24, 2012, from http://www.ers.usda.gov/Briefing/Rurality/WhatIsRural/

Vias, Alexander C., & Nelson, Peter B. (2006). Changing livelihoods in rural America. In William A. Kandel & David Louis Brown (Eds.), *Population change and rural society*. Dordrecht, Germany: Springer.

World Bank. (2008). World development report: Agriculture for development. Washington, DC: The World Bank.

S

Sanitation

Human health and well-being are highly dependent on clean drinking water and sanitation. Because human waste carries pathogens and chemical by-products, it can spread diseases and degrade the environment. Sanitation provides facilities and services that manage and dispose of human waste. The level of sanitation available to different populations in the Americas and Oceania varies widely and is often correlated with per capita income.

Humans excrete feces and urine as waste products that contain not only the by-products of digestion and metabolism but also micro-organisms. A wide range of bacteria and fungi are present in the human digestive tract and derive nutrition from their hosts, while we in turn benefit from their presence because they enhance our immune responses, provide some nutritional benefits, and can also protect us from being colonized by disease-causing pathogens. These bacteria and fungi are often referred to as *gut flora*. By contrast, disease-causing pathogens (including bacteria, viruses, and parasites) may be completely absent or present only in very low numbers that do not cause illness. They can occasionally, however, enter the digestive system and reproduce rapidly enough to overcome the human immune response and cause acute or chronic illness. Under these latter conditions, the feces of individuals infected by these pathogens are a contaminant source for further spread of disease. People can continue to excrete the pathogens for a considerable period of time after infection has occurred. (See table 1 on page 277.) Once people have been exposed to such pathogens, they are thus highly vulnerable to a range of serious infections over a protracted period of time.

In addition to pathogens, human waste can also contain chemical by-products and residues from the medicines we digest and the chemicals we are exposed to in our daily lives, including but not limited to personal care products, endocrine disruptors, plasticizers, agricultural chemicals, and heavy metals. Although the environmental risks associated with this group of contaminants in human waste may not necessarily be as great as point sources of heavy metals from industrial sites and landfills, for example, they can still be damaging to the environment. This damage can occur if human waste is released directly or transported by runoff into waterways, leaches into groundwater, or accumulates within the soil or on the ground surface. Unless it is managed effectively, therefore, human waste can be associated not only with the spread of diseases but also degradation of the environment.

Sanitation refers to the provision of facilities and services that manage and dispose of human waste. What is often referred to as an *improved* sanitation facility may include a flush or pour-flush toilet to a piped sewer, septic tank, or pit latrine; a ventilated improved pit latrine; a pit latrine with slab; or a composting toilet. These types of facilities are generally found in economies characterized by high to medium per capita incomes. By contrast, an *unimproved* sanitation facility can be: (1) a single private facility, such as a flush or pour-flush toilet where the outflow is channeled into an open sewer, drain, or waterway; an open pit latrine; a bucket; a hanging toilet or latrine (e.g., a lagoon latrine that comprises a basic "closet" overhanging a coastal lagoon or beach); (2) shared facilities of any type; and (3) open defecation. The costs associated with different types of sanitation vary significantly, so that improvements may be economically constrained for poor communities and those for whom access to infrastructure supplies is limited. This can be a major issue for isolated island populations across Oceania who are completely dependent on irregular delivery of materials by sea or air. Recent data suggest that costs per capita range

Table 1. Disease-Causing Organisms and Disease Symptoms and Durations

Organism	Concentration in Feces (number per gram)	Symptoms	Incubation Period	Duration of Illness	Duration of Excretion
Viruses					
Enteroviruses (polio, Coxsackie, and echoviruses)	1,000–10 million	Vary according to pathogen: respiratory illness, flulike symptoms, meningitis, diarrhea, encephalitis, paralysis	1–35 days	variable	2–16 weeks
Hepatitis A virus	100 million	Itchy skin, loss of appetite, nausea, vomiting, jaundice	15–50 days	1–2 weeks—several months	4–6 weeks
Rotaviruses	10 billion	Acute gastroenteritis with watery diarrhea	1–3 days	4–6 days	1–3 weeks
Bacteria					
Salmonellae	10,000–10 billion	Loose, watery diarrhea, muscle and joint pain	6–72 hours	3–5 days	4–5 weeks
Shigellae	100,000–1 billion	Bloody diarrhea with fever, reactive arthritis	12 hours–7 days	1–3 days	2 weeks
Vibrio cholerae	1 billion	Explosive watery diarrhea ("rice water stools"), vomiting, rapid dehydration, shock	9–72 hours	3–4 days	3–4 weeks
Parasites					
Crypto-sporidium	1 million–10 million	Copious watery diarrhea, abdominal pain	1–2 weeks	4–21 days	24 weeks
Giardia	1 million–10 million	Abdominal pain, bloating, greasy or watery stools, nausea	5–25 days	weeks—months	1–2 weeks

Source: Adapted from Rusin et al. (2000) and Moe (2002) as cited in Yates (n.d.).

from the equivalent of US$160 for sewer connection and septic systems to the equivalent of about US$52–60 for pour-flush toilets and latrines (WHO 2010).

The level of sanitation available to a population has significant implications for human health and well-being as well as for productivity. The risk of disease associated with unimproved sanitation increases with population density, so when unimproved sanitation occurs in urban areas, the risks are particularly high. Other issues relate to human dignity, particularly for women and girls who have to share facilities with perhaps hundreds of other people or who may have to wait until dark to go into fields to defecate. Both of these practices, particularly the latter, are not only demeaning, but also have associated risks of assault.

The importance of sanitation for human health and well-being was acknowledged by the World Summit on Sustainable Development in Johannesburg, South Africa, which in 2002 set a target of halving the proportion of people who do not have access to basic sanitation by 2015. At a global scale, 2.5 billion people are still without access to improved sanitation—including 1.2 billion who have no facilities at all and are forced to defecate in the open. Although this is not a widespread issue in developed countries of the Americas and Oceania, there are many populations in developing nations within the region where these global goals are particularly relevant. (See table 2 below.)

The impact of sanitation on people's lives is best illustrated using a number of examples from the Americas and Oceania. These include management of sanitation in response to endemic typhoid fever in Chile in the 1980s, a cholera epidemic in Peru in 1991, ongoing issues for island atoll communities in Kiribati, and compromised sewerage infrastructure in earthquake-affected Christchurch, New Zealand.

Chile

An endemic disease is one that is constantly present in a population. If typhoid fever is endemic, it is due to ongoing contamination of drinking water and/or food by sewage, exacerbated by poverty and high population density. In Santiago, Chile, for example, the incidence of typhoid was stable at approximately 50–80 cases per 100,000 population during the period 1950–1975. Between 1976 and 1983, however, endemic typhoid fever in Santiago shifted suddenly to being an epidemic, with up to 215 cases per 100,000 population and associated direct health costs equivalent to US$1.4 million per year (Bartone 1994; Chile Ministry of Health 2010). Epidemiological studies showed that 75 percent of those typhoid cases could be attributed to the irrigation of vegetable crops with sewage-polluted waters (Bartone 1994). Rather than a typical short cycle of disease transmission, the pathogens were transmitted by way of the

Table 2. Conditions of Sanitation by Location

Country, Area, or Territory	Improved (%)	Unimproved (%)	Shared (%)	Open Defecation (%)
Australia	100			
Canada	100			
Chile	96		3	1
Cook Islands	100			
Ecuador	92	3	2	3
Fiji	nd	nd	nd	nd
French Polynesia	100			
Kiribati	33	5	13	49
Marshall Islands	73	12	1	14
Mexico	85	9	2	4
Federated States of Micronesia	nd	nd	nd	nd
Nauru	50	23	26	1
New Zealand	100			
Niue	100			
Papua New Guinea	45		39	16
Peru	68	7	15	10
Samoa	100			
Solomon Islands	nd	nd	nd	nd
Tokelau	93		7	
Tonga	96		4	
Tuvalu	84		11	5
United States of America	100			
Wallis and Fortuna Islands	96			4

Source: WHO (2010).

Note: "nd" means there is no data available.

initial infected person or people, the transport of their sewage and consequent pollution of waterways, irrigation of vegetable crops with the contaminated water, ingestion of raw food receiving those waters, and reinfection of people who consumed the raw food. Such a long transmission cycle created challenges not only in first identifying the mode of infection but also in combating the disease. Although human health was a key concern, so too was the fact that the highly productive areas affected were generating around 40 percent of Chile's fresh fruit and vegetable exports. Emergency measures undertaken in 1986 addressed the issues of wastewater irrigation, with later efforts improving the sewerage infrastructure. Improved sanitation consequently increased from 87 to 96 percent, wastewater was intercepted and treated, and sewage discharge was relocated to minimize risks of infection. The impacts of these measures on typhoid morbidity were evident in two important trends: first, the epidemic was ultimately contained; and second, the number of cases per 100,000 population decreased well below the pre-1976 rates, when the disease had been endemic. (See figure 1 below.)

Peru

Cholera is a disease spread by contamination of water or food by human fecal material. It is associated with poverty, high population density, and often with cross-contamination between the water supply and sewerage systems. Six global pandemics occurred in the nineteenth century, originating in India. The seventh pandemic occurred in 1991, when seafood was contaminated with cholera off the coast of Peru and entered the human food chain first in Peru and then across South America. The source of contamination has been attributed to zooplankton populations off the coast of Peru. These plankton are natural hosts of the cholera bacterium, and it has been suggested that their distribution and particular abundance along the Peruvian coast in 1991 was a result of an El Niño event (Seas et al. 2000).

This outbreak was the largest cholera epidemic of the twentieth century. Peru happened to be particularly vulnerable at the time because it was experiencing political and economic instability with inflation at more than 700 percent (Rojas-Suarez 1992), population growth, and

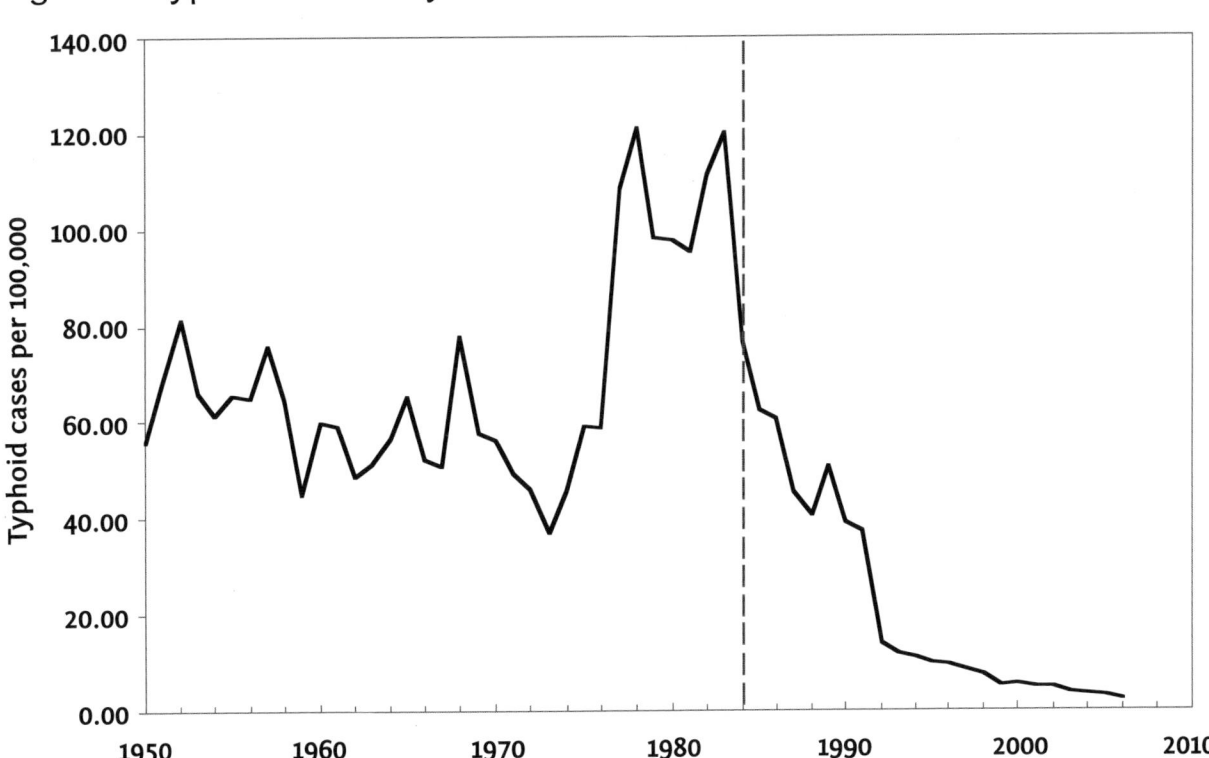

Figure 1. Typhoid Morbidity Rate in Chile, 1950–2006

Source: Chile Ministry of Health (2010).

The dashed line shows the effect of emergency measures put into effect in 1984.

rapid urbanization. Between 1961 and 1997, the population of the capital city of Lima, for example, increased from 1.2 million to 6 million. The development of infrastructure for water supply and sanitation could not keep pace with such rapid growth and urban migration. A significant proportion of people relied on unimproved sanitation or on drinking water contaminated by leaking sewers or by surface runoff polluted with human waste. When cholera arrived at the port cities of Lima and Chimbote, the lack of adequate sanitation, high population density, and poverty were the principal factors that led to 322,562 cases and 2,909 deaths across the country in 1991, and ultimately cost the equivalent of US$177 million in direct and indirect health costs. Fears of cholera cases reaching developed countries also led to trade embargoes and restrictions on tourism, which equated to further costs to the economy equaling close to US$771 million. Despite this, improvements to sanitation in Peru did not change significantly, with only a 10 percent increase in the use of improved sanitation occurring over the following seventeen years (WHO 2010). Open defecation practices, however, have almost halted over the same period of time.

If anomalously high populations of zooplankton associated with El Niño were indeed the primary source of cholera in the 1991 epidemic, then the risks to Peruvian cities and townships could be episodic but predictable.

Kiribati

Coral atolls have a distinct suite of climatic, geological, topographic, and demographic conditions that combine to make sanitation and water resources management the most challenging in the world. Water resources are extremely limited, with heavy reliance on rainwater and shallow groundwater. Kiribati is an island state in the Pacific Ocean comprising thirty-three islands spread over an exclusive economic zone of about 3.5 million square kilometers. The population totals 110,000 spread over a landmass of only 811 square kilometers. Tarawa atoll, where the capital city of South Tarawa is located, is highly urbanized with a population of 43,000. Sanitation in the past has been largely unimproved, including open defecation and the use of over-water latrines located immediately offshore of a beach (lagoon latrines). In 2004, 53 percent of the population of South Tarawa still defecated on the ocean beach or lagoon beach (Kingston 2004). Government-assisted programs in the 1970s introduced pit latrines; in a region characterized by reliance on shallow groundwater and highly concentrated populations, however, these latrines also represent significant sources of water contamination. Open dug wells consequently have become a severe hazard for human health. An additional issue, where domestic water supply is at risk from contamination, has arisen with the development of a limited reticulation system for urban water supply to South Tarawa. Groundwater is now pumped from a relatively large aquifer in the north of the atoll to South Tarawa, but along this pipeline numerous illegal breaches of the pipeline occur, providing sites for further contamination. The sites of fecal contamination are therefore widespread because there is connectivity between sites of fecal disposal and the marine environment, along the pipeline on the main atoll, and within the groundwater.

Poor sanitation has been identified as a causal agent of childhood illness and death in Kiribati, which has one of the highest rates of childhood mortality in the Pacific area. (See table 3 below.) Attempts to address this include

TABLE 3. Mortality Rates for Children Under Five Years in the Pacific Island States

Country	Total mortality rate per 1,000 population for children under 5 years			% deaths attributed to diarrheal diseases (2008 data only)
	1990	2000	2008	
Papua New Guinea	91	77	69	5
Kiribati	89	63	48	17
Tuvalu	53	42	36	1
Marshall Islands	48	39	36	9
Samoa	50	34	26	7
Tonga	22	20	19	6
Fiji	22	18	18	5

Source: WHO (2010).

locating sources of water for domestic use at a safe distance from villages and providing suitably designed latrines so that human excreta is not widely dispersed. In addition, in South Tarawa areas have been declared water reserves, set aside, free of human habitation and use, in order to optimize the quality of the underlying groundwater lens (the layer of fresh groundwater that floats on top of denser saltwater). Setting aside these reserves is, however, costly because traditional owners must be compensated. Foreign aid programs have supported the development of national strategies to address key sanitation and water supply issues for Kiribati. Although a range of institutional, social, and economic constraints means that the populations of these islands continue to be at risk, conditions appear to be improving.

Implications

The importance of improved sanitation for human health has been clearly recognized since 1854, when the English physician John Snow identified the source of a catastrophic cholera outbreak in London as fecal material from a broken sewer contaminating the water supply (Crosier 2011). Separation of water distribution and sewerage systems for urban areas then became an imperative for city planners throughout the developed world. The benefits of such an approach and the reliance on improved sanitation infrastructure are evident in public health records. One of the first cities to design, from scratch, an urban network of discrete water supply and sewerage pipelines was Christchurch, New Zealand. The public health record of the region within which Christchurch is located demonstrates the low incidence of illnesses associated with fecal-oral transmission (average of 190 cases per year per 100,000 population, 2000–2010). The Christchurch population faced significant challenges, however, when in September 2010, February 2011, and June 2011, three major earthquakes (magnitudes 7.1, 6.3, and 6.3, respectively; the February quake was the deadliest, killing 185 people) and over ten thousand aftershocks not only destroyed buildings but also extensively damaged the water supply and sewerage networks. Emergency provision of thousands of portable toilets, community education on personal hygiene, and a medical control and surveillance process ensured that—despite such widespread damage—there were no outbreaks of serious gastroenteric diseases. This series of events demonstrates that where the capacity exists, even under emergency conditions, appropriate containment and control of human waste is integral to maintaining optimal health and well-being.

Sara G. BEAVIS
The Australian National University

See also Gender Equality; Lima, Peru; Oceania; Pacific Island Environmental Philosophy; Rural Development (the Americas); Small Island States; Southern Cone; Urbanization; Water Use and Rights

Further Reading

Bartone, Carl R. (1994, December 19). Water pollution in Santiago: Health impacts and policy alternatives. In Joachim von Amsberg, Carl R. Bartone, Gunnar S. Eskeland & John A. Dixon (Eds.), *Chile: Managing environmental problems: Economic analysis of selected issues* (pp. 39–90). (Latin American and Caribbean Region Report No. 13061-CH). Washington, DC: The World Bank.

Chile Ministry of Health. (2010). *Incidenciade fiebre tifodidea y fiebre paratifoideaen Chile, 1950–2006* [Typhoid morbidity Rate in Chile, 1950–2006]. Retrieved November 29, 2011, from http://163.247.51.28/deis/vitales/Notificables/Tifoidea/Tifoidea.htm

Crosier, Scott. (2011). John Snow: The London Cholera Epidemic of 1854. Retrieved November 29, 2011, from http://www.csiss.org/classics/content/8

Kingston, P. A. (2004). *Surveillance of drinking water quality in the Pacific Islands: Situation analysis and needs assessment.* Geneva: World Health Organization.

Moe, Christine L. (2002). Waterborne transmission of infectious agents. In Christon J. Hurst (Ed.), *Manual of environmental microbiology* (pp. 136–152). Washington, DC: ASM Press.

Rojas-Suarez, Liliana. (1992, May). Currency substitution and inflation in Peru. Washington, DC: The International Monetary Fund.

Rusin, Patricia; Enriquez, Carlos E.; Johnson, Dana; & Gerba, Charles P. (2000). Environmentally transmitted pathogens. In Raina M. Maier, Ian L. Pepper & Charles P. Gerba (Eds.), *Environmental microbiology* (pp. 447–489). San Diego, CA: Academic Press.

Seas, Carlos, et al. (2000). New insights on the emergence of cholera in Latin America during 1991: The Peruvian experience. *American Journal of Tropical Medicine and Hygiene, 62*(4), 513–517.

World Health Organisation (WHO). (2010). World Health Statistics 2010. Retrieved November 29, 2011, from http://www.who.int/whosis/whostat/2010/en/index.html

Yates, Marylynn V. (n.d.). Introduction to waterborne pathogens. Retrieved November 24, 2011, from http://cws.msu.edu/documents/Yates_paper.pdf

Small Island States

Small island states—also called small island developing states (SIDS)—are small coastal countries that face major sustainable development problems, including environmental changes, population growth, urbanization, declining water supplies, and economic dependence on a narrow industrial base that usually consists of fishing and tourism. Their size, relative isolation, and lack of accessibility mean that they are extremely vulnerable to increases in energy costs, external financial shocks, and changes in export markets.

Small island states are distinctive in both their human and physical geographical characteristics. The term *small island states*—also called *small island developing states* (SIDS) or *island microstates*—refers to small coastal countries, some of which are low-lying. Despite tourist advertising that relies on romantic images of idyllic tropical coasts for promotion, the reality of small island states is that they face common sustainable development challenges (Hall 2010a). These comprise limited natural land-based resources, including water, food, and energy; remoteness from and limited access to major international markets and economic and political centers; growing populations; urbanization; high and increasing susceptibility to natural disasters; relatively fragile island and marine ecosystems; and economic dependence on a narrow range of industries and services (UN 2010).

The special sustainable development problems faced by SIDS were recognized formally by the international community for the first time at the United Nations Conference on Environment and Development (UNCED) held in Rio de Janeiro in 1992. Agenda 21, the action plan for sustainable development that resulted from the conference, stated, "Small island developing States, and islands supporting small communities are a special case both for environment and development. They are ecologically fragile and vulnerable. Their small size, limited resources, geographic dispersion and isolation from markets, place them at a disadvantage economically and prevent economies of scale" (UN 2010, iii). Although small island states can be found throughout the world, they are concentrated primarily in the Caribbean and in Oceania. In the Caribbean, the term refers to the following countries and regional groupings: Antigua and Barbuda, the Bahamas, Barbados, Belize, Cuba, Dominica, the Dominican Republic, Grenada, Guyana, Haiti, Jamaica, St. Kitts and Nevis, St. Lucia, St. Vincent and the Grenadines, and Trinidad and Tobago. In the Pacific, the term refers to the Cook Islands, Fiji, Kiribati, the Marshall Islands, the Federated States of Micronesia, Nauru, Niue, Palau, Papua New Guinea, the Independent State of Samoa, the Solomon Islands, Timor-Leste, Tonga, Tuvalu, and Vanuatu (UN 2010).

Islands are at the forefront of international public interest in sustainability. In the developed nations, public awareness of island states often has moved beyond the images of sun, sand, and surf presented in tourist brochures, thanks to media coverage of climate change issues that have bolstered awareness of SIDS' economic, social, and environmental circumstances (Gössling, Hall, and Scott 2009). In 2007, the Intergovernmental Panel on Climate Change (IPCC) projected that global sea levels will rise an additional 18 to 59 centimeters during the twenty-first century (Mimura et al. 2007). Many low-lying small island countries are no higher than a few meters above sea level, making them extremely vulnerable to rises in sea level. A large proportion of the population of many SIDS live in a low elevation coastal zone (LECZ), or the contiguous area along the coast that is less than 10 meters above sea level. Their situation is further complicated by a high coastline-to-land-area ratio. This means that many settlements—as well as critical infrastructure—are located on the coast and are increasingly vulnerable to erosion, storms and tidal surges, saline intrusion, and the intersection of groundwater with the surface, all of which can lead to inundation of low-lying areas. According to the Alliance of Small Island States' (AOSIS) Declaration on Climate Change, "climate change poses the most serious threat to our survival and viability, and . . . undermines our efforts to achieve sustainable development goals and threatens our very existence" (AOSIS 2009, 1). The threat of climate change to the Bahamas and the Caribbean islands, and to Pacific island states—particularly the Marshall Islands, Tuvalu, and Kiribati—has received significant coverage (Scott, Gössling, and Hall 2012).

Although the characteristics of small island states represent a major challenge with respect to sustainable development, their small size, clearly defined boundaries, and relatively small number of inputs and outputs also make them extremely significant case studies for sustainability research (Hall 2010a). For the biological sciences, and ecology and biogeography in particular, the confined natural systems of islands facilitate studying system dynamics and the impacts of humans and introduced species on them. Similarly, there is growing recognition of the opportunities islands provide to gain a better understanding of human ecology and well-defined political-economic systems, and the insights that such studies may bring. Small island states therefore have become major focal points for research on sustainability.

Environmental Importance

Islands play a pivotal role in the understanding of ecological processes. The Galapagos Islands, for example, were a source of inspiration for Darwin's theory of natural selection, and they continue to be an important natural-history research site (and tourist attraction) today. Islands are also important centers of biodiversity and environmental significance in their own right. Their relative isolation and well-defined ecological boundaries contribute to high degrees of endemism (the state of being unique to a particular place) as a result of speciation (the formation of new species due to factors that prevent interbreeding) and the presence of flora and fauna that otherwise may have become extinct in mainland areas. The characteristics of islands even have led to a theory of island biogeography that describes the relationship between a given area and the number of species within it (MacArthur and Wilson 1967).

The relative isolation of islands that may have protected them from human activities or the introduction of predators for thousands of years unfortunately has now been lost in many cases due to historical and modern migration and trade, and particularly because of the rapid movement of invasive species and diseases since the middle of the twentieth century (Quammen 1997). Information on changes over time in the number of threatened species is only available for a limited number of categories of animals (birds, mammals, and amphibia) for most small island countries. Taking these limitations into account, however, it is still apparent that the number of threatened species has increased in the first decade of the twenty-first century (Hall 2010b). In the Caribbean, the number of threatened animal species as a proportion of all animal species in a given country ranges from a low of 6.6 percent in Trinidad and Tobago to a high of 18.1 percent in Bermuda. The proportion of threatened animal species is generally much higher in the Pacific Islands, and ranges from a low of 14.8 percent in Tonga to 22.4 percent in French Polynesia (Hall 2010b). (The higher proportion may possibly be explained by a higher degree of endemism in the Pacific Islands.)

Given their limited area, however, growing populations and economic and environmental pressures have imposed significant constraints on island ecosystems. Studies of species-to-area relationships suggest that between 30 and 50 percent of a given community or ecosystem type needs to be conserved in order to maintain between 80 and 90 percent of species (Groves 2003). Only two Caribbean island states (the Cayman Islands, and Trinidad and Tobago) have designated more than 30 percent of their landmass as protected areas, although the Turks and Caicos Islands, Dominica, and Jamaica each have over 20 percent of their land area protected. In the Pacific, only Kiribati has set aside more than 30 percent of its land area for nature protection, while Tonga has a protected area of just over 25 percent (Hall 2010a). It is important to note that these figures refer to the overall area being conserved and not the proportion of specific ecosystems being set aside. Island ecosystems that are suitable for conversion to agricultural production tend to be the most underrepresented areas in conservation plans. Furthermore, despite the economic and environmental importance of marine resources—especially fish stocks—the proportion of marine area in the Caribbean and Oceania that is protected is much lower than that for terrestrial areas. In the Caribbean, Jamaica has the highest proportion of marine area set aside (3.56 percent), while in the Pacific, Palau has protected 8.74 percent of its marine territory (Hall 2010b). Given the threats posed to fish stocks in many island maritime areas by commercial overfishing, further development of protected marine areas would appear to be a high conservation priority.

Diasporas and Demographics

Nearly all of the island states of the Caribbean and the Pacific owe their political existence to the expansion of European empires, and the carving up of territory for economic and political purposes, between the sixteenth and early twentieth centuries. In some cases (particularly in the Caribbean), the formal colonial period lasted hundreds of years and left a lasting cultural and political heritage in terms of language, political organization, and economic relationships. In the Caribbean the colonial legacy also includes the presence of a substantial portion of the population with African heritage, whose ancestors were brought as slaves to work on plantations, or Indian populations that were originally brought as indentured labor by the British, French, and Dutch. Oceania also has some history of indentured labor migration, although not as well recognized internationally. For example, Fiji has a very substantial Indian population as a result of the use of Indian indentured labor in sugarcane production, and significant numbers of Polynesians were used as indentured or forced labor in Queensland, Australia, in the late nineteenth century, a process referred to as *blackbirding* (Rediker, Pybus, and Christopher 2007).

The substantial range of diasporas created because of the colonial histories of island states has meant that internal political representation and alliances may be based, at least in part, upon cultural and ethnic divisions. This is the case in Fiji, where there is a major political split between ethnic Fijians and Fijian Indians, and in French Polynesia, where there are significant differences between the indigenous population and the French settlers and their descendants. On the other hand, such diaspora also make for strong external economic relationships: the remittances from members of island populations who have moved abroad are an important part of the economies of many small island states.

On average, island states have relatively young populations (World Bank 2011), due in part to lower life expectancies, higher fertility rates, and high rates of emigration among the working-age populations. As of 2011 more than half of SIDS populations live in urban areas, with the Caribbean having one of the most highly urbanized populations in the world (World Bank 2011). Although there is wide variation among SIDS with respect to the share of population living in cities and towns (Trinidad and Tobago in the Caribbean has among the lowest proportion with 13 percent), urbanization is an increasingly common trend as people migrate to urban areas that are usually on the coastline, putting pressure on both coastal ecosystems as well as the settlements themselves (UN 2010). In the Pacific, Ebeye Island is the most populous island of Kwajalein Atoll in the Marshall Islands, with a population of over 15,000 and a population density of 38,600 per square kilometer as of 2007 (UN 2010)—a density much higher than the cities of developing countries in Africa or Asia.

Natural Disasters

Island states are especially prone to natural disasters, including tectonic events, such as earthquakes, tsunamis, and volcanic eruptions. The tropical location of many SIDS means they are subject to high-magnitude events such as cyclones, as well as significant climate variability. Climate change has exacerbated weather-related natural disasters, and cyclones, floods, and droughts have increased in frequency and intensity since the 1960s (Scott, Gössling, and Hall 2012). This has meant greater economic damages for larger numbers of people. The increased frequency of natural disasters has also restricted the ability of SIDS to recover between extreme events. Hydrometeorological disasters (for example, cyclones and tropical storms) are the most common and account for an estimated 45 percent of all SIDS natural disasters—although that percentage is even higher if related flooding, which accounts for an additional 25 percent of disasters, is considered (UN 2010, 8). Increasing population and expanding coastal urbanization, along with environmental degradation (such as mangrove loss), has made island states even more vulnerable to natural disasters that include both tectonic events, such as tsunamis, and cyclones (Scott, Gössling, and Hall 2012).

Between 1970 and 2006, Samoa, Saint Lucia, Grenada, Vanuatu, and Tonga were among the countries experiencing the highest relative economic losses on capital stock due to natural disasters. The impact of natural disasters is illustrated by the case of Samoa: due to the relatively small size of its economy, damages from a tropical storm and a forest fire in 1983, as well as three tropical storms in a row between 1989 and 1990, were estimated to have set its capital stock back more than thirty-five years (UN 2010). Such storms also place increased stress on the islands' biodiversity, an important consideration.

Water Supplies

A major sustainability challenge for island states is the quantity and quality of their freshwater supplies. Sea-level rise and flooding can lead to saltwater intrusion into freshwater aquifers, with the water supply being further compromised by the groundwater contamination and overextraction associated with urbanization, growing populations, and industrial demands. Some low-lying countries that comprise groups of small islands, such as Barbados, Kiribati, and Tuvalu, have chronically limited freshwater resources, low annual rainfall, and shallow water tables (UN 2010), but the amount of available renewable freshwater is declining in the majority of island states in the Caribbean and the Pacific (World Bank 2011). During droughts, water has had to be shipped to some islands and desalinization plants have had to be provided. In response, many SIDS are developing water conservation and management strategies (UN 2010).

Economics

Island states are economically vulnerable due to their distance from major markets, their susceptibility to natural disaster, and their narrow economic base and high level of imports, particularly with respect to fuel and food. They are also among the most trade-open economies in the world, a characteristic that has exacerbated their vulnerability to external financial shocks and changes in their export markets (UN 2010). The combination of geographical distance to markets, along with low trade and transport volumes, means that SIDS exports suffer from high logistical and transport costs. Increases in the price of oil and other energy sources make the relative cost of exporting even more problematic. As a result, SIDS typically have large external debts that are often unsustainable unless financed through external capital flows, such as official development assistance (ODA), foreign direct investment (FDI), and international private funds (IPF), combined with workers' remittances. Between 2000 and 2008, remittances accounted for 6–8 percent of SIDS gross domestic product (GDP). In 2005, Tonga, Haiti, Jamaica, the Dominican Republic, and Kiribati were among the top twenty remittance-receiving countries (as a percentage of GDP) in the world (UN 2010). The size of remittance flows to SIDS is increasingly vulnerable, however, as it depends on the state of the global economy and the capacity of migrant workers from SIDS to find employment in receiving countries, as well as economic activity in the SIDS themselves.

Along with tourism, SIDS economies rely heavily on their coastal and marine resources, especially fish stocks. In the Pacific, tuna fisheries make up more than 10 percent of GDP and over 50 percent of exports in some SIDS, and subsistence fishing supplies between 50 and 90 percent of the animal protein diet for people in rural areas and remote islands (UN 2010). Future food security is being challenged by the demands of a growing population and by the effects of climate change, especially ocean acidification and coral loss. Overfishing, illegal and unregulated fishing, and harmful fishing methods are damaging fish stocks severely, including high-value fish stocks, such as tuna (UN 2010).

Tourism

The majority of island states are relatively more dependent on tourism than other states (Hall 2010a). The level of tourism can vary widely among these states, but overall international tourism receipts accounted for 51 percent of the total value of exports from SIDS in 2007. This represents a substantial increase from the 42 percent recorded in 2000, which is striking compared to the less than 10 percent share in other developing countries (UN 2010). Although economically significant, the multiplier effect of tourism for island-state economies is limited by the high level of foreign ownership and vertical integration (an economic arrangement in which various elements of the tourism supply chain are united by a common owner), which leads to substantial economic leakage (Hall and Lew 2009). Tourism growth also is affected greatly by economic conditions in tourism-generating countries, exchange rates, and the availability of aircraft and cruise ship service. Given these circumstances, it is extremely difficult for SIDS to manage the volatility of tourism flows. Some SIDS have sought to diversify their tourism product base by focusing on ecotourism and medical tourism niches, and by encouraging tourist hotels to purchase local foods where possible. A long-term issue for many small island states, however, is that the development of tourism infrastructure, such as hotels, may occur on land that would otherwise be used for agriculture (Hall and Lew 2009). Furthermore, tourism also may compete for access to scarce water resources (Gössling et al. 2012).

The natural environment is important in attracting tourists to island states since in many cases tourism is the mainstay of island economies, but large numbers of visitors also provide extra pressures on natural resources and their conservation, as well as infrastructure such as sewage treatment facilities and water supplies. In Anguilla, the number of annual visitors is equivalent to a 30.5 percent increase in the permanent population, while in the Cayman Islands it is equivalent to a remarkable 89 percent (Hall 2010b). Yet the economic importance of tourism poses considerable challenges for conservation as well as for long-term responses to climate change. The difficulty for many island destinations is that tourism is often one of the few economic development opportunities available to them. At the same time, however, they also may be reasonably isolated from the source areas of international tourists and therefore may be highly vulnerable to any regulatory structures put in place to manage transport and aviation emissions, as well as increases in transport fuel costs (Gössling, Hall, and Scott 2009). Island destinations therefore find themselves positioned within a highly complex policy environment. While often they are committed to a path of future tourism development, they are also extremely vulnerable to both the contribution of tourism emissions to climate change as well as changes in tourism patterns and flows (Scott, Gössling, and Hall 2012). The transportation infrastructure that enables island tourism usually serves the inbound tourist market as well as the local population and businesses with respect to international accessibility. Any understanding of tourism's contribution to SIDS' sustainable development therefore needs to be able to account for both the environmental effects of tourism as well as the potential social and economic impacts of any loss of access to transport routes with respect to infrastructure use and economic contribution (Hall 2010a).

The Future

Island states face a difficult future. Climate change is one clear challenge, but growing populations, water and food security, and a narrow economic base also affect their long-term sustainability. Tourism has been an economic bright spot for many SIDS that may now be affected by climate-change mitigation efforts and consumer concerns over the environmental impacts of travel. The open economies of many island states have also made them vulnerable to external economic and financial shocks as well as changes in export markets. The final major challenge to SIDS is retaining their most educated residents. Migration and the diaspora are integral to island-state identity and ways of life. SIDS are eight times more likely to experience "brain drain" as a result of the emigration of their tertiary-educated populations compared with the world as a whole (UN 2010). Migration may provide a return in terms of much needed remittances and the development of business networks, but given the challenges that island nations face, retaining educated people and public-service and business positions is likely also essential to maintaining a knowledge base that will be vital for future adaptation and sustainability.

C. Michael HALL
University of Canterbury

See also Caribbean; Central America; Ecotourism (the Americas); Marine Ecosystems Health; Marine Preserves; Oceania; Pacific Island Environmental Philosophy; Parks and Protected Areas; Travel and Tourism Industry

Further Reading

Alliance of Small Island States (AOSIS). (2009). Declaration on climate change 2009. Retrieved February 29, 2012, from http://www.aosis.info/documents/AOSISSummitDeclarationSept21FINAL.pdf

Gössling, Stefan; Hall, C. Michael; & Scott, Daniel. (2009). The challenges of tourism as a development strategy in an era of global climate change. In Eija Palosuo (Ed.), *Rethinking development in a carbon-constrained world: Development cooperation and climate change* (pp. 110–119). Helsinki, Finland: Ministry for Foreign Affairs.

Gössling, Stefan, et al. (2012). Tourism and water use: Supply, demand, and security; An international review. *Tourism Management, 33,* 1–15.

Groves, Craig. (2003). *Drafting a conservation blueprint: A practitioner's guide to planning for biodiversity.* Washington, DC: Island Press.

Hall, C. Michael. (2010a). An island biogeographical approach to island tourism and biodiversity: An exploratory study of the Caribbean and Pacific Islands. *Asia Pacific Journal of Tourism Research, 15*(3), 383–399.

Hall, C. Michael. (2010b). Island destinations: A natural laboratory for tourism: Introduction. *Asia Pacific Journal of Tourism Research, 15*(3), 245–249.

Hall, C. Michael, & Lew, Alan A. (2009). *Understanding and managing tourism impacts: An integrated approach.* Milton Park, UK: Routledge.

MacArthur, Robert H., & Wilson, Edward O. (1967). *The theory of island biogeography.* Princeton, NJ: Princeton University Press.

Mimura, Nobuo, et al. (2007). Small islands. In Martin Parry, Osvaldo Canziani, Jean Palutikof, Paul van der Linden & Clair Hanson (Eds.), *Climate change 2007: Impacts, adaptation and vulnerability* (pp. 687–716). Cambridge, UK: Cambridge University Press.

Nurse, Leonard, & Moore, Rawleston. (2005). Adaptation to global climate change: An urgent requirement for small island developing states. *Review of European Community and International Environmental Law, 14*(2), 100–107.

Quammen, David. (1997). *The song of the dodo: Island biogeography in an age of extinctions.* New York: Simon & Schuster.

Rediker, Marcus; Pybus, Cassandra; & Christopher, Emma. (Eds.). (2007). *Many middle passages: Forced migration and the making of the modern world.* Berkeley: University of California Press.

Scott, Daniel; Gössling, Stefan; & Hall, C. Michael. (2012). *Tourism and climate change: Impacts, adaptation and mitigation.* New York: Routledge.

United Nations (UN), Division for Sustainable Development. (2010). *Trends in sustainable development: Small island developing states (SIDS).* New York: United Nations.

World Bank. (2011). *World development indicators 2011.* Washington, DC: International Bank for Reconstruction and Development/The World Bank.

Social Movements (Latin America)

Social movements are committed to advocating popular, grassroots interests to the government and the dominant culture in general. Although social movements are comprised of non-state actors who respond to immediate and specific concerns, in Latin America efforts to realize sustainable forms of development have become intertwined with the policy initiatives of leftist governments that share common goals of social justice and empowerment.

Social movements are groups of individuals or organizations that advocate for political or social change. Sometimes called *popular movements* because of their roots in subordinate populations, these movements typically challenge holders of power from the dominant sectors of society. Often they focus on the realization of civil or social rights and emerge in response to an immediate and specific crisis. Social movements are typically part of civil society and are known as "non-state actors." Rather than engaging in electoral campaigns or armed struggles with the goal of gaining direct control over governmental structures, social movements typically have more limited goals of influencing specific policies. Their force is often through an expression of numbers, commitment, and unity.

New Social Movements

In the 1990s sociologists began to speak of new social movements (NSMs) in order to distinguish them from older social movements that were typically rooted in traditional political parties, labor unions, or guerrilla insurgencies. Rather than engaging in a project of historical transformation aimed at controlling state structures, researchers interpreted NSMs as responding to specific crises with more focused and limited demands. While the old movements were commonly rooted in a Marxist understanding of class struggle, NSMs embraced the identity politics that emphasized issues of autonomy and democracy. Examples of new sociocultural actors engaging in these organizing efforts included gender rights and women's rights organizations, neighborhood organizations, human rights advocates, ecological activists, families of political prisoners and the disappeared, and advocates for indigenous peoples' rights and autonomy. (The preferred style throughout this encyclopedia is to lowercase the word "indigenous," but some authors [this author included] prefer the word to be capitalized. The word is kept lowercase here for consistency.) Initially, environmental concerns were just one of many issues, but media focus on climate change brought increased attention to the topic and related concerns including large-scale extractive mining and the consequences of petroleum-based economies. These concerns brought a sustainability discourse to the forefront.

Many scholars, including the Canadian professor of social and political science Judith Adler Hellman (1995), have challenged what researchers see as an artificial division between old and new movements. In particular, leftist scholars challenged an implicitly conservative ideological agenda in much of the research on NSMs, including an apparent desire to dismiss social class as a tool of analysis. The US economic and political anthropologist Marc Edelman (1999, 19–20), for example, notes that "old social movements" had not entirely ignored identity politics, and "new" movements had not discarded a class consciousness. Rather, these scholars urge the importance of considering how various forms of identity (including class, ethnicity, and gender) have interacted with each other in specific historical contexts.

Furthermore, activist undertakings that scholars championed as classic examples of new social movements engaged in the types of strategies and pressure tactics commonly associated with "old" social movements, including street demonstrations, electoral campaigns, and mass mobilizations specifically targeted to remove governments from power. Rather than solely engaging in class struggles or embracing the limited goals of identity politics, both the old and new movements repeatedly crossed these imaginary boundaries in order to transform hegemonic structures.

Initially, many scholars assumed that identity-based movements were compatible with neoliberalism because of their limited demands, and often conservative governments pursued policies based on that assumption. In what critics denounced as "multicultural neoliberalism," governments conceded ground on cultural issues such as recognition of indigenous languages and bilingual education programs, while simultaneously refusing to grant material benefits such as agrarian reform, increased wages, or housing (Hale 2002). Subsequent political events in the first decade of the twenty-first century challenged the assumptions of new social movement theory. Movements that scholars had interpreted as rooted in apolitical organizations with a loose hierarchy challenged exclusionary neoliberal governments. As class-based labor movements and political parties had previously sought to do, these new movements also opened up political spaces, articulated popular demands, and politicized issues (such as gender rights) that formerly had been confined to the private realm. Even the fundamental goals, strategies, and pressure tactics of NSMs remained similar to earlier movements in terms of engaging in demonstrations, strikes, and marches in order to wrestle concessions from the government.

Madres de la Plaza de Mayo

The Madres (Mothers) of the Plaza de Mayo was a group of women whose children "disappeared" during the Argentine military dictatorship's dirty war against political dissidents between 1976 and 1983. Frustrated with an endless search for their children, on 20 April 1977 the mothers gathered at the Plaza de Mayo in central Buenos Aires. The women publicly denounced the military government for their role in the disappearances of their sons and daughters. The mothers called for a public accounting of the reign of terror and punishment for those responsible for the crimes. These women departed from their gendered domestic spheres to play a decidedly visible and public role in denouncing human rights abuses. In a highly charged and repressive political environment, they employed their traditional roles as mothers as a mechanism of protest.

Scholars commonly depicted the Madres de la Plaza de Mayo as a classic example of a new social movement because they organized outside the structures of political parties and used their position as mothers for the limited and defined goal of freeing their children. As their struggle matured, however, they assumed more radical positions and began to engage broader political concerns. The mothers felt responsible to carry on their children's political work and advance the agenda that originally led to their disappearance. Furthermore, the experience of these women challenged the myth that motherhood is safe from political repression. When the women stepped outside their traditional and preassigned gender roles, they faced the same viciousness of repressive state apparatuses as did male dissidents. Away from the public eye, military officials often used the most brutal tools of rape and torture on dissident women.

Movimento dos Trabalhadores Rurais Sem Terra

Brazil's Movimento dos Trabalhadores Rurais Sem Terra (MST; Landless Workers' Movement) was one of Latin America's largest social movements and is an example of one that bridged the artificial divide between old and new movements. It formed in the late 1970s to defend the rights and lives of peasants who had been expelled from their lands. With 1.5 million members, the MST came to operate throughout much of Brazil. It was organized on an autonomous and nonhierarchical model in which grassroots members made decisions through discussion, reflection, and consensus. The MST had an eclectic ideology but was broadly governed by two basic principles: a struggle for land in order to diminish a bad quality of life in the city and to produce food, and a commitment to regaining dignity and cultural values, with freedom and liberty as the basis for a good society. The MST argued that land is part of nature and should belong to those who work it. They engaged in land occupations as a strategy to pressure the government for positive policy changes, including an agrarian reform that included access to land, health care, education, dignity, infrastructure, water, housing, and support for the young to stay on the land. More important than property rights was a true agrarian reform that would facilitate forms of production that would lead to food security and sovereignty. The MST opposed the use of biotech crops, chemical pesticides, and fertilizers because it gave more power to multinational corporations and took control out of the hands of the local farmers. Production was based on the principle "from each according to their ability, to each according to their effort." Their struggle was not just for themselves but for future generations as well.

The MST was part of the Via Campesina (Spanish for "Peasants' Way"), an international movement of about 150 organizations in 70 countries that represented about 200 million farmers from around the world. The Via Campesina was founded in 1993 to create a mechanism through which family farmers could make their voices heard in international debates on agricultural policies that directly affected their lives. The Via Campesina opposed corporate-driven agriculture that destroyed the environment and defended small-scale sustainable agriculture as a way to promote social justice and dignity. In 1996 the Via Campesina proposed the concept of food sovereignty as the right of communities to produce healthy food on their own land rather than engaging in patterns of neoliberal export economies that contributed to poverty and climate crises. The movement in particular defended women's rights and gender equality.

Confederación de Nacionalidades Indígenas del Ecuador

Activists formed the Confederación de Nacionalidades Indígenas del Ecuador (CONAIE; Confederation of Indigenous Nationalities of Ecuador) in 1986 with the goal of joining all indigenous peoples in the country into one large movement to defend their concerns and to agitate for social, political, and educational reforms. CONAIE's central and most controversial demand was to revise the constitution to recognize the "plurinational" character of Ecuador in order to incorporate the contributions of diverse populations into state structures, a proposal that elites repeatedly rejected as undermining the unity and integrity of the country. The movement's success in unifying and advancing an indigenous agenda gained it a reputation as one of the best-organized social movements in the Americas (Becker 2011).

In June 1990 CONAIE emerged at the forefront of a powerful uprising that paralyzed the country for a week. Indigenous activists blocked roads with boulders, rocks, and trees that paralyzed the transport system, effectively cutting off the food supply to the cities and shutting down the country. Frustrated by stagnated talks with the government over bilingual education, agrarian reform, and demands to recognize the plurinational nature of Ecuador, the uprising forced the government to negotiate their demands. CONAIE repeatedly led subsequent popular protests for land, economic development, education, and recognition of Indigenous nationalities.

In a shift in strategies from a focus on civil society to one on electoral campaigns, in 1995 CONAIE helped form the political movement Pachakutik to campaign for political office. Pachakutik identified itself as part of a new Latin American left that embraced principles of community, solidarity, unity, tolerance, and respect. Pachakutik opposed neoliberal economic policies and favored a more inclusive and participatory political system. In January 2000 indigenous leaders allied with lower-ranking military officials in a short-lived coup that removed president Jamil Mahuad from power after he had implemented unpopular neoliberal economic policies. What had once been seen as a primary example of a new social movement had shifted its strategy from organizing broad sectors of civil society to engaging in activities more representative of traditional political actors.

World Social Forum

From its first meeting in Porto Alegre, Brazil, in 2001, the World Social Forum (WSF) quickly grew into the world's largest meeting of civil society. From an assembly of 10,000 people (mostly from Latin America, France, and Italy) in 2001 who gathered to talk about creating a "globalization from below," the WSF grew dramatically, with 50,000 gathering in 2002; 100,000 meeting in 2003 and 2004; and 155,000 in 2005. With the slogan "Another World Is Possible," the forum featured speakers, workshops, panels, debates, marches, and cultural events. It provided an open platform for activists to discuss strategies of resistance to neoliberal globalization and to present constructive alternatives. Community organizers, trade unionists, young people, academics, and others met to rethink and recreate globalization so that it would benefit people, putting human rights, social justice, and ecological sustainability before profits.

The World Social Forum had its roots in earlier organizing efforts such as the 1992 Earth Summit at Rio de Janeiro, Brazil, and the First International Encounter for Humanity and Against Neoliberalism that the Zapatistas organized in Chiapas, Mexico, in 1996. Porto Alegre was a logical and favorable location for the WSF to meet, both because of municipal support from the governing leftist Partido dos Trabalhadores (PT; Workers Party) that was rooted in a history of trade unions and social movement organizing, and because its practice of participatory budgeting formed a positive model for civil society.

The WSF also provided an arena for perennial discussions regarding the relationship between civil society and political parties in organizing a social movement. With an emphasis on civil society, the WSF excluded political parties and military organizations from its discussions. With the rise of new left governments in Latin America during the first decade of the twenty-first century, many activists began to rethink the relationship between social movements and political parties. Although political parties could not mobilize massive demonstrations the way social movements can, social movements could not implement positive policy changes as governments can.

"Pink Tide" Governments and Extractive Industries

In 1998 Hugo Chávez won election as president of Venezuela, introducing a decade during which almost all of the South American countries subsequently elected "pink tide" governments with leftist tendencies. Chávez realized success through his appeals to the interests of marginalized sectors of society as he built what he called a Bolivarian revolution, which used Venezuela's petroleum wealth to redirect resources to the lower sectors of society.

Chávez represented the interplay between and merging of new and old movements. He was a career military officer, one of the few avenues for social advancement available to common people in Latin America. Chávez first burst on the political scene after a failed military-civilian coup d'état against the elected government of Carlos Andrés Pérez on 4 February 1992. The coup failed, but Chávez leveraged that exposure into his successful electoral campaign. Once in office, he challenged neoliberal governance by halting privatization, expanding social spending for education and health care, and increasing civil rights for women and marginalized peoples. While opponents derided Chávez for his authoritarian style of governance, he used governing structures to open significant spaces for grassroots social movements.

Chávez and other left-populist governments that followed him in Latin America funded their expansion of social spending through the extraction of natural resources. Leftist critics complained that pursuing such policies failed to establish a fundamental break with previous export-dependent economies. Environmental and social movement activists criticized the unsustainable nature of these policies, as well as the fact that local communities that bore the brunt of these endeavors rarely shared in their benefits. Protests against mineral extraction spread across the Americas, with both left and right governments arguing that large-scale mining was preferable to the alternatives because it was less ecologically damaging than small-scale artisanal mining.

In 2006 Bolivia's foreign minister, David Choquehuanca, introduced the *sumak kawsay* as a Quechua concept of living well, not just living better. Rather than focusing on material accumulation, it sought to build a sustainable economy. This perspective included an explicit critique of traditional development strategies that increased the use of resources instead of living in harmony with others and with nature. Rather than a neoliberal emphasis on individual and property rights, the *sumak kawsay* emphasized collective community interests. It entailed a new way of thinking about human relations that was not based on exploitation, and instead required a new relationship between economy and nature. Social movements embraced these ideas as a way to regain control over state structures to use them for the common good rather than for the profits of wealthy capitalists.

In one of many examples of the tensions between leftist governments and social movements, indigenous groups in Bolivia in 2011 marched against government plans to build a highway through the Isiboro-Sécure Indigenous Territory and National Park (TIPNIS) ecological reserve. Evo Morales, himself an indigenous person who leveraged his credentials as a leader of Bolivia's powerful social movements to election to the presidency in 2005, pressed for construction of the road because it was key to Bolivia's economic development. At first Morales refused to listen to protests that the road would destroy one of the world's most biodiverse regions, but social movement pressure forced him to change his policies. Leftist governments and social movements continued a complicated dance to realize mutual objectives of sustainable development that would benefit all peoples.

Marc BECKER
Truman State University

See also Amazonia; Bogotá, Colombia; Brazil; Central America; Corporate Accountability; Ecovillages; Fair Trade; Gender Equality; Guatemala City; Labor; Mexico City; Multilateral Environmental Agreements (MEAs); North American Free Trade Agreement (NAFTA); Organization of American States (OAS); Rio de Janeiro,

Brazil; Rio Earth Summit (UN Conference on Environment and Development); Rural Development (the Americas); Southern Cone

FURTHER READING

Baud, Michiel, & Rutten, Rosanne. (Eds.). (2004). *Popular intellectuals and social movements: Framing protest in Asia, Africa, and Latin America*. New York: Published for the International Instituut voor Sociale Geschiedenis, Amsterdam, by Cambridge University Press.

Becker, Marc. (2011). *Pachakutik: Indigenous movements and electoral politics in Ecuador*. Lanham, MD: Rowman & Littlefield Publishers.

Dangl, Benjamin. (2010). *Dancing with dynamite: States and social movements in Latin America*. Oakland, CA: AK Press.

Deere, Carmen Diana, & Royce, Frederick S. (Eds.). (2009). *Rural social movements in Latin America: Organizing for sustainable livelihoods*. Gainesville: University Press of Florida.

Eckstein, Susan. (Ed.). (1989). *Power and protest: Latin American social movements*. Berkeley: University of California Press.

Edelman, Marc. (1999). *Peasants against globalization: Rural social movements in Costa Rica*. Stanford, CA: Stanford University Press.

Escobar, Arturo. (2010). Latin America at a crossroads. *Cultural Studies, 24*(1), 1–65.

Fisher, William F., & Ponniah, Thomas. (Eds.). (2003). *Another world is possible: Popular alternatives to globalization at the World Social Forum*. London & New York: Zed Books.

Foweraker, Joe. (1995). *Theorizing social movements*. Boulder, CO: Pluto Press.

Hale, Charles R. (2002). Does multiculturalism menace? Governance, cultural rights and the politics of identity in Guatemala. *Journal of Latin American Studies, 34*(3), 485–524.

Harris, Richard L., & Nef, Jorge. (Eds.). (2008). *Capital, power, and inequality in Latin America and the Caribbean*. Lanham, MD: Rowman & Littlefield.

Hellman, Judith Adler. (1995). The riddle of new social movements: Who they are and what they do. In Sandor Halebsky & Richard L. Harris (Eds.), *Capital, power, and inequality in Latin America* (pp. 165–183). Boulder, CO: Westview Press.

Jaffee, Daniel. (2007). *Brewing justice: Fair trade coffee, sustainability, and survival*. Berkeley: University of California Press.

Miller, Francesca. (1991). *Latin American women and the search for social justice*. Hanover, NH: University Press of New England.

Petras, James, & Veltmeyer, Henry. (2011). *Social movements in Latin America: Neoliberalism and popular resistance*. Basingstoke, UK: Palgrave Macmillan.

Prevost, Gary; Campos, Carlos Oliva; & Vanden, Harry E. (Eds.). (2012). *Social movements and leftist governments in Latin America: Confrontation or co-option?* London: Zed Books.

Santos, Boaventura de Sousa. (2010). *Voices of the world*. London: Verso.

Smith, Jackie, et al. (2008). *Global democracy and the World Social Forums*. Boulder, CO: Paradigm Publishers.

Stahler-Sholk, Richard, & Vanden, Harry E. (2011). A second look at Latin American social movements. *Latin American Perspectives, 38*(1), 5–13.

Stahler-Sholk, Richard; Vanden, Harry E.; & Kuecker, Glen. (Eds.). (2008). *Latin American social movements in the twenty-first century: Resistance, power, and democracy*. Lanham, MD: Rowman & Littlefield.

Webber, Jeffery. (2011). *From rebellion to reform in Bolivia: Class struggle, indigenous liberation, and the politics of Evo Morales*. New York: Haymarket Books.

Wolford, Wendy. (2010). *This land is ours now: Social mobilization and the meanings of land in Brazil*. Durham, NC: Duke University Press.

Zibechi, Raúl. (2010). *Dispersing power: Social movements as anti-state forces*. Oakland, CA: AK Press.

Berkshire's authors and editors welcome questions, comments, and corrections. Send your emails about the *Berkshire Encyclopedia of Sustainability* in general or this volume in particular to: sustainability.updates@berkshirepublishing.com

Southern Cone

The southern portion of South America—the Southern Cone—includes a broad diversity of ecoclimates, from rain forest and mountain glaciers to fertile lowlands and deserts. The region is on a course toward increased political stability, regional integration, and socioeconomic development; however, the road ahead requires attention to social and environmental practices and policies as the area's societies attempt to balance growth and sustainability.

The expression *Southern Cone* refers to the cone-shaped area of South America located south of the Tropic of Capricorn. Although geographically this includes part of southeastern Brazil, in terms of political geography the Southern Cone has traditionally comprised Argentina, Chile, Paraguay, and Uruguay. Starting in the 1990s, and especially since the creation of the Southern Common Market in 1991, the term is often used to refer to a larger area also including Brazil and Bolivia. Countries of the region are dealing with sustainability issues in relation to such processes as increased development and population growth, intensification of agriculture, and expansion of mining activities and fossil fuel extraction. This also involves massive regional initiatives to develop transport and communication infrastructure to support the process of regional integration, which raises significant sustainability issues.

History

The countries of the Southern Cone achieved independence from Spain (or from Portugal in the case of Brazil) in the early nineteenth century, and by the 1870s the populations of most of them had doubled or even tripled. Starting in the mid-nineteenth century, Argentina, Chile, Uruguay, and Brazil attracted large-scale immigration, with Argentina alone receiving around 6 million European immigrants between the 1870s and 1930. Until the late nineteenth century, the region experienced ongoing civil and border wars. These included the Paraguayan War (1864–1870)—a traumatic conflict in which the allied armies of Brazil, Argentina, and Uruguay destroyed much of Paraguay's economy—and the War of the Pacific (1879–1883)— a war fought largely for the control of nitrate and other mineral deposits, in which Chile defeated Bolivia and Peru. Only in the last two decades of the nineteenth century did most of these countries develop into stable nation-states with clear territorial control, although border disputes among Southern Cone countries still persist. Some military confrontations also took place in the twentieth century, including the Chaco War (1932–1935) between Bolivia and Paraguay over the control of oil reserves and fueled by the activities of multinational oil companies.

Although during much of the twentieth century the Southern Cone as a whole was characterized by highly unstable politics, becoming particularly notorious for brutal military dictatorships in the 1970s, the histories of the individual countries vary considerably. While Argentina has faced almost continual institutional disruption and cyclical economic instability since the 1930s, Chile and Uruguay have maintained greater institutional stability. Since the 1980s, the return to democracy in the Southern Cone, along with the promotion of regional integration through the creation of the Southern Common Market in 1991, have created new possibilities for achieving political and economic stability in the region (OHCHR-UNDP 2004; UNDP 2004). These trends have been strengthened in recent years as a result of significant socioeconomic, institutional, and political transformations whereby the region has achieved a greater degree of autonomy in all these dimensions in the international domain. These trends include the emergence of Brazil as a world economic power, the regional impact of Brazil's emergence, and the increasing political assertiveness of the region's national governments, which among other outcomes led to the creation of the South American Union of Nations (UNASUR) in May 2008.

Geography

A wide diversity of ecoclimatic areas are found in the Southern Cone. The subtropical Andean region reaches its highest point at Aconcagua mountain (almost 7 kilometers) in Argentina; the Atacama Desert in Chile is one of the driest places in the world; forests in Argentina and Chile range from the subtropical to the subantarctic; large fertile plains (the pampas) stretch across southern Brazil, Uruguay, central-eastern Argentina, and the Patagonian steppes. The climatic spectrum is broad, with clearly defined seasons and high regional variability in annual precipitation, from a low of 100 millimeters in Patagonia to about 5,000 millimeters in Chile's Valdivian forest.

The Río de la Plata is the largest drainage basin in the region. Comprising the complex systems of the Paraná, Paraguay, Pilcomayo, Bermejo, Uruguay, and Río de la Plata rivers, it is the second-largest drainage basin in South America and the fifth-largest in the world. The basin contains the most densely populated areas of South America, including large portions of Brazil, Bolivia, Paraguay, Argentina, and Uruguay, and megalopolises and industrial centers such as São Paulo and Buenos Aires. The economic activities sustained by the basin account for over 60 percent of the combined gross domestic product of its constituent countries (OAS 2012). The basin has undergone large-scale transformation, especially through construction of massive dams such as Itaipú Dam, located on the border between Brazil and Paraguay. Itaipú remained the world's largest operating hydroelectric plant until the construction of the Three Gorges Dam in China in the early twenty-first century, and it supplies around 25 percent of Brazil's energy needs and over 90 percent of Paraguay's. Other large dams have been built in the basin, including the Yaciretá Dam on the Paraná River, located on the border between Argentina and Paraguay. In the context of the process of regional integration, the Southern Cone is undergoing a massive infrastructure program: the Initiative for the Integration of Regional Infrastructure in South America (IIRSA, its Spanish abbreviation). IIRSA involves the construction of hundreds of new projects, including dams, river transfers and hydroways, pipelines, railways, ports, and highways, among others. The implementation of this regional megaproject is set to introduce potentially irreversible social and environmental transformations, some of which are already underway and have prompted mounting social conflicts (Bank Information Center 2012; OLCA 2012).

Environmental Issues

The region's ecosystems have suffered extensive degradation and loss of biodiversity as a result of long-term anthropogenic (human-caused) transformations. Particularly serious are deforestation and resultant soil erosion and desertification caused by farming and overgrazing; construction of large-scale hydraulic works; and industrial and urban pollution of soil, air, and water. The massive dams in the region are thought to contribute to climatic change and play a part in the recurrent floods affecting Paraguay and northeast Argentina since the 1980s. Extensive agriculture and forestry have drastically transformed the landscape. This has led to the decline of much indigenous flora and fauna, notably the virtual extinction in large areas of the most valuable timber species, such as the *quebracho colorado* (*Schinopsis balansae*) or the *ñandubay* (*Prosopis affinis*), as well as indigenous fish such as the *mojarra de Valcheta* or "naked mojarra" (*Gymnocharacinus bergi*) and the *puyén* or *puye* (*Galaxias maculates*), and mammals including the *yaguareté* (*Panthera onca palustris*), the *capuchino* monkey (*Cebus apella*) the *puma* (*Puma concolor*), the Andean cat (*Oreailurus jacobita*), the *huillín* (*Lontra provocax*), and the *huemul* or South Andean deer (*Hippocamelus bisulcus*). The increase in single-crop farming (also called monocropping) since the late 1980s—particularly of genetically modified crops like soybeans but also others destined for the production of agrofuels, especially sugarcane—has triggered radical transformations over large areas, accelerating ongoing processes of soil erosion and pollution resulting from extensive use of agrochemicals.

Since the 1990s the region has seen rapidly expanding mining activities also, and even countries without a mining tradition, like Uruguay, are now active in the field. Chile and Bolivia currently depend on mining for around 23 and 12 percent of their gross domestic product, respectively, while the significance of mining is growing in the other Southern Cone countries as well (United Nations 2010). For instance, Argentina, Bolivia, and Chile control 85 percent of the known world reserves of lithium, a mineral at the center of the production of batteries for various uses, including mobile phones and electric cars (FUNDAMIN 2012). Argentina and Chile also have under development some of the world's largest copper, gold, and silver mines, a movement triggered by increasing demand for these metals from China and India. Mining activities are currently a major factor of environmental transformations in the region, particularly in the Andes Mountains, where there are ongoing disputes regarding the impact of open-pit mining and the use of hazardous substances like cyanide and mercury in mining processes, which are threats to both fragile glacier systems and water resources.

Other important environmental transformations in the region are connected with the expansion of technologies for energy production. Argentina and Brazil are the nuclear powers in the region, having a number of functioning nuclear energy plants and currently developing new projects. Most of these nuclear plants are located in the vicinity of large metropolises like Buenos Aires and Rio de Janeiro. Exploitation of fossil fuel reserves has also strained environmental stability, including extraction of the recently discovered gigantic reserves of oil off the shores of southern Brazil; the introduction of hydraulic fracturing (called fracking) technologies for the extraction of oil and gas, being used particularly in Argentina; and the expansion of offshore oil exploration near the Falkland Islands (in Spanish, Islas Malvinas), an area disputed by Argentina and the United Kingdom.

The actual or potential environmental impacts of these activities are not fully understood, and there is a significant degree of sensitivity that often precludes open discussion of these matters. Environmental agencies such as the United Nations Environment Programme have highlighted the urgent need for action on a number of fronts, especially in the designation and enforcement of protected areas to reverse ecosystem degradation and loss of biodiversity. Although the Southern Cone region has a long record of environmental protection and has contributed to the scientific understanding of environmental processes and their history, environmental concerns tend to rank low among government priorities. Despite the fact that there have been significant changes in this area since the 1980s, and environmental policy has become more important than in the past, most policy decisions related to environmental issues are still subordinated to powerful economic and political interests, and the region continues to be characterized by the prevalence of an agenda that privileges development and economic growth with little regard for sustainability. The Southern Cone is experiencing an unprecedented level of success in the consolidation of democratic institutions, regional integration, and socioeconomic development, which is likely to be facilitated with the rise of Brazil as a global player. One of the major challenges facing the region in this new context will concern the capacity of the local societies to cope with the rapid social and environmental transformations being unleashed by the process.

José Esteban CASTRO
Newcastle University

See also Amazonia; Andes Mountains; Brazil; Ecotourism (the Americas); Mining (Andes); Parks and Protected Areas; Rio de Janeiro, Brazil; Social Movements (Latin America); Travel and Tourism Industry

FURTHER READING

Bank Information Center. (2012). Latin America. Retrieved March 26, 2012, from http://www.bicusa.org/en/Region.4.aspx

Crosby, Alfred W. (1986). *Ecological imperialism: The biological expansion of Europe, 900–1900*. Cambridge, UK: Cambridge University Press.

Fundación para el Desarrollo de la Minería Argentina (FUNDAMIN). (2012). *El triángulo del litio: Argentina, Chile y Bolivia poseen más del 85% de las reservas mundiales de litio* [The lithium triangle: Argentina, Chile and Bolivia have over 85% of the world's lithium reserves]. Buenos Aires: FUNDAMIN. Retrieved March 26, 2012, from http://www.fundamin.com.ar/es/info/5-minerales-argentinos/315-el-triangulo-del-litio-argentina-chile-y-bolivia-poseen-mas-del-85-de-las-reservas-mundiales-de-litio.html

Initiative for the Integration of Regional Infrastructure in South America (IIRSA). (2011). Homepage. Retrieved March 12, 2012, from http://www.iirsa.org

Instituto, Herbert Levy. (1997). *MERCOSUR: Un atlas social, cultural y económico*. [MERCOSUR: A social, cultural, and economic atlas]. Rio de Janeiro: Instituto Herbert Levy and Manrique Zago Ediciones.

National Museum of Natural History. (2002). South America: Centres of plant diversity and endemism, VIII Southern Cone. Retrieved January 31, 2003, from http://www.nmnh.si.edu/botany/projects/cpd/sa/sa-viii.htm#geography

Observatorio Latinoamericano de Conflictos Ambientales (OLCA). (2012). Homepage. Retrieved March 26, 2012, from http://www.olca.cl/oca/index.htm

Office of the United Nations High Commissioner for Human Rights (OHCHR) & United Nations Development Programme (UNDP). (2004). *Compilación de observaciones finales del Comité de Derechos Económicos, Sociales y Culturales sobre países de América Latina y el Caribe (1989–2004)* [Compilation of final observations from the Committee of Economic, Social and Cultural Rights on the countries of Latin America and the Caribbean (1989–2004)]. Santiago de Chile: OHCHR-UNDP.

Organization of American States (OAS). (2012). Demografía de la Cuenca del Plata [Demographics of the Río de la Plata basin]. Retrieved March 26, 2012, from http://www.oas.org/dsd/plata/demograf%C3%ADaf.htm

Redford, Kent Hubbard, & Eisenberg, John Frederick. (1992). *Mammals of the neotropics: Vol. II. The Southern Cone: Chile, Argentina, Uruguay, Paraguay.* Chicago: University of Chicago Press.

United Nations. (2010). *Sustainable development in Latin America and the Caribbean: Trends, progress, and challenges in sustainable consumption and production. mining, transport, chemicals and waste management; Report to the eighteenth Session of the Commission on Sustainable Development of the United Nations.* Santiago, Chile. Retrieved March 26, 2012, from http://www.un.org/esa/dsd/csd/csd_pdfs/csd-18/rims/LAC_background_eng.pdf

United Nations Development Programme (UNDP). (2004). *La democracia en América Latina: Hacia una democracia de ciudadanas y ciudadanos* [Democracy in Latin America: Towards a citizens' democracy]. Buenos Aires: Aguilar, Altea, Taurus, and Alfaguara.

United Nations Environment Programme (UNEP). (2010). *Latin America and the Caribbean: Environment Outlook. GEO LAC 3.* Panama City: UNEP.

Sydney, Australia

4.39 million est. pop. 2011

Sydney is the most populous and well known of Australia's major cities. Despite its natural beauty, mild climate, and highly developed economy, Sydney faces major challenges in achieving long-term sustainability in issues like transport, greenhouse gas emissions, land use, and the population's impacts on the environment.

Sydney is a highly developed global city, blessed with a temperate climate and beautiful natural surroundings, such as pristine beaches and World Heritage national parks, as well as renowned arts and entertainment. Sydneysiders work in a rich, service-based economy. Sydney's collective sense of confidence arguably reached its peak with the hosting of the 2000 Olympic Games, regarded at the time as the most successful games ever held. Since then, despite considerable further growth, there has been much public questioning of Sydney's land use planning, transport system, and overall development direction. Even with all the obvious trappings of wealth, development, and its natural endowment, Sydney's long-term sustainability is not guaranteed.

A Long and Rich Aboriginal History

People have lived in the Sydney region for tens of thousands of years. At the time of the European settlement in the late 1700s, the Sydney area was home to the Cadigal people, comprising about thirty smaller bands or clans (City of Sydney 2012). There were at least three distinct language groups, and the clans had differing dialects, customs, and cultures. In 1788 the British government established a convict settlement in Sydney. Although records of the original numbers of indigenous people are not reliable, it is known that the population fell dramatically even within the first few years of settlement (less than one thousand by the early 1800s) due to the ensuing violence between indigenous peoples and settlers, and their susceptibility to European diseases (Kohen 2000). Despite the unfortunate history, Aboriginal culture remains an important part of Sydney's identity through the lives of the descendants of the Eora nation (1.2 percent of Sydneysiders have Aboriginal heritage), and the names of many suburbs, features, and landmarks come from this ancient culture. There are also thousands of indigenous heritage sites around Sydney, with midden deposits (cultural debris associated with human occupation), stone tools, weapons, and particularly extensive rock engravings.

Development

Although not the first governor of Sydney, the Scottish major-general Lachlan Macquarie (1762–1824), known as the "Father of Australia," succeeded in getting some form to the city by the early 1820s. British and Irish convicts constructed much of the public infrastructure. Macquarie is often credited with changing the area from a convict settlement to a free settlement (Karskens 2009). During the next two decades the city expanded into distinct suburbs, bolstered by the arrival of many more free settlers from Britain and Ireland. In 1842 Sydney was declared the first city in Australia. Sydney was a gateway in the 1850s to a more diverse group of arrivals as part of the first of the Australian gold rushes. In the late 1800s, Sydney's industrialization included steam-powered transport, promoting a further wave of settlement and growth. The city reached a population of about half a million at the start of the twentieth century (Aplin 2000). Untouched by major natural disasters or warfare throughout the twentieth century, Sydney grew steadily, with further periods of considerable immigration in the two decades after World War II. By the early-twenty-first century the population had reached 4 million (MCU 2011).

Geography and Natural Heritage

Greater Sydney lies in a large coastal basin, with the iconic natural Sydney Harbour at its center. (Note that the Sydney basin referred to here is not the Sydney Basin, the much larger area defined by geological characteristics.) The basin is bounded on the north and south by major waterways, and extends west approximately 40 kilometers to the Blue Mountains. These mountains and the national parks to the north and south contain vast areas of genuine wilderness regions. In fact, the Royal National Park, on Sydney's southern boundary, was established in 1879 and is one of the oldest national parks in the world (NSW Government 2012). The waterways, beaches, and national parks provide myriad outdoor recreation opportunities. Sydney Harbour, although declining as an industrial port, is still busy with maritime tourism and recreational pursuits and is the home to a thriving marine ecology.

Although the harbor and rivers that feed it are beautiful natural resources, the varied topography of Sydney and the legacy of its haphazard beginnings have combined to create transport and urban planning difficulties. Five to six major business districts are spread around the Sydney metropolitan area. Transport linkages between these central business districts are generally poor, with vehicle congestion costs conservatively estimated to be AU$3–4 billion per year and increasing.

Economy and Social Development

Sydney is the largest city in Australia, with an area of about 2,000 square kilometers, and is the capital of the most populous state (New South Wales), as well as being a significant global city in terms of trade and finance activities. The major employers in Sydney are the service industries such as health, education, business services, and retail and wholesale trade. Manufacturing and construction combined amount to less than 20 percent of the total employment (MCU 2011). Beginning around 2005 and still expanding, Australia has been experiencing a resources boom with very strong demand and high prices for mining commodities. Sydney and the New South Wales economy more widely have not directly received much of the economic growth and employment associated with the mining boom. Despite this, the unemployment rate in Sydney in 2011 was 5 percent (MCU 2011). Further, with the concentration of higher-skilled service jobs, in 2008 Sydney had the highest labor productivity (measured as gross value added per hour worked) of any Australian city (MCU 2011).

The negative side of the relatively strong economy, geographical layout, and poor long-term planning is Sydney's very high housing costs. Housing affordability is a major component of Sydney's high cost of living. The Economics Intelligence Unit (EIU) ranks Sydney as the sixth most expensive city in the world (MCU 2011). Sydney also ranks sixth in the EIU's livability rankings for 2011, with Melbourne ranked first.

The high per capita gross domestic product (GDP) of Sydney and its relative size of 4.4 million people in a country of 22 million contribute to varied and vibrant music, arts, education, and sporting scenes. Coupled with a population with very diverse backgrounds (40 percent of Sydneysiders were born outside Australia [Australian Bureau of Statistics 2012]), residents and visitors to Sydney enjoy rich cultural offerings. The 2011 census revealed that after English, the next most widely spoken languages in Sydney are Arabic and then Mandarin.

Local Sustainability

In world terms, air quality in Sydney is good, high-quality water is available by tap, health care is strongly supported by the government, and in general most Sydneysiders have a very high quality of life. Water availability was a major issue during the drought period, which lasted most of the first decade of this century. Because of the periodic El Niño phenomenon (a major climate fluctuation affecting the whole Australian continent relating to oscillations in the temperature of large areas of the Pacific Ocean), water security concerns led to the investment in a large desalination system for Sydney. Water use restrictions also saw Sydney's average per capita direct annual water use fall to about 85,000 liters, still a large amount of water (MCU 2011).

Changes in land use in the Sydney metropolitan area continue to be a source of tension. Considerable areas of market gardens and very significant general agricultural production in the relatively more fertile areas of western Sydney are increasingly under pressure from suburban sprawl. A rising population, the popularity of detached housing, and the lure of economic stimulus from new house construction are driving this change.

An independent report on climate change impacts in New South Wales raised some important issues for Sydney (Climate Commission 2012). Temperature rises are conservatively estimated to lead to a tripling of the number of days over 35°C for all of the Sydney area between 2008 and 2100. The temperature rises will be exacerbated in western Sydney because of an intensifying urban heat island effect. Given its large areas of bush reserves and national parks, Sydney is also not immune from the effects of bush fires, which are expected to become more prevalent with climate change (Climate Commission 2012). The sea level rise at Sydney since the late 1800s is estimated to be 0.2 meters. With a sea level rise of 0.5 meters, which is on the low side of global average estimates for 2100, what were historically regarded as one-in-a-hundred-years flooding events are estimated to be likely to occur several times each year. Although these anticipated impacts of climate change on Sydney are starting to be discussed, there is as yet no widespread recognition of the magnitude of the impacts, let alone a coordinated mitigation response.

Of the electricity supply for Sydney, approximately 90 percent is sourced from black coal–fired generators located outside the Sydney metropolitan area, resulting in about 3 tonnes of carbon dioxide equivalent (CO_2e) emissions per person per year. This dominant electricity source coupled with thermally inefficient buildings and an increasing desire for higher thermal comfort levels has caused a significant problem in the management of peak power loads. The issue is exacerbated by the high afternoon peak temperatures in summer and the gradual rise in the number of installed air conditioners.

Governance issues are the final major influence on local sustainability. Sydney is made up of more than forty local government areas. The New South Wales state government has primary responsibility for major aspects of Sydney, but the Australian government funding and policies also have important bearing on Sydney. The complexities (political, financial, and bureaucratic) of the three levels of government have for many years restricted the optimum planning and development of Sydney.

Wider Sustainability—Sydney's Footprints

To assess the true sustainability of a population in a city requires consideration of all the resources and impacts required to support that population (Lenzen and Peters 2010). The ecological footprint concept takes this principle and measures it in terms of productive land area required for a population. For the average Sydneysider, the carbon footprint associated with direct energy use and electricity is about one-third of their total carbon footprint of about 20 tonnes CO_2e (ACF and University of Sydney 2012). The other two-thirds of the footprint are the emissions embodied in food, materials, air travel, and all other goods and services that make up the average expenditure profile for Sydneysiders (Lenzen, Dey, and Foran 2004). Similarly, the total water footprint for an average Sydneysider is typically a factor of ten higher than the direct water-use footprint given above. The dominance of the indirect components of energy, carbon, and water footprints is a consequence of high affluence and development. There is a real challenge therefore in considering how we design, build, and manage cities not only to reduce the direct sustainability impacts but also to reduce these indirect impacts.

Outlook

The sustainable development of a large, modern, affluent city such as Sydney, in the strong sense of the definition of sustainability, has not yet been proven. If additional stressors are thrown in such as further population and economic growth, the attainment of its status as a "sustainable city" becomes even more challenging. Sydney's improvements in its sustainability performance in the near future will largely come down to governance and social development. Good decisions in such areas as appropriate technology, financing, planning, and equity will be needed to address the practical needs of transport, food provision, electricity generation, and better health. The final challenge will be to grow in social development terms but not in terms of the city's environmental footprint.

Christopher DEY
University of Sydney

See also Auckland, New Zealand; Australia; Labor; Mobility; Murray-Darling River Basin; Oceania; Perth, Australia; Public Transportation; Urbanization

FURTHER READING

Aplin, Graeme. (2000). From colonial village to world metropolis. In John Connell (Ed.), *Sydney: The emergence of a global city*. Oxford, UK: Oxford University Press.

Australian Bureau of Statistics. (2012). Australian census 2011. Retrieved June 22, 2012, from http://www.abs.gov.au/census

Australian Conservation Foundation (ACF), & University of Sydney. (2012). Consumption atlas. Retrieved June 18, 2012, from http://202.60.88.196/consumptionatlas

City of Sydney. (2012). Barani: Indigenous history of Sydney City. Retrieved June 18, 2012, from http://www.cityofsydney.nsw.gov.au/barani/themes/theme1.htm

Climate Commission. (2012). The critical decade: New South Wales climate impacts and opportunities. Retrieved June 12, 2012, from http://climatecommission.gov.au/wp-content/uploads/NSW-report_final_web.pdf

Karskens, Grace. (2009). The colony: A history of early Sydney. Sydney: Allen and Unwin.

Kohen, Jim L. (2000). First and last peoples: Aboriginal Sydney. In John Connell (Ed.), *Sydney: The emergence of a global city*. Oxford, UK: Oxford University Press.

Lenzen, Manfred; Dey, Christopher; & Foran, Barney. (2004). Energy requirements of Sydney households. *Ecological Economics*, *49*(3), 375–399.

Lenzen, Manfred, & Peters, Greg M. (2010). How city dwellers affect their resource hinterland. *Journal of Industrial Ecology*, *14*(1), 73–90.

Major Cities Unit (MCU). (2011). State of Australian cities 2011. Canberra, Australia: Department of Infrastructure and Transport. Retrieved June 15, 2012, from http://www.infrastructure.gov.au/infrastructure/mcu/soac.aspx

New South Wales (NSW) Government. (2012). Royal National Park. Retrieved June 12, 2012, from http://www.environment.nsw.gov.au/NationalParks/parkHistory.aspx?id=N0030

T

Toronto, Canada

2.6 million city est. pop. 2012; 9 million metropolitan area est. pop. 2012

Toronto, the capital of the province of Ontario, is the municipal core of Canada's Greater Golden Horseshoe region. Due to the efforts of provincial and local governance and civic society, the region has a history stretching back to the 1950s of making sustainable choices with respect to green space conservation—including a major greenbelt—and regional and community planning.

Toronto is a city within a very large, very diverse urban region in south-central Canada. The city itself is an amalgamation of several historical cities and towns, with a population of 2,615,000 in a land area of 630 square kilometers (Statistics Canada 2012). It has a continuous public waterfront trail along the shoreline of Lake Ontario, a ravine system that provides green space, a transit system, and a bike-friendly culture. The city has a strong commitment to tolerance and social welfare, complementing the provincial public health care and federal welfare systems. The city diverts from landfill much of its organic waste through yard waste collection and a household green bin program and successfully diverts recyclables. Making sustainability a part of everyday life and decision making is a challenge, but Toronto is moving in the right direction.

Toronto is the core of the Greater Golden Horseshoe region, named for its shape as it encircles the northern edge of Lake Ontario. The region has a population of 9 million (which is almost one-quarter of the entire population of Canada) and is expected to grow to 11.5 million by 2031 due to Toronto's role as Canada's gateway city for international in-migration (Ontario Ministry of Infrastructure 2006). This makes it by far the largest urban region in Canada (ahead of Montreal and Vancouver) and one of the largest urban regions in North America in population after regions centered in New York, Mexico City, and Los Angeles. As a rapidly growing region, sustainability concerns such as sprawl and affordable housing, commuting and traffic congestion, income inequality and distribution of services, natural system conservation and water quality, and farmland conservation and food security are high on the public agenda. To tackle these issues, in the first decade of the twenty-first century the provincial government created a 728,500-hectare greenbelt to protect source water, natural heritage systems, and agricultural land, along with a growth plan to direct population and employment growth to designated urban nodes served by an ambitious expansion in the road and transit system.

History

Toronto has grown from a center of First Nations gathering, trade, and settlement into modern Canada's hub for the banking and financial sector. (In Canada, First Nations refers to aboriginal peoples who are neither Inuit nor Métis.) Founded as the British colony of York in 1763, it is unique in its inland location on the Great Lakes system—the world's largest freshwater system—with direct access to the Atlantic Ocean through the Saint Lawrence Seaway. It is located in one of the most southern, fertile, and temperate zones in Canada. With Toronto at its center, the city-region has been planned and developed in a horseshoe-shaped arc close to the shoreline of the lake and northward along Yonge Street (which is said to be the longest road in the world and stretches from the center of the city on Lake Ontario to Lake Simcoe at what is now the urban-rural fringe of the metropolitan area in the north). This northern line of development along Yonge Street intersects with the Oak

Ridges Moraine, a significant landform in an otherwise flat topographical region. The moraine is a large glacial deposit dubbed the "rain barrel" of Toronto, which is underlaid by extensive aquifers and overlaid by the headwaters of the rivers flowing through the city to the lake (Bocking 2005). By the late 1980s the city's sprawling suburbs resulted in pressure to conserve the moraine, culminating in the creation of the Greenbelt in 2006. The Greenbelt builds on a history of landscape-scale protection in southern Ontario: most significantly the protection of the Niagara Escarpment (the granite shoreline of a prehistoric lake) that began in the 1970s—now a World Biosphere Reserve—and the planning for water management within all watersheds through conservation authorities that began in the late 1950s. The Greenbelt encompasses both the 190,000-hectare Oak Ridges Moraine Conservation Plan area and the 195,000-hectare Niagara Escarpment Conservation Plan area, with the rest of the land designated as Protected Countryside for conservation of the natural system and agricultural system. In addition, strong greenlands policies in the comprehensive plans of regional and local municipal plans provide a great deal of natural system protection.

Economy and Society

Toronto historically has had strong economic ties to the United States, which continues to be its largest trading partner (followed by Asia and the European Union). Toronto has been and continues to be a major manufacturing center in spite of global shifts in goods production that have reduced its automotive manufacturing base. It has a strong knowledge-based economy centered on finance, real estate, and business services. Its agricultural industries also make a strong contribution to the region's economy.

Toronto is one of the most demographically diverse places in the world, with people from over two hundred countries speaking more than 170 languages (Toronto, City of 2008). The challenge has been to create a livable environment for this diverse population, and although Toronto is not without its struggles, it is generally seen to be a safe and tolerant city. Many new immigrants live in relative poverty and face barriers to finding skilled work despite being highly educated. They are concentrated in a ring of 1960s-era suburbs—where access to transit and to stores and services is a problem—in the "in-between city" between the older, more well-to-do pre-war suburbs and the newer suburbs of the outlying areas (Young, Wood, and Keil 2011; Hulchanski 2010; United Way 2011). Where once Toronto had one of the best subway systems in the world, now the city is considered to be quite poorly served (in terms of mode, routes, and funding) due to lack of ongoing investment.

LiveGreen Toronto is a major sustainability initiative by the city's Environment Office. The initiative promotes a wide range of behavior changes for residents and businesses, including reduction of automobile commuting, incorporation of green roofs, improving stormwater management, and encouraging the community through grants and events to adopt sustainable behaviors (Toronto, City of 2012).

Waste reduction has been very successful in the city. Toronto's main landfill started to reach capacity in the 1990s, and the search for a new strategy triggered years of debate over what to do with the city's solid waste (Walker 1995). Although a new landfill site was finally announced in 2007, the effect of the debate has been a dramatic reduction in the amount of waste sent to landfill, with half of all residential waste already diverted through composting and recycling (Toronto, City of 2011).

Toronto has strong civil society groups and a typically progressive city government making a difference in sustainability issues, including addressing climate change, improving transit and housing, providing immigrant settlement services, funding food banks, and participating in local planning. Nongovernmental organizations such as the Toronto Environmental Alliance, the Center for City Ecology, and Evergreen shape the civic agenda and engage residents in city building (McBride and Wilcox 2005).

Planning and Development

Toronto was the home of the famous urbanist Jane Jacobs, who championed the city's livability in the 1960s at a time when US cities were being abandoned for the suburbs. Jane Jacobs wrote *The Death and Life of Great American Cities* (1961) in reaction to the evisceration of New York City in the 1950s by the slum clearance and expressway building led by US urban planner Robert Moses (Caro 1975). She came to Canada to avoid her sons' pending conscription into the Vietnam War, settled in Toronto, and soon became involved in stopping the Spadina Expressway, a major highway that would have sliced through what are now some of Toronto's most sought-after leafy neighborhoods (Alexiou 2007). Jacobs passed away in 2006, and her legacy is commemorated every year on the first weekend in May through Jane's Walks, an initiative that encourages residents to explore their neighborhoods and meet their neighbors (Jane's Walk 2010).

The city is also known for being part of the first metropolitan region in North America to create a coordinated plan for its thirteen cities: in 1954 it built the structure of roads and transit that still shapes the region today. In the 1970s the areas surrounding metropolitan

Toronto were organized into regional municipalities: York, Durham, Peel, and Halton regions each has its own comprehensive plan for contiguous growth within designated urban service areas to limit sprawl in rural areas. In 1998, through provincially mandated amalgamation, Metro Toronto and its cities became the City of Toronto.

Don Mills was planned in the 1950s as a self-contained suburb of the city of Toronto and the first of its kind in North America. It was the model for a generation of suburbs built at highway interchanges with bull's eye concentrations of apartment-style housing and shopping centers in the middle surrounded by decreasing densities of housing organized around elementary schools and a park system with industrial buildings at the outskirts. Don Mills is now being reimagined with the redevelopment of the central shopping mall into a contemporary lifestyle center that introduces through streets, a pedestrian orientation, and new condominium housing. Older single detached bungalow homes on generous lots are being rapidly turned over into very large homes and intensification of employment areas is occurring.

Since 2000 Toronto has experienced a condominium boom, from eight-to-ten-story mid-rises along designated avenues to thirty-to-eighty-story high-rises. The tall buildings are changing the face of the downtown area of the city. On one hand they exemplify sustainability by concentrating people in the existing downtown area and making use of existing infrastructure. On the other, they raise concerns about the long-term livability of high-rise neighborhoods due to poor urban design, isolation of superblock projects from the rest of the city, and the lack of family-sized units. At the same time there are established, leafy neighborhoods of homes built in the pre-war era served by streetcars. The centers of suburban cities in the region are also experiencing revitalization through condominiums and new retail formats—for instance, the City of Mississauga is in the process of changing from one whose city center is defined by a shopping mall to a vibrant, walkable, high-density urban core.

In many ways Toronto is a model of sustainability for the rest of the world in its tolerance for social and cultural diversity, conservation of green spaces and ecological function, economic prosperity, and strong governance.

Laura TAYLOR
York University

See also Architecture; Canada; Detroit, United States; Great Lakes and Saint Lawrence River; Mobility; New York City, United States; North American Free Trade Agreement (NAFTA); Public Transportation; United States; Urbanization; Vancouver, Canada

FURTHER READING

Amati, Marco, & Taylor, Laura. (2010). From green belts to green infrastructure. *Planning Practice and Research*, 25(2), 143–155.

Alexiou, Alice Sparberg. (2007). *Jane Jacobs: Urban visionary*. Toronto: HarperCollins.

Bocking, Stephen. (2005). Protecting the rain barrel: Discourses and the roles of science and the roles of science in a suburban environmental controversy. *Environmental Politics*, 14(5), 611–628.

Caro, Robert A. (1975). *The power broker: Robert Moses and the fall of New York*. New York: Vintage.

Hodge, Gerald, & Robinson, Ira M. (2001). *Planning Canadian regions*. Vancouver, Canada: UBC Press.

Hulchanski, J. David. (2010). *The three cities within Toronto: Income polarization among Toronto's neighbourhoods, 1970–2005*. Toronto: Cities Centre University of Toronto. Retrieved May 11, 2012, from http://www.urbancentre.utoronto.ca/pdfs/curp/tnrn/Three-Cities-Within-Toronto-2010-Final.pdf

Jacobs, Jane. (1961). *The death and life of great American cities*. New York: Vintage.

Jane's Walk. (2010). Homepage. Retrieved May 11, 2012, from http://www.janeswalk.com

McBride, Jason, & Wilcox, Alana. (Eds.). (2005). *Utopia: Towards a new Toronto*. Toronto: Coach House Books.

Ontario Ministry of Infrastructure. (2006). *Growth plan for the Greater Golden Horseshoe, 2006*. Toronto: Queen's Printer. Retrieved May 11, 2012, from https://www.placestogrow.ca/index.php?option=com_content&task=view&id=9&Itemid=12

Ontario Ministry of Municipal Affairs and Housing. (2005). *Protecting the greenbelt: The greenbelt plan*. Toronto: Queen's Printer. Retrieved May 11, 2012, from http://www.mah.gov.on.ca/Page189.aspx

Statistics Canada. (2006). 2006 Census: Portrait of the Canadian population in 2006: Subprovincial population dynamics. Retrieved May 11, 2012, from http://www12.statcan.gc.ca/census-recensement/2006/as-sa/97-550/p14-eng.cfm

Statistics Canada. (2012). Census profile: Toronto. Retrieved May 11, 2012, from http://www12.statcan.gc.ca/census-recensement/2011/dp-pd/prof/details/page.cfm?Lang=E&Geo1=CSD&Code1=3520005&Geo2=PR&Code2=35&Data=Count&SearchText=Toronto&SearchType=Begins&SearchPR=01&B1=All&GeoLevel=PR&GeoCode=3520005

Taylor, Zachary Todd, & van Nostrand, John. (2008). Shaping the Toronto region, past, present, and future. Retrieved May 11, 2012, from http://www.neptis.org/library/show.cfm?id=86&cat_id=11

Toronto, City of. (2008). Backgrounder: Release of the 2006 Census on ethnic origin and visible minorities. Retrieved June 18, 2012, from http://www.toronto.ca/demographics/pdf/2006_ethnic_origin_visible_minorities_backgrounder.pdf

Toronto, City of. (2011). 2011 waste diversion. Retrieved June 18, 2012, from http://www.toronto.ca/garbage/pdf/2011-graph.pdf

Toronto, City of. (2012). Toronto Environment Office. Retrieved June 18, 2012, from http://www.toronto.ca/teo/index.htm

United Way. (2011). Poverty by postal code 2: Vertical poverty, declining income, housing quality and community life in Toronto's inner suburban high-rise apartments. Retrieved May 11, 2012, from http://www.unitedwaytoronto.com/verticalpoverty/report/introduction/

Urban Strategies Inc. & Hariri Pontarini Architects. (2010). Tall buildings: Inviting change in downtown Toronto. Retrieved May 11, 2012, from http://www.toronto.ca/planning/tallbuildingstudy.htm#study

Walker, Gerald. (1995). Social mobilization in the city's countryside: Rural Toronto fights waste dump. *Journal of Rural Studies*, 11(3), 243–254.

Young, Douglas; Wood, Patricia Burke; & Keil, Roger. (Eds.). (2011). *In-between infrastructure: Urban connectivity in an age of vulnerability*. Vancouver, Canada: Praxis (e)Press. Retrieved May 11, 2012, from http://www.praxis-epress.org/availablebooks/inbetween.html

Travel and Tourism Industry

Travel and tourism grew exponentially following World War II. The concept of sustainable travel and tourism came about in the 1980s as a result of the industry's excesses, which included damage to local economies and local ecosystems. Sustainable tourism comprises economic efficiency, environmental conservation, and social equity. Although small-scale tourism developers and innovators have laid the groundwork for sustainable tourism, concerns remain, especially about cultural sites.

The travel and tourism industry initially gave rise to the development of mass tourism in the post–World War II era. Members of the industry, however, did not begin to adopt socially and environmentally responsible practices until the 1980s. There is an inherent paradox in the concepts of *the travel and tourism industry* and *sustainable tourism* because the former, through its excesses, has largely given rise to a need for the latter. Even decades after the industry has attempted to implement sustainable practices in the travel sector, however, the corporate scale of the tourism industry is often at odds with the more manageable scope that communities and environments need.

Experts define sustainable tourism in a variety of ways. The Greek sustainable tourism expert Haris Coccossis identifies three goals: economic efficiency, environmental conservation, and social equity (Mbaiwa and Stronza 2009, 335). Another way to define sustainable tourism is to analyze the relationships between the various parties involved: (1) the local participants—host communities, governments, and the environment—and (2) external participants—tourists, corporations, and nongovernmental organizations. The stronger the relationships between these six participants, the more likely they are to achieve sustainable outcomes. These relationships provide a basis for understanding the state of the travel and tourism industry throughout the Americas and in Oceania.

Corporate Evolution

Travel and tourism corporations in the Americas and Oceania played a key role between 1945 and 1980 in alienating many of the relationships that make up sustainable tourism. International airlines, often in tandem with hotel companies, undermined relationships between locals and visitors by creating large ecological footprints in host communities with massive hotels and airport facilities that generally accommodated large jets. Studies calculated models of economic development through tourism that showed a multiplier effect on local development. These studies did not predict the disparities with local scale, however, that left behind less compensation for locals and for environmental protection. To make matters worse, these studies rarely if ever considered the impact of mass tourism on local ecosystems.

Early tourism development, however, led to the first stage of sustainable development: regional planning for economic development across economies (including service and agricultural sectors). Global organizations such as the United States Agency for International Development (USAID), the World Bank, and the United Nations Educational, Scientific and Cultural Organization (UNESCO) originally commissioned studies on tourism planning because they recognized the connection between cultural preservation, economic development, and the need for regional versus larger-scale planning. These studies, however, did not necessarily integrate practices that respected the relationships between host communities, visitors, the environment, and corporations. Host governments have often chosen profits over long-term viability. They have emphasized economic development rather than protected the objects or sites of native peoples, known as *cultural patrimony*, and broken the bonds that create sustainable tourism (Addison 2008 offers a variety of examples).

The first environmental critiques of mass tourism's impacts on regional environments and the alienation of local populations in places as diverse as Acapulco and Venice came about in the late 1960s and 1970s. Small-scale tourism developers and innovators laid the foundations for sustainable tourism. The US philanthropist and conservationist Laurance Rockefeller took an incipient step toward sustainable tourism by siting small hotels near or within national parks throughout the United States and in the Caribbean (see Winks and Babbitt 1997). In the US state of South Carolina, the US developer Charles Fraser pioneered arguably the first sustainable resort, known as Sea Pines (see Shofner 2010–2011).

Current Practices

In the Americas mass tourism has traditionally dominated areas best known for sand and surf. Beginning in the first half of the twentieth century, US airline carriers such as Pan American began offering people affordable access from the United States to Mexico and the Caribbean. More recently there has been a significant shift: although US air carriers and hoteliers exert significant influence in the Caribbean basin, Spanish hoteliers and European charter companies have made access to more peripheral locations in the Americas and Oceania much easier.

At the local level, national, state, and municipal governments in emerging nations have made international access to peripheral locations easier. The Mexican government, for example, through its tourism development arm, Fondo Nacional de Fomento al Turismo (FONATUR), has maintained Cancún and Los Cabos, among other peripheral locations, for mass tourism. Cancún was home to over twenty-four thousand hotel rooms by 2006. The even more decentralized area known as the Riviera Maya soon surpassed Cancún in its number of rooms. These targeted development "poles," located in sparsely populated areas, have linked foreign tourism interests with state growth, often to the detriment of sustainable development. Cancún is now a metropolitan area with a wide-ranging periphery. According to the paradigm of sustainable relationships outlined above, state-driven tourism development, as a whole, has tended to privilege national development objectives over local residents' needs and concerns as well as to foster strong ties to the international tourism trade sector (Ward 2008).

One of the great questions regarding sustainable tourism concerns the management of growth. Applicants for hotel and resort development in Cuba, for example, have to pass through a gauntlet of at least a dozen agencies before the government approves a project. In Mexico, FONATUR exercises significant jurisdiction over its planned tourism committees, streamlining the process. Other resort developments, such as Punta Cana on the eastern coast of the Dominican Republic, developed under the direction of the Dominican businessman and hotelier Frank Rainieri and the US attorney and labor mediator Theodore Kheel, have used a multipronged approach to sustainable tourism development. On the one hand, price limits the tourists' footprint (as well as the number of residential developments) on the beaches fronting the Mona Passage between Puerto Rico and the Dominican Republic. The developers have supplemented this approach by using salt-resistant grasses on the golf courses and paying careful attention to the regional development of human resources, as opposed to relying on foreigners to manage and operate the resort (Ward 2008).

Other areas of the Americas have attempted to carve out niche markets like Punta Cana for "sustainable tourism." Costa Rica looms as one of the most prominent of these locations, boasting national environmental policies consonant with an emphasis on sustainable tourism practices. Sustainable tourism policies in the Caribbean basin should rely at the least as much on best practices as well as exclusionary pricing schemes to promote sustainable tourism. This approach demonstrates a strong commitment to local stakeholders, whose labor and livelihood is highly important to the development of peripheral regions.

Debates related to sustainable development have not excluded cultural tourism. Private advertising has been perhaps the most influential component of tourism development in emerging nations in the Americas. A 2007 contest to identify the New Seven Wonders of the World exemplifies this approach. In Peru, the results of this contest have pitted the development interests of the state, represented by President Alan Garcia, against those concerned with preservation of cultural patrimony. This conflict was nowhere more evident than at Machu Picchu. While preservationists called for greater attention to safeguarding the carrying capacity (the number of visitors the site can accommodate) of the Machu Picchu site, not to mention the fragile buildings, regional and national officials pushed for exponential increases in tourist numbers. The tilt toward mass tourism continued with plans to build a new international airport at Cuzco, which will further erode the impediment of distance for international tourists anxious to visit the Sacred Valley. Access versus preservation ultimately will be a principal concern for sustainable tourism in the twenty-first century.

Elsewhere in the Americas evidence is emerging that regionally oriented tourism, instead of internationally oriented tourism, could exercise a lighter footprint on the environment while at the same time benefiting local businesses and workers. In the mid-to-late 1980s, the Mexican tourism development agency, FONATUR, pressed forward with plans to develop twin tourism poles at Cabo San Lucas and nearby Loreto. While Cabo San Lucas attracted international attention, Loreto lagged behind. Recent research suggests, however, that local workers in Loreto have fared as well as their counterparts in Cabo San Lucas because a significant percentage of earnings in Cabo San Lucas leave the region en route to their international operators. Other factors also account for priorities in domestic tourism development over international tourism development. Cartagena, Colombia, boasts a high level of local Colombian ownership in the historic city, as well as on the beaches of Bocagrande. Although sprawl has enveloped this magnet of Colombia's poorest region, the Colombian Caribbean, the city remained relatively isolated (and visited primarily by Colombians) until the early twenty-first century, when drug-related violence began to decline.

Tourism in Oceania includes but is not limited to the Hawaiian Islands, Australia, and New Zealand. Much more so than the Caribbean, this area has served as a borderland between the tourists of two regions—in this case Asia and the Americas. Hawaii emerged as an early attraction for North Americans and later Japanese tourists. Japanese tourism to Australia continued strongly in the 1980s and early 1990s. In the late 1990s to the early twenty-first century, New Zealand parlayed its position on the silver screen, most notably in films such as the *Lord of the Rings* trilogy, into tourism success. The British sociologist Rodanthi Tzanelli (2004, 30) noted the transformation in New Zealand tourism in the late twentieth century and then again since the New Zealand filmmaker Sir Peter Robert Jackson's trilogy met wide acclaim: "Historically the country attracted adventurous European and Australian travelers. . . . [Yet the] generation of ties between local and global capitalist economy also contributed to an influx of foreign tourists, notably eco-tourists from Japan, Taiwan, Korea and Germany." Tzanelli (2004, 37) states that the transformation of New Zealand's traditionally eco-friendly landscapes into Middle Earth also transformed the nature and volume of tourism to New Zealand, noting that "[between] September 2002 and 2003, [*Lord of the Rings*]–induced tourism earned NZ$6.4 billion (US$4.4 billion) and the amount has been growing since." As in the case of Machu Picchu, state- and private-sector actors have been responsible for capitalizing on these opportunities that one day could run the same risk posed by the so-called tragedy of the commons (overuse or depletion of a shared, limited resource). In this case, external and internal actors must consider the long-term consequences of their stewardship over New Zealand's landscapes.

Outlook

If there is one virtue of the size of the travel industry, it is the scale on which sustainable practices and ideas can be diffused (see Kaplan 2008). Although various definitions of sustainable tourism exist, most stress the transcendence of environmental and social responsibility and a recognition of the relationships that exist within the tourism enclaves. In the main, the corporate scale of the travel industry has made it difficult, but not impossible, to adopt sustainable practices (see Carroll 1999).

Evan R. WARD
Brigham Young University

See also Amazonia; Australia; Brazil; Canada; Caribbean; Central America; Ecotourism (the Americas); Mobility; New Zealand; Oceania; Parks and Protected Areas; Rural Development (the Americas); Southern Cone; United States

Further Reading

Addison, Alonzo C. (2008). *Disappearing world: 101 of the Earth's most extraordinary and endangered places*. New York: Harper.

Carroll, Archie B. (1999). Corporate social responsibility. *Business & Society, 38*(3), 268–295.

Fondo Nacional de Fomento al Turismo (FONATUR). (2005). *30 años de inversion con buen destino* [30 years of investment with good outcomes]. Mexico City: FONATUR.

Joppe, Marion. (1996). Sustainable community tourism development revisited. *Tourism Management, 17*(7), 475–479.

Kaplan, Adam. (2008, May 1). Greening in the United States hotel sector: An exploratory examination (Master's thesis, University of Nevada–Las Vegas). Retrieved May 4, 2012, from http://digitalcommons.library.unlv.edu/cgi/viewcontent.cgi?article=1610&context=thesesdissertations

Mbaiwa, Joseph E., & Stronza, Amanda L. (2009). The challenges and prospects for sustainable tourism and ecotourism in developing countries. In Tazim Jamal & Mike Robinson (Eds.), *The SAGE handbook of tourism studies* (pp. 333–353). London: Sage Publications.

Organisation for Economic Co-operation and Development. (1980). *The impact of tourism on the environment: General report*. Paris: Organisation for Economic Co-operation and Development.

Shofner, Markham. (2010–2011). *Man, nature and new ideas: The legacy of Sea Pines Plantation* (Bachelor's thesis, Pomona College, Claremont University). Retrieved March 2, 2012, from http://ea.pomona.edu/wp-content/uploads/SHOFNER-thesis-final2.pdf

Telver, David J., & Sharpley, Richard. (2008). *Tourism and development in the developing world*. New York: Routledge.

Tzanelli, Rodanthi. (2004). Constructing the "cinematic tourist": The "sign industry" of *The Lord of the Rings*. *Tourist Studies, 4*(1), 21–42.

Ward, Evan R. (2008). *Packaged vacations: Tourism development in the Spanish Caribbean*. Gainesville: University Press of Florida.

Winks, Robin W., & Babbitt, Bruce. (1997). *Laurance S. Rockefeller: Catalyst for conservation*. Washington, DC: Island Press.

Berkshire's authors and editors welcome questions, comments, and corrections. Send your emails about the *Berkshire Encyclopedia of Sustainability* in general or this volume in particular to: sustainability.updates@berkshirepublishing.com

United States

The environmental history of the United States follows a distinct pattern: natural resource exploitation (mainly forests), which led to the development of the conservation movement, followed by concern about wilderness preservation before the modern environmental movement appeared in the post-World War II era. Today environmentalists are as much concerned by pollution, urban development, and climate change as with conserving and preserving wilderness.

The environmental history of the United States from European settlement to the present is a history of land and resource use based first on the exploitation of forests, wildlife, soils, grasslands, and minerals, followed later by conservation and resource management. Although native peoples had used the land for thousands of years prior to English settlement beginning in the seventeenth century, the rapid growth of population over the first three hundred years of European settlement took a toll on many resources. By the late nineteenth century, resource depletion sparked the conservation and preservation movements, which sought to manage resources—in the words of Gifford Pinchot, the first chief of the US Forest Service—for the "greatest good, of the greatest number, for the longest time," and to set aside lands for national parks and to preserve wildlife and wilderness. By the end of the twentieth century the environmental movement focused on environmental quality and justice and included the regulation of industrial pollution and urban development.

Over time, science has played an integral role in shaping the environment. It was initially used to exploit natural resources, starting with forests, but the conservation movement soon engaged science as a tool for developing resources more efficiently. The twentieth-century environmental movement used the sciences not only to manage resources but also to justify not developing them at all.

Natural Resource Exploitation

Forests were the first natural resource exploited and then brought under management in the United States. Raphael Zon, one of the first US foresters, observed, "No other economic and geographical factor has so profoundly affected the development of the country as forests" (Williams 1989, 4). Until the 1820s, European settlers looked upon forests as hindrances to be removed for agriculture, even though they often provided essential resources settlers needed. In a subtle shift in attitude, the growing demand for wood by the mid-nineteenth century led business people, land speculators, and even the federal government to view forests as just another agricultural commodity to be bought, sold, and harvested. Changes in saw technology and manufacturing made increased production possible. By 1850 the lumber industry had become the second-largest industry in the United States and remained among the top five industries until 1920. Census figures show that lumber production had been rising swiftly over the last half of the nineteenth century.

Forests provided more than just timber. They also provided habitat for essential game animals that provided meat for settlers and Native Americans alike and valuable skins and pelts for trade with European merchants. As early as 1604, French and British explorers began trading with Native Americans: French and British furs for knives, glasses, combs, hatchets, kettles, and food. Between 1700 and 1775, the beaver supplied over half of England's total fur imports, and eight other animals totaled another 40 percent of imports. The beaver and its habitats disappeared from the New England states, as did other associated species. Hunters exterminated the white-tailed deer in all of New England except Maine by 1890, along with the buffalo, the American elk, caribou, and moose from the region by then. Several tribes in New England had become dependent on European traders for food and European tools, which accelerated the rate at which animals were killed. This pattern of exploitation and extermination was repeated in other regions with other animals used for trade purposes, including otter (West Coast), buffalo (the Great Plains), and deer (the Southeast).

Agriculture also contributed to environmental problems. In the South, early dependence on commercial crops created a vicious cycle: because tobacco and cotton quickly rob the soil of nutrients, land had to be rehabilitated by being enriched with fertilizer or by being left fallow for several seasons, or new land had to be acquired. Impatient growers, who were focused on immediate profits rather than long-term planning, moved on to new land instead of developing environmentally beneficial practices. Commercial production led to the wasteful clearing of forests as farmers continually relocated. Clearing land of ground cover created soil erosion problems: waterways clogged with silt and vital topsoil lost.

The Conservation Movement

Just as forests were the first resource exploited, they were also the first resource protected. The dramatic increase in lumber production during the late 1800s, coupled with the visual evidence of how deforestation altered the landscape, created fear of a timber famine. The conservation movement of the late nineteenth century was a direct response to that fear. In the 1860s and 1870s, a small group of US scientists and political leaders, including George Perkins Marsh, Charles S. Sargent, and Carl Schurz, spoke out against the rapid deforestation, as well as the depletion of water, minerals, and soil. Interest groups, often founded and led by the wealthy, such as the American Forestry Association (forests), the Boone and Crockett Club (big game), and the National Audubon Society (birds), formed to protect specific resources; recreation groups like the Appalachian Mountain Club and the Sierra Club also became involved when industrial activities threatened the places where they hiked or camped. They deplored the unregulated exploitation of natural resources and called for government action on public land. Many favored conservation, or the sustained yield of renewable resources, such as water, trees, and game animals, and the careful, scientific management of both renewable and nonrenewable resources on a permanent basis. They petitioned Congress to take action. States like Wisconsin and New York, where large amounts of forest had been cleared for agriculture and lumber, set aside land to protect watersheds but did not actively try to improve or manage the land itself.

After years of such agitation, Congress responded by passing first the Forest Reserve Act in 1891 and subsequently the Forest Management Act in 1897; together these laws laid the foundation for federal land management. At the same time, government science bureaus (increasingly staffed by graduates of recently formed professional schools) were being established. Decisive action, however, began only during Theodore Roosevelt's presidency (1901–1909). His administration made scientific land management for utilitarian purposes (captured in Pinchot's "the greatest good" phrase) accepted policy. This policy also contributed to a split within the nascent conservation movement when the federal government approved construction of a dam in the Hetch Hetchy Valley of Yosemite National Park to provide water to the city of San Francisco: preservationists who wanted to leave the valley undeveloped no longer trusted the US Forest Service to protect federal lands and successfully agitated for creation of a separate national park system and bureau to manage those lands.

Federal conservation measures protected only public lands, however, not private lands. Clearing land for agriculture remained the biggest factor in altering the environment. Forest removal had caused flooding, soil erosion, and loss of wildlife and their habitats on land and in waterways, sometimes causing permanent changes. In 1911, out of concern for watershed protection, Congress passed the Weeks Act, which enabled the federal government to purchase private lands in the eastern United States for incorporation into the national forest system and to establish a federal-state cooperative framework for fire protection. In the 1920s, automobiles made forests and parks more accessible to more people. The internal combustion engine also helped mechanize farming and logging, although the ramifications of this were not immediately understood.

In the 1930s, President Franklin Roosevelt's administration, faced with the twin crises of the Great Depression and environmental overexploitation, expanded state-controlled management. Through programs such as this—and the Civilian Conservation Corps and the Tennessee Valley Authority and agencies like the Forest Service and the Grazing Service—the government tried to use science and commerce to reverse environmental damage on both private and public lands. Soil conservation became a major priority in the Great Plains and the South during the mid-1930s. The Agricultural Adjustment Act of 1933 created the Agricultural Adjustment Administration, which paid farmers to kill their animals and not to cultivate land. This allowed land to recover and raised prices of crops and farming produce. At the same time, the government purchased almost 5.7 million hectares of abandoned and exhausted farm and forest land in the eastern United States and initiated reforestation programs under the Weeks Act. Fire protection of forest lands expanded, bringing private associations and companies and private landowners into the federal-state framework, with the common goal of completely removing the danger of fire to the landscape to protect timber resources.

Wilderness Preservation and Environmentalism

Wilderness preservation and protection had grown along with the conservation movement, but they largely remained a secondary priority until the 1960s. Until then, scientific research provided a rationale for subduing the wild for the benefit of humankind. Between the two world wars, federal and state governments supported the systematic elimination of wolves and other predators from grazing areas, parks, and forests to increase big game populations for hunters. They built roads and lodging facilities in public parks and forest recreation areas to make wilderness more accessible to more people. During World War II and in the postwar era the federal government responded to the unprecedented demands for natural resources by relaxing regulations on public lands and cooperating with industry. The environment suffered proportionate injury from increased extraction activities such as mining and lumbering, from the introduction of chemical pesticides in agriculture, and from the discharge of industrial waste into waterways, landfills, and the air.

The tragedies of the Dust Bowl era had exposed the weakness of unlimited scientific exploitation. Conservationists' focus on efficient development of natural resources no longer provided all the answers. Ecologists began explaining how human activity affects the environment and that humans are part of the environment, not separate from it. In the early 1950s, the general public's growing interest in outdoor activity in a more natural environment fused with the science of ecology to create the environmental movement. The unfettered access to public forests and parks allowed private citizens to see how government was managing public lands and led some to begin questioning policies and practices they deemed harmful to the environment. Environmental consciousness grew exponentially in the 1960s, influenced by concerns such as nuclear radiation from the testing of atomic weapons, an unsustainable increase in the birthrate, and the Santa Barbara, California, oil spill of 1969. This new consciousness received its greatest expression with the organization of the first Earth Day in 1970, when thousands of people joined in marches across the nation, proclaiming "Give Earth a Chance."

Some historians have stated that the book *Silent Spring* is responsible for launching the modern environmental movement in the United States. Rachel Carson, a government scientist with the US Fish and Wildlife Service, had written several environmental books before publishing her most famous one, *Silent Spring* (1962), which decried society's overuse of pesticides. Many people read Carson's work; extensive news coverage about her book led to more widespread concern about science and technology and its unregulated application in addressing various environmental problems. In response to this and other public concerns, the federal government passed a series of laws aimed at cleaning up air and water pollution and protecting wilderness areas and wild and scenic rivers. This culminated in the passage of the National Environmental Policy Act in 1969, whose aim was to promote the enhancement of the environment by establishing a system of procedures and assessments that all federal agencies had to follow. From that point forward, government policy evaluated resources for both their aesthetic value and commercial value. Carson's critique also contributed directly to the establishment of the Environmental Protection Agency in 1972.

Silent Spring also helped transform the environmental community. Membership in organizations like the Sierra Club, the Wilderness Society, and the National Audubon Society greatly increased during the 1960s. Many housewives in the new consumer- and technology-oriented postwar era took up Carson's arguments, horrified at the hidden dangers they now perceived to be lurking around their homes. These environmental issues particularly attracted young people, many of whom were also involved in the student and/or civil rights movements. With their involvement came new energy and ideas, and the focus eventually expanded from wilderness to include urban environmental problems (Taylor 2002, 8–9).

All sides in the debate over the environment deployed scientific arguments to support their causes. Some scientists favored responding to ecological problems with increased human intervention, whereas others, like Carson, favored a reduction. Industry used its own scientific findings to support the status quo or the removal of regulations. When information about ecological damage reached the general public, however, it generated a passionate desire to reduce human intervention. Private organizations such as the Wilderness Society and the Sierra Club expressed a desire to limit or halt development in public wilderness areas and to set them aside for protection on behalf of the general public. Demands to protect nature became a major factor in the debate over the environment. In 1965, 17 percent of the US public questioned in a Gallup poll said they wanted the government to tackle air and water pollution. By 1970, this figure had risen to 53 percent. Between 1972 and 1976, other polls indicated that between 46 and 60 percent of the US public were very concerned about reducing pollution. "Polls also showed that most respondents were not willing to relax environmental standards to achieve economic growth, did not think that pollution control requirements had gone too far, and did not think we had made enough progress on cleaning up the environment to start limiting the cost of pollution control" (Taylor 2002, 10).

The discovery of toxic waste under the Love Canal neighborhood in the city of Niagara Falls, New York, in the late 1970s shifted the focus to urban environmental problems. The neighborhood had been knowingly built over a toxic waste dump site, which caused widespread health problems for residents. After local officials refused to take action, the federal government stepped in and paid to relocate residents and it also passed the so-called Superfund (the Comprehensive Environmental Response, Compensation, and Liability Act). This act was introduced in 1980 to pay for cleanup at sites where hazardous waste had been deposited (Gibbs 1982). Many have described this as the start of the environmental justice movement, which in the 1980s and 1990s was instrumental in working for a safer, fairer, and healthier environment for all.

In the 1980s, more and more environmental organizations were becoming huge, bureaucratic operations (many far removed from local issues) and were increasingly focused on national or international policies. Emboldened, environmental groups pushed for curbs on pollution—first for air and water in the 1950s and 1960s and then toxic chemical waste in the 1970s. They sought local, state, and federal laws to protect drinking water, clean up the air and waterways, and contain the spread of toxic chemicals. Environmentalists moved from reacting to a problem to preventing it through government regulation. If the government failed in its duty, environmentalists filed lawsuits to compel enforcement. This shift has left environmentalists at odds with industry leaders and quite frequently with the government agencies in charge of enforcing environmental regulations. Policy makers continually find themselves in a difficult situation: they must balance the economic needs of industry and of the local populations dependent upon it and with the ecological requirements of the land and the aesthetic and material needs of taxpayers in mind. Because all involved use scientific research to support their respective arguments, science, which had once provided answers, has now become part of the problem.

Such a scenario helps explain the decline of the timber industry in the Pacific Northwest in the 1990s. When a researcher discovered that the northern spotted owl population was declining to the point that it was declared a threatened species, his research revealed that this was the result of logging the old-growth forests on federal lands that were the owls' habitat. Environmentalists, loggers, scientists (some working for the government, some not), and government officials became embroiled in a sometimes violent battle that was oversimplified as one of "jobs versus owls." While loggers needed to be able to cut the trees for work and many forest managers argued that cutting all trees in the area was the best way to manage the land for timber, environmental activists filed lawsuits and staged protests to shut down logging activity and preserve the forests. The situation led the US Forest Service and other agencies to rethink how it managed its lands, and it contributed to its leaders' adoption of an ecosystem-level approach, which required assessing the land for all of its economic and aesthetic values, in order to properly manage its forests.

The Future

Since the end of the twentieth century and into the twenty-first, the major environmental issue concerning many groups has been climate change. Carbon dioxide emissions are the single greatest concern with regard to climate change, and emission levels in the United States are some of the highest in the world, with about 16 to 20 tonnes of carbon released per person annually (Black 2011). Despite this position as the world's leading emitter of greenhouse gases, the United States, along with Australia, was the only industrialized nation not to ratify the Kyoto Protocol, the internationally binding climate change agreement that went into force in 2005. Although Australia, under Kevin Rudd's Labor government, eventually signed the agreement in 2007, Canada abandoned the agreement in 2011 under prime minister Stephen Harper, aligning its greenhouse gas emissions goals with those of the United States, which objected to signing the protocol, in part, on the grounds that its economy would suffer as a result of the protocol's limitations on industrial output.

Rising energy consumption levels contribute to rising emission levels. To meet energy demands while also making the United States less dependent on foreign oil, some advocate increasing the use of coal, which is used to generate nearly 50 percent of all electricity in the United States but has a significant environmental impact from mining and burning it; building pipelines to move oil from Canada, although they would go through environmentally sensitive areas in the United States to processing sites; and injecting pressurized fluid into the ground to force out gas and petroleum through a process called hydrological fracturing (popularly known as "fracking"), despite growing evidence of its hazards. When in 2010 an oil well rupture in the Gulf of Mexico released 5.6–9.5 million liters of oil into the gulf per day for three months, many asked whether society's dependence on oil had become excessive and began demanding an increase in the use of renewable energy sources like wood and other biofuels, wind, and solar (BBC 2010). But despite the federal government providing research funding and tax incentives to develop and use renewable resources and licensing public lands for drilling and mining, it has yet to formulate a national energy policy.

Increasingly the environment, and especially climate change, is becoming a divisive issue in US policy making and politics. Changing climatic conditions have contributed to the deterioration of the health of forests, for example, which has led to debates over whether to increase timber harvests to reduce the chances of catastrophic wildfires while increasing the flow of water downstream from the dense timber stands. Yet the administrative process involved in planning and executing a timber harvest often can take several years because of lawsuits, by which time environmental conditions have changed and require a new plan.

Climate change and its potential impact on the environment entered popular consciousness when former US vice president Al Gore produced an award-winning film in 2006, *An Inconvenient Truth*, which explained and described the dangers and effects of climate change that would occur worldwide—including events such as rising sea levels and the melting of the polar ice caps—for a general audience. In the early twenty-first century, popular initiatives, such as ReduceCarbonFootprint.org and others, continue to drive change, as individuals and businesses voluntarily try to reduce their own impact on carbon dioxide emissions. But policy makers and politicians at local, regional, and federal levels must give environmental issues high priority if there is to be continuing progress in ensuring that the people of the United States have healthful air, water, and land as well as sustainable, safe environments.

James G. LEWIS
Forest History Society, Durham, North Carolina

See also Appalachian Mountains; Architecture; Canada; Chesapeake Bay; Columbia River; Detroit, United States; Great Lakes and Saint Lawrence River; Las Vegas, United States; Mexico; Mississippi and Missouri Rivers; New Orleans, United States; New York City, United States; North American Free Trade Agreement (NAFTA); Organization of American States (OAS); Phoenix, United States; Rocky Mountains; Yellowstone to Yukon Conservation Initiative (Y2Y)

FURTHER READING

Black, Richard. (2011, October 25). China "Won't follow US" on carbon emissions. *BBC News*. Retrieved October 25, 2011, from http://www.bbc.co.uk/news/science-environment-15444858

Bowler, Peter J. (1993). *The Norton history of the environmental sciences*. New York: W. W. Norton.

British Broadcasting Corporation (BBC). (2010, June 16). Q&A: Why estimates of the BP oil spill keep changing. *BBC News*. Retrieved October 25, 2011, from http://www.bbc.co.uk/news/10293952

Carson, Rachel. (1962). *Silent spring*. Boston: Houghton Mifflin Company.

Cohen, Michael P. (1988). *The history of the Sierra Club*. San Francisco: Sierra Club Books.

Fletcher, Thomas H. (2003). *From Love Canal to environmental justice: The politics of hazardous waste on the Canada–US border*. Peterborough, Ontario, Canada: Broadview Press.

Gibbs, Lois Marie. (1982). *Love Canal: My story*. Albany: State University of New York Press.

Goldenberg, Suzanne. (2011, June 28). How El Paso is beating the worst drought in a generation. *The Guardian*. Retrieved October 25, 2011, from http://www.guardian.co.uk/environment/2011/jun/27/water-conservation-el-paso-texas?INTCMP=SRCH

Graham, Frank, Jr. (1971). *Man's dominion: The story of conservation in America*. New York: M. Evans.

Hays, Samuel P. (1959). *Conservation and the gospel of efficiency: The progressive conservation movement, 1890–1920*. Cambridge, MA: Harvard University Press.

Lewis, James G. (2005). *The Forest Service and the greatest good: A centennial history*. Durham, NC: Forest History Society.

Limerick, Patricia Nelson. (1987). *The legacy of conquest: The unbroken past of the American West*. New York: W. W. Norton.

Merchant, Carolyn. (1989). *Ecological revolutions: Nature, gender, and science in New England*. Chapel Hill: University of North Carolina Press.

Mitchell, Lee Clark. (1981). *Witnesses to a vanishing America: The nineteenth-century response*. Princeton, NJ: Princeton University Press.

Petulla, Joseph M. (1977). *American environmental history: The exploitation and conservation of natural resources*. San Francisco: Boyd & Fraser.

Reisner, Marc. (1986). *Cadillac desert: The American West and its disappearing water*. New York: Viking Penguin.

Rome, Adam. (2003). Give Earth a chance: The environmental movement and the sixties. *Journal of American History, 90*(2), 525–554.

Taylor, Dorceta E. (2002). *Race, class, gender, and American environmentalism* (Gen. Tech. Rep.PNW-GTR-534). Portland, OR: US Department of Agriculture Forest Service.

Udall, Stewart. (1963). *The quiet crisis*. New York: Holt, Rinehart and Winston.

Williams, Michael. (1989). *Americans and their forests*. Cambridge, UK: Cambridge University Press.

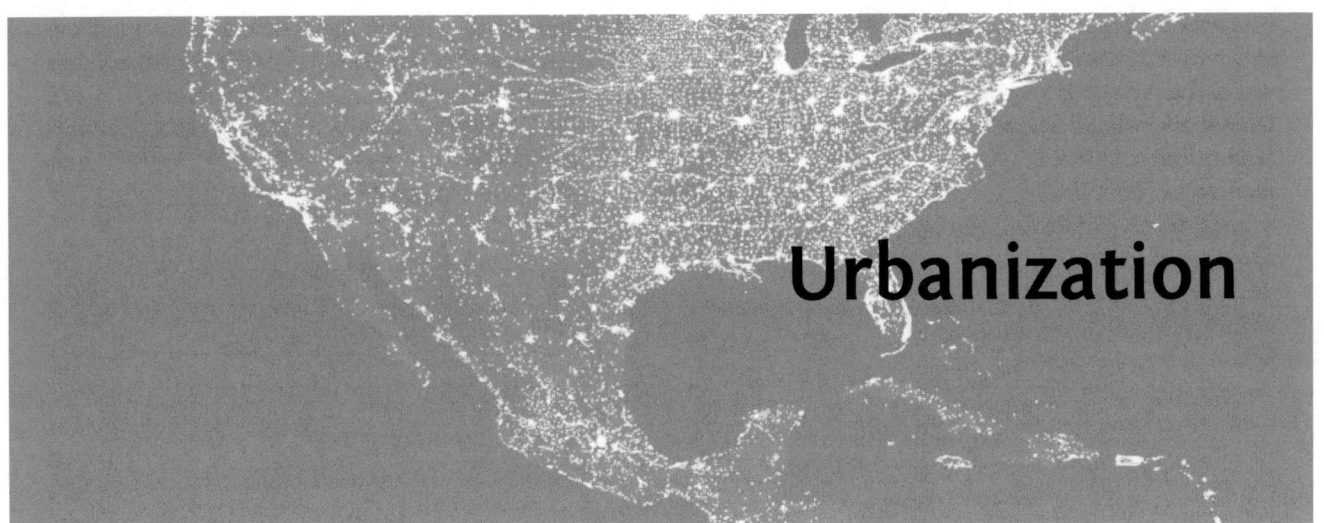

Urbanization

The people of the Americas and Oceania are among the most urbanized in the world, according to the United Nations. From precolonial cities to post–World War II suburbia, the process of urbanization has been the dominant spatial and demographic process across the two regions. Urbanization's impacts range from sustainability issues to socioeconomic inequalities to susceptibility to natural disasters. Researchers and planners have proposed solutions to these problems, some of which are already in place.

The urban population of the world in 2005 was 46 percent of the total population, according to the United Nations Department of Economic and Social Affairs (2010), Population Division, in their 2009 revision of world urbanization prospects. Population estimates project it will rise to 69 percent in 2050. North America is 81 percent urbanized with projections of 90 percent in 2050; 70 percent of the Central American population was urban in 2005, expected to rise to 84 percent in 2050. South America is even more urbanized, at 82 percent (with a 2050 projection of 91 percent).

Australia and New Zealand conform to the pattern found in the Americas, with a 2005 urbanization rate of 88 percent and a projection for 2050 of 93 percent. The various other island states that make up Oceania have highly variable rates of urbanization, but for the most part the absolute numbers involved are very small. The most urbanized nation is Nauru (100 percent urbanized), but the total population is only twenty-four thousand.

Current rates of urbanization are relatively low and relatively stable compared with, for example, sub-Saharan Africa, where rates in some countries increase at more than 5 percent annually. According to the United Nations, rates in Oceania between 2000 and 2005 rose 1.5 percent per year (1.4 percent in Australia and New Zealand), 1.4 percent in North America, 1.9 percent in South America, and 1.8 percent in Central America. Some countries in these regions have faster rates than this, such as Belize, Guatemala, Honduras, and Panama in Central America, which have rates of more than 3 percent; Paraguay and French Guiana in South America; and some, particularly Melanesian, island states in Oceania.

The Americas contain some of the largest cities in the world. In 2005 three of the five largest urban conglomerations were in the region—Mexico City, Mexico (18.73 million); New York–Newark, New Jersey, United States (18.865 million); and São Paulo, Brazil (18.675 million). Los Angeles, United States; Rio de Janeiro, Brazil; and Buenos Aires, Argentina, are other megacities in the region (defined as having a population of more than 10 million). Other major cities that feature in the top thirty urban conglomerations in the region include Chicago, United States; Lima, Peru; and Bogotá, Colombia. All of these cities have populations of more than 7 million. The largest city in Oceania is Sydney, Australia, with a 2005 population of 4.3 million.

Precolonial Urban Areas

Colonial and postcolonial waves of immigration, migration, and population growth spurred most of the processes of urbanization in the Americas and Oceania. A number of cities of significant size established themselves in the Mesoamerican and Andean civilizations of Central and South America before the colonial period. The most noteworthy of these are the Aztec city of Tenochtitlan, destroyed by the Spanish in 1521, who established Mexico City on the site in 1524, and Cholula, a major Aztec city, also in Mexico.

Colonial Cities

For much of the region the process of urbanization started with the arrival of European settlers. The timing of the start of this process varied considerably.

The Americas

The colonial period of the Americas commenced with the Spanish in the sixteenth century. The Portuguese, British, and French joined the Spanish across the continent, establishing many towns and cities. Tactics and methods of colonization varied, depending on each nation's policy and philosophy, but were largely detrimental to native populations whether intentionally (genocide and slavery) or unintentionally (the spread of new disease). Colonizers reduced native populations from an estimated 50 million to as little as 5 million within seventy-five years of first contact. The Spanish and Portuguese founded the earliest European cities in the Americas during the early sixteenth century. The English, French, and Dutch began colonization in the early seventeenth century.

Oceania

The colonial period in Oceania came later than in the Americas and involved fewer colonial powers. The Australian Bureau of Statistics estimates that the Aboriginal population declined after first contact with Europeans in 1788 from at least 315,000 (and possibly as many as 750,000) to approximately 93,000 in 1900. The first cities in the region were in Australia. The British founded Sydney in 1788 and Hobart in 1803. The British founded Port Moresby in Papua New Guinea in the late nineteenth and early twentieth centuries at a site that was a significant regional trading post prior to colonization. Port Moresby is the only significant urban area in Oceania outside Australia and New Zealand.

European Australia has always been one of the most urbanized populations in the world. In the late nineteenth century one-third of the population of just over 3 million lived in the six principal colonial cities. The largest at the time, Melbourne, had a population of 473,000 people. Australia arguably created the first example of suburban sprawl; Melbourne had a population 10 percent of that of London, England, the largest city of the nineteenth century, but covered the same land area.

Urban Expansion

Most cities in the region remained at fairly modest sizes (certainly by modern standards) throughout the seventeenth, eighteenth, and nineteenth centuries. The nineteenth and twentieth centuries bought significant social and economic changes to the region that resulted in substantial urban expansion, mass rural-to-urban migration, and immigration. This process was not uniform, but the Industrial Revolution and a process of economic liberalization were the two main drivers.

The Industrial Revolution

In North America the Industrial Revolution bought rapid and significant changes to urban areas in the nineteenth century. Agricultural mechanization, the loss of employment in rural environments, and an increase in labor demand in industrial cities pushed mass migration to urban areas. Labor markets opened up to successive waves of immigration.

New York grew from 313,000 to 4.8 million people between 1840 and 1910. Other parts of North America saw similar patterns of growth. Tensions between social equity and free market philosophies began in this period. Rapid economic expansion attracted people to the cities, but social development could not keep pace, leading to significant social and environmental problems.

Migration in Central and South America

Urbanization and industrialization occurred in the same way in most of South and Central America. Experts dispute the reasons for this development, but it is likely a result of different domestic and colonial policies and economic practices. More rapid urbanization occurred in South and Central America in the middle and latter parts of the twentieth century as a number of economies liberalized, changing rural land ownership and increasing labor demands in cities.

Rural–urban migration still occurs in much of the region. Rapidly expanding shantytowns with poor infrastructure, little development control, and little planning ring major urban areas. The populations of these towns run a high risk of disease, geological disaster (landslides, flooding, and earthquakes), and social disorder.

Impacts

Rapid urbanization resulted in significant environmental and social tensions in the cities. Poverty in urban areas has a harshness resulting from the lack of proximity to food production opportunities, pollution resulting from unregulated industrial processes, and uncontrolled human effluent. Poverty and the lack of access to power have been exacerbated by racial and ethnic inequality;

indigenous and black communities are likely to experience greater poverty than white European communities. Social and economic inequality is particular obvious in urban areas, where the close proximity of economic classes leads to social tensions. Economic inequality is measured using the "Gini coefficient"—a measure of inequality with a score of 0 being perfectly equal and 1 being perfectly unequal. According to the United Nations Human Settlement program, cities in Latin America have an average Gini coefficient of 0.5, which is the highest urban inequality of any region in the world. This level of inequality reflects poor governance and a lack of opportunity for the poor. Economic inequality is also relatively high in US urban areas when compared with Canadian and Australian cities. Economic inequality is correlated closely with a variety of social ills, including violent crime and social disorder.

The concentration of wealth and services in urban areas also increases the consumption patterns of a community, which affects sustainability at a global scale. The economies of cities by and large drive the global economic system and have far-reaching impacts removed from the cities' physical boundaries. In North America, Australia, and New Zealand, energy usage is lower per capita in urban areas than in rural communities because of the relative affluence of rural populations in these countries. Higher levels of wealth, services, and consumption elsewhere in the region raise energy use in urban areas.

Suburbanization

In many cities of the region the prevalent pattern of urbanization in the post–World War II era has been suburbanization. An expansion of the middle classes and the development of transportation technology allow for forms of urban development that are focused on the car as the primary means of transportation. These areas are of significantly lower density than seen in pre-car cities. The pattern and development of cities is often determined by the transportation options available to the residents. Development at a density that allowed people to access services becomes less important. Populations instead demanded space.

Railroads and Streetcars

The first transportation advance to significantly impact urbanization was the railroad. Railroads were not as influential to the layout of individual cities as other, later advances; they did extend economic development and city expansion into more areas previously excluded from the economic opportunities of trade and industry because of isolation. Cities in the US Midwest, for example, started to grow in the late nineteenth century as the railroad arrived.

The creation of streetcar networks in many American and Australian cities resulted in the planning and developing of spreading urban areas along the projected lines. This process started in the late nineteenth century and was a popular form of urbanization until the 1930s, when gasoline-fueled automobiles and buses became more popular and allowed more diffuse and unplanned expansion.

Development around streetcars kept urban areas relatively compact; individual communities had to be dense enough to support the streetcar lines economically. Suburbs developed with commercial centers around halts and stops, and residential areas around them. Most major cities in the region have examples of streetcar suburbs. The development of streetcars helped build many of the inner/early suburbs of major cities such as Montreal, Toronto, Los Angeles, Boston, Melbourne, Rio de Janeiro, and Mexico City.

A number of commentators see the streetcar suburbs as a model of sustainable development with their focus on pedestrian-friendly streets, compact development, and transit-oriented development (see for example Newman and Kenworthy 1999 or Dunay 2009). Cities such as Vancouver, Canada, and Curitiba, Brazil, are examples of transit-oriented development that has solved many social and environmental challenges found in modern cities. Particularly in older industrial cities in North America and Oceania, however, modern transport also started a process of socioeconomic separation between urban and suburban areas. Before mechanized transport, travel time limited the distance people could live away from urban centers. Once the streetcar developed, people were limited only by their ability to afford mechanized transport. The poor consequently settled in the urban cores and the wealthier moved farther out. The separation of socioeconomic classes in North America and Australia started in this period. In some cities this separation also became conflated with race as well as wealth.

Suburbia after 1945

The postwar period saw a rapid rise in affluence in North America and Australia, which coincided with a rapid increase in automobile use. Urban areas grew in population, but more notably in area. People's desire for home-ownership and backyards led to the suburban property and development boom.

Critics of suburbanization have pointed out its impact on sustainability. Jane Jacobs (1961), the US-Canadian writer and activist who campaigned against urban freeways in North America in the 1950s and 1960s, suggested that automobile-focused development reduces the social and community interactions that take place in thriving neighborhoods. More recently the US social critic and writer James Kunstler (1994) argued that the placelessness of suburbia creates social and health issues.

Cars also bring significant air quality challenges to urban areas. Los Angeles regularly exceeds healthy limits for a variety of pollutants related to car and truck emissions, such as low-level ozone, small particulates, nitrogen, and sulfur oxides. This level of pollution significantly increases bronchial complaints such as asthma, strokes, and measurable increases in mortality.

Tougher vehicle and industrial emission standards and a decline in industrial activity have improved air quality in many cities in North America. Latin America, where both car use and industrial emissions are increasing, has not seen the same trend. These increased greenhouse gas emissions significantly impact the health of populations in affected cities. Researchers predicted in 2006 that poor air quality in Mexico City; Santiago, Chile; and São Paulo, Brazil, between 2000 and 2020 will be responsible for 156,000 deaths and could cost US$21–$165 billion in health impacts (Bell et al. 2006).

Edge Cities

The US journalist and scholar Joel Garreau popularized the term *edge city* in his 1991 book, *Edge City: Life on the New Frontier*. The term refers to a growing trend in cities for commercial and retail development to move out of traditional business districts in urban centers into the expanding suburbs.

This trend creates car-focused "cities" linked to highway networks within the suburban fabric, which pull economic and social activity away from urban cores and spread out the urban area. Because of lower real estate prices and the car-focused nature of the development, these places tend to have low development and population density. Low density is frequently associated with many of the more environmentally unsustainable characteristics of modern cities. Private space rather than the public space of traditional urban areas—with malls and business parks rather than squares, streetscapes, and parks—characterize these areas. In extreme cases, such as in the US cities of Detroit and Los Angeles, the development of edge cities has in part contributed to the destruction of the central city as a functioning social and economic entity.

Although most commentators decry the unsustainable nature of the suburbs and exurbs around most cities, some critics, such as the US architects and scholars Ellen Dunham-Jones and June Williamson (2008), believe infilling, densification, repurposing, and redesigning can retrofit suburbia for sustainability.

The Edge in Latin America

The socially and economically marginalized—the poor who have migrated to the cities from rural areas seeking opportunity—have settled the suburban areas of cities in Latin America. These communities are often semilegal or illegal shantytowns. The rich still live predominantly in central areas.

Poor planning, inadequate housing, and a lack of government response to growing urban populations have led to these communities' development. Urban immigrants are too poor to afford land, and suitable affordable housing is not available legally. Adequate utilities and other infrastructure do not serve these communities, which immigrants have often built in unsuitable locations with high levels of geomorphological hazard. In Rio de Janeiro, Brazil, fifteen people died in 2010 where heavy rain caused landslides in a shanty community. The lack of planning and development control makes the impact of geological hazards much more significant than in more developed urban areas that have technical requirements and planning controls. Major earthquakes have hit urban areas in Haiti, Chile, and New Zealand. The 2010 earthquake in Haiti was magnitude 7.0 and hit 25 kilometers west of Port-au-Prince, an urban area of about 900,000. Whereas 300,000 people died in that earthquake, only 525 people died in the 2010 earthquake in Chile, which had a much greater magnitude (8.8) and affected major cities including the capital, Santiago, with a population of more than 4 million.

In the wealthier parts of Latin America (such as around the major cities of Mexico, Argentina, Chile, and Brazil) more affluent suburbs such as those found in North America have developed since the 1970s.

Solutions

Planners have proposed a number of solutions to the development of urban areas in more sustainable ways. These concepts hark back in many ways to aspects of colonial towns and early suburbs, which emphasized the public realm, civic space, and pedestrian-focused transit systems. They all share common themes of pedestrian-oriented traditional neighborhood planning and increased density and transit use.

Smart Growth

Smart growth developed from transportation- and community-planning traditions. Smart growth's principles prevent sprawl by designing new neighborhoods that promote mixed-use development, density, transit use, and the protection of ecological functionality in the form of open space, greenways, and the wise choice of development sites.

Critics have two main objections to smart growth. Some ecological economists observe that because we are already living beyond our ecological means, growth is always unsustainable, and smart growth therefore is an oxymoron (for example see Bartlett 2006; Warner 2006). The libertarian view of urbanization contends that the control over development required to implement smart growth is excessive interference in the free market (see for example the work of Randall O'Toole [2000] or Wendell Cox of the think tank Demographia [n.d.]). These commentators also claim that smart growth actually increases the problems it hopes to solve by increasing population density successfully but failing to encourage those people to use transit.

New Urbanism

The Congress for the New Urbanism formed in 1993 based on the idea that planners can design urban neighborhoods to encourage sustainable behavior. These principles look to a great degree to past urban forms. They promote a sense of community and walkability by keeping communities compact and diverse in use.

The main critics of New Urbanism, such as the US planning and urban development scholar Peter Gordon, believe the free market demonstrates that people prefer the suburbs and the freedom provided by car-based urban forms. These criticisms contradict the other, more practically observed criticism of New Urbanist projects: they are so popular that the expensive property prevents the diversity of economic class that the principles demand.

Transit-Oriented Development

Transit-oriented development (TOD) has a similar perspective but focuses on the urban system rather than individual neighborhoods. Mixed-use development concentrates at transit stops and interchanges. Many cities have implemented TOD in response to increasing transport inequity and congestion.

Curitiba, Brazil, is the most developed and integrated example of such planning. The Brazilian architect and later city mayor Jamie Lerner championed the process, which involved extensive public consultation, the development of local governance models, and high-quality design of a rapid transit system. The Rede Integrada de Transporte, a rapid bus network, supported the densification of development nodes. Many other cities around the region (and globally), most notably Bogotá, Colombia, have adopted the principles of Curitiba. Bogotá has developed a bus rapid transit system that employs many similar characteristics. Both these systems are designed to move large numbers of people around an urban system in frequent service rapid transit vehicles.

The Melbourne Principles

The United Nations Environment Programme International Environmental Technology Centre developed the Melbourne Principles, which provide a framework for the development of sustainable urban areas and cities, as a part of its Cities as Sustainable Ecosystems project. The International Council for Local Environmental Initiatives, an international local government network for sustainability, developed and sponsored these principles. The implications of these principles in planning and urbanization have been explored by two Australians, the environmental scientist Peter Newman and the sustainability expert Isabella Jennings, in their 2008 book *Cities as Sustainable Ecosystems*.

Outlook

All these solutions essentially seek to provide the same thing. They address the emergent problems of the car-driven free market response to planning that has resulted in urban, suburban, and exurban areas that are socially (lack of community, lack of public realm), ecologically (high carbon use, large land take, little provision for natural green space), and economically (expensive infrastructure, poor service provision, unattractive for small businesses) unsustainable. Emerging theories and development look to make modern cities sustainable and pleasant, efficient places to live.

Christopher LING
Royal Roads University

See also Architecture; Auckland, New Zealand; Bogotá, Colombia; Curitiba, Brazil; Detroit, United States; Guatemala City; Las Vegas, United States; Lima, Peru;

Mexico City; Mobility; New Orleans, United States; New York City, United States; Perth, Australia; Phoenix, United States; Public Transportation; Rio de Janeiro, Brazil; Rural Development (the Americas); Sydney, Australia; Toronto, Canada; Vancouver, Canada

FURTHER READING

Bartlett, Albert. (2006). Reflections on sustainability, population growth, and the environment. In Marco Keiner (Ed.), *The future of sustainability* (pp. 17–37). Dordrecht, The Netherlands: Springer.

Bell, Michelle L., et al. (2006). The avoidable health effects of air pollution in three Latin American cities: Santiago, São Paulo, and Mexico City. *Environmental Research, 100*, 431–440.

Butterworth, Douglas, & Chance, John K. (1981). *Latin American urbanization.* Cambridge, UK: Cambridge University Press.

Cervero, Robert. (1998). *The transit metropolis: A global inquiry.* Washington, DC: Island Press.

Demographia. (n.d.). Homepage. Retrieved April 3, 2012, from http://www.demographia.com/

Dunay, Andres. (2009). *The smart growth manual.* New York: McGraw-Hill.

Dunham-Jones, Ellen, & Williamson, June. (2008). *Retrofitting suburbia: Urban design solutions for redesigning suburbs.* Hoboken, NJ: John Wiley & Sons

Farr, Douglas. (2008). *Sustainable urbanism: Urban design with nature.* Hoboken, NJ: John Wiley & Sons.

Garreau, Joel. (1991). *Edge city: Life on the new frontier.* New York: Anchor Books

Gilbert, Alan, & Ferguson, James. (1998). *The Latin American city.* New York: Monthly Review Press.

Haas, Tigran. (Ed.). (2008). *New urbanism and beyond: Designing cities for the future.* New York: Rizzoli Publishing.

Jacobs, Jane. (1961). *The death and life of great American cities.* New York: Random House.

Kunstler, James. (1994). Geography of nowhere: The rise and decline of America's man-made landscape. New York: Free Press.

Mohl, Raymond. (1985). *The new city: Urban America in the industrial age, 1860–1920.* Wheeling, IL: Harlan Davidson.

Newman, Peter, & Jennings, Isabella. (2008). *Cities as sustainable ecosystems: Principles and practices.* Washington, DC: Island Press.

Newman, Peter, & Kenworthy, Jeff. (1999). *Sustainability and cities: Overcoming automobile dependence.* Washington, DC: Island Press.

O'Toole, Randall. (2000). *The vanishing automobile and other urban myths: How smart growth will harm American cities.* Camp Sherman, OR: Thoreau Institute.

Schwartz, Hugh. (2004). *Urban renewal, municipal revitalization: The case of Curitiba, Brazil.* Reston, VA: Higher Education Publications

United Nations Department of Economic and Social Affairs. (2010). *World urbanization prospects, the 2009 revision.* Retrieved March 3, 2012, from http://esa.un.org/unpd/wup/index.htm

Warner, Daniel M. (2006). Post-growthism: From smart growth to sustainable development. *Environmental Practice, 8,* 160–179.

Berkshire's authors and editors welcome questions, comments, and corrections. Send your emails about the *Berkshire Encyclopedia of Sustainability* in general or this volume in particular to: sustainability.updates@berkshirepublishing.com

Vancouver, Canada

2.1 million est. pop. 2006

Vancouver, British Columbia, is a Pacific Rim metropolis that has gained many economic advantages from being the terminal station of the Canadian Pacific Railway and a major West Coast port for trade between North America and Asia. Its planning agencies have developed innovative mechanisms for converting its downtown and environs into attractive tourist destinations and fulfilling its ambition to become the globe's greenest city by 2020.

Vancouver, an economic powerhouse and environmental pioneer in western Canada, has an urban population of 578,000 and a metropolitan population of more than 2,116,000 (2006 census). Known as a "city of neighborhoods," its demographic landscape features a population in which ethnic minorities (particularly Chinese) constitute over half of the total. Critical to Vancouver's growth in the last century was railroad executives' decision to locate the western end point of the Canadian Pacific Railway (CPR) in Vancouver, rather than Port Moody, in 1886. In that same year, Vancouver was incorporated as a small pioneer town with a few thousand inhabitants. At its founding, the CPR was granted 10.1 million hectares of land along the railway route across the prairies through the Pacific Rim wilderness and a large block of land in the center of what would become Vancouver's downtown (Wyn and Oke 1992). It played a powerful role in partnering with Vancouver's wealthy elites to segregate prominent business families from Vancouver's other socioeconomic classes and from East Asian immigrants. It also abetted the formation of a powerful urban growth coalition that controlled Vancouver's politics for more than three decades.

What distinguishes Vancouver is its trajectory from pioneer town to world-class city in less than a century. Blessed with a temperate rain forest climate, an abundance of natural resources (forests and precious metals), and transportation lines that reached the city limits, it has today become a magnet for Hollywood film production, in-migration of wealthy and aspiring families from East Asia, and an immense amount of tourist traffic from all over the world. No less important has been its success in seizing upon global extravaganzas like the 1986 World Expo and the 2010 Winter Olympics to boost its image in the world's eyes and build legacy projects that advance its city-building efforts.

Economy

Vancouver's economy has evolved quickly over its short history. In the mid-1800s, it established itself as the center of British Columbia's forest industry by virtue of the many milling operations in the vicinity. It also became an important commercial and trade magnet for British Columbia's mining industry. With its natural harbor, Vancouver was able in the late 1800s to take advantage of British Columbia's extensive natural resources to ship the wealth of the province's resource-based economy—primarily fishing, fur, forestry, and farming—as well as products delivered by rail from the Canadian prairie provinces to overseas markets in Europe and Asia.

Vancouver boasts one of the most diversified local economies also tied into the global economy by virtue of its trading network and seaport, generating more than C$75 billion in trade with 125 or more countries each year. Its port activities alone account for C$10.5billion in gross domestic product and nearly C$22 billion in economic output. Its twenty-first-century economy has built upon its natural geographic resources and temperate rain forest climate advantages to include not only international trade and natural resources, but substantial economic activity related to tourism, the film industry, and high technology.

The lure of Vancouver resides not only in its status as a world-class city with a vibrant, twenty-four-hour downtown. Its leisure environments, including Grouse Mountain, Stanley Park, Granville Island, and Queen Elizabeth Park are complemented by its beaches, parklands, ocean, and other leisure and entertainment venues, attracting more than a million tourists annually from around the world.

With its tax incentives and subsidies to film studios, its year-round mild climate, and diverse locales, Vancouver has become the second or third largest film production center in North America. It is second only to Los Angeles in television production and third behind Los Angeles and New York City in feature film production. Home to television series like *The X-Files, Millennium,* and *The Outer Limits,* it is the site of more than twenty feature films and forty or more made-for-television films produced annually. In 2010 the film and television industry spent C$1.5 billion in Vancouver (BC Film Commission 2011).

In tune with trends and changes in the twenty-first century's emerging computer, technology, and information economy, Vancouver's present economy has a galloping high-technology sector in software development, biotechnology, video game development, film animation, alternative energy technology (especially fuel cell development), Web companies, and space and defense technology. Its high-tech sector includes companies like Electronic Arts, Amazon, IBM, and MacDonald, Dettwiler and Associates. Key partnerships with major universities in the area, including the University of British Columbia and Simon Fraser University, as well as government-supported initiatives, like the National Research Council (NRC) Institute for Fuel Cell Innovation, assure Vancouver's leadership in cutting-edge, technology-driven industries for its growing urban and greater metropolitan economy.

Environment and Urban Planning

Since the 1970s, Vancouver has been a pioneer in transforming environmental concern among its inhabitants into significant policy advances. Prior to that decade, much of Vancouver's city politics was dominated by the economic growth agenda of a political coalition organized around a municipal party, the Non-Partisan Association (NPA), that continuously governed Vancouver from 1937 to 1972. During its three-and-a-half-decade hegemony, the NPA pressed what critics call a program of pro-business economic growth, downtown boosterism, and political cronyism that critics say disproportionately benefited Vancouver's West Side business elites and wealthy homeowners over the East Side's poorer ethnic and minority neighborhood inhabitants (Gutstein 1983; Yanarella and Lancaster in press). Not until the early 1970s was the NPA grip on City Hall power and politics broken by The Electors' Action Movement (TEAM), which defined itself as a more professional and civic-minded party with greater environmental consciousness and a more democratic planning ethic. With its new-found political power, TEAM's governance ushered in a new planning vision organized around the idea of the "livable city" and the deployment of new tools for transforming decaying industrial areas and undeveloped brownfield sites in the central district.

After Expo '86, politically progressive forces in Vancouver began to implement high design standards in the city's remaining undeveloped downtown areas around False Creek Inlet. By 1990, the first signs of this new planning ethic's success in targeting the environmental realm appeared in the "Clouds of Change" report, released in 1990 by a municipal task force charged with examining the risks to public health from air pollution and atmospheric change. In addition to triggering wider political concern about the consequences of global warming for Vancouver, it recommended that the city convert Southeast False Creek, a 32-hectare brownfield site heavily polluted by lumber and steel industries formerly located there, into a sustainable experiment utilizing energy-efficient technologies and innovative, ecofriendly, transit-oriented land-use policies.

From Livability to Sustainability to the Greenest City

As the last undeveloped brownfield site in the downtown area not yet redeveloped, the Southeast False Creek site became enmeshed in intense politicking by community activists, real estate developers and potential investors, and public officials. As TEAM's emphasis on "downtown first" and the "livable city" became embedded in Vancouver planning and politics, a significant change took place in the NPA's orientation to downtown planning and environmental policy. With the 2005 election of Sam Sullivan, the new NPA mayoral administration embraced a vague notion of urban sustainability by enunciating an "EcoDensity" vision and charter to advance Vancouver as a sustainable city built upon ecological design and population density. Under Sullivan's administration, efforts to bring the 2010 Winter Olympics to Vancouver came to fruition, and the Southeast False

Creek sustainable community was converted into the Olympic athlete village.

In 2008 Sullivan was succeeded as mayor by a Vision Vancouver–Committee of Political Electors (COE) coalition candidate, Gregor Robertson, who sought to fulfill two campaign promises: to channel the political energies of his new administration and majority council coalition into carving out a vision for sustainability that went beyond Sam Sullivan's EcoDensity agenda and to end homelessness in the Canadian city with the least affordable housing. His new sustainability strategy was grounded in a vision to rebrand Vancouver as a "green capital" and to make it into the "greenest city" in the world by 2020.

Implications

Arguably, Southeast False Creek, the symbol of a new consensus among Vancouver's municipal party, is the "greenest" urban implantation anywhere in North America—and indeed the globe—and a living laboratory for other cities to emulate. Sadly, Mayor Robertson's ambition to rid Vancouver of homelessness has fallen by the wayside, as Vancouver's green development has contributed only to increasing housing values and further marginalizing the homeless, unemployed, and working-class inhabitants of the green city by the sea.

Ernest J. YANARELLA
University of Kentucky

See also Auckland, New Zealand; Canada; Energy Efficiency; Labor; Mobility; New York City, United States; Public Transportation; Toronto, Canada; Travel and Tourism Industry; Urbanization

FURTHER READING

Berelowitz, Lance. (2005). *Dream city: Vancouver and the global imagination.* Vancouver, Canada: Douglas & McIntyre.

British Columbia (BC) Film Commission. (2011). British Columbia Film Commission production statistics 2010. Victoria, Canada: Ministry of Community, Sport & Cultural Development.

City of Vancouver. (2008a). EcoDensity: Vancouver EcoDensity Charter. Retrieved May 8, 2012, from http://vancouver.ca/commsvcs/ecocity/pdf/ecodensity-charter-low.pdf

City of Vancouver. (2008b). EcoDensity: How density, design, and land use will contribute to environmental sustainability, affordability, and livability: Project summary. Retrieved May 8, 2012, from http://vancouver.ca/commsvcs/ecocity/pdf/EcoDensity%20 Summary%20Report%20_web(1).pdf

Gutstein, Donald. (1983). Vancouver. In Warren Magnusson & Andrew Sancton (Ed.), *City politics in Canada* (pp. 189–221). Buffalo, NY: University of Toronto Press.

Harcourt, Mike; Cameron, Ken; & Rossiter, Sean. (2007). *City making in paradise: Nine decisions that saved Vancouver.* Vancouver, Canada: Douglas & McIntyre.

Ley, David. (1997). *The new middle class and the remaking of Central City.* New York: Oxford University Press.

McDonald, Robert A. J. (1996). *Making Vancouver: Class, status, and social boundaries, 1863–1913.* Vancouver, Canada: University of British Columbia Press.

Min, Christa; Eidse, James; & Kiessling, Lori. (Eds.) (2008). *Vancouver matters.* Vancouver, Canada: Simply Read Books/BLUEIMPRINT.

Punter, John. (2003). *The Vancouver achievement: Urban planning and design.* Vancouver, Canada: UBC Press.

Roger Bayley, Inc. (2010). *The challenge series: Millennium Water: The southeast False Creek Olympic Village – Vancouver, Canada.* Retrieved May 11, 2012, from http://www.thechallengeseries.ca/

Vancouver Greenest City Action Team. (2009). *Vancouver 2020: A bright green future: An action plan for becoming the world's greenest city.* Vancouver, Canada: City of Vancouver Mayor's Office.

Wyn, Graeme, & Oke, Timothy. (1992). *Vancouver and its region.* Vancouver, Canada: University of British Columbia Press.

Yanarella, Ernest J., & Lancaster, Robert W. (in press). Southeast False Creek, Vancouver, BC: The contradictions of sustainable development overcome? In Ernest J. Yanarella & Robert W. Lancaster (Eds.), *Getting from here to there: The politics of urban sustainability in North America.* London: Anthem Press.

Share the *Encyclopedia of Sustainability*: Teachers are welcome to make up to ten (10) copies of no more than two (2) articles for distribution in a single course or program. For further permissions, please visit www.copyright.com or contact: info@berkshirepublishing.com

W

Water Use and Rights

Recently developed nations of the Americas and Oceania have improved access to water due to substantial progress in reforming water rights and allocation systems. These systems are integral in managing water supply for diverse uses, but developing nations—particularly in Latin America and Oceania—are not faring as well. Unless nations recognize and act upon the universal human right to water, exploitation of water resources will continue.

The regions of the Americas and Oceania use water from different sources and in different patterns. Water rights—a collectively recognized claim to the use of water—also vary significantly within each region. Water usage is directly influenced by the regional characteristics and norms of individual nations with respect to conferring water rights. Considerable global attention has been given to the need to improve access to water by asserting that water is a human right, and during the twentieth century the developing areas of Central and South America have made significant progress toward this goal. Nevertheless, some nations have persisted in withholding this right due to financial barriers, conflict, and corruption. Without a basic recognition and enforcement of the human right to water, it is difficult to develop a system of rights to allocate and use water in developing nations that are adapting to globalization.

Water Use

Water use grew dramatically during the twentieth century, with total global water withdrawals projected to increase 23 percent between 1995 and 2025 (Rosegrant and Cai 2003). Water withdrawals refer to water that is removed from a source and returned at a later time, although the water returned may be of a different quality. In contrast, water consumption is the complete removal of water from a source. Freshwater sources include groundwater aquifers and surface waterways fed by runoff, snowmelt, and groundwater discharge. Brazil and Canada are two of the three countries worldwide with the largest supplies of freshwater resources. South America uses almost ten times the amount of surface water annually as the entire Oceania region, or Central America and the Caribbean combined (Gleick 2009). Seawater is also a freshwater resource in regions that have developed desalination treatment. The use of recycled or reused water is on the rise as well; Australia's utilization of these supply points as a supplement to traditional sources has increased 34 percent since 2006 (ANWC 2011a). Because precipitation varies significantly in terms of both time and area in Australia—which alternates between wet and dry years, and where on average 90 percent of precipitation is lost to evaporation and transpiration (ANWC 2005)—water availability and usage are often not in sync regionally. Roughly 80 percent of water used nationally is from surface-water sources, but reliance on groundwater is increasing due to impacts from climate change (ADSEWPC 2009). The United States uses half as much surface water as South America annually (WRI 2011), and about 80 percent of freshwater used is from surface-water sources, with the remaining supplied by groundwater (Barber 2009). Only a few reporting nations monitor groundwater use, and regional statistics are limited.

As discussed above, water use is either consumptive (water used in a way that prevents its return to watersheds or aquifers, usually through high evaporation or transpiration) or nonconsumptive (water used in a way that replenishes watersheds or aquifers). Activities such as fossil-fuel energy production, mining, manufacturing, and agriculture involve consumptive water use, unless the water is treated and recycled. Global consumptive use of water is projected to increase by 16 percent between 1995 and 2025 (Rosegrant and Cai 2003). Nonconsumptive uses include the production of hydropower, recreation, environmental protection, and some urban functions that include water recycling and water reuse programs. Nonconsumptive utilization is the most sustainable way to consume water, since it is used several times before its liquid form is lost to the atmosphere. Dwindling water-resource availability, in conjunction with projections of increased consumptive use, means that water-resource managers must prioritize nonconsumptive water-usage strategies to plan for future sustainability.

Nevertheless, nations continue to demand water from both categories. Statistics on water use are expressed as the proportion of water used by a given sector. Water use at the country scale is measured in units of cubic kilometers in most of the Americas and Oceania, and in units of acre-feet in the United States. It is also beneficial to understand water usage per person, or per capita, which is expressed in terms of cubic meters or liters in most of the Americas and Oceania, and in gallons in the United States. An individual requires an estimated minimum of 50 liters per day of water for personal well-being (Dubreuil 2006). Australians utilize the lowest amount of water per capita among developed countries, whereas the United States has the highest per capita consumption, followed by Canada. South America has the second highest level of total annual water withdrawals among four world regions, but the lowest level per capita. (See table 1 below.)

Agricultural, domestic, and industrial uses are the major sectors for which data are available in the Americas and Oceania. (See figure 1 on pages 326 and 327.) Statistics are less available in the Americas and Oceania on water usage attributable to energy production and environmental services, both of which are important subsectors of the global economy. In general, water usage is dominated by agricultural irrigation in the Americas and Oceania. Oceania's usage is chiefly in Australia, where 50 percent of consumptive water withdrawals are used for agriculture. Notably, however, Australia's water usage has declined by 25 percent since 2005 due to decreases in availability of water supplies (ANWC 2011b).

Understanding how to improve the sustainability of water usage has become a pressing concern among all regions and sectors, as issues such as potential climate-change impacts, geopolitical conflict, and population growth increase the difficulty of accessing a sufficient quality and quantity of water. In the Americas and Oceania, some countries and sectors have made a commitment to sustainable water use and have developed indicators to track progress toward this goal. These nations are using conservation, environmental protection, and usage fees (among other tools) to attain sustainable usage levels. Some water-rights advocates have suggested establishing an international authority that would require users conferred with water rights to use it sustainably. Such a proposal, however, is contentious, and in any case the validity of an international authority over sovereign nations is questionable. Without pathways to developing sustainable water-use goals, and implementation of effective policy mechanisms to achieve them, meaningful action toward preserving water resources and solving environmental-justice issues related to water access will proceed slowly.

Water Rights

Water rights are a collectively recognized claim to the use of water derived from within a hydrogeologic boundary, usually for a specified quantity or for a specific purpose. For example, an individual farmer may possess water rights for irrigation that specifies a particular volume or

TABLE 1. Annual Total and Per Capita Water Withdrawals by Region

Region	Annual water withdrawals in cubic meters per capita	Total annual water withdrawals (in cubic kilometers)
Central America and the Caribbean	600	100,742
North America	1,668	525,260
South America	471	164,619
Oceania	903	26,181

Source: WRI (2011).

North America has the highest annual water withdrawals by far among the regions listed above, in both total and per capita usage. Australia dominates annual water withdrawals in the Oceania region among reporting nations (Australia, New Zealand, Fiji, Papua New Guinea, and the Solomon Islands), each of which have quite disparate values for water use. The statistics shown reflect the most recent reports from nations with national water-usage data available.

Figure 1. Freshwater Withdrawal by Country and Sector

Source: Figure adapted from and by Gonzalez (2011); data from Gleick (2009).

Water usage as the proportion of freshwater withdrawals by region and sector is shown in the figure above. The size of each country's box represents its proportion of the regional population: for example, Australia's population is the largest in Oceania. Note that each region's statistics represent only those nations for which statistics are available, and are not inclusive of all nations comprising the region.

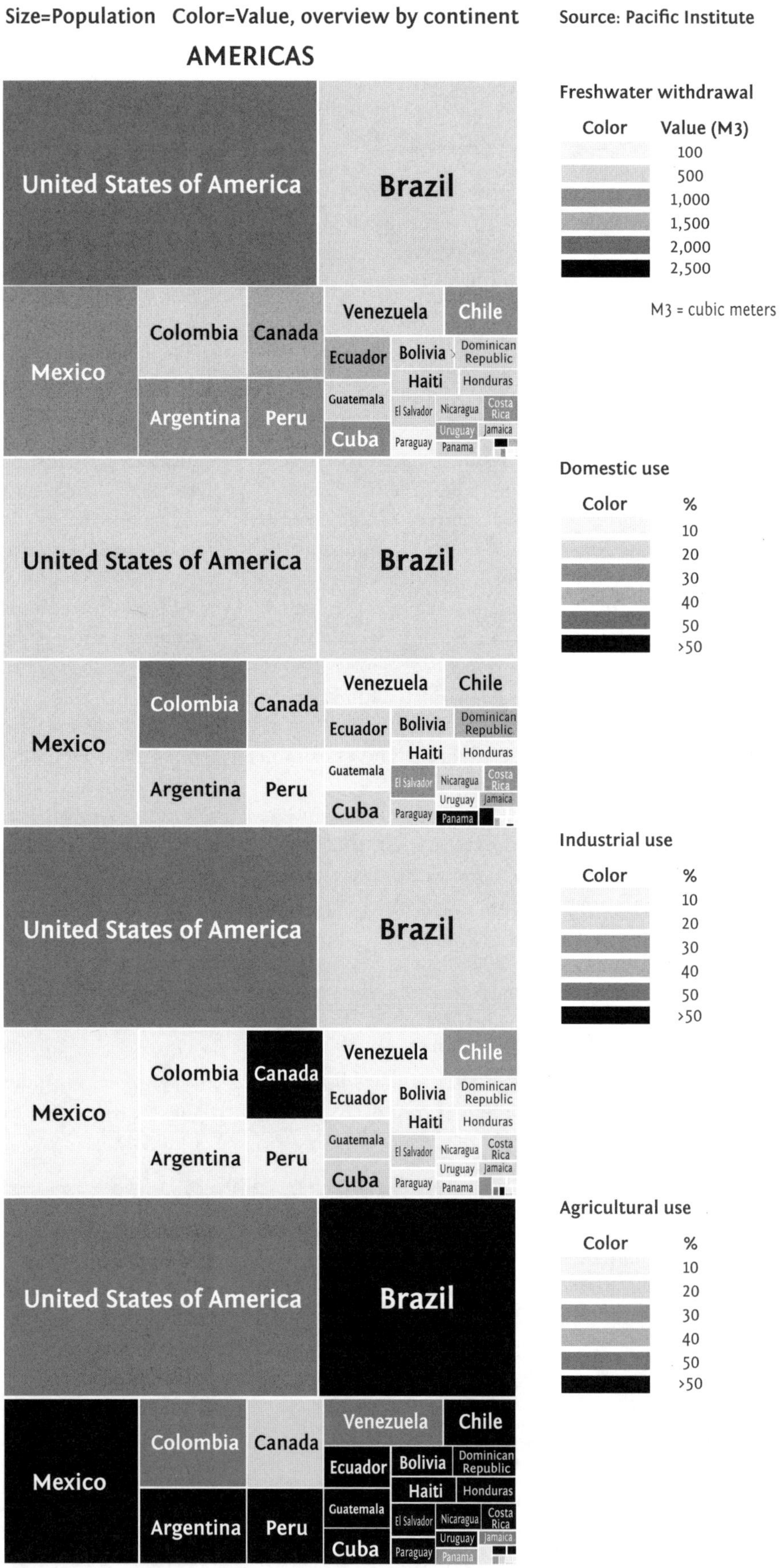
Size=Population Color=Value, overview by continent
Source: Pacific Institute
AMERICAS
United States of America
Brazil
Mexico
Colombia
Canada
Argentina
Peru
Venezuela
Chile
Ecuador
Bolivia
Dominican Republic
Haiti
Honduras
Guatemala
El Salvador
Nicaragua
Costa Rica
Cuba
Paraguay
Uruguay
Jamaica
Panama
Freshwater withdrawal
Color
Value (M3)
100
500
1,000
1,500
2,000
2,500
M3 = cubic meters
Domestic use
Color
%
10
20
30
40
50
>50
Industrial use
Color
%
10
20
30
40
50
>50
Agricultural use
Color
%
10
20
30
40
50
>50

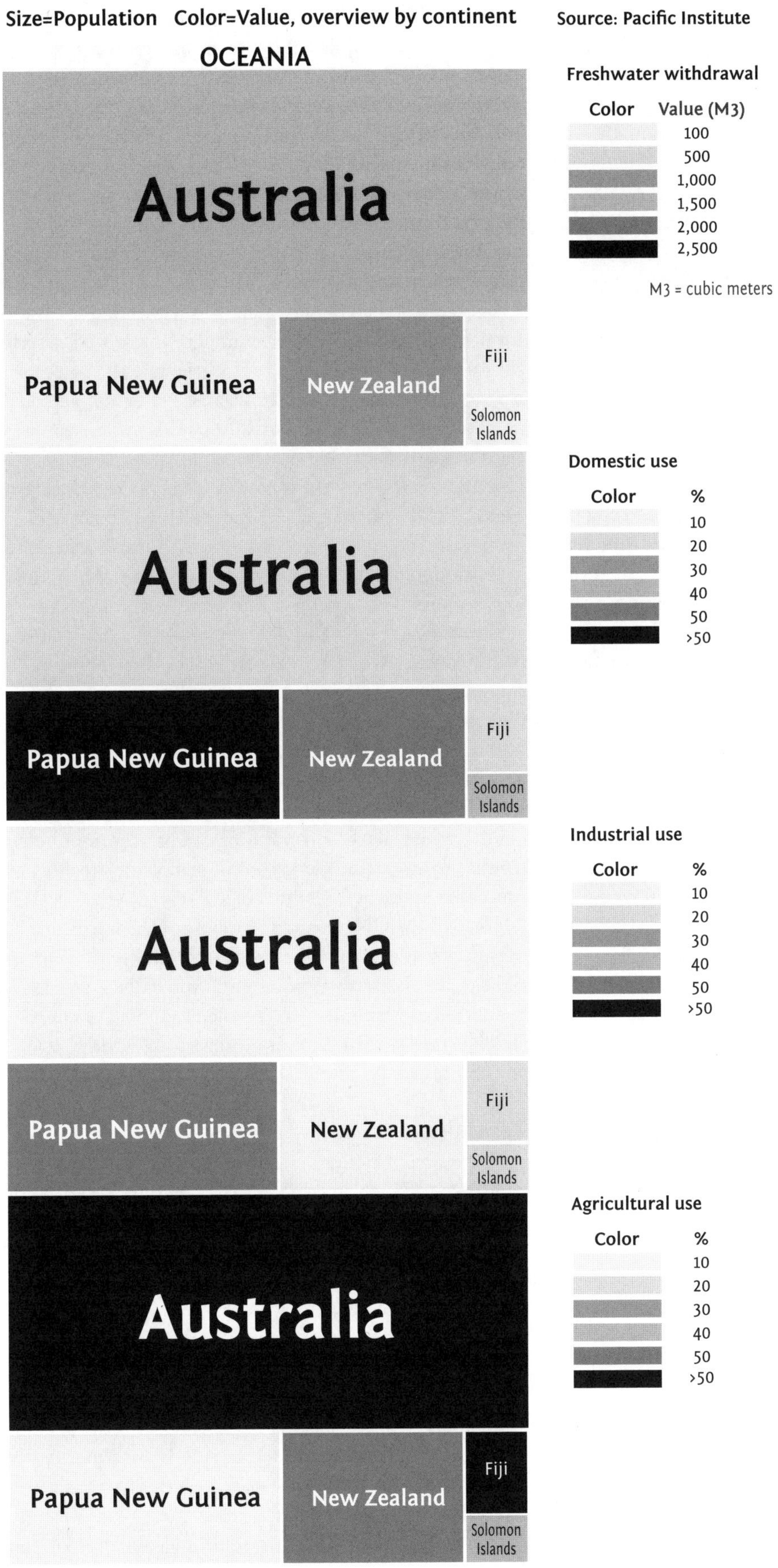

Size=Population Color=Value, overview by continent
Source: Pacific Institute
OCEANIA
Australia
Papua New Guinea
New Zealand
Fiji
Solomon Islands
Freshwater withdrawal
Color Value (M3)
100
500
1,000
1,500
2,000
2,500
M3 = cubic meters
Australia
Papua New Guinea
New Zealand
Fiji
Solomon Islands
Domestic use
Color %
10
20
30
40
50
>50
Australia
Papua New Guinea
New Zealand
Fiji
Solomon Islands
Industrial use
Color %
10
20
30
40
50
>50
Australia
Papua New Guinea
New Zealand
Fiji
Solomon Islands
Agricultural use
Color %
10
20
30
40
50
>50

flow rate that can be used during the growing season. Water rights vary considerably among regions and countries in terms of how they are conferred and implemented, based on the value a given society places on water. The right to water may be assigned seasonally, or on a permanent or temporary basis. A claim to the use of water also may be a nonformal, implied right—such as customary, traditional, or cultural rights that feature the participation of stakeholders (i.e., people with a vested interest in the resource) in the decision-making process. These kinds of rights function most successfully in areas where water use is directed toward one or two purposes, as in the island nations in Oceania where subsistence agriculture and urban uses are predominant.

Other claims to water may be defined more formally through statutory, local, or religious law (Pradhan and Meinzen-Dick 2010). Hybrid water rights consisting of a combination of societal norms and laws govern water use in many developing countries. Water rights that are defined by law are often expressed as being derived from property ownership. Decoupling water and property rights, however, allows for the establishment of institutional and financial structures that facilitate fair allocation of water rights. The means by which water rights are assigned is called *allocation*, and a water market is an allocation system utilized in many developed nations of the Americas and Oceania. Water markets may promote economic efficiency and sustainable environmental stewardship through their transactions of monetized, tradable water rights (Rosegrant and Cai 2003). Other water-allocation systems employed in these regions include regional surface-water transfer agreements and groundwater basin adjudication. Water rights and the systems used to allocate them influence political alliances and conflicts, economic productivity, human welfare, and ecosystem quality.

Human Rights and Water Rights

In the context of sustainability, water rights and allocation to communities, groups, or individuals are linked inextricably to the concept of the human right to water. Recognition of the human right to water is essential for the equitable and just allocation of this resource, and for establishing an ethical imperative over economic concerns. Equally important are the enforcement mechanisms applied to compel compliance with those rights, whether through the judiciary, the legislature, or other means. The history of the recognition of a universal human right to water is useful in understanding the evolution of water rights, particularly as developing nations in the Americas and Oceania strive to improve access to and quality of water for their populations.

Recognition of the human right to water and establishment of the requisite laws to ensure appropriate allocation has improved during the twentieth century, particularly in the recently developed regions of Latin and South America. Despite progress, historical conflicts and human-rights issues involving access to sufficient water in developing countries—including some island nations of Oceania—caused the UN to issue the International Covenant on Economic, Social and Cultural Rights General Comment Number 15 in 2002, which recognizes a human right to water (Salman and McInerney-Lankford 2004). General Comment Number 15 asserts that all humans are entitled to "sufficient, safe, acceptable, physically accessible and affordable water for personal and domestic uses" (Dubreuil 2006). This declaration was reinforced at the 2002 World Summit on Sustainable Development, where the UN's Millennium Development Goal (MDG) 7, Target 11 was established. MDG 7, Target 11 aims to improve access to drinking water and sanitation in the developing global community by reducing the number of people who were without access to water in 1990 by half (Palaniappan 2009). As of 2008, many countries in Latin America had met or were on track to meet this goal, but developing nations in the Oceania region were performing poorly (UN-Water 2008). A key impediment for these states is that agriculture, manufacturing, mining, and logging are increasing water usage without controls in place to maintain water quality, particularly in rural areas. As a result, polluted discharge and runoff are contaminating freshwater sources at an increasing rate (UN 2010).

In 2010 the UN expanded support of the human right to water by adopting a resolution recognizing the human right to drinking water and sanitation, calling on member nations for technical and financial support to improve water conditions in developing nations (Barlow 2010). Major economies in the Americas (such as the United States and Canada) and in Oceania (such as New Zealand and Australia) opposed the resolution and abstained from voting, citing procedural concerns over transparency, inclusiveness, and the legal implications of the resolution (Salman and McInerney-Lankford 2004). In contrast, water activists claimed that some major economies and their governments were pressured by private corporations and intergovernmental financial organizations to support policies promoting privatization market models in water servicing (Barlow 2010), a stance that is often inconsistent with the needs of undeveloped populations (Bakker 2011).

While the human right to water is internationally recognized and strides are being made in translating the normative basis for the UN's argument into legally binding obligations, many people in countries of the Americas and Oceania regions still struggle for adequate access to water. The human right to water differs from water rights, but the two have important connections, especially in the context of sustainable development and water rights (re)formation.

Water Rights in the Americas

In the Americas, nations such as the United States, Canada, Mexico, and Brazil support strong property rights, which extend to legally conferred water rights. Both Canada and the United States grant federally reserved rights for Indian reservations (or reserves in Canada), military installations, national parks, and forests. In Canada, Mexico, and the United States, water rights may be sold or traded individually or within a market structure. Water-rights allocation and enforcement programs may be poorly defined or still being developed in some countries of Latin and South America. Progress is lagging in these regions, but a few developing countries have emerged as successful examples of progressive and equitable water-rights policy development.

North America

Various forms of usufructuary water rights (the right to use and profit from water that is owned by the public as long as its value or quality is maintained) exist in the United States. Water rights are granted pursuant to state law and depend on the source of water. In the eastern United States, surface water rights are based on English common law and established by ownership of riparian land adjacent to a waterway (Totten, McClurg, and WEF 2005). The right must be exercised or be subject to assignment of lower priority or quantity. In contrast, surface water rights in the western United States are based on customary law (known as the doctrine of prior appropriation), in which the first to make a claim on water and put it to beneficial use receives the right, regardless of its proximity to land (Totten, McClurg, and WEF 2005). Those who fail to exercise their rights must relinquish them (known as the "use it or lose it" rule). Groundwater is not monitored in most of the western United States, and no federal groundwater management law exists, but groundwater rights are correlative in that property owners whose land overlies an aquifer have a right (governed by the principle of reasonable use) to utilize that water.

The US state of California employs a hybrid system, in which riparian rights supersede appropriative rights. California's water rights are conferred to a variety of users: the federal government has the majority of rights in terms of volume, followed by irrigation districts and private utilities (CSWRCB 2008). A geographic mismatch exists between the holders of water rights, water sources, and users that demand the water, creating a complex system for managing water resources.

Pueblo rights, which are conferred rights unique to North America, exist primarily in the southwestern United States and stem from Spanish-Mexican law, whereby the right to a waterway was conferred upon the community through which it passed (Cech 2010).

In the late twentieth century Mexico enacted new legislation to reform water-rights law incrementally, in response to the challenges presented by groundwater exploitation and geographic imbalances between supply and demand. The Mexican constitution holds that water is owned by the state; later amendments authorize the use of water as granted by qualifying authorities through concessions and a "user pays" system. Concessions are subject to review to ensure environmental protection, and are tradable within districts in a water market (Garduno 2005). Some indigenous communities in Mexico adhere to a "collective usufruct" system where supply is free and decisions are communal (Garcia 2007).

South America

In 2004 Uruguay amended its constitution by passing right-to-water legislation and prioritizing social needs over the imperatives of the economy, becoming the first country in the world to do so. The Latin American nations of Argentina, Chile, Colombia, Panama, and Peru have followed the example of Bolivia, Colombia, and Mexico and are engaged in similar successful campaigns to oust privatization regimes and amend their constitutions to improve access to water (WWAP 2009). One key challenge they face is developing an alternative model to manage their water resources successfully, based on defensible and ethical water rights and allocations systems.

Water Rights in Oceania

Oceania includes the continent of Australia as well as New Zealand and thousands of smaller islands, located across an area of approximately 8,112,000 square kilometers. Geographical, geological, geopolitical, and socioeconomic differences across this vast region define the hydrology and water-resources management of its member countries. These differences are further emphasized by distinct histories and cultures that have influenced the development of policies relevant to water and other natural resources.

Australia and New Zealand

In Australia, well-documented reforms in the latter part of the twentieth century resulted in a modernized water rights and allocation system. Water resources are managed through state conferred water-access entitlements that function as a license to a continuous share of water allocated by volume and seasonality. Regional water-supply entities and local municipal agencies are issued entitlements along with the industrial, mining, and agricultural sectors (ANWC 2011c). Building on the Council of Australian Governments' Water Reform Framework of 1994, the National Water Initiative (NWI) decoupled land and water rights in 2004 and expanded trading in a water market as the preferred entitlement-allocation mechanism. Reforms under the NWI also aim to provide water rights for indigenous Aboriginal peoples (Haisman 2005). The NWI recognizes environmental services as an equally important use of water in determining water-allocation programs, an approach that has highlighted the disparate needs and demands for water from various sectors. The challenge in reconciling the conflicting views of irrigators, the mining sector, and conservationists to develop a water-management plan acceptable to all parties is evident in the attempts by the Murray-Darling Basin Authority to do so between 2010 and 2012.

Guided by its Resource Management Act of 1991, New Zealand also allocates water based on reasonable-use criteria and allocation mechanisms (such as market-based systems, tradable permits, and court order) developed and administered by regional councils (Guerin 2003). Consents (known as "takes") for consumptive water use are issued on a first-come, first-served basis and apply for up to thirty-five years; they are reviewed approximately every ten years to ensure that minimum flows and the quality of the water resource are maintained (Guerin 2003). Water allocation has increased by more than 50 percent over the past decade, with the majority of consents issued for irrigation activities. Two-thirds of consents are granted from groundwater sources, 29 percent from surface-water sources, and the remainder from dams, lakes, and geothermal sources (Aqualinc Research Limited 2006). New Zealand's regional councils are challenged by the uncertainty of overallocated water resources, effects of land use changes, and the legal ambiguity of consent reviews and waiting lists, among other issues (Lincoln Environmental 2000). Adding further complexity to New Zealand's water-rights systems, a 322-kilometer stretch of the nation's coastal waters and freshwater estuaries is claimed by the indigenous Māori as tribal property, a claim that is being recognized as a form of customary rights (Rapaport 1999).

Micronesia, Melanesia, and Polynesia

The nations of Micronesia, Melanesia, and Polynesia historically have held customary rights to water, in which allocation is based on the indigenous cultural norm of access to sea, surface, and groundwater sources (Rapaport 1999). The Constitution of the Federated States of Micronesia affirms traditional property rights but contains no language referencing water rights. Traditional rights support the notion of correlative water rights, but without specific allocation programs, confusion arises as to who owns the rights to use the water that was previously managed collectively when these traditional rights are challenged. For example, the recent increases in foreign military forces being stationed in Guam (a Micronesian nation) and the accompanying water demands have brought attention to this very issue, causing the island nation to initiate water-rights legislation in 2007 and to consider privatization.

In the Solomon Islands (a Melanesian nation of one thousand islands) land is owned through customary law, and the state currently has no water policy or legislation that addresses water rights or usage. Customary law implies the "continued repetition of actions or practices by a collectivity in the conviction that they are legally binding," which "are often not enshrined in any written text" (Caponera 1992, 61). The mismatched and fragmented nature of multi-island water sources and users creates a complex puzzle for a government that does not prioritize water-resource management (KEW 2006). In another Melanesian nation, Papua New Guinea's Customs Recognition Act and its Water Resources Act recognize the state's right to use and control water as being consistent with customary water rights, making provisions for recourse should those rights be violated. Despite robust constitutional environmental-protection policy, recent extractive resource developments have tested the strength of customary water rights as developers operate with state authorization but contrary to customary rights of indigenous people. Moreover, extractive activities such as mining and logging have resulted in environmental degradation and other social and economic costs that have been borne by indigenous populations (Kalinoe 1998).

The Polynesian island nation of Samoa passed the Water Resources Management Act in 2008 to formalize how water rights are conferred and allocated, ranging from traditional village-scale water resource management to state-implemented payment for service models (KEW 2006). Because land ownership is still granted through customary law, many Samoans oppose state efforts to reach regional agreements managing water and implementing payment programs. While codification resolves the ambiguity associated with traditional and customary rights, it also introduces rigidity and undercuts the flexibility inherent in historically granted rights.

Sustainability for the Future

The impacts of climate change are creating a changing landscape of precipitation and hydrologic patterns and will require adaptive approaches to managing water. When coupled with excessive water withdrawal and usage, climate change can initiate responses or exacerbate existing problems such as rises in sea level, supply shortages, saltwater intrusion, and soil subsidence (a shifting downward of soil). Integrated water resource management (IWRM) is a body of principles and practices that emphasizes water equity, economic efficiency, and environmental integrity. The UN challenge to implement plans that incorporate this management paradigm usually has not been a priority in developing countries in Oceania and the Americas. Developing nations that reported their progress in formulating and integrating an IWRM plan either have plan preparation underway or have achieved minimal steps in initiating the plan process. The reasons for this delayed progress include low stakeholder participation and difficulty in mobilizing the resources required to implement IWRM. Brazil and Samoa, however, have completed and are in the process of implementing their IWRM plans, respectively, along with developed nations such as the United States, Australia, and New Zealand (UN-Water 2008). Meanwhile, Micronesian nations that included the Republic of Palau and the Marshall Islands hosted conferences aimed at investigating implementation of IWRM in 2011.

In addition to creating management paradigms, developing water sustainability indicators and information systems is necessary to track water usage, social justice, and policy-tool benchmarking. Technological systems comprise one component of the water-sustainability toolbox, but an equally important facet is the development of institutional capacity to govern water rights, allocation, and uses effectively. Water governance is a relatively new and poorly understood concept, but capacity building in this dimension of water-resources management is integral to effective, equitable, long-term change. Finally, it is critical for the global community to assert and advocate for the human right to water and for the reform of water rights. Essential components of this engagement include education and support of policies that induce humans to use and live with water in a sustainable manner.

Tiffany WISE-WEST
University of California, Santa Cruz

See also Amazon River; Australia; Canada; Columbia River; Great Lakes and Saint Lawrence River; Las Vegas, United States; Lima, Peru; Mackenzie River; Mexico City; Mississippi and Missouri Rivers; Murray-Darling River Basin; New Zealand; Oceania; Perth, Australia; Phoenix, United States; Sanitation; Small Island States; Sydney, Australia

FURTHER READING

Aqualinc Research Limited. (2006). *Snapshot of water allocation in New Zealand*. Wellington, New Zealand: Ministry for the Environment. Retrieved March 12, 2012, from http://www.mfe.govt.nz/publications/ser/snapshot-water-allocation-nov06/snapshot-water-allocation-nov06.pdf

Australia Department of Sustainability, Environment, Water, Population, and Communities (ADSEWPC). (2009). Water resources: Allocation and use. *Australian natural resources atlas*. Retrieved Mach 31, 2012, from http://www.anra.gov.au/topics/water/allocation/index.html

Australia National Water Commission (ANWC). (2005). *Australian water resources 2005*. Retrieved September 30, 2011, from http://www.water.gov.au/WaterUse/index.aspx?Menu=Level1_4

Australia National Water Commission (ANWC). (2011a). *National Water Initiative: 2011 assessment*. Retrieved March 29, 2012, from http://nwc.gov.au/reform/assessing/biennial/the-national-water-initiative-securing-australias-water-future-2011-assessment

Australia National Water Commission (ANWC). (2011b). Water use in Australia. Retrieved September 30, 2011, from http://www.nwc.gov.au/availability/use/australia

Australia National Water Commission (ANWC). (2011c). Allocations and entitlements. Retrieved September 30, 2011, from http://www.nwc.gov.au/markets/allocations-entitlements

Bakker, Karen. (2011). Commons vs. commodities: Political ecologies of water privatization. In Richard Peet, Paul Robbins & Michael J. Watts (Eds.), *Global political ecology* (pp. 347–370). New York: Routledge.

Barber, Nancy L. (2009). Summary of estimated water use in the United States in 2005 (US Geological Survey Fact Sheet 2009–3098). Retrieved April 7, 2012, from http://pubs.usgs.gov/fs/2009/3098/pdf/2009-3098.pdf

Barlow, Maude. (2010). Making water a human right. In Tara Lohan (Ed.), *Water matters: Why we need to act now to save our most critical resource* (pp. 104–113). San Francisco: AlterNet Books.

California State Water Resources Control Board (CSWRCB). (2008). eWRIMS Water Rights Search [Database]. Retrieved October 1, 2011, from http://ciwqs.waterboards.ca.gov/ciwqs/ewrims/EWServlet?Redirect_Page=EWWaterRightPublicSearch.jsp&Purpose=getEWAppSearchPage

Caponera, Dante A. (1992). *Principles of water law and administration*. Rotterdam, The Netherlands: A. A. Balkerma.

Cech, Thomas V. (2010). *Principles of water resources: History, development, management, and policy*. Hoboken, NJ: John Wiley & Sons.

Dubreuil, Celine. (2006). *The right to water: From concept to implementation*. Marseilles, France: World Water Council.

Garcia, Patricia Avila. (2007). Water and environment in one indigenous region of Mexico. In Petri Juuti, Tapio S. Katko & Heikki S. Vuorinen (Eds.), *Environmental history of water* (pp. 411–428). London: IWA Publishing.

Garduno, Hector. (2005). Lessons from implementing water rights in Mexico. In Bryan Randolph Bruns, Claudia Ringler & Ruth Meinzen-Dick (Eds.), *Water rights reform: Lessons for institutional design* (pp. 85–112). Washington, DC: International Food Policy Research Institute.

Gleick, Peter. (2009). *The world's water: The biennial report on freshwater resources*. Washington, DC: Pacific Institute for Studies in Development, Environment, and Security.

Gonzalez, Alberto. (2011). Tree map of freshwater withdrawal by country: A comparison between continents [Infographic]. Retrieved October 2, 2011, from http://www.circleofblue.org/waternews/2011/world/infographic-freshwater-withdrawal-tree-maps/

Guerin, Kevin. (2003). *Property rights and environmental policy: A New Zealand perspective* (New Zealand Treasury Working Paper 03/02). Wellington, New Zealand: New Zealand Treasury.

Haddad, Brent. (2000). *Rivers of gold: Designing markets to allocate water in California*. Washington, DC: Island Press.

Haisman, Brian. (2005). The impacts of water rights reform in Australia. In Bryan Randolph Bruns, Claudia Ringler & Ruth Meinzen-Dick (Eds.), *Water rights reform: Lessons for institutional design* (pp. 113–152). Washington, DC: International Food Policy Research Institute.

Hoekstra, A. Y., & Chapagain, A. K. (2007). Water footprints of nations: Water use by people as a function of their consumption pattern. *Water Resource Management, 2*, 35–48.

Kalinoe, Lawrence Kuna. (1998). *Water law and the nature of customary water rights in Papua New Guinea* (Doctoral dissertation, University of Wollongong, Wollongong, Australia). Retrieved September 20, 2011, from http://ro.uow.edu.au/theses/1862

KEW Consult Ltd. (2006). *Solomon Island Water Governance Programme: Report on visit to Samoa*. Retrieved October 7, 2011, from http://www.pacificwater.org/_resources/article/files/SI2%20-%20Visit%20to%20Samoa%20-%20Final%20Report.pdf

Lincoln Environmental. (2000). *Information on water allocation in New Zealand* (Report No. 4375/1). Wellington, New Zealand: Ministry for the Environment. Retrieved on March 12, 2012, from http://www.mfe.govt.nz/publications/water/water-allocation-apr00.pdf

Palaniappan, Meena. (2009). Millennium development goals: Charting progress and the way forward. In Peter H. Gleick, Heather Cooley & Mari Morikawa (Eds.), *The world's water 2008–2009: The biennial report on freshwater resources*. Washington, DC: Island Press.

Pradhan, Rajendra, & Meinzen-Dick, Ruth. (2010). Which rights are right? Water rights, culture, and underlying values. In Peter G. Brown & Jeremy J. Schmidt (Eds.), *Water ethics: Foundational readings for students and professionals* (pp. 39–58). Washington, DC: Island Press.

Rapaport, Moshe. (1999). *The Pacific Islands: Environment and society*. Honolulu, HI: Bess Press.

Rosegrant, Mark W., & Cai Ximing. (2003). Water development and food production: A global perspective. In Richard G. Lawford, Denise D. Fort, Holly C. Hartmann & Susanna Eden (Eds.), *Water: Science, policy, and management* (pp. 99–120). Washington, DC: American Geophysical Union.

Salman, Salman M. A., & McInerney-Lankford, Siobhan. (2004). *The human right to water: Legal and policy dimensions*. Washington, DC: The World Bank.

Totten, Glenn; McClurg, Sue; & Water Education Foundation (WEF). (2005). *The layperson's guide to water rights law*. Sacramento, CA: Water Education Foundation.

UN-Water. (2008). *Status report on IWRM and water efficiency plans for CSD16*. Retrieved October 24, 2011, from http://www.unwater.org/downloads/UNW_Status_Report_IWRM.pdf

United Nations (UN). (2010). *Millennium development goals report 2010*. Retrieved March 30, 2012, from http://www.un.org/millenniumgoals/pdf/MDG%20Report%202010%20En%20r15%20-low%20res%2020100615%20-.pdf

World Resources Institute (WRI). (2011). EarthTrends [Web portal]. Retrieved October 7, 2011, from http://earthtrends.wri.org/select_action.php?theme=2

World Water Assessment Programme (WWAP). (2009). *The United Nations world water development report 3: Water in a changing world*. Paris: UNESCO.

Berkshire's authors and editors welcome questions, comments, and corrections. Send your emails about the *Berkshire Encyclopedia of Sustainability* in general or this volume in particular to: sustainability.updates@berkshirepublishing.com

Y

Yellowstone to Yukon Conservation Initiative (Y2Y)

The Yellowstone to Yukon Conservation Initiative (Y2Y) is an international effort to conserve interconnected landscapes from Yellowstone National Park, United States, to Canada's Yukon Territory to ensure the survival of native species. The initiative has made globally significant innovations in large landscape conservation in the Yellowstone to Yukon region, but tensions between conserving world-famous natural values and extracting or otherwise developing significant natural resources also characterize the effort.

The Yellowstone to Yukon Conservation Initiative is a widespread collaborative effort to create long-term sustainability in the Rocky Mountains, the Columbia Mountains, and the Mackenzie Mountains that stretch from the Greater Yellowstone Ecosystem centered in northwestern Wyoming to the Arctic Circle in Canada's Yukon Territory. A nonprofit organization (y2y.net) based in Canmore, Alberta, with a field office in Montana coordinated the effort, which originated in December 1993 as a loose collaboration of conservationists and scientists. Yellowstone to Yukon is also increasingly being referred to as a region in the geographic sense in recognition of its shared geology, ecology, history, and current common endeavors. The Yellowstone to Yukon idea has also become a symbol for global efforts to protect interconnected landscapes to ensure the survival and resilience of robust populations of native species across a broad landscape. Y2Y is the abbreviation used interchangeably to describe all these facets; its meaning depends on the context of its usage.

Natural Values and Conservation Significance

The words *Yellowstone to Yukon* themselves have a conservation meaning in Western culture and some other parts of the world. Yellowstone is synonymous with national parks; the Yukon is synonymous with wilderness and wild animals. Actual conditions support these symbolic meanings. The Y2Y region contains the world's first national park (Yellowstone), the world's third oldest national park (Banff), the world's first "Peace Park" (abutting parks jointly managed across an international border) (Waterton-Glacier), and one of the world's largest national parks (Nahanni). These parks are all United Nations Educational, Scientific and Cultural Organization (UNESCO) World Heritage sites. The region also contains the oldest national forest in the United States (Shoshone), the largest and oldest legislated wilderness area complexes in the lower forty-eight US states (Bob Marshall and adjoining areas in Montana and the Frank Church–River of No Return/Selway-Bitterroot wildernesses in Idaho), the only two tribally designated wildernesses in the Unites States (Wind River Mountain Roadless Area, designated by the Eastern Shoshone and Northern Arapaho people in Wyoming, and the Mission Mountains Tribal Wilderness, protected by the Kootenai-Salish people in Montana). It also contains the Muskwa-Kechika Management Area in Northern British Columbia, which is a provincially legislated mix of wilderness parks and special resource-extraction management areas that have the long-term statutory objective of maintaining wilderness and wildlife.

The Y2Y region is home to all species native to western North America that were present at the onset of European colonization in the nineteenth century. These include iconic wildlife species such as the plains bison, bighorn and thinhorn sheep, moose, wolves, and wolverines. Native fish include globally important populations of cold water trout (bull and westslope cutthroat), and resident birds range from trumpeter swans and golden eagles to chickadees and dippers, as well as migratory species that include sandhill cranes and western tanagers. Because of the extraordinary wilderness and wildlife that persist in the Y2Y region in the twenty-first century, the area has been called the "wild heart of North America."

The symbol of Yellowstone to Yukon is the grizzly bear because it is an icon of wilderness and wildlife and because the survival of grizzly bears requires thoughtful society-wide conservation management. The species has been widely studied, and its conservation requirements are well understood. Grizzly bears are wide-ranging in nature, have low reproductive rates, need remote wilderness areas to rear their young in secure conditions that allow them to avoid conflict with humans, and require a vast interconnected landscape to avoid genetic isolation and inbreeding. These biological characteristics of the grizzly bear make it a useful "umbrella species" for conservation planning because it serves as a surrogate for the conservation of many other species. If the needs of grizzly bears are met, the needs of about 80 percent of other wildlife species are met too. The last surviving population of grizzly bears in the United States outside of Alaska is concentrated in the Y2Y region, and its survival is dependent on keeping that population connected to Canadian populations farther north; hence the need to think and act on a large scale, as with Yellowstone to Yukon.

Important intact gravel-bed river systems such as the Yellowstone River (the largest undammed river in the lower forty-eight US states) and many wild rivers in Canada support the natural attributes of Y2Y. Several rivers flow over the international border, including the Flathead River, on which pioneering research has been done to understand the function and central importance of intact gravel-bed rivers in the broader landscape. The Y2Y region has been called the "mother of rivers" because it serves as the headwaters for the Columbia, Missouri, Saskatchewan, Fraser, and Mackenzie river systems, as well as a headwater of the Colorado. These rivers account for most of the freshwater in western North America. This water tower function grows in importance with climate change, which is already causing glaciers to recede rapidly.

Human Dimensions: Settlement, Recreation, and Resources

The Yellowstone to Yukon region has been home to humans for more than ten thousand years. Aboriginal populations are distributed along the entire length of the mountain corridor as they have been since the retreat of glaciers from the Wisconsin Ice Age. Europeans did not reach the region until approximately 1750, and the initial engagement between peoples centered on the fur trade, which involved removing hides from the Y2Y region for sale to European and US East Coast markets. With the western expansion of railways in the last half of the nineteenth century came natural resource extraction and permanent settlements. Some of the largest mining operations in the world have occurred in the Y2Y region (Butte, Montana, and Crowsnest Coalfield in British Columbia), the first tall cement dam in the United States was built at Cody, Wyoming, and some of the world's largest dams for hydroelectricity are found on the Columbia and Peace river systems. Significant natural gas fields have been found and developed in northeastern British Columbia, Southern Alberta, and near Pinedale, Wyoming. Large-scale forestry operations have been established in British Columbia, in western Montana and Idaho, and in Alberta but are now in decline because most of the old growth has been liquidated and the trees grow back slowly. All of these resource-extraction activities tend to create economic prosperity for a period and severely fragment wildlife habitat and sometimes leave a toxic legacy. In the southernmost part of the Y2Y region, grassland environments in the rain shadow of the mountains attracted extensive cattle and sheep ranching. Ranching can compete with the needs of native ungulates (animals with hooves), conflict with predators, and affect the health of cold water streams and trout populations but also can preserve native grasslands.

The railways that shipped resources to external markets invariably followed the few low-elevation valley bottoms that cross the otherwise rugged north-south grain of the mountains of Y2Y. These rare valley bottoms also have the mildest climate; therefore they are at once the most biologically productive and the most attractive to human settlers. Farming is restricted to these few fertile valley-bottom areas. People built communities along the rail lines, and when paved roads came in the twentieth century, they usually paralleled the rail lines. The human population was initially concentrated in towns and cities or on large ranches. Even though ranching declined as an economic activity, with the expansion of automobile ownership in the last half of the twentieth century, the idea of subdividing rural lands for housing grew in popularity. Skiing also rapidly became popular, and second-home ownership in previously remote high places often accompanied resort developments. The growth of golf as a summer sport has created similar pressures in low-elevation areas. These development patterns significantly fragment wildlife habitat, sometimes with more severe impacts than ranching.

Reconciling Human Use with Natural Systems

The southern third of the Y2Y region (form Banff National Park, Alberta, to Wyoming) is the most populated zone and has the greatest number of protected areas. About 90 percent is public land. Within those lands, percentages of protection vary by jurisdiction, but in aggregate it is roughly 40 percent, protected by a variety of mechanisms. There are also significant private land conservation designations that likely account for about a sixth of the private land base, which is about 10 percent of the southern third of Y2Y. Taken together, the southern third of the Y2Y region is one of the world's most protected landscapes (Locke 2012b). Although impressive, this protection is not sufficient to achieve long term conservation. Studies show that at least half of any landscape should be protected in an interconnected way. In the Y2Y region this protection means that creatively managing the interface between wild nature and human development along low-elevation valley bottoms is central to keeping the Y2Y region connected for other species.

This need for valley-bottom wildlife connectivity led to globally significant conservation innovations. The busy Trans-Canada Highway traverses Banff National Park, and there were many animal-vehicle collisions in the early 1980s. To mitigate this carnage, a high fence combined with a series of wildlife-crossing structures built over and under the road have reduced wildlife collisions by 80 percent and still enabled animals to live their lives on both sides of the road (Highway Wilding n.d., 2). The Banff highway mitigations have attracted worldwide attention. This success has been replicated in part on the Kootenai-Salish Reservation on Highway 93 in Montana, and some similar structures have been built on highways near Pinedale, Wyoming. The death of wildlife along railways remains a serious problem, although fledgling efforts have begun on the Canadian Pacific Rail line in Banff National Park and along the Burlington-Northern line on the edge of Glacier National Park in Montana.

A large collaboration of land trusts that work cooperatively with the Y2Y organization is addressing the problem of habitat fragmentation from subdivisions in the southern part of Y2Y. Together the trusts acquire from willing sellers key valley-bottom parcels of private land that serve as links for grizzly bears between larger blocks of public land. This modification ensures maintenance (and in other places sets the stage for restoration) of wildlife connectivity at the Y2Y scale. Some ranchers have also voluntarily created conservation easements to prevent subdivision and fragmentation of their lands. Zoning of land to ensure open corridors for wildlife movement is used infrequently but effectively in Canada (e.g., Canmore, Alberta, where wildlife corridors are legally designated by law) but is very rarely done in the United States. Management of garbage through mandatory bear-proof containers in some communities in both countries has also helped to reduce the impact of human habitations on other species by reducing attractants.

Between Conservation and Industrialization

The northern part of the Y2Y region is one of the wildest places remaining on Earth. Differing worldviews drive a basic tension between those who see it as the last frontier whose natural resources should be exploited and those who see it as one of the last opportunities to protect vast wilderness areas and wildlife and the ability for native people to pursue their traditional livelihoods. In the Nahanni area of the Northwest Territories, a wild watershed that exceeds 35,000 square kilometers, this drama played out in the first decade of the twenty-first century. The result of a nine-year-long conservation campaign involving the Dehcho First Nations, conservationists, and Parks Canada was the expansion of a national park that now covers most of the watershed and is one of largest national parks in the world. An additional national park is actively being contemplated for its headwaters. A similar drama is playing out over the future of the vast 60,000-square-kilometer wilderness in the Yukon's Peel River watershed between First Nations and their wilderness conservationist allies on one side and the mining industry on the other. At the same time, the British Columbia government proposes a giant new hydro reservoir on the Peace River (at Site C near Fort St. John, British Columbia) and a new ski resort in the heart of a grizzly bear habitat in the Jumbo Mountain, which conservationists and some First Nations oppose.

In the 1990s, wolves from the Canadian portion of Y2Y were reintroduced to central Idaho and Yellowstone National Park. They have flourished, and the ecosystem has responded to the reduced grazing and browsing pressure from ungulates through a return of poplar forests and willows, which in turn support a wide variety of other species. Pressure from hunting and ranching interests, however, led to legislative removal of protection for wolves from the US Endangered Species Act in December of 2011. Administrative efforts to remove the Yellowstone population of grizzly bears from the list of endangered species have provoked litigation over disagreement about the long-term viability of the population. An administrative order by President Bill Clinton in the late 1990s that provided some important protection to officially designated roadless areas in US National Forests has survived fifteen years of litigation and political debate.

The sometimes international scale of issues in the Y2Y region is demonstrated by the case of the remote Flathead Valley (seen in the photograph by Harvey Locke on page •••). The Flathead River rises in Canada and flows south into the United States. An international conflict occurred over proposed open-pit coal mining and coal-bed methane development in the river's British Columbia headwaters, which is upstream from the Montana portion of Waterton-Glacier International Peace Park World Heritage Site. The government of Montana and that state's federal Senate delegation fought publicly with the government of British Columbia over this matter. A coalition of international nongovernmental organizations raised public awareness around the world of what they perceived to be a threat to a globally significant river valley and called instead for conservation of the area through a national park expansion and wildlife management area. The issue became very public. The prime minister of Canada and the president of the United States discussed the problem at the World Heritage Commission meeting in Seville, Spain, and dispatched a mission to investigate the threat. Fearing international protests at the 2010 Winter Olympics in Vancouver, the British Columbia government succumbed to pressure and announced a ban on oil and gas extraction and mining. Conservationists continue to advocate that the area be formally protected because it is still open to logging and off-road vehicle use and lacks a wildlife sanctuary. On the other hand, some local hunting and off-road vehicle users who drive forestry roads consider Y2Y to be an international conspiracy designed to deprive them of their chosen recreation (East Kootenay Residents Land Use Coalition n.d.).

The outcome of these conflicts is not clear. The enduring tension between conservation and industrialization of the landscape will continue to play out across the Y2Y region.

Outlook

Because of its vast scale, iconic species and landscape, and the advanced large landscape conservation strategies pioneered and implemented in the Y2Y region, the Yellowstone to Yukon Conservation Initiative has become the global icon of large landscape conservation efforts. The Y2Y idea has spawned many television programs, news stories, and books and has been the subject of doctoral and master's theses around the world. It has been emulated and adapted to local circumstances by similar initiatives on several continents, among them the Great Eastern Ranges Initiative in Australia, Two Countries–One Forest in the Northern Appalachians of Canada and the United States, and Baja to Bering which seeks to connect Baja, California to the Bering Sea along the Pacific Coast of North America. Through the International Union for Conservation of Nature World Commission on Protected Areas, Y2Y has also helped to nurture and advance a global community of large landscape conservation practitioners.

In the twenty-first century, the Y2Y region is of particular interest because it is at once a globally significant area for both conservation and resource extraction and features a growing human population that is drawn to the region for its natural amenities and its economic opportunities. It also supports an important tourism economy. The Y2Y region is valued also by people who live outside it, which engages national governments in the region's management and international treaties such as the World Heritage Convention. It also attracts outside interest from philanthropists and nongovernment organizations. Only a few regions on Earth attract intense interest at all these levels.

Climate change and its attendant impacts have only deepened the need for large landscape conservation strategies, especially ones that allow for species to adapt to warming temperatures by moving up-latitude and up-elevation. In a world where most conservation news is usually bleak, the Yellowstone to Yukon Conservation Initiative endeavors to stand as a beacon of hope for the reconciliation of humanity and nature in the twenty-first century.

Harvey LOCKE
Strategic Advisor, Yellowstone to Yukon Conservation Initiative

See also Canada; Columbia River; Ecotourism (the Americas); Mackenzie River; Multilateral Environmental Agreements (MEAs); North American Free Trade Agreement (NAFTA); Northwest Passage; Parks and Protected Areas; Rocky Mountains; Rural Development (the Americas); United States; Vancouver, Canada

FURTHER READING

Chester, Charles C. (2006). *Conservation across borders: Biodiversity in an interdependent world*. Washington, DC: Island Press.

East Kootenay Residents Land Use Coalition. (n.d.). Homepage. Retrieved May 3, 2012, from http://ekaccess.ca

Heller, Nicole E., & Zavaleta, Erika S. (2009). Biodiversity management in the face of climate change: A review of 22 years of recommendations. *Biological Conservation, 142*(1), 14–32.

Highway Wilding. (n.d.). Banff wildlife crossing research by numbers. Retrieved May 3, 2012, from http://highwaywilding.org/files/Highway%20Wilding%20research%20by%20numbers_21_March_2012.pdf

Hodgson, Jenny A.; Thomas, Chris D.; Wintle, Brendan A.; & Moilanen, Atte. (2009). Climate change, connectivity and conservation decision making: Back to basics. *Journal of Applied Ecology, 46*(5), 964–969. doi:10.1111/j.1365-2664.2009.01695.x

Konstant, W.; Locke, Harvey; & Hanna, J. (2005). Waterton-Glacier International Peace Park: The first of its kind. In Russel A. Mettermeier et al. (Eds.), *Transboundary conservation: A new vision for protected areas* (pp. 71–82). San Pedro Garza García, Mexico: Cemex-Agrupacion Sierra Madre-Conservation International.

Locke, Harvey. (1994). Preserving the wild heart of North America: The Wildlands Project and the Yellowstone to Yukon Biodiversity Strategy. *Borealis, 15*, 18.

Locke, Harvey. (2006). The need and opportunity for landscape scale conservation in the Yellowstone to Yukon region: A vision for the 21st century. In Alice Wondrak-Biel (Ed.), *Greater Yellowstone public lands: A century of discovery, hard lessons, and bright prospects* (pp. 99–108). Proceedings of the 8th Biennial Scientific Conference on the Greater Yellowstone Ecosystem. Yellowstone Center for Resources, Yellowstone National Park, Wyoming, USA. Retrieved April 23, 2012, from http://www.nps.gov/yell/naturescience/8thconferenceproceedings.htm

Locke, Harvey. (2009). Civil society and protected areas: Lessons from Canada. *The George Wright Forum, 26*(2), 101–128.

Locke, Harvey. (2012a). Transboundary cooperation to achieve wilderness protection and large landscape conservation. *Park Science, 28*(3), 24–28.

Locke, Harvey. (2012b). Unpublished raw data.

Locke, Harvey, & McKinney, Matthew. (2012). Flathead Valley Flashpoint. In Emma S. Norman, Alice Cohen & Karen Bakker (Eds.), *Water without borders: Canada, the US and transboundary water* (in press). Toronto: University of Toronto Press.

Locke, Harvey. (Ed.). (2012). *Yellowstone to Yukon: The journey of wildlife and art*. Golden, CO: Fulcrum Press.

National Park Service. (2011). A call to action: Preparing for a second century of stewardship and engagement. Retrieved April 23, 2012, from http://www.nps.gov/CallToAction

Nature. (2011). Think big. *Nature, 469*, 131. Retrieved April 23, 2012, from http://www.nature.com/nature/journal/v469/n7329/full/469131a.html

Newmark, William D. (1987). A land bridge island perspective on mammalian extinctions in western North American national parks. *Nature, 325*(6103), 430–432.

Noss, Reed F., et al. (2012). Bolder thinking for conservation. *Conservation Biology, 26*(1), 1–4.

Parks Canada Agency. (2000). *Unimpaired for future generations? Protecting ecological integrity with Canada's national parks: Volumes 1 and 2* (Report of the Panel on the Ecological Integrity of Canada's National Parks). Ottawa, Canada: Parks Canada Agency.

Patterson, Raymond M. (1999). *Dangerous river: Adventure on the Nahanni*. Erin, Canada: Boston Mills Press.

Salazar, Ken; Vilsak, Thomas J.; Jackson, Lisa P.; & Sutley, Nancy H. (2011). America's great outdoors: A promise to future generations: Report. Washington, DC: US Government Printing Office. Retrieved April 23, 2012, from http://americasgreatoutdoors.gov/report

Soule, Michael, & Terborgh, John. (1999). *Continental conservation: Scientific foundations of regional reserve networks*. Washington, DC: The Wildlands Project and Island Press.

Worboys, Graeme; Francis, Wendy L.; & Lockwood, Michael. (Eds.). (2010). *Connectivity conservation management: A global guide*. London: Earthscan.

Yellowstone to Yukon Conservation Initiative (Y2Y). (2012). Homepage. Retrieved April 23, 2012, from http://y2y.net/

Share the *Encyclopedia of Sustainability*: Teachers are welcome to make up to ten (10) copies of no more than two (2) articles for distribution in a single course or program. For further permissions, please visit www.copyright.com or contact: info@berkshirepublishing.com

Index

A

Aboriginal people, 29–30, 239
    European colonization and, 314
    Native Title and, 171
    See also **Australia**; **Sydney, Australia**
Agenda 21, 258–259, 261–262, 282
    See also **Rio Earth Summit (UN Conference on Environment and Development)**
Agriculture, Tropical (The Americas), 2–5
    agro-silvo-pastoral (ASP) systems, 3
    family agriculture, 3–4
    high-input agriculture, 2–3
    slash-and-burn agriculture, 3–4
Amazon River, 6–9
    climatic changes, historical, 6–7
    human colonization in, 7–8
    Pleistocene refuge theory, 7
    rubber economy in, 7–8, 43
Amazonia, 10–13
Andes Mountains, 14–16
    campesinos (peasants and rural farmers), 15, 63
Appalachian Mountains, 17–19
    Appalachian Trail, 18
    deforestation in, 18
Architecture, 20–24
    biomimicry, 23
    "cradle to cradle," 23
    Empire State Building, 22
    Fajardo, Sergio (mayor of Medellín, Colombia), 22
    Leadership in Energy and Environmental Design (LEED), 23, 132, 193
    Living Building Challenge, 23
    Manitoba Hydro Place (building), 21
    oil crisis of the 1970s and, 21
Argentina. *See* **Southern Cone**
Auckland, New Zealand, 25–28
    Auckland Plan, 27
    Māori people, 27
    Transition Towns, 27
    walking school bus (WSB) initiatives, 27
Australia, 29–34
    Bradfield scheme (inland irrigation project), 33
    Chaffey brothers (George and William), 30
    colonization of, 30–31
    Deakin, Alfred (prime minister), 30
    Flying Fox and Drifting Sand, 31
    invasive species in, 31
    irrigation in, 30–31
    Tasmanian tiger (thylacine), 30, 31
    See also Aboriginal people; *Man and Nature*

B

Bogotá, Colombia, 36–38, 317
    bus rapid transit (BRT) system in, 37
    Gini coefficient of, 37
Brazil, 39–46
    brazilwood, 41
    deforestation, 44–45
    domestication of plants and animals, 40, 41–43
    Gini coefficient of, 253
    gold rush, 44
    invasive species from, 42
    rubber in, 43
    São Paulo private car program, 45
Brundtland Report, 21, 258

C

Canada, 48–52
British North America Act (1867), 50–51
cod stock depletion, 48–49
deforestation in, 48
Hudson's Bay Company (HBC) and fur trade, 49
Keystone XL pipeline, 50
tar sand oil extraction, 49–50
Caribbean, 53–57
banana production, 56
non-native species, 54–55
sugarcane plantations, 55–56
Taino peoples, 54
Central America, 58–64
Columbian exchange, 59
Mayan people, 59, 156
Panama Canal, 60–61
See also under marine protected areas (MPAs)
Chávez, Hugo (president of Venezuela), 290
Chesapeake Bay, 65–66
Chile. *See under* **Sanitation**
See also **Southern Cone**
Columbia River, 67–69
dam impacts on salmon migration, 68
Commission on Sustainable Development (CSD). *See* **Rio Earth Summit (UN Conference on Environment and Development)**
Convention on Biological Diversity (CBD), 151, 181, 258
Corporate Accountability, 70–74
Asia Wage Floor Alliance, 72
Chentex factory, Nicaragua, 71
Fair Labor Association (FLA), United States, 71
Fair Wear Campaign, Australia, 72
Curitiba, Brazil, 75–76
bus rapid transit (BRT) system in, 248
Lerner, Jamie (mayor), 75, 317

D

Darwin, Charles. *See under* **Parks and Protected Areas**
Detroit, United States, 78–82
automotive manufacturing and, 79–80, 158
Bessemer steel process, 78–79
The Greening of Detroit (nonprofit organization), 81
immigrant residents in, 79
public transportation in, 80
Southwest Detroit Environmental Vision (SDEV), 81

Bold entries and page numbers denote encyclopedia articles.

E

E-Waste, 84–89
Australia and, 88
Bamako Convention 1991, 87
Basel Action Network (BAN), 86–87
Basel Convention 1989, 87
Electronics TakeBack Coalition, 87
rare earth elements (REE), 85–86
recycling of, 86
Ecotourism (the Americas), 90–91, 159, 235, 269
Ecovillages, 92–95
Crystal Waters Ecovillage, Queensland, Australia, 93–94
Dancing Rabbit Ecovillage, Missouri, United States, 93
Global Ecovillage Network (GEN), 92, 94
El Niño Southern Oscillation, 134–135, 141, 145, 219
Energy Efficiency, 96–100
in Australia, 99
in Brazil, 98
energy efficiency paradox, 97–98
Energy Star label, 98
rebound effect, 97
in United States, 98

F

Fair Trade, 102–104
coffee and, 103
Direct Trade vs., 103
Fairtrade Labelling Organizations International (FLO), 102, 103
Forest Management, 105–110
Montreal Process, 108–109
sustainable forest management (SFM), 105
sustainable forest management (SFM) certification, 108–109

G

Gender Equality, 112–115
Australia and, 113
Canada and, 113
gender and environmental roles, 112–113
Gini coefficient (measure of inequality from 0 to 1), 37, 253, 315
Global Environment Facility (GEF). *See* **Rio Earth Summit (UN Conference on Environment and Development)**
Great Lakes and Saint Lawrence River, 116–119
air pollution from ships in, 116
Boundary Waters Treaty of 1909, 117
Great Lakes Water Quality Agreements (GLWQA), 1972 and 1978, 117–118

Great Lakes Water Quality Initiative (GLI), 119
International Joint Commission (IJC), 51, 117, 118
invasive species in, 116
greenhouse gas (GHG) emissions. *See* air pollution *under individual city/country articles*; Kyoto Protocol of 1997
Guatemala City, 120–124
   air pollution in, 122
   forest management in, 122
   Transmetro, 122
   water management in, 121–122
Gulf of Mexico. *See* anoxia and hypoxia events *under* **Marine Ecosystems Health**; British Petroleum (BP) oil spill *under* **New Orleans, United States**

K

Kiribati island. *See under* **Sanitation**
Kyoto Protocol of 1997, 258, 260
   Australia and, 34
   Canada and, 51
   United States, refusal to ratify, 311

L

Labor, 126–128
   green labor, 128
   Industrial Revolution and, 126–127
   mining, 128
   timber, 127–128
Las Vegas, United States, 129–133
   air pollution, 130–131
   foreclosure rates, 130, 131
Leopold, Aldo. *See under* **Parks and Protected Areas**
Lima, Peru, 134–136
   air pollution in, 135
   public transportation in, 135
   waste disposal, 136
   water availability and treatment, 135–136
Limits to Growth, 21, 258

M

Mackenzie River, 138–140
   aboriginal peoples of, 138–139
   Foundation for a Sustainable Northern Future, 139–140
   Mackenzie Valley Pipeline Inquiry, 139
   Mining, 139
   water management, 139
Man and Nature, 32, 202
Māori people. *See under* **Auckland, New Zealand, New Zealand**
maquiladora program. *See* **North American Free Trade Agreement (NAFTA)**

Marine Ecosystems Health, 141–149
   anoxia and hypoxia events, 143
   biotoxin and exposure events, 143
   coral reef bleaching, 144–145
   disease events, 145
   disturbance predicting, 141–142
   mass mortality events, 144
   novel and invasive events, 145–146
   ocean acidification, 147
   oil spills and, 146
   physical forcing events, 144–145
   trophic disturbances, 143–144
Marine Preserves, 150–154
   Galapagos Marine Reserve, 152
   Great Barrier Reef Marine Park, Australia, 152
   Gwaii Haanas National Park Reserve, Canada, 151
   marine protected areas (MPAs), 150, 151, 153
   Papahānaumokuākea Marine National Monument (PMNM), Hawaiian Islands, 151
   Seaflower MPA, Colombia, 152
Marsh, George Perkins. *See Man and Nature*
Mayan people. *See under* **Central America**
Mexico, 155–160
   Border Environment Cooperation Commission (BECC) and, 158
   Cárdenas, Lázaro (president), 157
   ceiba trees in, 59, 156
   Detroit's economy and, 158
   Díaz, Porfirio (dictator) and the *porfiriato*, 157
   drug war in, 161
   ejidos (communal lands), 157
   Green Revolution in, 158
   Grupo de los Cien (Group of One Hundred), 158
   illegal immigration from Mexico to the United States, 158–159
   indigenous peoples of, 155–156
   North American Development Bank (NADB) and, 158
   pre-colonial agriculture in, 155–156
   Spanish colonization of, 156
   tourism in, 159
   Zapatista Army for National Liberation in Chiapas, 158
Mexico City, 161–165
   air pollution, 162–163
   Day Without a Car program, 163
   Ecobici program, 163
   Metrobus, 163
   Plan Verde (Green Plan), 163, 164
   thermal inversion of, 161
   traffic congestion in, 163
Mining (Andes), 166–169
   social and environmental changes, 167–168

Mining (Australia), 170–173
   Mabo v. Queensland 1992, 171
   sociopolitical factors, 167
   techno-economic factors, 171–172
   techno-environmental factors, 172–173
   See also Aboriginal people

Mississippi and Missouri Rivers, 174–176
   biofuel and, 175
   ExxonMobil pipeline burst and oil spill, 175
   preservation and restoration efforts, 175

Mobility, 177–180
   nonmotorized transportation, 178–179
   transit-oriented development (TOD), 178
   transportation integration, 177–178
   walkability index, 179

Multilateral Environmental Agreements (MEAs), 181–185
   Australia and, 182–183
   Brazil and, 183–184
   Canada and, 184
   Environment Protection and Biodiversity Conservation (EPBC) Act, 1999, 183
   national biodiversity strategies and action plans (NBSAPs), 181

Murray-Darling River Basin, 186–188

N

New Orleans, United States, 190–194
   British Petroleum (BP) oil spill, 191, 193
   flooding in, 190–191
   hurricanes Katrina and Rita, 191, 192, 193
   Make It Right Foundation, 193
   Master Plan, 192
   petroleum and oil drilling, 191

New York City, United States, 195–199
   greenhouse gas (GHG) emissions in, 198

New Zealand, 200–205
   European colonization, 202
   human settlement and, 200–202
   Māori people, 200, 201–202, 203
   Quota Management System (QMS), 202, 203
   Resource Management Act (RMA) 1991, 204
   sealing and whaling in, 202
   Treaty of Waitangi, 200, 202, 204
   Waitangi Tribunal, 202, 204

North American Free Trade Agreement (NAFTA), 80–81, 158, **206–209**
   Border Environment Cooperation Commission (BECC) and, 207
   Commission for Environmental Cooperation (CEC) citizen submissions, 151, 208
   maquiladora program, 158, 207
   North American Agreement for Environmental Cooperation (NAAEC), 207–208
   North American Development Bank (NADB), 207

Northwest Passage, 210–214
   Arctic Waters Pollution Prevention Act (AWPPA), 213
   climate change and, 211
   community impacts, 211–212
   indigenous peoples in, 211
   ship passage and, 210–211
   tourism and shipping, 212–213

O

Oceania, 216–221
   exploitation of resources, 216–217
   fertilizer extraction, 218
   indigenous peoples in, 217
   nuclear radiation in, 219
   World War II's effect on, 218–219

Organization of American States (OAS), 222–224
   Executive Secretariat for Integral Development Department of Sustainable Development (DSD), 223
   Inter-American Institute for Cooperation in Agriculture (IICA), 222
   Inter-American Institute for Global Change Research (IAI), 223

Our Common Future. *See* Brundtland Report

P

Pacific Island Environmental Philosophy, 226–231
   agroforestry, 228
   beach philosophy, 227
   coconuts, 229
   fishing practices, 227
   island of Pohnpei, 226–228, 229, 230
   Micronesia, 226–227, 228–230
   mountain philosophy, 227–228
   sakau plants, 228
   sakau rituals, 229
   seasonal diets, 227

Parks and Protected Areas, 232–238
   Darwin, Charles, 235
   indigenous peoples and, 223, 236
   Leopold, Aldo, 234, 236
   Roosevelt, Theodore, (president of the United States), 234
   social carrying capacity, 235
   See also Pinchot, Gifford

Perth, Australia, 239–241

Bold entries and page numbers denote encyclopedia articles.

Peru. *See* cholera in Peru *under* **Sanitation**; Lima, Peru; Machu Picchu *under* **Travel and Tourism Industry**

Phoenix, United States, 242–245
- Central Arizona Project (CAP) canal system, 243
- economic recession in, 243
- Hohokam people, 242
- solar energy in, 244
- water supply issues, 242, 243, 244

Pinchot, Gifford, 18, 234, 308

Public Transportation, 246–250
- bus rapid transit (BRT), 248
- rail systems, 248–249
- subways, 247
- water-based systems, 249

R

Rio de Janeiro, Brazil, 252–257
- Atlantic Rainforest, 252, 254
- *favela* settlements, 254–255
- Global Environment Facility (GEF), 259
- petroleum production and spills, 253
- sewage treatment in, 255
- transportation in, 255

Rio Earth Summit (UN Conference on Environment and Development), 45–46, 252, 258–263
- capitalism and, 261–262
- RIO+20, 252, 260
- shortcomings and criticisms, 259, 260, 262

Rocky Mountains, 264–265
- Continental Divide, 264

Roosevelt, Theodore. *See under* **Parks and Protected Areas**; **United States**

Rural Development (the Americas), 266–274
- boom-and-bust cycle, 269, 270
- brain drain phenomenon and, 273, 286
- *Democracy in America*, 270
- grassroots development and, 271
- import substitution industrialization, 267–268
- income remittances, 269–270, 273
- liberal economic approach, 268
- payment for ecosystem services, 272
- social capital and, 270–271

S

Sanitation, 276–281
- cholera in Peru, 279–280
- Christchurch, New Zealand, 281
- diseases and, 276–278
- Kiribati and, 280–281
- typhoid in Chile, 278–279

Silent Spring, 31, 310–311

Small Island States, 282–286
- economics of, 285
- freshwater availability in, 284–285
- natural disasters and, 284
- tourism and, 285–286

Social Movements (Latin America), 287–291
- *Confederación de Nacionalidades Indígenas del Ecuador* (CONAIE) (Confederation of Indigenous Nationalities of Ecuador), 289
- *Madres de la Plaza de Mayo* (Mothers of the Plaza de Mayo), Argentina, 288
- *Movimento dos Trabalhadores Rurais Sem Terra* (MST) (Landless Workers' Movement), Brazil, 288–289
- Pachakutik political movement, 289
- *sumak kawsay* perspective, 290
- *Via Campesina* (Peasants' Way), 289
- World Social Forum (WSF), 289–290

Southern Cone, 292–295
- Initiative for the Integration of Regional Infrastructure in South America (IIRSA), 293
- Itaipú Dam, 293
- Mining in, 294
- Río de la Plata, 293
- wars in, 292

swidden agriculture. *See* slash and burn agriculture

Sydney, Australia, 296–298
- Aboriginal cultures in, 296
- Macquarie, Lachlan (governor), 296

T

Toronto, Canada, 300–302
- the Greenbelt, 301
- Jacobs, Jane, 301
- LiveGreen Toronto, 301

Travel and Tourism Industry, 303–306
- filming of *Lord of the Rings* in New Zealand, 305
- Machu Picchu, Peru 305
- tragedy of the commons, 305

U

United States, 308–312
- agriculture in, 309
- conservation movement in, 309–310
- deforestation in, 308–309
- *An Inconvenient Truth*, 312
- oil extraction and spills in, 312
- Roosevelt, Theodore, 309
- Superfund Act, 311

Urbanization, 313–318
    air pollution and, 316
    Australia and, 314
    colonization in the Americas, 314
    colonization in Oceania, 314
    edge cities, 316
    Edge City: Life on the New Frontier, 316
    Gini coefficient, 315
    Industrial Revolution and, 314
    Melbourne Principles, 317
    railroads and streetcars (impacts of), 315
    smart growth, 317
    transit-oriented development (TOD), 315, 317

Uruguay. *See* **Southern Cone**

V

Vancouver, Canada, 320–322
    Canadian Pacific Railway (CPR), 320
    film production in, 321
    Southeast False Creek brownfield, 321, 322

W

Water Use and Rights, 324–332
    Australia and, 329–330
    consumptive vs. nonconsumptive use, 324–325
    human rights and, 328–329
    integrated water resource management (IWRM), 331
    Micronesia, Melanesia, and Polynesia and, 330–331
    New Zealand and, 330
    North America and, 329
    South America and, 329
    United Nation's Millennium Development Goal (MDG) 7, Target 11, 328
    usufructuary (i.e. use-based) water rights, 329
World Wide Fund for Nature (WWF), 152

Y

Yellowstone to Yukon Conservation Initiative (Y2Y), 334–338
    grey wolves, reintroduction of, 235, 337
    grizzly bears, importance of, 335, 337

Bold entries and page numbers denote encyclopedia articles.